The Invisible Hand
in Popular Culture

The Invisible Hand in Popular Culture

Liberty vs. Authority
in American Film and TV

PAUL A. CANTOR

UNIVERSITY PRESS OF KENTUCKY

Scholarly publisher for the Commonwealth,
serving Bellarmine University, Berea College, Centre College of Kentucky,
Eastern Kentucky University, The Filson Historical Society, Georgetown College,
Kentucky Historical Society, Kentucky State University, Morehead State
University, Murray State University, Northern Kentucky University, Transylvania
University, University of Kentucky, University of Louisville, and Western
Kentucky University.
All rights reserved.

Editorial and Sales Offices: The University Press of Kentucky
663 South Limestone Street, Lexington, Kentucky 40508–4008
www.kentuckypress.com

16 15 14 13 12   5 4 3 2 1

Library of Congress Cataloging-in-Publication Data

Cantor, Paul A. (Paul Arthur), 1945-
  The invisible hand in popular culture : liberty versus authority in American film
and TV / Paul A. Cantor.
     p. cm.
  Includes bibliographical references and index.
  ISBN 978-0-8131-4082-7 (hardcover : alk. paper) —
  ISBN 978-0-8131-4083-4 (epub) — ISBN 978-0-8131-4084-1 (pdf)
  1. Motion pictures—Political aspects—United States. 2. Television programs—
Political aspects—United States. I. Title.
  PN1995.9.P6C285 2012
  791.430973—dc23   2012029585

Manufactured in the United States of America.

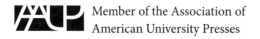 Member of the Association of
American University Presses

Resistance is futile.
   —The Borg Collective

Live Free or Die
   —New Hampshire license plate

Contents

PREFACE

But then are we in order when we are most out of order.

—William Shakespeare, *Henry VI, Part Two*

This study of popular culture focuses on the most American of all subjects: freedom. America is known as the land of the free, and "liberty" has been its rallying cry throughout its history, from the Revolutionary War and the Founding down to the present day. America was born in a rebellion, and its popular culture has embraced rebelliousness ever since. That explains America's peculiar fascination with truant children, from Tom Sawyer and Huck Finn to Bart Simpson and Eric Cartman. Many films and television shows have celebrated freedom in its characteristically American manifestations: the freedom to set one's own goals and go one's own way, the freedom to associate to solve common problems, the freedom to question authority and revolt against the establishment. But the ideal of freedom has often been challenged in American history, and it has clashed with other American values. In a series of case studies, I analyze the manifold ways in which American films and television shows have grappled with the question of freedom, often exposing its deeply problematic aspects, especially the tension between freedom and political order. The way the issue of freedom keeps coming up in different genres and time periods in popular culture is testimony to its centrality in the experience of the American people and their great experiment in democratic life.

I put this book together out of essays on popular culture that I wrote over the past ten years. All the previously published chapters have been thoroughly revised and rewritten for this volume, and in some cases substantially expanded. Two of the chapters, the ones on *Have Gun–Will Travel* and *Mars Attacks!*, are published here for the first time. To suggest what a rich panorama of artistic achievement American popular culture has to offer, the chapters cover a wide range of subjects. They are split evenly between film and television, and span roughly eight decades of material, from *The Black Cat* in 1934 to a few television series (*South Park, Fringe,* and *Falling Skies*) that are still ongoing (as of the 2011–12 season). I deal with several of the most important genres in pop culture. I devote a whole part to the Western, and I take up science fiction, Gothic horror, and film noir. I am interested in the issue of genre crossing, especially the intersection of the Western and science fiction, which I discuss in chapters 2 and 10 (in which I also discuss the fusion of the Gothic and science fiction). I treat the "high end" of popular culture: the work of celebrated directors such as John Ford, Martin Scorsese, and Tim Burton, as well as that of television writer-producers, such as Chris Carter and David Milch, who are highly regarded by sophisticated critics. But I have not avoided what is generally viewed as the "low end" of popular culture. I include a whole part on Edgar Ulmer, the King of the B-movies, and I have not shied away from discussing flying saucers, invading pod people, freakish superheroes, the Undead, and other mainstays of America's fertile mythic imagination. I even take up a surpassingly vulgar cartoon, in a chapter that delves into the potty-mouthed wisdom of the fourth graders of *South Park*.

This book is, then, wide-ranging but not systematic or comprehensive. I am not seeking to provide a historical overview of American popular culture and do not claim to have exhausted the subjects I discuss. Rather than attempting extensive coverage of whole fields of pop culture, I offer intensive readings of selected works. I am not a film or television historian, or a sociologist; my training is as a literary critic, and I concentrate on offering interpretations of the works I discuss. Still, I have chosen significant and representative moments in film and television history, of genuine interest in themselves, but also for what they can tell us more generally about American popular culture. I would be the first to admit that I have been highly selective in what I analyze, given my focus on the subject of freedom. Nevertheless, I hope that this book is enriched and enlivened by the way it jumps back and forth between film and television, different genres, and different time periods. At the same time, at the risk of some repetition, I have worked to keep each chapter self-contained, for readers who wish to concentrate on particular works.

The book is unified by its focus on the issue of freedom, and a number of common threads tie the chapters together. For example, several of the chapters deal with the tension between elites and common people in America. The *Have Gun–Will Travel* chapter explores the peculiar tendency of Hollywood elites to express their sense of superiority to ordinary Americans by fantasizing cosmopolitan heroes who are necessary to set right the injustices that supposedly occur routinely in small-town America. I argue that *Mars Attacks!* offers the inverse vision of America: it champions ordinary Americans for their ability to come together to overcome obstacles, while it debunks the elites who falsely claim to have the answers to all problems. The *Detour* chapter develops the idea that elitist European intellectuals, with their alien perspective on the United States, often misread both the country and its pop culture. Chapter 9 further pursues this notion of cultural elites misreading America—it examines the expert predictions that were made about the future of pop culture after 9/11 and shows how far off the mark they turned out to be.

The contrast that emerges in these chapters between elitist and populist visions of America points to a larger theme of this book—the difference between "top-down" and "bottom-up" models of order, an idea I outline and explain in the introduction. Reduced to its essentials, the question is: Are Americans better off running their own lives or submitting to the guidance and rule of various kinds of elites and experts? The opening section, on the Western, broaches the issue in terms of the perennial American debate about freedom versus order. For some of the works I discuss, such as *Have Gun*, freedom and order seem to be incompatible—order requires the very visible hand of a single hero to impose it on a chaotic and recalcitrant world of individuals pursuing their narrow self-interest (this is a "top-down" model of order). In other works, such as *Deadwood*, something akin to Adam Smith's invisible hand seems to produce social order. It emerges spontaneously out of the unregulated interaction of individuals, many of whom even appear to be criminals in the eye of the law (this is a "bottom-up" model of order with a vengeance). *Deadwood* suggests that freedom and order are compatible, and that ultimately only freedom can produce genuine social order.

The idea of spontaneous order, made famous by Austrian economist Friedrich Hayek, is, then, one of the organizing principles of this book. I argue that many works of American pop culture, in upholding freedom as an ideal, present what appears to be disorder as a deeper form of order. The heroes of American popular culture often do not seem to be orderly in any conventional sense. They are more inclined to break rules than to obey them. They are frequently mavericks, creative individuals who go against the crowd and chart their own course. But these seemingly disorderly characters often create the new orders that a country needs to keep making progress.

Because old orders have a tendency to rigidify and block progress, people who make up the rules as they go along can be valuable to society. This is especially true in the economic world, where the dynamic nature of business requires entrepreneurs who are always breaking existing molds in the process that the economist Joseph Schumpeter calls "creative destruction."[1] In American pop culture, Martin Scorsese's *The Aviator* and Trey Parker and Matt Stone's *South Park* are unusual for the way they take the side of entrepreneurs against the government officials who try to regulate them. In these works, government attempts to impose order and rein in economic activity have the effect of blocking progress, while visionary entrepreneurs, trying to improve life for their customers, usher in the order of the future. Both *The Aviator* and *South Park* suggest that the American people would be better off being left to their own devices, without government intervention in their lives. These works remind us of something that is often forgotten in discussions of freedom, that economic freedom is one of the most fundamental of all freedoms.

At the heart of the debate I explore in this book is a vital question: Is America great because of its national government or because of its people? Certainly, many films and television shows have celebrated the government of the United States and its leaders, and the grand achievements of the nation-state, the wars it has won and the vast public works it has helped construct (railroads, canals, dams, and so on). In this book, I highlight a countertradition in American popular culture, the disposition to question government authority and to celebrate the people who try to escape, thwart, or battle it to achieve freedom and thus a different kind of greatness. These free spirits may well be just as heroic as famous generals on the battlefield, or accomplish as much for the good of humanity as politicians. Several of the works I discuss, especially *Deadwood, Mars Attacks!,* and *South Park,* question the glorification of political leaders in American culture, particularly at the national level. Championing a localism that has always been a strong force in American politics, these works question whether the nation-state is the best form of government and consider the possibility that smaller units of organization might function more effectively, allowing greater freedom to ordinary people to run their lives as they see fit and achieve their own goals.

Thus, one subject I am examining in this book is the libertarian impulse in American popular culture. Libertarianism is a philosophy of freedom, and particularly endorses the free market as the best form of social organization.

The use of *libertarian* to describe a political position is fairly recent; it dates mainly from the mid-twentieth century.[2] But the roots of libertarianism lie in the eighteenth and nineteenth centuries, in what is often called the classical liberal tradition. (Given its insistence on limited government, this tradition must be distinguished from modern liberalism, which by contrast calls for big government.) In analyzing the libertarian aspects of some of the works I discuss, I draw upon classical liberal thinkers such as John Locke, Adam Smith, and Alexis de Tocqueville, and also on inheritors of this tradition in the twentieth century, including Austrian economists Ludwig von Mises and Friedrich Hayek. In almost all cases, I do not claim that the films and television shows I discuss were directly influenced by any of these thinkers. I mainly use their works to clarify and elucidate issues that I think are genuinely basic to American popular culture. The classical liberal thinkers are perennially relevant to discussing America because, throughout its history, they have profoundly influenced the development of the United States, including its political institutions and economic policies. This impact is epitomized by Locke's influence on the Founding Fathers. It does not matter whether individual movie directors or television producers have read Locke if he helped shape the America that they deal with in their works. The notions of freedom that circulate in American pop culture inevitably grow out of and remain related to the classical liberal tradition, and thus I feel comfortable drawing on it in my analyses. Still, I want to stress that I am not concerned with a programmatic or doctrinaire libertarian movement in film and television; that is why I refer merely to a libertarian "impulse." The only work that I discuss in this book that can properly be identified as libertarian is, I believe, *South Park*.

In exploring what is, broadly speaking, a libertarian strain in American popular culture, I am not claiming that it is the only strain, or even the predominant strain—only that it is a significant one.[3] Accordingly, several of my chapters, particularly those on *Have Gun–Will Travel* and *Detour,* deal with antilibertarian views, television shows or films that suggest that ordinary people, if left to their own devices, will run amok because of their greed, prejudice, and other character defects. In these works, the freedom that many Americans prize is viewed as anarchy, as a chaos of conflicting egoistic impulses that can only tear society apart. The ideal of freedom certainly has not gone unchallenged in American history. Nevertheless, it does have deep roots in American culture and keeps surfacing in films and television shows, sometimes in unexpected places. For example, one of the most persistent and vital traditions in American pop culture has been a peculiarly anarchic form of comedy, epitomized in the 1930s by the Marx Brothers and W. C. Fields (and even by the Three Stooges, on an admittedly lower level of artistic achievement). With their keen iconoclasm and healthy cynicism about authority, these comedians challenge silly laws, petty moralism, officious busybodies, social conventions, class distinctions, puritanical restrictions, intellectual pretensions, and other stultifying forces in society. In this book, *Mars Attacks!* and *South Park* are my examples of the anarchic power of comedy in American popular culture, with its tendency to smash idols, debunk the establishment, and release the energies of the American people in the name of "life, liberty, and the pursuit of happiness."

The anarchic impulse in popular culture is one reason why political elites in America have often—although not always—tried to constitute themselves as cultural elites as well. Elites who want to keep the American people in line fear the explosive energy of popular culture, its unruliness, its unwillingness to fit into established categories and tamely accept the dictates of authority. Ever since the nineteenth century, elites in America have been condemning various forms of popular culture for not measuring up to the norms of the traditional arts (often arts that originated in Europe). Popular culture has repeatedly been charged with being a force for disorder in society.[4] The elites who distrust freedom, and want, in particular, to impose order on what they view as the anarchy of free enterprise, tend to look down on popular culture as one more example of what goes wrong when ordinary people are allowed to have control over their lives. Elitists single out the worst of films and television and say, "Look what happens when people are left to themselves culturally, without the guidance of their betters." (Well, they rarely come right out and say this, but that is what they are thinking.) Over the years, one of the areas of American life that elites have most persistently wanted the government to regulate has been popular culture, especially film and television.[5] Elitists who profess to believe in democracy nevertheless have no faith in common people to make sound decisions on their own, even in a matter as simple as choosing the films and television shows they watch. How can people be trusted to choose their government if they cannot be trusted to choose their entertainment?

It would be very sad if American popular culture were as uniformly bad as many of its elitist critics claim. It would mean that freedom, which has worked well in many areas of American life, has failed in the realm of culture. That is one reason why I have searched out and focus on moments of sophistication and intelligence in American pop culture, even in some of its more vulgar manifestations. Many have tried to make Americans ashamed of what their pop culture has produced, but there is much that they can be proud of in the history of Hollywood. Films and television shows have been among America's most distinctive and important contributions to world culture. Contrary to what many critics insist, America's pop culture is one manifestation of its greatness. This is not to say that all of America's pop culture is great—far from it. It is to say that, as in other areas, the freedom and democratic spirit of America have provided the conditions that have allowed creative artists to flourish in popular culture. It is no accident that a democratic country has become a world leader in popular culture. The aristocratic heritage of Europe has at times acted as a brake on the development of its popular culture. By contrast, the United States, with the vast economic resources generated by its free enterprise system, has been a pioneer in many of the technological developments that have opened up new creative possibilities in film and television. Even European elites have at times come to appreciate certain aspects of American pop culture. Ever since Europeans became fans of Westerns in the nineteenth century, from James Fenimore Cooper's novels to Buffalo Bill's Wild West shows, the American frontier has exerted a peculiar fascination on the European imagination, precisely as a new image of freedom.

In short, freedom has worked well in American popular culture. Like all forms of liberty, it has been a freedom to fail as well as to succeed, and the history of Hollywood is littered with trash. But in most forms of culture the failures vastly outnumber the successes. Today we remember and cherish roughly a hundred Victorian novels and treat this period as a high point of cultural production. We forget the thousands of bad novels from the era, the potboilers and penny dreadfuls that have mercifully slipped down the memory hole of history. There is no simple formula for cultural achievement; genuine art is one of the greatest of human mysteries. Artistic success cannot be predicted or planned for in advance. Cultures seem to function best when they provide widespread opportunities for artistic creation and freedom to experiment with different possibilities in the hope of hitting upon a successful form. The mass entertainment system in the United States, for all the mediocrity it has generated, has managed to provide the broad base needed for genuine heights of cultural achievement.[6] Although by no means free of government regulation, the American film and television industries have been among the freest in the world. As a result, with all their shortcomings, they have at their rare best produced a body of work remarkable for its quality and variety.

Thus, American popular culture not only celebrates freedom; it is also itself an example of American freedom at its best and most vibrant. This is, of course, a controversial claim, especially in today's climate of opinion. The movement known as Cultural Studies and several other forms of contemporary critical analysis treat culture as a realm of unfreedom, dwelling on the constraints under which would-be creative people necessarily operate. These movements are, broadly speaking, historicist in approach. They view creators in all media as working within ideological horizons defined by the time period in which they live. In recent decades, cultural analysts have become increasingly obsessed with the prejudices and blind spots of artists, especially the way factors of race, class, and gender determine their outlook on the world and the content of their works. These critical tendencies are evident in the analysis of literature and the fine arts, but they are particularly pronounced in the study of pop culture. People laboring in film and television are said to be subject to an unusual array of forces that govern what they can produce, forces supposedly so powerful that many scholars in effect deny that any real creative freedom is possible in pop culture. The fact that films and television shows need to be popular supposedly means that would-be creators in these media become prisoners of the prejudices of the mass audiences they pursue. Needing to flatter their customers, these creators lack the freedom to challenge common opinion.

In the view of many cultural critics, the commercial nature of American pop culture is thus a strike against it. Even when they are not strictly speaking Marxists, they adopt a Marxist position: that American pop culture serves the cause of capitalism, working to make a potentially rebellious population content with its oppressed lot. Ever since the Frankfurt School of culture critique emerged in the 1940s, it has been fashionable to speak disparagingly of a culture industry in the United States and to view Hollywood as a dream factory. Pop culture is equated with mass culture and criticized for mass producing forms of debased entertainment to numb the American people into submission to their capitalist masters.

This understanding of cultural production, as plausible as it may initially sound, mistakes the average conditions in the entertainment industry for the only conditions.[7] It is certainly true that the majority of people producing films and television shows are not great artists or especially creative. Faced with all sorts of constraints, many of them financial, people working in

Hollywood are always tempted to make compromises, to sacrifice whatever artistic integrity they may have begun with, and to work within well-worn formulas that are supposed to deliver mass audiences. But even if most people in Hollywood lack artistic freedom, that does not mean that everyone does. Like all forms of historicism, this kind of culture critique treats a difficulty as if it were an impossibility. No one would deny that, given the demands of the entertainment industry, it is difficult to be genuinely creative in film and television. But one reason we are acutely aware of the widespread absence of creativity in Hollywood is precisely the fact that once in a while someone comes along who breaks the mold and shows what can really be accomplished in film or television. Hollywood's track record demonstrates that there is nothing inherent in pop culture that precludes creative freedom in film and television. As many of the figures I discuss in this book have proven, it is difficult but not impossible to buck the Hollywood system and achieve a high level of artistic success, even in genres that are thought of as the most formulaic (think of what David Milch accomplished in *Deadwood* with the seemingly moribund form of the TV Western). To aesthetic theorists, all the genuine achievements in popular culture have looked impossible—until someone achieved them. That is the difference between culture critics and creative artists. Where the critic sees insurmountable obstacles, the artist sees creative opportunities. Where the critic sees only imprisonment, the artist struggles creatively to find a path to freedom.

The creativity in American pop culture illustrates a general point about freedom. Freedom is not the ability to act without any constraints whatsoever. Given the constraints under which all human beings operate, freedom is the ability to choose how to respond to them. Faced with the Hollywood system, many people choose to compromise with it and work within its limitations, but others resolve to challenge the system, fight for their integrity, and stretch the limits of what can be done in film and television. Human nature being as complicated as it is, the choices in Hollywood are never quite this clear-cut and absolute. Most people combine moments of compromise with elements of integrity. The pop culture creators I discuss in this book are generally the ones who have produced some form of interesting work and were willing to struggle against the Hollywood system to do so. I take them seriously as artists and look carefully for what they have to say about important issues. I do not treat them as simply mirroring broader trends in American society or catering to the prejudices of their audiences.[8] There are too many ideological disputes within American pop culture for it to be

xviii Preface

viewed as mechanically reflecting some national consensus. As I show at many points in this book, individual films and television shows often carry on a dialogue with each other and dispute very basic issues. Sometimes I make a point about a given film or television show by contrasting its ideological position with that of mainstream pop culture. I am interested precisely in oppositional stances within American pop culture and therefore view many of the figures I discuss as mavericks, deliberately running counter to broader trends in film and television and in American society as a whole.

I cannot prove in advance that my approach is correct and that genuinely creative artists have been at work in film and television. The only proof is this book as a whole, in my detailed analysis of how artistically complex and ideologically sophisticated certain films and television shows can be. Many people have tried to give reasons why film and television are by nature inferior and unsophisticated media. They point to the fact that film and television are generally collaborative enterprises and do not allow for the individual creative genius that is supposedly responsible for all aesthetic achievement in literature and the fine arts. Or they raise concerns about the haphazardness of creation in the entertainment business, the fact that films and television shows are often produced on the fly and involve a good deal of scrambling to meet deadlines and budgets. How can a television show be a work of art if it was thrown together by a variety of hands and at the last possible moment?

In the introduction, I deal at length with these objections to taking pop culture seriously. On the one hand, it turns out that multiple authorship and haphazard production are more common in literature and the fine arts than is generally supposed. And, on the other hand, the chaotic conditions of production in Hollywood may sometimes result in improving its products in a process of trial and error, involving, among other factors, active feedback from audiences. Lurking behind many critiques of popular culture is the Romantic myth of the creative genius and the belief that such an artist can produce masterpieces only in godlike isolation, especially from the debasing effects of the marketplace. In film criticism, this myth takes the form of the auteur theory, the notion that there are a few great directors, such as Welles, Bergman, Fellini, and Kurosawa, who created their films single-handedly and in opposition to the commercial moviemaking system. I deal with the auteur theory in the introduction and in several of the chapters, especially chapters 2, 4, 5, and 8. I agree with the auteur theory insofar as it maintains that genuine artists can be found working in popular media. As a scholar of Romantic literature and a fan of William Blake, I have always been partial to the idea of the creative genius.

But the more I have studied film and television, the more I have come to realize that we do not need the notion of the solitary genius to authenticate genuine works of art. We are now told by art historians that some of the greatest Rembrandts were not in fact painted by Rembrandt, but by some of his very talented students, such as Govert Flinck. Perhaps the most famous example of a "decommissioned" Rembrandt is *The Man with the Golden Helmet* in Berlin. Long regarded as one of Rembrandt's masterpieces—and hence one of the greatest paintings of all time—the work was reattributed by the official Rembrandt Research Project in 1985 to a nameless imitator of the Dutch master. Suddenly it seemed to be a lesser work—and experts assumed that it would now fetch a fraction of its former estimated monetary value on the art market. And yet it is still the same painting—and still my favorite "Rembrandt." This is an example of how what is called the genetic fallacy can distort our view of art. How a work of art comes into being should not affect our judgment of its quality. As Svetlana Alpers has shown, Rembrandt set out to create what we now call "a Rembrandt," a painting with a certain look.[9] He was evidently able to teach his students how to produce such paintings. He operated a studio, out of which flowed a stream of "Rembrandts," some entirely by him, some entirely by his students, and some involving collaboration between him and his students. This form of artistic production was by no means unique to Rembrandt. Many of the greatest painters ran studios—Rubens is another notable example—and they left art historians charged with the difficult task of distinguishing the different hands in famous paintings. This is no doubt a fascinating and instructive enterprise, but does it really make a painting a lesser achievement to discover that two artists rather than one had a hand in its creation?

In studying art history, I was struck by the continual use of the word *studio,* and the connection with Hollywood did not escape me. The auteur theorists contrast the work of a few great directors with the mass production of the Hollywood studio system. And yet we know that some of the greatest paintings in history were products of a studio system. Many of the paintings that hang today in the hallowed halls of museums were originally done on commission, with the "big name" artists scrambling to complete them on time, often enlisting the aid of their students to meet the deadline. One can surely find many differences between the Rembrandt studio and Metro-Goldwyn-Mayer, but there are more similarities than many art historians would like to acknowledge. Cultural critics have developed a kind of reflex antipathy to any form of art that emerges out of commercial conditions. This anticommercial prejudice is so ingrained that it sometimes produces laughable statements, which betray a complete ignorance of cultural history. An actress defending her decision not to get involved in filmmaking said: "[Hollywood films] all seem to be about making money, and I don't find that terribly interesting. Today in our world, art has to be commercial. That's a really sad point of view. If Shakespeare had to be commercial, he wouldn't have written the things he did."[10] As any passing student of Renaissance drama could have told this actress, Shakespeare did write for a commercial theater company and was in fact the commercially most successful playwright of his day. He even became a stockholder in the company for which he wrote. Commerce and culture cannot simply be incompatible if the greatest author in any language wrote for a money-making operation.

In several of my chapters, I show that some of the legendary individual geniuses in Hollywood history did accept the commercial and collaborative nature of the entertainment business, even the studio system with all its faults. These artists sometimes openly admit that they profited aesthetically from the advice and suggestions of their colleagues and coworkers. In chapter 2, for example, I demonstrate that the *Star Trek* universe, which is generally thought to have sprung wholly formed from the lone genius of Gene Roddenberry, in fact developed out of a TV Western he wrote for, but did not create. In chapter 4, I offer evidence that one of the seemingly purest of contemporary auteurs, Tim Burton, acknowledges that he does not create his films single-handedly; he even expresses gratitude to his financial backers. Well after the initial publication of what is now chapter 8, I learned that the film *Detour* is not the pure invention of its director, Edgar Ulmer, but is based on a published novel and a detailed screenplay, both by Martin Goldsmith. The original French auteur theorists held up Ulmer as an example of a director who managed to place the stamp of his individual genius on all his films, no matter how cheaply or hastily produced. Now some film historians claim that Goldsmith should be regarded as the true auteur of *Detour,* since he made up the basic story and wrote much of the dialogue. I try to sort out the claims of Ulmer and Goldsmith in the appendix to chapter 8; but once again I would insist that, as an aesthetic object, the film remains the same, whether one, two, or any number of people created it.

The study of popular culture has suffered greatly from the genetic fallacy. Time and again academics have come up with theories that tell us in advance what films and television shows can and cannot do, supposedly because of the very nature of the media and the conditions that prevail in creating their products. Unfortunately, these theoretical perspectives can blind analysts to what has actually been accomplished in film and television. If you are certain in advance that nothing of artistic value can ever be achieved in these media, you will never make the effort needed to discover if you are wrong. Fortunately, enough great movies were produced in the course of the twentieth century to silence the skeptics about the medium, and a similar recognition of the artistic quality of the best television shows is beginning to spread, even in the academic world. As a sign of the times, Salman Rushdie created a stir in English newspapers when he announced: "I'm in this position where, for the first time in my writing life, I don't have a novel on the go, but I have a movie and a memoir and a TV series." It was indeed big news when a world-famous novelist decided to work on a science fiction series called *The Next People* for the Showtime TV network "in the belief that quality TV drama has taken over from film and is comparable to the novel as the best way of widely communicating ideas and stories."[11]

Ultimately, it is not critics with their theories who determine whether a medium is capable of producing genuine art; that is an issue for real artists to settle, when they decide whether to work in a given medium or not. What look like the inevitable limits of a medium to academics serve as challenges to artists, who are always searching for new outlets for their creativity, and hence push the envelope and break through seemingly established boundaries. In an interview, Trey Parker of *South Park* captured this spirit perfectly: "You can only say 'you can't do that' so many times to Matt [Stone] and me before we're gonna do it."[12] Many film theorists in the 1920s argued that cinema is by nature a silent medium. They insisted that talking pictures were not technically feasible and, even if they were, they would necessarily be inferior to silent movies in what is essentially a visual medium.[13] In 1927, *The Jazz Singer* proved that talking pictures could be made and succeed big time at the box office. In 1931, Fritz Lang's *M* put to rest forever the idea that sound effects could not be an integral part of a film's artistic impact and a powerful new cinematic resource. As frequently happens in the history of media, the artists proved the critics wrong.

Throughout this book, I have tried not to let theoretical presuppositions interfere with my appreciation and understanding of the works I discuss.[14] In the art world, if it looks like a Rembrandt, in some sense it is a Rembrandt.[15] Similarly, in the world of film and television, I am guided by the principle that if it looks like a work of art, it is a work of art, no matter how it came into being. In short, if I find coherence of form and content in a film or a television show, I treat it the way I would any serious work of art. My interpretations generally follow the pattern of what is known as close reading. Despite my theoretical disagreements with the New Criticism (outlined in the introduction), in practical terms I usually focus on how the parts cohere into a whole in the works I discuss. Since the works diverge significantly in terms of artistic quality, I do not expect the same degree of coherence in all the works I treat. Throughout the book I attempt to discriminate between first-rate works (such as *Deadwood*), worthy I believe to stand comparison with all but the greatest works in other media, and run-of-the-mill Hollywood entertainment (along the lines of *Earth vs. the Flying Saucers*). Without rehashing centuries of debate in aesthetics, I will simply state that I generally invoke traditional criteria of artistic excellence in my investigations. In discriminating among works, I look for the degree of complexity of plot, character, and theme, and other markers of genuine quality. I do not treat all the works equally. I reserve detailed analysis for the films and television shows that I believe can stand up to such intense scrutiny. But even mediocre films and television shows may repay serious study, if only to highlight what makes some other works superior.

Despite my attempt to avoid the genetic fallacy, in some cases I have looked into the conditions under which a given film or television show was produced and have taken those facts into account in my analysis. When possible, I have examined the stated intentions of the people who made the films and television shows, and sometimes I have factored that information into my interpretations. But basically in this book, I am looking at intentionality, not intentions. I reject "creationism" in aesthetic analysis. Modern biology studies organic form as having a design, without invoking the notion of a designer. That is, we do not need to know a Creator's intentions in order to understand the intentionality embodied in a given animal's form, how its parts fit together to achieve a functional and functioning whole. The theory of evolution tells us that something with intentionality of form can come into being by a random, seemingly undirected, and even messy process that occurs over time. While acknowledging all the differences between aesthetic and biological form, I believe that we can use the evolution of life as a model for the coming into being of much art (though not all)—an issue I discuss in the introduction.[16]

The creation of art may at times be an example of spontaneous order—

an achievement that does not have to take place in a single moment of perfectly planned creation. Instead it can involve a process, with the work evolving over time, in a feedback loop that requires a good deal of revision and correction; and a number of different hands may be involved in the process. Thus we should not reject the possibility of genuine art in popular culture simply because its conditions of production do not fit the Romantic model of the artist as solitary creator. As I show in the introduction, at times Romantic poetry itself did not fit this model. The auteur theorists were correct to find intentionality in popular culture and to treat individual films as works of art. Their mistake was to think that intentionality can be the product only of a single consciousness. As in many areas of human life, the working conditions in film and television can sometimes permit different people to collaborate in productive and aesthetically beneficial ways, in effect merging their individual intentions into a larger and more complex artistic intentionality.

Thus in many respects spontaneous order is the unifying idea of this book—popular culture often celebrates its power in American society and is itself an example of that power. In short, I am offering a bottom-up model of culture: genuine works of art often bubble up out of the most unlikely places, even the seemingly lowest strata of pop culture. For a variety of reasons, the greatest artistic energy can sometimes be found in the commercial media, which continually offer artists new opportunities for original and even groundbreaking work as well as the potential for substantial and sometimes spectacular financial rewards. The cultural elites who set themselves up as the analysts, evaluators, and custodians of art generally work with a top-down model of culture that mirrors their own elitism. Championing what they think of as elite culture, these critics imagine that aesthetic achievement can result only from artists working in splendid isolation, placed well above the hubbub of commercial life. These elitists cannot believe that commerce sometimes can give birth to art and infuse it with life. Just as the commercial world can be creative in economic terms, it can also be in aesthetic terms. The seeming chaos in film and television production sometimes—not always—results in genuine works of art.

The Hollywood system, with all its commercial demands, is, then, not simply a block to artistic impulses, although it surely is always a threat to them. The artists I discuss, especially John Ford, Tim Burton, Martin Scorsese, Chris Carter, and David Milch, have had to fight for their creative freedom in Hollywood, sometimes bitterly; but they have achieved it, at least as much as artists in any other media have. If, as the Marxists claim, Hollywood directors are subject to the demands of the American bourgeoisie, Rembrandt was no less dependent on the whims of Dutch burghers for the commissions that kept him in business. Again, freedom is not the absence of all constraints, but the option to struggle against them, and even to make them work in one's favor.[17] As disheartening as the spectacle of the average level of Hollywood's output may be, the best that has been created over the years in American film and television is really an edifying sight. It is a tribute to the vitality of popular culture and to what freedom in America—commercial freedom—can produce. If one took, for example, the twenty-five greatest movies produced by Hollywood in the twentieth century, they would, as a group, be comparable in artistic worth to a similar sampling from almost any other moment in cultural history, such as the twenty-five greatest Victorian novels or nineteenth-century Italian operas.[18]

It should not be surprising, then, that American popular culture has often celebrated the freedom that is the ground of its own artistic achievement. The greatest talents in film and television have been mavericks, and they have been attracted to the maverick heroes who have been admired in America from its beginnings in a revolutionary movement. Martin Scorsese is a movie entrepreneur; it is no accident that, in *The Aviator,* he identifies with Howard Hughes as a business entrepreneur, especially since one of Hughes's businesses was the motion picture industry. The creative spirits in popular culture value their freedom as artists, precisely because they have had to struggle so hard to achieve it. I have been guided throughout this book by the thought that no idea is more basic to America than freedom and that popular culture can teach us that freedom is a perpetual challenge, something valuable that we must constantly struggle to maintain in our world.

A Note on Organization

Each part of this book begins with a brief introduction that explains how the individual chapters fit together and what the part contributes to the book as a whole. It might, however, be helpful to give a preliminary outline of the book's structure here.

The introduction serves two purposes. First, it offers a methodological justification for the way I analyze individual films and television shows as works of art. It attempts to counter the many arguments that the conditions of production in popular culture prevent any kind of genuine artistic achievement in this realm. Second, it explains the idea of spontaneous order, which is central to this book and recurs in several of the chapters, especially the ones on *Deadwood, Mars Attacks!,* and *South Park.*

Part One deals with the most American of all genres, the Western, and the one that has traditionally been devoted to exploring the problematic nature of freedom. Taking up *The Searchers, Have Gun–Will Travel,* and *Deadwood,* I examine and contrast three very different visions of the relation between freedom and order in the Wild West as imagined in American popular culture.

Part Two takes up an improbable trio of subjects: *Mars Attacks!, The Aviator,* and *South Park.* But together they spotlight the libertarian strain in American pop culture. All three champion antiestablishment and antiauthority figures and give a dim view of government intervention in American life. The maverick creators of these works appear to sympathize with the maverick spirit that is basic to the popular conception of the American character.

Part Three offers Edgar Ulmer as a case study of the paradoxes and contradictions of American popular culture. For one thing, he was a European who more or less blundered into the world of Hollywood, and he therefore reveals how foreign influences are actually basic to American pop culture, despite its appearance of insularity. Ulmer could plausibly be offered as a prime example of the way the commercial system of Hollywood trapped and ruined a potential artist, and yet many film historians and theorists take the opposite view—that he was an auteur who triumphed artistically over the studio system. In my chapters on *The Black Cat* and *Detour,* I analyze how Ulmer's distinctive perspective on America as a European changed over the years, especially in his understanding of freedom and popular culture itself.

Part Four examines the interaction between popular culture and the larger world around it, focusing on the impact of 9/11 on American films and especially television shows, but dealing with other anxieties of the contemporary globalized world as well. I contrast what was predicted at the time of 9/11 for the future of American pop culture with what actually developed in the following years. The disasters of 9/11 were supposed to produce a new wave of patriotism and reunify pop culture in support of the American government. But in an illustration of the oppositional and contrarian nature of pop culture, many films and television shows have raised serious doubts about government reactions to 9/11, specifically the erosion of civil liberties as a result of the War on Terror. The way pop culture has reacted to 9/11 is one more chapter in the continuing story of how freedom has battled with other values in American history—security, order, stability—and thus this subject rounds out my discussion of the central issue of this book.

A Note on the Notes

Even though this book deals with seemingly nonacademic material, such as cartoons and flying saucers, it is a work of scholarship and the chapters are heavily annotated. General readers should feel free to skip the notes. As a scholar, I need to document my assertions wherever possible and acknowledge some of the scholarly controversies that have developed over the subjects I discuss, as well as anticipate objections to my argument and point out further lines of inquiry. Anyone outside the academic field of popular culture would be surprised to learn how much scholarship on the subject has already been published or how much archival material is available for studying individual films and television shows. I myself was amazed (and relieved) that I was easily able to obtain the screenplay of *Detour*, a film that was all but ignored by critics (and certainly by scholars) when it was released in 1945. My notes, as extensive as they may be, actually represent only a fraction of the research that went into the creation of this book. For those who are interested, I want to give my readers some sense of how serious the study of popular culture has become. At the same time, however, I am always worried that studying pop culture will become deadly serious and thus lose its peculiar charm—and enjoyment. Accordingly, I have tried to isolate the more scholarly side of my enterprise in the notes, while, as in my earlier book *Gilligan Unbound*, having some fun with (and sometimes at the expense of) the films and television shows I discuss in the body of the chapters. I believe that the academic study of the entertainment business should itself be entertaining.

INTRODUCTION

Popular Culture and Spontaneous Order, or, How I Learned to Stop Worrying and Love the Tube

A film may have its own unity, with its relationships coherent and its balance precise. But that the ultimate unity can be entirely foreseen is a dubious proposition: the distance between conception and delivery is so great, and the path between them so tortuous and unpredictable.... A film ... cannot be made in the mind and then transferred to celluloid precisely as conceived. One of the prime requirements for a film-maker is flexibility to improvise, and to adjust his conceptions to the ideas and abilities of his co-workers, to the pressures of circumstance, and the concrete nature of the objects photographed.

—V. F. Perkins, *Film as Film*

In studying popular culture, especially when working on my book *Gilligan Unbound,* I quickly ran into hermeneutical difficulties. I wanted to discuss television shows as works of art, to demonstrate how they present a meaningful view of the world in a skillful and sometimes even masterful manner. I was interested in how a sequence of television shows expressed changes in the way Americans perceived their place in the world and, more specifically, the way their attitudes toward globalization evolved. This project involved making statements such as: "*The Simpsons* portrays the national government negatively and celebrates a turn to the local and the global" or "*The X-Files* suggests that modern technology is at war with the power of the state." In short, like many of my colleagues, I surreptitiously imputed intentionality to something inanimate and truly unconscious—a television series. One could claim that in such circumstances saying "*The Simpsons*" is simply shorthand for saying "the team that created *The Simpsons,*" but I suspect that something more is at work here, an attempt to evade the difficult questions about intentionality and artistic purpose that analyzing a television show raises.

"Sailing to Byzantium" versus *The X-Files*

Our basic model of aesthetic intentionality in literature is the lyric poem. When William Butler Yeats sat down to write "Sailing to Byzantium," we like to think that he was free to shape the poem any way he chose. Thus, we want to say that the resulting poem was wholly the product of Yeats's intentions and his alone, and that means that every word in the poem is aesthetically meaningful.[1] One can therefore legitimately worry over the most minor details in a poem like "Sailing to Byzantium" and make something of the fact that Yeats chose to use one particular word rather than another. But is this kind of close reading appropriate for television shows, since they are not produced the way lyric poems are? No television show is created by a single author. Scripts are typically the product of a team of writers, and even the list of people officially credited with writing a given script does not include all those who had a hand in it. Writing for television resembles committee work rather than what we normally think of as artistic activity. Scripts generally involve compromises and may end up embodying different conceptions of the work in question, sometimes even contradictory ones.

Moreover, a script is only the rough blueprint for a television show. In the process of actually shooting the show, the director, and sometimes even cast members, modify the script, perhaps because it has led to problems in production or simply because on the spur of the moment they think that they can improve it. Even after it has been shot, a show has not taken its final form. Network executives, censors, and potential sponsors may well demand further changes before it can be aired. The result of the complicated production process of a television show is that the work that finally reaches the screen will never correspond exactly to the idea of the person who first conceived it and will often be quite remote from the initial conception.

It thus becomes problematic to speak of intentionality in the case of television shows because it is difficult to identify whose intentions one is talking about. Moreover, given the nature of the television industry, an element of contingency is inevitably introduced into the final product. As an interpreter one might, for example, try to make something of the darkening of the light in a particular scene and claim that it was intended to achieve a darkening of mood. But if one asked the producer about this particular "effect," he might say something like this: "It was two days till airtime, and we needed to finish the lakeside scene; I knew I was running out of light, but we were also running out of money, and I hoped nobody would notice the difference."[2] So much for any attempt to find the changed lighting of the scene aesthetically meaningful. In the course of researching *Gilligan Unbound,* I found many cases where developments in a television program could not be explained in terms of purely aesthetic considerations. In the second season of *The X-Files,* for example, Agent Dana Scully was abducted, possibly by aliens, and for several episodes the audience was wrapped up in the question of her fate. One might marvel at the ingenuity of the show's creators in mapping out this dramatic turn of events until one learns that, far from planning it in advance, they were scrambling to cope with the fact that Gillian Anderson, the actress who portrayed Scully, had become pregnant and was going to be unavailable for shooting in the middle of the season. For all that *The X-Files* managed to make of Scully's abduction, at root it was a plot device to cover over a production snag.[3] The more one reads about the history of shows like *The X-Files,* the more one realizes that this kind of improvising, rather than careful planning in advance, is typical of television production.

With considerations such as these in mind, I grew uneasy in the course of working on *Gilligan Unbound.* Was I falsely imputing aesthetic intentionality to shows like *The Simpsons* (1989–) and *The X-Files* (1993–2002)? Was I wrong to look for artistic unity in television shows when so many aspects of their creation point to a disunity of conception and an even greater disunity of the ultimate product? I had come to the study of popular culture with the training of a literary critic and had devoted much of my career to analyzing Shakespeare. Thus, it was natural that when I viewed television I was looking for masterpieces, for shows that use traditional artistic techniques to convey important truths about the world we live in. But can masterpieces be produced on a weekly schedule and a tight budget, and also please sponsors? My whole enterprise in *Gilligan Unbound* was haunted by the fear that I was illegitimately using categories derived from elite culture in my study of popular culture.

Nevertheless, despite everything I learned in the course of researching television shows, I could not ignore what had originally drawn me to some of them: an apparently high level of artistic achievement. In theoretical terms, the application of the concept of artistic intentionality to television shows seems dubious, but I could not help seeing signs of artistic intentions at work in some of them. Despite the general messiness of the medium, some of the shows seem extremely well crafted and, when carefully analyzed, appear to make coherent statements. Even the best of the shows do not achieve the artistic coherence of a perfect Yeats lyric, but that does not mean that one should label them incoherent. I began to ask: Is it fair to judge television programs by the standard of artistic coherence achieved in lyric poetry at its best? If I was having trouble applying the idea of artistic intentionality to television shows, perhaps the problem was not with the television shows but with the model of artistic intentionality I was using.

On reflection, it does seem inappropriate to use standards of artistic coherence derived from one medium to understand an entirely different medium. A thirty-two-line lyric poem is, at least in material terms, much easier to produce than a one-hour television program, and one can imagine the poem issuing from a single consciousness in a way that seems impossible for the television show, which must necessarily be a cooperative effort. Notice that this distinction is not simply one between elite culture and popular culture.[4] A lyric poem may not be the appropriate model for understanding a Shakespeare play either. Shakespeare was of course a great poet, and there is much that is poetic in his plays. Nevertheless, their conditions of production more closely resemble those of a television show than those of a lyric poem. As a dramatist, specifically a commercial dramatist, Shakespeare was working in a cooperative medium, and no doubt the finished form his plays took on the stage involved the kind of compromises we can observe in television production today. We do not have the detailed information about the production history of Shakespeare's plays that is available for television, but historical research has uncovered elements of contingency even in Shakespeare.

For example, we know something about the casting in Shakespeare's theater company. Its principal comedian was originally a man named Will Kempe, who specialized in comic dances and little dialogues with himself. When Kempe left Shakespeare's troupe—like a television actor today leaving a successful series—he was replaced by a man named Robert Armin, who excelled in different forms of comic business. Armin evidently sang well, and he also specialized in playing the part of a fool. This change in personnel in Shakespeare's company helps explain the fact that, in roughly the first half of his career, the chief comic figure in his plays was a clown, such as Launcelot Gobbo in *The Merchant of Venice,* whereas in the second half, Shakespeare switched to a fool, such as Touchstone in *As You Like It.*[5] This development may seem relatively insignificant until one realizes that one of Shakespeare's most distinctive strokes of genius—his inclusion of a fool in his greatest tragedy, *King Lear*—was not a move he pulled out of thin air. It is a good question: If Robert Armin had not replaced Will Kempe in Shakespeare's company, would the dramatist have come up with the brilliant idea of counterpointing Lear's tragedy with the Fool's comedy? We have reason to believe, then, that much like television writers today, Shakespeare wrote with specific actors in mind and sometimes tailored his plays to their peculiar talents.

Organic Form and Romantic Aesthetics

My efforts to reassure myself about the legitimacy of what I was doing in *Gilligan Unbound* thus led me to more general reflections about the nature of culture. Perhaps contingency is a more important factor in the artistic process than the example of lyric poetry would lead us to believe. In this regard popular culture may provide a better model for culture in general than the relatively elite activity of poetry. The domination of lyric poetry as our model of artistic creation is itself a historically contingent development. Poetry is one of the oldest of the arts, and it certainly had a considerable head start over television in offering a model of artistic activity. As early as Aristotle one can observe the tendency to think of all art as a form of *poiesis,* and his *Poetics* introduced the organic model of poetry and art more gener-ally—the crucial notion that a true work of art must form an organic whole. Given Aristotle's conception of organism, that means that in a true work of art every part has a function to play in the whole.[6] That in turn means that every part of a true work of art is there by design, not by chance. Aristotle was the first to try to theorize contingency out of the realm of art.[7] His organic model of art proved to be extremely durable and powerful, especially as a heuristic device. Precisely because critics were guided by the conception of the work of art as perfectly designed, they were impelled to study the often hidden ways in which such works hang together. Elements that might at first look anomalous in a work proved on closer inspection to have a role to play in its overall aesthetic logic.

Aristotle's organic model of art is so useful that it even survived one of the great revolutions in criticism, the shift beginning in the late eighteenth century from Classic to Romantic aesthetics. However much the Romantics revolutionized our conception of artistic form, they still maintained that it is organic in nature. In fact, they tended to make their argument against Classic conceptions of form by insisting that they are mechanical and only the new, Romantic conceptions are genuinely organic.[8] The Romantics opened up the concept of the organic unity of art, allowing for more complex forms of unification and for more heterogeneous elements to be unified, but they still remained true to the Aristotelian ideal of the artwork as perfectly designed. The difference is that the Romantics introduced the idea of artistic genius. The artwork takes organic form not because artists follow patterns inherent in the nature of the genre (as in the Aristotelian tradition), but because artistic geniuses shatter old models that have become mechanical and create new forms that restore life to their art.[9]

The Romantic reconception of organic form was developed in Germany and reached England chiefly in the writings of Samuel Taylor Coleridge, which were in many cases derived—even plagiarized—from German thinkers such as Friedrich Wilhelm Joseph Schelling and the Schlegel brothers.[10] Coleridge did much to establish the organic model of poetry in particular and art in general in the English-speaking world and was especially influential on the development of one of its chief incarnations in twentieth-century aesthetics, the New Criticism.[11] Our tendency to think of organic form in poetry as our model of art in general is largely the result of the way the New Criticism dominated American academics in the 1950s and '60s. The New Critics did not simply take lyric poetry as their model of art; more specifically, they operated with a certain kind of poetry in mind—the modernist lyric of T. S. Eliot and Yeats. They came to read not just all poetry but eventually drama and fiction as well on the model of works such as "The Love Song of J. Alfred Prufrock" or "Sailing to Byzantium."[12] It is remarkable how many genuine insights the New Critics were able to produce even though they were generalizing from a small sample of what actually constitutes literature. But the very specific nature of their model of artistic form leads to misperceptions when one tries to apply it to the realm of popular culture.

This is especially true because the New Criticism and the Romantic/modernist aesthetic out of which it grew were biased against popular culture from the start. In fact, both Romantic and modernist aesthetics defined themselves in opposition to popular culture. The very idea of a split between elite culture and popular culture is basically an invention of the late eighteenth and early nineteenth centuries.[13] Given economic, social, and political developments in the late eighteenth century, the Romantic generation was the first group of artists to confront mass commercial culture in the modern sense.[14] The Romantics found themselves competing in a newly developed cultural marketplace in which commercial success was replacing aristocratic and ecclesiastical patronage as the chief support for the arts. The Romantics' ideal of organic form became a weapon in their struggle with their competitors in the cultural marketplace. The Romantics identified organic form with what they now defined as elite or true culture and cordoned off a lower realm of popular or mass culture, which fails to measure up to the exalted standard of organic form. As Alvin Kernan formulates their position: "Isolated from society, exiled from and hostile to the world of industrial capitalism, they have spoken in poetry the truth and beauty known only to the imagination, defended the authentic human self with its ancient ways of thinking and feeling against science and crude utilitarianism, and created perfect works of art, organic in structure, crystalline in form."[15] Whereas the Romantics as geniuses could remain true to the purity of their inspiration and achieve perfection of organic design in their creations, they deemed the products of commercial culture imperfect because they are artistically impure.[16] Motives other than the purely aesthetic supposedly corrupt works of art produced for commercial markets. This Romantic attitude linked up with the idea of the autonomy of art developed by Kant in his *Critique of Judgment*. The Romantics claimed that true art could be produced only by the artistic genius operating in total independence and splendid isolation. Artists have to be relieved from the demands of the commercial world in order to be free to pursue their artistic vision and produce works that will be completely faithful to their own design and hence genuinely organic in form.[17]

If, however, artists are forced to work with commercial success as their motive, their vision will inevitably be compromised. They will have to introduce elements into their art to please others rather than themselves, and thereby corrupt the organic purity of their creations. The thrust of Romantic aesthetics is evident in the way that nineteenth-century critics tended to look down on the novel as a popular form, thinking it hardly a form of literature at all.[18] Created with a commercial market in mind, the novel was not viewed as authentic art, but rather as an impure form, filled with aesthetically extraneous elements whose only function is to please the public and sell copies. According to Romantic aesthetics, in a poem every word has an artistic function to perform in the work as a whole, but in a novel, many words are there simply because the novelist is being paid by the word.

In short, an anticommercial bias was built into the Romantic aesthetic from the start. Thus it is hardly surprising that when we apply a late form of that aesthetic, the New Criticism, to popular culture it looks suspect as an artistic realm. The Romantic heritage in our aesthetics has prejudiced us against popular culture. We assume that only if artists are given complete autonomy will they be able to achieve anything great. Unity of design demands a single designer, who out of his or her own inner depths molds the material into pure organic form. Accordingly, many of the institutions in our culture today are designed to shield artists from external pressures, particularly commercial ones. This is especially true of universities, foundations, and government granting agencies, which pride themselves on providing artists with financial support and thus freeing them from any need to please the public.[19] Supposedly this freedom will make their art better.

This glance at the historical development of our aesthetic assumptions helps clarify what is at stake in the debate over popular culture. When we find that the conditions of production in television are not the same as those in writing poetry, we assume that this is a bad situation and will make television less of an art form than poetry, perhaps not an art form at all. It is the Romantic ideal of the solitary genius that makes us wary of multiple authorship in television writing. We are also put off by all the elements of contingency involved in television production. We think that great works of art must be carefully planned in advance and are suspicious of any work improvised on the spur of the moment. And we are right to have these suspicions. Much of the greatest art was produced by individual geniuses who worked according to the Romantic aesthetic with an organic view of form in mind. Many great artists have complained about interference with their aesthetic autonomy and have become bitter when commercial demands intruded into what they hoped would be the self-contained world of their art.[20] This attitude prevails even in the realm of television. In researching *Gilligan Unbound*, I noted how frequently television producers railed against network executives who had interfered in the production process.[21] Like all artists, television producers crave a free hand to create their shows as they see fit. They do not want network executives or censors or sponsors telling them how to do their job, and they view outside interference as a source of corruption in their work. In many cases they are justified in this view. Network executives often fail to understand what television creators are trying to do, and shows would have been ruined if producers had not stood their ground and maintained their integrity as artists in the Romantic tradition. If the most creative talent in television distrusts conditions in the medium, surely critics trained in traditional elite culture can feel justified in their doubts about it. Certainly television produces enough trash programming every year to make anyone with taste wonder if there is not something inherently inartistic about the medium.

Yet I keep coming back to the fact that somehow television manages to produce works of genuine artistic quality. Which shows are authentic masterpieces is a matter of dispute—we are still in the comparatively early stages of television and hence are still sorting out its canon. But most people who take television seriously are willing to offer examples of what they think are its great shows. Since these shows are exceptional in quality, one might argue that their genesis must have been exceptional—that only when certain producers succeed in getting networks to respect their autonomy as creators does genuine quality television result. But the facts do not support this view. The shows people regard as the masterpieces of television were by and large produced according to the general rules of the medium. Although the most creative producers have repeatedly stood their ground against interference with their artistic integrity, they have also known when to yield to pressures from outside forces, commercial or otherwise. There is no simple correlation between the independence of television producers and the artistic quality of their shows. Producers with a relatively free hand have come up with artistic failures, while some of the best shows have been produced under the greatest commercial pressures.

Thus, although the ideal of the autonomy of art may be responsible for some of the greatest masterpieces in other media, television does not seem to offer evidence for its validity. This is reason to question not the ideal of the autonomy of art, but only the range of its applicability. It would in fact be surprising if all great art were produced according to the same formula. Thus far, when talking about the distinctive production process in television, we have been implying that insofar as it is distinctive, it has a negative effect on what is produced. But perhaps there is something in the process that is positive, that actually contributes to the artistic quality of the resulting product.

In Praise of Multiple Authorship and Improvisation

Consider the issue of multiple authorship in television. It is certainly true that too many cooks can spoil the broth, in art as well as life. The result of continually rewriting scripts is often to make them bland, to take out any originality and assimilate them to familiar patterns. But there is no reason why several minds coming together to write a script could not in some cases improve the final product. Different writers may bring different talents and strengths to the task and help to provide inspiration and encouragement to the others on the team. No writer—not even Shakespeare—is so great that he or she never makes mistakes and cannot benefit from some criticism and correction. Many television writers, far from wishing to be left alone, speak positively about script conferences and look forward to continual feedback on their work. The writers of *The X-Files,* for example, say how helpful Chris Carter, the creator-producer of the show, was to them in refining their original script ideas and making them work in the context of the series.[22] Upholders of the autonomy of art insist that in creation the individual art-ist knows it all and does it all. But this is not always true, even in the most rarefied realms of elite culture. Multiple authorship is not as uncommon in serious literature as the Romantic aesthetic would lead us to believe.[23] I am not just thinking of famous teams of authors, such as the English Renais-sance dramatists Francis Beaumont and John Fletcher. Multiple authorship was quite common in English Renaissance drama—another parallel between Shakespeare's medium and television.[24] From what we know of the rewrit-ing of plays such as Christopher Marlowe's *Doctor Faustus,* it seems that the Elizabethan Age even had its own script doctors.[25] Shakespeare himself may have served as one—we see his hand at work at a few points in a play called *The Book of Sir Thomas More*—and indeed, in the only dramatic passage we may have in Shakespeare's own handwriting, he is to our eternal frustration evidently working on somebody else's play.[26]

Even in the very bastion of the Romantic aesthetic—the writing of Romantic lyrics—artistic collaboration is not unknown. Wordsworth and Coleridge are among our models of the Romantic solitary genius, and yet they worked together on the volume of poetry that made them both famous, *Lyrical Ballads.* Although today each of the poems in this volume is credited to one author or the other, their handiwork was not distinguished in the original edition, and we now know that some of the poems were in effect joint productions—that some of the lines in the poems credited to Word-sworth were in fact written by Coleridge and vice versa.[27] Wordsworth and Coleridge were constantly commenting on each other's work and willing to take advice from each other, much to the benefit of the published work. Perhaps the most famous modernist poem is *The Waste Land,* which is, of course, ascribed to T. S. Eliot. But publication of the original manuscript has revealed that Ezra Pound's editing played such a role in the finished form the poem took that he might as well be credited as coauthor.[28] The degree to which Eliot was willing to accept Pound's editorial suggestions seems incredible to us, raised as we are on the Romantic aesthetic. Yet we must also admit that much of what we think of as the distinctively modernist character of *The Waste Land* results from Pound's efforts to edit the text down from Eliot's original inspiration.

Some might object that these are cases of solitary geniuses working together, and thus are quite different from the kind of collaboration characteristic of television, which often more closely resembles the case of a writer working with a commercial editor rather than a fellow artist. But even in this case, studies have shown that editors at commercial publishing houses have sometimes played an important role in the shaping of literary masterpieces. One of the most famous editorial collaborations in American literature involved novelist Thomas Wolfe and his editor, Maxwell Perkins of Charles Scribner's Sons. As Jack Stillinger writes: "Perkins's most publicized accomplishment . . . was the virtual creation of *Look Homeward, Angel* (1929) and *Of Time and the River* (1935) out of huge masses of manuscript that Wolfe had brought him in despair."[29] Thus, in considering multiple authorship we cannot draw a sharp line between elite culture and popular culture. And although multiple authorship may introduce contradictions into a work of art or result in a kind of "lowest common denominator" effect, it may instead, through the benefits of synergy or feedback, improve the ultimate product. The demands of the marketplace, far from always ruining literary works, have in many cases improved them. Commercial pressures can exercise a disciplining effect on artists, if only by forcing them to finish a work by a certain date or to keep it at a reasonable length. The record of art produced with foundation or government grants does not offer convincing evidence that being released from having to please the public is a sure path to greatness for an artist.[30] Thus, the fact that a popular medium such as television does not afford complete autonomy to individual artists is not an effective argument against it.

Rethinking the issue of contingency in television production leads to a similar conclusion. When we see producers scrambling to finish shows by a deadline, rewriting scenes up until the last possible moment, and jerryrigging special effects, it is hard for us to believe that what they are creating can be genuine art. This is especially true because of the way critics tend to approach artworks. They generally look to uncover a plan in the work, a pattern by which it is structured, and they assume that the artist had this plan fully elaborated before constructing it. What the critic discovers retrospectively, the artist must have divined prospectively.[31] It is natural for such critics to question the artistic potential of television as a medium when it does not seem to allow for this kind of advance planning.

But, once again, our knowledge of elite culture does not support this critique of popular culture. To be sure, we know many cases of artists who did in fact plan out their masterpieces well in advance, sometimes down to the smallest details. But for every example of the advantages of advance planning in the arts, we can find counterexamples of the advantages of improvisation. Many great literary masterpieces have been produced with deadlines fast approaching and the authors desperately struggling to finish them in the quickest way possible. Some artists seem to need the pressure of deadlines to produce their best work.[32] Some arts have incorporated improvisation as one of their fundamental principles. Think of the importance of improvisation in the careers of such musical geniuses as J. S. Bach, Mozart, and Beethoven. In short, many creators in the realms of elite culture have had to come to terms with an element of contingency in their art and have even learned to turn it to their advantage. Consider, for example, the role of the found object in surrealism.[33]

Slavic scholar Gary Saul Morson has argued that some authors have even made contingency the fundamental principle of their literary art—chiefly, in his view, Fyodor Dostoevsky and Leo Tolstoy. He shows that Dostoevsky, for example, allowed breaking stories in newspapers to alter the plot lines of a novel in the course of serial publication: "In *The Idiot,* real crime reports that first appeared between installments are read by the characters, who seem to be following the press along with the readers and the author. These real crimes shape characters' imagination, discussion, and future actions. Because those crimes took place after some sections of the work had appeared [in print], the reader recognizes that they *could not* have been part of an original plan, and that forces outside the author's control shape his work as it goes along."[34] This case is analogous to the way television shows often incorporate references to contemporary events at the last minute.[35] Morson shows that Dostoevsky deliberately created open-ended narratives, in which he himself did not know in advance in which direction the story was headed.[36] He in effect left the course of the action up to his characters, waiting until the last minute to see what decisions they would make and thus shape the outcome of the story. Morson argues that contingency becomes an aesthetic value in the novels of Dostoevsky; the open-ended narrative is a way of celebrating the reality of human freedom.

Thus, dealing with elements of contingency turns out to be something popular culture has in common with many forms of elite culture. It may be possible to eliminate all elements of chance from a brief lyric poem, but it is much more difficult to do so in a long novel. Some novelists have failed to catch minor changes in their works when typesetters accidentally introduced them in the printing process.[37] The larger the work, the more likely it will admit imperfections by the rigorous standards of tight, poetic form. But, for critics such as Morson, what looks like imperfection from the perspective of the Romantic aesthetic of organic form may be a higher kind of perfection according to a different aesthetic. The famous bagginess of the novel, which makes it seem loosely organized and even shapeless by comparison with lyric poetry, can also be viewed as a virtue and may be related to the novel's greater realism and, above all, its ability to capture a wider range of ordinary human experience. Insofar as contingency is an important element of human life, any form of art that strives to eliminate it risks becoming untrue to the way we actually experience our existence.[38]

The Feedback Model

Recognizing that contingency is an inevitable component of both life and art, many artists, even in elite culture, choose not to sketch out their plans in advance and prefer to develop them as they go along—to try a variety of possibilities and see what works and what does not. The alternative to a "perfect plan" model of artistic creation is a "feedback" model, in which the imperfections of a work of art are gradually corrected in a process of trial and error (or, according to Morson, sometimes even left in place to achieve a variety of effects). The feedback model is far more common in elite culture than the Romantic aesthetic would lead us to believe. Many artists crave contact with their audience precisely because of the valuable feedback it can supply.[39] Sometimes the audience is able to judge when artists are doing their best work more easily than they themselves can. For this reason, the way contemporary artists are shielded by institutional grants from the need to please an audience may actually have a deleterious effect on their art. Being free of the public's demands may be every artist's dream, but it can easily turn into a nightmare of aesthetic isolation, cut off from all sources of guidance and legitimate criticism, and perhaps even from the ultimate source of artistic inspiration itself.[40] There are many cases of artists who did their best work when they still felt a need to cater to their audience, and lost their way artistically when they began to feel that pleasing the public was beneath their dignity as autonomous geniuses.

If feedback from an audience is actually valuable to artists, popular culture has certain advantages over elite culture. In particular, many aspects of the production process in television that look dubious from the viewpoint of the Romantic aesthetic may turn out to work to the benefit of those who labor in the medium. What from one angle looks like harmful interference with the integrity of the artist in television from another angle looks like helpful feedback. Not all the advice from network executives is wrongheaded. Although their primary consideration may be the infamous bottom line, their very concern with audience reaction may sometimes lead them to suggest ways of genuinely improving programs. In my research on *Gilligan Unbound,* I was struck by the way successful television producers actively seek out feedback from all sources and look to it for guidance.

In the case of *The X-Files,* the producers discovered a new feedback mechanism: the Internet. They carefully monitored the many websites that had sprung up to discuss and celebrate the show and learned a great deal in the process. For example, in a first-season episode entitled "E.B.E." *The X-Files* introduced a new set of characters called the Lone Gunmen (Bruce Harwood, Tom Braidwood, and Dean Haglund)—three paranoid conspiracy theorists and computer experts who help the hero of the show, Fox Mulder (David Duchovny), in his struggle against the government. Glen Morgan and James Wong, the writers who thought up these quirky characters, felt that they were a failure and were ready to drop them from future episodes. But the Lone Gunmen caught on immediately with one of the core segments of the *X-Files* audience. As technological nerds, these characters appealed to precisely the fans who were among the first to take advantage of the Internet. Because of the popularity of the Lone Gunmen as judged by the *X-Files* websites, the producers decided to bring the characters back.[41] If the rest is not exactly television history, the quirkiness of the Lone Gunmen certainly contributed something to *The X-Files,* especially an element of humor that helped lighten the prevailing dark mood of the show. Somehow the show's audience, or a segment of it, was better able than the producers to sense the long-term contribution these characters might make to the series. The Romantic aesthetic tells us that giving in to audience demands can only corrupt an artist's vision. But the customer may occasionally be right, and artists who listen to their audience may learn to improve their art.[42]

As this example from the history of *The X-Files* reminds us, unlike many forms of art, a television series cannot be created all at once, but must of necessity be produced over long stretches of time—weeks at first, but over years if the series is successful. This is one reason that the television series does not fit the "perfect plan" model of artistic creation. But it is very well suited to the feedback model. Creating episode after episode, and unable to go back and alter earlier efforts in light of subsequent developments, television producers often find themselves in the embarrassing position of having introduced lapses in continuity into their shows, if not outright contradictions.[43] A devoted fan may have fun pointing out such inconsistencies, but they mark television shows as failures according to the strict demands of coherence imposed by the organic model of poetic form. But what a television series loses in coherence over the years it gains in its ability to experiment with new possibilities and discover ways to improve the show and expand its range. As the case of the Lone Gunmen in *The X-Files* demonstrates, in its long run a successful television series will often introduce new characters and see which ones click with its audience. Characters who prove to be unpopular will be dropped, and characters who are popular will see their roles expanded.[44] Although the addition of a popular character may not always improve a show artistically, it often does, and can sometimes revitalize the whole series.

Maintaining a strict division between elite and popular culture again proves impossible in the case of the serial character of much television production. Television did not invent the mode of serial production. It goes all the way back to the eighteenth century, when novels were first published in installments. This method of producing novels reached its peak in the Victorian era, when Charles Dickens led the way in making the serial novel the most popular and financially rewarding form of entertainment in England.[45] The novels we now study reverently in universities as masterpieces of fiction and, hence, elite culture were at the time of their creation serially produced and consumed, much like the weekly installments of shows on television today. We can observe the same feedback process at work in the Victorian novel. Novelists often killed off or otherwise disposed of characters who were proving unpopular with their audience and devoted more pages to those who were evidently increasing weekly or monthly sales.[46] Jennifer Hayward has argued that the serial in its many incarnations—the serialized novel, the comic strip, the movie serial with its cliff-hanger endings, the radio soap opera, the television soap opera and other forms of serialized television—is the distinctive form of modern culture.[47] The fact that serial production, by allowing for all sorts of audience feedback, facilitates communication between artists and their public may go a long way toward explaining the form's popularity.[48] Serially produced works will usually be looser in form and fail to achieve the level of artistic coherence possible in lyric poetry, but on the positive side they can be more experimental and pursue a wider range of possibilities in terms of both form and content. This is true whether one compares a Victorian novel or a television series with a lyric poem.[49] Observing the similarities in the way serial production functions in the nineteenth-century novel and in contemporary television is a good way of seeing how much elite culture and popular culture have in common.

Creationism versus Evolutionism

To place my argument about popular culture in a larger context, I want to examine briefly the broader implications of the contrast I have been drawing between the "perfect plan" model of artistic creation and the feedback model. The "perfect plan" model has its deepest roots in Western theology and the teleological understanding of the universe to which it is related. To think of artists planning out their works perfectly and in advance is to think of them on the model of God creating the universe, especially as understood in Christianity. According to this view, for any kind of meaningful structure to come into being and function, it must be the work of a single designer, who can bring all its elements into harmony. This way of understanding the world long dominated thought in a wide variety of areas. It seems natural to human beings to trace order anywhere they find it to some kind of single master planner, someone who brings the field into order in the first place.[50] In politics, this way of thinking produced the theoretical support for monarchy—the claim that a country is ruled best when a single authority is in place to give it order. In economics, this way of thinking leads to the belief that the government must intervene to introduce order into the marketplace—to set prices, for example, or, more generally, to impose restrictions on commerce in order to make the common good prevail. In biology, this way of thinking leads to what is called creationism, the idea that the perfection of form we observe in biological phenomena can be explained only as the work of a single divine creator. To borrow a term from economics, all these approaches to understanding order celebrate the virtues of central planning. They offer top-down models of order. Given the prevalence of this kind of thinking, it is understandable that it came to dominate aesthetics; the traditional idea of organic form in poetry is another way of celebrating central planning as the only route to order. As long as people thought that only a single, divine creator could be responsible for the order we see in the biological realm, it was logical to view order in the aesthetic realm as having a similar origin.[51] The ideal of central planning is actually more plausible in aesthetics than in any other realm. In poetry we can in fact observe poets at work and watch them achieve perfection of form as they carefully design their poems.

It is therefore not surprising that the central planning model of order survived in aesthetics long after it began to be challenged in other areas. Probably the most famous challenge to this way of thinking came in Charles Darwin's theory of natural selection. Darwin showed how the perfection we observe in the structure of animals and plants can be explained without recourse to the notion of a divine creator of that structure. His idea of natural selection is what we have been calling a feedback or bottom-up model of order. Evolution proceeds by what we now call random mutations, which lead to a proliferation of biological forms—experiments in life forms, as it were. In Darwin's view, the environment provides the feedback in this system, selecting out new forms that work and rejecting those that do not. If this sounds like my description of how a television series develops over time, with the audience accepting or rejecting innovations, that is just my point.[52] What looks anomalous from the viewpoint of traditional poetics fits the Darwinian model of how form can be perfected in a system that does not have a central planner, but instead evolves over time. Darwin provides a way of challenging traditional poetics by questioning its fundamental conception of organic form. Both Aristotelian and Romantic poetics stake their claims on the principle of organic form. But since Darwin we have come to understand that organic form need not be the result of conscious design or preplanning.

Franco Moretti and Gary Saul Morson have led the way in showing how Darwin's ideas can help us rethink our notion of literary form.[53] Drawing upon the work of Stephen Jay Gould, both have stressed how Darwin, as opposed to Aristotle, allows for an element of contingency in biological form.[54] The validity of Darwin's theory, in fact, hinges on our ability to find evidence of imperfection in biological form—elements of an organism that do not fulfill the Aristotelian criterion of being integral parts of the whole and that therefore do not appear to be the result of divine creation. The presence of vestigial organs in animals, for example, can be explained not by any theory of perfect design (since they, in fact, have no function), but only by reference to an animal's evolutionary history, and history is the realm of the contingent. As Gould writes:

Darwin invoked contingency in a fascinating way as his primary support for the fact of evolution itself. . . . One might think that the best evidence for evolution would reside in those exquisite examples of optimal adaptation presumably wrought by natural selection— the aerodynamic perfection of a feather or the flawless mimicry of insects that look like leaves or sticks. Such phenomena provide our standard textbook examples of evolutionary modification. . . . Yet Darwin recognized that perfection cannot provide evidence for evolution because optimality covers the tracks of history.

If feathers are perfect, they may as well have been designed from scratch by an omnipotent God as from previous anatomy by a natural process. Darwin recognized that the primary evidence for evolution must be sought in quirks, oddities, and imperfections that lay bare the pathways of history. Whales, with their vestigial pelvic bones, must have descended from terrestrial ancestors with functional legs. . . . If whales retained no trace of their terrestrial heritage, . . . then history would not inhere in the productions of nature. But contingencies of "just history" do shape our world, and evolution lies exposed in the panoply of structures that have no other explanation than the shadow of their past.[55]

If the biological realm allows for contingency of form, then, according to Moretti and Morson, literary form can admit contingent elements as well.

Darwin's revolution in how to conceive order was preceded by a revolution in economic thinking that we associate with Adam Smith and classical economics. Darwin himself admitted to having been influenced by classical economics in the person of Thomas Malthus, and in retrospect we can see that Malthus's theory of population was crucial to Darwin's understanding of natural selection.[56] Smith and his followers attacked central planning in its root economic form, the belief that only government intervention can achieve order in markets that would otherwise, if left to themselves, break down into chaos. Smith showed just the opposite—that markets are self-regulating and self-ordering, and it is government intervention that throws them out of balance and produces chaos. In Smith's analysis, the pricing mechanism of free markets produces the feedback that orders economic phenomena. Rising prices are a signal to producers to turn out more of a good, and falling prices are a signal to turn out less. The price mechanism thus works to bring supply into line with demand and thereby to make the market move toward equilibrium. When the government intervenes and tries artificially to raise or lower prices, it sends the wrong signals to producers, and that leads to surpluses or shortages in the market, which is to say, economic chaos.

Thus, in both Smith's economics and Darwin's biology, systems generate order from within themselves and on their own. In the traditional theological model of order, a force outside or above the system is necessary to intervene and introduce order into what would otherwise be chaos (the top-down model of order). In the Smith–Darwin model, a system becomes self-regulating through a feedback mechanism (the bottom-up model of order). Such a system does not achieve perfection all at once by an act of divine creation; rather, it is always striving toward perfection through a process of evolution—it is, in effect, self-perfecting rather than perfect. Austrian economist Friedrich Hayek has popularized the use of the term "spontaneous order" to describe this sort of system, and he did much to develop a general theory of spontaneous order, showing how the concept is applicable in a wide range of fields beyond economics and biology, from linguistics to law.[57] I have been trying to apply the concept of spontaneous order to popular culture. The realm of popular culture looks messy and disordered to us, and we have a hard time understanding how any kind of artistic form could emerge out of this apparent chaos. The idea of spontaneous order always seems counterintuitive to us; as human beings, we are evidently conditioned to attribute order to an individual who orders it. That is why the ideas of both Smith and Darwin (not to mention Hayek) encountered so much initial resistance and are rejected to this day by many people. But if one recognizes the various kinds of feedback mechanisms at work in popular culture, one begins to see how it can produce art out of chaos.

The Productions of Time

To return to my initial questions, if we find that authorship is as it were "corporate" rather than individual in television production, that does not rule out the serious study of television programs. As we have already seen, even in elite culture the concept of the single perfect author is perhaps best understood as a heuristic device. We may never encounter a work of literature actually produced entirely and perfectly by a single author, but it is useful to read literature and especially lyric poetry as if this were the case. We will find more in a literary work if we are looking for perfection in it. That is why the New Criticism, for all the dubious aspects of its theoretical foundations, proved to be fruitful in analyzing literature. Thus, when we turn to popular culture, even if we see that single authorship is not the norm of production, we can still "read" individual shows as if they had artistic integrity. This approach will help us to find whatever artistic merit they may in fact have.

In short, the typical critique of popular culture is a version of the genetic fallacy. By concentrating on how works of popular culture are produced, it prejudices us against taking the products seriously. But, as we have seen, in both elite culture and popular culture the genesis of a work does not necessarily tell us anything about its artistic quality. A work produced by a seemingly haphazard process may not turn out to be haphazard in form (by the same token, a perfectly planned work may turn out to be lifeless and dull). Instead of focusing on the original intentions of the creators in popular culture and worrying whether they have been carried out faithfully, we should dwell upon the intentionality of the finished product—whether in the end it has become, by whatever process, a work of art. We must beware of taking the perfectly unified lyric poem as our only model of aesthetic achievement. As studies of the novel increasingly reveal, a work of literature may embrace various forms of what would be regarded as imperfection in lyric poetry and still have aesthetic value. As Morson and Moretti have argued, novels may make those imperfections serve new artistic purposes. The same may be true of what are often considered to be the aesthetic shortcomings of popular culture. We should be careful about judging the new media of popular culture by the artistic standards of the older media of elite culture. We should instead be looking for the unprecedented aesthetic possibilities suddenly opened up whenever a new artistic medium comes along. In sum, we can take the artistic forms of popular culture seriously without assuming that they will conform to the norms of elite culture from the past. Indeed, the genuine excitement of studying popular culture may well be to discover the new conceptions of artistic form it is developing.

The spontaneous order model also helps us rethink our negative reaction when we encounter the element of contingency in television production.[58] We have begun to realize that to eliminate all contingency from art might well be to take the life out of it—especially now that Darwin has given us a concept of biological form that incorporates contingency, rather than banishing it, as the Aristotelian tradition tried to do. Another way of saying that television production inevitably involves an element of contingency is to say that it inevitably takes place over time, sometimes long periods of time.[59] In the model of a divine moment of perfect creation, time is seen as the great corrupting force. The world is perfect at the moment of creation and can only degenerate thereafter. A similar view is embodied in the idea of the moment of perfect poetic creation. Poets' visions are purest at the instant of inspiration, and any efforts to work out their original ideas over time and embody their visions in material form only lead them away from the initial perfection.[60] In the spontaneous order model, time is the friend rather than the enemy of creation. In both Adam Smith and Darwin, systems perfect themselves over time; and, on a smaller scale, the same process can be observed in the evolution of a television series. Rome was not built in a day, and neither was *The X-Files*.

None of this is to say that the conditions of television production *guarantee* high artistic quality and the automatic evolution of every show to perfection by its sixth or seventh season. Obviously from what we observe on television, something closer to the opposite seems to be the case. All I am claiming is that the typical conditions of television production do not simply *preclude* artistic quality, as some critics of the medium have argued.[61] As Hayward writes:

> The ability to alter narratives in response to the success or failure of subplots or characters is seen as negative because we have constructed ideologies of the "true" artist and writer as governed only by individual genius and never by the demands of the marketplace. . . . There is no inherent flaw in a kind of "just in time" production of stories; neither does this method preclude the inspiration of creative genius. Instead, both market forces and artistic gifts can work together to produce texts crafted by an individual or creative team but flexible enough to respond to good and relevant ideas from outside, whether in the form of audience response, news events, or other sources.[62]

We have seen some of the ways in which the various feedback mechanisms in television production can help to improve the quality of shows, but that still requires the talent of a creative producer to take advantage of the circumstances.[63] Because that talent is rare (although perhaps no rarer in popular culture than in elite culture), the overall level of aesthetic quality of television programs may remain low even while oases of genuine art spring up from time to time in the vast television wasteland.[64]

My main goal has been to identify and try to overcome the prejudices we have inherited from the tradition of Romantic aesthetics. This tradition has been anticommercial since its inception; the Romantics were the first to set up the autonomous creative genius in opposition to the vulgarity of the marketplace. In trying to rethink our view of popular culture, I have drawn upon the idea of spontaneous order, particularly because in its economic form it shows that commerce can be an ordering and, indeed, a creative force. The ultimate objection to popular culture is that it is commercial culture, and in the Romantic tradition commerce and culture are viewed as incompatible. But once we begin to think of popular culture—and perhaps culture in general—as a form of spontaneous order, we can begin to understand how commerce and culture can work together for their mutual benefit.[65] To put the matter in the most unromantic terms possible: just because a television show is a commercial success does not mean that it is an artistic failure.

Part One

FREEDOM AND ORDER IN THE WESTERN

Introduction to Part One

Anyone dealing with the subject of freedom in American popular culture has to come to terms with the Western. No genre is more closely associated with the celebration of freedom, and yet no genre does more to portray it as problematic. In the American imagination, the Western frontier has always been the place to which people go to achieve freedom and escape the shackles of society. Accordingly, the Western as a genre has traditionally been associated with the American spirit of rugged individualism. The Western hero is typically a loner, standing apart from the crowd, sometimes because of something shady in his past, sometimes because of his peculiar sense of mission, sometimes just because of his heroic virtue itself. The hero is frequently paired with a mirror image in the form of a villain, who equally stands alone, sometimes for unnervingly similar reasons. The fact that the line between the hero and the villain is sometimes difficult to draw in Westerns, at least in the more sophisticated ones, is a good indication that the genre does not simply celebrate freedom and individualism, but presents both concepts as deeply problematic.

The hero's status as a lone wolf often brings him into conflict with the very society he claims to represent or defend. The taming of the frontier is one of the central themes of the American Western, and the wolf is not a tame animal. A common Western plot involves the domestication of the hero, to make him fit into a community of less violent—and less heroic—people. Westerns frequently turn on the tension between freedom and order, between the individual and the community. The history of the Western is testimony to the fact that freedom has always been viewed as a challenge in America, something that cannot be achieved without great effort and great cost.

Critics often look down on the Western, regarding it as the prime example of pop culture at its worst, a form of crude and mindless entertainment. The movie and television industries have turned out thousands of Westerns over the years, and have necessarily relied on formulas and clichés in order to do so. Faced with the results, a critic can easily fall into the trap of saying that all Westerns look alike; that they endlessly recycle the same old material; and consequently that they have no aesthetic or intellectual value. This may well be true of the majority of Westerns; but, according to Aristotle's principle that the nature of a thing is the perfection of the thing, we should never judge a genre by its average specimens alone, but ultimately by its best. The Western has certainly had a checkered history, and its low points undoubtedly outnumber its high points—by a considerable margin. And yet no one can deny that the Western has had its high points, and, after a century of effort, the genre can boast of a significant number of masterpieces in its ranks, or at least genuine works of art.

Much can be learned from an extensive overview of the Western as a pop culture form; it is, for example, fascinating to trace the complex ways in which Westerns over the years have mirrored larger developments in American society. But much can be learned from an intensive approach to a genre as well; it allows for the kind of close reading and detailed interpretation that genuine works of art deserve. In this part, I concentrate on three well-known examples of the Western that I believe epitomize its potential and the issues with which it characteristically deals.

My first choice hardly needs justification. John Ford is without question the greatest maker of Westerns, and *The Searchers* is arguably the greatest of all his Westerns (and, I would add, one of the greatest movies in any genre). By comparing *The Searchers* to Greek drama (the *Oresteia*), as well as Greek epic (the *Iliad* and the *Odyssey*), I subject it to the most stringent aesthetic test possible, and I hope that I succeed in showing that the film is worthy of being discussed in this august company. *The Searchers* shows why it is inadvisable to draw a sharp line between elite culture and pop culture, and especially why one should not do so according to medium (theater versus film). We can learn a great deal by studying *The Searchers* and the *Oresteia* together. Ford's film helps to translate the issues Aeschylus explores into terms more familiar to us, thereby making the Greek drama come alive for us and seem less remote from modern experience. By the same token, Aeschylus' drama—and the Greek heroic tradition it represents—helps lift *The Searchers* out of a specifically American historical context, thus highlighting the universality of the problems the film confronts. Above all, turning to figures such as Agamemnon, Orestes, Achilles, and Odysseus as models of heroism gives us a fresh perspective on Ford's Ethan Edwards, freeing us from the overly narrow viewpoint of middle-class morality and allowing us to understand this complex and disturbing figure in the larger context of the epic and tragic traditions to which he properly belongs. In both Ford and Aeschylus the dramatic conflict centers on a frontier—the archetypal frontier between civilization and barbarism. And although they both fall back on certain stereotypes of the barbarian (oddly similar, despite the huge differences between their two cultures), Ford and Aeschylus ultimately subvert these stereotypes in the course of exploring the tragic foundations of civilization. In *The Searchers,* the freedom of the frontier hero is ultimately at odds with the civil order he helps to establish and protect.

What *The Searchers* is to the movie Western, David Milch's *Deadwood* is to the television Western—the greatest example of the genre. At a time when the Western was thought to be dead and buried on television, Milch did not simply revive the genre; he carried it to a level of complexity and profundity no one thought possible. While drawing upon familiar Western characters and motifs—who is more stereotypical than Wild Bill Hickok or Calamity Jane?—he virtually reinvented the genre, with some of the most original writing in the history of television. Even on the level of language itself, he forged a new idiom for *Deadwood,* a unique form of dialogue that moves seamlessly between poetry and profanity. My test for *Deadwood* is to discuss the show in terms of some of the most profound philosophical issues, specifically the state-of-nature thinking of Hobbes, Locke, and Rousseau. And *Deadwood* passes this test of intellectual seriousness. Milch himself has said that he conceived of the show as exploring the perennial political issue of "order without law." I argue that the central concepts of Hobbes, Locke, and Rousseau help clarify Milch's take on the American West, while *Deadwood* provides concrete dramatic illustrations of the specific issues the European philosophers debated. As I sometimes do in this book, I try to bring out the libertarian threads in Milch's thinking, or at least an antigovernment strain that pervades *Deadwood.* Milch's search for a principle of order without law becomes an examination of the possibility of human beings living together in freedom, independent of the nation-state, developing means to harmonize their interests without the intervention of government.

As for my central subject in this part of the book, *Have Gun–Will Travel,* I would not claim that it deserves to be ranked with *The Searchers* or *Deadwood* in the history of the Western, either in terms of artistic quality or cultural significance. Nevertheless, many regard it as the most literate and intellectually sophisticated of the classic TV Westerns of the 1950s and 1960s. It was my own favorite among Westerns at the time, indeed one of my favorites of all television shows when I was growing up. As a precocious—and, to be honest, pretentious—intellectual in my adolescence, I loved the fact that the show's hero quoted Shakespeare and consorted with the likes of Oscar Wilde. But despite the veneer of elite culture that originally attracted me to the show, now that I am older and somewhat wiser, I do not believe that *Have Gun* can hold up to the kinds of comparison to which I subject *The Searchers* and *Deadwood*. Accordingly, my test for *Have Gun* is to compare it to something more on the ordinary pop culture level and yet with at least a modicum of intellectual cachet, namely *Star Trek*.

When I began rewatching *Have Gun* on DVD, I became aware of an aspect of the series that could not have interested me when it originally aired. The supplementary material on the DVDs highlights the fact that a significant number of the episodes were written by Gene Roddenberry, who went on to become the legendary creator of *Star Trek*. When I discovered this, I thought, "This would make an interesting subject for a pop culture essay," but did nothing about it. A few years later and much to my amazement, I received an invitation from Hillsdale College to participate in a March 2009 symposium on the TV Western, and I was asked to speak specifically on Roddenberry's work on *Have Gun* and its relation to *Star Trek*. To this day, I do not know how anybody at Hillsdale could have known that I was interested in this peculiar subject, but in any event I jumped at the opportunity.

Allowing the comparison of *Have Gun* and *Star Trek* to lead me wherever it would, I found myself pursuing a number of intriguing lines of investigation in the history of pop culture. The fact that Roddenberry's work on *Have Gun* turned out to have significantly influenced his conception of *Star Trek* became an object lesson in the collaborative nature of creativity in television. Moreover, moving between what are normally thought of as two very distinct genres—the Western and science fiction—led me to question whether our generic divisions of pop culture really are as hard and fast as we sometimes think. The Western is generally regarded as a backward-looking genre, rooted in the past and hence conservative or even reactionary in its politics. Science fiction, by contrast, is generally regarded as a forward-looking genre, oriented toward the future and hence progressive or even radical in its politics. Roddenberry's vision of a technologically advanced, peaceful, and culturally tolerant future in *Star Trek* is a perfect example of the liberal utopianism that often characterizes science fiction. After all, the genre was popularized by a socialist—H. G. Wells. And yet my studies suggested that the science fiction world of *Star Trek* actually grew out of Roddenberry's work on the Western *Have Gun–Will Travel*.

My study of *Have Gun,* as well as my participation in the Hillsdale symposium, led me to reconsider my conventional assumption that the Western is conservative by nature. Upon reflection, I believe that our understanding of the politics of the Western has been unduly influenced and distorted by the fact that the two most famous stars of the genre—John Wayne and Clint Eastwood—have been associated in the public's mind with conservative causes. In actuality, the Western over the years has been open to all sorts of political viewpoints, many of them progressive and even left-wing. Although John Ford became increasingly conservative on foreign policy issues in his later years, for much of his career he can best be described as a New Deal Democrat, as epitomized by his film of John Steinbeck's *The Grapes of Wrath* or, for that matter, *Stagecoach,* with its nasty portrait of a criminal banker.

Viewing a wide variety of TV Westerns from the 1950s at the Hillsdale symposium, we were surprised by how seldom they fit the stereotype we had of the shoot-'em-up horse opera. In *The Rifleman,* for example, the single father raising his son on the violent frontier was constantly teaching the boy lessons in toleration and forbearance. In one episode, the Rifleman hires a crippled man on his ranch after his son shows signs of repugnance at the man's grotesque appearance, to condition the boy to accept strangers who look different. We were shocked to behold the degree of political correctness already at work in what we unthinkingly looked back upon as the Dark Ages of the TV Western. I found this impression strongly reinforced the more I studied *Have Gun.* The series fully anticipates the kind of Kennedy liberalism that Roddenberry went on to embody in *Star Trek. Have Gun* suggests that a progressive elite is necessary to counter the baleful effects of prejudice, bigotry, and other dark forces that dominate an unenlightened American heartland.

In each of the chapters in this part of the book, I pair a Western with something that is not a Western. My aim is to take the Western out of the trash-culture ghetto to which it is too often consigned. We sometimes become so obsessed with the Western as a genre that we see only its generic aspects and lose sight of subtle distinctions and its connections to broader cultural contexts. We need to be reminded that, at their best, Westerns tell basic human stories and explore fundamental human problems. And, although I discuss only three examples of the Western, I offer them as evidence of the wide range of political possibilities in the genre. *The Searchers* offers an unforgettable image of the rugged individualism of the lone hero, and yet ultimately calls this ideal into question, showing its tragic incompatibility with the progressive civilization he seeks to defend. *Have Gun–Will*

Travel also presents a rugged individual as its hero, but insists even more on his role as a defender of the weak, the oppressed, and the downtrodden. It suggests that a strong man is necessary to bring order to society, which in the absence of central control will degenerate into various forms of conflict and exploitation. By contrast, *Deadwood* is profoundly suspicious of elites who try to impose order on society from the top down. It explores the spontaneous impulses to order that emerge in ordinary human interaction, especially those involving commercial activity. The three Westerns I discuss are very different, and yet they are united in portraying the problematic nature of freedom on the American frontier.

1

THE WESTERN AND WESTERN DRAMA

John Ford's *The Searchers* and the *Oresteia*

> A wanderer, a fugitive
> driven off his native land, he will come home
> to cope the stones of hate that menace all he loves.
> —Aeschylus, *Agamemnon*

> your murdered kinsmen
> pleading for revenge. And the madness haunts
> the midnight watch, the empty terror shakes you,
> harries, drives you on—an exile from your city.
> —Aeschylus, *The Libation Bearers*

When critics praise John Ford's *The Searchers* (1956), they frequently reach for the words *epic* and *tragic* to describe it.[1] In the documentary that accompanies the film in the DVD Ultimate Collector's Edition, director John Milius says of Ford: "He's a storyteller, like Homer."[2] Critics rightly sense an affinity between the film and the literature of classical antiquity. They suggest that Ford is working on a Homeric scale, and captures the spirit of Greek tragedy in the way he shapes his characters' encounters with elemental forces and a cruel destiny. But few have systematically compared *The Searchers* with a particular ancient epic or tragedy.[3] I will use a detailed comparison with Aeschylus' *Oresteia* to bring out the thematic core of Ford's film. If *The Searchers* is a tragedy, it is specifically a tragedy of *revenge*, fundamentally the story of how its hero, Ethan Edwards (John Wayne), implacably pursues the Indian tribe that nearly wiped out his brother's family and kidnapped his niece, Debbie (Natalie Wood). As a revenge tragedy, the film has a venerable pedigree that includes many literary masterpieces, not the least of which is *Hamlet*. But to understand Ford's greatest Western, we can learn the most by going back to the very origin of Western drama and the earliest known revenge tragedy, Aeschylus' sole surviving trilogy, consisting of *Agamemnon, The Libation Bearers,* and *The Eumenides*. One advantage of viewing *The Searchers* against the background of Greek tragedy is that it allows us to move beyond the simplistic good guy–bad guy opposition of the conventional Western and view Ethan Edwards as a genuinely tragic hero, with all the moral complexity that implies.

Revenge Tragedy

Revenge is a perennially popular subject in both epic and tragedy. It is at the core of the earliest masterpiece of Western literature, the *Iliad*,[4] and can still be found in innumerable motion picture and television dramas today. Why is revenge so prevalent as a subject for drama? The pursuit of vengeance obviously provides the basis for an action-packed plot, but, more importantly, it raises serious issues of a particularly dramatic—and tragic—nature. Revenge is ultimately a *political* subject, or rather it allows an author to stage a confrontation between the prepolitical and the political, and thereby helps reveal the origin of politics as well as its limits.

Both the *Oresteia* and *The Searchers* focus on the story of a single family and how it generates the demand for vengeance, how it plunges the people involved into a potentially unending cycle of revenge. Revenge and the family are inextricably bound together in human history. As both the *Oresteia* and *The Searchers* show, the fundamental obligation of vengeance is to right a wrong against a kinsman (or kinswoman). Revenge is rooted in the historical moment when the family—or at most the extended family, the clan—was the basic unit of social organization. When families must rely on their own members to protect them, revenge assumes paramount importance as an ethical imperative. If you can reach for a phone to call the police, you no longer have to reach for a sword or a gun to right a wrong against your family. That is why the revenge ethic is characteristic of prepolitical situations and appears so often in the foundational literature of archaic peoples, from the Homeric epics to the Icelandic sagas, which generally chronicle heroes who have to make their own justice and become a law unto themselves. The issue of revenge takes us right to the heart of the difference between political and prepolitical association.

Very few of us today would react to the murder of a loved one by saying, "I have to go out and kill the person who did that with my own bare hands." The reason is that we have almost all been brought up to leave such matters to the law. We have been taught that to live in society is to accept the principle of civic justice. We have a legal system in place that is supposed to deal with crimes like murder. The police are supposed to arrest murderers, prosecutors are supposed to bring them to justice, the courts are supposed to convict and sentence them, and the prisons are supposed to punish them, perhaps even to execute them. Our very notion of being civilized has become bound up with the need to renounce revenge. We think of the cult of vengeance as characteristic of primitive societies; the impulse to take revenge seems positively atavistic in the contemporary world. For revenge, we might look to the blood feuds in the backlands of undeveloped countries or to the vendettas among criminals and mobsters in the underworld of our own society.

In short, in the modern political world, where legal institutions have been fully developed and are firmly in place, revenge seems like a throwback to the distant past. Why, then, are we still so interested in the subject that it continues to fill our movie and television screens? How was Ford able to create one of the great revenge tragedies of all time as recently as 1956? The answer seems to be that our sophisticated legal system can provide us with *civic* justice, but it cannot provide us with *poetic* justice, and we sense the gap between the two. The very notion of poetic justice points to the potential inadequacies of civic or legal justice; poetry must make up for the deficiencies of politics. The issue of revenge is one of the many areas where we have paid a price for the civilization we have embraced in order to avoid bloodshed and social chaos.[5] We have to renounce and suppress an impulse that is evidently deeply ingrained in human nature, or at least in human culture, and difficult to eradicate—the desire for swift, direct, and personal vengeance. To have an impersonal legal system deal with a crime against kinfolk may fail to satisfy the emotional needs of the injured parties. That is why even today we often hear of family members complaining bitterly about the procedural delays, the plea bargaining, the reduced sentences, the appeals, the pardons, and all the other compromises inevitably involved in the operation of any legal system.[6] Even in the most civilized society, aggrieved people will sometimes still demand an eye for an eye; they still want *blood*. It seems impossible to stifle completely the call for vengeance; it still lurks beneath the surface, even in our modern world with all its legal institutions. And if civilized society is no longer willing to satisfy this primal call for vengeance, literature and, more generally, the arts can recognize its force and acknowledge its claims in the symbolic form of stories and images.

That may be why we continue to use the phrase *poetic justice.*[7] Poets can still give us what civilized society denies us—images of a personal justice, a kind of elemental justice unmediated by modern legal institutions. Locked as we are into a world of impersonal justice, our culture, especially our popular culture, keeps offering us images of an old-style personal vengeance. Two of the most successful cinematic genres—the Western and the gangster movie—frequently focus on characters who take the law into their own hands or operate outside it, indulging their vengeful impulses often with great gusto, if not impunity. Perhaps the two greatest movies of all time, *Godfather I* and *II,* chronicle a grand cycle of revenge much as the *Oresteia* and *The Searchers* do. The revenge tragedy epitomizes the cathartic function of tragedy. By offering images of the kind of personal vengeance we have had to renounce in order to live in civilized society, revenge tragedy calls up and perhaps allows us to purge the powerful emotions we are continually forced to hold in check in our daily lives. Better to experience vicariously Charles Bronson acting out his vigilante impulses in the various *Death Wish* movies than to give vent to our own frustration in a world in which the police do not always do their job well. Over the centuries, the revenge tragedy has served as a kind of emotional safety value, allowing audiences to release in the safe and controlled environment of the theater the kind of emotions civilization requires them to suppress in real life for the sake of peace and social harmony.

But revenge tragedy can operate on an intellectual as well as an emotional level. In the hands of a great artist, it can help us think through the issue of revenge, which stands at the very foundation of political life. In the *Oresteia,* the polis, the political community, comes into being to end the cycle of family vengeance.[8] Revenge tragedies can pose anew for us and allow us to rethink *the* fundamental political question: the choice between a life of personal vengeance and a life of communal justice.[9] That may be the deepest ground of the dramatic power of the issue of revenge, and why time and again it proves to be a rich source of tragic subject matter. In Hegel's view, a tragic situation involves the conflict of two goods, one legitimate ethical principle clashing with another.[10] In such an ethical dilemma, the tragic hero has no way out without incurring guilt—no matter which course of action he chooses, he will violate one legitimate principle or another. Hegel's prototype of tragedy is Sophocles' *Antigone,* in which Antigone stands up for the principle of the family in her insistence on properly burying her brother Polyneices, while Creon stands up for the principle of the city in denying him burial as a traitor to Thebes.[11] Once both Antigone and Creon commit to their principles with stubborn integrity, a tragic outcome becomes inevitable. We can see why, in Hegel's understanding, revenge is tailor made as a subject for tragedy. It virtually calls for an author to dramatize the conflict between the unyielding revenge ethic and alternate principles, whether it be the Christian rejection of revenge, as in *Hamlet,*[12] or the turn to judicial solutions for righting wrongs, as in the *Oresteia.*

In Hegel's view, the most fertile ground for tragedy is a moment of historical transition, when a community is undergoing a fundamental change and an emerging ethic is poised to clash with the one it is displacing. The movement from a family- or clan-based society, with its revenge ethic, to a polis or political community, with its new notion of civic justice, is a perfect breeding ground for tragedy in Hegel's terms. The *Oresteia* portrays just such a historical moment.[13] And this may be its deepest point of contact with *The Searchers.* As in many of his films, Ford portrays the American West in *The Searchers* as a world in process, moving from a more primitive to a more civilized state, and that means from a world of families isolated and scattered on a savage frontier to a world of larger communities, in which law and order—civilization—may finally prevail.[14] In truly Hegelian fashion, the film turns on the clash between fundamentally opposed ways of life and focuses on liminal figures torn between the two, struggling to bridge them but at the same time exposing the gulf between them.

The *Oresteia* similarly centers on the conflict between civilization and barbarism, or, as Aeschylus formulates the polarity in the terms of his day, Greeks versus barbarians. Cowboys versus Indians in Ford turns out to be a reprise of Greeks versus barbarians in ancient epic and tragedy, and involves a similar degree of complexity in the opposition. Although *The Searchers* often falls into unfortunate Hollywood stereotypes of cowboys versus Indians, we will see that Ford rises above these conventional images and calls them into question, much as Aeschylus does with Greeks versus barbarians. Both works deal with the establishment of boundaries, but also with the dangerous crossing of thresholds. The *Oresteia* famously does so in the scene of Agamemnon fatally entering his palace. *The Searchers* does so equally famously in its opening and closing shots of a domestic portal opening onto a vast and potentially threatening wilderness. The problematic conflict between civilization and barbarism that lies at the heart of the *Oresteia* is also the thematic core of *The Searchers*. Only by taking seriously the genuinely epic and tragic elements in *The Searchers* can we fully appreciate Ford's achievement in the film and what sets it apart from conventional Westerns. As a Western, the film is, of course, a part of American culture, but viewing it in the larger context of world literature reveals its roots in the kind of perennial human dilemma we associate with the peaks of Greek epic and tragedy.

From Barbarism to Civilization

The *Oresteia* rests on the most spectacular and productive anachronism in the history of literature.[15] The trilogy asks us to believe that the heroic kingdom of Agamemnon is contemporaneous with a fully developed Greek polis in the form of Athenian democracy. In the course of three plays, we are swept from a palace in the twelfth-century B.C.E. Mycenaean era to a fifth-century B.C.E. Athenian courtroom, complete with a jury system, and we are evidently supposed to accept this mixing up of centuries without question.[16] We are so familiar with the *Oresteia* that it may be easy to overlook the audacity of Aeschylus' conception. But the very meaning of his trilogy lies in the huge temporal leap it both makes and tries to conceal. Aeschylus takes us in one jump from the archaic world of Homer's heroes to what for him was virtually the present day and hence a world of civilized institutions. Indeed, the *Oresteia* portrays the process of civilization itself, in its etymological sense of the movement of life into the city. The point of Aeschylus' grand anachronism is to bring into close conjunction what were for him Homeric antiquity and Athenian modernity, and thereby to show the superiority of the latter to the former. The Homeric heroes, who have lived as marauding lone wolves, must be herded into association with ordinary human beings, who will then get to decide the heroes' fate by the democratic principle of casting ballots. Tragedy emerges out of epic by placing the epic hero in a different ethical framework and forcing him to confront its new imperatives. The mythic heroes have been a law unto themselves, but in *The Eumenides* they must learn to accept the legal judgment of Athens. In an even more audacious move, Aeschylus brings the gods themselves within the jurisdiction of the city and shows them having to abide by its political authority. The *Oresteia* moves from the rule of the family clan to the rule of the polis. In the terms of the play, that means moving from the barbarism of the revenge ethic (championed by the old gods of the earth, the Furies) to the civilizing power of a law court (championed by the new gods of Olympus, Athena and Apollo). The city and its legal institutions come into being to bring a violent cycle of revenge to an end.[17]

The story of the House of Atreus that Aeschylus portrays in the *Oresteia* is not exactly the best advertisement for the family as a principle of human organization. In fact, this household, descended from the generations of Tantalus and Pelops, may well be the all-time dysfunctional family. As Aeschylus' imagery forcefully reminds us,[18] the House of Atreus is haunted by incidents of cannibalism in previous generations—a potent symbol of the way a family can turn in upon itself in a self-consuming and destructive manner. In the *Oresteia,* Aeschylus portrays the ongoing self-destruction of this family. In the background of the action lies the fateful step Agamemnon took as leader of the Greek expedition against Troy. To secure favorable winds for the voyage, Agamemnon was willing to sacrifice his daughter, Iphigenia, to the gods. As the trilogy opens, Agamemnon is finally returning home from Troy, and his wife Clytemnestra is waiting to kill him in revenge for his having killed their daughter. This brutal act places their son Orestes in a tragic dilemma in the second play, *The Libation Bearers.* As Agamemnon's son, he is called upon to avenge his father's murder and uphold the paternal principle. But to avenge his father, he must murder his mother and thereby violate the maternal principle. Orestes' situation is a textbook illustration of Hegel's concept of tragedy, and in fact the *Oresteia* was central to his formulation of the theory.[19]

Aeschylus shows that the family, left to itself, cannot solve its own problems. It seems only capable of producing an unending cycle of revenge, in which each new generation is doomed to repeat the crimes of its predecessors.[20] By the end of the second play of the *Oresteia,* we have encountered a father who killed his daughter, a wife who killed her husband, and a son who killed his mother. The story of Agamemnon and his family highlights the defects of the heroic world Homer portrays so nobly in the *Iliad* and the *Odyssey.* The Homeric heroes live in a largely prepolitical world. They come from different communities and therefore are not subject to a common law; ultimately they do not recognize any higher authority that could peacefully adjudicate their disputes. To be sure, the heroes often hold councils and engage in public debate; they appear to have procedures for arriving at mutually acceptable decisions. But it is striking how often their failure to agree threatens to erupt into violence. There is, of course, talk of kingship in the poems, but generally what we see is not the well-defined relation of a king to his subjects but the volatile relation of one king to another: "foreign" rather than "domestic" policy. Although Agamemnon is acknowledged as the leader of the expedition, and thus is a sort of king of kings, each Greek king has his own troops loyal to him and is therefore willing to go his own way if need be. That is the point of the dispute between Agamemnon and Achilles that begins the *Iliad* and that almost leads to disaster for the Greek cause when Achilles indignantly withdraws from battle as a result of being slighted by Agamemnon.

The fully developed polis—a community in which disputes are resolved by legal arbitration in an institutional setting—is virtually absent from the *Iliad* and only begins to emerge in the *Odyssey*.[21] Just as in the *Oresteia*, in Book XXIV Athena must intervene to put an end to a cycle of revenge that is beginning to emerge between Odysseus' clan and the families of the suitors he has violently slain upon his return to Ithaka. Homer's heroes are glorious in their willful independence and self-reliance, but they are consequently too quick to resolve their differences by resorting to force of arms; in an argument, their first impulse is to reach for their swords. The result, as Homer chronicles in the *Iliad* and the *Odyssey*, is that they bring down destruction upon themselves and their whole world. Odysseus alone manages to escape the cycle of destruction, but only because he is a different kind of hero—a more *political* one, someone who is intelligent and self-controlled enough to make the compromises necessary to survive in a hostile and violent world of proud and spirited warriors. The political character of Odysseus is shown by the fact that, unlike Achilles, he knows how to lie, and to lie well.[22]

The story of Agamemnon shadows the story of Odysseus in the *Odyssey*.[23] Aeschylus seems to have developed his *Agamemnon* as a kind of alternate *Odyssey*, the story of a disastrous return from the Trojan War to counterpoint Odysseus' successful return. Aeschylus uses Agamemnon's story to launch a critique of the revenge ethic that is characteristic of Homer's heroes, especially in the *Iliad*. The self-destruction of Agamemnon's house mirrors the self-destruction of the larger heroic world in Homer. In Homer's portrayal, Agamemnon is not completely admirable; but Aeschylus works to darken him further (Homer, for example, never speaks of Agamemnon's sacrifice of Iphigenia).[24] Above all, Aeschylus associates Agamemnon with the barbarian forces from the East he has been fighting against in Troy. To link Agamemnon with Asia, Aeschylus pairs him with a Trojan woman, Cassandra, when he returns home. The fact that he has brought a Trojan concubine with him back to Argos may be one of Clytemnestra's motives for killing him.[25] Cassandra, with her wild, nearly hysterical outbursts, produces the most "Asiatic" notes in the *Agamemnon*. It is she who speaks most vividly and extensively of the cannibalistic past of the House of Atreus and in general injects monstrous images into the play (152, lines 1224–27). She recalls with horror being raped by Apollo (155, lines 1286–91), thus introducing a powerful current of sexuality into the dialogue. She is the one who first speaks at length about the Furies, who come to represent the blood-lust of vengeance in the trilogy (150, lines 1189–99). Cassandra's truly prophetic character emerges in the way she speaks for all the irrational forces that threaten the discipline and order of civilized life and that are soon going to bring down Agamemnon. By companioning Agamemnon with her, Aeschylus suggests that the conquering hero has brought back an equivocal treasure from Troy and may have been fatally tainted by the very act of conquest.

The fact that Aeschylus gives these Asiatic associations to Agamemnon is important in light of the larger patterns of ancient Greek thinking. The opposition between West and East, Occident and Orient, Europe and Asia appears frequently in ancient Greek texts and corresponds to the opposition between Greek and barbarian.[26] This polarity appears as early as the *Iliad,* which stages a confrontation between the Achaeans, a European people, and the Trojans, an Asiatic people.[27] To be sure, the *Iliad* shows its true nobility as a war poem in the sympathy and admiration it displays for the "other side." Homer shows the Trojans worshipping the same gods as the Greeks,[28] and in general works to bring out their humanity and, indeed, their nobility, so successfully that some have argued that the Trojan Hector is the true hero of the *Iliad*.[29] Nevertheless, sometimes Homer contrasts the Trojans unfavorably with the Greeks and begins to articulate what was to become the stereotype of the barbarian.[30] Take, for example, the moment in Book IV when Homer juxtaposes the way the Greek and Trojan armies conduct themselves, beginning with the Greeks:

> You'd never think so many troops could march
> holding their voices in their chests, all silence,
> fearing their chiefs who called out clear commands,
> and the burnished blazoned armor round their bodies flared,
> the formations trampling on.
> > But not the Trojans, no . . .
> like flocks of sheep in a wealthy rancher's steadings,

thousands crowding to have their white milk drained,
bleating nonstop when they hear their crying lambs—
so the shouts rose up from the long Trojan lines
and not one cry, one common voice to bind them
all together, their tongues mixed and clashed,
their men hailed from so many far-flung countries.[31]

It is remarkable how much of the Greek-versus-barbarian stereotype
is contained in this single passage. It is even more remarkable how much
this contrast resembles the cowboys-versus-Indians stereotype in American
Westerns. The European Greeks represent rationality; the Asiatic Trojans
represent irrationality. The Greek troops prove their disciplined character in
the orderly way they march, silently obeying their orders and holding their
emotions in check. The Trojans, by contrast, are presented as subhuman
in their emotional outbursts and lack of order. The epic simile compares
them to animals, and all the noise they make suggests that they cannot be
organized into a disciplined fighting force. The subhuman character of the
Trojans is emphasized by the suggestion that they even lack language. They
come from so many different places that they cannot communicate in a common language and are reduced to barking and grunting at each other like
animals. The whole idea of the superiority of Greek to barbarian is summed
up in this single image of Achaean order versus Trojan disorder. And to
jump ahead for a moment to *The Searchers,* the same polarity prevails in
the way Ford contrasts the disciplined charges of the U.S. cavalry and the
Texas Rangers with the haphazard, hit-and-miss attacks of the Comanche
Indians (accompanied by their inarticulate war whoops).[32] The tendency
of Westerns to present Indians as virtually subhuman in their language is
notorious. They are commonly presented as speaking a pidgin English, and
their native languages are seldom treated with any respect (the Comanches
in *The Searchers,* for example, speak Navajo, not Comanche, simply because
Ford's extras were Navajo). The ways in which the cowboys in the Western
are presented as superior to the Indians are virtually identical to the ways
in which Greeks are presented as superior to barbarians in Homer and in
ancient Greek literature in general.

This negative stereotyping of the barbarian in Greek epic and the Indian
in the American Western is understandably very distasteful to contemporary
sensibilities, but we should pause and reflect before simply condemning
either Homer or Ford as racist. As I have suggested, Homer actually admires

the Trojans, and sometimes portrays them as superior to the Greeks.[33] We will see something similar in *The Searchers;* for the moment, note that Ford does not uncritically accept the traditional stereotyping of Indian linguistic inability, and, in fact, raises doubts about it. He supplies a pointed exchange between his hero, Ethan Edwards, and Scar (Henry Brandon), the Indian chief Ethan has been hunting down for years—an exchange that emphasizes their equality when it comes to language. In their first face-to-face confrontation, Ethan says to Scar: "You speak pretty good American for a Comanch." Moments later Scar comes back with: "You speak pretty good Comanch for a white man." Here cowboy and Indian are mirror images of each other.[34] As elsewhere in the film, Scar is presented on the same heroic level as Ethan; if they are not quite equals, they are legitimate rivals in the way that Achilles and Hector are in the *Iliad.* As we will see, Ford works to deconstruct any simple opposition between cowboys and Indians, and much the same can be said of Homer's treatment of Greek versus barbarian. And something similar is obviously happening in the *Oresteia,* where Aeschylus brings out the barbarian elements in Agamemnon.[35] If the titular leader of the Greeks in the Trojan War is revealed to have barbarian characteristics, then the standard opposition of Greek versus barbarian cannot be as hard and fast as it may at first seem. Even a great Greek hero carries the barbarian within him (much as Ethan does in *The Searchers*).

Aeschylus makes the plot of *Agamemnon* turn on the way the barbarian elements in Agamemnon come to the surface. Clytemnestra stage-manages his welcome to Argos so that he will publicly behave like an oriental despot according to Greek stereotypes.[36] She induces him to tread upon a luxurious tapestry, she prostrates herself before him in a kind of Asiatic slavishness, and she treats him like a god. Agamemnon himself comments on the barbarian character of his behavior in response:

> you treat me like a woman. Grovelling, gaping up at me—
> what am I, some barbarian peacocking out of Asia?
> Never cross my path with robes and draw the lightning.
> Never—only the gods deserve the pomps of honour.
> and the stiff brocades of fame.[37] (137–138, lines 912–916)

As if to clinch her casting of Agamemnon in the role of a barbarian ruler, Clytemnestra compares him to Priam, the King of Troy, and presents him as acting in contempt of the common people (138, line 930). In an effort to justify the murder she is about to commit, she successfully maneuvers Agamemnon into publicly committing an act of hubris.[38] Although Agamemnon protests against the way Clytemnestra treats him in barbarian fashion like a god, clearly something in him warms up to the role, exposing Asiatic tyrannical impulses in a Greek ruler.[39] Aeschylus goes on to portray Clytemnestra together with her lover Aegisthus acting like tyrants once they come to the throne, behaving with contempt for the law and all conventional restraints.[40] The fact that Aegisthus appears with bodyguards is in Athenian terms a clear marker of his having assumed the role of a tyrant.[41] He behaves impudently and tyrannically to the chorus at the end of the play, threatening them, calling them slaves, and flaunting his power over them. Evidently it was not just Troy that fell apart as a result of the ten years' war. Back in the Greek heartland, law and order have broken down, and murderous passions have been unleashed. The barbarism of the East has erupted within the palaces of the West, putting despotism in place of the rule of law.

Thus, at the core of his strategy of criticizing the ethos of revenge, Aeschylus associates murderous impulses with the non-Greek world, and indeed he presents them as the very antithesis of civilization and rational behavior, a holdover from a primitive stage of human development.[42] It is therefore appropriate that the chthonic deities, the Furies, emerge as the champions and patrons of the vengeance principle. Swarming over the stage, they are the wildest and most irrational forces that appear in the trilogy. They are opposed by Apollo, the god of light, and Athena, the goddess of wisdom. Aeschylus sets up a polarity that resembles Nietzsche's famous dichotomy in his *The Birth of Tragedy* between the Apollinian and the Dionysian, the rational versus the irrational.[43] As the new gods, the gods of the future, the Olympians, Apollo and Athena, stand up for civilization, while the old gods, the gods of the past, the Furies, stand up for the irrational impulses that need to be restrained for civilization to prevail.[44] Apollo associates the Furies with the cruel and primitive justice of the East:[45]

Go where heads are severed, eyes gouged out,
where Justice and bloody slaughter are the same . . .
castrations, wasted seed, young men's glories butchered,
extremities maimed, and huge stones at the chest,
and the victims wail for pity—
spikes inching up the spine, torsos stuck on spikes.
(239, lines 183–188)

The divine conflict comes to a head over the issue of whether Orestes must die for murdering Clytemnestra to avenge his father, with the Furies calling for Orestes' blood and Apollo seeking his pardon. But the gods seem incapable of arbitrating this issue among themselves. The Furies insist on the maternal principle, and Apollo insists just as adamantly on the paternal principle. The story of Agamemnon's murder by Clytemnestra and Clytemnestra's murder by Orestes thus seems to show why the family fails as a principle of social organization. It cannot settle its disputes except through bloodshed, and even then its divisions lead to unending violence, not a peaceful society.

In an Athenian drama, Aeschylus offers an Athenian court as the solution to the tragic dilemma created by the ethos of revenge and the contradictory divine commands it inspires.[46] The city is the successor to the family or the clan as the principle of social organization, and by providing an impartial form of justice, it promises to bring peace where the personal vendetta threatened to result in a war of all against all.[47] Aeschylus stresses the institutional aspects of civic justice.[48] Procedures are in place; and, above all, the contesting parties agree to abide by the verdict of the court, acknowledging the power of a higher authority that is impersonal and presumably impartial. The procedural aspect of the trial is emphasized by the casting of the ballots, especially by the fact that in the tie that results, Athena settles the dispute—according to an agreed-upon convention—by casting the deciding vote.[49] Moreover, the law allows for compromise.[50] Whereas a blood feud is a zero-sum game—the ultimate case of either winning or losing—civic justice tries to offer something to everybody. Orestes will not have to die to satisfy the Furies' thirst for vengeance, but they will not leave the court empty-handed. Athena promises that they will be accepted within the precincts of Athens and honored by the city.

The *Oresteia* portrays the family as failing in the act of incorporation. When Agamemnon attempts to reenter his home, he is destroyed, and the only successful acts of "incorporation" in the House of Atreus are typically acts of ingestion, the horrors of cannibalism that haunt the family. The city, by contrast, is a master of incorporation, finding a place for even the gods within its limits.[51] It is a sign of Aeschylus' wisdom that he realizes that the city cannot simply reject the irrational forces the Furies represent and try to expel them from its ranks. Rather, Athens must find a way to incorporate the Furies within its boundaries and make their power work for the city, not against it.[52] The fear they inspire must be channeled into awe for the power of the law.[53] Mera Flaumenhaft cleverly speaks of the movement "from

Furies to juries" in *The Eumenides*.[54] The Furies will supply the emotional basis for the rule of law that restrains their own murderous impulses. And bringing the gods within the jurisdiction of the city also helps to supply a divine sanction for its laws.

In Athena's grand speech about the founding of the court of the Areopagus, the *Oresteia* culminates in a vision of the triumph of civilization over barbarism, the rule of law over savagery:

> Now and forever more, for Aegeus' people
> this will be the court where judges reign.
> This is the Crag of Ares, where the Amazons
> pitched their tents when they came marching down
> on Theseus, full tilt in their fury, erecting
> a new city to overarch his city, towers thrust
> against his towers—they sacrificed to Ares,
> raised this rock from that day onward Ares' Crag.
> (262, lines 695–702)

Once again, Aeschylus harks back to the distinction between Greek and barbarian, as he recalls a mythic time when an invading force of Amazons from the Black Sea region had to be repulsed by an Athenian hero, Theseus. This victory of the forces of light over the forces of darkness will be repeated every time the power of the law prevails over the power of violent passion in an Athenian court. The *Oresteia* is a hymn to the civilizing power of the city and especially its legal institutions. But its vision of the triumph of the law over the violent passion of revenge is not naïve. The Furies may have given up on obtaining Orestes' blood, but they will remain in the city, a constant reminder that barbarism is not something to be found only outside its gates; rather, barbarism is incorporated into its foundations, ultimately dwelling in the human heart.[55]

The tragedy generated by the contradictory demands of the paternal and maternal principles within the family can be resolved in true Hegelian fashion only by lifting the issue to a higher plane, where the city as a more comprehensive community offers to mediate the conflict. The city achieves a higher synthesis than any god can provide on his or her own. Athens brings together the Furies and Apollo, the old and the new gods, all of whom are now to be honored by the city. The city is thus capable of offering a higher justice than the personal vendetta can ever provide. Athena emphasizes the importance of founding the city on the civilized principle of the rule of law, not the barbarian rule of violent force:

> The stronger your fear, your reverence for the just,
> the stronger your country's wall and city's safety,
> stronger by far than all men else possess
> in Scythia's rugged steppes or Pelops' level plain.
> Untouched by lust for spoil, this court of law
> majestic, swift to fury, rising above you
> as you sleep, our night watch always wakeful,
> guardian of our land—I found it here and now.
> (262, lines 714–721)

In the *Oresteia,* Aeschylus shapes the foundational myth of modern civilization. The grand dramatic sweep of the trilogy ultimately has one purpose: to drag the Homeric hero before a jury, to show that the seemingly irresolvable tragedies of the ancient heroic world can finally be settled only in a civilized court of law.[56]

"What Makes a Man to Wander?"

To bring the archaic heroic world into juxtaposition with the modern civilized world, Aeschylus, as we have seen, has to commit an almost grotesque act of anachronism in the *Oresteia.* All John Ford has to do in *The Searchers* is to move his cameras west. In the second half of the nineteenth century, the United States was one gigantic "geographic anachronism." The East was living in the world of Henry James; the West was living in the world of Homer (at least as popular culture portrayed it). The journey west in American literature has always been a journey into the past, into a more primitive world, a world that lacks both the advantages and the drawbacks of modern life. Western movies continue to present the West as the frontier between civilization and barbarism, and thus as a site where opposing ways of life clash—often tragically. *The Searchers* is the classic embodiment of this theme. Set in West Texas in the late 1860s and early 1870s, it portrays pioneers trying to establish a civilized community in the face of a harsh nature and hostile Indian tribes. But the barbarism the settler families confront is not simply a force external to their community. As in the *Oresteia,* barbarism is at work within the civilized community in *The*

Ethan Edwards (John Wayne) poised between civilization and barbarism on the frontier in John Ford's *The Searchers*. (Warner Bros./Photofest)

Searchers; indeed, it turns out that civilization needs a form of barbarism to defend itself against its enemies.

That is why Ethan Edwards has to be a rugged hero in the Homeric mold, with a strong streak of cruelty, an implacable will to revenge, and a well-developed capacity for killing his fellow human beings in cold blood. He has work to do, the work of protecting civilization, and that can be a nasty job. Much to the dismay of many critics, Ethan is not a nice guy, although he can be gentle with children and has an avuncular sense of humor. Ethan has been hardened by his experiences, particularly in war and in frontier combat. But he needs that hardness to deal with a harsh and hostile world. Homer's heroes are not nice either, because their world also does not allow them to be so. Ford's Western frontier is Homeric precisely because it is a world in which a man survives only by the strength of his own arms.[57] Like Homer and Aeschylus, Ford portrays a prepolitical world in all its epic and tragic grandeur, a world whose heroes can be savage in their self-reliance while at the same time providing the only bulwark against the triumph of barbarism over civilization.

In showing Ethan's dark side, Ford is working within a very old tradition that stretches back through Shakespeare to the ancient Greeks. Critics who insist on referring to Ethan as a villain have evidently forgotten what a *tragic hero* is.[58] Because the tragic hero is positioned at the flash point between conflicting ethical principles, from the perspective of one of the moralities he will inevitably appear to be flawed. If Ethan is torn between civilization and barbarism, and must incorporate some of the latter to defend the former, he is not going to appear perfectly virtuous according to the ordinary standards of domestic life. Even as a tragic hero is inevitably condemned by the standards of conventional morality, he raises doubts about the universal applicability of those standards by revealing dimensions of life beyond the conventional. You might not want to invite Ethan to the church picnic, but, then again, the same is true of Achilles or Agamemnon. Yet if you and your family felt threatened on the frontier, Ethan is exactly the kind of character you would want manning the barricades. As his nephew says when the Comanches are gathering to attack the homestead: "I wish Uncle Ethan was here."[59] Like Homer and the Greek tragedians, Ford understands that the tragic hero is a lion, not a pussycat, and a lion can create a lot of havoc if let loose in a city. Aeschylus uses exactly this image of a lion ravaging a peaceful community to suggest the problematic character of the tragic hero.[60]

By focusing on the issue of revenge, Ford highlights the prepolitical character of the world of *The Searchers*.[61] Ethan's unrelenting pursuit of the Indians who massacred his kinfolk must be understood in the context of the total absence of all the legal institutions we take for granted in modern communal life.[62] Ethan cannot expect Scar to be tried for rape and murder by a jury of his peers, because the chief's peers, rather than punishing him, would likely applaud him for what he did to Ethan's family. It may seem obvious, but it is important that Ethan and Scar do not belong to the same community and do not acknowledge any authority to whose higher jurisdiction they are both subject. If Ethan is going to bring Scar to any kind of justice, he has every reason to believe that he will have to be the one to do so.

Critics are correct to speak of the obsessive character of Ethan's quest for revenge, but they go wrong when they begin to speak of him as mad, even as clinically insane.[63] Ethan is no more—and no less—mad than Achilles. If, for example, we are seeking a precedent for Ethan's cruel treatment of fallen

Indians (shooting out their eyes, scalping them), we need look no further than Achilles' humiliation of Hector's corpse.[64] The fury that grips heroes in Homer, as well as in Greek tragedy, is a precise analogue for the obsession with revenge that takes possession of Ethan.[65] Although his behavior often seems mad in the eyes of men who are too prudent—or too cowardly—to follow him into danger, most of the time Ethan behaves quite rationally in his quest, often displaying cunning and shrewd calculation. He clearly cares about the amount of money he is expending on the search, and keeps a careful account of it: think especially of the scene where he retrieves his gold piece from Futterman (Peter Mamakos) after killing him.[66] When Ethan realizes that the Comanches have tricked him and his friends into leaving their families defenseless, he does not rush back home at once as the others do, but instead has the foresight to pause and refresh his horse for the long ride ahead. In this regard, he seems more like the thoughtful Odysseus than the rash Achilles. Unlike other characters in the story, Ethan rarely plunges into a situation without carefully thinking over his options and the odds of his surviving.[67] If he is in the grip of fury, it is almost always a controlled fury. His capacity for self-control culminates in the moving moment at the end when he decides to save Debbie instead of killing her.

I often wonder what some of Ethan's harshest critics think he should do when he returns to his brother's homestead and finds that his only relatives have been slaughtered—above all, his brother's wife, Martha (Dorothy Jordan), the woman he evidently was in love with in earlier days—and his two nieces kidnapped by the Indians who have already raped Martha. Should Ethan dial 911 and tamely report the crime to the police like a good citizen? There are no police in the world of *The Searchers* because there are no cities. The only authorities Ethan could appeal to are the U.S. cavalry and the Texas Rangers—neither the best representative of *civic* justice.[68] As we learn in the course of the film, the U.S. cavalry is a good killing machine, but it is rather indiscriminate in whom it kills, and, contrary to motion picture tradition, it can rarely be counted on to show up when and where it is needed.[69] The Texas Rangers are more Ethan's style. He becomes deputized as one of them and rides off with them initially to rescue his nieces, Lucy (Pippa Scott) and Debbie, and punish the Comanches. But, like Achilles, Ethan has a hard time taking orders from anyone,[70] even his old comrade, Captain Clayton (Ward Bond) of the Texas Rangers, who has a lot in common with him but refuses to pursue revenge with the same intensity and single-mindedness (perhaps because it was not *his* family that was massacred). Clayton himself acknowledges the difficulty of Ethan's situation when he admits that the pursuit of the Comanches is a job for more men than a company of Rangers—or fewer. In the absence of a frontier pacified by a massive military force from the federal government, the Homeric lone wolf has the best chance of tracking down the nomadic Indian tribe. Accordingly, Ethan sets off basically on his own, accompanied only by two young men, Martin Pauley (Jeffrey Hunter) and Brad Jorgensen (Harry Carey Jr.), who, as Ethan makes clear, must either follow his orders or return home.

Samuel Johnson Clayton is one of several liminal figures in *The Searchers* who help to define the border between civilization and barbarism. He is both a captain in the Texas Rangers and the local reverend. He can be heroic, courageous, and even bloodthirsty when he leads a troop into combat—he loves a good fight as much as the next man—but he also conducts funerals and weddings, presiding over the civilized rituals of domestic life and sanctifying them. With one foot in the realm of war and one foot in the realm of peaceful domesticity—symbolized by his quick changes of wardrobe—he embodies the ambivalence of the world Ford creates in *The Searchers*.[71] The fact that this admirable man respects Ethan is a clear indication of the truly heroic status Ford accords his protagonist. But Clayton's moderation—his unwillingness to take revenge as far as Ethan wants to—serves as a measure of the hero's extremism.

The figure of Captain Reverend Clayton sums up everything Ford is saying about the West in the process of being civilized. Even as Clayton is willing to resort to violence when necessary, he is a man of God and represents the pacifying power of religion, Christianity in particular. By contrast, Ethan twice interrupts Clayton's religious services, at the funeral for his brother's family ("Put an amen to it") and at the ill-fated wedding of Laurie Jorgensen (Vera Miles) and the hapless Charlie McCorry (Ken Curtis).[72] Ethan is not a man of peace—he openly says that after the Civil War ended, he refused to beat his sword into a ploughshare.[73] Unlike Reverend Clayton, Ethan displays a remarkable knowledge of Indian religion. In a gripping moment early in the film that helps define his character, Ethan shoots out the eyes of a murdered Indian because he knows that a Comanche would believe that this act will condemn the dead man to a life of wandering in the spirit world.[74] This is our first clue that Ethan is the right man for pursuing the Indians because he has so much in common with them.[75] Only because he understands their customs and beliefs will he be able to track them down. In the larger symbolic pattern of *The Searchers,* Ford is thus calling into question from the start any simplistic identification of cowboys with civilization and Indians with barbarism. Ethan must share in the barbarism of the Indians he opposes in order to deal with them successfully, and this "barbarism" turns out to be largely indistinguishable from the heroic life of the warrior that Ethan represents.

Another liminal figure who contributes to blurring the conventional line between cowboys and Indians, between civilization and barbarism, is Mose Harper (Hank Worden).[76] As a kind of Holy Fool, Mose stands outside normal social categories. When Ethan is explaining why he shot out the dead Comanche's eyes, Mose acts out his words in pantomime, and earlier he performs an abbreviated Indian dance when Ethan has figured out the strategy behind the Comanche cattle raid.[77] Mose wears a feather in his cap in imitation of Indians, and at a key moment in the story, he is able to go among the Comanches and obtain the information Ethan needs to track them down.[78] Half-crazed, Mose has a hard time fitting into polite society, but that is precisely his value for the settlers. An outsider himself, he has some kind of secret sympathy with the Indians that gives him insight into their movements. He is almost as nomadic as the Comanches themselves. But his ultimate dream is to settle down. All he asks in return from Ethan for his information about the Comanches is a place to live and a rocking chair in which he can, in true Western fashion, sit a spell. Mose reveals in comic form the poles between which the Western hero alternates—motion and rest. He is a man in perpetual motion who wishes only to settle down. As such, he is the comic equivalent of the tragic Ethan, who is torn between the attraction of home and the compulsion to avenge his family that keeps him moving on his quest.[79] Like the Indians he relentlessly pursues, Ethan seems condemned to a life of wandering forever.[80] In the dialectical terms of *The Searchers,* Ethan must always be on the move so that other people may eventually settle down and take possession of the land.[81] That is the deepest reason why in the famous ending of the film, Ethan cannot enter the Jorgensen home with his friends and kinfolk, but must walk off to become once again an isolated figure in the empty landscape out of which he emerged in the beginning.[82]

As a revenge tragedy, *The Searchers,* like the *Oresteia,* poses the question of the value of civilization in the starkest terms—the choice between personal vendetta and civic justice. Although Ford presents the search for vengeance as a heroic quest, he does not glamorize or glorify it. He leaves no doubt that it can become an obsession, poisoning a man's existence, and ultimately must be renounced as a way of life. Like Aeschylus, Ford highlights the cyclical character of revenge. We learn that Scar's raid on the Edwards homestead was in revenge for the murder of his two sons by white men. Thus, again like Aeschylus, Ford suggests barbarian origins to the revenge ethic. And who knows what the Comanches might do in retaliation for the murder of Scar? As long as we remain in the world of isolated families, clans, or tribes, the violence threatens to go on forever and to deny a safe and secure life to anyone on the frontier, cowboy or Indian. As much as this chaotic world brings out the heroism in people on both sides, Ford clearly suggests that the chaos must be brought to an end, if only for the sake of the women and the children, who unfortunately fall victim to masculine violence throughout the film—again on both sides. Like the doomed and self-destructive world of the Homeric epics, Ford's West has no future as long as it remains mired in the vendettas of the past. Ford follows Aeschylus' formula: the quest for revenge is heroic, but there is also something barbaric about it, and human beings must learn to rise above it.

Women and the Taming of the Frontier

Ford thus shows that the West must pursue the path of civilization, specifically the path of education; and in this process, women—with their devotion to their children and the next generation—have a great deal to contribute. Ethan's brother Aaron (Walter Coy) gives Martha credit for preventing him from abandoning their homestead in the face of all the threats to their lives: "She just wouldn't let a man quit."[83] Lars Jorgensen (John Qualen) points with pride to the fact that his wife used to be a schoolteacher. The men in the film, however heroic their stature, are noticeably deficient in education. Clayton spells *mount* "M-O-N-T-E," and Laurie Jorgensen points out that Martin Pauley spells her first name incorrectly with a "y." Martin can produce only one letter to Laurie in several years, a low level of literacy that nearly costs him her hand in marriage. He can barely read, and Laurie has to help him decipher an important note to Ethan. Throughout the story, women exert a civilizing influence on the men. Early in the film, Mrs. Jorgensen (Olive Carey) warns Ethan as he sets off on his search with Martin and her son Brad: "Don't let the boys waste their lives in vengeance."[84] And at the end of the film, Debbie brings out the civilized side of Ethan.[85] Women may seem helpless in the face of the violent world of *The Searchers* and wholly dependent on heroic men to protect them. But Ford presents a number of strong female characters in the film and has them speak out against irrational violence and in favor of a civilized way of life. As in many of his films, Ford suggests in *The Searchers* that if the West is ever to be civilized, women will play a major role in the process (as did, in fact, happen). In many respects, women stand for civilization in *The Searchers,* while the force of barbarism is represented largely by men.[86]

Nevertheless, the women in *The Searchers* are sometimes confronted by the choice between civilization and barbarism in a distinctively feminine and very practical form—when it comes to choosing their husbands (and women do appear to have that choice in this world). The fact that they almost of necessity prefer a peace-loving, tractable man over a warlike, violent man as a husband is perhaps the chief reason they exercise a civilizing force in society. Marriage is the most basic domestic institution and requires on the man's part a willingness to settle down and help raise a family, which is often incompatible with the kind of heroic quest that leads him away from hearth and home. That is why the hypermasculine hero, who holds many attractions for women, is not simply—or even regularly—preferred when it comes to the serious business of matrimony. This principle is illustrated in the back-story of a romantic triangle in the Edwards household that Ford hints at in the opening scenes. Evidently Ethan and Martha were once in love, if we are to judge by the way they still look at each other when he returns, and a number of other visual clues Ford supplies, such as Martha's tender caressing of Ethan's coat when she thinks that she is alone.[87] We cannot know for sure what really happened in the past, but from what we see of Ethan and Aaron, we can reconstruct a plausible explanation for why Martha chose the less impressive brother as her husband. Although she was more attracted to Ethan as a strong, heroic man, she realized that she could not get him to settle down to domestic life and that therefore Aaron, even though less of a man, would make the better domestic partner for her. As we see throughout *The Searchers,* Ethan is always running off to perform one heroic deed after another, whereas Aaron is the kind of man who stays with his family. In the story of Ethan, Aaron, and Martha, we see how women work to tame the men of the West. If a man wishes to marry and have a family, he will have to give up his heroic aspirations, or at least learn to moderate them and act in a more civilized, and less violent, fashion.

The story of Martin Pauley and Laurie Jorgensen develops this point more fully. By the end of the story, Martin is finally in a position to marry Laurie, but only because he has proven that he is different from Ethan, less violent and more domestic by nature. Laurie has been in love with Martin since childhood, and clearly wants to marry him. But for much of the film, he is too eager to leave her and accompany Ethan in the search for Debbie, thus time and again disappointing Laurie's hopes for their future together. Martin, although callow and naïve, is in his own way a heroic figure, and repeatedly shows that he is worthy to be Ethan's companion on the dangerous quest. It is after all Martin, and not, as we might have expected, Ethan, who finally kills Scar. But all along, Martin differentiates himself from Ethan as a searcher. For much of the movie, Ethan is more interested in killing Debbie than Scar; he cannot bear the thought of his niece becoming a savage. Martin, by contrast, makes it clear to Laurie that he has to go along with Ethan on the search precisely to prevent him from killing Debbie. A domestic motive—specifically the protection of a woman—is built into Martin's conception of the search. That shows his ultimate suitability as a husband for Laurie, even though the search forces him several times to abandon her.

Still, Martin faces an obstacle to his marrying Laurie, a rival in the person of Charlie McCorry. Ford brilliantly recreates the Ethan-Aaron-Martha triangle in the form of the Martin-Charlie-Laurie triangle.[88] A serious and sad story from the past gets reconfigured into a funny romantic entanglement in the present, a perfect example of how Ford mingles tragic and comic motifs in his story.[89] Laurie appears to be repeating Martha's original choice when she agrees to wed the oafish McCorry.[90] Everything tells her that Martin is the better man, but she obviously gets tired of waiting around for him and chooses Charlie simply because he is available and at her beck and call. The scene of the wedding offers all of Ford's regular symbols of civilized order—music, song, dance, ritual. As the presiding minister, Clayton even performs a quick change into formal clothes, and shuts down the bar. The way Ethan and Martin interrupt all this proper behavior confirms their status as borderline figures, who barely fit into polite civil society. As soon as Ethan shows up, the bar is once again open.[91]

With a chance to compare Martin and Charlie directly, Laurie realizes the error of her choice and cannot go through with the wedding. This abrupt decision leads to the most extended comic sequence in the film, the fight between Martin and Charlie. But given the way this romantic triangle resonates with the backstory in the Edwards household, the scene has serious undertones as well. We see civilization and barbarism mixed together.[92] On the one hand, there is a ritual quality to the way Martin and Charlie fight. Like adolescent boys in a shoving match, they observe the proper etiquette of the situation, as Charlie challenges Martin to step over a log. We sense that neither one is really going to get hurt. On the other hand, they both resort to dirty tactics, and the fight keeps threatening to get out of hand and lead to real injuries. The ritual barely contains the violence. Ford allows the serious tensions between aggressive males that often lurk beneath the surface in *The Searchers* to break out in a relatively harmless and therefore comic environment. But as funny as the scene may be, at the same time it presents *the* primal struggle: two men fighting over a woman. *The Searchers* portrays a remarkable sequence of masculine rivalries, mostly involving Ethan: Ethan versus Aaron, Ethan versus Scar, Ethan versus Martin, Ethan versus Clayton—the list goes on.[93] These rivalries run deep; they often involve a sexual component; and they sometimes have tragic results. The simmering rivalry between men—often over women—that runs throughout *The Searchers* finally erupts into open violence in the fight between Martin and Charlie.

Ford cannot resist showing that women just love this kind of scene. Ethan has to restrain Mrs. Jorgensen as a spectator, admonishing her: "Don't forget you're a lady." Then, in one of the most psychologically revealing moments in the film, Ford gives a full-face close-up of Laurie simply beaming at the sight of two men fighting for her hand in marriage. In Ford's presentation, women may generally seek to restrain the violent behavior of men, but at times they egg it on. This is the paradoxical position of women on the frontier—they want their men to be both violent and nonviolent. They need aggressive masculinity to protect them against hostile forces, but they also feel a need to tame that heroic disposition for the sake of raising children. Fortunately for Laurie, she is able to have the best of both worlds. The rival men in her life do not fight to the death over her and are willing, in a nonheroic and nontragic way, to let bygones be bygones. And in the long run, Martin turns out to be the happy medium between the violent hero and the peaceful domestic man. The domestic impulses that make Martin ultimately suitable as a husband for Laurie are no accident, but are in fact largely the product of her influence. As we see at several points in the film, Laurie has worked to domesticate Martin, to bring out his civilized side. His love for her forces him to become the tamer man she desires. This, Ford suggests, is one of the ways women contribute to making the West safe for civilization.

Accordingly, as Aeschylus does with Athena, Ford gives the great speech on the civilizing process in his story to a woman, Mrs. Jorgensen:[94] "It just so happens we be Texicans. A Texican is nothing but a human man way out on a limb. This year, and next, maybe for a hundred more. But I don't think it'll be forever. Someday this country is gonna be a fine good place to be. Maybe it needs our bones in the ground before that time can come." This is the tragic vision that unites the understanding of history in both the *Oresteia* and *The Searchers*. One does not have to go as far as equating Athens with Dallas or Houston to see that Aeschylus and Ford are dealing with fundamentally the same process: the emergence of the peaceful civic community out of the violent and chaotic reign of the clans. The blood of several generations may have to be sacrificed to make this goal possible, but in both Greek tragedy and the American Western, the end ultimately justifies the means. Civilization is built on the bones of the heroic pioneers who struggle against and out of barbarism. That is the fundamental tragedy of civilization.

To be sure, both Aeschylus and Ford shape a happy ending for their stories. The *Oresteia* is a good reminder that, contrary to popular opinion, Greek tragedies did not always end with the deaths of their heroes. Orestes survives in *The Eumenides,* even though he is a tragic hero. If other complete trilogies had survived from ancient Athens, we might be more used to the idea of a reconciliation of opposing forces taking place in Greek tragedy (Aeschylus' Prometheus trilogy evidently ended with Zeus and the suffering Titan somehow reconciled).[95] But although technically the *Oresteia* ends "happily," the conclusion of the trilogy hardly leaves the audience whistling a happy tune as they go home from the theater. The issues Aeschylus raises are so serious that we come away from the play not elated and overjoyed, but sobered and chastened. Aeschylus has laid bare the profound tensions and contradictions that lie at the core of civilized life, and no amount of reconciliation at the end can make us forget these tragic insights.

Similarly, the conclusion of *The Searchers* may look like a conventional Hollywood ending, incorporating many elements of reconciliation and even of romantic comedy. Debbie has been restored to her friends and relatives, and a marriage between Martin and Laurie may well be in the offing. Even Ethan has survived. One can easily imagine him having been killed in one way or another by the end. In the novel on which the film is based, the Ethan character does die at the hands of a Comanche woman, and Martin is left to rescue Debbie. Still, like the *Oresteia, The Searchers* is a sobering experience for the audience, and the way Ethan walks off alone at the end ensures that any cheering at the fates of Debbie, Martin, and Laurie will be muted. Like any real tragedy, *The Searchers* has given us a disturbing look into some of the fundamental dilemmas that lie at the heart of human life. The mere absence of the hero's death does not mean that we cease to be deeply troubled and unnerved by what we have seen happen in his story.

If anything, Ford's vision may be more tragic than Aeschylus.' He seems more troubled by what is lost in the civilizing process, as shown by the painful image he creates of Ethan's exclusion from the very world he has labored so hard to protect.[96] Ford seems more nostalgic for his heroic figures—he knows that they must be left behind, but at the same time he admires and celebrates them.[97] A sense of "there were giants in those days" pervades Ford's Westerns, even *The Searchers,* which gives perhaps his most uncompromising view of the violence and cruelty that went along with frontier heroics. And to his credit, Ford sees this heroism on both sides of the conventional divide between cowboys and Indians. As we have seen, and as many commentators have noted, Ethan and Scar are doubles, virtually mirror images of each other.[98] This becomes evident when they finally meet. As much as they hate each other, they feel a kind of grudging admiration as well, sensing that as heroic warriors they have more in common with each other than they do with the ordinary men in their respective "tribes." Despite this identification, however, Ethan takes a cruel satisfaction in working to wipe out the Indian culture he despises. In one particularly disturbing scene, he glories in killing bison just so the Comanches will have less to eat. In the deepest irony of *The Searchers,* Ethan does not realize that, if he succeeds in exterminating the Indians and their warrior way of life, he will simultaneously destroy his own reason for existence and end his career as a frontier hero. But Ford, of course, is aware of this irony and of the fact that he is pursuing what amounts to a Homeric theme: the self-destruction of an age of heroes. As Ethan walks off into the distance at the end of *The Searchers,* he is marching into the annals of history and legend, thereby bringing an entire era to a close.

I have tried to show the ways in which Ford shares Aeschylus' vision as a tragedian, with his similar understanding of the complex dialectic of civilization and barbarism—a vision that ultimately embodies a progressivist perspective, looking forward to the eventual emergence and triumph of civic life.[99] But, in the end, *The Searchers* is more elegiac in tone than the *Oresteia.* Especially in visual terms, it seems to be a melancholy reflection on the passing of a generation of heroes. As an elegy for a doomed but noble age, *The Searchers* is in some respects more like the *Iliad* than the *Oresteia*— an important reminder that Ford's greatest film is as much an epic as it is a tragedy. With its affinities to both the *Oresteia* and the *Iliad, The Searchers* is a true American classic, revealing what a high level of artistic achievement is possible in pop culture, even in one of its least respected genres. *The Searchers* is indeed a classic Western, but not a typical one. It tells the classic Western story of the hero as rugged individualist, battling elemental forces on the frontier. But Ford rejects the neat and comfortable ending of the typical Western, in which the lone-wolf hero eventually becomes tamed by the domestic community he is called on to defend. By isolating Ethan at the end of the film, Ford presents him as a tragic figure. Ethan represents the Western ideal of freedom in its purest form. Perpetually on the move, pushing the limits of the frontier, he charts his own course. But the self-reliance and gritty determination that make him a Western hero tragically leave him without a home at the end of *The Searchers*.

Like an ancient Greek playwright, Ford lays bare the tragic tension between the solitary hero and the political community. The critics who view Ethan as a villain or a madman have lost sight of the distinctive nature of the tragic hero. When they complain that he has violated one ethical principle or another, they forget that, according to Hegel, the tragic hero by definition must violate an ethical principle—that is inevitable, given Hegel's conception of a tragic situation as involving a conflict between two goods. Tragedy teaches us the incompatibility of ethical principles that we would like to think can be simply harmonized. Ethan is trapped on the borderline between civilization and barbarism. He finds that he cannot defend civilization without resorting to a form of barbarism disturbingly akin to what he is fighting. He pulls back from a complete plunge into barbarism when he refrains from killing Debbie, but he has been too tainted by his prolonged experience as a brutal avenger to be reintegrated into conventional domestic society. His freedom as a frontiersman is a double-edged sword. He does what the frontier hero must do to save the day, but he becomes emotionally and psychologically scarred in the process. In the story of Ethan Edwards, John Ford shows that freedom is integral to the heroic character, but it can be his curse as well. *The Searchers* leaves us with a troubling sense of how deeply problematic freedom can be, even—and especially—on the American frontier.

2

THE ORIGINAL FRONTIER

Gene Roddenberry's Apprenticeship for *Star Trek* in
Have Gun–Will Travel

> We stand today on the edge of a New Frontier—the frontier of the 1960s—a
> frontier of unknown opportunities and perils—a frontier of unfulfilled
> hopes and threats. . . . Beyond that frontier are the uncharted areas of
> science and space, unsolved problems of peace and war, unconquered
> pockets of ignorance and prejudice, unanswered questions of poverty and
> surplus. . . . I am asking each of you to be pioneers on that New Frontier.
> —John Fitzgerald Kennedy

Speaking these eloquent words on July 15, 1960, John Fitzgerald Kennedy
accepted the Democratic Party's nomination for president and set the tone
of his coming administration in terms he would return to repeatedly. In his
use of words like "frontier" and "pioneers," Kennedy's rhetoric was saturated
with the idiom of the American West, particularly appropriate when he was
looking forward to his cherished space program and specifically the race
against the Soviets to land a man on the moon. But the concept of the New
Frontier extended to every aspect of Kennedy's presidency. His foreign policy
also centered on the issue of frontiers. As an ardent Cold Warrior, he viewed
the United States as locked in a life-and-death struggle with communism,
which he pictured as a barbaric enemy pressing everywhere upon the borders
of the Free World, much the way the Indians were envisioned as impinging
upon the frontiers of civilization in the Old West. In his nomination speech,
Kennedy shows an acute awareness of frontiers: "Communist influence has
penetrated further into Asia, stood astride the Middle East and now festers
some ninety miles off the coast of Florida." In Kennedy's domestic policy,

the New Frontier took the form of a fight against prejudice, chiefly in his support of the civil rights movement, and a fight against poverty.

New Frontier Heroes

In offering himself as a New Frontier hero, Kennedy genuinely looked the part, almost as if he had come straight out of Hollywood central casting. His public image was pure Western—a combination of good looks, masculinity, youthful vigor, and strong leadership. Like a typical hero out of the Old West, he claimed to stand for justice, freedom, and concern for common people. But Kennedy's resemblance to a Western hero had its problematic aspects, which point to the tensions and contradictions in his presidency and the brand of liberalism he represented, what has been called "Kennedy liberalism." The typical Western hero of Hollywood and other forms of American pop culture is celebrated as a peacemaker, and yet he often seems trigger-happy, a bit too eager to reach for his gun to solve all problems. The heroic gunfighter often leaves a trail of death and destruction in his wake. Similarly, Kennedy positioned himself as a man of peace—after all, he founded the Peace Corps—but in his aggressive confrontations with communism, he brought the world to the brink of nuclear war in the Cuban Missile Crisis of 1962, and, in Southeast Asia, he pursued policies that eventually left the United States mired in the Vietnam War.

The Western hero is the champion of the weak against the powerful— the poor farmer against the cattle baron, for example—and yet he himself must often play the role of strong man to accomplish this task. He tends to set himself above common people in the very act of protecting them, claiming for himself extraordinary powers and the right to determine single-handedly what is good for the masses. Similarly, Kennedy championed freedom, particularly in contrasting the United States with the totalitarian-ism of big government in the Soviet Union, but in his economic and social policies at home, he often seemed to support big government himself. In issues such as civil rights, he seemed to think that only expanding the power of the federal government could secure the freedom of American citizens. His active domestic policy thus became the counterpart of his active foreign policy. He viewed government, especially in the person of a vigorous execu-tive, as necessary to protect people against any kind of oppression, foreign or domestic. Kennedy liberalism thus presents a paradoxical mix—a foreign policy of peace combined with aggressive anticommunism on all fronts, a celebration of freedom combined with a call for a more active executive and hence an expansion of the power of the presidency and government in general. These are precisely the paradoxes of the American Western. Its hero is often a strong man protecting the weak, shooting up bad guys in the name of peace and constantly stretching the power of the law in the name of upholding it.

If John Fitzgerald Kennedy mirrored the American image of the Western hero, his image was in turn mirrored in the popular culture of the 1960s in an iconic figure with a similar-sounding name—James Tiberius Kirk (William Shatner) of the television series *Star Trek* (1966–1969). As captain of the starship *Enterprise,* Kirk pursues a "foreign policy" remarkably similar to Kennedy's. He too is a Cold Warrior, determined to advance the cause of freedom throughout the galaxy. He is always working to thwart incursions by the totalitarian Klingons or Romulans into the space territories under the authority of the galactic equivalent of the United States, the United Federation of Planets.[1] Although Kirk constantly praises the virtues of diplomacy and the peaceful coexistence it can achieve and maintain, he is always ready to reach for his phaser or his photon torpedoes to deal with alien threats. At times he easily outdoes JFK—he brings not just Earth, but the whole galaxy, and possibly the entire universe, to the brink of destruction.

Kirk also pursues an active "domestic policy" in the galaxy, following Kennedy in championing the oppressed and downtrodden, and seeking to put an end to prejudice, ignorance, and poverty wherever he finds them. But his concern for the weak frequently leads Kirk to adopt the pose of the strong man, sometimes becoming virtually indistinguishable from the tyrants he opposes. Despite *Star Trek*'s famous Prime Directive, which dictates a policy of nonintervention on the part of a Federation starship in the development of alien peoples, Kirk repeatedly interferes in the life of the planets he visits, sometimes remaking alien civilizations from the ground up. Kirk's goal is always admirable: to free a people from bondage to superstition, religious idolatry, or some other form of ignorance and prejudice that enslaves them. But despite insistent rhetoric to the contrary, he characteristically views the civilizations he encounters around the galaxy as primitive, backward, and incapable of the self-development mandated by the Federation. He rarely hesitates to substitute his own enlightened vision for local beliefs—and does so more or less single-handedly and on his own initiative—all in the name of spreading freedom and democracy throughout the galaxy, in opposition to the totalitarian regimes represented by the Klingons and the Romulans.

As a result, *Star Trek* offers a vision of the future in which an intellectual, and specifically a scientific, elite will heroically bring the benefits of technology and the liberal idea of freedom and democracy to backward peoples all around the galaxy—whether they happen to want these benefits or not. Accordingly, Captain Kirk is always paired with his Science Officer, the brainy Mr. Spock (Leonard Nimoy), just as Kennedy was always linked to his Harvard brain trust, including McGeorge Bundy, John Kenneth Galbraith, and Robert McNamara. *Star Trek* highlights the tension at the heart of Kennedy liberalism, the uneasy alliance between a democratic, egalitarian spirit and a strong streak of intellectual elitism. As in the Kennedy administration, in *Star Trek* common people suffering from prejudice and oppression are the chief object of concern, but their liberation—and hence their destiny—rests in the hands of uncommon leaders. The leaders' expertise is necessary to save the day, thus elevating the intellectual elite to heroic, almost aristocratic status. That may explain why one of the most democratic administrations in American history is remembered today by the strangely aristocratic-sounding name of "Camelot."

Given all these parallels, it comes as no surprise to discover that *Star Trek*, like the Kennedy administration, routinely harked back to the American West. Viewers tuning into the show week after week were first greeted by the voice of Captain Kirk solemnly intoning the keynote of the series: "Space—the final frontier." The creator of *Star Trek*, Gene Roddenberry, said that he sold the concept to the NBC network as "*Wagon Train* to the stars," packaging it as the science-fiction equivalent of a TV Western very popular at the time.[2] One might at first be tempted to think that, given the timing, *Star Trek* derived its idea of space as the final frontier from JFK's New Frontier.[3] But, in fact, *Star Trek* had direct roots in an American Western that predated Kennedy's New Frontier by several years. Although Gene Roddenberry is today identified with *Star Trek*, before that series he had a significant career as a television writer dating back as early as 1954.[4] Roddenberry made a major contribution as a writer to one of the most successful of all TV Westerns, *Have Gun–Will Travel*, which ran on CBS from 1957 to 1963 and was consistently among the highest-rated programs on television. It is the fifth-longest-running Western in TV history.[5] In the show's six seasons, out of a total of 225 episodes, Roddenberry is credited as the writer of 24 of them. Viewing these episodes today, one is struck by how many of the ideas and motifs of *Star Trek* had their origin in the earlier Western. If space came to be the final frontier for Roddenberry—an inspired vision of the distant future—the original frontier for him was in U.S. terms the oldest frontier of them all, the American West.

Studying *Have Gun–Will Travel* can help us better understand *Star Trek*, as well as the Kennedy brand of liberalism that Roddenberry embraced and portrayed in both series. And the story of his involvement in *Have Gun* can change our view of the nature and history of both the Western and television more generally. It becomes a significant case study in the collaborative nature of television creativity and also a challenge to our assumptions about the sharp boundaries between different genres in popular culture. Finally, the many thematic connections between *Have Gun* and *Star Trek* call into question the common belief that the Western is by nature a politically conservative genre. If we can find anticipations of Kennedy liberalism in a TV Western that began in 1957, we must revise our picture of the history of pop culture. Liberal revision of the Western did not begin in the movies of the late 1960s, as is generally assumed, but was already flourishing in the heyday of supposedly simplistic shoot-'em-up horse operas on television in the 1950s.

Fast Gun for Hire

Have Gun–Will Travel was from the beginning regarded as the thinking man's Western.[6] Created by Herb Meadow and Sam Rolfe at the height of television's love affair with the genre, it was the most intelligent, sophisticated, and cultured of the classic TV Westerns, unrivaled in the quality of its writing until David Milch brought his series *Deadwood* to HBO in 2004. The hero of *Have Gun* is a man called simply Paladin (Richard Boone), "a knight without armor in a savage land," according to the show's memorable theme song. His very name conjures up images out of chivalric romance and hence the aristocratic and distant past.[7] He is a professional gunman, who sells his services to solve a wide variety of problems and disputes in cases where the use of force is likely to be necessary. Back in his home base of San Francisco, financed by his gunfighting income, Paladin leads the life of a cultivated gentleman, a combination of patron of the arts, gourmet, bon vivant, and playboy. But out on a job, Paladin is all business, one of the fastest draws in the West, with the military knowledge of a West Point graduate and the tracking ability of Indians (among whom he has lived and learned their languages and customs). Paladin is so versatile that in one episode he can trade blows with the British bare-knuckle boxing champion ("The Prize-Fight Story," episode #30), while in another he can trade witti-

Kirk and Spock rolled into one? Paladin (Richard Boone) in *Have Gun–Will Travel*. (Jerry Ohlinger's Movie Material Store)

cisms with Oscar Wilde during the author's lecture tour of the West ("The Ballad of Oscar Wilde," #51).[8] Although he is always prepared to kill in cold blood, Paladin also is capable of mercy and remorse. In an era of largely one-dimensional heroes in TV Westerns, Paladin stood out by virtue of the complexity of his character.[9]

Paladin is such a complex figure that in *Star Trek* terms, he can be viewed as a combination of Captain Kirk and Mr. Spock. Like Kirk, Paladin claims to be a man of peace and always tries to use diplomatic means to settle disputes and to avoid bloodshed if possible. But also like Kirk, Paladin has a proud and aggressive nature. He has a highly developed sense of honor and of his own dignity. He is quick to take affront at any challenge to his honor; he has a short temper; and he frowns upon any attempt to question his integrity and authority. Although he is disposed to keep out of a fight, once he gets into one, he is implacable in trying to win it. In short, like Kirk, Paladin perfectly embodies the paradox of the warlike man of peace. Sharing a kind of hypermasculinity with Kirk, Paladin also resembles him in his proclivity for womanizing.[10] Both heroes leave a trail of broken hearts wherever they go. Females of all types (of all species in Kirk's case) fall in love with the two as manly and exotic strangers, but unfortunately for these women, both Paladin and Kirk appear to live by the principle of "love 'em and leave 'em."

But for all these aggressive and erotic impulses, in many respects Paladin more closely resembles Spock.[11] He prides himself on governing his life by logic. He is extremely intelligent and learned, prizing reason above all other human attributes. Again like Spock, Paladin is often called upon to solve mysteries by the process of rational deduction. He is a champion of enlightenment, using reason to cut through the fog of superstition and prejudice. Paladin hates ignorance and groupthink. The mindless lynch mob is his greatest (and recurrent) enemy. Like Spock, Paladin often expresses a kind of aristocratic contempt for the average run of human beings, who fail to live up to his high standards of rationality.[12] Paladin's intellectual elitism links him to both the Kennedy administration and *Star Trek*. In his uncommon and highly cultivated nature, Paladin looks forward to another *Star Trek* hero, Captain Jean-Luc Picard. He was Kirk's replacement as the commander of the *Enterprise* in *The Next Generation* (1987–1994), Roddenberry's second go at a *Star Trek* TV series. Like Picard, Paladin is strangely bookish for an action hero. He likes to quote classical sources (Cicero in the original Latin in "The Golden Toad," #88), and words from Shakespeare as well as from Romantic and Victorian poets flow from his lips. All this intelligence, rationality, learning, and a highly developed taste for the classics of European culture heighten in Paladin the traditional paradox of the Western hero: he is an aristocratic figure serving democratic ends.[13]

Paladin resembles later Roddenberry heroes like Kirk, Spock, and Picard so closely that we must remind ourselves that Roddenberry did not create the central figure of *Have Gun–Will Travel* himself. Paladin was the brainchild of Meadow and Rolfe, and the character had taken its essential form before Roddenberry began writing for the series. Although Roddenberry wrote what are widely regarded as some of the best episodes of the show, his contributions as a writer were by no means unique, in either quality or the direction in which he develops the character of Paladin. For example, Roddenberry frequently has Paladin quote Shakespeare, but so do several of the other writers, and the most Shakespearean of all the episodes, a re-creation of *Othello* called "The Moor's Revenge" (#54), was written not by Roddenberry but by Melvin Levy.[14] What is really interesting about *Have Gun* for students of *Star Trek* is to see Roddenberry developing ideas for the later series while working within a formula originally established by Meadow and Rolfe. An important lesson in the collaborative nature of TV creativity can be learned from observing what are often viewed as the unique ideas of *Star Trek* incubating in an earlier series created by writers other than Roddenberry.

In its broad outlines, the formula for a typical *Have Gun* episode is very close to the *Star Trek* formula. Just as the *Enterprise* lands on an alien planet, Paladin typically rides into a Western community as a stranger in a strange land. The local inhabitants seem alien to him, and he seems alien to them. Dressed all in black, he stands out in a crowd in an ominous way, almost as if he had come from another planet. The locals typically distrust him as an outsider and are particularly suspicious of him because he fits their stereotype of an evil gunfighter, and they do not like a stranger interfering in their affairs. At the same time, the customs and conditions of the community are opaque to Paladin. Either the real power structure of the community is concealed, or some dark event in the past governs the present, or perhaps just the odd behavior of the inhabitants blinds Paladin to what is truly going on. Like the crew of the *Enterprise*, Paladin is challenged with uncovering the mysterious forces that rule the community into which he has wandered and thus breaking the impasse into which it has backed itself, or otherwise solving its problems, in the process often saving his own life or freeing himself from some form of imprisonment. Combining the talents of Kirk and Spock, Paladin must demonstrate his superiority by proving his adaptability to local conditions.

Paladin's great virtue is thus his cosmopolitanism. Like the crew of the *Enterprise,* he has traveled extensively and learned to size up an alien situation quickly. He does not possess the *Enterprise*'s convenient Universal Translator, but his command of languages is exceptional for his day. He knows a little Chinese, speaks several Indian languages, and in general has great skill at communicating with people apparently foreign to him. One of the keys to his repeated success is his tolerance. His wide travels have taught him an appreciation of, and sympathy for, different customs and ways of life. He therefore does not let prejudices stand in the way of his understanding and dealing with an unfamiliar situation.

Roddenberry himself recognized the parallels between *Have Gun* and *Star Trek* when he was trying to sell another science fiction series to NBC and argued that the success of the Western augured well for his new project:

> *Assignment: Earth* could also be called *Have Gun–Will Travel 1968!* Yes, I'm quite serious, and should know what I'm talking about. As well as being co-creator of *Assignment: Earth* I also was head writer of *Have Gun–Will Travel.* The prime dramatic ingredients of the two shows are almost identical—both shows feature a slightly larger-than-life main character, who sallies forth weekly from a familiar "home base" to do battle with extraordinary evil in an action-adventure format. As top HG-WT writers were aware . . . , there were a surprising number of "science fiction" ingredients in the character of Paladin. Certainly for a person living in 1872, his remarkable knowledge, attitudes and abilities were very much that of a man from "another place" or "another time." In fact, one of Paladin's most effective dramatic tools and charms was his detached and superior, sometimes almost condescending, perspective from which he viewed the fallible world about him.[15]

Roddenberry is shrewdly peddling his wares to NBC here, but he still displays keen insights into the character of Paladin and the nature of *Have Gun* in general, and reveals that he thought of himself as in some sense already writing science fiction when he was working on the earlier Western.

The structural parallels between *Have Gun* and *Star Trek* point to the key thematic similarity between the two series: celebrating toleration as the central and universal virtue. When Roddenberry was concerned that Paramount's *Star Trek* films were deviating from his original conception, he tried to get the franchise back on course by writing a long letter to the producer who had replaced him in the film series, Harve Bennett. He stated clearly what he regarded as the fundamental principle of the *Star Trek* universe (as its creator, he was convinced that he ought to know):[16] "to be different does not mean something is ugly or to think differently does not mean that someone is necessarily wrong."[17] These words could serve equally well as the motto of the typical *Have Gun–Will Travel* episode. Like the crew of the *Enterprise*, Paladin repeatedly finds himself caught between warring factions or tribes or ethnic groups, and is forced to negotiate their differences and show that, for all their obvious oppositions and divisions, deep down they have something in common, which can provide the basis for their living together in peace and prosperity.

Learning to live with difference is thus the central theme that unites *Have Gun* with *Star Trek*. Both series constantly teach the need to overcome prejudice, especially hateful and harmful stereotypes. Sam Rolfe took pride in this aspect of his series: "We couldn't have an actor, say, come out and tell a whole town that they're prejudice[d] toward religion or ethnics. But we were able to tell the same story without using those words—such as prejudice, and viewers kept tuning in each week not because they liked the fiction, but because they knew it was true. . . . They couldn't admit that prejudice was next door, but could accept a drama that was."[18] To be sure, both series often fell into the trap of perpetuating stereotypes even while seeking to combat them. Although both could lay claim to feminist credentials in seeking to provide positive images of powerful women, particularly in positions of authority traditionally reserved for men, they also often presented women in demeaning stereotypes, partially as a result of Paladin's and Kirk's incorrigible womanizing, and also because of a tendency to exoticize female characters, often depicting them as irrational and incapable of living up to masculine standards of discipline.[19] The record of both series in portraying race is also equivocal. In *Have Gun*, the role of Hey Boy (Kam Tong), a porter in Paladin's hotel who is effectively his servant, is an example of orientalist stereotyping. As his name indicates, Hey Boy is infantilized and placed in a subordinate position. He is frequently portrayed as superstitious and often embodies the stereotype of the Inscrutable East. But a number of episodes give Hey Boy a more active role and are clearly meant to emphasize Paladin's respect for Chinese culture in all its ancient wisdom.[20] Similarly, Paladin is repeatedly shown to be a friend of the Indians, and he often defends their interests while displaying a genuine knowledge of their culture.[21] And yet by contemporary standards, *Have Gun* is painfully stereotypical in its portrayal of what we now call Native Americans, sometimes presenting them as little better than ignorant and cruel savages.[22]

Much the same can be said of the treatment of race in *Star Trek*. Roddenberry prided himself on offering a multicultural, multiracial view of the future, and the show became famous for presenting the first interracial kiss—between Kirk and Lieutenant Uhura (Nichelle Nichols)—on prime time network television.[23] And yet, as many commentators have pointed out, the command structure of the *Enterprise,* and of the United Federation of Planets more generally, remained predominantly white. Racially darker figures, like the Klingons and the Romulans, tended to be presented in a negative light. There can be no question that both *Have Gun–Will Travel* and *Star Trek* fail to meet contemporary standards of political correctness.[24] But it is important to remember that by the standards of their own day, both shows were progressive on issues of race and gender—and were deliberately intended to be so. Thus, in analyzing Roddenberry's apprenticeship in *Have Gun–Will Travel* for the creation of *Star Trek,* one can see how he learned to write effective parables of the need for toleration and of the appreciation of what is today called diversity.

The Armenian Helen of Troy

Of all the stories Roddenberry wrote for *Have Gun–Will Travel,* perhaps the one most clearly linked to *Star Trek* is a first-season episode called "Helen of Abajinian" (#16).[25] The title is clearly intended to recall Helen of Troy, as is the name of a third-season episode of *Star Trek,* "Elaan of Troyis" (#57). The exotic dance performed by the eponymous heroine of "Helen of Abajinian" is very similar to one in the pilot of *Star Trek,* "The Cage" (#1). If one were looking for Roddenberry's personal obsessions in *Have Gun* and *Star Trek,* his fascination with the Helen of Troy archetype would be a good place to start. Roddenberry seems to have been fixated on stories about beautiful, exotic women who are the source of conflict among aggressive males, driving them to distraction, if not destruction.[26] One way in which Paladin proves to be a forerunner of Captain Kirk is that he must learn how to use the female of the species to bring peace rather than war to men, and to do that, he must learn to channel the sexual power of women for constructive purposes. That perhaps explains why some of Roddenberry's most persistent fantasies seem to have involved the domestication of a Helen of Troy figure.[27]

In "Helen of Abajinian," a wealthy winemaker named Sam Abajinian (Harold J. Stone) has hired Paladin to rescue his daughter, Helen (Lisa Gaye), whom he thinks has been abducted by a young cattle rancher named Jimmy O'Riley (Wright King). In the Roddenberry universe, it turns out that the man rather than the woman is the victim. Helen has run off with O'Riley in a scheme to lure him into marriage. In a typically conflicted situation, Paladin must mediate among a whole series of opposing forces. He must get O'Riley to want to marry Helen, and at the same time reconcile Abajinian to having Jimmy as a son-in-law and Jimmy to having Sam as a father-in-law. Paladin's task is complicated by a whole set of ethnic and other differences that cut across the battles between the sexes and between the generations. As a grape grower, Sam has a farmer's mentality, while Jimmy is locked into thinking like a cattle rancher. As a result, they quarrel over questions of land use in a fashion typical of the Western. Moreover, Jimmy is presented as a straitlaced, mainstream American, whereas Abajinian is a colorful Armenian immigrant, speaking with a heavy foreign accent and accompanied by a couple of ethnic sidekicks named Gourken (Vladimir Sokoloff) and Jorgi (Nick Dennis). Sam has all sorts of Old World notions, including an extreme conception of honor, that make it difficult for him to deal with American customs. The episode thus tests Paladin's cosmopolitanism, and fortunately he rises to the challenge. He can speak a little Armenian, he appreciates the fine points of Armenian cooking, and he can match and even surpass Sam when it comes to downing a potent Armenian brew. Above all, when negotiating his fee, Paladin demonstrates a complete command of Old World haggling that earns him the respect of the farmer: "My friend, you bargain like an Armenian."

As Shakespeare's *Othello* demonstrates, ethnic differences can be the stuff of tragedy, but as *The Merchant of Venice* shows, they can also be played for comedy. "Helen of Abajinian" illustrates how easily jokes can be generated out of the confusion and misunderstanding produced by ethnic differences. The episode even contains jokes at the expense of Kurds, which must have been truly baffling to an American audience in the 1950s. The only way Paladin can prevent ethnic conflict from leading to tragedy is to get the characters to laugh at their differences, which ultimately means getting them to laugh at themselves. His smooth cosmopolitanism facilitates that result. *Have Gun–Will Travel* was generally a serious show, dealing with weighty issues, but it had many humorous moments. In several of his scripts, Roddenberry displayed a particularly light touch among the writers, foreshadowing the comedy that was to liven up *Star Trek*. As we can see in "Helen of Abajinian," comedy often served Roddenberry as the means of overcoming the tragic potential of ethnic difference.

Dealing with O'Riley turns out to be easier for Paladin than dealing with Sam Abajinian. After all, he has the power of Helen's innate sexuality working for him. It is her exotic dance that finally wins the day in a scene that was to become fairly common in *Star Trek* ("starship crew turned on by interplanetary sexpot"). But Paladin makes sure to give a deeper significance to what might otherwise seem to be a merely sexual attraction. He displays the kind of archaeological knowledge that was to become Spock's stock-in-trade: "Ancient Armenia was at the crossroads of the world." Referring to Greece, Persia, and Minoa, Paladin teaches O'Riley a lesson in Roddenberry's favorite subject, universality: "These dances, O'Riley, are a language. The most compelling, understandable, universal language of mankind." This kind of cross-cultural communication is what Paladin has been trying to facilitate throughout the episode. O'Riley has been puzzled by the—to him—strange customs of the Armenians ("women don't chase men"). But Paladin carefully shepherds him to the point where he makes a Roddenberryan declaration of the acceptance of difference: "Just 'cause they don't do things like my people, that don't mean they ain't real down-to-earth folks too." By the same token, O'Riley expects some multicultural indulgence himself; when Paladin tells him that bathing before one's wedding is an Armenian custom, the young man insists: "I've got my customs, too." By the end of the episode Paladin has brought peace to all the warring parties in the valley. In a final display of his ability to bargain like an Armenian, he negotiates a generous dowry for O'Riley from the skinflint Abajinian. With Paladin's help, the man is ready to settle down with the woman, the son-in-law with the father-in-law, and the cattle rancher with the farmer. In the terms of *Star Trek*, they are ready to live long and prosper.

Liberalism in the Desert

"Helen of Abajinian" was a standout episode of *Have Gun–Will Travel* and earned Roddenberry a Writer's Guild award for the best-written TV Western script in 1957.[28] It was the kind of offbeat, change-of-pace episode that was later to characterize *Star Trek* at its best. A more typical *Have Gun* episode Roddenberry penned, the third-season "The Golden Toad" (#88), explores similar issues and also can be linked to *Star Trek*. Paladin once again wanders into a situation rife with divisions and tense with strife. He has come to aid a Mr. Webster (Kevin Hagen), who is in danger because he discovered an ancient Indian treasure on his property. Bitter over having been sold "no good, dried-out land" by townspeople who failed to warn him of the drought in the area, Webster is determined to keep the treasure for himself. The opposition to Webster in the town is led by a woman named Doris (Lorna Thayer), who is the big landowner in the region. Proud that her "family has owned this valley since '32," Doris speaks, as do many of the antagonists in the series, like a feudal aristocrat: "This is my valley—if it weren't for me, none of you would be here." Doris claims that she retained the mineral rights to the land she sold to Webster, and thus is entitled to her share of any gold he has discovered. This is the kind of standoff Paladin typically has to deal with—people fighting over property, mineral rights, buried treasure, and willing to kill each other for financial gain. As in an earlier episode Roddenberry wrote, "Yuma Treasure" (#14), he takes a very dim view of the obsessions generated by greed. All that Webster has actually found is a golden toad, some kind of ancient idol that the vanished Indians once worshipped; but everyone assumes that it is part of a larger treasure hoard.

Because he is free of the vice of greed, Paladin figures out what the ancient artifact really signifies. The worship of an amphibious creature like a toad must point to the presence of water somewhere in the area. By dynamiting the cave Webster has been searching, Paladin sets free an underground river that can irrigate the entire valley and end the drought. That is the true treasure of the ancient Indians—not a barren metal but the fertilizing power of nature. Having earlier solved the riddle of the golden toad, Paladin has, in fact, surreptitiously gone off to the county seat and secured the water rights to the underground river. But unlike the greedy townspeople, Paladin has no intention of exploiting anybody, and announces at the end: "In order to promote peace and increase the population in the valley, which of course will serve my interests also, additional shares will be given to each married family at no extra charge." Paladin's proclamation sets off a frenzy of marriages in the valley, including that of Doris to Webster.

Once again Paladin has saved the day and brought peace and prosperity to warring people, and he has done so by following Roddenberryan principles. Consumed by greed, the townspeople fall prey to the power of ancient myth. They believe that a buried treasure must be gold. But Paladin, with his enlightened mind, looks for a natural explanation for the ancient myth and finds it in the purely natural power of water, which ultimately will mean much more to the townspeople than any traditional treasure. Notice also the Kennedy liberalism in Paladin's approach, a middle way between communism and capitalism. Paladin owns the water rights, but he exercises them in a civic-minded fashion, and in the process manages to further his self-interest while aiding the townspeople. Several episodes of *Have Gun–Will Travel* focus on the issue of water rights, including the first one Roddenberry wrote for the series, "The Great Mojave Chase" (#3). For the liberal Roddenberry, water rights symbolize everything that can go wrong under capitalism, the ability of one individual to monopolize a resource that ought to be available to all. Roddenberry is deeply suspicious of capitalism, which he views as chiefly taking the form of robber barons.[29] His scripts for *Have Gun* are filled with big landowners who act like local tyrants, imposing their will on the common people, who are dependent on the rich for their livelihood.

What makes Roddenberry a liberal, rather than a communist, is that he still has a limited faith in private enterprise and does not simply offer public ownership as the solution to the problem of, for example, water rights. Like a good Kennedy liberal, he searches for a way to reconcile private ownership with public good, and he offers Paladin as a model. In both "The Golden Toad" and "The Great Mojave Chase," Paladin represents a strong and competent outside force that can intervene in a community and break up its monopolies of ownership. In both episodes Paladin behaves more like a government official than a private businessman; above all, he does not arise spontaneously from within the community but must enter it as an outsider. In the grand progessivist tradition of Teddy Roosevelt, he is a trust buster. The chief point is that Paladin is detached from local interests and prejudices and is thus able to see the big picture. Positioned above the competing local interests, he has the objectivity to come up with a solution that is beneficial to all, not just to a single individual. In this respect, Paladin foreshadows the world of *Star Trek*, where purely commercial interests are generally treated with contempt and the public-spiritedness of quasi-governmental figures like Kirk and Spock is constantly offered as the alternative to the senseless greed of businesspeople and other wealthy figures.[30]

Witch Hunt on the Frontier

"The Golden Toad" may also be seen as a prototype of a *Star Trek* episode in the way that Paladin finds a purely rational solution to the riddle of an ancient myth. In several *Star Trek* episodes, Kirk and Spock have to demystify ancient myths, and they often have to solve a kind of riddle to do so.[31] This enlightenment spirit is evident in one of Roddenberry's less successful scripts for *Have Gun,* the second-season "Monster of Moon Ridge" (#63), the only Halloween episode the series ever attempted. Pushing the limits of genre, Roddenberry tries to turn a Western into a horror story. Unfortunately, in the process he loses the believability that is usually the hallmark of his scripts. The episode threatens to become laughable when we hear talk of werewolves and vampires intruding into the American frontier. The West was wild, but not *that* wild. Nevertheless, the episode is noteworthy from a thematic standpoint in any comparison with *Star Trek.* The story begins with an interesting exchange between Paladin and Hey Boy, which reflects the orientalist stereotype of the East as superstitious and the West by contrast as rational. When Hey Boy learns that Paladin is going off on a dangerous mission that may involve supernatural forces, he gives his friend what purports to be a dragon's tooth to protect him. Paladin sets the keynote of the episode when he speaks for the enlightenment spirit of America: "Hey Boy, your new country has a much stronger potion for driving off evil—equal parts reason and daylight."

Paladin heads off to a remote town, where rumors of a monster on Moon Ridge have left the locals on edge, their guns loaded with silver bullets. Paladin keeps laughing off the rumors and scorns the superstitions of the town. When he tells the sheriff, "Salem witch burners would be very happy in your town," he tips us off to the deeper political significance of the episode. As is particularly evident in Arthur Miller's famous play *The Crucible* (1953), throughout the 1950s the term *witch hunt* was a code word for McCarthyism, the overzealous pursuit of communist infiltration in government and other positions of importance in American society.[32] Hollywood was particularly sensitive to the issue of McCarthyism because of the infamous blacklisting of several well-known screenwriters for alleged communist sympathies. Whenever Roddenberry is dealing with superstition and the irrationality of mob psychology, he often has in mind the way anticommunist zealots like Joseph McCarthy were able to manipulate American public opinion against people with any evidence of left-wing sympathies and connections in their past.[33]

But "Monster on Moon Ridge" turns out to be a more general parable on the evils of persecution and prejudice. Paladin discovers that the monstrous apparitions on Moon Ridge have been created by a woman named Maria (Shirley O'Hara), who is trying to ward off strangers in order to protect her simpleminded son and the equally simpleminded daughter of a neighbor with whom he likes to play. As Paladin says, the woman feels that she has been "run out of town by ignorance and prejudice" and now believes that she must exploit the superstitious fear of the townspeople if she is to keep the youngsters safe from ridicule and contempt. The focus of the episode is on Paladin's extraordinary composure in the face of the apparitions. Here he is at his most Spock-like; he behaves just as coolly as the logical Vulcan does repeatedly in similar circumstances in *Star Trek*. Faced with what appears to be an old crone, and ever the Shakespearean, Paladin sees the theatricality of the situation: "It's *Macbeth*—enter the First Witch."[34]

Confronted by Paladin's unflappability, Maria finally tells him, "I was afraid of you. You have no respect for witches." In one of the show's more feminist moments, Paladin replies, "Well, I do have respect for some things—courageous, intelligent women, for example." As always, Paladin's great strength is his freedom from prejudice, which translates into a freedom from superstition as well. Maria ends up celebrating the debunking power of Paladin's enlightened mind: "Materialize an apparition on a broomstick in front of him and he'll ask it to sweep the floor." The same could be said of Mr. Spock and Captain Kirk. A number of *Star Trek* episodes turn on the refusal of the *Enterprise* crew to be taken in by ghostly apparitions and attempts to manipulate their minds.[35] This theme apparently meant a great deal to Roddenberry. In "Moon Ridge," it prompts one of the most didactic endings in any of his *Have Gun* scripts. Paladin announces that the real monsters are the townspeople who would make fun of the young boy and girl simply because they are different. Despite his usual enlightenment commitment to spreading the truth, in this case Paladin has no interest in disabusing the town of its frightening illusions: "Ignorant and prejudiced people like to be deceived and I think they deserve it when they are. Why confuse them with the truth?" This is the kind of condescension toward common people that Roddenberry himself notes in Paladin in his letter promoting his *Assignment: Earth* project. Perhaps something of Roddenberry's own attitude toward his fellow human beings surfaces in the script here as well.

Indian Indians

The link between prejudice and superstition, and Roddenberry's contempt for both, is the thematic core of another one of the change-of-pace episodes he wrote for *Have Gun*, the third-season "Tiger" (#89). In planning the second season, Sam Rolfe had contemplated sending Paladin off to foreign countries to extend the range of his adventures.[36] The scripts had already given him backstories that placed him formerly in exotic lands such as India and China, to which he might eventually return. But the economics of production and the fear of tampering with a successful formula were to keep Paladin squarely in the American West for the six-season run of *Have Gun*. But if Paladin could not go to India, perhaps India might come to him, and Roddenberry showed his versatility as a writer by supplying just the right script for the purposes. In "Tiger," Paladin is summoned to Argus, Texas, by a refugee from British India named John Ellsworth (Parley Baer). Ellsworth needs a tiger hunter, and Paladin evidently was legendary as such in his earlier days in India. Ellsworth is the standard local tyrant of *Have Gun* scripts. He thinks that his wealth gives him the right to order anybody around, even Paladin: "I can buy and sell people like you, Mr. Gunman." He treats the servants he has brought with him from India with disdain, and sadistically enjoys tormenting a romantic couple among them by at once encouraging and frustrating their love.

Ellsworth behaved even more abominably back in India. Pursuing his sport as a hunter, he wounded a tiger that, in its rage, went on to kill over a hundred people in Bengal. Ellsworth shows his contempt for humanity by saying offhandedly, "Maybe I am responsible for a few miserable natives dying." By contrast, Paladin is sympathetic to the natives: "I always found the Bengalis to be a gentle people." Ellsworth is now paying for his arrogance. He believes that he is the victim of a Bengali curse and firmly expects that he will be killed by a tiger. He has come to Texas to get as far away as possible from India and any tiger habitat. The episode works to create something of a supernatural aura around the threat to Ellsworth, but in typical Roddenberry fashion it ends up demystifying the curse. A tiger does show up, but it belongs to a traveling circus and is a harmless pet. Nevertheless, like Oedipus, Ellsworth runs squarely into his fate precisely by trying to avoid it. So consumed is he by superstition that merely hearing the roar of the tiger on the loose frightens Ellsworth into running off a cliff to his death. As in "Monster on Moon Ridge" and many *Star Trek* episodes, Roddenberry supplies a purely natural explanation for what at first appears to be a supernatural event.

What distinguishes an otherwise run-of-the-mill script in "Tiger" is the way Roddenberry has fun playing with ethnic stereotypes. Paladin can, of course, speak a little Hindi when he meets Ellsworth's servant Pahndu (Paul Clarke), but they quickly switch to English for the following exchange when Pahndu realizes his mistake in trying to bar Paladin from access to his master:

Pahndu: I thought you were one of the natives here.
Paladin: Natives? Oh yes, a quaint lot.
Pahndu: Very strange, and I'm afraid dangerous.
Paladin: Only when restless.

Here white Americans are subjected to the prejudices normally invoked in scripts about Indians or other exotic foreigners. Roddenberry is enjoying reversing perspectives and standing stereotypes on their head, something *Star Trek* does all the time. "The natives are restless" is a cliché of jungle adventure stories, typically spoken by white explorers of the Africans or Asians or South Americans they are hunting down or otherwise trying to exploit. Here the Easterner Pahndu turns the tables on the Westerner Paladin, who plays along with the game. As a civilized Indian having come to the wilds of Texas, Pahndu looks on Americans as the dangerous natives. Moreover, he finds American customs quaint and puzzling. He asks Paladin about a strange rite he refers to as a "box dance." It takes even the quick-witted Paladin a moment before he realizes that Pahndu is asking him about that most American of customs, the square dance.

In a reversal of orientalist disparaging of the East, Pahndu reacts to news that a Texas mountain lion is too small to be mistaken for a tiger: "Even in animals, this is an inferior continent." Roddenberry also plays with the ambiguity of the word *Indian* in the episode. The townspeople refer to Pahndu as "Ellsworth's Injun" and challenge him: "Tell us again what tribe you're from." By the time Roddenberry is through ringing the changes on ethnic stereotypes, we come away from "Tiger" not agreeing with Rudyard Kipling that "East is East, and West is West, and never the twain shall meet," but rather wondering how to keep East and West clearly distinct in our minds if an Indian can be an Injun and Paladin a restless native. By shifting us back and forth between Eastern perspectives on the West and Western perspectives on the East, Roddenberry uses "Tiger" to teach a lesson in cultural relativism. The multicultural perspectivism of the episode is a harbinger of many *Star Trek* scripts to come.

How to Handle a Lynch Mob

"Tiger" is a story of prejudice appropriately punished by superstition. The very close-mindedness in Ellsworth that leads him to treat the Bengalis with contempt makes him susceptible to believing that they have the power to put a curse on him. As early as in his writing for *Have Gun–Will Travel,* Roddenberry was focusing on the dangers of close-mindedness, especially insofar as it manifests itself in forms of groupthink, such as superstition. We have already seen him critical of the witch-hunt mentality; a related theme, basic to the Western, is the lynch mob. Many episodes of *Have Gun* take up this theme, including several of Roddenberry's scripts.[37] The best of these is "Posse" (#82), in the third season. The plot is familiar, but Roddenberry gives it a novel twist. Wandering as usual, Paladin comes upon a seemingly pitiful and helpless saddle tramp and makes camp with him. But Dobie (Perry Cook) is in fact a murderer and has come up with a clever plan to shift his guilt onto Paladin when they are both found by the posse that has been hunting for the tramp. While Paladin is not paying attention, Dobie makes things look as if Paladin has overpowered him and even succeeds in planting the murder weapon in Paladin's saddlebags.

The story generates the powerful dramatic tension that always comes from watching an innocent man on trial for his life in illegal and unjust proceedings. Paladin has to use all his considerable wits to escape the attempt to hang him, and only a slip of the tongue by Dobie reveals his guilt and exonerates Paladin. The episode explores all the issues a lynching usually raises in Westerns.[38] Once again the story features a local tyrant—a cattle baron named McKay (Denver Pyle)—who flaunts his power by dominating the deliberations of the posse and overruling the sheriff whenever he wants.

But Roddenberry puts the emphasis on an unusual aspect of the situation: Paladin's heroic refusal to be rattled by the danger of his circumstances. For Roddenberry the episode becomes a case study of how to deal with the psychology of a lynch mob. Paladin again plays a Spock-like role, keeping cool in circumstances that would drive most people to fall apart emotionally.[39] In response to any provocation, he maintains his rationality and is determined to stand or fall with the power of logic. When the sheriff questions his behavior, saying, "An innocent man would be begging now, mister," Paladin logically replies, "So would a guilty one." In Paladin's analysis, the real danger he faces is the irrationality of mob behavior. By refusing to beg for his life, he is pursuing a deliberate strategy: "I'd rather give this gathering a chance to do some thinking." That is why he will not give the mob the emotional display it craves: "A good lynching needs tears and screams and terror—the more excitement, the less thinking." Paladin is an astute analyst of lynch-mob psychology and understands that it depends on a process of scapegoating and victimization: "The ideal victim is mentally or emotionally ill. . . . Lynchers have to be content with people that are merely a little bit different—little people, the weaker they are, the better."[40]

Roddenberry thus returns to his central goal of defending the right to be different. He condemns mobs because they constitute their identity by defining themselves in opposition to a lone victim who is somehow different. They are like a pack of animals ganging up on the weakest member of the group and killing it. Thus Paladin must be at his strongest in this episode. If he shows any sign of weakness, the pack will turn on him. He is, in fact, at his most aggressive and sarcastic in "Posse." In circumstances in which most people would feel compelled to humble themselves and beg for mercy, Paladin bristles with pride and speaks with utter contempt for the men who hold his life in their hands. When the posse members finally realize their mistake, they go ahead and lynch Dobie anyway, thus confirming Paladin's contempt for them as a mob. His last words in the episode are "Heaven help us from what men do in the name of good." Paladin is a strange kind of American hero. Although he usually stands up for the rights of common people, he does so from an aristocratic perspective, which often involves contempt for their judgment, especially when it manifests itself in any form of groupthink. The more "common" the thinking, the more Paladin despises it. For Roddenberry, the problem seems to be that common people, mired in their commonality, will not allow individuals to be different.

Roddenberry thus crafts a distinctive take on the standard Western lynch-mob plot. Ordinarily in such a story, Dobie would have been saved at the end, at least for a fair hearing in a courtroom. The posse would have learned the error of its ways and balked at trying to lynch two men in one day. Frequently the leader of the lynch mob would have been discredited, perhaps by having been revealed to be evil in some way, with an ulterior motive for lynching the particular victim. But, although McKay has some elements of the typical wealthy villain in *Have Gun*, Roddenberry insists on making him a semi-sympathetic character. He gives McKay a long speech eloquently defending the need to resort to vigilante justice. In words that resonate with a brand of Western rhetoric familiar from Ford's *The Searchers* (1956), McKay talks of how difficult it was to create civilization on the frontier. He goes on to say, "It wasn't the law that done that. A lot of hard work, sweat, a few guns, a couple of ropes." McKay thus explains why he and his men are taking the law into their own hands: "That's why we got more faith in trees than courthouses." Roddenberry does not want McKay to come across as an *evil* man. Recall Paladin's saying, "Heaven help us from what men do in the name of good." He does not question the sincerity of McKay or his fellow vigilantes. That makes his critique of groupthink all the more powerful. The recurrent witch hunts and lynch mobs in Roddenberry's scripts point to the problem with common people—when they think in common, they automatically assume that what they are doing is for the common good, and thus they may end up doing evil in the name of good. In his scripts Roddenberry frequently juxtaposes a brave individual who is right against a crowd that finds strength in numbers and blunders into wrong. This is a motif Roddenberry was later to develop in many *Star Trek* episodes.

The Night before Christmas

A story that epitomizes the foreshadowing of *Star Trek* in *Have Gun–Will Travel* is "The Hanging Cross" (#15), an only partially successful attempt at a Christmas episode in the first season (it was first broadcast on December 21, 1957). The story is vaguely reminiscent of *The Searchers;* it deals with the attempt to recover a white child who has been stolen by Indians. Paladin is working for a rancher named Nathaniel Beecher (Edward Binns), yet another of the unending sequence of tyrannical rich men in *Have Gun*. (Paladin appears to be the only human being uncorrupted by money in the series, perhaps because he uses it to enjoy himself, not to exercise power.) Beecher throws his weight around in the community by throwing his money around. At a key moment in the plot, he gets his ranch hands to follow his lead by threatening to fire them all. Sounding like a frontier Bertolt Brecht, Beecher cynically says of his economic control over his hands: "The belly always wins out." The great grief of Beecher's life is that his son, Robbie (Johnny Crawford), was kidnapped when very young by the Sioux. As the story opens, Beecher has located a boy he believes to be his long-lost son among a traveling band of Pawnees and has taken him against his will back to the ranch. Naturally Paladin speaks Pawnee and can serve as Beecher's interpreter in talking to the boy, who is extremely uncomfortable in his new and unfamiliar surroundings.

The episode becomes yet another study of Paladin mediating between different ethnic groups, in this case the classic Western opposition between the cowboys and the Indians. Beecher speaks contemptuously of Paladin as an "Indian lover," but it turns out to be fortunate that he is, because only his closeness to the Indians allows him to negotiate with the Pawnees once they steal the boy back. To the Pawnees, Paladin is known as "he who rides with many tribes," and they trust him. Paladin is once more cast as the cosmopolitan man who is uniquely qualified to bridge the gap of cultural difference.

Roddenberry evidently took his task of writing a Christmas episode seriously. "The Hanging Cross" is one episode in which Paladin voluntarily hangs up his gun and refuses to use it to solve the problems he is dealing with. On Christmas Eve, he truly becomes a man of peace. At a Christmas celebration, he gives a long speech in praise of peace that is a model of the sort of wordy oration Captain Kirk is given to in *Star Trek*. Beecher plays the role of Scrooge in the Christmas scenes. Although he does not quite get around to saying "Bah, humbug!," he does complain about having to listen to "preachin' from a gunslinger." Despite Paladin's heroic pacification efforts, the episode appears to be building up to a bloody climax. Beecher and his hands come to the Pawnee camp itching to recapture the boy and to punish the Indians, in particular to hang their chief. But at the last minute, not the U.S. cavalry but the remaining townspeople come to the rescue. Led by women and children, they interrupt the violent confrontation that is developing and spread Christmas cheer among the heathen, carrying baskets full of holiday food. Under the circumstances, even Beecher cannot bring himself to commit violence, and as a reward for his forbearance, he receives proof in the form of a ring that the boy really is his son. If we have not yet figured out that we are watching a Christmas episode, in the final moments, the gallows Beecher has had erected casts the shadow of what is clearly a cross in Paladin's path. It is unusual to see such a conventionally Christian symbol in a Roddenberry script. But it is, after all, Christmas.

Roddenberry even has Paladin take a stab at explaining Christmas to the Pawnees, reassuring them that this is the one night of the year when the white people honor their children and thus can be trusted. As usual, Paladin brings peace and hope to people for whom war and despair had seemed to be looming. He displays a genuine sympathy for the plight of the Pawnees and is prepared to take their side in the conflict. And yet the Pawnees pay a great price for the solution Paladin comes up with. They must surrender the boy, not just physically but culturally. He had been stubbornly refusing to speak anything but Pawnee, but by the end of the episode he seems proud to have learned how to say "Christmas." As we saw Paladin do with Sam Abajinian, he uses the leverage he has gained with Beecher to negotiate a good deal for the Pawnees, getting them 500 acres of Beecher's land. But in order to settle on this land, the Pawnees are obviously going to have to abandon their traditional nomadic way of life, specifically their warrior ways. The 500-acre grant smacks of a reservation. There is something pater-nalistic about Paladin's solution to the Indians' problems. He is playing the traditional role of the Great White Father.

The Intellectual as Superhero

"The Hanging Tree" thus highlights the tensions at the heart of *Have Gun–Will Travel.* As we have repeatedly seen, Paladin heroically fights for the common good, but he typically expects to be the sole person to dictate the precise terms in which it will be formulated. He enters a different world each week as a stranger and uses his outsider status to assess objectively what is wrong with that world. The local inhabitants are incapable of doing so on their own by virtue of their belonging there and thus being captive to a certain set of traditions, prejudices, and closed horizons. Paladin typically ends up remaking the communities he visits, with the welfare of the inhabit-ants in mind and guided by liberal democratic principles. Nevertheless, in the name of freedom and democracy, he usually sets himself up as superior to the community he is helping, imposing his own solution on it and often expressing open contempt for the people who run it and the way it under-stands its own interests. In all his travels, Paladin never seems to come upon a functioning community, with a set of decent political institutions that make it capable of self-government.[41] The local authorities he deals with are almost always corrupt, or too weak to handle a crisis. The premise of *Have Gun* seems to be that ordinary human beings left to themselves will destroy each other in senseless conflicts, chiefly over property, prejudice, and honor. This Hobbesian war of all against all seems to require the force of a Leviathan like Paladin to bring peace.[42] Paladin has to be the man on the horse, the great leader who can bring the common people out of bondage, but always on his own terms. And standing behind his benevolence, and underwriting it, is the power of his gun, which he does not hesitate to use when necessary (and, of course, he makes the decision when exactly to use it).

In making such decisions unilaterally, Paladin epitomizes the intellec-tual elitism that characterized both *Star Trek* and the Kennedy administra-tion. As we have seen, Roddenberry himself spoke of Paladin's "detached and superior, sometimes almost condescending, perspective from which he viewed the fallible world about him." For all his sympathy for common people, Paladin is *not* a man of the people. Despite his capacity for violent action, he is, in fact, an intellectual hero. That is why the *Have Gun* writers, including Roddenberry, always have him quoting classics of literature and philosophy, as if he were a college professor. He is the sort of hero a writer can love, a hero who loves writers. Paladin is an intellectual's idea of what a hero should be, or rather, the kind of hero an intellectual would like to be if only he had the power. Free of common people's prejudices and intellectual limitations, Paladin knows what is truly good for humanity and nobly struggles to achieve a better world for his fellow human beings. No wonder Roddenberry found it easy to project himself into the character Meadow and Rolfe had created.[43]

For the same reasons, Roddenberry readily identified with both Kirk and Spock.[44] All three figures embody an intellectual writer's fantasy of himself as a superhero. Like many authors, Roddenberry fancied himself morally and intellectually superior to his fellow human beings—"the fallible world about him"—and assumed that, given the power and the opportunity, he could prove his superiority, much to the benefit and admiration of all humanity. If one is looking for a personal touch in Roddenberry's vision of Paladin and Kirk, evidently he especially liked to fantasize about a hypermasculine hero so irresistible to women that they would constantly throw themselves at his feet in worship.[45] Both *Have Gun* and *Star Trek* gave Roddenberry a chance to play out his fantasy life on national television, while at the same time enjoying the moral satisfaction of teaching uplifting lessons in toleration to an admiring public.

There is one more way in which the intellectual's image of his ideal superhero can teach us something about liberalism, and it is evident in Roddenberry's impulse to divide up between Kirk and Spock the character elements that were originally combined in Paladin. Spock best embodies the liberal intellectual's dream of himself—a perfectly logical, detached, and disinterested creature, free of all human passions, capable of coming up with purely rational and scientific solutions to human problems. Spock is the liberal intellectual as social engineer. His calm demeanor reflects the liberal's inclination to deny that aggressiveness is natural to human beings, or at least to minimize its role in human life. In the liberal vision, aggressiveness is an atavistic impulse, left over from the bad old days, the undemocratic ages during which wolfish aristocrats imposed their wills on sheepish people. Throughout *Have Gun–Will Travel*, aggressiveness is for bullies, and Paladin's mission is evidently to rid the Wild West of bullies.

And yet paradoxically, as we have seen, Paladin is a bit of a bully himself, not averse to throwing his own weight around and unfailingly answering aggressiveness with more aggressiveness. Both *Have Gun* and *Star Trek*—and the liberalism they reflect—are premised on the ideas that the only thing that cannot be tolerated is intolerance and that prejudice can be eliminated only by force. Thus the liberal hero ends up in a dilemma. He very much needs his aggressiveness, and yet on some level he must deny it and present himself as a man of peace. In *Star Trek,* Spock turns out to be insufficient as a hero and must always be paired with Kirk, who can supply the element of aggressiveness lacking in the overly rational Spock. Captain Kirk is the living embodiment of the paradoxes of liberalism.[46] He speaks all the time in favor of harmony and cooperation, and yet he is one of the most competitive men imaginable (this aspect of his character is reflected in his compulsive womanizing). He claims to be a tolerant man, but he will not tolerate challenges to his authority as captain of the *Enterprise.* In political terms, Kirk is ambitious for office and continually fights to stay in power. He reveals the aggressiveness that a political man must have if he is to gain power and accomplish anything in the public sphere. This is one more way in which Kirk mirrors his model, John Kennedy, and highlights a contradiction in liberal politicians: their unwillingness to acknowledge their own aggressiveness, even though it is necessary to fuel their ambition and drive their liberal programs.

Liberals tend to exempt themselves from their view of humanity as hopelessly mired in the prejudices and aggressiveness of the past. But if everyone else is corrupted by base motives like greed and ambition, why should we expect liberals alone to be free of these human foibles? As we have seen, *Have Gun–Will Travel* asks us to believe that every rich man in the West is corrupted by money except Paladin. The record of liberal politicians like John Kennedy in office raises genuine doubts about whether their high-minded goals insulate them from the traditional failings of ambitious men. Paladin comes too close to revealing the contradictions at the heart of the liberal character. By dividing up Paladin into Spock and Kirk, Roddenberry was to some extent able to conceal these paradoxes and to maintain in Spock the purity of the liberal's self-image as intellectually superior and free from ambition and aggressiveness. Thus *Have Gun* in many respects offers a more complex view of the world than *Star Trek* does because Paladin is a more problematic figure than either Kirk or Spock.[47] Contrary to Roddenberry's intentions, the conjunction of *Have Gun* and *Star Trek* may teach us a lesson in the dangers of a peculiar kind of liberal self-righteousness. Convinced of the purity of his motives and the justice of his cause, a heroic figure may develop a new form of the arrogance of power, perhaps as destructive as the old aristocratic pretensions. Unacknowledged and thus working below the surface of consciousness, a hero's pride may tempt him into overestimating his capabilities and lead him into perilous situations. This certainly happens to Paladin. Often he must shoot his way out of situations into which his pride has gotten him. As it turns out, "the knight without armor in a savage land" is still a warring knight and still capable of savagery himself.[48]

Who Created *Star Trek*?

The extent to which Roddenberry's scripts for *Have Gun–Will Travel* anticipate his later work on *Star Trek* may surprise fans of the science fiction series. They like to idolize him as the sole creator of *Star Trek*, the visionary genius who single-handedly brought science fiction to television against overwhelming odds. In his public statements, Roddenberry did very little to discourage this exalted view of his role. But if many of his ideas for *Star Trek* developed in the course of his writing for *Have Gun*—if, for example, the character of Paladin helped shape his conception of Kirk and Spock—then Herb Meadow and Sam Rolfe in effect contributed to the genesis of *Star Trek*. After all, they created Paladin, and in writing for their series Roddenberry was working within parameters they set up. In addition, the themes and motifs of the episodes Roddenberry wrote for *Have Gun* are very similar to what we find in episodes by the other writers for that series. Given my focus on Roddenberry in this chapter, I have discussed in detail only the *Have Gun* episodes he wrote, but I could make basically the same points by looking at the work of the other writers, who just as regularly came up with scripts about lynch mobs, water rights, overweening cattle barons, persecuted minorities, and women for Paladin to charm.

I have followed a different procedure in referring to episodes of *Star Trek* here. For the later series I have *not* restricted myself to episodes that were specifically written by Roddenberry. He took a writing credit for surprisingly few of the seventy-nine original *Star Trek* episodes.[49] My assumption, however, has been that, whether or not Roddenberry is credited with writing a particular episode, they all reflect his influence. As the creator-producer of *Star Trek*, he came up with the basic framework for the series, formulated instructions for anybody writing scripts for it, and enforced those guidelines carefully. As a hands-on producer, he worked closely with all the writers, sometimes throwing out suggestions to them, always shepherding their scripts through production—a process that in television necessarily involves a great deal of rewriting, which Roddenberry often did without taking a writing credit for himself.[50] According to all accounts, every *Star Trek* episode bears the stamp of Gene Roddenberry. That is why, in talking about his vision in *Star Trek,* one does not have to restrict oneself to scripts that officially carry his name. But that means in turn that the scripts Roddenberry wrote for *Have Gun–Will Travel* all bear the stamp of Herb Meadow and Sam Rolfe. And one must not discount the efforts of a variety of producers and script editors who undoubtedly (and largely anonymously) worked with Roddenberry to polish his scripts as they made their way to the air. If we recognize Roddenberry's influence on all the writers who worked on *Star Trek,* then we must acknowledge the influence of the creators of *Have Gun–Will Travel* on him as a writer for the earlier series and thus by extension their ultimate influence on the later series. Whatever his fans may think, *Star Trek* did not spring magically out of Roddenberry's solo imagination.[51]

As we have already seen, when he thought it would help, Roddenberry tried to pass himself off as "head writer" of *Have Gun–Will Travel,* even though Sam Rolfe has made it clear that no such position ever existed.[52] A good deal of evidence suggests that throughout his career, Roddenberry had a tendency to take more credit for his writing accomplishments than he fully deserved.[53] We need to do a better job of putting his achievement in perspective. For *Have Gun* he was part of a very talented team of writers (several of whom also went on to write for *Star Trek*).[54] More generally, in working on the Western, he was teamed with producers and directors, all of whom played a significant role in making the series a success. The record shows that in the case of *Have Gun,* its star, Richard Boone, was unusually active for an actor in shaping the development of the series and insisting on maintaining its quality. He even directed many episodes himself.[55] By the same token, actors like William Shatner and Leonard Nimoy clearly put their stamp on *Star Trek* and surely deserve some of the credit for the success of the series.[56]

In sum, like any TV series, *Star Trek* was not the one-man show Roddenberry's admirers often take it to be. We tend to come to popular culture with a paradigm of solitary authorship ultimately derived from Romantic poetry.[57] We want to picture television writers on the heroic model of the lonely, misunderstood genius we are familiar with from the self-image of poets like Byron and Shelley. But the fact is that, like most of pop culture, television is very much a collaborative medium, and it succeeds precisely by pooling the talents and resources of many creators at once. In a moment of candor in 1965, Roddenberry himself acknowledged this aspect of pop culture in a letter to a colleague: "In fact, it seems that our business violates the one basic rule of all businesses, i.e. that committees can never accomplish anything. In almost any other work, creativity always ultimately reduces itself to one man doing the job. Here we have a half dozen or more creators, all contributing. The producer can guide them but he dare not do much more."[58] The history of both *Have Gun* and *Star Trek* confirms this understanding of the collaborative nature of creativity in television. It does not call into question Roddenberry's creativity to point out that, in working on both shows, he was not operating alone but constantly depended on and learned from his colleagues, repeatedly benefiting from their advice and example and often drawing upon their ideas. Perhaps Roddenberry's true genius was his knack for taking advantage of the pool of creative talent in Hollywood.[59]

Science Fiction—Forget about It

The links between Roddenberry's work on *Have Gun* and his creation of *Star Trek* bear on another issue that has been raised, the question of whether he truly was a science fiction writer. It may seem preposterous to wonder whether the creator of arguably the most popular science fiction vehicle of all time should be legitimately regarded as a science fiction writer. But there are, in fact, legitimate grounds for controversy here. David Alexander, the writer of *Star Trek Creator*, the authorized biography of Roddenberry, goes out of his way to establish Roddenberry's credentials as a science fiction writer, asserting, for example (with somewhat limited evidence), that Roddenberry's interest in science fiction went all the way back to his youth.[60] Once *Star Trek* made Roddenberry famous, he eagerly claimed admission to the fraternity of science fiction writers and took great pride in his friendships with giants in the field, such as Isaac Asimov and Arthur C. Clarke. But at least one critic, Joel Engel, in his decidedly unauthorized biography of Roddenberry, has argued that the creator of *Star Trek* became a science fiction writer by accident. Engel points out that the bulk of Roddenberry's early writing for television was for cop shows and Westerns, and that he wandered into the area of science fiction simply in his continuing search for a successful TV formula. Engel questions the depth of Roddenberry's familiarity with traditional science fiction and claims that Roddenberry had to pump friends and colleagues for knowledge in the area when he finally set about working up *Star Trek*.[61]

The fact that we have seen Roddenberry developing the basic elements of *Star Trek* while working on a TV Western does raise some doubt about how fundamental science fiction was to his vision as a writer. Roddenberry's anxiety about his credentials as a sci-fi writer may explain why, as we have seen, he chose to baptize Paladin retroactively as a science fiction figure, almost as if he were trying to reassure people that he had been writing science fiction all his life; *Have Gun* just looked like a Western. But elsewhere, Roddenberry reversed his position, claiming that what makes *Star Trek* good is *not* its science fiction aspects. Amazing as it may sound to his admirers today, he instructed his authors not to think of themselves as writing science fiction when working for the show. Consider these excerpts from a long memo he wrote to the agent of one of his *Star Trek* writers:

> We are asking of the writer no more than any other new show asks and must have, i.e. study what is available on the lead characters, his attitudes and methods, the secondary characters, the inter-relations, and those basic things you would have whether this was the beginning of a Western, hospital drama, or cops and robbers. . . . *At this point, we not asking [the writer] to write science fiction!* We are asking him to give us quality in how he draws his characters, in making our regular people act and interact per our format with which he has been amply provided, to give them the "bite" of their individual styles, to have the Captain (like Matt Dillon or Dr. Kildare even) *act* like what he is, and above all, *again forgetting science fiction,* have everybody use at least simple Twentieth Century logic and common sense in what they look for, what they comment on, what surprises them, how they protect themselves, and so on.[62]

I quote this memo at length not just for the shock value of seeing Roddenberry telling one of his authors to forget about writing science fiction.[63] It is a fascinating document—a rare opportunity to see in writing the kind of detailed instructions show runners have undoubtedly been giving orally to writers ever since the beginning of television. As Roddenberry continues, we see clearly that he conceived of *Star Trek* on the model of another TV Western, *Gunsmoke* (1955–1975): "For example, as you will see in the script, we are in an Earth-like city which stopped living some centuries ago.

And yet, as they land there, no one comments on the strange ancient aspect of it. For God sakes, if Matt Dillon came upon an Indian village which had been deserted for even three or four years, he or Chester or someone would at least be aware of that fact."[64] Evidently, in thinking about a good show, Roddenberry asked himself, "What would Matt Dillon do?"[65] In general, in analyzing good writing, he abstracted from the question of genre. To him the same rules of exposition, character development, plot construction, and believability govern Westerns, hospital dramas, cop shows, and science fiction alike.

In what would today be called the *Star Trek* Bible, the Writer-Director Information Guide that Roddenberry prepared for anyone interested in working on the show, he makes his position clear: "Science fiction is no different from tales of the present or the past—*our Starship central characters and crew must be at least as believably motivated and as identifiable to the audience as characters we've all written into police stations, general hospitals, and Western towns."* [66] The loyal science fiction fans of *Star Trek* might be shocked to see Roddenberry's formulation of the prime directive that governed the scripts. He laid down the law of what makes for a bad *Star Trek* story in these terms: "They fail what we call our 'Gunsmoke–Kildare–Naked City Rule'—would the *basic story,* stripped of science fiction aspects, make a good episode of one of these shows?"[67]

In view of this evidence, the question inevitably arises: if in his own mind Roddenberry was stripping scripts of their science fiction aspects in order to determine their quality, how basic could science fiction have been to his conception of *Star Trek?* Maybe his calling it "*Wagon Train* to the stars" was more than just a selling pitch to NBC. A great deal of evidence suggests that Roddenberry thought that a good television show is simply a good television show, whether it be science fiction, a Western, a hospital drama, or a police story. His work on *Have Gun–Will Travel* demonstrates that he was capable of getting across the same messages in a Western that he later preached in *Star Trek.* In fact, Roddenberry prided himself on the way he and his fellow writers were able to work social justice messages into early Westerns:

> We *can* be proud of TV writers. Although forced to compromise with commercial censorship since the beginning of television, they have always managed to insert into their scripts messages that "to be different is not necessarily to be evil" and many other similar

concepts which historians may someday see as quite important in helping pave the way for the youth and social revolutions going on in America today [1968]. . . . I cannot help but believe that these "messages" skillfully inserted even in the early Westerns we . . . wrote . . . had over the years a cumulative effect on the attitudes of people like my own rather strange relatives in our small Georgia home town. This was done constantly by almost every writer I know and . . . the steady flow of these ideas could not have helped but soften prejudice and intolerance to a point where the current and larger breakthroughs became possible.[68]

There could be no clearer evidence of the fact that for Gene Roddenberry the Final Frontier grew out of the Old West.

The Death of the Western—and Its Resurrection

The *Have Gun–Star Trek* connection can shed light on another controversy, the question of the death of the Western. The Western was by far the most popular genre on television during the 1950s and '60s, but by the 1970s, it had virtually disappeared from the airways, returning only sporadically since and never regaining its former popularity.[69] The simple fact is that television became saturated with Westerns, and the American public became bored with them. But all sorts of deeper reasons have been offered for the television audience becoming disenchanted with Westerns by the end of the 1960s. Some have argued that the Western as a genre was hopelessly locked into an antiquated ideology that made it impossible for the form to adapt to the massive changes in American society that occurred in the course of the 1960s. Some writers have insisted that the TV Western of the 1950s was a fundamentally conservative or even reactionary genre, fixated on the past and promoting traditional American values, such as patriotism, respect for the law, and rugged individualism. Such critics argue that the Western, with its roots in nineteenth-century America, was a vehicle for expressing the ideology of capitalism and thus could not handle the intellectual challenges posed by the New Left in the late 1960s to traditional American ideals.[70] In particular, the unpopularity of the Vietnam War is said to have undermined old notions of patriotism and made Americans uncomfortable with the way Westerns had traditionally portrayed Indians and other nonwhite people as the enemies of civilization.[71]

Some of this may be true, but what we have seen in *Have Gun–Will Travel* raises doubts about this account of the death of the TV Western and the notion of its inability to adapt to changing conditions in America. The way *Have Gun* is linked to *Star Trek* shows that it was already anticipating the pop culture trends of the 1960s. Fans of *Star Trek* should not be troubled by learning that the roots of Roddenberry's vision of the future lie in a TV Western of the 1950s. The point of the comparison is to see how thoroughly the people who produced *Have Gun* were working to transform the Western into something more modern and more liberal. *Have Gun* involved a reconception of the Western, radically transforming its ideology and subverting the genre from within. The show, in fact, inverted a long-standing polarity of American pop culture, the elevation of the small town over the big city.

Traditionally American pop culture in general, not just the Western, celebrated the small town as the site of authentic moral virtues, and by contrast portrayed the big city as a source of moral corruption. An archetypal American plot involves a virtuous character leaving his or her home in a small town, becoming seduced by the artificial glitter of the big city, and losing his or her moral goodness in the stews of urban vice and sin.[72] Given the way the Western traditionally pictured progress on the frontier, it served as a bastion of the American ideal of the small town. The ultimate good in the classic Western is settling down, putting down roots, creating order in the wilderness, precisely in the form of a typical American small town. This process involves taming the frontier, plowing the fields, putting up fences, and eventually erecting the central symbols of small-town order: a schoolhouse, a courthouse, and a church.[73] The villains of traditional Westerns are nomads—the Indians, of course, but also white men without roots, such as itinerant gunfighters and gamblers, the sort of characters who ride into a town and wreak havoc with its attempts to develop law and order. That is why even cattlemen are often suspect in the traditional Western. They do not lead the stable existence of farmers. To be morally good in the traditional Western one must ultimately learn to stay put—"to sit a spell," as the heroes like to say.

Have Gun–Will Travel inverts the traditional polarity of American pop culture and champions the big city over the small town. Now the small town is the site of corruption, and it can be saved only by a sophisticated hero from the big city. This reevaluation of the small town versus the big city in American pop culture reflects a new understanding of the nature and basis of virtue. In the older view, virtue is understood as a moral absolute, embodied in traditional conceptions of good inherited from our forebears and hence best learned and practiced in a small-town atmosphere. The narrow horizons of the small town help to inculcate and maintain the traditional moral virtues, whereas the wider horizons of the big city can only confuse and disorient people with a new range of moral options. Once moral virtue is no longer viewed as an absolute but is reconceived as toleration for a wide variety of ethical positions, small-town thinking becomes the antithesis of virtuous behavior, and only the big city, with its diversity of human types, can breed the authentic virtue of tolerance.[74]

Accordingly, Paladin is urban and urbane, sallying forth each week to teach lessons in enlightened morality and justice to the benighted backwaters of rural America. He is everything the villain used to be in the traditional Western, which explains why he inverts even its color symbolism and shows up dressed in black. He is an itinerant gunfighter and even a gambler, never once contemplating settling down in the towns he passes through.[75] He would not dream of it—they are too boring and devoid of everything that makes his life meaningful back in the big city of San Francisco—the opera, the ballet, the theater, the fine restaurants with their wine lists, and all the fancy women, not to mention his corps of tailors. Paladin comes to a small town not to learn from it, but to set it right. The more I have thought about it, the more I have realized how appropriate it is from a Hollywood perspective that Paladin comes from California. Paladin is California's gift to the American heartland—the cosmopolitan man who can save it from all the problems created by the small-mindedness of its small towns. *Have Gun* maps America the way many intellectuals do to this day. All the virtue is on the coasts, and in the middle is a sink of land-locked ignorance and prejudice.[76] Paladin does what Hollywood has in effect been doing for decades. He brings sophistication to the American hinterland, saving it from its narrow horizons and opening its eyes to the modern enlightened world. Paladin's virtue is precisely his mobility—just what was regarded as a vice in a traditional Western, or at least as something deeply problematic. In *Have Gun*, the man with no attachments to the community is paradoxically presented as the person best positioned to save it, despite his lack of local knowledge. Unlike the traditional Western hero, Paladin has no attraction to family life and thus no interest in putting down roots. Only because he has no disposition to settle down can he solve the problems of the simple folk who are stuck in their small towns.[77] *Have Gun* shows what the heartland of America looked like to liberal intellectuals in Hollywood in the 1950s.[78]

The liberalism of *Have Gun–Will Travel* runs so deep that its West seems to be really the South. The small towns it portrays are the home of lynch mobs, corrupt sheriffs, and local bosses, all mired in a web of prejudice—exactly the image of the South held by 1950s liberals. Many of the problems Paladin encounters are explicitly said to have their origins in the aftermath of the Civil War.[79] It is remarkable how many civil rights issues *Have Gun* managed to transpose from the South to the West. We can see what really preoccupied liberals in the 1950s, the very issues that were to animate the Kennedy administration in the 1960s—and *Star Trek* as well.[80] The small towns Paladin enters are usually governed by some form of WASP elite, whose power he must break in order to make justice prevail. "Diversity" is the keynote of the series.[81] For example, in a third-season Roddenberry story called "Charlie Red Dog" (#91), Paladin brings law and order to a town by offering it a Navajo Indian (Scott Marlowe) as its new marshal.[82]

Again and again, *Have Gun* shows that local authorities, precisely by virtue of being local, are incapable of dealing with the problem of prejudice. And the show stresses that it will take force, violent force, to overcome prejudice. This is exactly the logic that in the 1950s led increasingly to calls for the federal government to intervene in the South on civil rights issues. Paladin's recurrent role as a savior from outside reflects the liberal program of allowing the federal government to override the traditional power of the states and local communities to govern themselves in such areas as education. *Have Gun–Will Travel* marks a turning point in American pop culture, a switch from the traditional reliance on local self-governance to a new faith in the power of an outside force, usually the federal government, to right all the wrongs in America. In the traditional Western, the small town typically manages to pull itself together in the end to solve its problems on its own (albeit usually under the leadership of a lone hero who may be a bit of an outsider). This is precisely what no town seems able to do in *Have Gun*.[83] Moving freely among the states, and transcending all local attachments, only Paladin can deal with what Kennedy called the "unconquered pockets of ignorance and prejudice." Paladin is an apt image of the 1950s liberal's hope for the federal government to save the American heartland from itself.

In its systematic inversion of traditional American values, *Have Gun–Will Travel* anticipated the revisionist Westerns of the late 1960s and 1970s. The third-season episode "Night the Town Died" (#99, directed by Richard Boone, written by Frank R. Pierson and Calvin Clements) is one of the more radical scripts, portraying a small town that has been consumed by its prejudices, destroying itself in a McCarthy-style witch hunt for traitors in its midst.[84] Although Paladin manages to deal with the town's immediate problems, there is no sense of renewal at the end, as would be characteristic of a traditional Western. This is after all the night the town *died*. The episode even looks like a Sergio Leone Spaghetti Western. The town's streets are deserted, with tumbleweeds blowing by a ruined buckboard wagon. The episode exemplifies the tendency of the series as a whole to deconstruct traditional Western myths, indeed to deconstruct the traditional Western town itself.

Thus *Have Gun–Will Travel* shows that the TV Western in the 1950s was fully able to adapt to America's changing understanding of itself.[85] In *Have Gun*, Roddenberry was dealing with the same issues he was later to treat in *Star Trek*. The earlier Western was just as capable as the later sci-fi show of criticizing racial intolerance and capitalist greed. This fact helps us to see that the Western did not die; it merely migrated and mutated. As the *Have Gun–Star Trek* connection suggests, the Western was reborn in science fiction, as well as in other genres, like the cop show, which beginning in the 1970s often took the form of an urban Western.[86] Perhaps we trouble ourselves too much over questions of genre in television. In practice, it turns out to be an exceedingly fluid concept. As strange as it sounds today, *Have Gun–Will Travel* was not originally conceived as a Western. Meadow and Rolfe had in mind a series in a contemporary setting, in which a soldier of fortune would offer his services every week wherever he was needed in a troubled world. It took network executives to convince them to develop their concept as a Western.[87] Similarly, the germ of Roddenberry's idea for *Star Trek* was much closer to a Western, a series embodying "his vision of a giant dirigible set in the late 1800's manned by a multiethnic crew traveling the world righting wrongs and doing good."[88] It is a tribute to the creativity of television writers that they seem to be able to develop their vision in any setting, adapting to commercial considerations and working in whichever genres are currently fashionable with the networks.[89]

Thus perhaps it is unnecessary to trouble ourselves over the question of whether *Star Trek* is really a Western in disguise. As we have seen, the "final frontier" rhetoric of the series is related to the "New Frontier" rhetoric of the Kennedy administration. And this rhetoric of the frontier is deeply rooted in American experience. From its origins, America has been a nation confronted with the problem of the frontier. The basic vehicle for Americans to deal with their frontier experience has been the Western, first in nineteenth-century fiction since James Fenimore Cooper and then in twentieth-century movies and television. The Western is arguably America's most distinctive contribution to world culture. It comes as no surprise, then, that the Western should have influenced both John Kennedy and *Star Trek*. The Western may at first seem like a nostalgic and backward-looking genre and hence an unlikely candidate for influencing the most futuristic and forward-looking of genres, science fiction (or the most futuristic and forward-looking of U.S. presidents, John Kennedy). And yet, precisely because it focuses on the frontier, the Western has always dealt with breaking boundaries and learning to cope with experiences that are fundamentally new and unprecedented. The *Star Trek* motto—"to boldly go where no man has gone before"—has also always been the keynote of the Western. In short, the convergence of *Have Gun–Will Travel* with *Star Trek*—and the Kennedy administration—reflects the centrality of the West in American experience.

3

ORDER OUT OF THE MUD

Deadwood and the State of Nature

> *Deadwood* is a show about how order arises out of the mud. That's what you see in the opening credits, and that's what you see as the story moves forward: men coming together out of the most limited motives to create something larger than themselves. Order is provisional and mysterious. It requires a temporary suspension of immediate concerns in the interest of an agreed-upon fiction about a better tomorrow.
> —David Milch, *Deadwood: Stories of the Black Hills*

> You cannot do political philosophy on television.
> —Neil Postman, *Amusing Ourselves to Death*

The Western, with its setting on the frontier between civilization and barbarism, has throughout its history provided a vehicle for exploring a fundamental American problem: the difficult choice between freedom and law. Do we want to live free of the shackles of the law, even at the risk of society descending into anarchy and violence—everything we fear when we speak of lawlessness? Or are we willing to give up our freedom so that law and order will prevail in society, under the aegis of a strong government? The abstract dilemma of freedom versus law is concretely embodied in many of the standard Western plots, which typically pit a lone individual against the combined forces of society. Some Westerns celebrate the rugged individualism of the gunfighter and his freedom to chart his own course. Others show how problematic the free-ranging and free-wheeling outlaw can become and champion imposing law and order on the frontier community. Sometimes, as we saw in *The Searchers,* a Western presents the tension between the individual and the community as tragic. Sometimes, as we saw in *Have Gun–Will Travel,* a Western offers a single strong man as the only way of imposing order on a community incapable of governing itself properly. One reason that the Western has played a central role in American popular culture is that it takes us straight to the heart of the great American experiment: to found a nation on the basis of the principle of the freedom of the individual. American democracy rests on the hope that there is a way out of the freedom–law dilemma, that freedom and order might be made compatible under the rule of law.

Hobbes, Locke, Rousseau

The Western thus in effect investigates a fundamental question of political philosophy, the issue of the state of nature (a state of freedom) and its relation to civil society (a state of law). We do not usually associate the Wild West with European political philosophy. Yet in his *Second Treatise of Government* (1689), John Locke, one of the most important state-of-nature theorists, speaks of "the wild woods and uncultivated waste of America."[1] In fact, he makes more than a dozen references in this work to America, many of them specifically to Indians, even going so far as to claim, "In the beginning all the world was America."[2] Locke is carrying on a debate with the first modern state-of-nature thinker, Thomas Hobbes, who in *Leviathan* (1651) also speaks of "the savage people in many places of *America.*"[3] The third most famous figure in the state-of-nature debate, Jean-Jacques Rousseau, tells "the story of a chief of some North Americans" in his *Second Discourse* (1755).[4] Evidently America was very much on the mind of the European thinkers who reflected on the state of nature.

These inquiries into the state of nature attempted to conceptualize the prepolitical existence of humanity: life without codified laws, public officials, or other manifestations of government power. Imagining human life without political institutions offers a way of analyzing the need for, and value of, such contrivances. One can truly say, "Tell me a philosopher's evaluation of the state of nature, and I will tell you his evaluation of the nation-state." In *Leviathan,* Hobbes presents such a horrific portrait of the state of nature as a war of all against all that he ends up endorsing any form of government, no matter how absolute, as better than none. Hobbes prefers law over freedom. By contrast, in creating an attractive portrait of the state of nature as idyllic, peaceful, and noncompetitive, Rousseau in his *Second*

Discourse raises serious doubts about the legitimacy of civil society as an alternative, especially given its economic, social, and political inequalities. Rousseau prefers freedom over law.[5] In his *Second Treatise of Government,* Locke crafts an image of the state of nature roughly midway between the extremes of Hobbes and Rousseau—less warlike than in Hobbes but more competitive and conflicted than in Rousseau. As a result, Locke's version of the state of nature allows him to legitimate political authority while still reserving the right to criticize the specific forms it takes. Locke hopes to combine freedom with law, offering a law-abiding state as the guarantor of the freedom of its citizens.

If the existence of America influenced state-of-nature thinking in Europe, the writings of Hobbes, Locke, and Rousseau in turn influenced the political development of America. All three philosophers have had an impact on American political thinking, specifically that of the Founding Fathers. Locke is generally credited with being the chief theorist behind the principles embodied in the United States Constitution, such as the separation of powers.[6] Accordingly, it is not surprising that American popular culture has sometimes shown the influence of Hobbes, Locke, and Rousseau, especially in the Western.[7] This influence, whether direct or indirect, is particularly evident in the HBO television series *Deadwood* (2004–2006), created by writer-producer David Milch.[8] Widely recognized as one of the most sophisticated shows in the history of television, *Deadwood* is thoughtful, intelligent, and as close to philosophical as popular culture ever gets.[9] In interviews, DVD commentaries, and his book about the series, *Deadwood: Stories of the Black Hills,* Milch has been unusually forthright in discussing the show. As a result, we have a rare opportunity: to study the philosophical underpinnings and implications of a television show as explicitly formulated by its creator.[10] At the same time, analyzing *Deadwood* helps clarify the issues at stake in the debate among Hobbes, Locke, and Rousseau about the state of nature.

Milch was attracted to the story of Deadwood, a mining camp in the late 1870s in what is now South Dakota, by a unique set of circumstances. In 1875, rumors began to spread of gold finds on Indian land in the Black Hills. Because of the U.S. government's treaty with the Sioux, this land belonged to them and was outside federal jurisdiction (the state of South Dakota did not exist at the time). Thus the people who poured into the Deadwood camp in search of gold and other ways to make their fortune were there illegally to begin with and were not subject to any government authority—municipal, state, or federal. Almost the first words we hear in the first episode of the series come from a jailed criminal in Montana saying wistfully: "No law at all in Deadwood?"[11]

The situation in Deadwood thus allowed Milch to explore a subject that came to fascinate him during years of working on television police dramas such as *Hill Street Blues* (1981–1987) and *NYPD Blue* (1993–2005): the potential disjunction between law and order. As Milch wrote:

> A misapprehension that can distort one's understanding of Dead-wood—and the world in which we live today—arises from the way that law and order are commonly conjoined. The phrase "law and order" can easily create the impression that these two very different social phenomena arise from a common human impulse, or that they are somehow one and the same. Law and order are not the same. It is common for us to try to retrospectively apply the sanction of law to the things we do to maintain order. Our desire for order comes first, and law comes afterward.[12]

In short, what intrigued Milch about Deadwood is the way a motley group of human beings, pursuing—sometimes viciously—their own self-interest could, in the absence of any legal institutions or established government, nevertheless manage to organize themselves into a community and pursue some form of common good. One of the actors in the series, W. Earle Brown, formulates clearly its central question: "The whole show is about the need for community, and in that community that's built in complete chaos, how does order form, how does law form?"[13] Or to formulate the issue another way: Can human beings spontaneously arrive at rules that make possible and facilitate their productive social interaction, or are they dependent on the central authority of the state to create and enforce law and only thereby to make life in society feasible?

Thus the way Milch creates in *Deadwood* "an environment where," in his words, "there was order and no law whatsoever" allows him to raise the same question that is at the heart of state-of-nature thinking: how does the prepolitical existence of humanity define the parameters of political life?[14] If there can be order without law—if human beings can find ways of organizing their social life safely and productively in the absence of the state—then the state cannot claim to be the sole source of human order and must respect the independently evolved order of society. In short, the idea of order without law sets limits on state authority and creates room for freedom. If, however, there can be no order without law, then the state, as the sole source of social order, can lay claim to unlimited authority and absolute power, leaving freedom in jeopardy.[15]

Al Swearengen: Nasty, British, and Short

The latter alternative is the core of Hobbes's state-of-nature teaching and his doctrine of absolute sovereignty. Hobbes espouses the position Milch rejects. He equates law with order, arguing that all social order, all lawfulness in society, is ultimately the result of positive law, law made and maintained by the state. To be sure, Hobbes talks about "natural law" and the "laws of nature," devoting chapters 14 and 15 of *Leviathan* to the subject, and thus seems to allow for some kind of prepolitical social order. But "natural law" quickly turns out to be a fiction in Hobbes's account:

> For the Laws of Nature (as *Justice, Equity, Modesty, Mercy* . . .) of themselves, without the terrour of some Power, to cause them to be observed, are contrary to our naturall Passions, that carry us to Partiality, Pride, Revenge, and the like. And Covenants, without the Sword, are but Words, and of no strength to secure a man at all. Therefore notwithstanding the Laws of Nature, . . . if there be no Power erected, or not great enough for our security; every man will and may lawfully rely on his own strength and art, for caution against all other men.[16]

In short, in Hobbes, natural law is revealed to be unnatural ("contrary to our naturall Passions") and wholly ineffectual on its own. In his view, only by creating the Leviathan State are human beings able to achieve any kind of reliable social order, and for Hobbes an unreliable order is no order at all. Hobbes's blanket endorsement of a centralized political authority and his basic indifference to the distinctions among the different forms authority might take are exactly the results Milch is trying to avoid when he insists that order is separable from law and preexists it.[17]

Thus we need to resist the strong temptation to describe the vision of *Deadwood* as simply Hobbesian, even though several commentators have used just that adjective.[18] To be sure, *Deadwood* is filled with violence, and one aspect that sets it apart from most television series is the fact that from its very first episode, it conditions us to believe that any character might be suddenly killed at any moment. Under these circumstances, it seems at first apt to apply to the show the words with which Hobbes famously describes the state of nature—as a state of "continuall feare, and danger of violent death; And the life of man, solitary, poore, nasty, brutish, and short."[19] People who frequent the Gem Saloon, owned by the local boss, Al Swearengen (Ian McShane), may indeed find that life in Deadwood is "nasty, brutish, and short," but, aside from the obvious fact that the camp is far from poor, Milch's most basic point in the series is that human life is *not* solitary, but takes communal forms even in the absence of the state and in the midst of bitterly divisive economic and social forces. As Milch says, "there's an inevitability in our natures which draws us to some form of organization."[20] Milch rejects Hobbes's vision of the state of nature as solitary because he realizes that if community is not in some sense natural to human beings, then they will be hopelessly subject to the dictates of the Leviathan State, the artificial construct created to correct the defects of the state of nature.[21]

Nevertheless, despite Milch's fundamental difference from Hobbes, life in Deadwood shares many characteristics with the state of nature portrayed in *Leviathan*. Milch may want to show that community is natural to human beings, but he does not wish to portray it as coming easily to them. In his view, human beings must struggle to achieve community and must overcome many potential sources of conflict to do so. On the sources of that conflict, Milch and Hobbes are in remarkable agreement. Hobbes identifies three forces that lead to the war of all against all in the state of nature: "So that in the nature of men, we find three principall causes of quarrell. First, Competition; Secondly, Diffidence; Thirdly, Glory. The first, maketh men invade for Gain; the second, for Safety; and the third, for Reputation."[22] The same array of forces is at work in Milch's Deadwood. Hobbes writes: "if any two men desire the same thing, which neverthelesse they cannot both enjoy, they become enemies."[23] That is exactly what happens in Deadwood. The characters fight, often to the death, over women as well as gold, land, and other forms of wealth and property. In addition, both Hobbes and Milch see murderous violence arising from the radical insecurity of living without a clear government authority in place. Because any man may be attacked by any other at any time, he must forestall his potential enemies and attack them first.

Life in Deadwood continually follows this model of the preemptive strike. In season 1, episode 2, contrary to the traditional image of the honorable gunfighter, Wild Bill Hickok (Keith Carradine) draws first and shoots a man who has not yet reached for his gun, merely because he senses—correctly, as it happens—that the man meant to kill him. Many of the episodes turn on the issue of whether to neutralize an enemy by killing him before he can kill you. This issue reaches its apex on the communal level in the third season, when the "native" citizens of Deadwood, under Swearengen's leadership, must decide how to respond to the appearance in town of the mining magnate George Hearst (Gerald McRaney), who draws upon his great wealth to build up a private army of Pinkerton agents, which he increasingly employs to impose his will on the camp. All of Al's instincts tell him to strike first against Hearst and his army. Swearengen begs a meeting of Deadwood's elders to tell him why he should not undertake a preemptive strike while he still has a chance of defeating Hearst's continually strengthening forces.

We can readily understand why these men fight over the same desired object or to defend themselves or to protect their family and property. But the violence in Deadwood becomes widespread because it often seems irrational and unmotivated—men fighting, it seems, merely for the sake of fighting. But here, like Hobbes, Milch uncovers the deepest source of instability in any community: masculine pride and aggressiveness. Milch portrays Deadwood as a community of alpha males who are constantly fighting to establish their individual dominance, to maintain a pecking order in the town. Hobbes explains this situation with his typical clear-sightedness: "For every man looketh that his companion should value him, at the same rate he sets upon himselfe: And upon all signes of contempt, or undervaluing, naturally endeavours, as far as he dares (which amongst them that have no common power, to keep them in quiet, is far enough to make them destroy each other,) to extort a greater value from his contemners."[24]

Here Hobbes explains for us the fight between Swearengen and the ex-lawman and businessman Seth Bullock (Timothy Olyphant) that begins the second season of *Deadwood,* as well as the violent struggles between Hearst and a host of other characters in the series. This violence always seems disproportionate to its ostensible and proximate cause in some minor incident. As Hobbes puts it, men "use Violence . . . for trifles, as a word, a smile, a different opinion, and any other signe of undervalue, either direct in their Person, or by reflexion in their Kindred, their Friends, their Nation, their Profession, or their Name."[25] Because of all these sources of sensitivity, Deadwood is a powder keg. Given the underlying struggle for domination in the town, the slightest incident may trigger an outbreak of murderous violence. The most powerful image of this situation is the titanic battle in

Al Swearengen (Ian McShane) keeps a watchful eye on developments in *Deadwood*. (Jerry Ohlinger's Movie Material Store)

the third season between Swearengen's henchman, Dan Dority (W. Earle Brown), and Hearst's bodyguard, Captain Turner (Alan Graf), which ostensibly takes place because Dority spoke disrespectfully to Hearst. Dority and Turner fight to the death not only for their own prestige and honor but also as the representatives of their masters' power struggle to rule the camp.[26]

"I'll Settle for Property Rights"

The extent of the agreement between Milch and Hobbes on the sources of violence among human beings only highlights their more fundamental difference. For Hobbes, only the institution of the Leviathan State can end the cycle of violence in the state of nature. By contrast, *Deadwood* shows that, even in the absence of government, human beings have motives for and means of limiting their violence on their own, which is another way of stating Milch's principle that order is possible without law. Here is where Milch displays his greater affinity with Locke, who, unlike Hobbes, conceives of forms of order in the state of nature. The crux of the difference between Hobbes and Locke can be seen in the issue of property.[27] For Hobbes, there is no property in the state of nature: "Where there is no common Power, there is no Law: where no Law, no Injustice. . . . It is consequent also to the same condition, there be no Propriety, no Dominion, no *Mine* or *Thine* distinct; but onely that to be every mans [sic] that he can get; and for so long, as he can keep it."[28] It is entirely characteristic of Hobbes that he views the right to property as created only by the state. If the state creates the right to property, then it can take that right away at will—a key example of what Hobbes means by the state's absolute sovereignty.[29]

By contrast, Locke argues that the right to property exists in the state of nature and thus preexists the state or any communal action: "I shall endeavour to show how men might come to have a property in several parts of that which God gave to mankind in common, and that without any express compact of all the commoners."[30] For Locke, rather than the state being the origin of property, property becomes in effect the origin of the state: "The great and chief end, therefore, of men's uniting into commonwealths and putting themselves under government is the preservation of their property."[31] Since in Locke's account the right to property exists prior to the state, he sets limits on its treatment of private property. If the express end of government is to protect the right to property, it cannot legitimately seize property at will. Locke's vision of limited government as opposed to Hobbes's absolute sovereignty follows from his argument that the right to private property exists prior to the nation-state:

> But though men when they enter into society give up the equality, liberty, and executive power they had in the state of nature into the hands of the society, . . . yet it being only with an intention in every one the better to preserve himself, his liberty and property—for no rational creature can be supposed to change his condition with an intention to be worse—the power of society . . . can never be supposed to extend farther than the common good, but is obliged to secure every one's property by providing against those . . . defects . . . that made the state of nature so unsafe and uneasy.[32]

In contrast to Hobbes, then, Locke offers an example of what Milch means by order without law. Although Locke eventually concedes that the state is necessary to *secure* property rights, he insists that they can develop in society without the intervention of the state. This may seem like a trivial distinction—both Hobbes and Locke view the state as ultimately necessary—but, if one looks at the conclusions they draw from their contrasting understanding of property, the difference is very important. Locke's conception of the state of nature as allowing for property rights gives him a basis for evaluating different forms of government and championing those that secure property rights as opposed to those that violate them with impunity.

Locke's argument for a right to private property prior to the formation of the state grows out of his theory of self-ownership:

> Though the earth and all inferior creatures be common to all men, yet every man has a property in his own person. . . . The labour of his body and the work of his hands, we may say, are properly his. Whatsoever then he removes out of the state that nature hath provided and left it in, he hath mixed his labour with, and joined to it something that is his own, and thereby makes it his property. It being by him removed from the common state nature hath placed it in, it hath by this labour something annexed to it that excludes the common right of other men.[33]

Locke's argument applies particularly to land as property. He maintains that the value of land does not reside solely in the land itself but, more importantly, in what is done with it. If someone fences in and cultivates a piece of land, he thereby increases its productivity and adds to its value, and that in turn entitles him to its use and makes it his own. As Locke puts it: "As much land as a man tills, plants, improves, cultivates, and can use the product of, so much is his property."[34]

The key to Locke's defense of property rights is that he does not view the dividing up of the world into private property as a zero-sum game. It may seem that by making a piece of land his own, a man is depriving the rest of humanity of something valuable. But Locke stresses the way an owner improves a piece of land by laboring on it and thereby increases the general stock of humanity. He even offers a mathematical demonstration of his point:

> He who appropriates land to himself by his labour does not lessen but increase the common stock of mankind; for the provisions serving to the support of human life produced by one acre of enclosed and cultivated land are—to speak much within compass—ten times more than those which are yielded by an acre of land of an equal richness lying waste in common. And therefore he that encloses land, and has a greater plenty of the conveniences of life from ten acres than he could have from a hundred left to nature, may truly be said to give ninety acres to mankind; for his labour now supplies him with provisions out of ten acres which were by the product of a hundred lying in common.[35]

Here is the magic of private property for Locke: if ten acres of cultivated land are more productive than one hundred acres of uncultivated, then a farmer who appropriates ten acres of land to himself will nevertheless effectively provide his fellow human beings with the benefit of at least an additional ninety acres of land.[36] Hobbes conceives of the state of nature as a zero-sum game, a realm of scarcity in which people have to struggle over severely limited goods. Locke, by contrast, offers the increased productivity of land once it is in private hands as a way of generating a new abundance in the state of nature that works to everybody's benefit and creates a common interest in having land owned privately.

Locke and the Old Homestead

We can now see the root of the difference between Locke and Hobbes. Locke can imagine an economic order independent of the political order. Economic logic can dictate as complicated a social development as the dividing up of the world into private property, even in the absence of a government to enforce the results. Locke's argument for the priority of economic order over political is the most important example of what Milch means by order without law, and perhaps a clearer way of formulating the idea. In Hobbes's view, human beings left to themselves will simply start killing each other, and only the Leviathan State can stop them.[37] In Locke's more optimistic view, human beings left to themselves will set to work cultivating their gardens (the killing starts much later). Locke makes his difference from Hobbes explicit: "And here we have the plain difference between the state of nature and the state of war which, however some men have confounded, are as far distinct as a state of peace, good-will, mutual assistance, and preservation, and a state of enmity, malice, violence, and mutual destruction are one from another."[38]

Milch displays his affinity with Locke on the priority of economic over political order in a pointed exchange between his two heroes in season 1, episode 4. Wild Bill Hickok has a vision of the future of Deadwood: "Camp looks like a good bet. . . . They'll get the Sioux making peace. Pretty quick you'll have laws here and every other thing." In Milch's terms, Hickok makes the mistake of viewing law as the prerequisite of all social order. Seth Bullock replies to Hickok's political vision with a more basic economic consideration: "I'll settle for property rights." In the process of laboring on a house for his family and thus building for the future, Bullock realizes the importance of the economic foundations of society. He is not interested in grand political visions; he wants his economic circumstances clarified and determined before he will worry about political issues, and he believes that Deadwood can find ways to settle property disputes on its own.

The emphasis on property rights is the most Lockean aspect of *Deadwood* and comes naturally to a show dealing with a gold rush, a situation in which the fundamental issue for most people is staking out claims to mining territory.[39] Milch shows that even in the absence of conventional legal institutions, Deadwood is able to evolve ways of establishing and arbitrating property rights, or, as he puts it, "institutions can organically develop."[40] We learn in the first episode that a land deal in Deadwood is ratified by spitting in one's palm and shaking hands with the other party. Precisely because legal methods of enforcing contracts are unavailable in Deadwood, its citizens take the customs they have evolved for making deals very seriously.[41] For all the force and fraud that interfere with honest commerce in Deadwood, a basically functioning economic community still prevails, in which people can roughly rely on each other's word—or handshake—in a business deal. With no legal authorities to fall back upon, the citizens of Deadwood are very careful about such matters as evaluating gold strikes and assaying gold itself. Since no business can take place in an environment of complete hostility and distrust, it is to everyone's advantage to observe at least a minimum of civility and probity in their dealings with each other. George Hearst is usually gruff and insensitive in his treatment of other people, but he tries to be ingratiating in his business deals, working to cover over his hostility when he concludes the purchase of the mine of Alma Garrett Ellsworth (Molly Parker): "Advancing your interest, Mrs. Ellsworth, mine, and all others, what we do here seems natural and proper" (3.12). "Common economic interest" is about as close as we get to a definition of natural law in *Deadwood*, a definition very much in the spirit of Locke.

Deadwood even operates with a Lockean definition of property. The premise of the series is that a mining claim is yours as long as you actively work it.[42] When Claggett (Marshall Bell), a representative of the territorial government, arrives in the camp, he makes this policy official: "The territory respects the statutes of the Northwest Ordinance, which state that a citizen can have title to any land unclaimed or unincorporated by simple usage. Essentially if you're on it and improve it, you own it" (1.9). This passage is so close to Locke's analysis of property that it sounds as if he deserves a writing credit for *Deadwood*. Actually, this scene is evidence of Locke's profound influence on the development of American political institutions. The Northwest Ordinance did, in fact, establish this principle of land ownership precisely because the governing powers in Washington, D.C., were thoroughly familiar with Locke and his arguments for private property.[43] Even if Milch were not familiar with Locke's writings on the subject, his thorough knowledge of American history led him in a Lockean direction in his treatment of the issue of property in *Deadwood*.

Commerce Tames the Alpha Male

The Lockean understanding of property in *Deadwood* points to a larger Lockean spirit in Milch's economic and political understanding of the American West. The show reflects Locke's hope that economics might trump politics, that the peaceful and cooperative spirit of commerce might triumph over the warlike and divisive impulses of political life. As we will see, David Milch is no friend of capitalism in the form of big business and cannot be described as a champion of the free market. Nevertheless, for someone who is deeply suspicious of businesspeople, he is surprisingly open to arguments for the positive effects of commerce on human relations. In *Deadwood* commerce is the chief force that works to produce order without law. Above all, it seems to be the only force that can get the alpha males to set aside their differences, give up their fighting to the death, and work together for their mutual benefit.

The way in which economic logic can dictate social peace is most clearly evident in the career of Al Swearengen. In the incredible rogues' gallery Milch created, Swearengen is the greatest rogue of all, and the most fascinating and complex character in the series.[44] As the owner of the Gem Saloon, he hardly seems to be a model citizen. He is involved in crooked gambling and prostitution, and we quickly learn that he is also guilty of shady land deals and runs a gang of highway robbers. He is responsible for a whole string of murders in the opening episodes. He has a hot temper and is brutal in his treatment of women and subordinates. A perfect example of an alpha male, he seeks to dominate all around him and regards himself as the unofficial ruler of Deadwood. In short, in the early episodes he shows every sign of being the chief villain in the series and the most destructive force in the community.

Yet in the course of the series, Swearengen emerges as the chief architect of order without law in Deadwood. Of all the many alpha males in town, he is the most rational and the most able to control his emotions, especially his anger. He realizes that, when economic necessities demand it, he must restrain his violent impulses and work for peace. When it appears that Deadwood may be annexed to the Dakota territory, thus becoming subject to the rule of outside forces, it is Al who organizes the influential citizens of the camp to respond to the threat. One day he announces to the elders of the camp, "Be in my joint in two hours—we're forming a fuckin' government" (1.9). He is constantly working to get the other powerful males in town to recognize their mutual self-interest and unite against their common enemies from outside the camp.

In the first season of *Deadwood*, one might well think that Milch was setting up a simple contrast between Al Swearengen as villain and Seth Bullock as hero. But the intellectual complexity of the series is evident in the way that Swearengen, the criminal, turns out to be a force for order in the community, while Bullock, the lawman, turns out to be a force for disorder. Although Bullock is genuinely good-hearted and well intentioned, he cannot control his emotions, especially his anger and his pride. Bullock is as much of an alpha male as Swearengen, and their rivalry comes to a head in a brutal fight at the beginning of the second season. But it is Swearengen who realizes that they need to work together against the outside forces threatening the camp. He swallows his pride in order to make the conciliatory gesture of returning Bullock's guns to him and thereby to solidify an alliance with a man he initially distrusted and despised (Swearengen even backs Bullock for sheriff of Deadwood). Swearengen continually struggles to calm Bullock's hot temper and get him to act rationally in the complicated circumstances in which they find themselves. In the third season, Swearengen is willing to take calmly a terrible insult from Hearst (he chops off one of Al's fingers), whereas Bullock, provoked by mere words, hauls Hearst off to jail by the ear, thereby threatening to ruin Swearengen's delicate negotiations with Hearst. Bullock has to learn to trust Swearengen. Silas Adams (Titus Welliver), one of Swearengen's henchmen, sums up the paradox of his character: "When he ain't lyin', Al's the most honorable man you'll ever meet" (3.12).[45] In the figure of Swearengen, Milch seems to be suggesting that one does not need high-minded, public-spirited motives to become a pillar of the community.

In line with Locke, then, and in contrast to Hobbes, Milch shows how human beings, following their economic interests, can find ways to control their anger and their pride—and thus their violent impulses—and achieve forms of social order even in the absence of the state. The citizens of Deadwood quickly reach the point where they themselves realize that killing each other is simply bad for business. This idea is further illustrated in the series in the role of Sol Starr (John Hawkes), Bullock's partner in a hardware store in Deadwood. Unlike Bullock, who is a lawman at heart, Starr is born and bred a merchant. He is always quoting his Viennese father, spouting maxims such as "you reduce costs buying in volume" (2.3). Because he thinks predominantly in economic terms, Starr becomes one of the chief peacemakers in Deadwood. In the opening episodes, he labors mightily to mediate between an angry Bullock and a suspicious Swearengen. What ought to be a simple economic transaction—Bullock and Starr want to buy land for their hardware store from Swearengen—threatens to erupt into a Hobbesian battle until Starr gets both Bullock and Swearengen to calm down and settle their differences. Generally good things happen in Deadwood when cooler economic minds prevail over the hot tempers of the aggressive males in the camp.[46] The hardware store represents the contribution commerce has to make to the Deadwood community. As Starr advertises his wares: "These are quality items. They meet these folks' needs. They're being offered at fair mark up" (1.1). Without presenting Milch as the Milton Friedman of the Western, one may note many instances in *Deadwood* of the market being portrayed as a positive force in the community. When a rival bordello opens in town and Swearengen raises the prospect of colluding to set rates, the new madam, Joanie Stubbs (Kim Dickens), tells him, "As far as pussy, Al, we'll want to let the market sort itself out" (2.3). In the second season, Hearst's geologist and advance man, Francis Wolcott (Garrett Dillahunt), proclaims, "it's always preferable to allow the market to operate unimpeded" (2.4).

To be sure, Wolcott turns out to be the creepiest villain in the series, and Milch presents the business policies he pursues on Hearst's behalf in an extremely negative light. But these policies could justifiably be described as the very opposite of the way a free market operates. Hearst is trying to buy up mining claims in an effort to create a monopoly and does so not by straightforward market means, but instead by using force, fraud, and political influence. Hearst represents the intrusion of outside forces, on a national scale, into the local marketplace of Deadwood. Here we see Milch's distrust of large-scale business allied with the state, as opposed to the small-scale, independent entrepreneurship he generally admires. And when Hearst learns of the gruesome way in which Wolcott has murdered several prostitutes, he fires him and drives him to suicide—not because of any moral outrage, but simply because Wolcott's behavior is bad for business. Many of the best outcomes in *Deadwood* happen for the "wrong" reasons—that is, not out of moral idealism but out of the apparently crudest material motives. Milch views this seeming paradox as characteristic of America, and a cause for celebration, not condemnation. He wants us to be clear-eyed about America and to recognize how its vices are bound up with its virtues: "None of us want to realize that we live in Deadwood, but all of us do. . . . After first recoiling in horror, we come to love the place where we live, in all of its contradictions. . . . American materialism, in all of its crassness and extravagance, is simply an expression of the fact that we have organized ourselves according to a more energizing principle than any civilization that came before us."[47] From what we see in *Deadwood*, that "energizing principle" is the market economy. The best example of order without law is the free market.

The Gold Standard

Milch's grudging respect for the material motives of humanity is reflected in his distinctive treatment of the motif of gold in *Deadwood*. Generally in

American popular culture, money is viewed as the root of all evil, and the gold rush serves as an archetype of greed at its worst (think of Charlie Chaplin's great 1925 silent film on the subject). At times, gold may seem to be the central villain of *Deadwood*. Many men and women die as a result of their quest for it, or ruin their lives and destroy their families in the process. Yet in trying to give a fuller picture of the human condition, Milch insists that gold can function as an agent of civilization. He is well aware from his study of American history that the West would never have been settled or developed as rapidly as it was without a series of gold rushes, from California to Alaska. Gold becomes the central symbol in *Deadwood* of order without law:

> The initial transactions of gold for drink or gold for sex give rise to a more complex social order that is traced in the development of Deadwood. Everyone in town takes up a position in a social order that is based on the premise that gold has value. . . . The agreement to believe in a common symbol of value is really a society trying to find a way to organize itself in some way other than, say, hunting or killing. . . . Agreeing on this single symbol of value has allowed us to organize our individual energies on a wider scale. If we've got to barter wheat for barley and barley for shoelaces, everybody is going to fight, "I worked seven months on these shoelaces and you're going to give me one sheaf of wheat!"[48]

The evolution of gold as a medium of exchange is a prime example of the self-organizing power of society and its remarkable ability to replace violent confrontation with cooperative and mutually beneficial transactions.

In a particularly interesting plot twist, Milch shows how gold can work to solve the bitter problem of prejudice in society, a problem of which he has been acutely aware in all his television series. The community of Deadwood is saturated with prejudice of the most noxious and virulent kind—against Indians, Jews, blacks, the Chinese, women, and many other categories. Milch clearly deplores this aspect of human behavior. He shows that economic self-interest is one of the few forces in human nature that is powerful enough to overcome prejudice.[49] The people of Deadwood, as anti-Semitic as they are, accept Sol Starr, a Jew, once they realize that he is good for the economy of the town. Hearst's monomaniacal obsession with gold makes him a kind of monster, indifferent to the most basic human concerns, but, on the bright side, it also makes him indifferent to the color line. He employs a black cook and forces the classiest hotel in Deadwood to let her live on the premises. He is willing to deal with her son and violate all social taboos by having a private dinner with him, only because gold is at stake between them. Milch articulates the ambivalent nature of our desire for gold:

> Yet the process of abstraction that Hearst embodies, which is symbolized in gold, is also at the very heart of what makes us human. It's the best in us, as well as the worst, and it is often both at the same time. . . . Hearst sees the power of gold . . . in the way [it] can eliminate the stickier aspects of our human particularity. That's why Hearst can befriend Odell, the son of his black chef, Aunt Lou. Odell has discovered gold in Liberia. For Hearst, the agreed-upon value of gold is the root of all civilized behavior. It mandates a calculus of utility that trumps even the most deep-seated prejudice.[50]

It is remarkable to hear a television writer describe gold as "the root of all civilized behavior," not of all evil. In the actual episode, Milch develops the point at length in a dialogue between Hearst and Odell (Omar Gooding): "Before the color [gold], no white man . . . no man of any hue, moved to civilize or improve a place like this, had reason to make the effort. The color brought commerce here and such order as has been attained."[51] In the spirit of Locke rather than Hobbes, Hearst sees commerce, not the Leviathan State, as bringing order to human society:

> *Hearst:* But for that gold, you'd never have sat at my table. And for the effrontery in your rising up, except that you'd showed me the gold, I'd've shot or seen you hanged without a second thought. The value I gave the gold restrained me, you see, your utility in connection with it. . . . Gold confers power, and that power is transferable. Power comes to any man who has the color.
> *Odell:* Even if he is black.
> *Hearst:* That is our species' hope—that uniformly agreeing on its value, we organize to seek the color. (3.7)

With all his failings as a human being, Hearst nevertheless gives the most eloquent expression of the great Lockean hope of *Deadwood:* that commerce might bring human beings together in peace by overcoming all the dark Hobbesian forces that set them at war with one another.

If human beings can develop a widely accepted medium of exchange out of their commercial transactions among themselves—a complex task of social coordination—then they can find other ways on their own of living together peacefully and productively. Gold provides an excellent example of bottom-up, rather than top-down order. It spontaneously evolved as a medium of exchange as a product of market forces and is not the result of government action—in sharp contrast to any paper currency, which needs to be made legal tender by legislative fiat and thus is imposed on society from above.[52] Milch explicitly draws a connection between gold and the spirit of Lockean liberalism in *Deadwood:*

> Yankton, the capital of Dakota territory, was a creation of the Indian agencies. It was the governmental bureaucracy, with all that that implies. When Deadwood came into being, it threw everything off. Provided with an abundant source of economic security of which any man could partake [gold], the Black Hills settlers and miners had returned to the traditional distrust of government and a renewal of pride and self-sufficiency, which the oligarchy in Yankton had never endorsed. Mining was a real industry as opposed to this sterile instrument of suppression, this paper fiction whose only real use was to steal from the Indians.[53]

As a student of American history, Milch seems to be aware that throughout the nineteenth century both government currency and treaties with the Indians were sometimes not worth the paper they were printed on. He thus views paper money as an instrument of government oppression and gold as a site of resistance to it. As such, gold is perhaps the best representative of spontaneous order and the independence of the economic order from the political.

Prepolitical or Postpolitical?

Jean-Jacques Rousseau's radical reconception of the state of nature provides a different philosophical perspective on *Deadwood*. Rousseau would call into question the claim that *Deadwood* offers any insight into the state of nature. His challenge to the show is evident in his criticism of the thinkers who preceded him in analyzing the state of nature, specifically Hobbes and Locke. As Rousseau wrote:

The philosophers who have examined the foundations of society
have all felt the necessity of going back to the state of nature, but
none of them has reached it. Some have not hesitated to attribute to
man in that state the notion of the just and unjust, without troubling
themselves to show that he had to have that notion or even that it was
useful to him. Others have spoken of the natural right that everyone
has to preserve what belongs to him, without explaining what they
meant by *belong*. . . . All of them, finally, speaking continually of
need, avarice, oppression, desires, and pride, have carried over to
the state of nature ideas they had acquired in society: they spoke
about savage man and they described civil man.[54]

Rousseau argues that previous philosophers were not radical enough in con-
ceiving the state of nature. For example, Hobbes posits vanity and pride in
his natural men; that is what drives them into the war of all against all. But,
according to Rousseau, vanity and pride can arise only in the midst of civil
society, where men can compare themselves with each other; these vices
cannot arise in the isolated condition of natural men. Rousseau comes up
with a vision of natural man stripped of all the characteristics he believes
are acquired only in society, including speech and reason. The result is that,
in civilized terms, Rousseau's natural man is virtually subhuman, enjoying
the peace and happiness of a grazing animal.

Rousseau's version of the state of nature thus raises a serious intellectual difficulty about *Deadwood*. The townspeople may well be seeking
a fresh start in Deadwood, but they come to the camp with a great deal of
baggage, intellectual as well as emotional.[55] This fact calls into question the
idea that Deadwood portrays a prepolitical community. Although for the
moment there may be no legally constituted authorities in the camp, its
citizens operate with clear models of traditional political order. When they
put Jack McCall (Garrett Dillahunt), the assassin of Wild Bill Hickok, on
trial, they know ahead of time what a courtroom looks like—for example,
that it requires a judge and a jury. They do not need to invent the institution from the ground up. When they start to organize as a community,
they know that a municipality requires a mayor. Milch himself says of the
meeting in Al's saloon: "They start to act governmental."[56] How could they
act "governmental" if they had not already observed government in action?

Although the citizens of Deadwood may momentarily revel in the
absence of law in the camp, from the very beginning they anticipate being

brought back into the United States and act accordingly. In the very first episode, A. W. Merrick (Jeffrey Jones), the editor-publisher of the local newspaper, says, "We will be restored to the bosom of the nation." The characters in *Deadwood* are temporarily living outside the jurisdiction of any government, but they all have had the experience of living under political authority, they know what it entails, and they anticipate returning to that condition, with varying degrees of eagerness or reluctance. Rousseau would argue that the world of the law and the state is a shadowy presence throughout *Deadwood,* always hovering on the horizon as a either a memory or an anticipation, and in any case a guidepost. Washington, D.C., is mentioned with surprising frequency in Deadwood for a town that is supposed to be without a nation-state.

The Rousseauian argument that *Deadwood* does not portray a truly prepolitical community suggests an alternative way of understanding the series, one still compatible with Milch's idea of order without law. Perhaps Milch's Deadwood is best understood as a postpolitical community, one consisting of people who have for one reason or another deliberately fled the state and who seek to live free of its stifling and inhibiting laws. They know full well what a state is and are quite familiar with its institutions, but—at least temporarily—they welcome the chance to operate without a government and see what they can achieve on their own. Their choice to live free of government becomes clear when some citizens in Deadwood imitate the state institutions they remember and start to reimpose regulations on the community. For example, after a fire breaks out in town, the people of Deadwood decide to create the office of fire marshal. With a typically bureaucratic sense of self-importance, Charlie Utter (Dayton Callie) takes his new post very seriously and starts bossing around the other people in town. Faced with the imposition of fire regulations on his establishment, Tom Nuttall (Leon Rippy) balks: "That's the kind of shit that ran me out of Wilkes-Barre" (1.11).[57] In his protest against government meddling in his affairs, Nuttall speaks for the spirit of independence that created Deadwood in the first place.

From this perspective, the political treatise most relevant to *Deadwood* may well be James C. Scott's *The Art of Not Being Governed: An Anarchist History of Upland Southeast Asia.* In a study focused on the hill peoples of Southeast Asia, Scott argues that ethnic groups usually offered as examples of true primitives—people living in a precivilized and prepolitical state— are really refugees from centralized monarchies in the valleys, states that oppressed and exploited them, chiefly with high taxes and forced labor. As Scott sums up his argument:

> In the valley imagination, all these characteristics are earlier stages in a process of social evolution at the apex of which elites perch. Hill peoples are an earlier stage: they are "pre-" just about everything: pre–padi cultivation, pre-towns, prereligion, preliterate, pre–valley subject. As we have seen at some length, however, the characteristics for which the hill peoples are stigmatized are precisely those characteristics that a state-evading people would encourage and perfect in order to avoid surrendering autonomy. The valley imagination has its history wrong. Hill peoples are not pre-anything. In fact, they are better understood as post–irrigated rice, postsedentary, postsubject, and perhaps even postliterate. They represent, in the longue durée, a reactive and purposeful statelessness of people who have adapted to a world of states while remaining outside their firm grasp.[58]

In short, Scott argues that when we see a people living without a state, we should not automatically assume that they are at some primitive stage of development, as yet culturally incapable of forming a state. They may well have already experienced what it is to live under state control, rejected that regimented way of life, and sought an alternative, often by literally running for the hills.

At several points, Scott draws parallels between the region he is discussing and the frontier in the American West; and indeed Deadwood, set in the Black Hills, is a good example of the kind of hill community Scott has in mind. His description of the frontier of the Chinese empire fits Milch's Deadwood perfectly: "a pandemonium of adventurers, bandits, speculators, armed traders, demobilized soldiers, poor migrants, exiles, corrupt officials, fugitives from the law, and refugees."[59] Scott thus provides a new way of understanding the phenomenon Milch calls "order without law." Scott documents in great detail how people who have experienced the worst aspects of state control can find ways to lead ordered lives without the rigid controls of government apparatus. In particular, Scott dwells as Milch does on the economic aspects of this nongovernmental order. He emphasizes the role of commercial trade, especially the fact that hill peoples typically have access to resources greatly desired and/or needed by the valley states they border, valuable commodities they can use to gain leverage with their more powerful neighbors (and thus maintain their independence). The role of gold in *Deadwood* is an obvious example of this strategy.

Given the economic exchanges that typically occur between hill and valley, Scott points out that the boundary between stateless people and those living in states is extremely permeable and ever-changing. People will leave states when the tax burden and other government impositions become too great, but they may well return when conditions ease and the benefits of living under government again outweigh the costs. In conventional state-of-nature thinking, the social contract is a "once and for all" proposition. Once people enter into a social contract, they supposedly leave the state of nature forever. Scott's way of thinking suggests that the social contract is perpetually being negotiated and renegotiated. People break the social contract and slip out of the state when its burdens become too oppressive, but they will always consider returning when conditions become favorable again. In conventional state-of-nature thinking, the social contract may appear to be the hypothetical construct of the political theorist. But in his study of hill peoples, Scott suggests that whether to live in a state is a genuine decision human beings make when they rationally weigh their alternatives. Scott's account helps explain what might at first appear to be the peculiar relation of the characters of *Deadwood* to the state. Despite possessing good reasons for having effectively moved out from under governmental authority, they are constantly considering the possibility of getting back into the United States, and carefully calculating the costs and benefits of doing so. The characters of *Deadwood* have the mobility, versatility, and adaptability that Scott claims is characteristic of hill peoples everywhere.

The idea of Deadwood as a postpolitical rather than a prepolitical community provides an answer to a Rousseauian critique of Milch's conception of order without law. As long as Milch concentrates on economic examples of order without law, he is on solid ground. Gold as a medium of exchange is an excellent case of a social ordering arrived at purely as a result of market forces, with no government intervention or legal postulation. When Milch shows underlying economic forces leading to social organization in Deadwood, it does not matter if the townspeople are following models derived from their prior existence in civil society. (Sol Starr, for example, cites economic maxims originating in Old World Vienna.) These models themselves evolved independently of government action and represent a perennial human possibility of society producing order out of its own commercial transactions. One should not demand that the citizens of Deadwood go through the laborious process of rediscovering for themselves what makes gold superior as a medium of exchange (its independent value in alternate uses, its comparative rarity, its durability, its malleability, its transportability, its divisibility, and so on). All that matters is that, for Deadwood, gold, as it has for much of humanity, represents a medium of exchange people have arrived at on their own—not one imposed on them by a government and its laws regarding legal tender. In the area of economics, Milch successfully shows that human beings are able to order their lives "naturally"—that is to say, spontaneously, without the intervention of government and laws.

Town with Pity

A Rousseauian critique of *Deadwood* for failing to provide insight into a prepolitical condition may be countered with Scott's notion of the postpolitical, but Rousseau's *Second Discourse* can still provide insights into the series. One of Rousseau's distinctive contributions to state-of-nature thinking is his claim that natural man is characterized by the trait of pity, a point he makes in explicit contrast to Hobbes:

> There is, besides, another principle which Hobbes did not notice, and which—having been given to man in order to soften . . . the ferocity of his vanity, or the desire for self-preservation before the birth of vanity—tempers the ardor he has for his own well-being by an innate repugnance to see his fellow-man suffer. . . . I speak of pity, a disposition that is appropriate to beings as weak and subject to as many ills as we are; . . . and so natural that even beasts sometimes give perceptible signs of it. Without speaking of the tenderness of mothers for their young and of the perils they brave to guard them, one observes daily the repugnance of horses to trample a living body underfoot.[60]

Milch is Rousseauian in his insistence that pity—fellow feeling—is innate to humanity and one of its most basic emotions. Compassion, particularly for the physical suffering of fellow human beings, is remarkably pervasive in Deadwood, especially for such a rough-and-tumble camp. What most surprises us in Al Swearengen as we learn more about him is that this brutal man actually has a tender side, often strangely conjoined with his cold-bloodedness. At the end of the first season, he carries out a mercy killing of the ailing Reverend Smith (Ray McKinnon), and at the end of the third, for what can only be described as sentimental reasons, he cannot bring himself to kill "Trixie the whore" (Paula Malcomson) on Hearst's orders (although he is willing to kill another one of his prostitutes as a substitute).

The outbreak of smallpox in the first season is the first occasion for Deadwood to organize itself as a community.[61] The heroic actions to save lives on the part of Doc Cochran (Brad Dourif) and Calamity Jane (Robin Weigert) reflect the best side of humanity as Milch views it—a genuine concern for the welfare of other human beings. The specific contribution of women to life in Deadwood, especially toward the nurturing and educating of children, reflects a Rousseauian view of compassion as essential to human sociability. The events that bring the community of Deadwood together at the end of the second season—the funeral of Seth Bullock's stepson William (Josh Eriksson) and the marriage of Alma Garrett and Whitney Ellsworth (Jim Beaver)—also make a Rousseauian point about the importance of domestic sympathies to social life. As in *The Searchers,* there is a long tradition in the Western of presenting women as the great civilizing force on the frontier, and *Deadwood* follows that pattern. The building of a new schoolhouse in the third season—an archetypal Western moment—is one of the central symbols of the growth of civilization in Deadwood.

"What Some People Think of as Progress"

The deepest way in which Rousseau is relevant to *Deadwood* is that, of the three principal state-of-nature thinkers, he has the gravest doubts about the value of civilization. Rousseau calls into question the triumphalism of the state-of-nature narratives in both Hobbes and Locke. They view the movement from the state of nature to the state of civil society as progress, a distinct improvement in the human condition. By contrast, Rousseau does not believe in the inevitability of the movement from the state of nature to civil society, and he is not at all convinced that this transition should be called "progress." He insists that the movement out of the state of nature, far from being a necessary development, as Hobbes and Locke present it, resulted from a "chance combination of several foreign causes which might never have arisen and without which [man] would have remained eternally in his primitive condition."[62] Moreover, Rousseau argues that even after humanity left the state of nature, its development might have stopped at a stage well short of the full-blown nation-state, and humanity would have been happier as a result.[63]

Human beings in Rousseau's state of nature live in peaceful harmony, largely because they are scattered in the forests and hardly have anything to do with each other. There are no alpha males in Rousseau's state of nature and therefore no violence and, in fact, no competition whatsoever. In contrast to Hobbes, Rousseau views the state of nature as a realm of abundance; and in contrast to Locke, he views the development of property as generating artificial scarcities among human beings.[64] To sum up the differences: Hobbes argues that there can be no order without law created by the state; Locke argues that a limited economic order is possible independent of any law made by the state, but it ultimately can be secured only by the state; Rousseau argues that order is fully possible without law in the state of nature. In fact, for Rousseau, law actually generates disorder; the attempt to suppress the passions by laws only succeeds in inflaming them.[65]

Because Rousseau's state of nature is so much more attractive than that of Hobbes or even Locke, his writings serve as a powerful indictment of existing governments, and they helped to fuel modern revolutionary movements, beginning in America in 1776 and France in 1789. Rousseau's state of nature offers a model of human freedom and autonomy. To be sure, Rousseau explicitly denies that the message of his work is "Back to Nature!"[66] Rather, he presents the state of nature as a kind of Paradise Lost.[67] But his political writings are devoted to the difficult task of recapturing as much of the positive aspects of the state of nature as is possible in modern civil society. He is highly critical of the way civic institutions have distorted human nature, especially through the inequalities a modern economy creates, with its property rights and division of labor. The most famous sentence Rousseau ever wrote is the beginning of *The Social Contract:* "Man is born free, and everywhere he is in chains."[68]

Deadwood embodies a similar skepticism about the value of government and modern civilization. It may present the town's movement toward developing municipal institutions and being incorporated into the United States as inevitable, but it questions whether this truly constitutes progress, an improvement in the lives of Deadwood's citizens. In the spirit of Rousseau, Milch raises doubts about the triumphalism of the traditional Western. The standard pattern of the Western portrays the closing of the frontier, the bringing of civilization to the Wild West. Typically, a lawless community, overrun by rampaging gunfighters, must be tamed by a brave lawman or two in concert with civic-minded businessmen, a crusading newspaper editor, and a beautiful schoolmarm waiting in the wings to educate a new generation of law-abiding city dwellers.

One can hear this standard narrative of progress in the historical fea-
turette "Deadwood Matures," included in the DVDs of the third season. The
historians tell a familiar tale of the town's march toward civilization, sparked
by technological developments such as the telegraph and the railroad, as
well as the growth of civilizing influences such as the schoolhouse and the
theater.[69] A kind of Hegelian optimism informs these narratives—events in
the West happened in the way they had to happen and no other outcome
could have been better. Civilization must be good because it is what history
led to. Elements of the Western myth of progress are present in *Deadwood,*
especially in the third season, when outside forces truly begin to transform
the town. But Milch himself evaluates this transformation quite differently:
he refuses to view it simply as progress. *Deadwood,* in fact, dwells upon what
is lost when a town makes the transition to civilization and becomes part of
the nation-state. What is lost is freedom.[70]

The second season of *Deadwood* begins with Al Swearengen observing
the new telegraph poles going up in the town and ruefully commenting,
"Invisible messages from invisible sources, or what some people think of as
progress." Al is right to be skeptical about the benefit to Deadwood of becoming connected to the outside world. Its citizens will be kept better informed
of gold prices in the East, and Dan Dority hopes that baseball scores will
now be more readily available. But the telegraph will also allow the East
to exert greater control over the West and proves to be the harbinger of a
federal takeover of Deadwood. The upside of Deadwood's initial isolation
is its local autonomy. The bureaucratic and corporate forces that invade the
town in the second and third seasons take away the camp's control of its
own destiny and have little concern for the welfare of its citizens. Politicians
and businessmen eye Deadwood as a place to plunder. The government
officials who come to Deadwood are mostly looking to be bribed. With no
intention of settling in the town themselves, they plan on governing it from
afar, with little or no knowledge of what is actually going on there. George
Hearst, as the representative of big business in the series, wishes to add the
Deadwood camp to his far-flung mining empire. He wants to extract as
much gold as he can from the Black Hills as fast as possible. At the end of
the third season, he leaves Deadwood as abruptly as he arrived at the end
of the second. He cares nothing about the town, speaking with contempt
of the "small-mindedness and self-interested behavior that's so pervasive
in this shithole" (3.6).[71]

During the first season of *Deadwood,* one might well have thought that no one could be more evil or worse for the town than Al Swearengen. It is a measure of Milch's doubts about the so-called civilizing process that by the third season, Al has become a sort of hero in *Deadwood* for leading the resistance to the outside forces trying to "modernize" the town. We certainly start rooting for him in his struggles against Hearst, and the mining magnate becomes the new villain in the series, chilling us with a degree of cold-bloodedness that Al could not muster on his worst days. What are the differences between Swearengen and Hearst that make the latter the greater villain in Milch's eyes and ours?[72] Swearengen is a tyrant, but he is Deadwood's own tyrant. As a homegrown boss, he is by nature limited in his evil. When Al kills someone, he usually has to look him—or her—straight in the eye. In general, he has to live with the consequences of his evil deeds. He lives among the very people he preys upon. This fact does not stop him from preying upon them, but it does moderate the way he treats them. He never kills indiscriminately. In reality, Al is a better man than his carefully cultivated public image as a cutthroat would suggest. Despite giving the impression that he is purely self-interested, he actually takes a certain civic pride in Deadwood, and from the balcony of the Gem Saloon he secretly watches the public life of the town with a sort of seigniorial satisfaction.

By contrast, Hearst embodies all the dangers of a man who seeks to rule people as a complete stranger to them. The quality Milch associates with Hearst is abstraction. He has one goal in life—to find and extract gold from the earth—and Milch acknowledges that this ability to abstract, to disregard all other considerations, gives remarkable energy to Hearst's economic endeavors. But it also means that he is blind to ordinary human concerns and tramples over anyone standing in his way. Unlike Swearengen, Hearst does not know the men he has killed, and he always acts through intermediaries. He tries to keep as much distance as possible between him and the dirty deeds that make his business empire possible. For Milch, Hearst stands for the tyranny of abstraction, and he symbolizes everything that is questionable about life in the modern nation-state, which places the seat of power remote from the communities it rules.

Deadwood begins as a small town, the locus of small business, with impoverished men trying to make their fortunes in mining, accompanied by entrepreneurs like Bullock and Starr, who hope to make their living by providing necessary goods and services to the miners. Milch shows much that is questionable about the economic behavior that goes on in the isolation of this small town. Yet he seems to find it preferable to what happens when big government and big business invade Deadwood. As we have seen, there is something self-regulating about economic life in Deadwood, where everybody knows everybody else and people deal with each other face to face. It is the facelessness—the abstraction—of big government that Milch seems most to question. Big business presents the same problem. Hearst represents corporate interests, and therefore Swearengen and others see no point in killing him, because other shareholders in his corporation would simply take his place. Hearst's almost magical invulnerability in the third season symbolizes the implacable power of corporate, or what might be better called state or crony, capitalism. What troubles Milch is the alliance between big government and big business that generates, and is in turn generated by, the nation-state.[73] In the modern nation-state, power is simply too abstract and too remote from the people, radiating from a system that has lost touch with ordinary human beings and their actions as individuals.[74] What Milch most objects to is the spectacle of an aloof and self-interested elite trampling over local interests.

Government as a Necessary Evil

Deadwood is filled with antigovernment comments that are almost libertarian in spirit. Washington especially comes in for criticism, because it is the unit of government furthest removed from the people it tries to rule and therefore lacks the crucial knowledge of local circumstances needed to rule well. With regard to the U.S. government's treatment of the Indians, Swearengen sarcastically remarks: "deep fucking thinkers in Washington put forward that policy" (1.3). Even one of the corrupt politicians from Yankton, Hugo Jarry (Stephen Tobolowsky), speaks with contempt of the federal government, specifically its attempts to hide its own corruption and incompetence: "Washington harasses us for our difficulties in distribution to the Indians, thereby distracting the nation at large from Washington's own fiscal turpitudes and miasms" (3.9). Jarry also complains about the ignorance of his fellow federal bureaucrats in Yankton: "They're too busy stealing to study human nature" (2.5). Milch clearly shares his characters' skepticism about the federal government; he notes, "I'm always amazed when people say, 'Congress has adjourned and they have accomplished nothing.' A congressional term that accomplishes nothing is what the Founding Fathers prayed for. They wanted to keep the government canceling itself out, because it's in the nature of government to fuck people up."[75]

Deadwood shows how predatory government is on all levels. Nothing Swearengen can do on his own to rob the townspeople can match the ambitious plans of the new municipal government to fleece them. The leading citizens get together under Al's leadership to raise the money to bribe officials in Yankton to let their mining claims stand. The first thing that the newly "elected" mayor, E. B. Farnum (William Sanderson), proposes is a scheme to extract money from the unwitting townspeople: "Couldn't our informal organization lay taxes on the settlement to pay the bribes?" Farnum hits the nail on the head when he defines the nature of government: "Taking people's money is what makes organizations real, be they formal, informal, or temporary" (1.9). With government activity epitomized by raising taxes to pay bribes, it is no wonder that politicians acquire a dubious reputation in *Deadwood.* Wolcott is the most repulsive character in the entire series, and yet even he insists on dissociating himself from the public sector: "I am a sinner who doesn't expect forgiveness, but I am not a government official" (2.10). Milch certainly shows that a great deal of chicanery and outright cheating goes on in Deadwood when business is unregulated. But the problem with offering the government as a solution to these economic problems is that the would-be regulators are far more corrupt than the people they are supposed to regulate. Milch presents government as basically petty theft on a grand scale. A government's ability to extract money from people dwarfs what any individual criminal can accomplish.

Perhaps the most eloquent discourse on the nature of government in *Deadwood*—a ringing statement of the postpolitical creed—is delivered by Swearengen's rival saloon keeper, Cy Tolliver (Powers Boothe), on the occasion of Yankton's attempt to question the validity of the town's mining claims: "Who of us here didn't know what government was before we came? Wasn't half our purpose coming to get shed of the cocksucker? And here it comes again—to do what's in its nature—to lie to us, and confuse us, and steal what we came to by toil and being lucky just once in our fuckin' lives. And we gonna be surprised by that, boys, government being government?" (2.5). Despite such negative views of government in *Deadwood,* Milch seems to acknowledge its necessity, and even the idea that the town must be incorporated into the nation-state. Civilization, after all, requires some sacrifices, even of our natural freedom. In the most Rousseauian comment in the series, Swearengen tells his henchman Dority, "From the moment we leave the forest, Dan, it's all a giving up and adjusting" (3.2). But even with this concession, Milch, like Swearengen, gives a less than ringing endorsement of the power of government: "The politicians will always screw you, but there are circumstances in which we would rather have them around."[76]

This quotation from Milch seems to epitomize the attitude of *Deadwood* toward government, especially the nation-state. Government is at best a necessary evil, but we must be skeptical about its claims to serve the public interest and always remain vigilant to resist its perennial tendency to increase its power and encroach upon personal freedom. The closer power can be kept to a local level, the better. Milch's faith in order without law ultimately puts him in the camp of those, like Locke, who believe in limited government, perhaps radically limited government. Maybe the dilemma of freedom versus law can be resolved along the lines of the U.S. Constitution, which attempts to limit government power, secure the freedom of its citizens, and impose the rule of law even on the government itself. Moreover, the federalism of the constitutional system offers some hope of people retaining power at local levels.

Whether or not one agrees with these conclusions, one must acknowledge the sophistication of the economic and political thinking in *Deadwood*. The show is Hobbesian in the way that it analyzes the sources of violence in human interaction. The show is Lockean in the way that it portrays the establishment of property rights and the resulting commerce as civilizing forces in society. And the show is Rousseauian in the doubts that it raises about the standard narrative of the triumph of the nation-state as progress. To try to sum up *Deadwood*'s complex philosophical position: the show is basically Lockean in its faith in the self-organizing power of society, while it maintains a Hobbesian anxiety about the fragility of social order together with a Rousseanian skepticism about civilization's ultimate value.[77] In combining elements of Hobbes, Locke, and Rousseau, *Deadwood* exemplifies the seriousness and thoughtfulness of the Western at its best. Such is the remarkable result when Thomas Hobbes, John Locke, and Jean-Jacques Rousseau meet Wild Bill Hickok and Calamity Jane on the American frontier.

Part Two

MAVERICK CREATORS AND MAVERICK HEROES

INTRODUCTION TO PART TWO

This part deals first with flying saucers and a trailer-trash family in Kansas, then with a billionaire aviation tycoon and his conflict with a U.S. senator, and finally with four potty-mouthed children from Colorado. Thus, at first sight its unity may not be entirely obvious, especially when compared with the other parts of the book, one of which deals with a single genre (the Western), another with a single figure (Edgar Ulmer), and the last with a single historical moment (9/11 and its aftermath). Nevertheless, the chapters in this part go right to the heart of this book's subject: the tradition of challenging authority in America and championing free individuals—in short, the American conception of the hero as maverick. The term *maverick* comes out of the American West, where it referred to unbranded cattle, and one of the most successful television Westerns was named *Maverick*. The archetypal American hero has roots in the Western frontier and is distinguished by his maverick qualities—his determination to go his own way and his unwillingness to play by the conventional rules. As we saw in discussing Gene Roddenberry in chapter 2, the spirit of the Western has a way of migrating into other pop culture genres. We should not be surprised to find it resurface in a science fiction movie that begins with a cattle stampede (*Mars Attacks!*), or in the story of an authentic American hero in *The Aviator* (after all, we call Howard Hughes an aviation *pioneer*), or even in a cartoon (*South Park* provides a comic counterpart of *Deadwood*, with the same spirit of anarchy and flouting of authority, as well as the amazing ability of its children to match the likes of Al Swearengen curse word for curse word).

Despite many differences, the three works I discuss here have much in common, especially a kind of transposed frontier spirit and a focus on rejecting and rebelling against the establishment. *South Park* is, of course, antiestablishment at its core and has drawn fire from educational, moral, and religious authorities of all stripes. *Mars Attacks!* takes the side of ordinary Americans against the Washington establishment, which patronizes them and tries to run their lives for them. At first glance, the Howard Hughes of *The Aviator* would seem to be an establishment figure himself. Rich and powerful, in command of a business empire, he appears to be the kind of big man who pushes little people around. But in the manner of a typical Martin Scorsese film, *The Aviator* focuses on Hughes as a perpetual underdog, fighting first the Hollywood establishment, then the aviation industry establishment, and finally the biggest establishment of them all, the U.S. government.

Without getting too biographical in approach, it would be easy to see affinities between the maverick creators of these works and the maverick heroes they champion. Martin Scorsese is one of the most fiercely independent spirits ever to work in the American film industry, and one of the most creative. He is legendary for his artistic integrity, and he has made some of the most original films in Hollywood history. Tim Burton is also one of the rare directors who has put the stamp of his individual genius on all his films, and like Scorsese he has often had to fight the Hollywood establishment in order to do so. The creators of *South Park*, Trey Parker and Matt Stone, would probably not be classed by media historians in the same league as Scorsese and Burton. Yet in many respects they fit the model of the auteur and might even be called the Orson Welles or the Charlie Chaplin of the cartoon world. They created *South Park* on their own, write the scripts, supervise the production process for each episode, compose some of the songs, and even voice many of the characters themselves. In terms of language and subject matter, they have pushed the envelope in television as much as anyone who has ever worked in the medium, and have had to struggle with network executives to achieve their creative freedom.

Scorsese, Burton, and Parker and Stone constitute solid evidence that American popular culture should not be judged by its lowest common denominator. They have shown that Hollywood rules, however rigid they may appear, are made to be broken. To be sure, all four have had to compromise at various points in their careers, and have had to accept the interference of their corporate bosses in their creative work. They have not always been able to get exactly what they wanted on the screen. Nevertheless, because of their willingness to fight for what they believe in, they have produced genuinely original and creative works. Considering how innovative and audacious these works have been, we should marvel at what these artists have managed to get away with in Hollywood, rather than complain about the commercial restraints on their creativity. They have not had any magic formula that guaranteed their success, and, given their backgrounds, no one could have predicted how much they have accomplished. At key moments in their careers they have been lucky, but only in the sense that they were fortunate to be given a chance to make a given movie or television show. They still had to prove themselves and demonstrate the truth of the principle that "talent will out." The careers of Scorsese, Burton, and Parker and Stone show that one can be a maverick and still make it in Hollywood. As much as they have struggled at times with the commercial system of production, they have also profited from it—both financially and artistically. Hollywood has made them rich, and has also given them the financial and other resources they need to practice their craft. Burton, as well as Parker and Stone, have spoken with gratitude—and even some amazement—about the amounts of money that Hollywood has been willing to put at their disposal.

Scorsese, Burton, and Parker and Stone have all benefited from the free enterprise system in the United States, especially the freedom to take chances in one's chosen profession and see what one can accomplish. Each in his own way has lived out the American dream, coming from ordinary and undistinguished origins and rising to the top of his field. It is appropriate, then, that they celebrate the American principle of liberty in their work. Accordingly, this is the part of my book that focuses most clearly on the libertarian impulse in American film and television. Of all the figures I discuss in this volume, I believe that only Parker and Stone identify themselves as libertarians (Chris Carter of *The X-Files* has occasionally referred to himself as a "left libertarian"). Indeed, *South Park* explicitly and emphatically defends free enterprise and makes fun of the way capitalism is routinely demonized in the American media. I doubt that Scorsese thinks of himself as a proponent of capitalism, and yet *The Aviator* insightfully portrays the visionary nature of the entrepreneur and takes his side against government efforts to regulate his activities and stifle his creativity. The fact that Scorsese could identify with Howard Hughes specifically as a motion picture entrepreneur probably helped generate the broader sympathy for a businessman hero that makes *The Aviator* unusual among American films.

South Park and *The Aviator* share a distrust of government intervention in the marketplace. In particular, they both show that government actions that claim to be in the public interest are often done at the urging of private interests behind the scene. In a form of unfair competition, one company gets the government to take action against another, often in an attempt to create a government-sanctioned monopoly. Thus neither *South Park* nor *The Aviator* is simply pro-business. A common error about libertarians is to think that, because they support free enterprise, they are always on the side of any business, especially big business. But as *South Park* makes clear, libertarians support big business only when it has grown big by means of legitimate market competition. When big business gets in bed with big government to seek protection and aid, libertarians are the first to condemn what they call corporate welfare or crony capitalism. The "Gnomes" episode of *South Park* is particularly valuable for showing that libertarians do not unthinkingly side with big business against small. Rather libertarians distinguish between businesses (big or small) that are willing to compete freely in the market and those (again, big or small) that exploit their government connections to eliminate or reduce competition. In its portrayal of the battle between TWA and Pan Am, *The Aviator* draws the same distinction, one that Adam Smith had made in 1776 and that is fundamental to genuine free market thinking.

I do not see any form of specifically economic libertarianism in *Mars Attacks!*, but it certainly shares the antigovernment and antiestablishment spirit of *The Aviator* and *South Park*. Burton's movie is filled with a democratic respect for the self-organizing power of the American people and confidence in their ability to take care of themselves. *Mars Attacks!* gives a vicious portrait of America's political, scientific, media, and military elites and suggests their utter irrelevance to ordinary life in the United States. They are shown to be out of touch with what is important to average Americans. In a crisis, the common people in the film must act to save themselves, and they draw upon their pop culture to do so. *Mars Attacks!* reverses the position we saw in *Have Gun–Will Travel* in chapter 2. In that show's vision of the United States, a broad-minded and cosmopolitan figure from the cultural elite (based, like Hollywood itself, in California) is necessary to protect small-town Americans from themselves and their own small-mindedness. In *Mars Attacks!* the cultural elite is exposed as a sham, and people from the heartland of America band together across racial and ethnic lines to rally to their own defense in the absence of any effective leadership from Washington.

The Aviator and *South Park* share this suspicion of elites who claim to be concerned about the common people but are really interested only in maintaining their own power and social status. *South Park* particularly attacks the Hollywood elite and the stars' relentless campaigning for politically correct causes about which they can feel smug and self-satisfied. But the show also satirizes politicians such as Al Gore, who seize on alarmist issues as a way of clinging desperately to their celebrity and feeding their vanity (see especially the tenth-season episode "Manbearpig"). *The Aviator* explores the paradox of wealthy elites who condemn money-making activities because they want to preserve their elevated status against up-and-coming entrepreneurs such as Hughes. Ultimately, what the three works I discuss in this part share is a bottom-up rather than a top-down vision of America. They all take the side of the little guy, with the understanding that in the face of big government even the biggest businessman is a little guy. They question the ability of the government to run the world effectively or fairly and turn to individuals to get things done and save the day. *South Park* offers the only example in this book of something approaching programmatic libertarianism, but *Mars Attacks!* and *The Aviator* embody what I speak of more loosely as the libertarian impulse in American popular culture.

My continuing effort to show that popular culture can be taken seriously in artistic and intellectual terms is most severely challenged in this part, especially when I am dealing with a movie as silly as *Mars Attacks!* or a television show as vulgar as *South Park*. But I persist in my claim that what is often cordoned off as elite culture is nevertheless relevant to popular culture. In the *Mars Attacks!* chapter, I use Alexis de Tocqueville's *Democracy in America* as a reference point and argue that Tim Burton shares with the French thinker an appreciation of the importance of localism in democracy. In the *Aviator* chapter, I draw upon the ideas of free market economics, including works by Adam Smith, Ludwig von Mises, and Friedrich Hayek, to illuminate the movie's understanding of entrepreneurship. I also draw upon these ideas in the *South Park* chapter, and try to place the show in a tradition of philosophical comedy that goes back as far as Aristophanes, Socrates, and Plato. I use Rabelais and Mark Twain to suggest that *South Park*, with all its profanity and blasphemy, harks back to some distinguished cultural antecedents. Parker and Stone did not invent the fart joke. It has a long and venerable history, stretching back through Twain and Rabelais all the way to Aristophanes' *The Clouds*. Works that are venerated today as exemplars of elite culture are sometimes as vulgar as contemporary comedies, and were in their own day condemned as profane, obscene, and blasphemous. *South Park* may be my best example of how the high and the low are often inextricably intertwined, not just in popular culture, but in culture more generally.

4

MARS ATTACKS!

Tim Burton and the Ideology of the Flying Saucer Movie

> I am obliged to confess I should sooner live in a society governed by the first two thousand names in the Boston telephone directory than in a society governed by the two thousand faculty members of Harvard University.
> —William F. Buckley Jr.

Tim Burton's wacky sci-fi film *Mars Attacks!* (1996) is not considered one of the highpoints of his career. Although the movie took in over $100 million worldwide in its initial release, it was judged a box-office failure, given that it was budgeted for roughly the same amount and its backers were hoping for another blockbuster from the director of *Batman* (1989). Moreover, critics generally did not review *Mars Attacks!* favorably. Speaking for many of his colleagues, Kenneth Turan of the *Los Angeles Times* wrote, "*Mars Attacks!* is not as much fun as it should be. Few of its numerous actors make a lasting impression and Burton's heart and soul is not in the humor."[1] From the moment of its conception, the movie risked falling victim to what literary critics call the fallacy of imitative form. Burton set out to recreate the cheesy flying saucer movies of the 1950s. True to his mission, he ended up with a cheesy flying saucer movie. How much could one have expected from a film that turns out to have been based on a set of bubble-gum trading cards that depict Earth being invaded by a particularly nasty bunch of Martians?[2]

I myself was disappointed with *Mars Attacks!* when I first saw it. At the time I was a devoted Burton fan. I was particularly struck by the consistency of his achievement, having been impressed by each of his first six feature films: *Pee-wee's Big Adventure* (1985), *Beetlejuice* (1988), *Batman* (1989), *Edward Scissorhands* (1990), *Batman Returns* (1992), and *Ed Wood* (1994).

For me, *Mars Attacks!* broke this streak and left me wondering whether Burton had lost his magic touch. But like a good Bordeaux—and unlike bubble gum—*Mars Attacks!* has, at least for me, improved with age. I would still grant that it has more than its share of silly moments and cheap jokes. What changed my opinion of it, however, was realizing that it has something important to say. It is not just a random exercise in recreating 1950s flying saucer movies; it is a serious critique of the pro-government ideology they embodied.

The Federal Government to the Rescue

While Burton may seem to be following closely the formula of his cinematic models in *Mars Attacks!*, in fact he is inverting and deconstructing it. As products of a Cold War mentality, the 1950s flying saucer movies generally expressed a faith in the goodness of America's political, military, and scientific elites and their capacity to save the nation from all threats. By contrast, *Mars Attacks!* systematically and mercilessly debunks the elites who claim to be able to protect America. It turns instead to the country's cultural underclass, so despised by those elites, and shows that people often dismissed as "trailer trash" are capable of defending themselves. Always sympathetic to the underdog and the marginalized figure—from Pee-wee to the Penguin—Burton expresses a Tocquevillian confidence in the power of ordinary Americans to associate on their own to deal with any problem. In *Mars Attacks!* all the top-down efforts by the authorities in Washington to respond to the Martian invasion fail utterly, while pockets of outcasts, misfits, and losers around the country spontaneously come together in a bottom-up effort to defeat their enemies from outer space. As Bill Warren writes, "The leaders of Earth are helpless; it's up to the little people to save the day."[3] *Mars Attacks!* is Burton's tribute to American pop culture in one of its more vulgar manifestations—the flying saucer movie—and is at the same time a celebration of the power of pop culture itself to save America. In the end, the Martians are defeated not by the combined wisdom of America's scientists and the might of its military, but by the music of Slim Whitman, a yodeling country-and-western singer who virtually defines lowbrow taste in America.

To appreciate the polemical thrust of *Mars Attacks!*, the most fruitful point of comparison is Fred Sears's *Earth vs. the Flying Saucers* (1956). This is the film that Burton mentions most frequently in his comments on *Mars*

Attacks!, and it provides more models for the plot elements and the special effects of his movie than any other sci-fi classic of the 1950s. Moreover, it offers perhaps the purest distillation of the political ideology that informed this moment in Hollywood history. This was the height of the Cold War, when fears of communist aggression from both the Soviet Union and the People's Republic of China gripped America. Anxieties focused, of course, on the threat of nuclear annihilation, but Americans were also worried about real and supposed attempts to subvert their institutions from within by communist infiltrators, spies, and traitors. By the 1950s, movies had begun to reflect and capitalize on these widespread concerns. Imaginary stories of extraterrestrial aliens invading Earth became convenient vehicles for expressing fears that America might be facing real threats from foreign powers and perhaps internal subversion as well.[4]

In Cold War ideology, the bulwark of American defense against all these threats was the government of the United States. Movie after movie—not just sci-fi films—celebrated the competence, courage, and integrity of federal officials, particularly if, like the FBI, they combated communism.[5] Perhaps at no point in American history has the federal government inspired as much confidence as it did in the 1950s. In World War II, the federal government had successfully led the battle against enemies in Europe and Asia, and the United States had emerged from the conflict as unquestionably the strongest nation in the world economically and militarily. American triumphs in World War II were attributed to many factors; one of the most important was American scientific and technological superiority. The United States' development of the atomic bomb was credited with having ended the war with Japan, and this Manhattan Project became a powerful symbol of the federal government's ability to achieve whatever it set out to do, provided it devoted enough resources to the task and was able to mobilize the nation's scientific elite behind it.

In view of all the skepticism about nuclear power today, one must make an effort to recall how widely and enthusiastically atomic energy was embraced in the 1950s as the solution to the world's problems. The "Atoms for Peace" program, touted by the federal government, promised to translate wartime technological triumphs into peacetime dividends.[6] The respect and, indeed, the awe with which most Americans were taught to view atomic energy in the 1950s epitomized the pro-government ideology of the day.[7] The federal government, the military, and the scientific elite had banded together to create this new power, which was supposed to lead the country into a glorious future. What these three forces had in common in the 1950s was the aura of expertise they projected. On all issues, from politics to economics to technology, the ordinary people of America were supposed to defer to the experts, who knew what was best for them. Science has never enjoyed more prestige in American culture than it did in the 1950s; grandfatherly Albert Einstein had become the poster boy for the goodness of nuclear physics. The prestige of the federal government and the prestige of science fed off each other; the one endorsed the other. The federal government began to support science at unprecedented levels of peacetime funding, while scientists flocked to work for the federal government, directly or indirectly, and lent their authority as experts to government programs.[8]

The notion that ordinary Americans have to rely for protection on a benevolent alliance of military and federal government officials with scientific experts is at the ideological heart of the 1950s flying saucer movies. These films generally present the American people as helpless in the face of an alien invasion, overwhelmed by superior technology, which renders their ordinary weapons useless, especially their firearms. In *Earth vs. the Flying Saucers,* for example, average Americans appear largely in the form of mobs, fleeing alien attacks in total panic. They seem completely incapable of organizing themselves into any kind of reasonable response to the threat. In particular, they cannot rely on any local authorities to protect them. The police, for example, do not have anything approaching the technology needed to counter the aliens. *Earth vs. the Flying Saucers* is typical in presenting an ordinary traffic cop on a motorcycle as a comically inept figure. He gets involved in the struggle with the space invaders, but makes a fool of himself by thinking that his revolver will be effective against them. The aliens end up sucking out his brain, puny as it is.

Another classic of the genre, William Cameron Menzies's *Invaders from Mars* (1953), carries this denigration of local authorities to an extreme. This movie is unusual because it tells the story from the viewpoint of an adolescent boy, who witnesses an alien invasion unfold before his eyes. The lesson he must learn is to distrust all the local authorities he has been brought up to respect, including his own family. *Invaders from Mars* follows a formula later made famous by Don Siegel's *Invasion of the Body Snatchers* (1956): the aliens systematically take over the minds of human beings one by one, in this case by implants in their necks.[9] The boy watches with horror as first his father and then his mother become zombified by the aliens and turn against him. When he goes to the local police station to get help, he discovers that the police chief has been taken over by the aliens as well.[10] The boy finds that he can rely only on a social worker to protect him by making him in effect a ward of the state. As a representative of the Department of Health, this woman symbolizes the need to replace the traditional family as a source of authority with a rational bureaucracy. The woman is, after all, a medical doctor, an expert, and thus better able to care for the child's welfare than his own mother and father. And the force that ultimately saves the boy and the whole world is the United States military, which manages to marshal the technological resources to defeat the Martians.[11]

Reliance on the U.S. military and federal, as opposed to local, authorities is almost as prominent in *Earth vs. the Flying Saucers*. The film is filled with important-sounding federal government programs and agencies, many with links to the military, such as Operation Skyhook, the Air Intelligence Command, the Hemispheric Defense Command, and the Internal Security Commission. Somehow even the Bureau of Standards and the Bureau of Meteorology get involved in fighting the space invaders. As this array of bureaucracies suggests, *Earth vs. the Flying Saucers* offers a union between science and the military as the salvation of America. The hero is a scientist named Russell Marvin (Hugh Marlowe), who is portrayed as a superior form of human being. As he himself says of his testimony as to the existence of UFOs, "There is a qualitative difference when you're a scientist."[12] Although Marvin encounters a few difficulties working with the military top brass, on the whole they form an effective alliance to defeat the aliens, and he is as militaristic as the generals. The film underscores the lesson about the dangers of appeasement learned from the run-up to World War II. Marvin says bitterly of the alien invaders, "They'll sail into Washington in broad daylight and expect us to capitulate when they land." But not in Cold War America, according to *Earth vs. the Flying Saucers*. One of the generals reassures Marvin: "When an armed and threatening power lands uninvited in our capital, we don't meet them with tea and cookies."

The film emphasizes the need to respond to the alien threat as a nation. The aliens try to make contact directly with Dr. Marvin and wish to deal with him alone. Here a general in the Pentagon draws the line: "If we are to be confronted with a hostile and unknown power, any decision to meet with them must be made at the cabinet level." Accordingly, the film tells us, the secretary of state and the secretary of defense must fly back to Washington before any action can be taken. Nevertheless, Marvin decides to go ahead and meet with the aliens on his own. In another moment that seems to denigrate the family in the name of the nation-state, his new bride chooses to report him to the government agent assigned to shadow him, telling Marvin, "But it's not your job alone." Again and again the film asks us to put our faith in Washington, D.C. Above all, it stresses the unique ability of the federal government to respond to the technological challenge posed by the alien invaders. When they succeed in shooting down U.S. satellites and destroying a missile base, the portentous voice-over narration intones, "An aroused public demanded an answer. And the federal government dedicated the strength of all its branches to the task of finding one."

The speed with which the federal government manufactures weapons to combat the aliens is reminiscent of the Manhattan Project. With the help of other scientists, Marvin comes up with the idea for an ultrasonic gun that will knock the flying saucers out of the skies. He promises that, "with enough scientific and engineering help, we could construct a working model in a very short time." In the very next scene, Marvin has his prototype ready for testing. He quickly discovers that an electromagnetic gun is more practical than an ultrasonic. As for mass-producing the experimental weapon, once again the voice-over reassures us: "From all parts of the globe, under top priority, came every facility and scientific help the governments of the world could furnish." The movie's faith in government knows no bounds. My favorite moment comes again in the voice-over narration, when the federal government has less than two weeks to evacuate the citizens of Washington in the face of a planned alien attack: "Although the authorities and the military worked miracles, when the tenth day dawned more than 60 percent of the people of Washington were still in the metropolitan area." Here *Earth vs. the Flying Saucers* inadvertently supplies a more accurate appraisal of Washington's competence. It is, indeed, a miracle any time the federal government manages to accomplish as much as 40 percent of what it claims to be able to do.

Earth vs. the Flying Saucers hammers home the lesson that many political pundits were preaching in the 1950s. Technological developments during and after World War II, especially the dawning of the Atomic Age, supposedly had altered the human condition fundamentally, to the point where ordinary human beings were said to be no longer capable of running their own lives. Scientific and technological challenges, especially of a military kind, could only be handled at the national level, and Americans were made to feel grateful that they had a federal government devoted to their welfare and protection, with the vast resources needed to promote those ends. Of course, *Earth vs. the Flying Saucers* is only one movie, and it offers a particularly rosy image of government omnicompetence and a particularly dim view of the capacities of ordinary citizens. Other alien invasion movies complicated the ideological picture. As we have seen, *Earth vs. the Flying Saucers* suggests that scientists and the military can easily form an alliance. Other 1950s sci-fi classics raise doubts about this possibility and show the two forces at odds.

For example, in *The Thing from Another World* (1951), directed by Christian Nyby and produced by Howard Hawks, when an alien being lands in the Arctic, the military leader and the scientist confronted by it differ over how to deal with the threat.[13] The Air Force captain wants to protect humanity by annihilating the alien being, but the scientist views the situation as a valuable opportunity to expand human knowledge and wants to preserve the Thing and learn how to communicate with it. The scientist is convinced that the Thing is a superior life form, free of the corrupting effects of human emotion (one hint that the alien may symbolize the threat of what was then regarded as "soulless" communism). But the scientist is proven wrong when the Thing tries to kill him, thus vindicating the military position. In the great Cold War debate—recall that *The Thing* came out during the Korean War—the movie clearly sides with the advocates of a forceful military response to communist aggression and criticizes those who sought any kind of détente with the other side.[14]

Robert Wise's *The Day the Earth Stood Still*, which came out in 1951 as well, also sets scientists at odds with the military, but this film champions the former over the latter. In this movie, a visitor arrives from another planet to warn the people of Earth about the dangers of their reckless and destructive militarism, especially now that they have developed atomic weapons. The military authorities, with their knee-jerk hostility to anything alien and an overconfidence in their own power, bring Earth to the brink of destruction. Only the scientists work toward a peaceful and productive rapprochement with the alien visitor. *The Day the Earth Stood Still* makes a strong pacifist statement, and the film has been viewed as subversive of American Cold War ideology.[15] Considering just these three classics of the genre makes it clear that a wide range of views on central Cold War issues was available in the 1950s flying saucer movies.

Yet despite their divergence in opinion, these three films—and many others from the era—converge on one point: Ordinary people cannot solve their problems on their own and must depend on some kind of higher authority to protect them, whether it be scientific or military or some combination of the two.[16] *The Day the Earth Stood Still* rejects the blatant nationalism of the other two films, but only by offering a supranational solution to human problems. The film holds up the United Nations as an ideal, and the scientists are pointedly from all different countries, constituting an international brotherhood ready to save humanity. In this respect, the film resembles the world government fantasies of H. G. Wells, who hoped that scientists might band together and use their technological superiority to force the rest of humanity into peace.[17] *The Day the Earth Stood Still* builds up to a long and tendentious speech by the alien Klaatu (Michael Rennie), who patronizingly informs humanity that intelligent life elsewhere in the universe has long since renounced violence by surrendering their sovereignty to all-powerful robots who automatically enforce peace on their planets. Whatever lesson *The Day the Earth Stood Still* teaches, it is not one of human freedom.[18] Indeed, it seems to teach the ultimate Hobbesian lesson—that avoiding violent conflict is so important we must surrender our autonomy to a Leviathan power.[19] Wise's film seems to go further than any other 1950s sci-fi classic in asking Americans to bow down before the altar of a scientific elite.

The Hobbesian slant of *The Day the Earth Stood Still* suggests how the extraterrestrial invasion films of the 1950s can be linked to the Westerns we examined in Part One. By destroying the institutions of government, the alien invaders threaten to return Americans to the state of nature and the Hobbesian war of all against all. These films generally show civil society dissolved and collapsing into complete anarchy in the absence of effective control from the federal government. By merely raising the specter of social chaos, the flying saucer movies supplied an ideological grounding for the authority of the nation-state. For all their differences, the films as a group reflect the way the U.S. government was able to exploit the Cold War fears of the American people to increase its power over their lives.

But as we saw in *Deadwood,* Thomas Hobbes's understanding of the state of nature is not the only one. John Locke, for example, does not regard the state of nature as a condition of pure anarchy. He views civil society as capable of existing independent of the state and credits ordinary people with being able to achieve complex forms of economic organization on their own. The alien invasions create what I referred to in chapter 3 as a postpolitical community, leaving open the possibility of Americans finding ways of dealing with disaster on their own initiative, with no help from government. As we will see, Tim Burton shares with David Milch the idea that order is possible without law, that even, and perhaps especially, in the face of a catastrophic breakdown of government institutions, the resourcefulness and resilience of ordinary people will save the day.

Debunking the Elite

It is not surprising that Burton, with his antiestablishment impulses and his sympathy for the little guy, found the message of 1950s flying saucer movies unacceptable and that when he came to parody them he completely reversed their ideological polarities, championing ordinary Americans over the elites that view them with contempt. But before plunging into a serious political analysis of *Mars Attacks!*, I should acknowledge how absurd this enterprise may seem at first sight. On the face of it, *Mars Attacks!* is a very silly movie. Burton himself said of it, "On the depth chart, it's like a *Love Boat* episode."[20] In the face of this kind of statement from the film's creator, it may seem pointless to probe *Mars Attacks!* for any kind of political message. Moreover, far from sounding like a critic of 1950s flying saucer movies, Burton has professed himself a fan, saying, "I grew up with this kind of movie. They're in my blood."[21] He especially admires the work of Ray Harryhausen, who did the special effects for *Earth vs. the Flying Saucers:* "I love the old Ray Harryhausen movies, so a lot of this [*Mars Attacks!*] draws inspiration from those."[22] As with all his films, Burton set out to create a distinctive look for *Mars Attacks!*, and for that purpose he stuck close to his 1950s models. He particularly admires Harryhausen's mastery of stop-motion animation and talks about that in his interviews more than he does about any message in *Mars Attacks!* It would be easy to conclude from the interviews that, for Burton, the movie was purely an exercise in recreating the visual style of films he enjoyed in his childhood.

Burton has, however, made some statements that hint at a polemical thrust to *Mars Attacks!*, particularly when he mentions the historical-political context for the film: "It was during the Gulf War, when the media seemed to have taken it to another level—wars having titles and theme music—and I found it kind of disturbing. I felt like these characters were just a cathartic shakeup of that kind of thing."[23] This comment strongly suggests that Burton saw the nationalism and militarism of the Cold War being revived by the enthusiasm for U.S. military adventures sparked by the Gulf War and that he wanted to take some of the wind out of the government's sails. This idea is supported by the fact that Burton's principal creative collaborator on the film was British screenwriter Jonathan Gems. As a foreigner, Gems was well positioned to take a critical stance on American institutions, as he himself explained: "There's a certain kind of joy in the way the Martians just come and smash everything up. I was a punk in London and we always used to do pranks. So here you get the Martians taking the piss out of society."[24]

Gems identifies the antiestablishment spirit of *Mars Attacks!,* and further comments by Burton pick up the theme, particularly when he talks about the trading card series that inspired the film: "I remembered those cards from types of cards I had as a kid. I just liked the anarchistic spirit of them. Jonathan has sort of an anarchistic spirit himself, I think—being British and living in America and having an alien perspective of it, which I sort of have myself."[25] For anyone wishing to give an antigovernment reading of *Mars Attacks!,* it is encouraging to hear the words *anarchistic* and *anarchic* repeatedly in Burton's comments on the film: "I was feeling really strangely about things at the time, about America—everything just seemed really off-kilter to me, and I think that was a partial dynamic of what I liked about the material. I was just feeling more anarchic, and that was the energy I liked in it—I saw that in the Martians."[26] With its disrespect for authority, *Mars Attacks!* is Burton's contribution to a long tradition of anarchic comedy running throughout the history of American popular culture, a tradition perhaps best epitomized by the films of the Marx Brothers and W. C. Fields.[27]

Burton's talk of anarchism takes us to the thematic core of *Mars Attacks!* and its fundamental difference from its 1950s models. The original flying saucer movies were the very opposite of anarchistic in spirit. Their message was that, in the face of foreign threats, Americans had to get behind their government and work together as a nation to stave off alien destruction of their institutions. By contrast, in Burton's own account, *Mars Attacks!* takes a perverse joy in portraying just that destruction: the annihilation of Congress, the humiliation and murder of the president, and a literal downsizing of the military when a particularly aggressive U.S. general is miniaturized by a Martian and then stomped underfoot. Evidently what attracted Burton to the Martians is precisely their lack of respect for American institutions. He speculated that the iconoclasm of the film may explain why it did better abroad than at home: "I actually felt European audiences understood it much better or seemed to get it better. They didn't seem to have that American egotism of, 'You can make fun of some things, but you can't quite make fun of other things.'"[28]

Mars Attacks! is unrelenting in its mockery of American elites, including all the categories familiar from the 1950s sci-fi movies—the politicians, the military, and the scientists. But Burton adds one more element to the establishment—media stars—and their narcissism provides a clue to the nature of all the elites in the film. Jason Stone (Michael J. Fox), a vain news anchor for GNN (a thinly disguised CNN), is mainly concerned about how to use the Martian invasion to advance his career. He is dismayed when his girlfriend, Natalie Lake (Sarah Jessica Parker), scoops him on a rival network with an interview with the government's chief scientist, Donald Kessler (Pierce Brosnan). Lake is just as vain as Stone, and even dumber. The fact that her show, *Today in Fashion,* gets to air the main interview about the Martians is the film's comment on the shallowness of media coverage in America. Everything is reduced to the level of fashion and show business, even an Earth-threatening invasion from Mars. Stone and Lake are career-conscious media celebrities, and their vanity is the key to understanding all the elites in the film. Almost all the representatives of the establishment are portrayed as vain, more interested in their own celebrity and popularity than in public service or the common good.

In the media-dominated world the film portrays, the White House press secretary, Jerry Ross (Martin Short), seems to have the status of a cabinet official. Indeed, he exercises more influence on the president than anybody else. The prominence of the press secretary reflects the corruption of politics by television. All the establishment figures are chiefly concerned with how they appear on television and how it will affect their status as celebrities. Kessler goes on Lake's daytime talk show and openly flirts with her. A high-ranking general (Paul Winfield) is thrilled to be televised greeting the Martians at their first contact with the human race. And, of course, President James Dale (Jack Nicholson) is obsessed with his television appearances, carefully orchestrating his every move with Ross's advice. He is overjoyed to be the one to announce the Martians' arrival on television: "The people are going to love it."[29] He instructs Ross to have a speech written for him that will be statesmanlike and historical and yet still ingratiate him with the American people, ordering up "Abraham Lincoln meets *Leave It to Beaver.*" The 1950s flying saucer movies built up the Washington establishment by suggesting that the leaders are knowledgeable, public-spirited, and genuinely concerned with America's welfare. *Mars Attacks!* shows them to be self-centered, devoted only to advancing their own careers, and concerned more with show than with substance.

The elites in the film generally consist of beautiful people—fashionably dressed and superficially elegant and sophisticated. The First Lady, Marsha Dale (Glenn Close), frets over redecorating the White House. Taffy Dale (Natalie Portman), the president's daughter, comes across as a spoiled brat, but no more spoiled than the rest of the establishment. They all lead a life of privilege and self-indulgence. Jerry Ross sneaks prostitutes into the White House; the fact that he takes them to what is called the Kennedy Room suggests that higher officials have followed the same path. The establishment figures present themselves as raised above the level of ordinary Americans, but the film exposes that act to be a sham. They are hypocrites, standing up for morality in public while pursuing sexual affairs in private. One of the film's most effective satirical devices is to have Jack Nicholson play both the president and a sleazy real estate developer named Art Land. Land becomes a double for Dale, and the obvious suggestion is that the president is as much of a con man as his gambling casino counterpart. At one point, Land insists to his wife, Barbara (Annette Bening), "I'm not a crook. I'm ambitious. There's a difference." But the film suggests just the opposite, and the echo of Richard Nixon in Land's statement cements the idea that ambition is indistinguishable from crookedness in the Washington establishment.

The film undercuts the idea that any form of integrity can be expected from the nation's elites; but it goes further, suggesting that to the extent that they are at all guided by principles, they are in fact misguided. It does an especially good job of capturing the smug, self-satisfied political correctness of the elites in Washington. *Mars Attacks!* is filled with the high-sounding rhetoric of multiculturalism.[30] The most obvious difference from the 1950s flying saucer movies is that the aliens are initially welcomed with high hopes by the establishment instead of being treated with suspicion and hostility. In the face of some doubts about the Martians' intentions, the scientist, Kessler, repeatedly assures the president about the aliens: "They're peaceful. An advanced civilization is by definition not barbaric." Pierce Brosnan may have been chosen to play the scientist because, as an Englishman, he reminds us of Michael Rennie's role as the alien Klaatu in *The Day the Earth Stood Still.* Kessler makes similarly patronizing remarks about the human race in comparison to the Martians: "They're an advanced culture—therefore peaceful and enlightened. . . . The human race, on the other hand, is an aggressively dangerous species. I suspect they have more to fear from us than we from them." This way of speaking reverses the pro-Earth, pro-America chauvinism of the typical 1950s flying saucer movie, almost as if Klaatu had now moved into the White House as the president's chief science advisor. Kessler is relentless in his multicultural embrace of the Martians: "We must be open to them," he says. "We need a welcome mat, not a row of tanks." The president uses his announcement of the Martians' arrival to pursue a similar multicultural agenda, telling the American people, "We have become one planet and soon will be one solar system."

We are so used to this kind of talk in our culture that it may be difficult to believe that the film is satirizing it, but events in the movie repeatedly undercut the apparently high-minded rhetoric of the establishment figures, who are made to look ridiculous in their blind faith in the aliens' benevolence. Even after the Martians slaughter the greeting party sent to welcome them, Kessler sticks to his claims on their behalf: "I know this seems terrible, but let's not be rash." The film emphasizes the absurdity of Kessler's position by counterpointing it with a more pragmatic response by an old-style general named Decker (Rod Steiger), who is a throwback to the trigger-happy military figures of the 1950s movies. Decker's advice to the president concerning the Martians is concise and to the point: "Let's nuke them now." His disgust with Kessler's views registers when he leaves a meeting speaking with a crescendo of contempt: "liberals, intellectuals, peacemongers, idiots!"[31] Yet even in the face of Martian violence, Decker does not prevail, as Kessler finds a way of explaining the initial disaster by falling back on his relativism: "This could be a case of cultural misunderstanding."[32] The president seizes on this excuse for the Martians, and when he gets a chance to speak with them he too relies on cultural relativism: "Our customs may be strange to you, but we mean no harm." The president's motives for pursuing a peace policy with the Martians soon become clear: he thinks that it will be popular with the public. When the Martians make the apparently peaceful gesture of asking to be permitted to address Congress, Dale readily grants the request, and proclaims, "It's a great victory for our administration."

Unfortunately, however, the Martians use the opportunity to kill everybody in Congress, thus vindicating Decker's initial hostility to them. But even with all the evidence that the Martians cannot be trusted, Dale makes one last effort to strike a deal with them when they finally break all the way into the White House situation room. His speech is quite moving, and Nicholson delivers it with conviction: "Why be enemies? Because we're different? Is that why? Think of the things we could do. Think how strong we would be. Earth and Mars together. There is nothing that we could not accomplish. Think about it. Think about it. Why destroy, when we can create? We can have it all or we can smash it all. Why can't we work out

Interplanetary diplomacy in Tim Burton's *Mars Attacks!* Martian on the left; Jack Nicholson on the right. (Jerry Ohlinger's Movie Material Store)

our differences? Why can't we work things out? Why can't we just all get along?" One might think that the film endorses this eloquent speech, but, once again, the context makes Dale's posturing laughable. The Martians respond by simply killing him.

Mars Attacks! portrays a political establishment so absorbed in its own ambitions that it loses sight of the public interest and so bewitched by its own multicultural rhetoric that it loses touch with reality and proves incapable of dealing with a genuine alien threat. For all the vaunted power of the American military, it can do nothing to halt the Martian invasion.[33] When a government fails at its most basic task—protecting its people—it loses its legitimacy. Dale's efforts to reclaim his authority after the disasters that happen on his watch, especially the annihilation of Congress, are pitiful, epitomized by one of the signature lines of the film: "I want the people to know that they still have two out of the three branches of government working for them, and that ain't bad." Having failed as commander in chief, Dale has to fall back on partisan politics and the tired old claims of what government does for its citizens: "I want the people to know that the schools will still be open, okay, and I want the people to know that the garbage will still be carried out, and I want a cop on every corner, which incidentally we would already have if they had listened to me last election." In the face of the threatened annihilation of humanity, routine campaign promises ring hollow. The satire of the Washington establishment in *Mars Attacks!* culminates in this image of the moral and intellectual bankruptcy of the political class in America.

Tocqueville and American Civil Society

Disgusted by the corruption he sees in Washington, Burton moves beyond the Beltway, to the rest of America, to find a saving remnant. The geography of *Mars Attacks!* provides a key to understanding the film. Several scenes are set in the heartland of the United States—Kentucky and Kansas—and Burton evokes the traditional view that virtue is to be found in rural America. But he does not operate completely within the conventional paradigm that presents rural existence as superior to urban.[34] From the beginning, *Mars Attacks!* alternates between two cities—Washington and Las Vegas—with Nicholson in his dual role presiding over both and providing a connection between the two. It is almost as if Burton is suggesting that the United States has two capitals, Washington as its political capital, Las Vegas as its entertainment capital (in fact, it claims to be the entertainment capital of the world). In a reversal of normal expectations, Burton prefers the entertainment capital to the political. Las Vegas is still Sin City in the film, focused on gambling, sex shows, and rampant real estate development. But in contrast to Washington, Las Vegas comes across in *Mars Attacks!* as a genuine city of the American people. Unlike Washington, Las Vegas gives the people what they want; its purpose is, after all, to entertain them. The Vegas of *Mars Attacks!* actually has a lot in common with the American heartland and is populated by basically the same kind of people. In both places, average Americans are shown working together—especially as families—and are therefore ultimately capable of defending themselves and what they value in life—especially their families. In the eyes of the cultural elite, places like Kansas and Las Vegas represent everything that is contemptible about America, epitomized by the lowbrow entertainment beloved by country bumpkins and rubes. But in Burton's view, the cultural elite are out of touch with genuine human values; it is the ordinary people in the cultural backwaters of the county who understand what really matters in life and are willing to stand up for it. That is why *Mars Attacks!* champions local areas in the United States against the national government.

In this respect, *Mars Attacks!* recurs to the original conception of the United States propounded by the Founding Fathers and to the genuine spirit of federalism. The Constitution was designed precisely so that the federal government would not be all-powerful and intrude in every aspect of life in America. The document limits the powers of the federal government and reserves many governmental functions to the individual states and even smaller political units. A long-standing principle of American government is that power is better exercised at local levels, where the authorities are more in touch with and more responsive to the needs and demands of the people. Perhaps the most acute analyst of the American regime, the Frenchman Alexis de Tocqueville, argued in *Democracy in America* that the diffusion of power and authority in the United States is a key to its success. If democracy is in its essence self-government, Tocqueville was struck by the capacity of ordinary Americans to govern themselves, especially their penchant for forming associations to deal with their problems on their own, with no guidance from Washington, D.C.[35] Tocqueville celebrated the vibrancy of civil society that he saw in America, the fact that many problems were dealt with outside the formal political system by people banding together voluntarily:

> Americans of all ages, all conditions, all minds constantly unite. Not only do they have commercial and industrial associations in which all take part, but they also have a thousand other kinds: religious, moral, grave, futile, very general and very particular, immense and very small; Americans use associations to give fêtes, to found seminaries, to build inns, to raise churches, to distribute books, to send missionaries to the antipodes; in this manner they create hospitals, prisons, schools. . . . Thus the most democratic country on earth is found to be, above all, the one where men in our day have most perfected the art of pursuing the object of their common desires in common.[36]

It is striking how many of the activities that Tocqueville regarded as the province of private associations in the United States are now viewed as the legitimate (and perhaps even the inevitable) responsibility of the federal government ("hospitals, prisons, schools"). Tocqueville recognized that it is a great temptation in a democracy to turn over all activities beyond the capacity of individual human beings to government authorities. But he regarded that course as leading to the loss of freedom and the emergence of tyranny:

> A government could take the place of some of the greatest American associations, and within the Union several particular states already

have attempted it. But what political power would ever be in a state to suffice for the innumerable multitude of small undertakings that American citizens execute every day with the aid of an association?

It is easy to foresee that the time is approaching when a man by himself alone will be less and less in a state to produce the things that are the most common and the most necessary to his life. The task of the social power will therefore constantly increase, and its very efforts will make it vaster each day. The more it puts itself in place of associations, the more particular persons, losing the idea of associating with each other, will need it to their aid. . . . Will the public administration in the end direct all the industries for which an isolated citizen cannot suffice? . . . will the head of the government have to leave the helm of state to come hold the plow?[37]

I do not know whether Tocqueville would have enjoyed 1950s flying saucer movies, but it is safe to say that he would have been troubled by their implicit claim that the complexities of the Atomic Age mean that ordinary Americans are now incapable of managing their own lives and must rely instead on the wisdom of government experts.[38] Prophetic in so many respects, Tocqueville was at his most acute in foreseeing the erosion of freedom as a result of the increasing reliance on government to solve problems:

The morality and intelligence of a democratic people would risk no fewer dangers than its business and its industry if the government came to take the place of associations everywhere. . . .

A government can no more suffice on its own to maintain and renew the civilization of sentiments and ideas in a great people than to conduct all its industrial undertakings. As soon as it tries to leave the political sphere to project itself on this new track, it will exercise an insupportable tyranny even without wishing to; for a government knows only how to dictate precise rules; it imposes the sentiments and the ideas that it favors, and it is always hard to distinguish its counsels from its orders.[39]

Here Tocqueville outlines what Friedrich Hayek was later to call the road to serfdom.[40] Anticipating Hayek, he argues that the national government, precisely by virtue of its remoteness from the people and their specific circumstances, lacks the local knowledge necessary to deal with their problems, knowledge that is—almost by definition—more likely to be available to local authorities or the people themselves. Moreover, the larger the sphere of a government's authority, the more general are the rules by which it operates, leading it to impose "one size fits all" solutions for problems when the solutions really need to be tailored to the local circumstances. Most important, Tocqueville worries what the effect of relying on the national government will be on the character of the American people. He fears that they will lose their spirit of self-reliance, which is precisely what distinguishes them among the peoples of the world. Tocqueville's analysis of the healthy tendency of Americans to form associations lays the foundation for the concluding chapters of *Democracy in America.* There he expresses his concern about the possibility of a soft despotism emerging in the United States if the American people, in the hope of making their existence easier and happier, allow their national government to keep expanding its powers and its ability to regulate every aspect of their lives.[41]

Trusting Trailer Trash

I do not know if Burton is at all familiar with Tocqueville's writings, but *Mars Attacks!* takes a Tocquevillian view of democracy in America, grounding it in the self-reliance of the American people, not the omnicompetence of their government. To be sure, the film cannot be accused of giving an overly optimistic portrait of the common people of America. In the Kansas scenes, it focuses on an extended and somewhat dysfunctional family, who can only be described as trailer trash—indeed, they live in a trailer. They are an urban liberal's worst nightmare. "They cling to their guns, or religion, or antipathy toward people who aren't like them, or anti-immigrant sentiments," to use the words of a famous urban liberal.[42] Although they live in Kansas, they seem more like southern rednecks, a point emphasized by having Joe Don Baker, often cast as a good old boy, play the patriarch of the clan, Mr. Norris. His favorite son has the southern-sounding name of Billy-Glen (Jack Black). The son volunteers for anti-Martian duty at his army base. When he finally goes into battle against the invaders, he is true to the redneck tradition, shouting at them: "Die, you alien shitheads." As this remark suggests, political correctness is not a hallmark of the Norris clan. They are prejudiced, with not a hint of multicultural openness to the aliens. Seeing them on television, Norris says, "Martians—funny-lookin' little critters, ain't they?" Unlike the establishment figures in the film, Norris is hostile to the aliens from the beginning: "Any of them Martians come around here, I'm going to kick their butts." The Norris family members are strongly committed to protecting their home and proudly lock and load their many guns to do so. They know where to take a stand against the Martians: "I tell you one thing—they ain't getting the TV." As a tight-knit family, they close ranks against the rest of the world. Although they admire the military, they have no respect for the Washington elite. When the grandmother (Sylvia Sidney) sees what the Martians do to her representatives in the Capitol building, her only response is to say "They blew up Congress" and laugh.

In sum, in *Mars Attacks!* the Washington establishment presents itself as tolerant, open-minded, cosmopolitan, and devoted to saving the world; the Norris clan is bigoted, close-minded, parochial, and devoted to saving its own family and TV. And yet the movie seems to take the Norrises' side. For one thing, they are right about the Martians and willing to take action against them. The movie seems to suggest that there is something healthy about the ordinary human prejudice in favor of one's own. If you care about something deeply, you will know how to defend it. In *Mars Attacks!* the common men and women are concerned with protecting not their egos and their public images, but something far more basic and real, their families, and that seems to bring out the best in people. In one of the subplots, an African American ex-boxer in Las Vegas named Byron Williams (Jim Brown) is struggling to be reunited in Washington with his divorced wife (Pam Grier) and their children. At the film's climax, he becomes a hero by fighting the Martians with his bare fists in the hopes of getting back to his family. Most important, the attempt by Richie Norris (Lukas Haas) to save his grandmother from the Martians leads to the discovery that Slim Whitman's yodeling will splatter their brains. The president's effort to forge a cosmic alliance with the Martians accomplishes nothing; it is only Richie's attempt to rescue someone in his immediate family that ends up saving the world.

Mars Attacks! thus rejects the conventional opinion that the ordinary people of America would be helpless in the face of a disaster or a crisis like a Martian invasion, unable to save themselves without the vast resources of the federal government working on their behalf. In fact, the film shows, the American people are remarkably resourceful and especially good at improvising.[43] The fact that someone may be uneducated or unsophisticated does not mean that he or she is stupid, and in real-life situations common sense can often be more useful than expertise. The Washington establishment's response to the invasion is hampered by its ingrained assumptions, especially its multicultural ideology, and its overreliance on technology, such as a computer to translate Martian. The ordinary Americans in the film are able to think outside the box, perhaps because they are outside the establishment. No expert would ever think of using yodeling to destroy the Martians—where is the scientific proof that it works?—but Richie is quick to recognize the potential of his unconventional weapon. The motif of an unexpected means of destroying the Martians goes all the way back to the first story of interplanetary conflict, H. G. Wells's *The War of the Worlds* (1898), where the Martians, lacking immunity to terrestrial germs, are killed off by nothing more complicated than the common cold.[44] Burton no doubt thought that Slim Whitman's music was almost as common—and as much in the air—as the cold virus, and thus it offers another case of something very ordinary preventing the Martians from conquering the Earth.

The Slim Whitman surprise ending adds another twist to Burton's championing of the common people of America against the elites who look down on them. The members of the Washington establishment we see in the film would not be caught dead listening to a Slim Whitman album. Thus they would never discover that it could defeat the Martians. The film shows that the elite keep themselves entirely separate from the common people they claim to champion. Despite all the complicated intercutting of plots in *Mars Attacks!*, the elites and the common people almost never interact. The White House scenes show that when tourists show up, they are kept carefully cordoned off from what really happens in the building (the joke in the film is that the White House inhabitants are not allowed to interfere with the tours). The film pointedly portrays the lack of interaction between the elites and the common people when a scene between the African American mother and her children ends, and Jerry Ross pulls up in the neighborhood in a limousine. He has arrived just to pick up a prostitute, and indeed the only ordinary person in the film admitted to the inner precincts of the White House is a prostitute (Lisa Marie Smith) brought by Ross (she actually is an alien disguised as a prostitute). In *Mars Attacks!* the elites keep their distance from the common people, except when they want to exploit them.[45]

Thus, the common people in *Mars Attacks!* are forced to rely on their own resources. The trailer trash are appropriately saved by their trailer trash culture, and not just their beloved Slim Whitman albums. Much of the effective resistance to the Martians comes from members of the underclass precisely in their stereotypical underclass roles. Byron Williams is modeled on Mohammad Ali—he is African American and a Muslim and has fought

Sonny Liston. He is the stereotypical down-and-out ex-boxer, reduced to working as a greeter in a Las Vegas casino. The cultural elite in America looks down on boxing as a vulgar sport, not to be mentioned in the same breath as politically correct sports in America like tennis and soccer (who ever heard of a "boxing mom"?). But Williams is able to use his fists to keep the Martians in check. Meanwhile, his adolescent sons back in Washington are presented as stereotypical streetwise youth. Coming from a broken home, they play hooky from school and use the time to play video games like Space Invaders. The establishment would frown upon their devoting themselves to video games instead of books, but it turns out that they are thereby preparing themselves for the real-life challenges they will face. Their truancy pays off when they come up against the Martians during a school field trip to the White House. Only the boys are able to pick up the Martians' ray guns and know how to use them to kill the invaders—thanks to their video game experience.

Boxing, video games, country and western music—all these mainstays of American pop culture prove to be the mainstays of the defense against the Martians. In perhaps the wackiest development of the plot, pop singer Tom Jones, playing himself, turns up in Las Vegas and joins the coalition against the aliens. Jones's performance in the film may be the most remarkable. One might describe it as self-parody, but in fact he really is just playing himself, and he is of course totally at home in Las Vegas. With the smoothness of a veteran Vegas performer, he takes everything in stride, reacting as if nothing unusual is happening, even when the world is literally crashing down around him. Perhaps it helps that his signature tune is called "It's Not Unusual" (which he sings twice in the film).[46] Jones's unflappability symbolizes the ability of ordinary people to stay calm in a crisis. Whatever happens in America, the show must go on, especially in Las Vegas. In a telling moment that recalls hundreds of B-movies, the boxer asks Jones, "You know how to fly a plane?" and Jones replies without missing a beat, "Sure. You got one?" There in a nutshell is the resourcefulness of the common man (if Jones is not exactly the common man, he is the quintessential common man's entertainer). The way the Las Vegas forces band together to fight the Martians becomes emblematic of the common men and women of America associating in their own defense. They know when a threat is real, and they respond to it as real people. It is perhaps the deepest irony of Mars Attacks! that it presents the show business world of Las Vegas as more genuine than the political world of Washington, D.C.

Still, *Mars Attacks!* does not give a flattering portrait of the American people, even though it takes their side against the Washington establishment. Burton's movie makes fun of everybody. It may show that the hawks within the military are better judges of the Martians than the doves are, but it still caricatures their hawkishness and makes General Decker look ridiculous. Similarly, Burton does not romanticize the ordinary people in *Mars Attacks!* He does not, for example, present them as hidden geniuses or especially heroic in character. In fact, he portrays them with all their foibles because the point is to show them precisely in their ordinariness. The movie is not trying to find a new elite within the American people, but merely to suggest that in their ordinariness, the people are able to muddle through, even in extraordinary circumstances. "Muddle through" is the operative term here. The triumph of the ordinary Americans over the Martians is accidental. The Washington establishment prides itself on its superior wisdom and, above all, on its ability to plan for every contingency. Time and again, the elite in effect claims to the American people, "We have a plan, and you don't. You can rely on us." *Mars Attacks!* reminds us that government plans are likely to fall apart in the face of genuine crises and disasters. No government can ever anticipate and plan for the full range of contingencies. When confronted by the inevitable chanciness of the world, it is better to rely on improvisation, and that is what ordinary Americans, with their Yankee ingenuity, have to offer.

Mars Attacks! is deeply Tocquevillian in the way that it insists that America is much more than its governing elites, that the human resources of the country are spread widely, and unpredictably, throughout its population and territory—not concentrated in Washington. The film may appear to be unrelentingly cynical and iconoclastic, but in fact it expresses a democratic faith in the basic decency and capability of the American people.[47] Moreover, the film goes out of its way to suggest the multiethnic and multiracial character of the American people. The Washington elite may preach multiculturalism in the abstract from their remote, privileged position, but the common people actually live out multiculturalism in their lives. To be sure, the Norris clan appears to be bigoted (although mainly against Martians). But the film opens with a Filipino family living on a farm in the middle of Kentucky who evidently get along with their mainstream American neighbors, thus suggesting that the United States has generally welcomed at least one kind of aliens in its midst. A little later in the film, in an image of racial and religious harmony, Byron Williams, an African American Muslim, is being photographed with a group of white nuns. The little band that gathers toward the end of the film to fight the Martians in Las Vegas is almost as multiethnic as a platoon in a Hollywood World War II movie, including Williams, the very ethnic Danny DeVito character, and the Welshman Tom Jones.[48] Apparently, with no guidance from the Washington elite, different races and ethnic groups in America can get along with each other, especially when they have an enemy in common.[49]

The different races and ethnic groups in the film come together in Las Vegas, which is presented as a kind of melting pot, bringing exotic cultures into the American mainstream, including the giant pyramid of the Luxor hotel and casino in which Williams works, dressed up "like King Tut," in the words of the DeVito character.[50] By the end of the film, with all the carnage, the only group left to play the U.S. national anthem at a Washington ceremony is a Mariachi band, giving a peculiar ethnic twist to the occasion. American popular culture has always been multicultural in nature and has often been quicker than elite culture when it comes to assimilating foreign influences.[51] The country-and-western star Slim Whitman was not alone in incorporating Swiss yodeling into his singing style. The multiculturalism of song, dance, and other folk arts is one reason why the film suggests that we cannot appreciate the vitality of the American people if we leave popular culture out of the picture. Las Vegas, with its uncanny ability to assimilate and amalgamate foreign cultural elements, is as important to a full understanding of what constitutes America as Washington is. Elitism often takes a cultural form and looks down on the entertainment of the common people as vulgar. By contrast, *Mars Attacks!* is a kind of backhanded compliment to one genre of pop culture, and it presents pop culture as one of the great resources of the American people.

In sum, Burton suggests that on some fundamental level, America *is* its pop culture. If you want to see what Americans truly are, look at what they enjoy in common. The vulgarity of Las Vegas and other forms of popular entertainment may alienate cultural elites, but it does give Americans something to share as a people. *Mars Attacks!* shows Americans at home in their popular culture, feeling comfortable with their Slim Whitman albums, their video games, and their boxing memories. The fact that Americans live on the level of their popular entertainment means that different racial and ethnic groups share a culture. Boxing unites Catholic nuns with African American Muslims. Burton sees the positive side of pop culture and does not share the contempt that cultural elites express for it. To be sure, he maintains a critical distance from popular forms of entertainment. By its very nature, *Mars*

Attacks! makes fun of cheesy flying saucer movies, and within the movie Burton emphasizes the tackiness of American pop culture, with his focus on Slim Whitman and Las Vegas lounge acts. Burton himself is not a B-movie director. And yet he sees nothing wrong with B-movies and has never gotten over his childhood love of creature features. His remarkable mythic imagination has fed on the world of horror movies, sword-and-sandal epics, and other popular genres of the 1950s and '60s. His roots lie deep in American pop culture, and *Mars Attacks!* is his tribute to it. It is an equivocal tribute, one that acknowledges all the limitations of popular forms of entertainment; but in the end one gets the feeling that Burton thinks that Americans should put their faith in their pop stars rather than in their elected officials. I understand why critics have generally criticized *Mars Attacks!*, but I hope that my analysis might lead some to reconsider their opinion of the film. It has a manic energy and in its own wacky way is an impressive achievement. It reminds us that film genres embody certain ideologies, and working within a genre can be a way of subverting it and offering an alternate ideology. The look of *Mars Attacks!* may have its origins in nothing more than bubble gum cards, but the thinking behind the film ultimately goes back to Tocqueville, the original spirit of American federalism, and a serious vision of the self-organizing power of the American people.

Epilogue: The Auteur from Burbank

Mars Attacks! is seldom discussed at length in general assessments of Burton; but, with its self-consciousness about genre, it can help us understand what distinguishes him as a filmmaker. His career is paradoxical. He is an auteur who is oddly at home in Hollywood. He is the very definition of a maverick director, with a unique vision of the world, a quirky and even bizarre visual style that is instantly recognizable as his and his alone. One can truly speak of a Tim Burton film in the way one can speak of an Alfred Hitchcock film. He has put his stamp—and even his name—on films that he did not direct, such as *Tim Burton's The Nightmare before Christmas* (1993). Yet despite the idiosyncratic and intensely personal character of his films, Burton has often succeeded in connecting with mainstream movie audiences. Most of his films have done well at the box office, and he has several blockbuster hits to his credit, from *Batman* to *Alice in Wonderland* (2010), which made over $1 billion worldwide. As Kristine McKenna writes in the preface to her *Playboy* interview with Burton: "It's odd that director Tim

Burton keeps finding himself at the helm of big-budget studio blockbusters, because he's really not the type. Trained as a fine artist and described
as a shy, withdrawn loner, he has indie filmmaker written all over him."[52]
Somehow Burton has reconciled the commercial demands of Hollywood
with his integrity as an artist. Perhaps his secret lies in the fact that, while
he is often critical of Hollywood, he does not have a blanket contempt for
it. Recognizing the economic realities of the entertainment business, he has
generally been willing to work with Hollywood, rather than simply struggling against it, as many would-be auteurs have done.

Indeed, as much as any other director, Burton has managed to work
within the commercial system and still make the movies he wants to make.
He says so in an interview: "Movies obviously cost a lot, even if you're doing
a low-budget movie, and I try to keep that in mind all the time and not be
somebody who's thinking, 'I'm an *artiste!* Leave me alone!' I try to be responsible, because that's a lot of money they're giving me. But at the same time, I
don't have real trouble having to do something I didn't want to do."[53] Burton
has a love-hate relationship with the Hollywood film industry. He grew up
in the Los Angeles area (specifically in Burbank), totally absorbed as a child
in the world of film. He was enchanted by the products of Hollywood, but
he soon became disenchanted with how they are made once he began to
work in the film business, chiefly in the Disney studio in his early days. He
was frustrated by all the attempts to impose conformity on creative artists.
Fortunately, Burton had so much talent and, with luck, so much early success that he has generally been able to get financial backing for his projects
even when they must have struck studio executives as odd, if not insane.

Burton has had to learn how to live within the financial constraints of
Hollywood, but he has always dwelled within its imaginative borders, that
is, the genres that divide up the Hollywood landscape. He thus presents the
paradox of a Hollywood outsider who very much works within Hollywood
traditions. As *Mars Attacks!* exemplifies, his films are steeped in Hollywood
history—and mainstream commercial Hollywood, not the twilight zone of
art films. Ever since *Pee-wee's Big Adventure,* his movies have been filled with
references to, and echoes of, earlier movies.[54] Sometimes his cinematic allu-
sions can be regarded as homage to his predecessors; sometimes he seems to
be making fun of Hollywood clichés. Sometimes it is hard to tell the difference. Burton has a strong command of Hollywood genres and works within
them, if only to subvert them. That is one reason why he is able to connect
with mainstream audiences, despite the idiosyncrasy of his creative vision.

He does not make conventional movies, but he knows all about movie conventions and how to use them to reach an audience.

Despite his occasional setbacks and frustrations, Burton's career is a testimony to the wealth of opportunities offered by American pop culture to creative talent, as long as it can prove itself. He has demonstrated time and again that creativity does not demand freedom from all constraints whatsoever, financial or artistic. He recognizes that moviemaking does not occur in a vacuum. Although he clearly is a case of what is called individual genius, and is evidently a loner by temperament, he has accepted the nature of film as a collaborative medium. He has developed productive working relationships with screenwriters (such as Jonathan Gems), individual actors (such as Johnny Depp), and with other contributors to the filmmaking process (such as composer Danny Elfman). In his interviews, he has even acknowledged the contribution that his financial backers have made to his creativity and is grateful for all the money that has been placed at his disposal over the years, instead of complaining, like many directors, that it should have been more—and with no strings attached. In contrast to many artists, Burton feels that he needs limitations to bring out his creativity: "it's almost like humans need boundaries. It needs to be in a framework, it needs to be held in check with other elements. . . . For me, there's no such thing as unlimited resources in movies—you need boundaries."[55] He also recognizes that other people may have something to contribute to perfecting his films. As he says in an interview about *Batman Returns,* "It's good for me to be questioned about certain things; I think it's healthy for me not just to spin off into the cosmos."[56]

Burton often gives his actors considerable latitude to develop their roles and, unlike some directors, he does not speak of them with contempt or assume they are his enemies: "With *Pee-wee's Big Adventure* and *Beetlejuice* I was working with actors like Paul Reubens, Michael Keaton, and Catherine O'Hara. They're so good at improvisation that most of those movies wound up being improvised. I get excited by actors who can surprise you."[57] Contrary to the common understanding of the auteur, Burton is not a control freak. Although he makes use of storyboards, he does not try to create a whole film in his head before he starts shooting and then expect the actors and other contributors to follow his instructions slavishly to realize his vision exactly as he foresaw it.[58] Instead, he views filmmaking as a process to which people other than the director contribute meaningfully, and that involves a large element of contingency. As he says, he likes to be surprised, and the results show in the often surprising character of his films, the quirkiness that endears him to audiences and critics alike. In harmony with the antiestablishment, antigovernment attitude of *Mars Attacks!*, Burton does not like playing the role of an autocrat. He does not insist on having a movie perfectly planned out in advance, but seeks instead the spontaneity of creation that comes only from improvisation and feedback on the set. His embrace of the often chaotic working conditions in the film business accords with the anarchic political spirit of *Mars Attacks!* Whether in life or in art, Burton likes to see things shaken up.

In short, despite going his own way in his films, Burton does not set himself up in simple opposition to the Hollywood community. He freely acknowledges his debts to earlier filmmakers, and not the usual pantheon of famous auteurs like Orson Welles, but the run-of-the-mill Hollywood directors who made the movies that he grew up with and that inspired him. In *Ed Wood,* he paid tribute to one of those directors, a man who made one artistic and commercial flop after another. Yet on some level, Burton identifies with Ed Wood.[59] In his movie, Burton includes a scene that improbably pairs Wood with Welles, reminding us that the two were, after all, in the same business, and that, if the auteur principle produced the greatest film of all time (*Citizen Kane,* 1941), it also produced the worst (*Plan 9 from Outer Space,* 1959).[60] Burton may be a maverick director, but he is at the same time acutely aware of his place in Hollywood history and in the Hollywood community. As in many of his movies, in *Mars Attacks!* he is self-consciously working within a Hollywood genre, but that becomes not a brake on his creativity, but a spur to it. To be sure, many directors have become captive of the genres that the commercial demands of Hollywood have imposed on them, genres that lock them into formulaic plots and dialogue. But that does not mean that we should speak, as cultural pessimists, of the prison house of genre. For someone as talented as Burton, a given genre becomes a jumping-off point, a chance to show, for example, that he can do something with the flying saucer movie that no one ever imagined before. As in all the arts, creative freedom in Hollywood is not absolute, but a matter of working within artistic traditions and reshaping them to one's own vision. Burton's love-hate relationship with the flying saucer genre in *Mars Attacks!* tells us something about creativity in popular culture. An artist can work within the constraints and traditions of popular culture and still maintain a critical perspective on its conventions and ideologies. What prevented Burton from making just another routine flying saucer movie was his own creativity.

Genuine artists are not overwhelmed by their sources; they triumph over prior works by reimagining them.

Tim Burton's career has not conformed to the common image of the director as auteur. He has not, like some divine demiurge, brought his films into existence in a single act of perfect advance planning, by himself, with no reference to prior models. Instead, he has worked with other creative talent in a process that evolved over time and involved revision, experimentation, improvisation, and sheer scrambling to deal with the inevitable contingencies and accidents of film production. Even the best of his creations have not sprung Athena-like from his head, but have their roots deeply embedded in Hollywood tradition. As he himself insists, the man who made *Mars Attacks!* is not an *artiste,* but very much a product of American popular culture and a tribute to its vitality. It is no accident, then, that Burton chose to celebrate that vitality in *Mars Attacks!*

A Note on *Independence Day*

One of the reasons why *Mars Attacks!* failed to do as well as expected at the box office is that it had the bad luck to be released in the wake of the big summer blockbuster of 1996, Roland Emmerich's *Independence Day.* As another space-invaders movie, the Emmerich film is remarkably similar in plot and several motifs to *Mars Attacks!,* and stole its thunder with movie audiences. Burton had no idea that the other movie was being made and was shocked to see it: "I was surprised how close it was, but then it's a pretty basic genre I guess."[61] Despite some humorous moments, *Independence Day* takes very seriously the subjects that *Mars Attacks!* makes fun of. At the time, it was hard not to think that Burton had set out to parody Emmerich's work, as he himself admitted: "it almost seemed like we had done some kind of *Mad* magazine version of *Independence Day.*"[62] The fact that the Emmerich movie had struck a responsive chord in the American people, stirring patriotic feelings, made *Mars Attacks!* seem all the more blasphemous when it came out. Indeed, it came across as an assault on the hallowed American institutions *Independence Day* had just celebrated.

Like *Mars Attacks!, Independence Day* alternates between scenes of political, military, and scientific elites from Washington, D.C., and scenes of ordinary people in America responding to the crisis of an alien invasion. It similarly features trailer trash, offering at one moment a veritable flotilla of mobile homes converging on a remote military base. Like *Mars Attacks!,*

Independence Day has several important African American characters; Will Smith plays one of the heroes, Captain Steven Hiller. The 1950s flying saucer films, like many movies of the day, were predominantly, if not exclusively, white in their casts. Both *Mars Attacks!* and *Independence Day* show that racial and ethnic minorities have a contribution to make to American life. In Emmerich's film, Judd Hirsch and Jeff Goldblum play identifiably Jewish characters, a father-and-son pair named Julius and David Levinson, who are central to the plot.

In *Independence Day,* just as in *Mars Attacks!,* the underclass plays an important role in responding to the invasion. For example, a stripper named Jasmine Dubrow (Vivica Fox) rescues the First Lady (Mary McDonnell) from a downed helicopter. The first death blow to an alien spaceship is delivered by a character named Russell Casse, played by Randy Quaid at his grungiest. Casse heads the main trailer trash family in the film and earns his living in the unglamorous job of crop-duster pilot. Goldblum plays a brilliant scientist who has been reduced to working as a satellite technician for a cable TV company, whose subscribers are mainly concerned about how the space invaders have interfered with their reception of *The X-Files.* And yet it is David Levinson—not the establishment scientists with their gleaming laboratories and their white coats—who comes up with the means to defeat the aliens. In a clever updating of Wells, Levinson uses a computer virus, rather than a cold virus, to destroy the invaders.

In short, *Independence Day* shares with *Mars Attacks!* the idea that people outside the elites in America are capable of dealing with a crisis, rising to the occasion to contribute to the struggle against alien powers. The difference between the two films is that in *Independence Day* the common people work in concert with the Washington elites, not, as in *Mars Attacks!,* on their own. As we have seen, in *Mars Attacks!* the elites are carefully cordoned off from the common people, but in *Independence* Day the lives of the two groups keep intersecting, to the benefit of both. Julius Levinson marvels at the ease with which he and his son gain access to the White House in the middle of a world crisis. Moreover, the Emmerich film does not debunk the Washington elites. Although it does portray a couple of rotten apples in the federal barrel, it generally pictures the political and military leaders as decent people and dedicated public servants. President Thomas J. Whitmore (Bill Pullman) is an especially heroic character, who eventually climbs into a fighter plane to fly sorties against the alien spaceship. Russell Casse may come across as a misfit and a loner, ridiculed by his peers for his claim that he was once abducted by aliens, but he used to be an air force fighter pilot in the Vietnam War, and his prior military training saves the day. In *Independence Day,* the military is the great American equalizer. It ultimately brings together the president and the crop duster in the same fighter squadron.

Rather than suggesting, as *Mars Attacks!* does, an opposition between the American people and the elites who govern them, *Independence Day* does everything it can to portray a harmony between the Washington establishment and common men and women. In that respect, it is a throwback to the patriotic spirit of the 1950s flying saucer movies, except that it shows more respect for common people, especially minorities. The flattering image that *Independence Day* creates of the unity of the American nation helps explain its great success with mainstream movie audiences. Given the film's celebration of government authorities, Burton may not have been unhappy that he had inadvertently produced a *Mad* magazine version of it in *Mars Attacks!* In any case, the almost simultaneous appearance of *Independence Day* and *Mars Attacks!* in 1996 shows that, decades after its movie debut, the flying saucer genre remained open to a wide range of ideological possibilities.[63]

5

FLYING SOLO

The Aviator and Entrepreneurial Vision

The first thing a genius needs is to breathe free air.
—Ludwig von Mises, *The Anti-Capitalistic Mentality*

Martin Scorsese is the cinematic champion of the underdog, even when that person happens to be the richest man in the world. That explains how *The Aviator* (2004) fits into the impressive body of work Scorsese has created in his long and distinguished career as a director. At first glance, the billionaire aviation tycoon Howard Hughes would not appear to be the sort of subject that would attract Scorsese. As a rich and powerful businessman, a handsome playboy, and a media celebrity, Hughes seems to be the archetypal top dog. He is exactly the kind of person a typical Scorsese protagonist can only dream of becoming. A Travis Bickle (*Taxi Driver,* 1976) or a Rupert Pupkin (*King of Comedy,* 1983) stares at public figures like Hughes and is driven to commit crimes in the hope of entering the charmed circle of their publicity. Scorsese is the great poet of the American underclass, focusing on the loners, the losers, the misfits, and the malcontents, those on the outside of society, desperately struggling to get in. As an Italian American, he has often dwelled in particular on the plight of immigrant subcultures as they try to fit into the mainstream of American society, culminating in his dark tribute to the immigrant experience in *Gangs of New York* (2002). Howard Hughes would seem to be the opposite of all this. Stepping right out of the American heartland, he was born in Texas and inherited a fortune and hence social respectability. As a record-setting aviator, Hughes seems cut out of the mold of the quintessential all-American hero, Charles Lindbergh—and hence worlds removed from a typical Scorsese psychotic criminal like Max Cady (*Cape Fear,* 1991).

Slumdog Billionaire

Yet *The Aviator* manages to turn Howard Hughes into a trademark Scorsese underdog, the Jake LaMotta of the aviation industry. Scorsese's Hughes is a street fighter, sometimes a bully and always a scrapper. He is portrayed as continually at odds with the establishment, whether in Hollywood or the aviation industry, and ultimately he runs afoul of the law and finds himself pitted against the U.S. government itself.[1] Despite the fact that he is surrounded by beautiful women and at times an adoring public, the film reveals him to be at heart a loner and a misfit, even a freak. To be sure, in pursuing his ambitions, Hughes is far more successful than the typical Scorsese protagonist, and he does accomplish what they can only dream of doing. Yet in the end Hughes is just as tormented as Travis Bickel, Rupert Pupkin, and Jake LaMotta.[2] Like these earlier Scorsese figures, he pursues his dreams obsessively, compulsively, monomaniacally, and therefore cannot remain content even when he achieves his goals.

Still, Scorsese finds something triumphal, and perhaps even redemptive, in Hughes's tortured psyche because it is, after all, the source of his creativity. Precisely because the world does not satisfy him, Hughes is always out to change it and improve it. His obsessive perfectionism continually drives him to new heights of achievement. He wants the perfect motion picture, the perfect airplane, and even the perfect woman, and in each case he keeps on molding and remolding reality to make it fit his visionary expectations. Scorsese uses Hughes's story to explore the thin line between madness and genius, and ultimately shows that the line cannot be drawn clearly. Hughes's psychological obsessions make his achievements possible, but in the end poison them and incapacitate him. The artist as madman, the madman as artist—here is Scorsese's deepest point of identification with Hughes and the reason why he is able to give such a sympathetic portrait of a figure who could easily be presented in a very negative light.

Scorsese obviously saw a great deal of himself in Hughes, and with good reason. As an independent filmmaker who bucked the Hollywood studio system, as a perfectionist who kept reshooting scenes and reediting film footage, thereby continually going over budget, Howard Hughes was the Martin Scorsese of his day. As Scorsese himself describes Hughes: "When he made *Hell's Angels* (a picture I've always loved), he was a truly independent filmmaker, and he literally spent years and a small fortune trying to get it right."[3] Many of Scorsese's films have drawn on autobiographical material,

most obviously whenever he deals with Little Italy, the New York neighborhood in which he grew up. But it is remarkable how in turning to what at first
seems to be subject matter utterly alien to his own immigrant background,
Scorsese nevertheless found in Hughes a mirror of his own struggles as a
creative artist. The Hollywood scenes of *The Aviator* are probably as close
as we will ever come to seeing *Raging Director: The Martin Scorsese Story.*

The Entrepreneur as Visionary

As a result of Scorsese's identification with Hughes as a filmmaker, *The
Aviator* offers something rare in a Hollywood movie: a positive portrait of
a businessman. In the typical Hollywood production, whether in motion
pictures or television, the entrepreneur often appears as a villain.[4] People
engaged in business are generally presented as greedy, corrupt, uncaring, and
willing to do anything for the sake of profit. They typically cheat customers,
employees, colleagues, and investors, despoil the environment, subvert the
due process of law, and commit all kinds of crimes. In one mystery after
another, the murderer turns out to be a businessman, trying to eliminate
a rival, cover up an earlier misdeed, or just make a buck at the expense of
his fellow human beings. In opposition to these kinds of capitalist villains,
Hollywood offers a variety of altruistic, public-spirited heroes, who put the
common good above their narrow economic interests. Public prosecutors,
the police, government officials of all kinds, together with an army of social
workers, investigative journalists, environmentalists, and other do-gooders,
are presented as necessary to rein in the antisocial impulses of private enterprise. Oliver Stone's *Wall Street* (1987)—which ironically immortalized
Gordon Gekko's phrase "Greed is good"—is only an extreme example of the
negative image of business that Hollywood usually projects.[5]

   Scorsese himself has participated in this antibusiness trend in American
popular culture. In movies such as *The Color of Money* (1986) and *Goodfellas*
(1990), he portrays the corrupting effects of the profit motive and works to
link the world of business with the world of crime. As part of his sympathy
for the underdog or little guy, he has generally adopted a left-wing attitude
toward big business and corporate America, namely that it is evil and corrupt and leads to the big fish preying on the little fish. But in *The Aviator*
Scorsese seems to strike off in a new direction and look at the positive side
of business for a change, perhaps because he is dealing in part with his
own business, filmmaking. The story of Howard Hughes allows Scorsese

to portray the entrepreneur as visionary and creative, even heroic. Hughes was, of course, heroic in a conventional Hollywood sense. As a pioneer in aviation and a daring aviator himself, often serving as the test pilot for his own innovative planes and setting speed and distance records, Hughes was obviously courageous in the way in which the traditional Hollywood hero normally is. With the title of *The Aviator,* one could imagine Scorsese's film assimilating Hughes to conventional Hollywood models of the heroic aviation pioneer, from Charles Lindbergh to Amelia Earhart to John Glenn. Hughes had the right stuff. But although the heroic aviator archetype is integral to Scorsese's portrayal of Hughes, the movie reveals much more than his raw courage in an airplane.

Scorsese's Hughes is also heroic as a businessman, displaying a different kind of courage in his willingness to take economic risks—above all, with his own money. *The Aviator* is unusual among movies in capturing what it is to be an entrepreneur, a genuine innovator in business. Scorsese's Hughes is creative in all his activities, not just in his work as a filmmaker. What unites his activities in the film and aviation industries is his ability to predict the future. He is always alert to emerging technological possibilities and the new demands of consumers, and he is willing to bet his own money on what he thinks the wave of the future will be. In most movie portrayals, the business executive has nothing to contribute to the common good, and in fact makes money only by cheating, defrauding, or otherwise exploiting the public. By contrast, *The Aviator* presents Hughes as a progressive force in two industries, someone who gives the public what it wants (for example, talkies rather than silent movies) and, more remarkably, correctly anticipates what the public would want if it were made available (for example, transcontinental and transatlantic flights in reliable, fast, and comfortable aircraft).

Thus, even though Scorsese may share the left-wing political opinions typical of Hollywood, *The Aviator* in many respects celebrates the spirit of free enterprise and embodies libertarian views. One may profitably interpret the film in terms of concepts derived from classic defenders of the free market, such as Adam Smith, and also draw on the work of the Austrian School of economics, whose chief representatives are Ludwig von Mises and Friedrich Hayek. The emphasis in Austrian economics on the special role of entrepreneurs and their ability to deal with the risk and uncertainty endemic to economic life makes it particularly relevant to understanding *The Aviator.* Scorsese is unlikely to have been influenced by Smith, Mises, Hayek, or any other libertarian thinker; nevertheless, he may share their understanding of freedom. There has always been a rebellious and antiestablishment streak in his movies that suggests an affinity with libertarianism. In *Gangs of New York* and *The Aviator* Scorsese seems to be focusing on the government—especially the federal government—as a prime enemy of liberty. In many ways the most distinctive—and libertarian—aspect of *The Aviator* is the way it champions the lonely figure of the private businessman against the vast oppressive apparatus the federal government brings to bear on him. Normally in Hollywood movies this figure is the villain, and a noble representative of the government—often a congressman or a senator—is necessary to bring him to justice.[6] *The Aviator* reverses this Hollywood stereotype, casting a crusading senator as the corrupt villain and a businessman as the victim of government injustice. Usually in American popular culture the government is presented as the solution to all our problems ("There ought to be a law"), and we almost never encounter the idea that free market forces might instead be the answer. By contrast, *The Aviator* seems to suggest that the government itself is the problem, and the entrepreneurial spirit is presented as the key to improving the world. I do not wish to associate Martin Scorsese with Ayn Rand, but I will say that not since the courtroom scene in *The Fountainhead* (1949) has a Hollywood movie vindicated the philosophy of rugged individualism as forcefully as *The Aviator* does in the Senate hearing scene.

Hermeneutical Issues

Before turning to a detailed analysis of the film, I want to take up briefly two preliminary but important issues of interpretation, one involving Martin Scorsese, the other Howard Hughes. I have been talking about *The Aviator* as if it were simply a Martin Scorsese creation and he were solely and completely responsible for its content. In fact, *The Aviator* is a rare example of Scorsese becoming involved in a film project that he did not initiate himself. The actor who plays Hughes, Leonardo DiCaprio, was the driving force behind doing a film on the subject and worked closely in developing the screenplay with John Logan—a talented and successful writer whose screen credits include *Gladiator* (2000), *The Last Samurai* (2003), *Any Given Sunday* (1999), and *Star Trek: Nemesis* (2002). Scorsese was not even the first choice to direct the film, but when Michael Mann backed out (he stayed on as coproducer), DiCaprio wisely approached the director he was working with on *Gangs of New York*. Thus, the story of *The Aviator* had largely taken shape before

Scorsese started to work on the film, as we can see from his own description of Logan's screenplay: "He had written a character who was both tragic and triumphant, whose brilliance was inseparable from his mania, whose vulnerability was inseparable from his callousness, whose private vision of perfection drove him forward and stopped him dead in his tracks, and then drove him forward once more. Which is to say that *The Aviator* was a portrait of the artist, writ large across the landscape of 20th century America."[7]

Clearly, many of the ideas I have been attributing to Scorsese he found already embodied in the script that was handed to him. Thus, any full account of *The Aviator* must acknowledge Logan's contribution to the creative process, as well as DiCaprio's. Film is a collaborative medium, and despite the attractions of French auteur theory, one cannot regard any movie as the product of a single creator. Auteur theorists focus on directors and are particularly hostile to the Hollywood star system, which they believe corrupts American moviemaking. Too many Hollywood films, they claim with some justification, are made to satisfy the needs and demands of their bankable stars. But in the case of *The Aviator,* the star around whom the movie was built and financed had an unusually active role in its development, and everyone involved, including Scorsese, has credited DiCaprio with having positively influenced the final product. As we saw Tim Burton acknowledge in chapter 4, sometimes actors can help make films better; they are not always a force for evil in the movie business, as the auteur theorists imply. Just as Burton formed a productive relationship with Johnny Depp, Scorsese has benefited from working with particular actors, including De Niro and DiCaprio.

Even with all these qualifications, however, it is still reasonable to talk about *The Aviator* as a Martin Scorsese film. As I have shown, it fits into his body of work as a whole and reflects many of his characteristic preoccupations as a filmmaker. And of course the finished motion picture bears the unmistakable stamp of his unique cinematic genius. The genesis of *The Aviator* is an excellent example of the creative serendipity that is more typical of popular culture than we like to think. We might wish that *The Aviator* were a project that Martin Scorsese had carefully planned out himself from start to finish. But in fact he was handed a script that was tailor-made for his distinctive vision of the world, and, what is more, gave him a chance to develop that vision in new directions. The happy result was one of Scorsese's most successful movies—artistically, critically, and commercially—and, although he was not single-handedly responsible for it, one may still say that the film carries his full endorsement and embodies his view of the world.

The other issue I must confront is the question of the accuracy of the movie's portrayal of Hughes. It appears that we will never know the truth, the whole truth, and nothing but the truth about the real Howard Hughes. His life has become surrounded by so many myths, mysteries, mystifications, fabrications, and lies that we will probably never be able confidently to separate fact from fiction in his case. *The Aviator* is grounded in a great deal of research into Hughes's life, and draws particularly on Charles Higham's biography (the movie, however, offers a much more positive interpretation of Hughes than the book does). DiCaprio studied newsreel footage of Hughes in preparing for the role, as is particularly evident in the Senate hearing scene. Substantial newsreel clips from the hearing survive, which allowed DiCaprio to imitate Hughes's behavior on this occasion quite closely (in addition, much of the dialogue in this scene is transcribed verbatim from the recorded testimony). At the same time, *The Aviator* takes some artistic liberties with the historical truth. The hearings were not televised, and Hughes's persecutor, Senator Owen Brewster (Alan Alda), was only a member of the Senate committee, not, as the film claims, its chairman. With exceptions such as this, *The Aviator* is in general true to the facts about Hughes that can be determined; but like any work of art it makes a selection from and an interpretation of those facts, and thus ends up emphasizing certain aspects of Hughes's life at the expense of others.

Insofar as I have been able to sort out the historical facts, I would say that the Howard Hughes we see in *The Aviator* is generally a more admirable and attractive figure than the real Howard Hughes. The mere fact that the film deals with only the first half of Hughes's career—before he completely withdrew from public life and became a bizarre recluse—means that we view him in a more favorable light. *The Aviator* does acknowledge the dark sides to Hughes's character and presents some of his more questionable deeds, but it does so in the larger context of treating him as a hero rather than a villain. Thus I want to make it clear that I am discussing a fictionalized portrait of Hughes, the Howard Hughes of Scorsese's film, not the real Howard Hughes. The historical Hughes would be a much more dubious choice as a poster child for free enterprise. Particularly in the second half of his career, when he earned most of his money from secret defense contracts, he became part of the military-industrial complex and hence largely a partner of the federal government, even its creature, not someone who heroically stood up to it. For much of his career, Hughes was a beneficiary of crony capitalism. Still, although the real Howard Hughes was not truly a good model of a free market entrepreneur, this fact does not refute the idea that the film embodies libertarian views. For the purpose of analyzing *The Aviator* as a Scorsese film, what matters is how it portrays Hughes, not what Hughes was really like. In fact, by comparing the historical Hughes with the film's significantly idealized portrait of him, one gets a sense of what Scorsese was trying to emphasize: namely, the heroic side of the entrepreneur.

In sum, when I use the phrase "Scorsese's Hughes" or just plain "Hughes" in this chapter, it should be read as shorthand for the more cumbersome phrase "the fictionalized image of Howard Hughes shaped by Martin Scorsese, John Logan, Leonardo DiCaprio, and other contributors to *The Aviator*—an image based in a mass of historical facts about the real Hughes but departing significantly in artistic ways from the full truth about Hughes insofar as it can be determined." In short, I am writing about a character in a movie, not a historical figure, and it is that character I am claiming is a celebration of the entrepreneur in a libertarian spirit.

Risking One's Own Money

The Aviator begins with a brief prologue, which suggests that the source of Hughes's lifelong obsession with cleanliness and health can be found in his childhood and his relation to his overprotective mother. The film then jumps ahead to Hughes as a young man, soon after the death of his parents left him extremely wealthy as the owner of Hughes Tool Company. Hughes is in southern California making *Hell's Angels* (1930), a film about World War I flying aces and their aerial combat. We get our first glimpse of Hughes the perfectionist, as he does everything he can to make the movie on a truly epic scale. He has assembled "the largest private air force in the world" (6) for the picture.[8] As the story begins, he has decided that an unprecedented number of twenty-four cameras is still not enough to shoot the aerial combat scenes the way he wants them—he needs two more. In his quest for the elusive additional cameras, he approaches one of the grandest of movie moguls, Louis B. Mayer (Stanley DeSantis), and the film introduces the motif of Hughes's ongoing battle with the establishment. Mayer treats him with contempt as an outsider in Hollywood and dismisses him with the curt comment "MGM isn't usually in the practice of helping out the competition" (8).

Thus, from the start the film presents images of Hughes's visionary power and his iron will in making his dreams come true. His first words in the film, as he deals with technical problems with the aircraft, are appro-

Howard Hughes (Leonardo DiCaprio) combines flying and filmmaking in Martin Scorsese's *The Aviator*. (Miramax/Warner Bros./Photofest)

priately "Don't tell me I can't do it! . . . Don't tell me it can't be done!" (3). These words could serve as the defining motto of the Howard Hughes of *The Aviator*. At every step of the way, he refuses to compromise and accept the seemingly practical solution that, according to conventional wisdom, the situation demands. For example, after Hughes concludes that he needs clouds in the background to make the excitement of aerial combat visible to movie audiences, he waits months—despite mounting costs—for the proper weather conditions to materialize. After finally finishing *Hell's Angels*—well behind schedule and over budget—Hughes is on the verge of releasing it in theaters when he discovers the first talking picture, *The Jazz Singer* (1927) with Al Jolson. Without hesitation, Hughes announces to his weary business manager Noah Dietrich (John C. Reilly): "You see, this is what people want. Silent pictures are yesterday's news, so I figure I have to reshoot *Hell's Angels* for sound" (22–23).

Hughes's perfectionism is vindicated when *Hell's Angels* turns out to be a critical and a commercial success. But as we see throughout *The Aviator,* Hughes pays a price for perfection, in this case literally, in terms of how much money it costs him to keep reworking *Hell's Angels* to meet his high standards. Fortunately for Hughes his inheritance ensures that he has enough money to pursue his dreams, as he tells Dietrich: "My folks are gone now *so it's my money*" (4). *The Aviator* keeps emphasizing this point—that Hughes's own money is at stake in his artistic and business ventures. It is not just that he is a visionary—"Leave the *big ideas* to me" (10)—it is even more important that he has the courage of his convictions and is willing to put his money where his mouth is. Even when he borrows money to finance his enterprises, he puts up all his personal assets as collateral. To raise the money to finish *Hell's Angels,* he instructs Dietrich: "Mortgage Toolco. Every asset" (26). The results could be disastrous, as his second-in-command tells him: "If you do that you could lose everything" (26). As a businessman, Hughes is a gambler, and he plays for high stakes. He does not simply risk some of his money; again and again he risks it all. *The Aviator* distinguishes itself from most movies about business by constantly reminding us why entrepreneurs are rewarded: it is for taking risks, and the biggest winners are often those who take the biggest chances.

The motif of "one's own money" runs throughout *The Aviator* and develops a moral dimension. Hughes makes many daring decisions, and he often makes them on the spur of the moment and by himself, against the advice of others. At times he appears to be erratic, eccentric, or irresponsible. But, the film implies, as long as it his own money that he is risking and he is willing to bear the consequences himself, he has the right to act as he does. In the last main plot sequence in the film, when Hughes is building the giant flying boat that he called the Hercules and that a skeptical public came to know as the Spruce Goose, the moral basis of his business conduct alters precisely when, as a defense contractor, he starts risking taxpayers' money. *The Aviator* would truly be a libertarian film if it were suggesting that Hughes's eagerness for government contracts was what in the end corrupted him, but I am not sure that the film goes that far. But it does raise doubts about his business morality only when he enters the world of big-government spending, and when factors like bribery become more important in winning contracts than genuine economic competitiveness. Hughes is able to vindicate himself at the Senate hearings only when he returns to the motif of one's own money, as he tells the committee: "You see the thing is I care very much about aviation. It's been the great joy of my life. So I put my own money into these planes. . . . I've lost millions, Mr. Chairman" (179).

The Nature of the Entrepreneur

Beyond the moral dimension of risking one's own money as a business principle, *The Aviator* suggests that doing so makes one a better entrepreneur. In his struggle to get *Hell's Angels* right, Hughes reveals what is driving him to perfection: "My *name* depends on this picture. If it doesn't work, I'm back to Houston with my tail between my legs, making goddamn drill bits for the rest of my life" (10). Hughes's personal pride is bound up with his personal fortune, and we see that the fact that he has such a personal stake in his business enterprises makes him a much better steward of the money he has at his disposal. If he were spending other people's money, as government bureaucrats do, he would have less incentive to be careful with it. In such circumstances, if he made a mistake, he would not suffer the financial consequences himself, and if he made the right decision, he would not reap the financial reward. But as *The Aviator* shows, Hughes is a true entrepreneur—he plays a high-stakes game in which he stands to lose or gain millions personally.

The film thus displays a solid grasp of the libertarian understanding of the entrepreneurial function in the free market, a point made cogently by Mises when he distinguishes the true entrepreneur (who invests his own money) from the mere manager (who handles other people's money):

> Society can freely leave the care for the best possible employment of capital goods to their owners. In embarking upon definite projects these owners expose their own property, wealth, and social position. They are even more interested in the success of their entrepreneurial activities than is society as a whole. For society as a whole the squandering of capital invested in a definite project means only the loss of a small part of its total funds; for the owner it means

much more, for the most part the loss of his total fortune. But if a manager is given a completely free hand, things are different. He speculates in risking other people's money. He sees the prospects of an uncertain enterprise from another angle than that of the man who is answerable for the losses. It is precisely when he is rewarded by a share of the profits that he becomes foolhardy because he does not share in the losses too.[9]

When people complain about the "obscene" profits entrepreneurs make, they conveniently forget about the appalling losses they risk at the same time. Entrepreneurs are fundamentally rewarded for taking risks, indeed for living with a level of risk that most people would find utterly unacceptable. *The Aviator* shows clearly that Hughes's great financial successes were constantly haunted by the prospect of financial disaster. The movie grasps the difference between a true entrepreneur and a mere manager; indeed, it shows Hughes always concentrating on the big investment picture while leaving the details to his managers. In portraying Hughes as willing to make a big business decision, stick to it, and accept the personal consequences, *The Aviator* celebrates the authentic courage of the entrepreneur.

One would think that more Hollywood filmmakers would appreciate the role of the entrepreneur, given the fact that filmmaking is one of the most entrepreneurial of businesses.[10] Huge amounts of money are made and lost in Hollywood as producers try to anticipate what entertainment the fickle public wishes to see. The entrepreneurial character of *The Aviator* itself is stressed in an article appropriately entitled "This Year, the Safe Bets Are Off" by Patrick Goldstein.[11] He discusses what distinguished the five Oscar nominees for best picture in 2004: "They were largely financed by outside investors. . . . Most of the nominees aren't even classic outside-the-system indie movies. They're artistic gambles financed by entrepreneurs. . . . *The Aviator,* though released by Miramax, was financed largely by Graham King, who was responsible for roughly $80 million of the film's $116-million budget (the rest coming from Miramax and Warner Bros. Films)." Ironically, the chief reason it was hard to raise the money to make *The Aviator* was Scorsese's reputation as a difficult director who has trouble respecting schedules and budgets. Goldstein cites King: "He says *The Aviator* met with rejection everywhere, even with DiCaprio attached to star. Everyone was scared that Scorsese would be uncontrollable." As it turned out, despite wildfires on location in California that interrupted shooting, Scorsese managed to finish the film on schedule in November 2003 and without large cost overruns. Still, everyone involved in the film had reason to feel grateful to King for his $80 million gamble on the project. Goldstein writes of the way DiCaprio showed his gratitude: "Hanging in King's office in Santa Monica is a framed picture of the star kneeling in front of one of the film's biplanes, with the hand-scrawled inscription: 'To Graham, thank you for being the only one to have the [guts] to make my dream a reality.'"[12] Goldstein adds his own tribute to King: "It's no wonder why King alone has produced three best picture nominees in the last five years: *The Aviator, Gangs of New York* and *Traffic.* Unlike the studios, King, who bankrolls his films by selling off the rights in foreign territories, is in the risk-taking business." The story of the making of *The Aviator* neatly parallels the story the film itself tells. Indeed, it is the same story of the courage of an entrepreneur in risking large sums of his own money on a film he believes in. As we saw in the case of Tim Burton in chapter 4, the financial backers in the film industry can play a positive role in moviemaking and are not totally incapable of recognizing and supporting artistic talent when they see it.

The Way of the Future

In the matter of anticipating consumer demand, *The Aviator* also celebrates the intellectual qualities of the entrepreneur. As we have seen, the key to Hughes's success is his orientation toward the future. He immediately sees that the arrival of talkies has made the silent movie obsolete, and he acts accordingly without hesitation. He is a great pioneer in aviation because he is always asking himself what the public wants and how airline service could be improved. He builds TWA into a major airline by following his vision of the future: "We build a plane that flies *above* the weather and we could get every man, woman and child in this country to feel *safe* up there. . . . An airplane with the ability to fly into the substratosphere—across the country—across the world. . . . Now that is the future" (37). At the end of *The Aviator,* right after Hughes has finally gotten the Spruce Goose to fly, he is still thinking about the future of aviation, as he turns his mind to the potential of jet aircraft for commercial use. This is one of the points where the film departs from historical accuracy. The real Howard Hughes was, in fact, slower than his competitors in equipping his airline with jet aircraft.[13] But to strengthen its presentation of the entrepreneur as visionary, *The Aviator* shows Hughes one step ahead of his competition even in this area:

"I've been thinking about something. Something new—*jet airplanes*. . . . Whoever can start utilizing jet technology on commercial airlines is gonna win all the marbles. . . . We gotta get into it. Jets are gonna be the way of the future. The way of the future. The way of the future. The way of the future. . . ." (189–190). *The Aviator* emphasizes Hughes's role as a forward-looking entrepreneur by offering these as his last words in the film. It ends with him repeating this phrase over and over again, while his aides hustle him off so that no one can see him finally plunging into madness. In the film's view, Hughes was a victim of what is now called obsessive-compulsive disorder (OCD), and the perfectionism that made him succeed in business was rooted in a pathological condition that eventually drove him out of his right mind.[14]

The film links Hughes's madness to his genius by suggesting that it is what makes him think outside the box. He does not behave the way ordinary people do, and he does not think the way they do either. When he orders a meal, it must be "New York cut steak, twelve peas, bottle of milk with the cap on" (42)—twelve peas, no more, no fewer, arranged symmetrically. Here his childhood obsession with order and cleanliness comes into play, and it makes him appear weird. But the same obsessiveness is at work when he sets out to produce the world's fastest plane: "The rivets have to be completely flush, every screw and joint countersunk. No wind resistance on the fuselage. She's gotta be clean, Odie" (36). In short, it is precisely because Hughes is a misfit that he stands out from the crowd. He is always doing what is least expected of him and proves the value of a contrarian stance in economic matters. Once again, *The Aviator* develops a portrait of the entrepreneur that is familiar in libertarian thinking in general and Austrian economics in particular. Here is Mises's classic description of the entrepreneur:

> The real entrepreneur is a *speculator*, a man eager to utilize his opinion about the future structure of the market for business operations promising profits. This specific anticipative understanding of the conditions of the uncertain future defies any rules and systematization. It can be neither taught nor learned. If it were different, everybody could embark upon entrepreneurship with the same prospect of success. What distinguishes the successful entrepreneur and promoter from other people is precisely the fact that he does not let himself be guided by what was and is, but arranges his affairs on the ground of his opinion about the future. He sees the past and present as other people do; but he judges the future in a different

way. In his actions he is directed by an opinion about the future which deviates from those held by the crowd.[15]

The Aviator is fully in accord with Mises's conception of the entrepreneur. By acknowledging that there may be an element of madness in entrepreneurial genius, it emphasizes the individuality of great business leaders, the uniqueness of their vision, the fact that they simply do not see the world the way ordinary people do.[16]

Patrician Socialists

While celebrating the visionary power of the entrepreneur, *The Aviator* also does a remarkable job of identifying the sources of opposition to this creativity and originality. As the representative of the future, the entrepreneur is constantly running afoul of all the representatives of the past, members of the establishment who have a vested interest in seeing that the status quo remains undisturbed. In *The Aviator* the establishment consists of three principal forces: old money, big business, and big government. Hughes ends up in conflict with old money as a result of his affair with Katharine Hepburn (Cate Blanchett), who, according to the screenplay (66), comes from a "patrician Yankee clan." When the actress brings Hughes home to her "ancestral Connecticut manor" (66) to meet her family, he cannot fit into this upper-class environment and is rejected by the Hepburns as a nouveau riche upstart. Here is another point at which the film departs from historical accuracy. To emphasize the contrast between Hughes and the Hepburns, it downplays the fact that Hughes was not exactly nouveau riche, having inherited a great deal of money himself. And his family did send him to an exclusive New England boarding school in the Boston area (Fessenden).[17] But the film may be allowed some poetic license here for the sake of creating a dramatic contrast and making an important point about old money. Moreover, with his roots in Texas and California and his stake in the motion picture and aviation industries, Hughes does represent the brash new economic forces from the West Coast and the Southwest that challenged the supremacy of the East Coast establishment in twentieth-century America.

    The Aviator presents this struggle as a cultural war. Hughes represents the new popular culture of Hollywood, while the Hepburns represent the old elite culture of New England, with its ties to Europe. Even though Katharine

Hepburn is a movie actress, from her first appearance she makes it clear that she prefers traditional drama to film: "I adore the theater. Only alive on stage" (33). The Hepburn family looks down on Hughes as crass, uncultivated, and uncouth, as a kind of mechanic who has no appreciation for art and all the other finer things in life. He reads "flying magazines" (actually aviation journals); they "read books" (71–72). In the arts, the Hepburns keep current with all the fashionable contemporary trends. The painter in their little artist colony is "abstract of course," and they sit around debating the merits of Goya versus Picasso and quoting Jean Cocteau about Edith Piaf (68, 72–73). The film presents the Hepburns as affected snobs of the worst kind. The screenplay reads, "Welcome to Fenwick where all the blood is blue and all the jaws are clenched" (68). Clearly we are meant to sympathize with Hughes in this scene. For once, he seems to stand for normality in the midst of all this aristocratic pretension and pseudointellectualism.

Like Burton's *Mars Attacks!*, *The Aviator* is suspicious of people who are hostile to American pop culture. Such attitudes smack of cultural elitism and may translate into a form of political elitism as well. What is most interesting about the presentation of the Hepburns in *The Aviator* is their politics. Although they are wealthy and upper-class, they are left-wing in their political opinions. In fact, almost the first thing Mrs. Hepburn says to Hughes at the dinner table is, "We're all socialists here!" (68). In practical political terms, the Hepburns are Democrats and partisans of Franklin Delano Roosevelt and his New Deal, with all its antibusiness policies. Mrs. Hepburn announces to Hughes with all her aristocratic hauteur, "I will not have sniggering at Mr. Roosevelt at my table" (69). Roosevelt was, of course, from an old, established, socially prominent, East Coast family himself. The idea that aristocrats might be socialists and favor antibusiness policies may at first appear strange. But as several libertarian thinkers have argued, the extreme left and the extreme right often meet in their distrust and hatred of the free market.[18] Like socialists with their commitment to central planning, aristocrats believe in a static social order and reject the supposed messiness and chaos of the free market. *The Aviator* explores the socioeconomic dynamic of "aristocratic socialism" by the contrast it draws between Hughes and the Hepburns.

We tend to lump the wealthy together into a single class, but *The Aviator* suggests that how one acquires one's wealth makes a great difference. The Hepburn family scene culminates in a pointed exchange between Hughes and his hosts:

Ludlow: Then how did you make all that money?

Mrs. Hepburn: We don't care about money here, Mr. Hughes.

Howard: That's because you have it.

Mrs. Hepburn: Would you repeat that?

Howard: You don't care about money because you have it. And you've always had it. My father was dirt poor when I was born—. . . . I care about money, because I know what it takes out of a man to make it. (74)

The Aviator suggests that those who are comfortably born into money take it for granted. The wealthy entrepreneur, by contrast, has made his money by his own efforts and appreciates both the money itself and the struggle it takes to accumulate it. Understanding how markets work, the entrepreneur will be in favor of economic freedom and oppose government policies that limit the flexibility he needs to respond to ever-changing market conditions. The representatives of old money are hostile to economic change because they worry that it can only undermine their upper-class status. Hence, old money may paradoxically support socialist or antibusiness policies because they hamstring the entrepreneurial activities that lead to the formation of new money. To preserve its privileged position, old money may favor government intervention in the market that hinders the accumulation of new wealth by the next generation. The sociological analysis implicit in the Hepburn family scene in *The Aviator* is subtle and accords with libertarian thinking on the subject. In exploring the conflict between old money and new, the film complicates our understanding of social class and reminds us that just because people are wealthy, they do not necessarily share a common interest or the same opinions about economic policy. Hughes is in many respects at his most sympathetic in this scene, which shows how Scorsese can treat even a wealthy man as an underdog. And where else has Hollywood ever portrayed supporters of Franklin Delano Roosevelt so unsympathetically?[19]

The Senator from Pan Am

The other source of opposition to Hughes in *The Aviator* is the sinister alliance between big business and big government. The film builds to a climax with Hughes's struggle against the efforts of Pan Am in collusion with a U.S. senator to keep TWA out of the international airline business.

The Aviator thus ends on a distinctively libertarian note, as it dwells on the confrontation between the heroic individual and the Leviathan State.[20] As Hughes himself puts it when being cross-examined by Owen Brewster, "I am only a private citizen, while you are a Senator with all sorts of powers" (170). In the contrast it draws between Hughes and Juan Trippe (Alec Baldwin), the president of Pan Am, *The Aviator* again differentiates what many analysts, Marxist and otherwise, mistakenly lump together. Not all people engaged in business are alike; some are genuine entrepreneurs and serve the public, while others use the power of the government to stifle free competition and hence innovation. Trippe represents the business establishment, which is comfortable working with the government and its regulations, especially when the regulatory powers of the government can be exploited to entrench a company's market position. In contrasting Hughes with Trippe and TWA with Pan Am, *The Aviator* suggests that there are two approaches a business can use to dominate an industry. TWA under Hughes's leadership gains its market share the legitimate way, by providing the public with what it wants in an economically efficient manner. Pan Am under Trippe's leadership exemplifies the dark side of business. Using its influence with the government to restrict access to its markets, it does not have to worry about being competitive in the services it offers.[21] *The Aviator* clearly distinguishes between genuinely competitive business practices in a free market environment and monopolistic practices in an environment of government regulation.

    The Aviator presents Hughes as fighting explicitly against the principle of monopoly: "No one airline should have a *monopoly* on flying the Atlantic. That's just not fair! . . . [Juan Trippe] owns Pan Am. He owns Congress. He owns the Civil Aeronautics Board. *But he does not own the sky. . . .* I have been fighting high hat, Ivy League pricks like him my whole life" (105). *The Aviator* adopts the concept of monopoly familiar in libertarian think-ing. Unlike Marxists, libertarians do not view monopoly as the inevitable outcome of economic competition and the ultimate stage of capitalism. On the contrary, they view it as the opposite of capitalism, a holdover from the precapitalist system known as mercantilism, in which governments granted special privileges to businesses, often chartering them as the exclu-sive proprietors in a given field. The script of *The Aviator* makes it clear that Senator Brewster's Community Airline Bill has nothing to do with capitalism. It is instead based on a European socialist model of national-ized industries: "Senator Brewster is saying that domestic competition will kill expansion into the global market—because the nationalized foreign carriers, like Air France and Lufthansa, can offer lower fares 'cause they don't have to *compete*, right? So, hey, let's get rid of all that messy competition and have a *nationalized* airline of our own. And, hey, why don't we make it Pan Am?" (116).

In his private meeting with Hughes before the hearings, Brewster tries to present himself in typical big-government fashion as the friend of the consumer:

> *Howard:* You think it's fair for one airline to have a monopoly on international travel?
> *Brewster:* I think one airline can do it better without competition. All I'm thinking about is the needs of the American passenger. (145)

At the actual hearing, Hughes is able to cut through Brewster's rhetoric and focus on the real reason behind his legislation: "This entire bill was written by *Pan Am executives* and designed to give that airline a *monopoly* on international travel!" (175). *The Aviator* supports the claims of many opponents of government intervention in the market—that the agencies created to regulate the market become clients of the very businesses they are supposed to be regulating.

At its heart, *The Aviator* thus champions the American principle of free market competition against European socialism and the model of nationalized industries. At the hearing, Hughes demolishes the pretense of big government to represent the public interest and shows that corrupt senators like Brewster are simply serving one private interest (Pan Am) at the expense of another (TWA). The film clearly suggests that the public interest is in fact better served by an economic system in which genuine entrepreneurs are free to compete with each other to introduce innovations in the marketplace. In the Senate hearing scene, *The Aviator* brilliantly plays with a Hollywood stereotype.[22] When one sees anyone hauled before a Senate committee on charges of corruption, one normally expects to find the public-spiritedness of the government triumph over the greed of the private individual. But Scorsese uses all his cinematic powers to craft a scene that shows just the opposite, revealing what often turns out to be the reality behind the illusion of big-government benevolence. One company is simply using its influence with the government to gain an unfair advantage over a legitimate competitor.

The Invisible Hand

In the way in which *The Aviator* differentiates the good business executive from the bad, it provides a useful reminder that free market thinkers are not lackeys of big business, as Marxists often try to portray them. Libertarians do not uncritically support business executives; they defend a system that forces those in business, often against their will, to compete with each other in serving the interest of consumers. Libertarian thinkers are acutely aware that many corporate executives resent the harsh discipline of the marketplace and turn to governments to relieve them from competitive pressures by granting them economic privileges. Libertarians champion only the true entrepreneur, who accepts the challenge of competing in an open market. For that very reason, libertarians are suspicious of big business, which, as *The Aviator* shows, is often all too eager to collude with big government to eliminate competition. That is one of the central claims of Adam Smith's *The Wealth of Nations*. Smith defended free trade and other free market principles, but he often speaks of those in business in extremely negative terms. In fact, he is no friend of people in business because he is a friend of free markets. He believes that these individuals must be forced into free competition. In his view, their natural inclination is to seek out economic privileges from governments.

Smith sees the baleful influence of business leaders behind the protectionist policies of the European regimes of his day, as well as the mercantilist doctrine that stood in the way of free trade:

> That it was the spirit of monopoly which originally both invented and propagated this doctrine, cannot be doubted. . . . In every country it always is and must be the interest of the great body of the people to buy whatever they want of those who sell it cheapest. The proposition is so very manifest, that it seems ridiculous to take any pains to prove it; nor could it ever have been called in question, had not the interested sophistry of merchants and manufacturers confounded the common sense of mankind. Their interest is, in this respect, directly opposite to that of the great body of the people. . . . It is the interest of the merchants and manufacturers of every country to secure to themselves the monopoly of the home market.[23]

Most people do not realize that Smith traces the lack of freedom in the marketplace to what he calls "the monopolizing spirit of merchants and manufacturers."[24] In the way it portrays the battle between Hughes and Trippe, *The Aviator* offers a concrete illustration of this basic principle. Many people have a hard time grasping the fact that free market thinkers support capitalism but not necessarily individual capitalists—especially when they turn out to be working against the very principle of the free market. Libertarians argue that free market principles are needed precisely to discipline individuals in business, to prevent them from seeking out unfair advantages at the expense of legitimate entrepreneurs.

This disciplinary power of the market is one way of formulating Smith's famous principle of "the invisible hand." Smith argued that the best social order is not one that attempts to pursue the public good directly. Far preferable is an order in which human beings are free to pursue their private good as they themselves understand it. The larger good of the public will emerge out of this free competition in pursuing private goods. As Smith writes in one of the best-known passages in *The Wealth of Nations:*

> As every individual, therefore, endeavours as much as he can both to employ his capital in the support of domestick industry, and so to direct that industry that its produce may be of the greatest value; every individual necessarily labours to render the annual revenue of the society as great as he can. He generally, indeed, neither intends to promote the publick interest, nor knows how much he is promoting it. By preferring the support of domestick to that of foreign industry, he intends only his own security; and by directing that industry in such a manner as its produce may be of the greatest value, he intends only his own gain, and he is in this, as in many other cases, led by an invisible hand to promote an end which was no part of his intention. Nor is it always the worse for the society that it was no part of it. By pursuing his own interest he frequently promotes that of the society more effectually than when he really intends to promote it. I have never known much good done by those who affected to trade for the publick good.[25]

This passage might serve as a gloss on *The Aviator*. The film shows that those who claim to be pursuing the public good are often hypocrites, secretly pursuing their own private good behind a façade of respectability and stifling the entrepreneurial activity that is the only real source of progress. In its complicated and ambivalent portrait of Howard Hughes, the film makes a fundamental libertarian point: one does not have to be a morally good person in order to serve the public good. Scorsese's Hughes has many faults. He is ambitious and vain, with a compelling need to be the center of attention. He is a fierce competitor, who is often willing to resort to unscrupulous means to achieve his ends. He is not public spirited in any conventional sense. On the contrary, he is always looking out for himself, interested primarily in his own fame and fortune. Yet *The Aviator* suggests that in pursuing his private obsessions, Howard Hughes ended up benefiting the public. He advanced two of the great arts of modernity—aviation and the motion picture—and thereby helped build the world of the twentieth century. One is reminded of another famous passage in Smith: "It is not from the benevolence of the butcher, the brewer, or the baker, that we expect our dinner, but from their regard to their own interest. We address ourselves, not to their humanity but to their self-love."[26] This doctrine may sound cynical, but it is also realistic. There are many fantasy elements in *The Aviator*—it is, after all, in part about the dream factory of Hollywood—but, as we have seen, it is rooted in an unusually solid grasp of economic reality. It offers one of the fullest, most complex, and most insightful portraits of the nature of the entrepreneur ever to appear in a film. And in celebrating the visionary career of Howard Hughes, *The Aviator* becomes one of the great American motion pictures because it celebrates the freedom and the entrepreneurial spirit that made America great.

6

CARTMAN SHRUGGED

The Invisible Gnomes and the Invisible Hand in *South Park*

> Tho' ye subject bee but a fart, yet will this tedious sink of learning ponderously philosophize.
>
> —Mark Twain, *1601*

The first few times I watched *South Park* (1998–) I thought it was the silliest show I had ever seen on television. But my students were finding my references to *The Simpsons* getting old (this was in the late 1990s), and they insisted that *South Park* was on the cutting edge of television comedy. So I kept watching the show until I began to realize that there is more to it than its relentless obscenity and potty humor. It can be brilliantly satirical, and, perhaps most important, it consistently defends freedom against its many enemies today, on both the left and the right. But despite the fact that the show won me over, I can still sympathize with its many vocal critics. I feel their pain. Watching a bunch of fourth graders see how many times they can use a given four-letter word in a single episode is not the most edifying of spectacles and requires some justification from anyone who claims to have a serious interest in pop culture.

High Philosophy and Low Comedy

To mount a high-minded defense of the show's low-minded humor, one might go all the way back to Plato to find a link between philosophy and vulgarity. Toward the end of his dialogue the *Symposium*, a young Athenian nobleman named Alcibiades offers a striking image of the power of Socrates. He compares the philosopher's speeches to a statue of the satyr

Silenus, which is ugly on the outside but which, when opened up, reveals a beautiful interior: "if you choose to listen to Socrates' discourses you would feel them at first to be quite ridiculous; on the outside they are clothed with such absurd words and phrases. . . . His talk is of pack-asses, smiths, cobblers, and tanners. . . . so that anyone inexpert and thoughtless might laugh his speeches to scorn. But when these are opened, . . . you will discover that they are the only speeches which have any sense in them."[1]

These words characterize equally well the contrast between the vulgar surface and the philosophical depth of the dialogue in which they are spoken. The *Symposium* contains some of the most soaring and profound philosophical speculations ever written. And yet in the middle of the dialogue the comic poet Aristophanes comes down with a bad case of hiccups that prevents him from speaking when his turn comes. By the end of the dialogue, all the characters except Socrates have consumed so much wine that they pass out in a collective drunken stupor. In a dialogue about the spiritual dimension of love, Plato thus suggests that, however philosophical we may wax in our speeches, we remain creatures of the body and can never entirely escape its crude bodily functions. In the way that the *Symposium* moves back and forth between the ridiculous and the sublime, Plato seems to be making a statement about philosophy—that it has something in common with low comedy.[2] Both philosophy and vulgar humor fly in the face of conventional opinion.

I am not sure what Plato would have made of *South Park*, but his Silenus image fits the show quite well. *South Park* is one of the most vulgar shows ever to appear on television, and yet at the same time it can be one of the most thought-provoking. Its vulgarity is the first thing one notices about it, given its obsession with farting, shitting, pissing, vomiting, and every other excretory possibility. As Plato's dialogue suggests, it is all too easy to become fixated on the vulgar and obscene surface of *South Park*, rejecting out of hand a show that chose to make a Christmas icon out of a talking turd named Mr. Hankey. But if one is patient with *South Park* and gives the show the benefit of the doubt, one finds that it takes up one serious issue after another, from environmentalism to animal rights, from assisted suicide to sexual harassment, from presidential elections to U.S. foreign policy. And the show approaches all these issues from a distinctly libertarian perspective. If anything, *South Park* can become too didactic, with episodes often culminating in a character delivering a speech that offers a surprisingly balanced and nuanced account of the issue at hand.

Before dismissing *South Park,* we should recall that some of the greatest comic writers—Aristophanes, Chaucer, Rabelais, Shakespeare, Jonson, Swift—plumbed the depths of obscenity even as they rose to the heights of philosophical thought. The same intellectual courage that emboldened them to defy conventional proprieties empowered them to reject conventional ideas and break through the intellectual frontiers of their day. Without claiming that *South Park* deserves to rank with such distinguished predecessors, I will say that the show descends from a long tradition of comedy that, ever since ancient Athens, has combined obscenity and profanity with philosophy. There are almost as many fart jokes in Aristophanes' play *The Clouds* as there are in a typical episode of *The Terrance and Phillip Show,* the cartoon within a cartoon often presented in *South Park.* In fact, in the earliest dramatic representation of Socrates that has come down to us, he is making fart jokes as he tries to explain to a dumb Athenian named Strepsiades that thunder is a purely natural phenomenon, not the work of the great god Zeus:

First think of the tiny fart that your intestines make.
Then consider the heavens: their infinite farting is thunder.
For thunder and farting are, in principle, one and the same.[3]

Thus, in characterizing *South Park,* it would not be wholly inappropriate to evoke a variety of elite culture precedents and call the show Aristophantic, Chaucerian, Rabelaisian, or Swiftian.[4] Like Aristophanes or Swift, Trey Parker and Matt Stone (the show's creators) relentlessly satirize political leaders, portraying them as bumbling idiots and exposing their hypocrisy, pretentions, and hidden agendas.[5] Like Chaucer or Rabelais, Parker and Stone ridicule religious authorities, again focusing on their hypocrisy, but also having fun with the absurdities of church dogma and doctrine. In short, for all its vulgarity, *South Park* descends from a long and distinguished tradition of calling into question the prestige of political and religious elites. As several commentators have noted, perhaps the best adjective for describing *South Park* is *carnivalesque.* The eminent Russian critic M. M. Bakhtin used this word in his groundbreaking analyses of the work of Rabelais.[6]

Bakhtin discusses the ways in which Rabelais drew upon the popular culture of his day to develop his trenchant satire of political, ecclesiastical, and other authorities in his *Gargantua and Pantagruel.* Bakhtin is particularly interested in the kinds of carnival festivities that broke up the daily monotony of medieval life throughout Europe—customs, ceremonies, rituals, pageants, and comic shows that allowed the common people to mock the authorities who ruled them and thus temporarily to escape their yoke, if only on an imaginary plane. In the midst of a repressive culture, carnival opens up a space of imaginative freedom. Central among such carnivalesque elements in European culture was the Feast of Fools, in which a King of the Fools was chosen, a commoner jokingly elected to a position of eminence. This inversion of conventional hierarchy, in which the low is made high, goes to the heart of the carnival spirit. By parodying the standard symbols of power—for example, placing a crown on the head of a fool—carnival customs call into question the rigid stratification of the social order. Carnival cuts elites down to size by making fun of them and challenging the all-pervasiveness of their rule.

Such customs have a liberating effect, if only by momentarily giving ordinary people a glimpse of different ways of ordering the world. The festive spirit of carnival seeks a temporary release of the energies of the body ordinarily suppressed by political and ecclesiastical elites. A momentary indulgence in food, drink, and sex is the polar opposite of the repression that was normally imposed on common people in the medieval Christian world. In its own cartoonish way, *South Park* similarly fulfills a carnivalesque function, inverting the hierarchies that dominate the contemporary world, pointing to a liberation of repressed impulses, and challenging the political, moral, and religious establishment. With his rotund body, his playacting, his love of birthday parties, and his insatiable appetites, Eric Cartman is a perfect emblem of the carnival spirit.[7] He is the pint-sized Falstaff of the cartoon world.[8]

Bakhtin especially notes the way in which linguistic excess performs a liberating function in Rabelais's prose. Rabelais broke out of the narrow limits of polite literary discourse and drew upon the vast resources of the language of the people—regional dialects; professional jargon; slang of all kinds; and, above all, curse words and obscenities. To read most serious literature, one would never know the enormous range of vocabulary a living language has to offer. Rabelais revealed how many words a language has to describe bodily functions, words one never hears in polite conversation. Consider the linguistic cornucopia that results when Rabelais has Gargantua's governesses pay tribute to his male member, glorious even when he is still a child: "And they amused themselves by rubbing it between their hands like a roll of pastry, and then burst out laughing when it raised its ears, as if the game pleased them. One of them called it my pillicock, another my ninepin, another my coral-branch, another my stopper, my cork, my quiverer, my driving-pin, my auger, my dingle-dangle, my rough-go stiff-and-low, my crimping iron, my little red sausage, my sweet little cocky."[9]

In a whole chapter devoted to what might be decorously described as anal hygiene, Rabelais really lets the subterranean powers of language loose, as he waxes poetic:

Shittard,
Squittard,
Crackard,
Turdous,
Thy bung
Has flung
Some dung
On us.
Filthard
Cackard,
Stinkard,
May you burn with St. Anthony's fire
  If all
  Your foul
  Arseholes
  Are not well wiped ere you retire.[10]

This is just the kind of language that critics complain about when they hear it in *South Park*. The show's exuberance of language has a similar function: to shock us out of our linguistic habits, and hence our habits of thought, by confronting us with the way people really speak.[11] In particular, Parker and Stone have an excellent ear for the way children talk among themselves, and *South Park* continually reminds us that the words they pick up on the street go well beyond the vocabulary the little tykes are supposed to have at their command.

As Bakhtin demonstrates, another way the carnival spirit performs its subversive function is to create new perspectives on the world by shaking us out of conventional frameworks. For example, in *Gargantua and Pantagruel*, we are often asked to look at the world through the eyes of giants, allowing Rabelais to play with the size of things, reducing some by making them look smaller and celebrating others by making them look larger.[12] For example, medieval Christianity had denigrated the human body, diminishing its value by picturing it as small, ugly, deformed, and wretched. Rabelais's giants, by their very size, celebrate the energies of the human body and its enormous capacity for enjoyment. In one of the most emblematic moments in Rabelais, the infant but gigantic Pantagruel epitomizes the liberating spirit of the Renaissance by breaking out of the cradle that tries to confine him: "Then he broke that cradle of his into more than five hundred thousand pieces with a blow of his fist, which he struck at the middle of it in his rage, and swore that he would never go back into it."[13] When Rabelais wants to diminish the Catholic Church in his readers' eyes, he literally reduces its size compared to Gargantua. In book 1, chapter 17, the giant is so large that, when he takes a fancy to the bells of the Notre Dame Cathedral in Paris, he can simply carry them home to hang on the neck of his horse. So much for the grandeur of the Catholic Church.

In the comic tradition of Rabelais and Swift, *South Park* uses extremes of size for comic and satiric effect. For example, in the first-season episode "Mecha-Streisand" (#112), a gigantic Godzilla-like Barbra Streisand symbolizes the inflated egos and overblown reputations of celebrities in our culture, as well as the undue influence that they exert on public opinion.[14] The eleventh-season episode "Lice Capades" (#1103) takes the opposite approach. It cuts environmental catastrophism down to size by imaging it in terms of a Lilliputian community of lice, who act out an overblown end-of-the-world scenario while perched on the head of one of the schoolchildren. The episode is reminiscent of the famous chapter 32 of book 2 of *Gargantua and Pantagruel,* when the author enters Pantagruel's mouth and finds an alternate world of people living there who are unaware of anything beyond its borders.

Out of the Potty Mouths of Babes

At the heart of *South Park* is another way of reversing perspectives and inverting conventional hierarchies: viewing the world through the eyes of children. The series fundamentally works by showing that children are wiser than adults. In *South Park* the adults often act like children while the children act like adults—a perfect example of carnivalesque turning the world on its head. Precisely because the children are not yet fully socialized into adult life, they see the world differently and are free of many social prejudices and pretentions. While the adults think that they already have all the answers,

Super Best Friends celebrate the holidays in *South Park:* And the little children shall lead them. . . . (Comedy Central/Photofest)

the children of *South Park* continually ask questions and raise doubts about the conventional wisdom of the community. As children, they are eager to explore their world and are open to new experiences, which lead them well beyond the limited intellectual borders of their small town.

In taking seriously the child's perspective on the world, *South Park* is heir to an old American tradition, which stretches back at least as far as Mark Twain and his classic American heroes, Tom Sawyer and Huckleberry Finn. It is surprising how few critics have noted the affinities that link Parker and Stone with Twain, but perhaps people are reluctant to acknowledge that a venerable American brand of humor stands behind anything as vulgar as *South Park.*[15] Like Parker and Stone, Twain viewed the child's perspective as distinctively American in its openness and lack of conventional social prejudice. When Twain wanted to call into question the idea that slavery is natural, he paired the young Huck Finn with the escaped slave Jim. Huck has been taught all his life that slavery is morally right, but, removed from the everyday context of his community, he gradually learns to see with fresh eyes and eventually concludes that slavery is morally wrong.[16] As in *South Park,* in the world of Tom Sawyer and Huck Finn the children are wiser than the adults precisely because they do not unthinkingly accept the common opinions of their day (a refusal symbolized in both worlds by various forms of truancy from school). Twain deliberately chose to make children *the* representative figures in his portrayal of America. Viewing the United States as a land of freedom and a place where people could make a fresh start in life, Twain saw children as best capturing the true spirit of America. A similar process of thought stands behind Parker and Stone's decision to tell their stories from the perspective of fourth graders. What seems at first to be a childish obsession with potty humor in *South Park* is simply the reverse side of the childlike openness of its characters to fresh perspectives, and that is what gives the show its affinities to Twain and the long tradition of philosophical comedy.

One might object that the mere presence of children in some of Twain's best-known fiction is not enough to link him with *South Park* and its strong brew of profanity, obscenity, blasphemy, and other violations of linguistic and social decorum. To be sure, the climate of opinion in Twain's day did not allow him the freedom of expression that the creators of *South Park* have enjoyed. Obviously, Twain could not use four-letter words in books that he intended to be read in polite society, as well as by children. It is, however, interesting to note how many times Twain refers to profanity in books such as *Adventures of Huckleberry Finn,* almost as if he were indicating that he would have used such language if he had been permitted to. Phrases such as "[he] used considerable many cuss words" or "He cussed away, with all his might" or "give them a solid good cussing" appear regularly in *Huckleberry Finn.*[17] Huck Finn might sound a lot more like Eric Cartman if Twain had not been inhibited by nineteenth-century literary proprieties.

If one sets aside the issue of diction and surveys Twain's career in terms of subject matter, one finds that he shared many interests—even obsessions—with Parker and Stone. Like them, he took controversial positions on many of the hot political issues of his day. *South Park* has questioned America's military involvement in a number of foreign countries, including Iraq and Afghanistan. Twain similarly was disturbed by the aggressive and expansive foreign policy that the America of his day pursued in such areas as the Philippines. He did not wish to see the United States become an imperialistic power, and Parker and Stone appear to share that concern.

On religious issues, Twain also adopted controversial positions, and he got away with a good deal of satire of the church in works such as *A Connecticut Yankee in King Arthur's Court*. But again, given the climate of American opinion in his day, he had to be careful about expressing heretical opinions and free thinking in public. As a result, some of Twain's most daring and provocative religious satire did not see the light of print during his lifetime. The book project generally known as *The Mysterious Stranger* was not published until after his death, and then only in a heavily edited and distorted edition. From what we now know of the various versions of this text Twain left behind, we can see that it has many affinities with the religious satire in *South Park*, and in particular it shares Parker and Stone's fascination with the figure of Satan and their animus against Catholicism.

To see a nineteenth-century precedent for *South Park* in a classic American writer, the best place to turn is a peculiar work of Twain's entitled *1601*. Written in a faux Elizabethan English dialect, this brief piece purports to be a conversation among a number of legendary figures from the era, including Shakespeare, Ben Jonson, Francis Bacon, Walter Raleigh, and Queen Elizabeth herself. Twain peppers their dialogue liberally with most of the famous four-letter words. For example, he describes an awkward pause in the conversation this way: "There was silent uncomfortableness now; 'twas not a good turne for talk to take, sith if the queene must find offense in a little harmless debauching, when pricks were stiff & cunts not loath to take the stiffnesse out of them, who of the companie was sinless?"[18] The story features a fart joke that Parker and Stone would envy, as Raleigh inelegantly but forcefully trumpets his presence in courtly society: "Then delivered hee himself of such a godless & rocke-shivering blast that all were fain to stop their ears, & following it did come so dense & foul a stink that that which went before did seeme a poor & trifling thing beside it. Then saith he, feigning that he blushed and was confused, *I perceive that I am weak to-daie & cannot justice doe unto my powers*; & sat him down as who sholde say, *There, it is not moche; yet he that hath an arse to spare lette hym fellow that, an' he think he can*."[19] Beyond the sheer vulgarity of its language, *1601* anticipates *South Park* in the way it treats elites. Twain, much like Parker and Stone, enjoys cutting famous people down to size, demonstrating that great cultural icons were ordinary human beings, subject to the same bodily functions as common people. In a brash and characteristically American gesture, Twain does not allow himself to be intimidated by the most august figures of European elite culture, its very royalty, so to speak, but instead treats them with a healthy dose of democratic irreverence. *1601* gives a rare glimpse into the really nasty and reductive side of Twain's humor. It reads just like an episode of *South Park.*

Speaking the Unspeakable

The example of Twain helps to place *South Park* in a broader cultural context. He was extraordinarily successful as an author in commercial terms and quickly became a fixture of American popular culture. Tom Sawyer and Huck Finn are true American archetypes. But, perhaps precisely because of his popularity, Twain was generally looked down on by the cultural elite of his day.[20] His works were condemned for all sorts of reasons during his lifetime, and yet several of them have come to be regarded as masterpieces of American literature. This is a common pattern: works condemned as mere popular culture when they are published, works that were censored or even banned originally, go on to become classics.[21] This pattern is especially characteristic of comic works. Comedy makes fun of people—that is its nature. As Aristotle stated in his *Poetics,* comedy portrays people as worse than they are and makes them look ridiculous.[22] To laugh at people is to feel superior to them. Comedy can thus be downright vicious. The contemporaries of a given comedy may well be offended by it, especially when they are the objects of its ridicule and feel threatened by it. Only the passage of time can soften the initially savage blows of satiric comedy and allow later generations to put up on a pedestal authors who were originally viewed by their angry contemporaries as being deep down in the gutter.

Thus the people who condemn *South Park* today for being offensive need to be reminded that comedy is by its very nature offensive.[23] It derives its energy from its transgressive power, its ability to break taboos, to speak the unspeakable. Comedians are always pushing the envelope, probing to see how much they can get away with in violating the speech codes of their day. Comedy is a social safety valve. We laugh precisely because comedians momentarily liberate us from the restrictions that conventional society imposes on us. We applaud comedians because they say right out in front of an audience what, supposedly, nobody is allowed to say in public. Paradoxically, then, the more permissive American society has become, the harder it has become to write comedy. As censorship laws have been relaxed and people have been allowed to say and show almost anything in movies and television—above all, to deal with formerly taboo sexual material—comedy writers such as Parker and Stone must have begun to wonder if there is any way left to offend audiences.

The genius of Parker and Stone was to see that in our day a new frontier of comic transgression has opened up because of the phenomenon known as political correctness. Our age may have tried to dispense with the conventional pieties of earlier generations, but it has developed new pieties of its own. They may not look like the traditional pieties, but they are enforced in the same old way, with social pressure and sometimes even legal sanctions punishing people who dare to violate the new taboos. Many of our colleges and universities today have speech codes, which seek to define what can and cannot be said on campus and in particular to prohibit anything that might be interpreted as demeaning someone because of his or her race, religion, gender, disability, and a whole series of other protected categories. Sex may no longer be taboo in our society, but sexism now is. *Seinfeld* (1989–1998) was perhaps the first mainstream television comedy that systematically violated the new taboos of political correctness. The show repeatedly made fun of contemporary sensitivities about such issues as sexual orientation, ethnic identity, feminism, and disabled people. *Seinfeld* proved that being politically incorrect can be hilariously funny in today's moral and intellectual climate, and *South Park* followed its lead.[24]

The show has mercilessly satirized all forms of political correctness—anti–hate crime legislation, tolerance indoctrination in the schools, Hollywood do-gooding of all kinds, environmentalism and anti-smoking campaigns, the Americans with Disabilities Act, the Special Olympics—the list goes on and on. It is hard to single out the most politically incorrect moment in the history of *South Park,* but I will nominate the fifth-season episode "Cripple Fight" (#503). It portrays in gory detail what happens when two "differently abled" or, rather, "handi-capable" boys named Timmy and Jimmy square off for a violent—and interminable—battle in the streets of South Park.[25] The show obviously relishes the sheer shock value of moments such as this. But more is going on here than transgressing the boundaries of good taste just for transgression's sake.

A Plague on Both Your Houses

This is where libertarianism enters the picture in *South Park.* The show criticizes political correctness in the name of freedom. That is why Parker and Stone can proclaim themselves equal opportunity satirists: they make fun of the old pieties as well as the new, ridiculing both the right and the left insofar as both seek to restrict freedom. "Cripple Fight" is an excellent example of the balance and evenhandedness of *South Park* and the way it can offend both ends of the political spectrum. The episode deals in typical *South Park* fashion with a contemporary controversy, one that has even made it into the courts: whether homosexuals should be allowed to lead Boy Scout troops. The episode makes fun of the old-fashioned types in the town who insist on denying a troop leadership to Big Gay Al (a recurrent character whose name says it all). It turns out that the ostensibly straight man the Boy Scouts choose to replace Big Gay Al is a pedophile, who immediately starts to abuse the boys by photographing them naked. As it frequently does with the groups it satirizes, *South Park,* even as it stereotypes homosexuals, displays sympathy for them and their right to live their lives as they see fit. But just as the episode seems to be simply taking the side of those who condemn the Boy Scouts for homophobia, it swerves in an unexpected direction. Standing up for the principle of freedom of association, Big Gay Al himself defends the right of the Boy Scouts to exclude homosexuals. An organization should be able to set up its own rules, and the law should not impose society's notions of political correctness on a private group. This episode represents *South Park* at its best—looking at a complicated issue from both sides and coming up with a judicious resolution of the issue. And the principle on which the issue is resolved is freedom. As the episode shows, Big Gay Al should be free to be homosexual, but the Boy Scouts should also be free as an organization to make their own rules and exclude him from a leadership post if they so desire.[26]

This libertarianism makes *South Park* offensive to the politically correct, for, if applied consistently, it would dismantle the whole apparatus of speech control and thought manipulation that do-gooders have tried to construct to protect their favored minorities.[27] With its support for freedom in all areas of life, libertarianism defies categorization in terms of the standard one-dimensional political spectrum of right and left. In opposition to the collectivist and anticapitalist vision of the left, libertarians reject central planning and want people to be free to pursue their self-interest as they see fit. But in contrast to conservatives, libertarians also oppose social legislation; they generally favor the legalization of drugs and the abolition of all censorship and antipornography laws. Because of the tendency in American political discourse to lump libertarians with conservatives, many commentators on *South Park* fail to see that it does not criticize all political positions indiscriminately, but actually stakes out a consistent alternative to both liberalism and conservatism with its libertarian philosophy.[28]

Parker and Stone have publicly identified themselves as libertarians and openly reject both liberals and conservatives.[29] Parker has said, "We avoid extremes but we hate liberals more than conservatives, and we hate them."[30] This does seem to be an accurate assessment of the leanings of the show. Even though it is no friend of the right, *South Park* is more likely to go after left-wing causes. In an interview in *Reason,* Matt Stone explained that he and Parker were on the left of the political spectrum when they were in high school in the 1980s, but in order to maintain their stance as rebels, they found that when they went to the University of Colorado in Boulder, and even more when they arrived in Hollywood, they had to change their positions and attack the prevailing left-wing orthodoxy. As Stone says: "I had Birkenstocks in high school. I was that guy. And I was sure that those people on the other side of the political spectrum [the right] were trying to control my life. And then I went to Boulder and got rid of my Birkenstocks immediately, because everyone else had them and I realized that those people over here [on the left] want to control my life too. I guess that defines my political philosophy. If anybody's telling me what I should do, then you've got to really convince me that it's worth doing."[31]

Defending the Undefendable

The libertarianism of Parker and Stone places them at odds with the intellectual establishment of contemporary America. In the academic world, much of the media, and a large part of the entertainment business—especially the Hollywood elite—anticapitalist views generally prevail.[32] As we saw in chapter 5 on Martin Scorsese's *The Aviator,* studies have shown that those who are engaged in business are usually portrayed in an unfavorable light in films and television.[33] *South Park* takes particular delight in skewering the Hollywood stars who exploit their celebrity to conduct liberal or left-wing campaigns against the workings of the free market (Barbra Streisand, Rob Reiner, Sally Struthers, and George Clooney are among the celebrities the show has pilloried). Most of the celebrities who are shown in *South Park* are impersonated ("poorly," as the opening credits keep reminding us), but even some of those who have voluntarily chosen to participate have been treated shabbily. Clooney, for example, who helped the show originally get on the air, was reduced to barking as Stan's gay dog, Sparky, in the first-season episode "Big Gay Al's Big Gay Boat Ride" (#104). Like Tim Burton, Parker and Stone seem to enjoy taking Hollywood icons down a peg or two. They share Burton's contempt for all the elites who set themselves up as superior to ordinary Americans. In an interview in 2004, Parker said of Hollywood, "People in the entertainment industry are by and large whore-chasing drug-addict fuckups. But they still believe they're better than the guy in Wyoming who really loves his wife and takes care of his kids and is a good, outstanding, wholesome person. Hollywood views regular people as children, and they think they're the smart ones who need to tell the idiots out there how to be." In Parker's description of the typical Hollywood mentality, we can recognize the attitude toward the American heartland that we saw Gene Roddenberry adopt in *Have Gun–Will Travel*. Stone joins Parker in criticizing this patronizing elitism: "In Hollywood, there's a whole feeling that they have to protect Middle America from itself. . . . And that's why *South Park* was a big hit up front, because it doesn't treat the viewer like a fucking retard."[34]

South Park is rare among television shows for its willingness to celebrate the free market and even to come to the defense of what is evidently the most hated institution in Hollywood, the corporation. For example, in the ninth-season episode "Die Hippie Die" (#902), Cartman fights the countercultural forces who invade South Park and mindlessly blame all the troubles of America on "the corporations." Of all *South Park* episodes, the second-season "Gnomes" (#217) offers the most fully developed defense of capitalism, and I will attempt a comprehensive interpretation of it in order to demonstrate how genuinely intelligent and thoughtful the show can be. "Gnomes" deals with a common charge against the free market: that it allows large corporations to drive small businesses into the ground, much to the detriment of consumers. In "Gnomes" a national coffee chain called Harbucks—an obvious reference to Starbucks—comes to South Park and tries to buy out the local Tweek Bros. coffee shop. Mr. Tweek casts himself as the hero of the story, a small-business David battling a corporate Goliath. The episode satirizes the cheap anticapitalist rhetoric in which such conflicts are usually formulated in contemporary America, with the small business shown to be purely good and the giant corporation shown to be purely evil. "Gnomes" systematically deconstructs this simplistic opposition.

In the standard narrative, the small business operator is presented as a public servant, almost unconcerned with profits, simply a friend to his customers, whereas the corporation is presented as greedy and uncaring, doing nothing for the consumer. "Gnomes" shows instead that Mr. Tweek is just as self-interested as any corporation, and he is in fact cannier in promoting himself than Harbucks is. The Harbucks representative, John Postem, is blunt and gruff, an utterly charmless man who thinks that he can just state the bare economic truth and get away with it: "Hey, this is a capitalist country, pal—get used to it." The irony of the episode is that the supposedly sophisticated corporation completely mishandles public relations, naïvely believing that the superiority of its product will be enough to ensure its triumph in the marketplace.

The common charge against large corporations is that, with their financial resources, they are able to exploit the power of advertising to put small rivals out of business. But in "Gnomes," Harbucks is no match for the advertising savvy of Mr. Tweek. He cleverly turns his disadvantage into an advantage, coming up with the perfect slogan: "Tweek offers a simpler coffee for a simpler America." He thereby exploits his underdog position while preying upon his customers' nostalgia for an older and presumably simpler America. The episode constantly dwells on the fact that Mr. Tweek is just as slick at advertising as any corporation. He keeps launching into commercials for his coffee, accompanied by soft guitar mood music and purple advertising prose; his coffee is "special like an Arizona sunrise or a juniper wet with dew." His son may be appalled by "the metaphors" (actually they are similes), but Mr. Tweek knows just what will appeal to his nature-loving, yuppie Colorado customers.

"Gnomes" thus undermines any notion that Mr. Tweek is morally superior to the corporation he is fighting; in fact, the episode suggests that he may be a good deal worse. Going over the top as it always does, *South Park* reveals that the coffee shop owner has for years been overcaffeinating his son, Tweek (one of the regulars in the show), and is thus responsible for the boy's hypernervousness. Moreover, when faced with the threat from Harbucks, Mr. Tweek seeks sympathy by declaring, "I may have to shut down and sell my son Tweek into slavery." It sounds as if his greed exceeds Harbucks'. But the worst thing about Mr. Tweek is that he is not content with using his slick advertising to compete with Harbucks in a free market. He also goes after Harbucks politically, trying to enlist the government on his side to prevent the national chain from coming to South Park. "Gnomes" thus portrays the campaign against large corporations as just one more sorry episode in the long history of businesses seeking economic protectionism—the kind of business-government alliance that Adam Smith criticized in *The Wealth of*

Nations. Far from the standard Marxist portrayal of monopoly power as the inevitable result of free competition, *South Park* shows that it results only when one business gets the government to intervene on its behalf and restrict free entry into the marketplace. It is the same story we just saw played out between Pan Am and TWA in *The Aviator.* Like Scorsese's film, *South Park* does not simply take the side of corporations. Rather, it distinguishes between those businesses that exploit government connections to stifle competition and those that succeed by competing honestly in the marketplace.

The Town of South Park versus Harbucks

Mr. Tweek gets his chance to enlist public opinion on his side when he finds out that his son and the other boys have been assigned to write a report on a current event. Offering to write the paper for the children, he inveigles them into a topic very much in his self-interest: "how large corporations take over little family-owned businesses," or, more pointedly, "how the corporate machine is ruining America." Kyle can barely get out the polysyllabic words when he delivers the ghostwritten report in class: "As the voluminous corporate automaton bulldozes its way. . . ." This language obviously parodies the exaggerated and overinflated anticapitalist rhetoric of the contemporary left. But the report is a big hit with local officials, and soon, much to Mr. Tweek's delight, the mayor is sponsoring Proposition 10, an ordinance that will ban Harbucks from South Park.

In the ensuing controversy over Prop 10, "Gnomes" portrays the way the media are biased against capitalism and the way the public is manipulated into antibusiness attitudes. In a television debate, the boys are enlisted to argue for Prop 10 and the man from Harbucks to argue against it. The presentation is slanted from the beginning, when the moderator announces: "On my left, five innocent, starry-eyed boys from Middle America" and "On my right, a big, fat, smelly corporate guy from New York." Postem tries to make a rational argument, grounded in principle: "This country is founded on free enterprise." But the boys triumph in the debate with a somewhat less cogent argument, as Cartman sagely proclaims, "This guy sucks ass." The television commercial in favor of Prop 10 is no less fraudulent than the debate. Again, "Gnomes" points out that anticorporate advertising can be just as slick as pro-corporate advertising. In particular, the episode shows that people are willing to go to any length in their anticorporate crusade, exploiting children to tug at the heartstrings of their target audience. In a wonderful parody of a political commercial, the boys are paraded out in a patriotic scene featuring the American flag, while the "Battle Hymn of the Republic" plays softly in the background. Meanwhile the announcer solemnly intones, "Prop 10 is about children. Vote yes on Prop 10 or else you hate children." The ad is "paid for by Citizens for a Fair and Equal Way to Get Harbucks Out of Town Forever." *South Park* loves to expose the illogic of liberal and left-wing crusaders, and the anti-Harbucks campaign is filled with one non sequitur after another. Pushing the last of the liberal buttons, one woman challenges the Harbucks representative with the question "How many Native Americans did you slaughter to make that coffee?"

Prop 10 seems to be headed for an easy victory at the polls until the boys encounter some friendly gnomes, who give them a crash course on corporations. At the last minute, in one of the most didactic of the *South Park* concluding-message scenes, the boys announce to the puzzled townspeople that they have reversed their position on Prop 10. In the spirit of libertarianism, Kyle proclaims something rarely heard on television outside of a John Stossel report: "Big corporations are good. Because without big corporations we wouldn't have things like cars and computers and canned soup." And Stan comes to the defense of the dreaded Harbucks: "Even Harbucks started off as a small, little business. But because it made such great coffee, and because they ran their business so well, they managed to grow until they became the corporate powerhouse it is today. And that is why we should all let Harbucks stay."

At this point the townspeople do something remarkable: they stop listening to all the political rhetoric and actually taste the rival coffees for themselves. And they discover that Mrs. Tweek (who has been disgusted by her husband's devious tactics) is telling the truth when she says, "Harbucks Coffee got to where it is by being the best." As one of the townspeople observes, "It doesn't have that bland, raw sewage taste that Tweek's coffee has." "Gnomes" ends by suggesting that it is only fair that businesses battle it out not in the political arena, but in the marketplace, and let the best product win. Postem offers Mr. Tweek the job of running the local Harbucks franchise, and everybody is happy. Politics is a zero-sum, winner-take-all game in which one business triumphs only by using government power to eliminate a rival; but in the voluntary exchanges that a free market makes possible, all parties benefit from a transaction. Harbucks makes a profit, and Mr. Tweek can continue earning a living without selling his son into slavery. Above all, the people of South Park get to enjoy a better brand of coffee. Contrary to the anticorporate propaganda normally coming out of Hollywood, *South Park* argues that, in the absence of government intervention, corporations prosper by serving the public, not by exploiting it. As Ludwig von Mises makes the point: "The profit system makes those men prosper who have succeeded in filling the wants of the people in the best possible and cheapest way. Wealth can be acquired only by serving the consumers. The capitalists lose their funds as soon as they fail to invest them in those lines in which they satisfy best the demands of the public. In a daily repeated plebiscite in which every penny gives a right to vote the consumers determine who should own and run the plants, shops and farms."[35]

The Great Gnome Mystery Solved

But what about the gnomes, who, after all, give the episode its title? Where do they fit in? I never could understand how the subplot in "Gnomes" relates to the main plot until I was lecturing on the episode at a summer institute, and my colleague Michael Valdez Moses made a breakthrough that allowed us to put together the episode as a whole. In the subplot, Tweek complains to anybody who will listen that every night at 3:30 a.m. gnomes sneak into his bedroom and steal his underpants. Nobody else can see this remarkable phenomenon happening, not even when the other boys stay up late with Tweek to observe it, not even when the emboldened gnomes start robbing underpants in broad daylight in the mayor's office. We know two things about these strange beings: (1) they are gnomes; (2) they are normally invisible. Both facts point in the direction of capitalism. As in the phrase "gnomes of Zurich," which refers to bankers, gnomes are often associated with the world of finance. In the first opera of Wagner's Ring Cycle, *Das Rheingold,* the gnome Alberich serves as a symbol of the capitalist exploiter—and he forges the Tarnhelm, a cap of invisibility.[36] The idea of invisibility calls to mind Adam Smith's famous notion of the "invisible hand" that guides the free market.[37]

   In short, the underpants gnomes are an image of capitalism and the way it is normally—and mistakenly—pictured by its opponents. The gnomes represent the ordinary business activity that is always going on in plain sight of everyone, but which people fail to notice and fail to understand. South Park's citizens are unaware that the ceaseless activity of large corporations like Harbucks is necessary to provide them with all the goods they enjoy in their daily lives. They take it for granted that the shelves of their supermarkets will always be amply stocked with a wide variety of goods and never appreciate all the capitalist entrepreneurs who make that abundance possible.

What is worse, the ordinary citizens misinterpret capitalist activity as theft. They focus only on what people in business take from them—their money—and forget about what they get in return, all the goods and services. Above all, people have no understanding of the basic facts of economics and have no idea of why those in business deserve the profits they earn. Business is a complete mystery to them. It seems to be a matter of gnomes sneaking around in the shadows and mischievously heaping up piles of goods for no apparent purpose. Friedrich Hayek noted this long-standing tendency to misinterpret normal business activities as sinister:

> Such distrust and fear have . . . led ordinary people . . . to regard trade . . . as suspicious, inferior, dishonest, and contemptible. . . . Activities that appear to add to available wealth, "out of nothing," without physical creation and by merely rearranging what already exists, stink of sorcery. . . . That a mere change of hands should lead to a gain in value to all participants, that it need not mean gain to one at the expense of the others (or what has come to be called exploitation), was and is nonetheless intuitively difficult to grasp. . . . Many people continue to find the mental feats associated with trade easy to discount even when they do not attribute them to sorcery, or see them as depending on trick or fraud or cunning deceit.[38]

Even the gnomes do not understand what they themselves are doing. Perhaps *South Park* is suggesting that the real problem is that people in business themselves lack the economic knowledge that they would need to explain their activity to the public and justify their profits. When the boys ask the gnomes to tell them about corporations, all they can offer is this enigmatic diagram of the stages of their business:

Phase 1	*Phase 2*	*Phase 3*
Collect Underpants	?	Profit

This chart encapsulates the economic illiteracy of the American public. They can see no connection between the activities entrepreneurs undertake and the profits they make. What those in business actually contribute to the economy is a big question mark to them.[39] The fact that entrepreneurs are rewarded for taking risks, correctly anticipating consumer demand, and efficiently financing, organizing, and managing production is lost on most people. They would rather complain about the obscene profits of corporations and condemn their power in the marketplace.

The "invisible hand" passage of Smith's *Wealth of Nations* reads like a gloss on the "Gnomes" episode of *South Park*:

> As every individual, therefore, endeavours as much as he can both to employ his capital in the support of domestick industry, and so to direct that industry that its produce may be of the greatest value; every individual necessarily labours to render the annual revenue of the society as great as he can. He genuinely, indeed, neither intends to promote the publick interest, nor knows how much he is promoting it. By preferring the support of domestick to that of foreign industry, he intends only his own security, and by directing that industry in such a manner as its produce may be of the greatest value, he intends only his own gain, and he is in this, as in many other cases, led by an invisible hand to promote an end which was no part of his intention. Nor is it always the worse for the society that it was no part of it. By pursuing his own interest he frequently promotes that of the society more effectively than when he really intends to promote it. I have never known much good done by those who affected to trade for the publick good.[40]

"Gnomes" exemplifies this idea of the "invisible hand." The economy does not need to be guided by the very visible and heavy hand of government regulation for the public interest to be served. Without any central planning, the free market produces a prosperous economic order. The free interaction of producers and consumers and the constant interplay of supply and demand work so that people generally have access to the goods they want. Like Adam Smith, Parker and Stone are deeply suspicious of anyone who speaks about the public good and condemns the private pursuit of profit. As we see in the case of Mr. Tweek, such people are usually hypocrites, pursuing their self-interest under the cover of championing the public interest. And the much-maligned gnomes of the world, the corporations, while openly pursuing their own profit, end up serving the public interest by providing the goods and services people really want.

The Wal-Mart Monster

The dissemination of an earlier version of this chapter on the Internet brought the wrath of the anticorporate intelligentsia down upon me. I was accused of having sold my soul for a double latte. For the record, I do not even drink coffee.[41] I had already noticed that, whenever I lectured on *South Park* at college campuses, nothing infuriated my audiences more than my explication of "Gnomes" with its implicit championing of Starbucks. I am somewhat mystified by the way this particular episode provokes so much indignation, but I think it has something to do with the defensiveness of intellectual elites when confronted with their own elitism. What many intellectuals hold against capitalism is precisely the fact that it has made available to the masses luxuries formerly reserved to cultural elites, including their beloved mocha cappuccinos.[42] From the time of Marx, the left argued unconvincingly for roughly a century that capitalism impoverishes the masses. But the general economic success of capitalism forced the left to change its tune and charge that free markets produce too many goods, overwhelming consumers with a dizzying array of choices that turns them into materialists and thus impoverishes their souls rather than their bodies.[43] Parker and Stone regularly do a marvelous job of exposing the puritanical character of the contemporary left. It does not want people to have fun in any form, whether laughing at ethnic jokes or indulging in fast food. In an interview, Stone excoriates Rob Reiner for this latter-day Puritanism: "Rob Reiner seems like a fun-killer. He just likes to kill people's fun. He supported a proposition in California that raised taxes on cigarettes. It's like, Goddamn it, quit killing everyone's fun, Rob Reiner! There's such a disconnect. It's like, Dude, not everyone lives in fucking Malibu, and not everyone has a yacht. And some people like to have a fucking cigarette, dude. Leave them alone. I know you think you're doing good, but relax."[44]

Having had the audacity to defend Starbucks, in its eighth season *South Park* went on to rally to the cause of Wal-Mart, using an even more thinly disguised name in an episode called "Something Wall Mart This Way Comes" (#809).[45] The episode is brilliantly cast in the mold of a cheesy horror movie. The sinister power of a Wal-Mart-like superstore takes over the town of South Park amid lengthening shadows, darkening clouds, and ominous flashes of lightning. The Wall Mart exerts "some mystical evil force" over the townspeople. Try as they may, they cannot resist its bargain prices. Just as in "Gnomes," a local merchant starts complaining about his inability to compete with a national retail chain. In mock sympathy, Cartman plays syrupy violin music to accompany this lament. When Kyle indignantly smashes the violin, Cartman replies simply, "I can go get another one at Wall Mart—it was only five bucks."

Widespread public opposition to the Wall Mart develops in the town, and efforts are made to boycott the store, ban it, and even burn it down (the latter to the uplifting strain of "Kumbaya"). But like any good monster, the evil Wall Mart keeps springing back to life, and the townspeople are irresistibly drawn to its well-stocked aisles at all hours ("Where else was I going to get a napkin dispenser at 9:30 at night?"). All these horror movie clichés are a way of making fun of how Wal-Mart is demonized by intellectuals in our society.[46] These critics present the national chain as some kind of external power, independent of human beings, which somehow manages to impose itself on them against their will—a corporate monster. At times the townspeople talk as if they simply have no choice in going to the superstore, but at other times they reveal what really attracts them: lower prices that allow them to stretch their incomes and enjoy more of the good things in life. To be evenhanded, the episode does stress at several points the absurdities of buying in bulk just to get a bargain—for example, ending up with enough Ramen noodles "to last a thousand winters."

In the grand horror movie tradition, the boys finally set out to find the heart of the Wall Mart and destroy it. Meanwhile, Stan Marsh's father, Randy, has gone to work for the Wall Mart for the sake of the 10 percent employee discount, but he nevertheless tries to help the boys reach their objective. As they get closer, Randy notes with increasing horror, "The Wall Mart is lowering its prices to try to stop us." He deserts the children when he sees a screwdriver set marked down beyond his wildest dreams. He cries out, "This bargain is too great for me," as he rushes off to a cash register to make a purchase. When the boys at last reach the heart of the Wall Mart, it turns out to be a mirror in which they see themselves. In one of the show's typical didactic moments, the spirit of the superstore tells the children: "That is the heart of Wall Mart—you, the consumer. I take many forms—Wal-Mart, K-Mart, Target—but I am one single entity: desire." Once again, *South Park* proclaims the sovereignty of the consumer in a market economy. If people keep flocking to a superstore, it must be doing something right, and satisfying their desires. Randy tells the townspeople, "The Wall Mart is us. If we like our small-town charm more than the big corporate bullies, we all have to be willing to pay a little bit more." This is the free market solution to the superstore problem—no government need intervene. The townspeople accordingly march off to a local store named Jim's Drugs and start patronizing it. The store is so successful that it starts growing, and eventually mutates into—you guessed it—a superstore just like Wal-Mart. *South Park* has no problem with big businesses when they get big by pleasing their customers.

Working for the Man

Parker and Stone acknowledge that they themselves work for a large corporation, the cable channel Comedy Central, which is owned by a media giant, Viacom. In the *Reason* interview, Stone says, "People ask, 'So how is it working for a big multinational conglomeration?' I'm like, 'It's pretty good, you know? We can say whatever we want. It's not bad. I mean, there are worse things.'"[47] Anticorporate intellectuals would dispute that claim and point to several occasions when Comedy Central pulled *South Park* episodes off the air or otherwise interfered with the show in response to various pressure groups, including Viacom itself.[48] The most notorious of these incidents involved Parker and Stone's attempt to see if they could present an image of Mohammed on television.[49] They were deeply disturbed by what had happened in 2005 in Denmark and around the world when the newspaper *Jyllands-Posten* published cartoon images of Mohammed. Threats and acts of violence from Muslims turned the event into an international incident. As staunch defenders of the right to free speech and free expression, Parker and Stone set out to establish the principle that Americans could—in the spirit of satire—show whatever images they wanted to on television. Unfortunately, Comedy Central refused to air the very tame images of Mohammed that Parker and Stone had wanted to show, even though the network at other times had no problem with showing viciously satirical images that they crafted of other religious figures, such as Jesus, Buddha, and Joseph Smith.[50] This incident probably represents the low point of Parker and Stone's relations with Comedy Central and certainly left them with extremely bitter feelings about their bosses.

But despite this kind of interference, the fact is that Comedy Central financed the production of *South Park* from the beginning and thus made it possible in the first place. Like Tim Burton, Parker speaks with gratitude of the financial support he and Stone have received from the corporate world, with specific reference to their film *Team America: World Police* (2004): "At the end of the day, they gave us $40 million for a puppet movie."[51] Over the years, Comedy Central has granted Parker and Stone unprecedented creative freedom in shaping a show for television—not because the corporate executives are partisans of free speech and trenchant satire but because the show has developed a market niche and been profitable. Acting out of economic self-interest, not public spiritedness, these executives nevertheless furthered the cause of innovative television. *South Park* does not simply defend the free market in its episodes—it is itself living proof of how markets can work to create something of artistic value and, in the process, benefit producers and consumers alike.

South Park is a wonderful example of the vitality and unpredictability of American pop culture. Who could have imagined that such a show would ever be allowed on the air, or would become so popular or last so long, or would have such an impact on American pop culture? To this day, I watch an episode like the sixth-season "The Death Camp of Tolerance" (#614) and wonder how it managed to emerge out of the world of commercial television. The imaginative freedom of the show is, of course, first and foremost a tribute to the creativity of Parker and Stone. But one also must give credit to the commercial system that gave birth to *South Park*. For all the tendencies toward conformism and mediocrity in American pop culture, the diversity and competitiveness of its outlets sometimes allow creativity to flourish— and in the most unexpected places.

Part Three

EDGAR G. ULMER

The Aesthete from the Alps Meets the King of the B's

INTRODUCTION TO PART THREE

Edgar G. Ulmer is a fascinating, if minor, figure in the history of American popular culture. Although his work as a director was almost forgotten during his lifetime, he has come to occupy a respectable place in film criticism. In terms of achievement, I would rank him somewhere between Orson Welles and Ed Wood. Like Welles, Ulmer made a splash with his feature film debut in Hollywood. *The Black Cat* is no *Citizen Kane* (1941), but it is an impressive movie, and, like Welles, Ulmer uses the techniques of German expressionist cinema to tell a tale of psychological obsession. Again like Welles, Ulmer never fulfilled the promise of his first film. Welles ran into trouble in Hollywood because of his repeated failure to stay within budgets and his inability to deliver completed films on time. Ulmer had the opposite problem. He became so well known for being able to operate on shoestring budgets and weeklong shooting schedules that he was typecast as a B-movie director. Hence the comparisons with Ed Wood. If Ulmer never made a film as bad as the infamous *Plan 9 From Outer Space* (1959)—widely regarded as the worst movie ever made—he did come up with the likes of *The Man From Planet X* (1951) and *The Amazing Transparent Man* (1959)—sci-fi films that shared the late-night hours in the early days of television with some of Wood's efforts. Weak scripts, continuity lapses, recycled stock footage, cheap props, and lame special effects—Ulmer's films share these elements with Wood's. Both Ulmer and Wood always had to scramble to make their movies, especially to find financial backing. For different reasons, the same came to be true of Welles.

Critics argue continually about where to place Ulmer in the ranking of directors. Was he, like Welles, a cinematic genius, whose genuine artistic aspirations were thwarted by a philistine Hollywood community always obsessed with the bottom line? Or was he more like Wood—someone with only pretentions to cinematic genius, whose ambitions outran his talent? After studying Ulmer's films, I am convinced that the truth lies somewhere between these two extremes. In any event, Ulmer's career can teach us much about the heights and depths of working in Hollywood—both of which he experienced. Ulmer often felt frustrated by the censorship and commercial constraints to which his filmmaking was subject in Hollywood. His career certainly does not exemplify the Romantic image of the artist, with the freedom to create as he sees fit, unfettered by financial or other external considerations. Yet, by dint of his talent and persistence, Ulmer did manage to have a long and productive career as a filmmaker. Many have argued that he left behind a distinguished body of work. That would have been impossible without the resources placed at his disposal by a movie industry that—grudgingly—give him the support he needed to be creative.

In one respect, Ulmer is the odd man out in this book—a situation in which he often found himself throughout his lifetime. All the other main figures I discuss were born in the United States, but Ulmer was born in what is now the Czech Republic and at the time was a province of the Austro-Hungarian Empire. One might then ask what he is doing in a book on *American* popular culture. Including Ulmer is a useful reminder that the notion of a *native* American culture has always been problematic. America is a land of immigrants, and waves of foreigners coming to its shores over the years have made the country what it is. Especially when analyzing the growth of the motion picture industry, we must take into account the contribution of immigrants to its development. We often refer to this industry simply as "Hollywood," reflecting our belief that it is the most distinctively American of all the arts. By the 1930s, when Ulmer began making films on his own in Hollywood, it had become the dominant force in the world in the movie industry. But in the preceding three decades, when the industry was first developing, cinema may have been the most international art form in history, one that managed to leap over national borders with ease. There were several reasons for this situation, but the primary one is the simple fact that for their first three decades movies were silent, thus eliminating the language barrier that normally separates one nation's art from another's. Movies could be filmed in any language, with their written titles then translated for any nation's market. As a result, in its formative years the motion picture industry could draw upon talent from any nation. Many of the great pioneering efforts in the cinema came out of France, Germany, and Italy, with countries such as Sweden, Denmark, England, the Soviet Union, and Japan not far behind in contributing significantly to the art of the motion picture.

By the second decade of the twentieth century, Hollywood began drawing upon foreign talent, including directors, cinematographers, set designers, and actors and actresses. It very quickly became questionable whether one can speak of a *native* American movie industry in any simple sense. This situation was compounded by the fact that the entrepreneurs in the industry, who developed its financial, marketing, and distribution practices, were mainly European immigrants, mostly Jewish in origin. Moreover, the audience in the early days of the motion picture in America contained a large proportion of immigrants. Not speaking English, they had difficulty understanding stage plays or popular fiction, but they could sit back and enjoy the wordless action of silent movies. With so many foreigners involved in the making and viewing of movies in America, it should come as no surprise that the films produced often incorporated foreign perspectives and dwelled on immigrants' experiences in the United States. Continuing to import talent and ideas from all over the world, Hollywood has never lost its ties to foreigners or its interest in immigration as a theme. Perhaps the greatest of all films, *Godfather I* and *II,* are centrally concerned with the fate of immigrants as they try to adapt to the American way of life. The two most significant U.S. filmmakers in the second half of the twentieth century—Francis Ford Coppola and Martin Scorsese—both identify themselves as Italian Americans.

Thus, in his status as an immigrant, Ulmer is actually typical of much of American popular culture, and he provides a good illustration of how foreign perspectives have contributed to its development. Ulmer forces us to rethink our analytical categories in other respects. The course of his career raises doubts about our belief that we can easily distinguish elite from pop culture. Ulmer had two, apparently contradictory, nicknames in Hollywood: "the aesthete from the Alps" and "the king of the B-movies." The first points to the fact that he was steeped in European elite culture and had a command of philosophy, literature, and classical music. His early training was with Max Reinhardt, the grand figure of German theater in the first half of the twentieth century, and with movie directors such as F. W. Murnau, the master of German expressionism in the cinema. Many aspects of Ulmer's films reflect his cultural erudition—for example, his use of expressionist sets, camera angles, and lighting, or the remarkable classical music scores he commissioned. But the man who made a film called *Carnegie Hall* (1947) as a labor of love also cranked out one called *Girls in Chains* (1943), and the latter title is unfortunately more characteristic of his output. Ulmer truly earned the title "king of the Bs." He worked in just about every genre of low-budget, lowbrow Hollywood film: the horror movie, film noir, science fiction, the pirate adventure, the sexploitation movie, the Western, the sword-and-sandal epic, the oriental fantasy, the nudie flick, even the ethnic musical (both Ukrainian and African American!). The man who early in his career in Hollywood worked with Murnau on *Sunrise* (1927), regarded by some as the most beautiful movie ever made, was eventually reduced to making films with such titles as *Goodbye, Mr. Germ* (1939) and *Babes in Bagdad* (1951–1952). With its artistic ups and downs, Ulmer's career provides an illuminating case study of the intersection between European high modernism and American popular culture at its most basic and most vulgar.

Analyzing Ulmer's checkered career can thus help explore the question, is film a form of art, or merely a commercial enterprise, or a strange combination of the two? With his admiration for Murnau, Ulmer clearly had aspirations of becoming a cinematic artist and sought creative control as a director. But almost all his movies were made under severe financial constraints and with the sole aim of making money, thus forcing him to cut corners artistically and pander to the taste of his audience. He ended up laboring on what was known as Poverty Row in Hollywood, working not for the major studios, but for small companies that imposed on him low budgets and tight shooting schedules. Given the circumstances, it is a wonder that his films are generally as good as they are. In the 1950s, Ulmer became one of the darlings of the auteur film theorists in France, serving as an example of a director who, despite all the obstacles, managed to impose his distinctive vision on a wide range of films. Having been influenced by these theorists, I will argue that Ulmer's movies do embody a personal view of the world and can be analyzed as aesthetic wholes. But the more I learned about how they were created, the more I came to have my doubts about the pure auteur theory. I raise the issue of Ulmer as auteur particularly in the appendix to chapter 8, on *Detour.*

In analyzing Ulmer, I concentrate on what I—and many others—regard as his two best films, *The Black Cat* and *Detour.* This choice allows me to write about two of the most significant genres of American pop culture—the horror movie and film noir—and trace their links to European culture. I would not call either movie an artistic masterpiece; but, if one judges them by the standards of their respective genres, they hold up very well to this day and are in fact generally regarded as among the best works in each category. Both movies have their faults and limitations, and even their cheesy, low-budget aspects, but I do them the courtesy of taking them seriously and trying to bring out their intellectual side. In the case of *Detour,* I demonstrate Ulmer's affinity with the thinking of the Frankfurt School, particularly the ideas of Theodor Adorno and Max Horkheimer. I relate *The Black Cat* to a long-standing European tradition of insisting on the cultural inferiority of the United States. Much to my own surprise, I even found myself drawing parallels between Ulmer and Martin Heidegger. *The Black Cat* is a good example of the "diamond in the rough" character of popular culture. If one gives it a chance, what seems at first to be a trashy movie may have something serious and enlightening to say.

One aspect of Ulmer's movies I find particularly interesting is the fact that the contrast between elite culture and pop culture becomes thematic in several of them. It was undoubtedly a subject that was very much on his mind as he contemplated his own situation in Hollywood. *The Black Cat* self-consciously juxtaposes the cheap melodrama of American pulp fiction with the serious European tragedy Ulmer is trying to tell in the film. Ulmer draws on his experience as a European immigrant in America to meditate on the differences between his birthplace in the Austro-Hungarian Empire and his adopted home in the United States. In *Detour*, Ulmer even more pointedly draws a contrast between elite and popular culture, by taking up the story of a classical pianist who is forced to turn to jazz to earn a living (a theme he also explores in *Carnegie Hall*). The critique of mass culture implicit in this situation is related to a broader critique of Hollywood as a dream factory developed in the film. This critique is what unites Ulmer most closely with the Frankfurt School. In both *The Black Cat* and *Detour*, Europe is associated with elite culture (modernist architecture and classical music), while America is associated with pop culture (pulp fiction and jazz). Ulmer's films reflect the fact that much of the elitist critique of American pop culture is a product of European émigrés and thus expresses an alien perspective on the United States.

At the same time, however, Ulmer's career follows a classic American pattern, the story of a penniless immigrant who comes to America and, against all odds, becomes a success in Hollywood. To be sure, Ulmer did not equal the achievements of his friend Billy Wilder, but he did get to make dozens of movies and earned an honored place in film history. Although a foreigner, Ulmer, like many immigrants in Hollywood, had enough of a feel for his adopted country to please American audiences in their most homegrown genres, including the horror movie and film noir. The original audiences of *The Black Cat* and *Detour* undoubtedly had no idea that the films they enjoyed had been made by a highly cultivated Austro-Hungarian intellectual with an interest in Freud, Jung, and Bauhaus architecture.

Europeans may condemn American pop culture as unsophisticated, and yet, as Ulmer's career illustrates, they have often played a direct role in its development. Supposedly vulgar genres in American pop culture, such as the horror movie and film noir, turn out to have their roots in the rarefied world of German expressionism.

But like many other immigrants in Hollywood, Ulmer maintained a certain distance from America and was never fully accepted into the motion picture mainstream. In many respects, he became an isolated and alienated figure, and that alienation is often reflected in his films, particularly *Detour*. Ulmer may have lived the American dream, but it often looked more like a nightmare to him. He had his finger on the pulse of America in terms of its taste in B-movies, but, to vary the metaphor, he carried a lot of European baggage with him to Hollywood. Being forced to cater to lowbrow tastes as a B-movie specialist may have increased his highbrow disdain for the very pop culture in which he had to make his living. Ulmer embodies many of the paradoxes of American popular culture I explore in this book. He was a European working in the most American of genres, an aesthete operating in the most commercial end of the movie industry, a would-be auteur forced to compromise at every turn in making his movies.

Ulmer thus has a distinctive take on the subject that is at the center of this book—freedom in America—and the two films studied in this part reveal the ambivalence of his response. When he made *The Black Cat* in 1934, he appeared to be on the verge of a brilliant career in Hollywood. The film centers on the contrast between Europeans and Americans. Although the film is patronizing in the image it creates of Americans as culturally naïve, Ulmer is equally critical of European elite culture. He images it as satanic, self-destructive, and doomed. In this, the one film Ulmer ever made as a featured director for a major studio (Universal), he seems optimistic about America and its potential. He in effect celebrates America's freedom from the entangling and disabling past of Europe, a continent then still obsessed by and mired in the conflicts that caused World War I. In *The Black Cat*, European elites seem to represent the destructive power of the past, while ordinary Americans represent the creative power of the future, thus in effect validating Ulmer's move to the New World.

By the time Ulmer made *Detour* in 1945, he surely knew that his early promise as a Hollywood wunderkind would never be fulfilled. He had become a journeyman director, respected in the industry for his professionalism but virtually unknown to the public and not in any great demand.

Detour may well reflect Ulmer's disillusionment with the adopted homeland that had at first seemed to offer him so much. In the tradition of film noir to which it belongs, *Detour* is a deeply cynical and bitter movie. It exposes the American dream as an illusion and a lie. It systematically deconstructs one of the great images of American freedom: the open road, specifically the road west. Ulmer's highways seem to stretch endlessly off into empty distances. Ulmer's affinity with the Frankfurt School in *Detour* reveals that he is looking at America with European eyes in this film. The freedom that is often celebrated in America appears, as it often does to Europeans, as chaos in *Detour,* a ceaseless wandering and homelessness that can end only in destruction. In *The Black Cat,* Ulmer seems to side with ordinary Americans against a sophisticated (but corrupt) European elite; in *Detour,* he adopts a European elitist perspective on ordinary Americans. The film debunks all the hopes on which America's self-image as the land of the free is founded—the idea of a fresh start, of succeeding in one's chosen profession, of building a new life in a new land. In *The Black Cat,* Ulmer presents Americans as naïvely optimistic, but he also shows them, unlike his Europeans, to be capable of leaving the past behind and moving on in a psychologically healthy way. The Americans of *Detour* have lost their ability to escape the past; on the contrary, they are all dragged down by their personal histories of failure. All their efforts to begin life anew—epitomized by the characters' heading for California—are inevitably frustrated and come to nothing. *The Black Cat* is a story of American newlyweds on their honeymoon; in *Detour* the young couple never manage to get married. Men and women are figuratively and literally at each other's throats in the film. Every fresh start in *Detour* turns out to be a false start.

The promise of a fresh start is, of course, precisely the hope that America has always held out, especially to immigrants. If *The Black Cat* is Ulmer's equivocal tribute to an America that had recently opened up new creative opportunities to him, the image of America as a wasteland in *Detour* is his revenge for its failure to fulfill its promises to him. In both films, Ulmer's European perspective on America helps to reveal how deeply problematic freedom can be. Yet at the same time, the fact that the Hollywood Ulmer came to despise nevertheless made it possible for him to make two films by which he is remembered today as an artist suggests that America does not break all its promises to its immigrants. *The Black Cat* and *Detour* are proof that creativity is possible in American popular culture, even on its margins and in its most debilitating circumstances. Ulmer's career illustrates just about every obstacle that can stand in the way of artistic achievement in commercial culture, and yet ultimately it is a tribute to the ability of a talented and determined individual to be creative in any system of production. In the end, the aesthete from the Alps managed to fulfill himself as the king of the B-movies.

7

THE FALL OF THE HOUSE OF ULMER

Europe versus America in the Gothic Vision of *The Black Cat*

The American public apparently does not want us to give screenplays a natural ending, because movie fans really do not want motion pictures like the books from which they are adapted. . . . In Europe a realistic production is considered splendid entertainment by the masses, even though it is a stark tragedy. In America, however, every picture must end with the hero and heroine dying in each other's arms. They must live happily ever after, but life isn't like that.
—Carl Laemmle Sr., *Universal Weekly*

The horror story is one of the many exotic goods that Americans have traditionally imported from Europe. This was already true in American Gothic fiction in the early nineteenth century; the situation persisted even in the twentieth century and the new medium of cinema.[1] To be sure, the horror movie seems at first to be a quintessentially American phenomenon—a rite of passage for American teenagers and a genre in which America has come to dominate the world. It is due to American movies that the faces of Dracula and the Frankenstein monster are known all around the globe. Yet both these creatures were originally the creations of European authors (Bram Stoker for Dracula and Mary Shelley for the Frankenstein monster). Even as motion picture figures, they can be traced back to European precursors in German expressionist cinema—*Nosferatu* (1922) for *Dracula* (1931), and *The Golem* (1920) and *Metropolis* (1927) for *Frankenstein* (1931).

Importing Horror

An excellent example of the equivocally American character of the horror movie is *The Black Cat* (1934), one of the highlights of the groundbreaking

horror series that the Hollywood studio Universal turned out in the 1930s.[2]
Several commentators regard it as one of the greatest achievements in the
genre.[3] As its title indicates, *The Black Cat* was intended to evoke the spirit
of America's most famous native exponent of the horror story, Edgar Allan
Poe.[4] But at the same time, the movie was made to capitalize on the popularity of Universal's two most famous—and exotic—horror movie stars, an
Englishman named William Henry Pratt, who had adopted the very Euro-
pean-sounding stage name of Boris Karloff, and a Hungarian actor with the
equally European name of Bela Lugosi.[5] The director of the film, Edgar G.
Ulmer, was an émigré from the defunct Austro-Hungarian Empire who had
worked with several German expressionist film directors, including the great
F. W. Murnau.[6] The film has a European feel in all its aspects, including the
art direction and the casting of the minor roles (Ulmer drew upon fellow
émigrés to fill several of the parts).[7] With its abstract, geometric sets, unusual
camera angles and tracking shots, and artful use of light and shadow, *The
Black Cat* at times looks like pure German expressionism on the screen.[8]
The musical score is one of the most remarkable in Hollywood history for
its unabashed use of European classical music, with passages from Bach,
Beethoven, Brahms, Chopin, Liszt, Schubert, Schumann, and Tchaikovsky,
often used as Wagnerian leitmotifs to highlight the action.[9]

   Thus, one of the greatest of American horror movies appears upon
closer inspection to be European through and through. Moreover, the film
turns out to have Europe as a theme. It stages a confrontation between the
Old World and the New and attempts to define the one way of life by comparison with the other. Ulmer draws upon the European Gothic tradition to
create a ruined castle for the twentieth century, a haunted house shadowed
by the new horrors of the modern world, specifically the nightmare of the
Great War, 1914–1918. Faced with the task of creating an American horror
movie, Ulmer had a brilliant idea. He realized that if Americans wanted to
see something horrific in 1934, all they had to do was to look across the
Atlantic to a European landscape permanently scarred by World War I. But
at the same time, as a sophisticated European himself, Ulmer could not avoid
a certain condescension in the way he portrays his American protagonists in
the film.[10] He sees something childish in his Americans, with their naïveté
and lack of culture.

   Ulmer thus joins a long line of Europeans who regard the United States
as offering an alternative to Europe as a way of life and a challenge to its
assumptions. If Americans have been fascinated by Europe as the source

of their culture, Europeans have been obsessed with America as "the child that got away," the offspring of Europe that rebelled against it and in many ways went on to surpass it, but only by taking culture in a democratic direction that Europeans, with their aristocratic traditions in the arts, view with disdain. Like many Europeans, Ulmer could not help treating Americans with a mixture of admiration and contempt. Yet in the end he seems to turn to them as the only hope of escaping, as he himself had just done, from a Europe morbidly fixated on its own conflicted past and becoming self-destructive in its obsessions. *The Black Cat* is a fascinating case study of how Europeans looked to Americans at one moment of cultural history and how Americans looked to Europeans—all in a film created by a man who, as an émigré filmmaker, was moving between the two worlds himself.[11]

The Haunted House of Edgar Ulmer

The Black Cat tells the story of Peter (David Manners) and Joan Alison (Jacqueline Wells), an American couple who have come to Central Europe for their honeymoon. Boarding the Orient Express, they are thrown together in the same train compartment with a cultivated European gentleman, a Hungarian psychiatrist named Vitus Werdegast (Bela Lugosi). Soon they transfer to a bus and set off with Werdegast to their hotel; he is headed for the home of an old friend, an architect named Hjalmar Poelzig (Boris Karloff). In a rainstorm, the bus overturns; the driver is killed and Mrs. Alison is injured; and Werdegast takes the young couple to Poelzig's house. Due to this series of accidents, the Americans get caught up in a European power struggle, as Werdegast fights bitterly to revenge himself on Poelzig for wrongs done to him fifteen years earlier.

The backstory of the revenge plot emerges only gradually in the course of the movie, and it turns out to be rooted in the horrors of World War I.[12] The ill-fated bus driver (George Davis) sounds the keynote of the film when he narrates a grim travelogue for his passengers just before his own death: "All of this country was one of the greatest battlefields of the war. Tens of thousands of men died here. The ravine down there was piled twelve deep with dead and wounded men. The little river below was swollen, red, a raging torrent of blood."[13] The driver's catalogue of the carnage of the Great War culminates in his description of Fort Marmaros, "the greatest graveyard in the world." It turns out that Poelzig commanded Marmaros, and we later learn that he sold out the fort to the Russians, saving his own skin but sending thousands of men to their deaths and condemning the others to imprisonment in Siberia. Werdegast was one of those prisoners; after fifteen years he has returned to get his revenge on the man who betrayed him and his country. He has tracked Poelzig down to his magnificent new home, a showcase of modernist architecture constructed on the ruins of Fort Marmaros.

Upon this very real foundation of the horrors of the war, Ulmer builds one Gothic element upon another. Werdegast has come back not only to avenge his wrongs, but also to regain his wife and daughter. After the war, Poelzig told Werdegast's wife that he was dead and stole her from him, marrying her and running off with her and the daughter she had with Werdegast; both wife and daughter are named Karen (Lucille Lund). To his horror, Werdegast now learns that his wife is dead, and he suspects that Poelzig killed her. What he can see with his own eyes is that Poelzig has embalmed her corpse and keeps it in a display case in a room of the old fort that lies beneath his house. Earlier we have seen several other dead women mysteriously on view in the fort's nether regions. *The Black Cat* consists of a series of increasingly disturbing revelations. Eventually Werdegast learns that his daughter did not die, as Poelzig originally claimed. Instead the architect went on to marry his stepdaughter, and in the course of the film he kills her, too, intending to add her to the gruesome collection he keeps below his house.

To the Gothic motifs of necrophilia and incest, Ulmer adds satanism to the morbid mix of Poelzig's perversions. The architect is the high priest of a satanic cult, and, with a Black Mass scheduled for the night of the full moon, he decides to take advantage of the accident that has brought Joan Alison within his grasp and to use her as a sacrifice in the ceremony. Much of the movie is devoted to a battle between Poelzig and Werdegast over the fate of the young and innocent Americans, played out literally and figuratively as a chess match. At the last minute, Werdegast manages to rescue Joan from Poelzig's evil clutches. In the ensuing combat between them, Werdegast overpowers his mortal foe with the help of his faithful servant, Thamal (Harry Cording). Together they stretch the architect out on his own embalming rack, and the crazed doctor proceeds to flay him alive, to tear the skin from his body, "slowly, bit by bit," while Poelzig can only howl like an animal. Werdegast shows the Alisons the way out of what has come to seem like a madhouse to them. He then pulls the "red switch," initiating a self-destruction sequence in the old fort, which is mined with dynamite. The Americans barely escape in time to watch Werdegast achieve his revenge

Vitus Werdegast (Bela Lugosi) and Hjalmar Poelzig (Boris Karloff) reminisce about old times in Edgar Ulmer's *The Black Cat*. (Jerry Ohlinger's Movie Material Store)

(though at the cost of his own life)—he blows Poelzig and his "rotten cult" sky-high.

Even in this bare summary, the plot of *The Black Cat* seems extraordinarily daring, especially for the 1930s, and one wonders how Ulmer managed to get some of the film's elements past studio censorship.[14] Such a story of father-daughter incest would still be shocking today.[15] The Black Mass is vividly realized on the screen, centering on a crooked, modernistic cross, with Ulmer using every cinematic trick he had learned from German expressionist cinema. The scene would have done Murnau himself proud. But *The Black Cat* has more to offer than just shock value. Its horror does not depend on monsters or special effects. It is psychological, growing largely out of Poelzig's fiendish obsessions.[16] Moreover, the horror is ultimately rooted, as we have seen, in something very real—the horror of the Great War.[17]

In an interview with Peter Bogdanovich, Ulmer traced the genesis of *The Black Cat* back to a conversation he had in the 1920s with the novelist Gustav Meyrinck (best known for having written *The Golem*): "Meyrinck at that time was contemplating a play based upon Doumont, which was a French fortress the Germans had shelled to pieces during World War I; there were some survivors who didn't come out for years. And the commander was a strange Euripides figure who went crazy three years later, when he was brought back to Paris, because he had walked on that mountain of bodies. I thought it was an important subject, and that feeling was in the air in the twenties." Ulmer went on to explain that he made *The Black Cat* in order to counter falsely idealistic views of the war that had prevailed in Europe: "because I did not *believe* the literature during and after the war, on both sides: in Germany *and* in England, it was very much the heroic thing, where enemies were friends like you never saw before."[18] To show the true horror of World War I, Ulmer turned to the Gothic tradition and shaped an unnerving parable of Europe in the aftermath of a monstrous conflict, a whole continent that seems incestuously turned in upon itself, in love with death and headed toward an orgy of self-destruction.

Chez Poelzig is immediately recognizable as the haunted house of the Gothic novel cleverly transposed to a modern setting, a sort of Bauhaus version of Castle Dracula.[19] Beginning with Horace Walpole's *The Castle of Otranto* in the eighteenth century, the Gothic novel is typically set in a ruined castle, which symbolizes the waning power of the Old Regime. The crumbling of the castle shows that the aristocracy is in decay, and yet its walls are still powerful enough to imprison a young hero and/or heroine. The castle usually has a dungeon below, in which unspeakable acts can take place, forms of torture hidden from the prying eyes of the outside world. Ghosts often walk the castle's corridors, reminders of ancestral crimes committed on the premises; and the building may be filled with moldy tombs and surrounded by a melancholy graveyard. The haunted castles of the Gothic novel embody the nightmare of the European Enlightenment: a powerful image of the way the Old Regime crushed freedom, of a past that stubbornly refused to let go, of a world of death that would not make room for the living.

Ulmer manages to maintain the Gothic symbolism of the haunted castle in *The Black Cat* while adding a few modern touches of his own. As seen from afar and in interior shots, Poelzig's creation is a model of modernist architecture, with sleek lines, geometric forms, and a number of up-to-date gadgets, such as an intercom system and digital clocks. But this triumph of modernist art literally and figuratively rests upon a dark foundation. As Werdegast describes it: "The masterpiece of construction built upon the ruins of the masterpiece of destruction, the masterpiece of murder. The murderer of ten thousand men returns to the place of his crime." Poelzig's architectural wonder conceals the dungeon-like vaults of the old Fort Marmaros. It is truly a haunted house, redolent of its master's crimes, suffused with "an atmosphere of death," as Werdegast explains. In one of the most famous lines in the film, when Poelzig learns that his telephone is not functioning, he says: "You hear that, Vitus? The phone is dead. Even the phone is dead." The dynamite that lies under the fort, threatening to blow it up at any moment, is an emblem of the psychological tension between Werdegast and Poelzig that figuratively is just waiting to explode in the course of the movie.

Gothic Archetypes

The dungeon-like corridors in the depths of the old fort conceal reminders not only of Poelzig's military crimes during the war, but also of his sexual crimes since. As we have seen, he keeps the embalmed corpses of women (presumably sacrifices at earlier satanic ceremonies) on display in glass cases in the rooms of the old fort. As he explains to Werdegast about his long-lost wife: "You see, Vitus, I have cared for her tenderly and well. You will find her almost as beautiful as when you last saw her." A frightening caricature of the modernist aesthete, Poelzig is obsessed with the female form: "I wanted her beauty always." The key element in Poelzig is his possessiveness; he prefers the embalmed woman to the living one, because only in that state can he make her completely his own and enjoy her in a state of perfection forever.[20]

There is something profoundly compulsive about Poelzig's behavior. He is fixated on the past and obsessively keeps coming back to it. As Werdegast realizes, in building his home Poelzig has deliberately returned to the scene of his crime; and he also collects women like trophies. In his obsessions, he descends from a long line of Gothic villains who represent the dead hand of the past trying to maintain its grip on the living. He is a kind of vampire, who preys upon young women and can hardly wait to drain them of their blood and make them immortal in his possession.[21] At the deepest level of the movie, this is Ulmer's symbol of the way World War I drained the lifeblood out of European culture and fixated it on death. Werdegast is just as implicated as Poelzig in this world of death. He speaks of the Russian prison he has returned from as a place "where the soul is killed slowly." Poelzig hurls this claim back at him in one of his few sympathetic speeches: "You say your soul was killed and that you have been dead all these years. And what of me? Did we not both die here in Marmaros fifteen years ago? Are we any the less victims of the war than those whose bodies were torn asunder? Are we not both the living dead?" "The living dead" is a term used of vampires—the Undead—and here the Gothic symbolism of *The Black Cat* merges with the very real issue Ulmer treats in the film, the way World War I scarred the European psyche. Everyone in Europe is now a victim of the Great War, caught up in the poisonous atmosphere of death it spread throughout the continent. Poelzig goes on to challenge Werdegast: "We shall play a little game, Vitus. A game of death, if you like." In Ulmer's portrayal, postwar Europe has become the grim playing field for a grand—and grue-some—game of death.

The vampire motif of *The Black Cat* is linked to the motif of father-daughter incest, another one of the disturbingly Gothic elements in the film. Incest epitomizes the transgressive force of the Gothic, its implacable urge to go beyond all boundaries, especially the bounds of conventional law and morality. Incest generally comes in two forms in the Gothic, with opposed symbolic valences: brother-sister incest and father-daughter incest. Brother-sister incest is symbolically rebellious—it represents the revolt of the younger generation against the older, the breaking of a fundamental taboo in a quest for absolute happiness (the perfect union of like with like). This symbolism runs throughout Romantic poetry and fiction, especially in the writings of Lord Byron, and the motif culminates in truly operatic fashion in the Siegmund-Sieglinde story in Richard Wagner's *Die Walküre*. Father-daughter incest reverses the symbolic thrust of brother-sister incest. It represents the unwillingness of the older generation to yield to the younger. The father who sexually possesses his own daughter is refusing to turn her over to the next generation and allow her a life of her own. If brother-sister incest represents all the revolutionary forces that were sweeping through Europe from the late eighteenth century on, father-daughter incest represents the Old Regime against which they were rebelling.

Percy Shelley's play *The Cenci* is a good example of the Romantic archetype of father-daughter incest. Filled with Gothic paraphernalia of dungeons and prisons, the play tells the story of Beatrice Cenci, an innocent young maiden who is raped by her father, the vicious Count Cenci. Symbolically linked with the Catholic Church through his alliance with the Pope, the aristocratic Cenci is a perfect image of the Old Regime in all its oppressive power and obsession with stifling the live-giving forces of the young. Cenci is a kind of vampire, unnaturally prolonging his own vital force by preying upon his daughter.[22] By the same token, vampirism is symbolically a form of father-daughter incest, as is clear in the Dracula myth in its many incarnations. Count Dracula—another predatory aristocrat—represents an older generation that will not make room for the new. The vampire is an older man who exerts a hypnotic fascination over a young woman, thereby coming between her and the young man she has fallen in love with. Using the greater sophistication that comes with age, the aristocratic vampire makes the young boyfriend look callow by comparison and attracts away the young woman. Dracula comes to her at night and merges with her in her bed, mixing his blood with hers and thereby artificially prolonging his own life. The sexual symbolism of the vampire has long been recognized, and its political symbolism as well. It is no accident that in traditional vampire stories the monster is always an aristocratic figure: *Count* Dracula.[23] As an undead creature, centuries old, emerging out of a ruined castle to suck the blood of the young, the figure of the vampire sums up the Gothic nightmare of a revolutionary Europe haunted by frightening memories of its aristocratic past, a past that simply refuses to die.

The traditional vampire myth splits the ambivalent image a young woman has of her father into its two "pure" sides: the benevolent and the malevolent parent. A woman is likely to have mixed feelings about her father. Insofar as he nurtures her, she looks up to him; but insofar as he stands in the way of her independence in life—her marriage to a younger man—she fears him. The vampire is the "evil twin" in the father archetype, the parent who will not allow his children to flourish on their own. As is clear in Bram Stoker's original *Dracula,* and in many of the film versions of the story, the myth typically pairs the vampire with an opponent who represents everything good about the older generation, a benevolent father figure. In Stoker's version, Abraham Van Helsing, though obviously not the same age as Dracula, still stands for the older generation and must use its greater wisdom not to prey upon the young, but to nurture them and liberate their energies. In contrast to Dracula, Van Helsing does not show a sexual interest in the young women he is called upon to protect. Instead he labors to thwart the vampire's designs upon them and to free them from his spell. The enduring power of the vampire myth rests partly on the way it captures the intergenerational psychodynamics of family life.

Strictly speaking, *The Black Cat* is not a vampire story, but it seems reasonable to think that a movie coming out of Universal and starring Bela Lugosi might show the influence of the 1931 box office hit *Dracula.* The pairing of Poelzig and Werdegast is modeled on that of Dracula and Van Helsing. Poelzig is the evil father archetype. He has married his own stepdaughter, and he keeps Karen Werdegast imprisoned in his house. Evidently he will not even allow her out of the bedroom, and he kills her when he discovers that she has disobeyed him and crossed its threshold. For Joan Alison he plays the role that Dracula does for the young women in his story. Although frightened by Poelzig, Joan also seems fascinated by his aristocratic bearing and his sophistication (her husband offers the older man little competition in these areas). Clearly Poelzig means to possess her and prevents her from leaving his home. Thus, it becomes necessary for Werdegast to help her. He uses the wisdom that comes with age to free her from Poelzig's spell (it is appropriate that Werdegast is a psychiatrist). The callow young man she loves, Peter Alison, has no chance of saving her on his own. Thus, in the symbolic pattern of *The Black Cat,* Werdegast at first sight seems to represent the good side of the parent archetype—during the film's crisis he addresses Joan as "dear child"—with Poelzig representing the evil side.[24]

The Black Cat complicates this simple opposition by suggesting that, deep down, Poelzig and Werdegast are mirror images of each other. Unlike Van Helsing in *Dracula,* Werdegast does at times display a sexual interest in the young woman he is supposed to protect. In the early scene in the train compartment, a dozing Peter Alison opens his eyes to catch Werdegast caressing his wife's hair. Werdegast hastily explains that she reminds him of his own wife, Karen. Since "Karen" is also the name of his daughter, one can say that in his attraction to Joan, Werdegast, like Poelzig, is confusing his daughter with his wife. In any case, he is showing interest in a woman young enough to be his daughter. Evidently, in the original shooting script, Werdegast was an even more ambiguous figure, explicitly battling with Poelzig to possess Joan.[25] Even in the film as it presently exists, both Peter and Joan at one point or another regard Werdegast as in league with Poelzig and hence as their enemy. In his obsessiveness, he becomes a double for Poelzig. He is also fixated on the past, and by the end of the film Werdegast is just as crazed as his antagonist, and ultimately just as destructive.

Innocents Abroad

The genius of *The Black Cat* lies in the way it maps the Gothic psychodynamics of the family onto a political landscape. At the heart of the film stands a conflict between the older and the younger generations, and the older generation must destroy itself if the younger is to be freed. What is fascinating about the film is the way Ulmer identifies the older generation with Europe and the younger with America, thus creating an allegory of European-American relations in the post–World War I era. America is the child of Europe, but a child that needs to get free of its parents or go down to destruction with them. Poelzig represents the satanic temptation of the European past, the force of the Undead trying to draw the youth of America into its vampiric grasp. Werdegast represents a more benign aspect of European culture, willing to let America go free. Poised between these two antagonists, the Americans are presented as naïve and unsophisticated compared to the Europeans.[26] When Werdegast asks Joan Alison if she has ever heard of satanism, she stares at him with a blank expression, as if to say, "What in the world are you talking about?" The Americans have evidently led sheltered lives and have been shielded from the kinds of shattering experiences the Europeans have undergone, especially in the war. By comparison with the world-weary Europeans, the Americans seem like children. Implicitly drawing a contrast with his American guests, Poelzig reproaches Werdegast: "Come, Vitus, are we men or are we children?" Werdegast is capable of cold-bloodedly skinning alive a fellow human being; Peter Alison winces when he simply has to watch the doctor injecting his wife with a sedative.

Although the Americans are genuinely frightened by what they see of the Europeans, in their ignorance and superficiality they tend to laugh off whatever seems foreign and strange to them. Unable to pronounce a German name, Joan jokingly refers to Poelzig as "Mr. Pigslow."[27] But Poelzig is no laughing matter. The Americans in the film may think that they are in a comedy—they are, after all, on their honeymoon—but they have, in fact, wandered into a tragedy, a deeply European tragedy that they, as Americans, are incapable of understanding. In a strange way, *The Black Cat* fits into the familiar American genre of "innocents abroad" (to use the title of one of Mark Twain's works). In the nineteenth century, American authors such as Nathaniel Hawthorne and Henry James were exploring the impact of European culture on Americans who travel across the Atlantic. Ulmer's trick was to reconfigure the "innocents abroad" theme by developing it in the context of a horror story out of the European Gothic tradition.[28]

The most striking fact about the Americans in *The Black Cat* is the amount of time they spend unconscious. They are barely able to stay awake throughout most of the film. Both Joan and Peter fall asleep in the opening sequence in the train compartment. Joan is knocked out in the bus crash and must be carried unconscious to Poelzig's house. That night the Alisons are both shown sleeping, while the wide-awake Werdegast and Poelzig begin their cat-and-mouse game. Given a "powerful sedative" by Werdegast to help her rest, Joan seems to be sleepwalking when she first gets up and meets Poelzig. Speaking later of the bus crash, she says, "I don't remember anything after that." She faints twice in the course of the action; Peter is knocked unconscious twice, first by Werdegast's servant and then by Poelzig's majordomo (Egon Brecher). The suggestion seems to be that Americans are largely unconscious of what is happening in Europe. As an émigré to the United States, Ulmer may have wanted to give Americans a wake-up call about the European tragedy. His movie points to the genuine horror in Europe, a continent still playing out the feuds that sparked World War I, making Europe a dangerous powder keg of violence just waiting to explode again.[29] *The Black Cat* suggests that, unfortunately, Americans would not recognize a European horror story even if they wandered right into the middle of it. With World War II breaking out in Europe barely five years after the release of *The Black Cat*, Ulmer turned out to have been prophetic about Europe's potential for catastrophe.[30]

The contrasts Ulmer develops between Europeans and Americans are not all to the advantage of the latter. To be sure, the Europeans in *The Black Cat* are deeply neurotic, obsessive-compulsive, and self-destructive, not to mention downright evil and even satanic, while the Americans are free, open, good-natured, and optimistic. But at the same time the Europeans are clearly more interesting than the Americans. The Europeans are intelligent, cultured, and artistic, while the Americans are bland, prosaic, and more than a little bit obtuse. This contrast emerges clearly when Poelzig, Werdegast, and Peter Alison formally introduce themselves to one another. Poelzig is "one of Austria's greatest architects" and Werdegast is "one of Hungary's greatest psychiatrists." Alison's introduction starts off auspiciously but quickly collapses; he describes himself as "one of America's greatest writers—of unimportant books." Alison is, in fact, a writer of mass-market mysteries, and the film implicitly contrasts his cheap melodramatic stories with the genuine European tragedy that unfolds before his uncomprehending eyes.[31] Ulmer develops the European–American opposition in terms of a contrast between elite and popular culture. The Europeans are consistently associated with elite culture: they perform elaborate rituals in Latin to the music of J. S. Bach. Alison's roots, by contrast, are in American pulp fiction, and he seems bewildered by the rarefied aesthetic environment he encounters in Europe.

Confronted, for example, with the brilliance of Poelzig's architectural achievement in the modernist house, Alison says to Werdegast, "I suppose we've got to have architects, too, but if I wanted to build a nice, cozy, unpretentious insane asylum, he'd be the man for it." Alison's low assessment of Austrian modernism actually displays a good deal of American common sense. Poelzig *is* mad, and his house reflects his mania. Still, there is a strong element of cultural philistinism in Alison's failure to appreciate the subtleties of Poelzig's art. On a basic level, Hjalmar must show Peter how to use a stylish Art Deco radio (and what comes on is Schubert's *Unfinished Symphony*). On a more profound level, Alison is blind to the depth of the evil all around him. Listening to talk of the black cat and its connection to deathless evil, Alison can only say, "Sounds like a lot of supernatural baloney to me." In another one of the film's most famous lines, Werdegast pointedly replies, "Supernatural, perhaps. Baloney, perhaps not." Then, echoing Hamlet's famous words to Horatio, Vitus adds, "There are more things under the sun," calling attention to Alison's limited horizons. In Ulmer's vision, American innocence and optimism transform into dangerous ignorance and naïveté.

The contrast between Europeans and Americans is neatly summed up in the fact that Werdegast and Poelzig play chess, while Alison can merely claim that he "used to play a very good hand of poker." Ulmer emphasizes the cultural superiority of Europe by representing it in terms of Bauhaus architecture and Freudian psychoanalysis, two avant-garde movements that had come out of Europe and were being introduced into the United States in the 1930s, largely as a result of European émigrés like Ulmer himself. Psychoanalysis and modernism in architecture were still rather exotic phenomena for the kind of audience Ulmer could expect for *The Black Cat,* and he does a good job of connecting the two. Poelzig's house is at once a representative of modern architecture and a kind of Freudian symbol. The gleaming house up above, with its orderly, geometric structure, represents the rational ego; the dungeon-like fortress down below, with all its darkness and grim reminders of Poelzig's madness, represents the hidden depths of irrationality in the id.[32]

Coming from the world of the Austro-Hungarian Empire, Ulmer no doubt admired the extraordinary achievements of his compatriots in the fields of architecture and psychoanalysis.[33] Yet the complexity of *The Black Cat* can be seen in the way that Ulmer links both phenomena to the aftermath of World War I and even suggests that there is something potentially satanic about them. The unprecedented new opportunities that arose for architects to rebuild Europe after World War I were sadly made possible by the unprecedented scale of the destruction the war had caused throughout the continent. In that sense, as we have already seen in Werdegast's description of Poelzig's house, modernist architecture rested on the ruins left by the Great War. Moreover, the radical character of the break modernist architects made with traditional styles and modes of building reflected their profound disillusionment with the whole of Western civilization. The cultural traditions of Europe had failed to halt the catastrophe of the Great War; many Europeans wondered at the time if perhaps these traditions had even contributed to it. The contempt that modernists in all the arts displayed for traditional culture was rooted in their sense that it had let Europe down in a crisis. That is why there was a strong strain of nihilism in European modernism, even in its architecture, which seemed concerned as much with tearing down the old Europe as with building a new one.[34]

The war similarly gave a new impetus to psychoanalysis. Could this new science account for the violence that had suddenly taken the whole continent of Europe by surprise? Surely there was something lurking undiscovered in the depths of the human psyche of which people had been unaware. Psychoanalysts began to probe beneath the surface of the human mind in an effort to uncover the hidden sources of violent behavior and war. It is no accident that Freud's *Group Psychology and the Analysis of the Ego* came out in 1921. With his theory of the primal horde, the Austro-Hungarian scientist was seeking, among other things, an explanation for the catastrophe that had just befallen Europe. The thrust of Freudian psychoanalysis was to suggest that irrational, aggressive impulses are always lurking just below the surface of the rational ego, even in ordinary, law-abiding citizens.

Appropriately as the work of an Austrian and a movie that features a psychiatrist, *The Black Cat* reflects this Freudian understanding of human aggressiveness.[35] Two respected professionals, a doctor and an architect, turn out to be monstrously mad, harboring murderous impulses. What is extraordinary about the Black Mass scene is the utter ordinariness of the participants. The men all appear to be respectable members of society; in their evening clothes, they look mostly like middle-class businessmen. The women look just as decent; we see nothing of the stereotype of the grotesque witch in the scene. As the participants in the Black Mass put on their robes, they could be getting ready for a college commencement. Ulmer's point seems to be that the most ordinary human beings can be hiding satanic impulses in their breasts.[36] But this kind of psychoanalytic insight can itself be demonic. In seeking out the causes of evil and perversion, psychoanalysis gives us a glimpse into the abyss and risks unnerving and disorienting us with its revelations of human depravity. A strain of nihilism thus links modern architecture and psychoanalysis in the film, symbolically reflected in the way that Poelzig and Werdegast form mirror images of each other. For much of the film they act like opponents, but eventually Werdegast gets caught up in his rival's cult.[37] Representing the new cultural aristocracy of modern Europe, architect and psychiatrist are both ultimately satanic. In this way Ulmer carries the Gothic tradition forward into the twentieth century.[38] In a strange way, Ulmer portrays European high modernism as rooted in the horrors of World War I and, as a result, bordering on the brink of madness, ready to plunge into a nihilistic abyss.[39]

We come away from *The Black Cat*, then, with a disturbing and conflicted response. We sense that, compared to Peter and Joan Alison, Werdegast and Poelzig have seen much deeper into human life. But we are not convinced that the Europeans are better off for all their insights into the depths of human evil. They seem to have been corrupted by their encounter with evil, perhaps even driven insane. The Americans might be healthier for turning their backs on this glimpse into the heart of darkness. Early in the film, Peter Alison has already sensed that something has gone terribly wrong with his honeymoon and vows never to leave North America again and expose himself to European horrors: "Next time I go to Niagara Falls." The epilogue to the film stresses the limited character of American experience, how it is closed off from the European experience of tragedy and remains confined to the commonplace and everyday. Returning on a train from his ordeal, Peter finds a newspaper review of his latest thriller, *Triple Murder:* "Mr. Alison has in a sense overstepped the bounds in the matter of credibility. These things could never by the furthest stretch of the imagination actually happen. And we would wish that Mr. Alison would confine himself to the possible, instead of letting his melodramatic imagination run away with him." Ulmer is obviously having fun with his audience here, using the cheap melodrama of Alison's fiction to set off the genuine European tragedy he has just portrayed in his movie.[40] Indeed, "there are more things under the sun" than American popular fiction comprehends. American book reviewers can imagine only two possibilities: stories of everyday reality or fantastic melodrama. The American imagination is cut off from the true horrors of human existence that European culture has for centuries been daring to explore. As a novelist, Peter Alison is no Fyodor Dostoevsky.

Ulmer seems to be self-conscious about his own peculiar position—working in the pop culture genre of the horror movie while trying to tell a deeply serious tale of European tragedy. That may be why he chooses to juxtapose pop culture with elite culture in his movie. He shows that, as Americans, his hero and heroine cannot understand the very story that Ulmer, as a European, has tried to tell. Yet he also suggests that Americans would be better off turning away from the tragedy of Europe.[41] The ability of Americans to build a better future seems to depend on their shutting themselves off from the tortured European past. Peter and Joan share a remarkable talent for forgetting, of going through the most horrific experiences and remaining unscathed and unscarred. At the end of what ought to have been a deeply traumatic experience for them, they are prepared to laugh it off and get on with their lives. In this respect they contrast sharply with the Europeans Werdegast and Poelzig, who go to their destruction precisely because they cannot forget the past and move on.[42]

The View from Europe

In the end, *The Black Cat* is an oddly self-reflexive film. As an American film made by a European that deals with the differences between America and Europe, it is a work that in effect meditates on its own origins. Ulmer was a European émigré making a film for the American market, and he drew upon everything that he had learned from European cinema to do so. The film becomes strangely autobiographical, or at least self-referential, dealing with what it means to move between Europe and America. Working on the film made Ulmer acutely aware of his European cultural heritage, and yet he chose to portray how problematic that heritage had become by the 1930s for Americans, whose best hope lay in looking forward rather than back in history. The film is a kind of elegy to a European elite culture that seemed to have killed itself off in the cataclysm of World War I and its aftermath. But it is also a tribute to Ulmer's new homeland, the United States, with all its optimism and moral decency and what he hoped might be its immunity to the European disease of corrosive nihilism.

Ulmer's conflicted feelings about his own film surface in what was originally intended to be the ending of *The Black Cat:* as Paul Mandell writes, "The film ends on a light note, but the ultimate in-joke never made the release print. When the Alisons hail a passing bus, the driver was scripted as being none other than Edgar Ulmer, disguised in white beard and goggles. Speaking in Austrian [*sic*], he eyeballs the couple and shakes his head contemptuously. 'Will you take us to Vizhegrad?' asks Peter. 'I'm not going to Vizhegrad,' replies Ulmer. 'I'm going to a sanitarium to rest up after making *The Black Cat* in fourteen days!'"[43] Here is cinematic self-reflexiveness with a vengeance—a moment straight out of Mel Brooks's bag of tricks rather than F. W. Murnau's. With its postmodern archness, this epilogue would have broken the dark mood of the film in a way that the playful scene that really ends it does not.[44] Still, in this projected epilogue, we do catch something of Ulmer's self-consciousness about working in the world of American pop culture. Having grown up in the very different world of European high modernism, he is now in Hollywood making a crazy horror movie on an absurdly short shooting schedule, and it has driven him nearly crazy himself. We can feel both Ulmer's humorous sense of detachment from his work on the film and his concern that the pressures of filmmaking can lead a true artist to madness. Ulmer shows that he is aware that *The Black* Cat is merely a work of mass entertainment, and yet at the same time he hints at how obsessively he labored on it. His mixed feelings about being a European artist working in American pop culture seem to cry out in this would-be comic epilogue.[45]

Ulmer is not unique in his ambivalent view of America from a European perspective. Over the years, many European observers have shared his sense that democratic America has purchased its freedom from the nightmares of Europe's aristocratic and conflicted past only at the expense of its cultural development. In perhaps the best analysis ever written of the United States, Alexis de Tocqueville, writing in the nineteenth century in *Democracy in America,* argues that Americans will have a difficult time equaling European cultural achievements in the arts and sciences.[46] The European tradition of dwelling upon America's lack of elite culture continued unabated into the twentieth century, in such movements as the Frankfurt School's critique of mass entertainment in the United States as a soul-destroying culture industry.[47]

To focus on a single important example: in Martin Heidegger's thought, America functions as an image of everything that Europe is not. It may seem bizarre to link a horror movie like *The Black Cat* with the author of *Being and Time,* and yet the symbolic geography of Heidegger's philosophy bears a curious resemblance to the imaginative map of Ulmer's film. Like Ulmer, Heidegger sees Europe as poised between two hostile and uncomprehending world powers, Russia to the east and America to the west.[48] Also like Ulmer, Heidegger sees Europe as tragically on the brink of perishing of its own self-destructive tendencies: "This Europe, in its ruinous blindness forever on the point of cutting its own throat, lies today in a great pincers, squeezed between Russia on one side and America on the other. From a metaphysical point of view, Russia and America are the same; the same dreary technological frenzy, the same unrestricted organization of the average man."[49] Heidegger's equation of Russia and America may seem odd, but it rests on the idea that these two gigantic nations became the bastions of the common man and antiaristocratic leveling in the twentieth century and thus threatened to undermine centuries of authentic European elite culture. Heidegger's vision is actually far more extreme than Ulmer's, and yet in Werdegast's account of the Great War and his Siberian imprisonment, *The Black Cat* does present Russia as an even more immediate threat to European culture than America; its prison system has destroyed the soul of a cultivated Central European like Werdegast.

Heidegger dwelled upon the dual threat to Europe from the East and the West:

> We have said: Europe lies in a pincers between Russia and America, which are metaphysically the same, namely in regard to their world character and their relation to the spirit. What makes the situation of Europe all the more catastrophic is that this enfeeblement of the spirit originated in Europe itself. . . . All things sank to the same

level. . . . Intelligence no longer meant a wealth of talent, lavishly spent, and the command of energies, but only what could be learned by everyone. . . . In America and in Russia this development grew into a boundless etcetera of indifference and always-the-sameness. . . . Since then the domination in those countries of a cross section of the indifferent mass has become . . . an active onslaught that destroys all rank.[50]

Heidegger spoke these words originally in a lecture delivered at the University of Freiburg in the summer of 1935, that is, roughly one year after Ulmer created *The Black Cat*. As different as the German philosopher and the Austrian American filmmaker undoubtedly were, when they looked at the world in the 1930s they seem to have shared a common sense of European culture in peril.[51] Both Heidegger and Ulmer saw the decay of the aristocratic culture of Europe as proceeding hand in hand with the rise of a democratically leveling culture in the great non-European world powers of the day. With Heidegger in mind, we begin to find something ominous in the way Ulmer portrays the blandness of his Americans in *The Black Cat*. On the meta-level in the movie, American pop culture is obliterating European elite culture—the mass-produced mystery novel is taking the place of the European Gothic tale.

The European ambivalence toward the New World is encapsulated in a brief poetic tribute to America written by Johann Wolfgang von Goethe in 1827 called "To the United States":

America, you're better off than
Our continent, the old
You have no castles which are fallen
No basalt to behold.
You're not disturbed within your inmost being
Right up till today's daily life
By useless remembering
And unrewarding strife.

Use well the present and good luck to you
And when your children begin writing poetry
Let them guard well in all they do
Against knight- robber- and ghost-story.[52]

Drawing upon the same Gothic conventions, Goethe contrasts Europe with America in exactly the terms Ulmer uses in *The Black Cat*. Goethe seems to be celebrating the fledgling United States precisely for the way it differs from Europe. With its castles in ruins, Europe is the land of the dead past; for Goethe, America is the land of the living present. Europe remains in the grip of unproductive memories and "unrewarding strife." Cut off from the nightmares of the European past, America will have the freedom to shape the future. But a hint of condescension is mixed with Goethe's admiration for the United States. When he thinks of Americans, he thinks of children. He hopes that they will be spared the nightmare of ghost stories (*Gespenstergeschichten*), as well as tales of knights (*Ritter*) and robbers (*Räuber*). Yet Goethe's friend and colleague Friedrich von Schiller was famous for a play called *Die Räuber*, and what is Goethe's own masterpiece, *Faust*, if not the greatest of all *Gespenstergeschichten?* The European imagination had fed itself for generations precisely on tales of knights, robbers, and ghosts. Goethe's brief ode to the United States thus quietly sounds a cautionary note. The absence of castles in America points to something lacking in its imaginative horizons. Without antique monuments—a meaningful past and symbols rooted in tradition—how will America find nourishment for its artistic imagination?

Drawing upon European sources of inspiration for an American horror movie, Ulmer was perhaps troubled by the same question. He suggests that Americans might do well to sever their cultural ties to Europe, but at the same time he demonstrates exactly how important those ties have always been to the flourishing of culture in America. We think of Hollywood as an American institution, and yet a look at the film community in the 1930s shows it populated by boatloads of European directors, cinematographers, screenplay writers, actors and actresses, and technicians, without whom the movie industry as we know it would have been impossible. Ulmer hoped to warn Americans against their cultural links to Europe, and yet in *The Black Cat* he introduced them to strange new European imports, such as Bauhaus architecture and Freudian psychoanalysis. Along with all the other European émigrés who directed horror movies in the 1930s, he helped make the avant-garde cinematic techniques of the German expressionists part of the Hollywood mainstream. In the end, Ulmer's aim in *The Black Cat* is internally contradictory—to create a European movie to argue for the cultural independence of America. Fortunately for him and us, this self-defeating quest resulted in a horror movie masterpiece, an unusually thoughtful product of Hollywood that reflects on the relation of popular to elite culture.

8

AMERICA AS WASTELAND IN *DETOUR*

Film Noir and the Frankfurt School

> It is easier for me to say this, coming from Europe, an area where nature
> can be seen as friendly and domesticated, unlike the USA, where nature
> is seen as either to be exploited or to be fled to as a relief from civilization.
> I am continually shocked by the unhumanized nature in this country, no
> parks, no formal gardens. Nature never intended human beings to live in
> the USA—only in just a little bit of Europe and in New Zealand.
> —W. H. Auden, *Lectures on Shakespeare*

In the history of film noir, Edgar G. Ulmer's *Detour* (1945) occupies an
honored place, appearing on many short lists of the classics of the genre,
and frequently cited as the director's best work.[1] At the time Ulmer made
the movie, he was operating on the fringes of the motion picture industry, virtually as an independent producer. Although *Detour* was famously
made in six days and on a low budget, Ulmer delivered a professional piece
of work, showing why he came to be known as the King of the B-Movies.[2]
Despite some signs of haste and cheapness in the production, *Detour* is an
excellent example of film noir.[3] In terms of technique, Ulmer makes use of
many film noir conventions: voice-over narration, unusual camera angles,
and an effective use of lighting that harks back to his training in the 1920s,
when he worked with F. W. Murnau at the peak of German expressionist
cinema. In terms of subject matter, *Detour* tells a typical noir tale of an ordinary, basically decent man who, through a quirk of fate, is drawn into a web
of crime, chiefly as a result of a chance encounter with a femme fatale. The
story unfolds quickly, with a strong sense of inevitability, as every step the
hero takes to avoid his doom only brings him closer to it.

A film noir encyclopedia conveniently offers a summary of the plot of *Detour:*

> Al Roberts is a pianist in a New York nightclub where his girl friend, Sue, is a singer. The two plan to marry, but Sue is ambitious and leaves for "stardom" in Hollywood. Left alone, Roberts calls her one night and Sue tells him that she works as a waitress. He decides to hitchhike West and join her. Eventually, he is picked up by Haskell, who is carrying a lot of cash and driving all the way to Los Angeles. Haskell talks about a female hitchhiker who scratched him viciously when he made a sexual advance. Later, he goes to sleep while Roberts drives. When it begins to rain, Roberts attempts rousing Haskell to put up the convertible top, but Haskell is mysteriously dead, although his head hits a rock when Roberts accidentally causes the body to fall out of the car. Roberts, believing the police will never accept his innocence, hides the body and drives on alone. The next day Roberts picks up Vera, initially unaware that she is the same woman who scratched Haskell. Questioning him about the man's death, she does not believe Roberts' story but agrees to remain silent if he will follow her plans. Arriving in Los Angeles, they rent a room; and Vera plans that Roberts will sell the car using Haskell's identity. But when she discovers that Haskell was the heir of a dying millionaire and that his family has not seen him for years, she plans to pass Roberts off as Haskell. That night they quarrel about this scheme, and Vera runs into the other room threatening to call the police but collapses drunkenly on the bed with the telephone cord entwined about her neck. Roberts pulls on the cord from the other side of the locked door, inadvertently strangling her. Without even seeing his fiancée, Roberts flees to Reno, where he sits in a diner and reflects on the strange circumstances that have put him in such a hopeless situation.[4]

Deconstructing the American Dream

Even in such a bare summary, the bitterness and cynicism of *Detour* are clearly evident. The film systematically deconstructs the American dream. The hero's quest for happiness—to find simple contentment with the woman he loves—leads only to his corruption and eventually to his destruction (he is being arrested as the film ends). Like any good American, Roberts (Tom Neal) wants to make a better life for himself, and his chance encounter with Haskell (Edmund MacDonald) seems to give him the opportunity, providing him with all the external signs of success in American terms: a luxury automobile, a fancy suit, and a wad of cash in his pocket. Roberts seems able to trade places with the outwardly successful Haskell; he can step right into Haskell's clothes: they fit him perfectly. But all these newly acquired material goods turn out to be a burden to Roberts and are what trap him into committing further crimes.

The full polemical thrust of Ulmer's film becomes evident when one realizes that he is using *Detour* to restage a particular archetype of the American dream. As a hitchhiker headed for California, Roberts is following Horace Greeley's immortal injunction to Americans: "Go west, young man." But no pot of gold, real or metaphoric, awaits Roberts at the end of the California rainbow.[5] His girlfriend, Sue (Claudia Drake), has preceded him to Hollywood and failed to achieve her dream of becoming a star as a singer. Haskell turns out to be a two-bit chiseler and gambler, whose dream of a big payoff at a West Coast racetrack ends with his body lying somewhere in the Arizona desert. Vera (Ann Savage), who dreams of making a fortune with a con game at the expense of the legitimate heirs in the Haskell family, ends up strangled in a hotel room. Everywhere one looks in *Detour,* the American dream, particularly of striking it rich, turns into a nightmare, and the West—traditionally the land of opportunity in American mythology—is revealed to be in truth the land of shattered dreams.[6]

Thus *Detour* is an anti-Hollywood film in both a general and a specific sense. It serves as a counterweight to the typical product of the Hollywood dream factory. Ulmer inverts a standard pattern of Hollywood romance, in which a young couple must go their separate ways in order to pursue their independent goals in life, but in the end are happily reunited, usually with their goals accomplished and their love intact and even deepened as a result of the obstacles they have encountered and overcome. That Ulmer had the narrative clichés of Hollywood romance in mind is evident in the script of *Detour.* At one point Roberts is contemplating how things might work out with Vera, and imagines a variety of stock Hollywood happy endings: "If this were fiction, I would fall in love with Vera, marry her, and make a respectable woman of her. Or else she'd make some supreme Class-A sacrifice for me and die. Sue and I would bawl a little over her grave and make some crack about there's good in all of us."[7] The implication of these lines is clear: "If this were fiction. . . . but it isn't." Ulmer establishes the realism of his film by contrasting it with the fantasy and sentimentality of standard Hollywood melodrama.[8]

But Ulmer goes further—he is debunking not just the generic Hollywood version of the American dream, but the dream of Hollywood itself. Early in the story, Sue decides to advance her singing career by leaving New York for the West Coast: "I want to try my luck in Hollywood." Roberts tries to prevent her from pursuing this empty dream: "Don't you know millions of people go out there every year and wind up polishing cuspidors?" Aware of the deceptive allure of Hollywood, Roberts later tries to console Sue over the phone when she finds that reality does not measure up to dreams in California: "Those guys out in Hollywood don't know the real thing when it's right in front of them." At the beginning of the film, Roberts thinks that he can distinguish reality from illusion, even if Hollywood talent scouts do not know the real thing when they see it. But as he journeys west, Roberts gradually loses his grip on reality and allows himself to be drawn into pursuing a dream as false as anything generated in Hollywood.

By creating an anti–fantasy film, Ulmer is criticizing Hollywood for serving up illusions to the American public, always telling them that their dreams will come true if they just try hard enough and get a lucky break or two. He is specifically criticizing Hollywood for offering itself as its most potent fantasy. The greatest myth the film industry ever created is the myth of being discovered in Hollywood (preferably at Schwab's Drugstore) and becoming a star overnight. We know how a movie like *Detour* would have ended in the hands of the average Hollywood studio. Sue would get her big break as a singer, make the most of it, and use her newly acquired wealth to get Roberts out of his predicament. In the last scene, he would be making his long-delayed debut as a concert pianist at Carnegie Hall, with Sue in the audience cheering him on. But at every turn Ulmer thwarts the plot expectations his audience has inherited from standard Hollywood fare. "This is the way life really is," he seems to be saying, "not the way you see it in the movies."[9]

Eminent Émigrés

It would be easy to give a straightforward biographical interpretation of *Detour*.[10] Ulmer had more reason than most to distrust the Hollywood dream: for a time he lived it, and then suddenly he lost it all. Having emigrated to Hollywood in the early 1930s after some earlier experience in the film industry, Ulmer got his big break when Universal chose him to direct *The Black Cat* (1934)—a major assignment, considering the fact that it was to be the first project to unite the studio's two most famous horror movie stars, Bela Lugosi and Boris Karloff. *The Black Cat* was a triumph for Ulmer. Many consider it one of the most sophisticated and powerful horror movies ever made; and, more to the point, with Lugosi and Karloff giving perhaps their best screen performances, and certainly their best together, the film was a box office success: it "proved to be Universal's hit of the season, with a profit of $140,000."[11] Ulmer's future in Hollywood seemed bright. But, in a turn that eerily anticipates the lurid plot twists of his own later movies, Ulmer had an affair with the wife of a nephew of Carl Laemmle, the head of Universal. The resulting divorce and Ulmer's marriage to the woman he loved led to his being banished from the Universal lot. Laemmle was so powerful in the industry that Ulmer was effectively exiled from Hollywood for over a decade, thus sending him off on his checkered career as a more or less independent filmmaker, or at least one operating largely outside the major studio system. Thus, Ulmer had personal experience of the elusiveness of the Hollywood dream, and reason to criticize a system that had at first embraced and then rejected him. One could justifiably read *Detour* as the work of a man bitterly disillusioned with Hollywood, determined to get his artistic revenge with a film that exposes the illusory character of the typical Hollywood fantasy and presents Hollywood itself as the biggest illusion of them all.

But even though *Detour* may have grown out of Ulmer's personal experience, to view the film as solely a product of his private vendetta against Hollywood would be to reduce its power. To see how *Detour* transcends merely personal issues, we need to place it in the larger cultural and intellectual context of its day. In retrospect *Detour* appears to be an act of what has come to be known as culture critique. In its attitude toward America in general and Hollywood in particular, Ulmer's film displays remarkable affinities with the thinking of the Frankfurt School. Discussing *Detour* and the Frankfurt School together will illuminate the two: the ideas of the Frankfurt School will help clarify what Ulmer is saying about Hollywood in *Detour,* and Ulmer's film will in turn help us understand the impulses behind the Frankfurt School and the whole movement of culture critique.

The Frankfurt School is named after the location where the members of the Institute for Social Research (*Institut für Sozialforschung*) first gathered. Founded in Frankfurt am Main, Germany, in 1923, and Marxist in its orientation, the Frankfurt School nevertheless drew on the whole German intellectual tradition, including Kant, Hegel, Nietzsche, and Heidegger, and also was heavily influenced by Freud. Among the figures associated with the Frankfurt School over the years were Theodor Adorno, Walter Benjamin, Erich Fromm, Max Horkheimer, Leo Lowenthal, and Herbert Marcuse.[12] Because the Frankfurt School associates were left-wing intellectuals (several of the founders were members of the Communist Party), they were forced to flee Nazi Germany in the 1930s, especially since many of them were Jewish or of Jewish ancestry. Those who managed to leave Germany safely generally emigrated to the United States, mostly settling in New York, but some moving on to Los Angeles.[13] Adorno, for example, ended up living during World War II in the Brentwood area of greater Los Angeles, and Horkheimer in Pacific Palisades, thus placing them just west of Hollywood.[14] As refugees from Nazi Germany, the Frankfurt School members were generally welcomed by the Hollywood community and thus had something in common with Ulmer in terms of their initial experience of the United States.[15]

The Culture Industry

The central work of the Frankfurt School is *Dialectic of Enlightenment* by Horkheimer and Adorno, first published in German in 1944 as *Dialektik der Aufklärung*. The best-known chapter of this book, and the one most relevant to *Detour*, deals with Hollywood—"The Culture Industry: Enlightenment as Mass Deception." As this title indicates, Horkheimer and Adorno set out to present Hollywood as a fountain of illusions, just the sort of dream factory Ulmer has in mind in *Detour*: "The culture industry perpetually cheats its consumers of what it perpetually promises. The promissory note which, with its plots and staging, it draws on pleasure is endlessly prolonged; the promise, which is actually all the spectacle consists of, is illusory: all it actually confirms is that the real point will never be reached, that the diner must be satisfied with the menu. In front of the appetite stimulated by all those brilliant names and images there is finally set no more than a commendation of the depressing everyday world it sought to escape."[16] In general, the Frankfurt School marks a turn in twentieth-century Marxism from an economic to a cultural critique of capitalism. The Frankfurt School thinkers were smart enough to see that orthodox Marxism was losing the economic argument against capitalism. Traditionally Marxists had claimed that capitalism would lead to the progressive impoverishment of the masses. By the 1940s, despite the significant setbacks of the Depression, the standard of living of workers in capitalist countries had risen substantially since the days of Marx—Adorno speaks of "the greater abundance of goods within reach even of the poor."[17] The idea of "the poor with a greater abundance of goods" is one of those marvelously paradoxical concepts twentieth-century Marxists have come up with. It was especially difficult for someone moving from Europe to Southern California to conclude that Americans were materially worse off because of capitalism. Adorno and other members of the Frankfurt School had to find a way of showing that the abundance of commodities capitalism produces is in fact bad for the masses—that, although people seem to be materially enriched by capitalism, they are really being spiritually and culturally impoverished.[18] The work of the Frankfurt School came to focus on culture critique, on analyzing the harmful effects of the commercial culture of capitalism, especially insofar as it takes the form of mass culture.

Accordingly, "The Culture Industry" attempts to show that motion pictures, with their links to commercial advertising, are the capitalist equivalent of totalitarian propaganda. In an argument that has become familiar and widely accepted, Horkheimer and Adorno claim that the motion picture industry manipulates and even controls the American public. It gives the appearance of merely providing people with what they want, but in fact it creates the desires that it claims to be satisfying. In the view of Horkheimer and Adorno, Hollywood is always foisting unwanted products onto a gullible public: "It is claimed that standards were based in the first place on consumers' needs, and for that reason were accepted with so little resistance. The result is the circle of manipulation and retroactive need in which the unity of the system grows ever stronger. . . . The man with leisure has to accept what the culture manufacturers offer him" (121, 124). Horkheimer and Adorno present American audiences as the passive victims of an all-powerful entertainment industry that manipulates them as cleverly (and cynically) as fascist dictators. In a remarkable variant of the moral equivalence argument, they claim that "the bourgeois . . . is already virtually a Nazi" (155). Later they compare "the spread of popular songs" to the rapid diffusion of Nazi propaganda slogans (165), and in a truly bizarre passage they equate the radio transmission of a Hitler speech with an NBC broadcast of Arturo Toscanini conducting a symphony (159).[19]

The Big Casino

The Frankfurt School's view of the American public offers many parallels to the vision of life in the United States that Ulmer develops in *Detour*. Critics have often noted the passivity of the characters in film noir and particularly in *Detour*—the way their lives seem to be governed by forces beyond their control. The characters in *Detour* seem incapable of generating authentic desires. They are always setting their goals on the basis of the models that American society offers them, and, as we see quite literally in the case of Roberts, their aim becomes to step into the shoes of the other guy only because he is a type admired by the community. Ulmer strongly suggests that Hollywood is the principal source of these images of desire, shaping the dreams that govern the average person's life. Similarly, Horkheimer and Adorno view the entertainment industry as capitalism at its most exploitative, inducing people to spend their hard-earned money on forms of amusement that they could easily do without and that they never wanted in the first place.[20] But for the Frankfurt School the sinister role of capitalism extends beyond merely dumping unwanted goods on a hapless public. Itself the ultimate expression of capitalism, the entertainment industry seeks to provide an ideological justification for capitalism, to help make the system as a whole function and sustain its power over the masses.

To accomplish this purpose, as the Frankfurt School understands it, the entertainment industry must reconcile the masses to the system that exploits them and thus prevent them from even thinking about rebelling against it. With this end in view, Hollywood creates a mass cultural myth of hope, tantalizing the American people with the prospect of bettering their lives and escaping from their downtrodden condition. Hollywood manufactures a picture of society as a kind of giant lottery in which anyone might win the big payoff. The vast majority of individuals in the capitalist system may have to live with being exploited and accept their passive roles as losers, but if they can be bombarded with striking images of winners, of people who have been lucky enough to beat the system, they can live on in hope that they too might someday cash in on good fortune and join the magic circle of the successful. Horkheimer and Adorno see that the culmination of this image of society as a lottery is the myth of success in Hollywood itself. A key passage in "The Culture Industry" is worth quoting at length:

Al Roberts (Tom Neal) and Vera (Ann Savage) learn that life is a big gamble in Edgar Ulmer's *Detour*. (PRC/Photofest)

Not everyone will be lucky one day—but the person who draws the winning ticket, or rather the one who is marked out to do so by a higher power—usually by the pleasure industry itself, which is represented as unceasingly in search of talent. Those discovered by talent scouts and then publicized on a vast scale by the studio are ideal types of the new dependent average. Of course, the starlet is meant to symbolize the typist in such a way that the splendid evening dress seems meant for the actress as distinct from the real girl. The girls in the audience not only feel that they could be on the screen, but realize the great gulf separating them from it. Only one girl can draw the lucky ticket, only one man can win the prize, and if, mathematically, all have the same chance, yet this is so infinitesimal for each one that he or she will do best to write it off and rejoice in the other's success, which might just as well have been his or hers, and somehow never is. . . . Increasing emphasis is laid not on the path *per aspera ad astra* (which presupposes hardship and effort), but on

winning a prize. . . . Movies emphasize chance. . . . [Moviegoers] are
assured that they are all right as they are, that they could do just as
well and that nothing beyond their powers will be asked of them.
But at the same time they are given a hint that any effort would be
useless because even bourgeois luck no longer has any connection
with the calculable effect of their own work. (145–146)

Just like Horkheimer and Adorno, Ulmer portrays an America obsessed
with the lottery idea, of striking it rich. Haskell is literally a gambler; significantly, the horse he intends to bet on at Santa Anita is named "Paradaisical"
[*sic*], pointing to the American hope for heaven on earth. But all the main
characters in *Detour* are, in one way or another, gamblers, and Sue's story
suggests that Hollywood may be the biggest gamble of them all. Ulmer wants
to efface the distinction between gambling as an illicit or illegal activity and
gambling as a part of everyday life in America—perfectly symbolized by the
way the decent citizen, Roberts, seamlessly steps into the role of the bookie,
Haskell. Vera and Roberts play cards to pass the time while waiting to sell
Haskell's car. And the film is narrated from Reno, Nevada, where Roberts
ends up in his effort to escape Los Angeles—Reno, the capital of legal gambling in the United States at the time *Detour* was made. When one adds
up all the instances in the film, Ulmer seems to be presenting gambling as
the American way of life, or rather the idea that the American way of life is
fundamentally a gamble.

Mechanical Reproduction

The core of the Horkheimer-Adorno critique of American culture is that
it is a mass phenomenon and that in order to reach wide audiences the
entertainment industry has to mechanize and merchandise culture. Here
they were drawing upon Walter Benjamin's well-known essay "The Work of
Art in the Age of Mechanical Reproduction."[21] Benjamin argues that in the
modern world the work of art is losing its unique aura because it is being
reproduced ad infinitum by a capitalist economy—packaged, advertised, and
thus commodified. Adorno, who was a musicologist and a composer, was
particularly interested in how this process was playing out in the world of
music. He adamantly defended the virtues of live performance; he objected
to presenting the musical classics in recorded form. As we have seen in his
strange equation of Hitler and Toscanini, he even objected to radio broad-

casts of live performances. Adorno believed, with some justification, that only when people are physically present at a live performance can they experience the full impact of the music. He was not impressed by the counterargument that radio and records were making classical music available to multitudes of listeners in a way that was impossible in the nineteenth century.[22] For Adorno, great classical music is inevitably compromised by any effort to make it widely accessible. He was struck by the fact that radio stations play both classical and popular music and was disturbed by hearing performances by Toscanini right next to performances by Guy Lombardo (143).[23]

Adorno believed that America was corrupting the sublime achievements of European composers by effacing the distinction between classical and popular music: "The jazz musician Benny Goodman appears with the Budapest string quartet, more pedantic rhythmically than any philharmonic clarinetist, while the style of the Budapest players is as uniform and sugary as that of Guy Lombardo" (136). Here Adorno actually claims that the playing style of the Budapest String Quartet was contaminated by contact with American popular culture. Above all, he inveighed against jazz, America's distinctive contribution to world music.[24] For Adorno, jazz summed up everything that is vulgar and debased in American culture, and he was particularly appalled by jazz arrangements of classical music: "No Palestrina could be more of a purist in eliminating every unprepared and unresolved discord than the jazz arranger in suppressing any development which does not conform to the jargon. When jazzing up Mozart he changes him not only when he is too serious or too difficult but when he harmonizes the melody in a different way, perhaps more simply, than is customary now" (127).

One would not expect to find this kind of sophisticated argument about classical music translated into cinematic terms, especially in a B-movie, and yet that is just what Ulmer does in *Detour*.[25] As the film opens in a roadside cafe in Nevada, the first music we hear comes from a jukebox—the Benjaminian technological nightmare par excellence. Roberts reacts violently to the jukebox music and wants it turned off. He is upset because the song reminds him of his lost love, Sue, but, almost as if he were a member of the Frankfurt School himself, he also seems to be reacting against the sheer mechanical reproduction of the music. In the first of the many flashbacks that make up the movie, we see by contrast Roberts performing live as a pianist in a small jazz combo with Sue as the vocalist. But when the set is over and Roberts is performing for himself, he is playing classical music—Chopin's Waltz in C-sharp Minor, op. 64, no. 2. Sue addresses him: "Mr. Paderewski,

I presume. It's beautiful. You're going to make Carnegie Hall yet, Al." Ulmer sketches in the background quickly, but the basic story is clear. Roberts has aspirations of being a great classical pianist like Paderewski and performing in the high temple of classical music, Carnegie Hall. But for the moment, his aspirations are thwarted and he must earn a living playing jazz for the paying customers in a cheap nightclub. Ulmer reinforces the point: the next scene begins with Roberts playing Brahms's Waltz in A-flat Major, op. 39, no. 15, but after a few bars he begins to jazz it up, launching into a full-scale boogie-woogie version of Brahms's original delicate melody. Roberts earns a ten-dollar tip from a nightclub patron for prostituting his art and Brahms's. It almost seems as if Ulmer had been reading Adorno.

But Ulmer did not need Adorno to teach him about classical music. It was his lifelong passion, and he was extremely knowledgeable about it. His daughter, Arianné Ulmer Cipes, reports that at one time he wanted to be a conductor; perhaps as compensation for not becoming one, he sometimes used a baton when directing his actors.[26] He was friends with some of the most famous classical musicians of the twentieth century. For example, the Hungarian conductor Fritz Reiner was godfather to Ulmer's daughter. With Reiner's connections, Ulmer made the film *Carnegie Hall* (1947), which features a remarkable number of major figures in classical music, including Jascha Heifetz, Arthur Rubinstein, Gregor Piatigorsky, Leopold Stokowski, Bruno Walter, Ezio Pinza, Lily Pons, and Reiner himself. Although low budgets constrained Ulmer, he tried to make the most of the musical scores in his movies. *The Black Cat,* for example, contains some of the most effective and inventive uses of classical music in any Hollywood score.[27] It draws upon some classical warhorses, such as Tchaikovsky's *Romeo and Juliet* and Bach's Toccata and Fugue in D Minor, but it also includes unusual orchestrations of solo piano works, which are used in Wagnerian fashion as leitmotifs—for example, Liszt's Sonata in B Minor and Brahms's Rhapsody in B Minor, op. 79, no. 2.

Civilization and Barbarism

It may be hard to believe that the man who created movies with such titles as *Girls in Chains* (1943), *The Man from Planet X* (1951), *The Daughter of Dr. Jekyll* (1957), *Naked Venus* (1958), and *The Amazing Transparent Man* (1959) was a highly cultivated aficionado of classical music, but Ulmer certainly was. This fact helps suggest an explanation for the otherwise puzzling affinities between Ulmer and the Frankfurt School. Sometimes the resemblances can be uncanny. Ulmer's daughter describes his background: "He was a European intellectual who had based most of his thinking on the great minds of the German language, only to find that it led to a stupid monster of an Austrian painter named Hitler. For the rest of his life he tried to understand how civilization could end up in barbarism." This formulation seems to echo Benjamin's famous statement in his "Theses on the Philosophy of History": "There is no document of civilization which is not at the same time a document of barbarism."[28] Horkheimer and Adorno offer a similar formulation of their task in *Dialectic of Enlightenment:* "It turned out, in fact, that we had set ourselves nothing less than the discovery of why mankind, instead of entering into a truly human condition, is sinking into a new kind of barbarism" (xi). But despite what appear to be verbal echoes of the Frankfurt School in reports of Ulmer's thinking, I have been unable to uncover evidence of any direct link between him and Horkheimer or Adorno. I would not, however, rule out the possibility because, through the Hollywood connection, their circle of acquaintances probably overlapped.

Setting aside the question of direct or indirect contacts between Ulmer and Horkheimer or Adorno, we do know that the three men grew out of the same intellectual and cultural milieu and thus might well have been expected to think alike, especially about the United States. The similarity between Ulmer and the members of the Frankfurt School went well beyond a common passion for Austro-German classical music. Ulmer also grew out of the same political tradition; his daughter says that "he was part of the socialist revolutionary beliefs of his European era." Ulmer was well educated—in his youth he studied architecture and philosophy in Vienna. His daughter points out that "he loved Thomas Mann, Schiller, and Goethe." Thus, he had the same literary tastes as the Frankfurt School. The mention of Thomas Mann is especially significant, since Adorno was closely associated with Mann. For example, he helped with the musicological details of Mann's novel *Doktor Faustus* (1947), which tells the story of a twelve-tone composer, loosely modeled on Arnold Schoenberg. In short, even if Ulmer never heard of Horkheimer and Adorno, his intellectual profile was remarkably similar; in the 1930s, he was known around Hollywood as "the aesthete from the Alps."[29]

Thus, Ulmer together with Horkheimer and Adorno provide examples of products of European elite culture reacting to the vulgarity of American popular culture. All three were well positioned to be critical of culture in the United States, to measure it by the sophisticated standards of European culture and find it wanting. But as outsiders they also were prone to misunderstand and misinterpret American culture. However intelligent and insightful they may have been, they sometimes lacked an insider's feel for American culture; it was easy for them to miss its nuances and hence whatever complexities it might embody. Their reaction to American popular culture was also colored by their status as displaced persons in the United States (this was truer of Horkheimer and Adorno than of Ulmer, who came to America earlier and more voluntarily). Having been plunged into an alien environment—and what could be more alien than the bizarre world of Hollywood?—they inevitably had problems adjusting, and it is no wonder that they found themselves repelled by many American phenomena. Their largely grim vision of America reflected their own alienation. In *Detour,* Ulmer portrays America as a land of lonely drifters, homeless and perpetually on the move. This may have corresponded to the reality of America (particularly during the Depression),[30] but it corresponded even more closely to Ulmer's own situation as a European émigré. Having left his homeland to come to the United States and then finding himself exiled from Hollywood, he must have experienced a strong sense of displacement, which then translated into his film noir vision of individuals alienated from the landscape and the community.[31]

This dark vision of the rootlessness of America is perhaps the most interesting point of convergence between Ulmer and the Frankfurt School. Europeans have always been struck by the mobility of Americans and have often reacted negatively to it. What looks like freedom to Americans looks like chaos to Europeans. Coming from more centrally ordered and hierarchical societies, many Europeans have difficulty appreciating the quintessentially American desire to be able to go one's own way. In particular, Europeans are often puzzled by Americans' devotion to—some might say their obsession with—their cars. Europeans prefer trains, with their fixed routes and rigid timetables, whereas Americans long for the freedom of the open road— significantly called the freeway in Los Angeles. Europeans frequently sing the praises of public transportation while condemning the extravagance and wastefulness of that most private of vehicles, the automobile. Socialists in particular hate the automobile; for them it has often served as the ultimate symbol of capitalism. All this suggests why the Frankfurt School members who ended up in Southern California must have felt—despite the climate—that they had been plunged into some kind of hell specially reserved for European socialists. Woody Allen has shown in *Annie Hall* (1977) that for someone who cannot drive, Los Angeles is indeed hell, and Adorno never learned to drive.[32] It is therefore revealing that Adorno often reacts negatively to precisely those aspects of American culture that center around the automobile.

On the Road Again

Adorno's book *Minima Moralia* (1951)—written during his stay in Los Angeles in the mid-1940s and, hence, right at the time of *Detour*—is filled with reflections on the peculiar mobility of Americans and its effect on their culture. When Adorno looks at the United States, what he sees is a country criss-crossed by empty roads: "[The roads] are always inserted directly in the landscape, and the more impressively smooth and broad they are, the more unrelated and violent their gleaming track appears against its wild, overgrown surroundings. They are expressionless. . . . It is as if no-one had ever passed their hand over the landscape's hair. It is uncomforted and comfortless. And it is perceived in a corresponding way. For what the hurrying eye has seen merely from the car it cannot retain, and the vanishing landscape leaves no more traces behind than it bears upon itself" (48). Adorno could see the positive side of this kind of scene, mentioning the "beauty of the American landscape: that even the smallest of its segments is inscribed, as its expression, with the immensity of the whole country" (49). Still, as a European used to a densely populated countryside, he was obviously intimidated by exactly what Americans have always cherished—the wide-open spaces from sea to shining sea.

Adorno was also repulsed by what he saw growing up alongside all those endless American roads: the culture of motels and drive-in restaurants. He inveighs against the poor service in the United States, contrasting American technical efficiency with the old-fashioned elegance he was used to in Europe:

> The division of labour, the system of automatized facilities, has the result that no-one is concerned for the client's comfort. No-one can divine from his expression what might take his fancy, for the waiter no longer knows the menu. . . . No-one hastens to serve the guest, however long he has to wait. . . . Who would not prefer the "Blauer Stern" in Prague or the "Österreichischer Hof" in Salzburg, even if he had to cross the landing to reach the bathroom, and was no

longer woken in the small hours by unfailing central heating? The nearer the sphere of immediate physical existence is approached, the more questionable progress becomes, a Pyrrhic victory of fetishized production. (117)

This passage reveals how much Adorno's critique of America grows out of unabashed nostalgia for an aristocratic European past.[33] His ultimate nightmare is a peculiarly American institution, the drugstore lunch counter: "the drugstore, blatantly a shop, behind whose inhospitable counter a juggler with fried-eggs, crispy bacon and ice-cubes proves himself the last solicitous host" (117). As Nico Israel writes, "The word 'snob' flies off of the page in passages like these."[34] Adorno may have a legitimate point about the shabbiness of American tourist establishments, but it seems odd for a Marxist to use the standard of European luxury hotels, the exclusive preserve of a wealthy elite, in order to condemn the simple lunch counters of 1940s America, which tried to make restaurant food available at a price anybody could afford. As in his criticism of the music broadcasting and recording industry, Adorno seems to condemn America principally for making available to the masses (albeit in adulterated form) what was reserved for a privileged elite in Europe.

Home on the Range

Ulmer does not seem to share Adorno's snobbishness and elitism,[35] but he does have a very similar vision of America. *Detour* opens with a shot of an empty road stretching out to the horizon in an empty landscape, and that scene becomes typical of the film.[36] *Detour* revolves around the automobile. The plot centrally deals with the efforts of Roberts and Vera to sell a stolen car. That eventually takes them to the most distinctively American of all institutions—the used-car lot. Much of the film consists of characters talking in a moving car, first Roberts and Haskell, then Roberts and Vera. Hitchhiking from the East Coast to the West, Roberts becomes the perfect symbol of American mobility. In Ulmer's distinctively European vision of the United States, there is nothing between New York and Los Angeles— just a vast wasteland. Like the Frankfurt School refugees, Ulmer lived a bicoastal existence in America, with New York and Los Angeles essentially constituting the sum total of his experience of the United States. At most in *Detour* one finds Reno between the coasts, "the biggest little city in the world," as its famous advertising sign proclaims (glimpsed in the film)—a sort of reproduction of Los Angeles or New York in the middle of the desert, which is to say in the middle of nowhere.

It is extraordinary how empty the American landscape is in *Detour*—miles and miles of bleak and inhospitable terrain. All Roberts encounters on his journey west are gas stations, motels, roadside cafes, and finally the one locale that sums up everything Adorno despised about America—a drive-in restaurant, where he and Vera can eat without ever leaving their car.[37] Above all, Roberts must always keep moving. For him life in America has turned into an endless journey, and as the film concludes he is being picked up by a passing police car. Ulmer presents Roberts as epitomizing the rootlessness of America. When he tries to settle down in an apartment with his "wife," Vera, it is, of course, a complete sham. Vera can only sarcastically refer to it as "home sweet home." Roberts spends most of the film separated from his real fiancée, Sue, and they are forced to communicate—or not communicate—by phone. When Roberts finally manages to get to the West Coast, he finds that he is still separated from Sue: "Far from being at the end of the trip, there was a greater distance between Sue and me than when I started out!" There are no families anywhere in *Detour*—in Ulmer's vision, America is a land of atomistic individuals. The truck driver (Pat Gleason) looking for companionship who approaches Roberts at the beginning of the film stands for all Americans: "I ain't got nobody at all." In the eyes of a European socialist, this is the ultimate result of American capitalism—it destroys community and isolates the individual.

It would, of course, be wrong to dismiss Ulmer's vision in *Detour* simply as a European misperception of America. The United States *is* a land of highways, motels, and roadside restaurants, and the mobility of Americans is genuinely one of their distinguishing characteristics. The vision of America as perpetually on the move is by no means restricted to European observers. An episode of the television series *The X-Files* entitled "Drive" (1998) is very similar to *Detour* in the way it allegorizes the American landscape. Due to a government experiment gone awry, the main character of the story must keep moving in a speeding car; and, just as in *Detour*, he must specifically keep heading west until he reaches California (with even more disastrous results—in this case, his head explodes when he "runs out of west," as the episode puts it).[38] *The X-Files* is an American television show, but it is just as capable as any European source of identifying rootlessness as the fundamental condition of the United States. Still, in evaluating the truthfulness of Ulmer's vision of America in *Detour*, it is worth bearing his European origins in mind. Even for a film noir, *Detour* presents an extraordinarily bleak view of the United States, and one might with some justification question whether the American landscape is quite as empty as Ulmer pictures it or as devoid of positive human interaction. What is quite literally absent from Ulmer's view is the American heartland—just the portion of the landscape with which a bicoastal European émigré is least likely to be familiar.[39]

Under European Eyes

Thus, while granting a degree of genuine insight into the American condition to both Ulmer and the Frankfurt School—a perceptiveness enabled precisely by their position as outsiders—one must also wonder whether their status as aliens did not also work to color, cloud, and even distort their view of the United States. Horkheimer and Adorno sometimes seem to be devoid of sympathy for American culture. They appear to be tone deaf to its distinct accents; they seem to miss the point of a Donald Duck cartoon in a way that someone native to the American scene would not.[40] Above all, their insistence on the uniformity of American popular culture is exactly the reaction of someone positioned outside a culture, someone who lacks an insider's ability to differentiate among its productions.[41] It is ironic that much of the academic study of American popular culture to this day is still heavily influenced by the approach developed by Horkheimer and Adorno back in the 1940s as displaced persons in the United States. We should not ignore their largely negative judgments about American culture, but we need to take such judgments with a grain of salt, when we realize how much they were rooted in European cultural elitism and specifically a haut-bourgeois nostalgia for an aristocratic past.

Similar doubts arise about the validity of the film noir vision of America—and not just in the case of Ulmer's *Detour*. We tend to think of film noir as an American cultural development; and, to be sure, the classic noir films were generally made in Hollywood and have American settings. Their plots were often derived from American detective novels, such as *The Maltese Falcon* and *The Big Sleep*.[42] But if one views the director as central to the creation of a movie, suddenly film noir begins to look about as American as apple strudel. Many of the great noir films were directed by Europeans, including, to name just some of the most famous in addition to Ulmer: Curtis Bernhardt, John Brahm, Michael Curtiz, William Dieterle, Alfred Hitchcock, Fritz Lang, Rudolph Maté, Max Ophuls, Otto Preminger, Robert Siodmak, Josef von Sternberg, Charles Vidor, Billy Wilder, and William Wyler. However American the subject matter of film noir may seem to be, it was often presented through European eyes behind the camera, and the formal characteristics of the genre owe more to European than to American directors, above all, to the masters of German expressionist cinema.[43]

Why is it important to stress the European roots of film noir? Many film analysts have treated the genre as indigenous to the United States and hence as an accurate reflection of the realities of life in twentieth-century America.[44] Certainly the dark vision and even nightmarish quality of these films give a glimpse into the American psyche and its fears and anxieties when confronted with some of the traumatic developments of the 1930s, 1940s, and 1950s, such as the Depression, the rise of totalitarianism, World War II, the Cold War, and the threat of nuclear annihilation. Yet one must be careful in talking about the "realism" of film noir given that the genre is so highly stylized and so clearly involves imposing a set of narrative and other conventions on its subject matter.[45] To the extent that these conventions were European in origin, they may have distorted the American reality that they purported to represent. In short, in viewing film noir we may not be getting, as some critics have supposed, an unmediated look into the heart and soul of America. Rather, because in film noir we are often looking through European eyes, we may be getting an unduly negative and pessimistic view of the American way of life. Film noir may be one more example of a long tradition of European anti-Americanism, or at least a tendency to fault the United States for failing to measure up to European standards of civilization and culture.[46]

Here the parallels between Ulmer's *Detour* and the Frankfurt School are genuinely informative, since in both cases we can see how the very sophistication of European observers can blind them to whatever is positive in American commercial culture. It tells us something about film noir that a classic of the genre corresponds so closely to the vision of America in the work of a group of German left-wing intellectual émigrés. This consideration helps explain the otherwise curious fact that the supposedly American genre of film noir has a European name. It is well known that it took the French to "discover" film noir and establish it as a topic for serious aesthetic analysis. Perhaps a European sensibility was needed to appreciate film noir critically because the genre embodied a European sensibility in the first place. The alienation that European film noir directors portray as characteristic of Americans may be their own alienation as refugees projected outward onto what was for them a foreign landscape. A typical film noir depicts characters who feel lost in a bewildering world in which familiar guideposts have disappeared and they no longer know the rules of the game. What is this if not the archetypal experience of a European refugee in 1940s America? In creating a classic of American cinema in *Detour,* Edgar Ulmer drew deeply upon his European experience as a displaced person.

Appendix: Who Is the Author of *Detour*?

When I originally wrote and first published this chapter, I was unaware that *Detour* is based on a novel of the same name, which was written by Martin Goldsmith and published in 1939. In 1944, Goldsmith sold the movie rights to the story to Producers Releasing Corporation (PRC). He went on to write the screenplay and is listed as the author in the credits to the film. I should have made note of this fact, but like many commentators on *Detour* I was so interested in the film as a work by Ulmer that I failed to consider the possibility that someone else might have had a hand in its creation. As it happened, none of the books on film noir that I consulted at the time referred to Goldsmith's contribution as novelist and screenplay writer. The neglect of Goldsmith is a good example of the potentially distorting effect that the auteur theory may have on the history of film. The French theorists who "discovered" Ulmer in the 1950s presented him as the epitome of their concept of the auteur: a director who managed to impose an individual and idiosyncratic visual style on his films, despite working with severely limited resources—a true artist with a unique vision of the world that can be traced from one film to another in his checkered career.

Having been heavily influenced by the auteur approach to Ulmer, I was surprised when rewriting this chapter to learn from Noah Isenberg's book on *Detour* that its plot and many of its thematic motifs can be traced back to a literary source. This fact obviously forces us to reconsider the common view that Ulmer was the sole creator of *Detour*. More specifically, it seems at first to offer strong evidence against my claim that the film embodies a European sensibility. If its basic plot elements must be credited to an American author, how European can *Detour* be? Fortunately, I had acknowledged in the original version of this chapter that film noir was heavily influenced by American sources, especially the hard-boiled detective fiction of authors such as Raymond Chandler and Dashiell Hammett.[47] As its style clearly shows, Goldsmith's novel grows out of this tradition. One can hear the voice of the standard private dick when Goldsmith's hero says, "Why, that car was so hot, whoever drove it would have to wear asbestos drawers."[48] Thus, the genesis of *Detour* actually illustrates the widely accepted theory of the dual origins of film noir I have been presenting: *Detour* is a European director's recreation of a work of American hard-boiled fiction. I decided therefore to let this chapter stand largely in its original form, but to add an appendix analyzing what Goldsmith's contribution to *Detour* might tell us about the film. I was pleased to discover that the novel was reprinted in 2006—presumably in response to interest in Ulmer's film, since the cover of the reprint uses the original poster for the movie, not the novel's original cover. In addition, I found that *Scenario: The Magazine of Screenwriting Art* had published Goldsmith's screenplay in 1997, thus facilitating comparisons among the original novel, the screenplay, and the movie version of *Detour*.

Scenario offers the *Detour* screenplay in a polemical spirit: "Martin Goldsmith adapted the screenplay from his own novel, and his shooting script was written before a director was even hired! So why is *Detour* always and solely credited to Edgar Ulmer?"[49] In a brief, unsigned essay entitled "Auteur Detour," the journal goes on to insist that "only a slavish devotion to the director-as-auteur-theory . . . would allow for the view that *Detour* is the work of anyone other than Martin Goldsmith" (181). But *Scenario* offers very little evidence for this claim, relying mainly on quoting this dubious argument from C. R. Portz in his essay "The Working Class in Film Noir": "Goldsmith was from New York City, Ulmer from Vienna. Ulmer was a set director, Goldsmith a novelist. Ulmer spoke very poor English, Goldsmith was a fast-talking cynical New Yorker. Goldsmith was hanging out with other writers such as John Fante, Jim Thompson, and James Cain. Ulmer was making musicals. If Ulmer had been the controlling force on *Detour*, it would have been an extremely different film" (181). Following the logic of Portz's argument, one might suppose that if Ulmer had been fully in charge of *Detour*, it would have ended up a musical, perhaps a Viennese operetta. The absurdity of this claim is obvious. As the auteur critics have convincingly shown, *Detour* bears the unmistakable stamp of Ulmer's visual style. Portz's evidence is largely irrelevant, highly selective, and sometimes just plain wrong. Ulmer did not speak "very poor English"; as his interviews show, he was fluent in English, although he spoke it with a heavy accent. As for the issue of associates, Ulmer's acquaintance with the likes of F. W. Murnau, Max Reinhardt, and Fritz Reiner probably trumps Goldsmith's pairing with John Fante, Jim Thompson, and James Cain.

264 Edgar G. Ulmer

Scenario is no doubt correct in emphasizing Goldsmith's role in the genesis of *Detour,* but one begins to suspect that *The Magazine of Screenwriting Art* is indulging in a little special pleading for its profession when it goes to the extreme of denying the director any role in the film's creation. *Scenario* seems to assume that, if one can locate a novel or a well-written screenplay behind any film, then the writer, not the director, must be credited as its creator. According to this logic, *The Searchers* (1954) is not the creation of John Ford, but of Alan LeMay (the novelist) or Frank Nugent (the screenwriter); and Mario Puzo, not Francis Ford Coppola, is the auteur of *Godfather I* (1972) and *II* (1974). This approach flies in the face of everything we know about the art of moviemaking.

Moreover, *Scenario* may not have its facts right. Isenberg, who seems to have researched the matter with greater care, gives a different account of the genesis of the shooting script of *Detour:*

> What [Goldsmith] produced was an elaborate, meandering text that would have required shooting a film with a run time of some two and a half hours; indeed, more than twice the length of the sixty-eight minutes to which the film would finally be restricted. With seasoned input from associate producer/writer Martin Mooney, who had many PRC productions under his belt, and from Ulmer himself—who would later take much of the credit and rather emphatically dismiss Goldsmith's novel as "a very bad book"—the script was pared down to a manageable length. Entire sections had to be tossed out, others radically revised.[50]

Isenberg's account raises a serious question about what exactly *Scenario* published. The journal speaks indiscriminately of the "screenplay" and the "shooting script" of *Detour,* but which did they publish? In his biography of Ulmer, Stefan Grissemann supports Isenberg's account of the genesis of *Detour* and outlines several stages in the evolution of its screenplay. He claims that Goldsmith's original version was 144 pages long and that the second version was reduced to 69 pages.[51] The version that *Scenario* published is 42 pages long, with double columns and fairly large type, suggesting that it may be the second version, perhaps the shooting script rather than the original screenplay, which means in turn that this version may already embody Ulmer's contributions.

Contrary to what *Scenario* says, Grissemann insists that once Ulmer was assigned to *Detour* he did have a role in shaping the script. Grissemann quotes

Ulmer's wife, Shirley, saying that he rewrote the script daily while the film was being made. Grissemann claims that Ulmer and Goldsmith in fact quarreled about the changes the director was making, particularly about the large cuts on which he insisted. As evidence for this point, Grissemann cites the fact that years later, in the 1960s, when Ulmer contacted Goldsmith about remaking *Detour,* the novelist insisted on restoring the story lines Ulmer had cut.[52] To turn the tables on Portz: Grissemann's account suggests that if Goldsmith, rather than Ulmer, had been the controlling force on *Detour,* it would have been an entirely different film—something much closer to the novel.

The controversy over the authorship of *Detour* shows how complicated, and even murky, such disputes can become. Ulmer's own account is terse: "Martin Goldsmith, the brother-in-law of Tony Quinn, wrote a very bad book called *Detour.* I took it to Martin Mooney, and rewrote the script."[53] *Scenario* counters with the testimony of Ann Savage, the actress who played Vera. Praised for her performance, she replied, "I must also give Mark Goldsmith credit.... It was all there in the script" (181). But, as Isenberg points out, on another occasion, Savage gave the credit to Ulmer: "Without his direction, *Detour* would have been just another B."[54] That Hollywood personalities may make inconsistent statements about film history should come as no surprise.

On balance, Isenberg's and Grissemann's accounts of the genesis of *Detour* seem truer to the norms of Hollywood production. Screenplay and story credits in the movie industry are legal fictions, often a matter of delicate contract negotiations and later disputes and Screen Writer's Guild arbitration. Thus, the fact that Goldsmith is solely credited with the screenplay of *Detour* does not mean that he was in fact its sole author. *Scenario* claims that Ulmer had no hand whatsoever in the shooting script. It would be very unusual in Hollywood for a film's director not to have any role in shaping its shooting script. The main point is that neither Goldsmith nor Ulmer should be credited as the sole author of *Detour.* The film was, as is typical in Hollywood, a collaborative effort.

As Isenberg and Grissemann explain, the movement of *Detour* from novel to screenplay to movie was a process of progressive compression, during which much of Goldsmith's material was jettisoned for the sake of greater focus. In the novel, Sue's story is as fully developed as Al's. The book alternates between scenes of Sue's experiences in Hollywood and Al's efforts to join her there. Even the screenplay gives more scenes to Sue than the movie does. The result of all this editing down is to make the film focus on Al's highway journey in a way that the novel and even the screenplay do not.[55] To be sure, the highway setting is in the novel. Its hero, named Alexander Roth, does say early in the story, "Instantly I realized that I was safe as long as I was on the highway and moving," and later he speaks of the "three thousand miles of highway separating me from Hollywood and Sue."[56] The screenplay also includes the highway setting; it opens with a scene of Al hitchhiking, and it calls for this landscape: "A desolate expanse of desert highway with the setting sun on the horizon, and, in the foreground, a dusty joshua tree with a great vulture perched on it."[57] In short, Ulmer's "desolate highway" comes from Goldsmith, but by eliminating so many other scenes from the novel and the screenplay, Ulmer made the open road the focus of *Detour* in a way that Goldsmith did not.[58] This result is, of course, partly the inevitable outcome of moving from the page to the screen. Obviously, Ulmer's film dwells on and elaborates the visual aspects of the highway setting in a way that Goldsmith's novel and screenplay cannot.[59] Thus, the notion of *Detour*'s reflecting Ulmer's European obsession with America as a nation of highways remains valid. It is Ulmer's cinematic visualization of the story that creates the distinctive image of America as a wasteland in *Detour*. The seeds of this image are present in the novel and the screenplay, but it took Ulmer's vision as a director to make it blossom—and that vision was European.

To Goldsmith's credit, he does develop one aspect of the story in the novel as fully as Ulmer does in the film—the critique of Hollywood. Because of all the scenes unique to the novel in which Sue has to deal with vain actors and corrupt agents, Goldsmith actually takes the anti-Hollywood theme further than Ulmer does. The idea of Hollywood as a dream factory is, if anything, even more pronounced in the novel. Sue talks at length about her disillusionment with the film community: "Then that wave came over me, that sudden suspicion it was all a hoax, a frame-up by the publicity-greedy studios and the Chamber of Commerce to lure people out here, away from their regular jobs, their families and friends. The lies of the movie maga-zine's [*sic*], the lush literature of railroad companies and the exaggerated salaries the press agents announced, all combined to bait one of the foulest traps imaginable. And I was one of the little mice it had captured."[60] The unreality of Hollywood is encapsulated in Sue's vision of her Hollywood apartment: "You felt that if you stood in the center of the living-room and shouted: 'Strike it, boys!' the whole place would fold up and disappear like a set in a very few seconds."[61] Passages such as these remind us that it did not take German émigrés from the Frankfurt School to figure out that not everything in Hollywood should be taken at face value. As several critics have noted, Goldsmith's book has much in common with Nathaniel West's homegrown anti-Hollywood novel *The Day of the Locust* (1938), which also stresses the illusory character of the movie industry.[62]

Thus, despite Ulmer's evident contempt for Goldsmith's novel, he did derive something from it, especially its treatment of Hollywood (although Ulmer hardly needed Goldsmith to teach him about the dark side of the movie business). Even some of the visual details in *Detour* most praised by auteur theorists turn out to be indebted to Goldsmith. Many critics have noted the moment in the film when Vera falls asleep while Al is driving; the position of her head exactly parallels that of Haskell when he similarly dozes off earlier in the film. This visual echo is supposed to be a sign of Ulmer's genius as a director, but it is clearly spelled out in Goldsmith's novel: "The girl must have been pretty tired because she fell asleep not twenty minutes after she stepped into the car. She lay sprawled out with her feet on her little overnight-case and her head resting against the far door—like Haskell."[63] Another famous visual moment in *Detour* is the flashback that is generated out of Al's image reflected in the car's rearview mirror. This visual effect is, in fact, specified in the screenplay.[64] Given the uncertainty about Mooney's and Ulmer's contributions to the version of the screenplay published by *Scenario,* we cannot be sure if this visual touch should be credited to Goldsmith. All one can say with certainty is that the published screenplay is a professional job, containing many efforts to visualize specific cinematic effects, some of which Ulmer followed in the finished product.

Even this brief analysis of the journey of *Detour* from novel to screenplay to film provides an object lesson in the pitfalls of the auteur approach to cinema. Like many, I originally allowed my enthusiasm for Ulmer to blind me to Goldsmith's significant contribution to the film. It is tempting to romanticize Ulmer as the lonely, misunderstood, underrated bad-boy genius of Hollywood—a director who struggled single-handedly against the entire motion picture industry to create something artistic rather than commercial. But in fact Ulmer worked within the Hollywood system (even if on its fringes); and, like many directors, he benefited artistically from collaborating with others in the creation of his films. As recent commentators have stressed, Martin Goldsmith deserves a place in the story of *Detour.* Anyone who wishes to study *Detour* seriously needs to read Goldsmith's novel and screenplay. Neglecting this material, one risks attributing to Ulmer artistic decisions that were at least in part guided by Goldsmith.

Having acknowledged Goldsmith's contribution, one should, however, make an important aesthetic distinction. Goldsmith's *Detour* is a second-rate novel, whereas Ulmer's *Detour* is a first-rate film. I very much doubt that anyone today would read Goldsmith's novel with interest if it were not connected to Ulmer's film. It is a common pattern in artistic history to find first-rate works being created out of second-rate sources. Many people are surprised to learn that Shakespeare created very few of his plots on his own; he generally worked with material from earlier fiction, poetry, and even drama. A good measure of Shakespeare's genius is to compare his version of *King Lear* with his many sources, including the old play on the subject from which he took several of the most important details of his plot. In the case of Alfred Hitchcock, scholars have carefully studied the literary sources for many of his movies and noted how he consistently improved upon them.[65] Perhaps we can go so far as to suggest that it is a law of artistic history that great works of art are usually based on second-rate sources. There is, after all, generally little reason—and little maneuvering room—to recreate a great work of art in another medium, although it has occasionally been done, as witness Verdi's *Otello* and *Falstaff*. Drawing on second-rate sources can liberate an artist to produce something new and brilliant, far surpassing the original.

Ulmer is not in the league of Shakespeare, or even Hitchcock, but he is superior to Goldsmith as an artist. Thus, we should not let our discovery of the sources of *Detour* undermine our sense of Ulmer's achievement in the film. Today people who read Goldsmith's novel do so only after having seen Ulmer's film, usually several times, since they are mostly Ulmer scholars. Thus, it is difficult to avoid viewing Goldsmith's novel through the lens of Ulmer's film. We inevitably pick out and emphasize just those elements that Ulmer himself chose to highlight, and may be tempted to credit those emphases to Goldsmith in the first place. It is fair to say that Goldsmith's *Detour* contains as much of a critique of Hollywood as Ulmer's. But when it comes to the vision of America as a wasteland of highways, it is doubtful whether anyone reading Goldsmith's novel on its own would come away with that impression. For that view, one needs the stark and powerful images that Ulmer dwells on in the film.[66] Even though these highway images are nascent in Goldsmith's novel, just reading it would not fix them in one's mind. These highway images are, however, exactly what sticks in one's mind after watching the movie version of *Detour*. Thus, the film's distinctive view of America as a wasteland should still be credited mostly to Ulmer and related to his European perspective and his visual style as a director.

Part Four

9/11, GLOBALIZATION, AND NEW CHALLENGES TO FREEDOM

INTRODUCTION TO PART FOUR

The terrorist attacks of 9/11 tested the resilience of America in many areas, even in popular culture. The heavy loss of life at the World Trade Center and the Pentagon evoked a complex reaction of grief, anger, and bewilderment in the American people. The difficult moment generated all sorts of anxieties about the future of America. Still, it was surprising how quickly the media commentators turned to the question of the future of popular culture. Within a day or so, the experts were speculating about how 9/11 would change the course of movies and television. They were all sure that it would, and quickly a consensus emerged that American pop culture would shake off years of irony and cynicism and return to the kind of patriotism and championing of traditional values that characterized World War II movies. A few voices cautioned against jumping to conclusions so soon after the shocking events, and it was hard not to detect a hint of special pleading in the media prophets. Many seemed to be certain that the effect of 9/11 would be to bring about whatever changes in American pop culture they themselves had long desired.

I found it strange that people were worrying about the future of movies and television at a time when many more important issues were at stake. I remember wondering, "On December 8, 1941, did anybody care how Pearl Harbor was going to affect their favorite movie stars?" Subsequent research has taught me that in fact concerns about popular culture, especially the movie industry, did surface almost immediately after the U.S. entry into World War II. I should have realized that in a moment of national crisis, the fate of movies and television would be on the minds of many Americans. In my work on the subject, I had noticed that cultural issues had begun to trump political issues in the United States or, rather, that cultural issues had become the new political issues. The fact that the future of movies and television came up so frequently in the anxious discussions about the consequences of 9/11 was proof that culture had become a central concern in twenty-first-century American public discourse.

I did, at least, immediately realize the importance of the post-9/11 debates about pop culture. Accordingly, I began to collect articles on the subject as they appeared, especially from my favorite source, *TV Guide*. My archival efforts saved many prophecies that might have otherwise gone down the memory hole of history, particularly since the people who made them have little motivation to recall them today. I quote extensively from this mini-archive in chapter 9.

The story of the relation between 9/11 and popular culture has much to teach us, and I can touch on only a few of the principal issues in this part. First and foremost, the many predictions made in September 2001 about the fate of films and television provide an object lesson in the unpredictability of popular culture. The media pundits predict one thing; the creative people in the media often go off in an entirely different direction. To give just one example: In the fall of 2001 many experts were saying that 9/11 would spell the doom of reality TV programming. But a decade later, reality TV is more prevalent than ever. In retrospect, the premature obituaries for reality TV look like a case of wishful thinking. The pundits who confidently predicted its demise disliked reality TV and used the occasion of 9/11 to deal it what they hoped would be a deathblow.

This is a good example of how members of the cultural elite who take it upon themselves to pronounce sweeping judgments on popular culture often turn out to be out of touch with the American people. These pundits talk about popular culture as if it were something monolithic and easy to comprehend in simple formulas. They want to say, "X has happened in the real world; Y will be the result in popular culture." But the responses to 9/11 in American film and television illustrate the fact that popular culture can be a very complex phenomenon that often confounds the simplifications of the experts. Pop culture does not march in lockstep with the world around it. That is another way of saying that pop culture remains a realm of human freedom. Because movies and television shows are sometimes made by genuinely creative individuals, the form they take is in principle unpredictable. I acknowledge that media experts were under enormous pressures in the wake of 9/11, but the way they confidently made predictions that we now know were far off the mark should teach humility to anyone aspiring to be a cultural prophet.

The aftermath of 9/11, especially the War on Terror it provoked, raises many of the questions about freedom that have been central to this book. We began with a part on the Western that analyzed the tension between freedom and order in America's vision of itself on the frontier. We saw that Americans value their freedom, above all, their ability to go it alone, but they also recognize the dangers of that kind of liberty and worry that it may lead to violence and prove incompatible with a settled social order. The importance of the Western in popular culture reflects its ability to explore the trade-offs between freedom and order that run throughout U.S. history. The War on Terror has revived this age-old American debate in a particularly urgent form. In the face of international terrorism, do Americans have to sacrifice some of their cherished freedom—especially traditional civil liberties—in order to be protected against new threats to social order? Or, to rephrase the question: has the War on Terror asked Americans to give up the very freedom it is supposed to be defending? These are not simple questions, and they do not have simple answers. To the credit of American popular culture, post-9/11 films and television shows have sometimes responded to these questions with subtlety and insight, appreciating the complexity of these issues and trying hard to sort out solutions to what they recognize to be genuinely deep dilemmas. In this section, I discuss the way some films and television shows have responded to what they perceive to be new threats to freedom in the wake of 9/11.

Immediately after 9/11, many commentators expressed the hope that popular culture would become a cheerleader for American values and a booster for defending them against foreign threats—in short, that it would return to its predominant mode during World War II and the Cold War. In fact, movies and television shows have not generally fallen into this one-sided response. They have instead chosen to air both sides of the debate over freedom versus order. One of my favorite shows, *The X-Files,* the one I discuss at greatest length in my earlier book, *Gilligan Unbound,* became one of the initial subjects of the post-9/11 debate about popular culture. Many commentators singled out *The X-Files,* with its powerful antigovernment message, as an example of the kind of program that would have to go in light of 9/11. Go it did, in the spring of 2002, but whether it left the air *because* of 9/11 is a question I examine in this part. I argue that the commentators who proclaimed the irrelevance of *The X-Files* in the wake of 9/11 missed the fact that the show was in fact profoundly relevant to what happened on 9/11—so much so that, in March 2001, in its spin-off, *The Lone Gunmen,* it even came eerily close to predicting the exact details of the attack on the World Trade Center in a way that spooked several government agencies (not to mention the *X-Files* producers themselves). Far from fading into obscurity, as its critics confidently predicted, *The X-Files* has remained a fundamental reference point in American popular culture. In the decade since it ended, *The X-Files* has spawned a remarkable series of imitations, strongly suggesting that it still resonates with the anxieties of the American people. And, as I show in my analysis of its concluding episode, "The Truth," *The X-Files,* in a way that is deeply rooted in American tradition, chose to champion freedom and civil liberties in the wake of 9/11.

Together with other international developments, 9/11 forced Americans to rethink their self-conception as a nation with open borders. As we saw in the previous chapters on Edgar Ulmer, immigrants have always contributed greatly to American popular culture, and it has accordingly often portrayed immigration in a favorable light. But the issue of immigration turns out to be a variant of the broader issue of freedom versus order. The success of immigrants in the United States is one of the greatest tributes to the freedom it offers its citizens. But over the years, many Americans have wanted to restrict immigration, viewing it as a threat to order in the United States. In the increasingly globalized world of the late twentieth and early twenty-first centuries, the issue of immigration has come to the fore in American politics. The threat of international terrorism has only increased some Americans' anxieties about the porousness of U.S. borders. In my final chapter, on what I call "un-American Gothic," I analyze a number of television shows, beginning with *The X-Files,* that reflect American fears about globalization and specifically immigration. I argue that television shows about imaginary invasions by extraterrestrial aliens encode very real concerns about illegal aliens in America. Again to the credit of American popular culture, these programs strive to avoid oversimplifying the issues they raise and instead recognize the genuine complexity of the immigration question. They present their aliens as monstrous, but at the same time they frequently display sympathy for these aliens precisely for being alienated, that is, for not fitting in to the American mainstream.

The immediate effects of 9/11 on American pop culture were quite noticeable. Some movies halted production, some television shows retooled, comedians became very cautious about what they made fun of—all because, understandably, no one in the media wanted to offend the sensibilities of the American people. But the long-term substantial changes that the experts predicted at the time failed to materialize. Rather quickly, movies and television basically returned to business as usual. A decade later, movies and television shows that portray government agencies and activities unfavorably are probably more prevalent than they were in the 1990s. The paranoid conspiracy mode of *The X-Files* has become routine on American TV. The domestic consequences of the War on Terror, together with the prolonged U.S. involvement in Iraq, Afghanistan, and other countries, has generated new concerns about the overextension of government power. In short, 9/11 did not cause American popular culture to settle into a straightforward and comfortable support of U.S. government policy, as many media pundits in 2001 predicted it would. Some might regret this outcome, but I take it as evidence of the resilience of American popular culture. Faced with great pressures to conform, many creative people in movies and television maintained their oppositional stance. At its best, pop culture has always reflected freedom of thought in America and has refused to bow to conventional opinion, including the prevailing government ideology. While recognizing that freedom has its problematic aspects, American popular culture has nevertheless chosen to speak up on behalf of the liberty that is the nation's most precious heritage. In that respect, the response to 9/11 in movies and television exemplifies a long-standing and admirable American tradition.

9

THE TRUTH IS STILL OUT THERE

The X-Files and 9/11

> What does this science fiction have to do with anything?
> —Special Agent Kallenbrunner, "The Truth"

From the beginning it was difficult to separate the significance of the events of 9/11 from the significance of the media representation of them. The impact of what happened that day was bound up with the fact that it largely took place on live television, with the whole world watching. The terrorists who planned the attack no doubt were counting on media coverage to magnify its impact and thus to achieve their sinister purposes. With the media rushing to cover such a shocking event, their commentary quickly turned into meta-commentary, as they began to discuss not just the event itself, but also how they were covering it. Within days, if not hours, of the event, media commentators began speculating about how 9/11 would affect American popular culture. At times, the talking heads on television seemed concerned as much about the cultural impact of 9/11 as about its political, economic, and military implications.

The End of Irony?

Under the stress of a profoundly traumatic event, the media experts were understandably tempted to make apocalyptic pronouncements. Soon a consensus seemed to emerge: *after 9/11, American popular culture would never be the same again.*[1] Cynicism about America was out; patriotism would return to movies and television. The mood of the moment was crystallized in a *Time* magazine article by Roger Rosenblatt entitled "The Age of Irony

Comes to an End" (September 16, 2001). In words that resonated throughout the mediasphere, Rosenblatt powerfully argued that "one good thing could come from this horror": Americans would wake up from three decades of insisting that "nothing was to be believed in or taken seriously." In opposition to a postmodernist attitude that "nothing was real," the events of 9/11 would serve as a reality check for Americans: "The planes that plowed into the World Trade Center and the Pentagon were real. The flames, smoke, sirens—real." From this perception, Rosenblatt went on to predict a return to patriotism: "The greatness of the country: real."[2] Rosenblatt's eloquent rhetoric struck a responsive chord in America, especially among those who had long felt that movies and television were letting down their country, failing to offer images embodying its traditional values and instead debunking its icons of national greatness. The heroic responses to the 9/11 crisis by firefighters, police, military personnel, and ordinary citizens were genuinely inspirational and, many commentators argued, would serve as new and invigorating models for American popular culture. Many predicted that the traditional all-American hero would soon be returning to movie and television screens.[3]

The events of 9/11 certainly had an immediate impact on television. In the first few days following, broadcasting schedules had to be hastily reshuffled. For example, the Fox Network cancelled a showing of the movie *Independence Day* (1996) advertised for September 15. The movie's trademark shot of the White House exploding was exactly what Americans did not want to see so soon after witnessing all-too-similar disasters in the real world.[4] Late-night talk show hosts such as David Letterman and Jay Leno were candid about their reluctance to go ahead with their normal comedy routines at a time when the nation was more inclined to grieve than to laugh.[5] To focus on a trivial reflection of a very serious situation: the wacky family sitcom *Malcolm in the Middle* (2000–2006) had to retool. Since its beginning the show had featured a subplot involving Francis (Christopher Masterson), the oldest son in the family, being exiled to a military academy. The show mercilessly satirized this institution as fascist, with a particularly repellent commandant named Edwin Spangler (Daniel von Bargen), a grotesque caricature of an authoritarian personality. When the sitcom began its third season on November 11, 2001, it took only a week for the show to find a way for Francis to flee the military school and head to Alaska to work at a resort. I may have been the only person to make anything of this development at the time—the country had more important things on its mind—and

I have never seen any explanation from the producers of the series. Yet I cannot help thinking that Commandant Spangler was a casualty of 9/11. In its own small way, *Malcolm in the Middle* confirmed what commentators like Rosenblatt had argued. After 9/11, one of the most cynical shows on television now drew the line at making fun of the military in any form.

The mainstream of popular culture—especially television—may have changed its tone in the immediate aftermath of 9/11, but the spirit of the American people is not easily contained and controlled. The cultural elites had passed a death sentence on irony, but it was by no means clear that the American public was ready to carry it out. Popular culture always has a way of colonizing new media, especially when they offer greater freedom of expression. As a result, since the 1990s a good deal of American popular culture has migrated to the Internet. And it was to websites and e-mail that one had to turn in mid-September 2001 to get a fuller picture of how Americans were reacting to the terrorist attacks and to see that, despite everything else they had lost, Americans had not lost their sense of humor.

One hesitates to repeat in print the obscene and cruel jokes that almost immediately began circulating about Osama bin Laden via e-mail, and the computer-generated graphics suggesting how to deal with him and al-Qaeda soon proved that American ingenuity—and irony—were still very much in play. Irony began to resurface in semirespectable public venues with surprising speed. The splendidly irreverent and politically incorrect satirical online newspaper *The Onion* quickly decided not to pull its punches. As early as its September 26, 2001, issue, it ran several tasteless but hilarious headlines: "U.S. Vows to Defeat Whoever It Is We're at War With," "American Life Turns into Bad Jerry Bruckheimer Movie," and "Hijackers Surprised to Find Selves In Hell: 'We Expected Eternal Paradise for This,' Say Suicide Bombers." By October 4, *The Onion* was even making fun of the national obsession with how the events of 9/11 would affect popular culture in a story headlined "A Shattered Nation Longs to Care about Stupid Bullshit Again." As the article explained:

> Three weeks after the horrific attacks that claimed more than 6,000 lives, many Americans are wondering when their priorities will finally be in the wrong place again. Some are wondering if their priorities will *ever* be in the wrong place again.
>
> "In the aftermath of this horrible tragedy, people find themselves cruelly preoccupied with the happiness and well-being of their loved

ones, unconcerned with such stupid bullshit as the new Anne Heche biography or Michael Jackson's dramatic comeback bid," said Dr. Meredith Laufenberg, a psychologist and family therapist at UCLA Medical Center. "Who knows how long it will be before things are back to normal?"[6]

In short, the cultural elite may have prematurely proclaimed the end of irony because they were looking in the wrong places in an American popular culture that had found new outlets and had become increasingly decentered and diversified. But even the mainstream media could not do without irony for long. I would date the official end of the end of irony to a much-publicized exchange on NBC's *Saturday Night Live* (September 29, 2001) between the show's executive producer Lorne Michaels and then New York City mayor Rudolph Giuliani. Seeming to reflect the somber mood of a chastened entertainment industry, Michaels was seeking official sanction to return to business as usual in comedy from the man who more than anyone had come to personify the agony of New York in the wake of 9/11. Michaels soberly asked the mayor, "Can we be funny?" In a soon-to-be legendary reply, Giuliani said with a straight face, "Why start now?"[7] We were expecting Giuliani to answer as the mayor of New York, perhaps saying something statesman-like: "We have been through a lot, Lorne, but we do need to maintain our sense of humor." But instead, Giuliani replied as "the mayor of New York," a character in a comedy sketch scripted for him by the *SNL* writers.

Here was irony in its most postmodern form: Giuliani self-consciously playing himself, and playing himself for laughs. And for most New Yorkers, as well as most of the nation, this exchange showed that irony can be cathartic. Precisely because it gives us some distance on our emotions, it can help us come to terms with them. The commentators calling for the end of irony had forgotten that it has a healthy role to play in any culture. That is why irony has such a long history, stretching back at least as far as the ancient Greeks. Before calling for the end of irony, commentators might have remembered that its most famous practitioner was a man named Socrates.

From what we saw of *South Park* (1998–) in chapter 6, it should come as no surprise that it quickly chose to deal with 9/11 and its aftermath, and to do so with irony and irreverence. Just two months after 9/11, on November 7, 2001, the show aired an episode called "Osama bin Laden Has Farty Pants" (#509), in which it contrived to send its four young heroes to

Afghanistan to confront their counterparts among Afghani children.[8] As its title indicates, this episode takes the terrorist leader, who by this time had been elevated in the media to quasi-mythic status, and treats him with the utmost contempt, cutting him down to size with the force of sheer ridicule. The show suggests that the best way to deal with bin Laden would be just to kill him, in as humiliating a fashion as possible. Accordingly, *South Park,* in full Looney Tunes mode, casts bin Laden as Elmer Fudd and Cartman as Bugs Bunny and subjects the terrorist to one embarrassing scene after another, culminating in the exposure of the tininess of his genitalia. Finally, bin Laden is executed by an American soldier putting a gun to his head, in a moment that eerily anticipated his actual fate ten years later.

At the same time, however, the show satirizes various forms of what it presents as overreaction to the terrorist threat in the United States. It shows the boys forced to wear gas masks to school and subjected to the sort of searches that were becoming mandatory in many areas of American life. A television news report speaks of how "more and more cases of terrorist-related AIDS continue to grow." The episode repeatedly points to the exaggerations, distortions, and misinformation being spread by the media in the wake of 9/11. It also makes fun of the political rhetoric that 9/11 generated. The boys are in Afghanistan to return a goat sent from there by four children, in return for the four dollars the American children had sent to Asia on the recommendation of President Bush. Ever the diplomat, Cartman explains to the Afghani children about the goat: "It was choking on the sweet air of freedom in America, so we brought it back to your crappy country."

At a time when Americans were honestly wondering how people from other countries could possibly hate the United States, *South Park* had the daring to suggest that the reason might be that the United States was involved in military operations all around the world. Considering how soon this episode aired after 9/11, it is remarkable how far it goes in challenging received opinion on terrorism. One of the boys even expresses sympathy for terrorists when he first arrives in Afghanistan: "No wonder terrorists come from places like this! If I grew up here, I'd be pissed off, too!" The boys try to defend the United States to the Afghanis: "Do you really think your civilization is better than ours? Your people play games by killing animals, and oppress women!" But *South Park* allows the Afghani child to make a sharp retort: "It's better than a civilization that spends its time watching millionaires walk down the red carpet at the Emmys!" Even the American boys have to admit, "He's got us there, dude."

As we saw in chapter 6, *South Park* can be surprisingly evenhanded in treating issues, and here it distinguished itself by considering how the war in Afghanistan must have looked to the other side. Nevertheless, even *South Park* felt compelled to end this episode on a patriotic note. One of the boys rescues an American flag from desecration in Afghanistan and says, "America may have some problems, but it's our home. Our team. And if you don't want to root for your team, then you should get the hell out of the stadium." This may sound like a cop-out, but actually *South Park* makes an important point. One can be patriotic and still question some of the policies and attitudes of one's country. Here, as elsewhere, the show insists that to be critical of America is not necessarily to be anti-American. In the climate of opinion generated by 9/11, it was useful to remind Americans of their long tradition of tolerating dissent on the most heated and controversial political issues.

Perhaps the most significant and complex case study of the impact of 9/11 on American popular culture is provided by *The X-Files* (1993–2002). In its eight-season run leading up to the fall of 2001, *The X-Files* exemplified what media critics had in mind when they complained about a negative attitude toward government in American popular culture. One of the show's mottoes was "Trust No One," and that meant especially trust no one in government. The show features two FBI agents, Fox Mulder (David Duchovny) and Dana Scully (Gillian Anderson), who are presented as heroic, but only because of their independence from the government—their constant willingness to disobey the orders of their superiors and go it alone in their pursuit of truth and justice. Over the years, *The X-Files* portrayed the FBI and other government agencies, such as the Federal Emergency Management Agency (FEMA), as alternately incompetent or sinister. In the seemingly contradictory terms of the show, government agencies are either incapable of handling the simplest problems or involved in complex conspiracies and cover-ups. In the central plot arc of the series, the FBI and other government agencies are shown to be manipulated by a shadowy syndicate masterminding a projected alien takeover of the planet, which involves, among other nefarious schemes, the federal government spying and experimenting on American citizens against their will and without their knowledge. *The X-Files* raises doubts about the conduct of the U.S. government throughout the Cold War, often presenting its actions as morally equivalent to those of its evil enemies. In a number of episodes, the show takes a cynical attitude toward the first Gulf War, even going so far as to suggest that Saddam Hussein was a puppet of the United States—indeed, its creation.

Thus, if any show was going to run into problems with a changed American public in the wake of 9/11, it was going to be *The X-Files,* and Fox chose to delay the beginning of its ninth season by several weeks. In the event, its ratings plummeted in the 2001–2002 season, with the show averaging 8.5 million viewers, down from 13.2 million in the previous season and from a peak average of 18.3 million in 1996.[9] By January 2002, the creator-producer of *The X-Files,* Chris Carter, could see the handwriting on the wall and made the decision to pull the plug on the series. When its last episode aired in May 2002, many commentators chose to view *The X-Files* as another casualty of 9/11. In a thoughtful—and appreciative—article on the show, Andrew Stuttaford argued that 9/11 had relegated *The X-Files* to the dustbin of history: "the *X-Files* is a product of a time that has passed. It is a relic of the Clinton years as dated as a dot-com share certificate, a stained blue dress or Kato Kaelin's reminiscences." Echoing Rosenblatt and other media pundits, Stuttaford accused the series of not taking life seriously, pointing to its "cynicism, irony, and a notable sense of detachment." He added, "This is a show where, for all the drama, no one seems genuinely involved—even with each other. . . . This is Po-Mo Sci-Fi. . . . It is *Seinfeld* with flying saucers, another show, ultimately, about nothing. Nothing serious, anyway." Invoking 9/11 as having transformed the world, Stuttaford dismissed the series as having become irrelevant in the twenty-first century: "The *X-Files* was a show for self-indulgent, more complacent times, an entertainment for *before.*"[10]

TV Prophets of Doom

Sorting out causality in the realm of culture is notoriously difficult, and an argument like Stuttaford's risks falling into the fallacy of *post hoc, ergo propter hoc.* Merely because the popularity of *The X-Files* began to decline after 9/11 does not prove that a change in the American public's attitude toward government was responsible for the show's demise. To his credit, Stuttaford admitted that other factors may well have been at work. Nine seasons is a long time for any television series to survive. *The X-Files* is in fact the longest-running science fiction show in TV history (by comparison, the original *Star Trek* lasted only three seasons). Well before 9/11, media critics began wondering whether the 2001–2002 season would—and should—be the last for *The X-Files.*[11] Many argued that the show had suffered a significant decline in quality ever since its fifth season, or at least since its seventh. For a show that often depended on the shock value of its episodes, *The X-Files* was running out of novel plot twists. Moreover, casting problems threatened to doom the show once its stars, David Duchovny and Gillian Anderson, began to lose interest in continuing in their roles. In the eighth and ninth years of the show, this uncertainty left its creators unable to plan out whole seasons in advance, as they had done so successfully in the past. Duchovny's absence from all but the final episode of the ninth season was probably enough by itself to sink the series. The attempt in the eighth season to introduce two new FBI agents to pick up the slack from Mulder and Scully never really caught on with *X-Files* fans. In short, the show had probably run its course by the 2001–2002 season, and attempts to attribute its demise to a post-9/11 change in mood in the American public probably overemphasize the importance of sociopolitical factors.

More to the point, if Stuttaford's thesis were correct, *The X-Files* should by now have long since slipped off the pop culture map. Instead, a significant segment of the public continues to be very interested in the show. *The X-Files* has been highly successful in syndication and is still rebroadcast regularly on several channels in the United States and on the BBC in Britain. DVDs of the show have also sold very well in various forms of packaging and repackaging. Despite Stuttaford's confident prediction, *The X-Files* has not gone the way of Kato Kaelin, ending up as a mere footnote in pop culture history. On the contrary, *The X-Files* has emerged as a permanent feature of the American pop culture landscape. New television shows and movies continue to draw upon its legacy and refer to it in implicit and explicit ways.[12] Far from being made outdated by 9/11, *The X-Files* actually pioneered a model of what post-9/11 popular culture would be like. Some critics were saying this even in the immediate aftermath of 9/11. An October 23, 2001, *New York Times* article on how horror movies might have to change after 9/11 quotes Robert J. Thompson, a professor of media and popular culture at Syracuse University: "The horror movie is going to move away from the age of Godzilla, which personified this enormous threat of atomic power to destroy things. . . . Instead, it's going to be much more on the 'X-Files' model, where the villain is elusive and perhaps conspiratorial."[13]

Perhaps *The X-Files* did not generally receive the credit it deserves for modeling the post-9/11 world because media pundits did not want to face up to a disturbing truth: the show had predicted a new age of international terrorism with uncanny accuracy. *The X-Files* is one of the darkest and most unnerving shows in the history of television, especially in the way it dwells on the nightmare aspects of globalization. Its horror stories often focus on how the increasing dissolution of national borders is unleashing new and terrifying forces in the contemporary world, forces that threaten to undermine and destroy the American way of life. *X-Files* plots often deal with the migrant as monster and the monster as migrant. In episode after episode, various forms of alien creatures, whether extraterrestrial or not, penetrate U.S. borders and have to be hunted down by Mulder and Scully. The show rests on the premise that in the age of globalization, the nature of the threat to the United States has undergone a fundamental transformation. Gone are the Cold War days when America had faced a single, clear-cut enemy in the form of the Communist bloc and the central fear was of nuclear annihilation. *The X-Files* accurately reflected the fact that by the 1990s, the enemies of the United States were no longer coming neatly packaged in the form of hostile nation-states like the Soviet Union.

Again and again *The X-Files* suggests that in a globalized world, threats will take more shadowy, diffuse, and mysterious forms, difficult to pin down and hence difficult to deal with. Many episodes center on the threat of terrorism, both international and domestic, and the line between the two is often difficult to draw. *The X-Files* is especially interested in bioterrorism, and several episodes portray the threat of plague and other forms of disease being spread around the globe by sinister but unidentifiable forces. As I summed up the basic situation in *The X-Files* in a book published in September 2001:

> *The X-Files* portrays a kind of free-floating geopolitical anxiety that follows upon the collapse of the clear-cut ideological divisions of the Cold War. . . . [It] presents a post–Cold War world that, far from being polarized in terms of nation-states anymore, is interconnected in all sorts of clandestine and sinister ways that cut across national borders. . . . The central image of threat during the Cold War was a nuclear explosion—destruction that starts at a clear central point and spreads outward. The central image of threat in *The X-Files* is infection—a plague that may begin at any point on the globe and spread to any other—thanks to international air travel and all the other globalizing forces at work today.[14]

Does this sound like a television show that is irrelevant in the post-9/11 world?

In fact, when the events of 9/11 were quickly followed by the anthrax scare, and scenes of personnel in hazmat suits decontaminating whole buildings suddenly filled the airwaves, the real world seemed to have been plunged into an *X-Files* episode. I remember thinking at the time not how outdated the series was, but how prophetic it had turned out to be. Life seemed to be imitating art in the form of *The X-Files*. But the most prophetic moment the show produced came not in the series itself, but in its spin-off, *The Lone Gunmen* (2001). The titular characters are three paranoid conspiracy theorists who run a tabloid that seeks to expose various forms of government cover-ups and evil deeds. Introduced in the first season of *The X-Files* as aides to Mulder in his FBI investigations, the characters were treated semi-comically and became very popular with fans of the show. Eventually the *X-Files* team decided to give the Lone Gunmen their own series, produced by the same people who had made the parent show successful (Chris Carter, Frank Spotnitz, John Shiban, and Vince Gilligan).

The new series debuted on March 4, 2001, with a pilot episode punningly entitled "Pilot" because it deals with piloting an airplane. Incredible as it sounds, the episode portrays an attempt to pilot a commercial airliner into the World Trade Center in order to create an international incident. Of course the episode does not get all the details right—it involves a Boeing 727 rather than a 757 or a 767, and the fictional flight is heading for Boston's Logan Airport, not departing from it. Still, the resemblance of the fictional story to the actual events of 9/11 was chilling for anyone who, like me, remembered the *Lone Gunmen* episode on that fateful day in September. It seems to me very odd to claim that 9/11 demonstrated the irrelevance of *The X-Files* to the twenty-first century when the creators of the show had anticipated the details of the disaster better than anyone else in the twentieth century, including U.S. intelligence agencies.

To be sure, in the TV episode, the plane headed for the World Trade Center is being piloted not by Islamic terrorists, but by remote control, and at the last moment the Lone Gunmen succeed in freeing the regular pilots to fly the 727 on their own. The plane merely grazes one of the Twin Towers, and disaster is averted. As for the explanation of the "terrorism," true to the conspiratorial worldview of *The X-Files*, in the *Lone Gunmen* episode the plot has actually been hatched by a faction within the U.S. government. As the father of one of the Lone Gunmen explains it: "The Cold War's over, John, but with no clear enemy to stockpile against, the arms market's flat. But bring down a fully loaded 727 into the middle of New York City and you'll find a dozen tin-pot dictators all over the world just clamoring to take responsibility and begging to be smart-bombed."[15] In their commentary on the *Lone Gunmen* DVD set, the producers of the show talk about how difficult it was for them just to view the episode after 9/11. Frank Spotnitz says, "I actually couldn't bring myself to even look at the episode again until I sat down to prepare for this interview today." They regret having presented a plot so close in its details to 9/11 as if it had been planned by the U.S. government itself. Commenting on the episode's explanation of the events depicted, one of the producers says, "The irony is there are people out there who believe this to be true"—referring to all the conspiracy theories about the 9/11 attacks having been executed by the U.S. government, not by Islamic terrorists.

The deeper irony is that the existence of this *Lone Gunmen* episode has itself fueled conspiracy theories about 9/11. Refusing to accept the idea that the anticipation of 9/11 in this television show could have been a mere coincidence, conspiracy theorists have offered the episode as proof that some people in the United States must have known about the World Trade Center plot ahead of time.[16] Some theorists have seized upon the fact that, like *The X-Files*, *The Lone Gunmen* was broadcast on the Fox Network, which is owned by the wealthy and powerful media mogul Rupert Murdoch. These people insist that Murdoch must have been actively involved in producing the episode, perhaps trying to warn the public about what turned out to be the 9/11 terrorist attacks, perhaps trying to create disinformation about them in advance. There could be no better example of art and life blurring together than the way in which the pilot episode of *The Lone Gunmen* has become woven into conspiracy theories about 9/11. In this case, television has become part of the reality it is supposed to be merely representing.

But if we are to believe the *Lone Gunmen* producers—and I think that we should—they were as shocked as anybody by what happened on 9/11. In the DVD commentary, Spotnitz says of the morning of 9/11: "My first thought was the *Lone Gunmen*. . . . 'I hope this has nothing to do with what we did on television six months ago. . . . I hope we weren't somehow guilty of inspiring this.'"[17] Given the amount of time that was required to prepare for the 9/11 attacks, Spotnitz and his colleagues were safe in assuming that they were innocent of having contributed in any way to what happened. Nevertheless, they are troubled by their strange "prediction" of the World Trade Center disaster. A number of government authorities, in defense of their failure to anticipate 9/11 and their lack of any contingency plans for dealing with this kind of attack, have said that such a terrorist act was unimaginable. And yet in working on the *Lone Gunmen* pilot, the *X-Files* team did imagine it.[18] As

Spotnitz says about his assumptions at the time, "If we thought about something like this happening, then the government certainly has thought about something like this happening. When it actually happened in real life, six months after this was broadcast, I just was shocked that there was nothing in place . . . to prevent something like this from happening." Unfortunately, the events of 9/11 confirmed not only the *X-Files* vision of the rise of global terrorism, but also its vision of the U.S. government's inability to deal with this development. The kind of bureaucratic infighting and snafus *The X-Files* frequently portrays in the FBI and other government agencies turned out to be all too real. As subsequent investigations revealed, various government agencies had reason to believe that a terrorist attack was imminent in September 2001, but their failure to share their information and other errors prevented them from doing anything to forestall the disaster.

"The Truth" At Last

Perhaps, then, those who chose to dismiss *The X-Files* in the wake of 9/11 were shooting the messenger. Far from being wrong about the world we now live in, *The X-Files* had portrayed it all too accurately. Disturbed by what they saw in that mirror, critics decided to blame the representation for what it revealed about the underlying reality it was representing. As the series approached its final episode, many commentators seized the opportunity to proclaim its irrelevance in the post-9/11 era, but they never bothered to analyze the episode itself.[19] They thereby missed a chance to see whether *The X-Files* might have anything important to say about the post-9/11 world.

Watching "The Truth" air on May 19, 2002, I was so caught up in the excitement of seeing the last-ever episode of *The X-Files* that I was unable to view it critically. Seeing it years later on DVD, I would have to say that "The Truth" is not an example of *The X-Files* at its dramatic and intellectual best. Chris Carter and his crew were trying to accomplish too many things at once in this episode. As drama it suffers from being overburdened with retrospective exposition, nostalgia, and the sheer emotional weight of making the last show. Oddly enough, in light of the criticism of the show at the time, the strongest aspect of the final episode is its contemporary relevance. Unwilling to go down without a fight, Carter came out swinging in "The Truth." At a time when movies and television were heeding the media pundits and trying to avoid any content that might be considered antigovernment, the final episode of *The X-Files* remains true to the series' motto of

"Trust No One." "The Truth" has turned out to be almost as prophetic as the "Pilot" episode of *The Lone Gunmen*. Just as the Bush administration's War on Terror was ramping up, *The X-Files* chose to deliver a timely warning against its tendency to disregard civil liberties and to deprive people of their fundamental legal rights.

In "The Truth," Mulder breaks into a secret government facility and is put on trial for supposedly killing a soldier in the attempt. The episode is largely devoted to showing how brutally Mulder is treated in detention and how unjustly he is treated during the trial. Early in the episode, he is kept incommunicado in a military prison. The parallels with the U.S. government's detention facility for terrorist suspects in Guantánamo Bay were obvious at the time and have become only stronger as more information has emerged about how the government has treated its prisoners at the Cuban base.[20] Mulder is being held in secret, with no access to legal counsel and no way to communicate with his friends and allies. In the opening sequence, he is brainwashed by vicious military guards, who, in Orwellian fashion, keep asking him, "What are you thinking?"[21] He is deprived of sleep, beaten, and tormented in an effort to break his spirit and get him to confess his guilt. At a time when most Americans were not inclined to think too closely about what their government was doing in Guantánamo, *The X-Files* was confronting them with images of what can happen when there is no public scrutiny of the treatment of prisoners.

Mulder's friends at the FBI, including Scully and Assistant Director Walter Skinner (Mitch Pileggi), finally find out that he is, in Skinner's words, "being held . . . indefinitely," and are able to come to his aid. But they seem virtually helpless in the face of a coalition between the military and the FBI to ensure that Mulder is convicted. FBI deputy director Alvin Kersh (James Pickens Jr.) has always had it in for Mulder; and he is told by General Mark Suveg (William Devane) that he will preside over Mulder's trial. Suveg makes Kersh's task clear: "I want a verdict—a guilty verdict." Then, in typical *X-Files* fashion, he ominously adds, "There are forces inside the government now that a man would be foolish to disobey." This seems to be Carter's comment on a political turn for the worse in post-9/11 America.

As for Mulder's trial, it is a classic case of a kangaroo court. In the director's commentary on the episode in the DVD set, Kim Manners says that Carter's model for the trial was the Australian movie *Breaker Morant* (1980)—a powerful story of military subordinates taking the fall for the misdeeds of their imperialist superiors. In "The Truth," every aspect of the trial

A post-9/11 kangaroo court in "The Truth," the series finale of *The X-Files*. (Everett Collection)

is stacked against Mulder. Skinner tries hard to defend him, but any appeal he makes to traditional legal safeguards is rejected by the court. Finally, in exasperation, he says to Kersh, "This isn't a secret tribunal; as you so kindly informed me, it's a court of law." But Kersh immediately counters that it is "a military court of law," and it turns out to be a secret tribunal of the worst kind. No written record is being kept at all of the proceedings. The government is never able to produce the body of the soldier Mulder is charged with killing (which would, in fact, be impossible, since Mulder's "victim" is one of the show's invincible "supersoldiers" and hence cannot be killed). Even when Scully comes up with incontrovertible forensic evidence that the corpse the government claims is Mulder's "victim" is a fake, Kersh refuses to accept her expert testimony. He finally delivers the court's verdict: "Acting fairly and impartially, this panel finds the defendant guilty." But fairness and impartiality are exactly what the episode demonstrates are absent when the government is able to try people in secret, outside the normal justice system.

Condemned to death by lethal injection, Mulder is rescued by his FBI allies (in one of several plot developments in the episode for which the viewer is insufficiently prepared, Kersh inexplicably comes to Mulder's aid and helps him escape). Instead of fleeing to safety through Canada, Mulder heads with Scully to one of the series' favorite locations, the deserts of New Mexico (site of the infamous UFO incident at Roswell in 1947 and hence where the story all begins for *The X-Files*). Here the episode's plot gets murky, especially for anyone unfamiliar with *X-Files* mythology. In a remote mountain cave, Mulder finds none other than the chief villain of the series, the sinister Cigarette Smoking Man (William B. Davis). We had every reason to believe that he had been killed off in an earlier episode, but somehow he survived and somehow he has made it to this mountain retreat, where he is cared for by an old Native American woman.

None of this action is well explained, and at this point the plot appears to be driven by considerations not of narrative logic but of thematic symbolism. The most striking fact about the scene is that the hitherto urbane Cigarette Smoking Man, at home in the corridors of power in Washington, D.C., has retreated to a mountain cave in New Mexico. In President Bush's October 7, 2001, address on the first U.S. military operations in Afghanistan, he had famously said, "Initially the terrorists may burrow deeper into caves and other entrenched hiding places."[22] Because of its initial implausibility, I offer this interpretation with some hesitation, but in the mountain cave scenes of "The Truth," the Cigarette Smoking Man appears in some weird way to be standing in for Osama bin Laden.[23] He has traded in his standard-issue government bureaucrat's business suit and adopted the pose of a shaman. He is referred to as a "wise man" and looks the part of some Eastern sage with his newly flowing long hair. At the climax of the episode, two military helicopters blast him into flaming oblivion by firing missiles into his retreat. Exactly this kind of scene was very much on the American public's mind at the time this episode aired. The U.S. government was promising to deliver a similar blow to bin Laden in his mountain hideaway in Afghanistan.

I am not sure exactly what point *The X-Files* was trying to make by linking the Cigarette Smoking Man with Osama bin Laden, but a connection that seems logically weak is extremely strong visually in the episode (and television is a visual medium). Just look at these mountain cave scenes with the sound turned off and ask yourself whether what you are seeing was more appropriate to Afghanistan than to New Mexico at the time the show was broadcast. The best I can do to articulate the connection would be this: Native Americans, especially the long-vanished Anasazi peoples referred to in this episode, figure prominently in *X-Files* mythology. The show criticizes what it regards as a contemporary American empire by linking it with the conquest and extermination of native tribes in the course of creating the American nation-state. If "The Truth" is pairing Afghanistan with New Mexico, the suggestion would be that the United States was doing to a Third World people in Asia in 2002 what it had done to natives in America throughout the nineteenth century—namely, using its technological superiority to wipe them out.

As for the destruction of the Cigarette Smoking Man, it seems to be an illustration of the principle of blowback, which was on many people's minds in connection with 9/11. The United States had originally armed and trained the mujahideen in Afghanistan; terrorists were now using those weapons and skills against the United States. Similarly, throughout *The X-Files,* the Cigarette Smoking Man had participated in one government operation after another directed against indigenous peoples around the world, operations that sometimes bordered on genocide. In the final episode, the government weapons he helped unleash against the world come back to destroy him with a kind of rough justice.

As often happens in *The X-Files,* opposites come to be equated. Governments turn out to be the mirror images of the evil opponents they rail against; sometimes governments generate the very enemies they fight. In "The Truth," the Cigarette Smoking Man has retreated to his cave because unusual mineral deposits in the area will protect him against the aliens and the government's supersoldiers. He explains to Mulder, "Indian wise men realized this over two thousand years ago. They hid here and watched their own culture die. The original shadow government." These words take us back to the beginning of the episode, when Skinner explains that the secret facility Mulder broke into, the Mount Weather Complex, is "where they say our so-called shadow government is installed." Two shadow governments—the episode is bookended by images of leaders hiding out in mountain caves, protecting themselves while appearing to be indifferent to the fate of their own people. Ever willing to play two sides against each other, the Cigarette Smoking Man moves between these two worlds, the government at the center of power and the remote native tribes on the periphery. In response to 9/11, there was much speculation about where American leaders would go to keep safe during a national emergency. *The X-Files* could not resist calling attention to the irony of the fact that our nation's leaders might be hiding in mountain caves even as they were directing air strikes against terrorist leaders hiding in mountain caves in Afghanistan.

The finale of *The X-Files* is characteristic of the series as a whole in the way it blurs the line between the persecutor and the persecuted, showing that the victim is the mirror image of his killer. The protean Cigarette Smoking Man, who had already played many contradictory roles in the series, represents at once both the government and the forces it wants to suppress. In seeking to annihilate him, the government is trying to eliminate the destructive forces it originally set loose itself. In a world of terrorist blowback, the mountain cave scenes of "The Truth" make a kind of rough sense. After all, in bombing Afghanistan, the United States was trying to wipe out terrorist forces it had originally armed and trained back in the 1980s in an effort to push the Soviet Union out of the country.

Bush, Batman, Bauer, and Blowback

If we had any lingering doubts about the contemporary relevance of the final episode of *The X-Files* when it first aired, they have been dispelled by the evidence of a deleted scene that can be found in the DVD version. We now know that "The Truth" was originally intended to conclude with a scene of President Bush in the White House overlooking the Washington Monument (they cast a remarkable look-alike named Gary Newton in the role). Handed a note that evidently tells him that Mulder has escaped, Bush says, "What do you want me to do? I was told this was being handled. The truth is out there now." The camera then pans to the other figure in the room, and it turns out to be one of the members of Mulder's kangaroo court. Indeed, he is the most sinister of the judges, the one who had been identified by the psychic, Gibson Praise (Jeff Gulka), as an alien and the clandestine orchestrator of Mulder's railroading in court; in the quaint terminology of *The X-Files,* he is known as the Toothpick Man (Alan Dale). It is this dark figure who was originally going to conclude the episode and hence *The X-Files* as a whole with ominous words that evoke two of the show's mottoes: "The truth has always been out there, Mr. President. The people just don't want to believe."

Even by the normally harsh standards of *The X-Files,* this scene is extraordinarily cynical about the U.S. government. It is the only time in the long history of the series that a U.S. president is shown actively engaged at the heart of the great conspiracy the program purports to chronicle. By having Bush speak the words "What do you want me to do?," the show suggests that the U.S. president is merely the puppet of shadowy forces of which the American public is willfully ignorant. One of the commentators on the deleted scene says, "I'm so happy we cut this scene," and perhaps this decision is evidence

that even *The X-Files* felt a need to exercise some self-restraint in the wake
of 9/11. Yet further comments on deleting the scene suggest that the real
reason for doing so was aesthetic, not political. The producers wanted to
end the episode and the series with the highly emotional exchange between
Mulder and Scully that brought the original broadcast to a close. But whatever the reason for deleting the Bush scene was, its mere existence gives
some insight into the political attitudes of *The X-Files* and emphasizes how
much it was engaged with the realities of the post-9/11 world. Precisely when
media pundits were calling for movies and television to get on board with
the program and become cheerleaders for Team America, *The X-Files* had
the courage to remain true to its long-term mission of providing a voice of
dissent in popular culture. In sum, even though the plot and the symbolism
of the final episode of *The X-Files* are often murky and perhaps inconsistent,
it is still clear that the series was engaging with some of the fundamental
issues that had been raised by 9/11 and its aftermath. The attitude the show
took toward those issues may not have pleased media pundits at the time,
and they had every right to criticize the show's position, but it was unfair to
say that *The X-Files* had simply been made irrelevant by 9/11.

As for the prediction of a total transformation of American popular
culture after 9/11, very little of what the pundits prophesied in the fall of
2001 has come to pass.[24] As we have seen, in the immediate weeks and
months after 9/11, there were many signs of film and television producers altering their plans in an effort to avoid upsetting and displeasing a
traumatized American public. But as for the long-term effects of 9/11 and
its aftermath, films and television seem to have become more cynical than
ever about government.[25] I originally wrote this chapter in the summer of
2008 and chose that moment as a representative sample of American pop
culture. The biggest blockbuster of that season was the new Batman movie,
The Dark Knight, a film that in its scenes of urban destruction on a mass
scale clearly evokes 9/11. Insofar as it is an allegory of a post-9/11 world, it
suggests that the good guys have become virtually indistinguishable from
the bad guys. Batman (Christian Bale) must operate outside the law and
resort to the tactics of the villains in Gotham City in order to combat them
successfully.[26] In particular, the Caped Crusader must rely on morally and
legally dubious practices, such as kidnapping foreign citizens on foreign soil
and eavesdropping on a massive scale on the citizens of Gotham City in the
name of protecting them. The Joker (Heath Ledger) is a chilling portrait of
a terrorist, a man who is not interested in money or any of the other usual

goals of criminals, but who is destructive because "some people just want to watch the world burn." The Joker is actually shown triumphing in the film, because he manages to turn the most upright man in Gotham City, District Attorney Harvey Dent (Aaron Eckhart), into Two-Face, a crazed vigilante who seeks vengeance at any price. After Dent dies, the only way justice can prevail in the world of the film is for the authorities to cover up his crimes to preserve the myth of his being a decent and just civic official. *The Dark Knight* may end up endorsing the need to violate civil liberties in order to combat terrorism, but its portrait of government officials comes very close to what *The X-Files* typically shows.[27]

Two other popular superhero movies in the summer of 2008—*Iron Man* and *The Incredible Hulk*—portray the federal government in general and the military-industrial complex in particular in a sinister light. In both cases, the government literally produces monsters and unleashes them to wreak havoc on its own cities on a scale that dwarfs the devastation of 9/11. *Iron Man* explicitly connects the operations of the U.S. military-industrial complex with terrorist threats coming out of Afghanistan from a group called Ten Rings. Both movies provide powerful metaphors of geopolitical blowback. A third blockbuster hit of summer 2008, *Indiana Jones and the Kingdom of the Skull* was reviewed with this opening line: "Steven Spielberg's fourth Indiana Jones adventure is the best very special episode of *The X-Files* ever!"[28] Spielberg's film heavily borrows its plot elements from *The X-Files*, with references to the 1947 Roswell incident, alien autopsies, and extraterrestrial forces colonizing the Earth in earlier periods of history. The film is cinematically nostalgic, with a loving recreation of the 1950s as it was visualized in film, including a teenage hangout, perfect in all the details. It takes us back to the "simpler" days of the Cold War and even features that great treat of 1950s films, a nuclear explosion. But the film does not take a 1950s attitude toward the 1950s. The main villains are from the Soviet Union, but it portrays FBI agents as their moral equivalents. Just as in *The X-Files*, the McCarthyism of the FBI is presented as the mirror image of the Stalinism of the KGB.[29]

The popular Fox series *24* (2001–2010) is frequently offered as the alternative to *The X-Files* and an example of a patriotic response to 9/11.[30] The show celebrates the actions of a government counterterrorist unit and makes a hero out of Jack Bauer (Kiefer Sutherland) for risking everything, including his own family, to foil terrorist plots against America. But *24* is much closer to *The X-Files* than it may at first appear. Bauer is much like

Mulder and Scully—he succeeds not because of, but in spite of, the government agencies he works for and with. *24* goes just as far as *The X-Files* ever did in showing how bureaucratic incompetence and infighting hamstring government efforts to deal with terrorism. Bauer is, if possible, even more insubordinate than Mulder and Scully, and even more of a lone wolf and a loose cannon. Both *The X-Files* and *24* suggest that the government is completely dependent on mavericks among its agents in order to protect America against its enemies. Following its own rules and procedures, the government would succumb to bureaucratic gridlock. Only the determination, initiative, and resourcefulness of independent-minded agents can save the day. Even within government, a sort of free enterprise principle is necessary to accomplish anything. The highly centralized, top-down control of bureaucratic organizations cannot respond well to crises. Only the bottom-up, flexible responses of agents in the field can adapt to rapidly changing circumstances and prevent disasters.

As for the portrait of government leaders in *24,* it did offer a very attractive model of a president in the figure of David Palmer (Dennis Haysbert), but it went on to show Palmer assassinated on the orders of his successor, Charles Logan (Gregory Itzin). In Logan, *24* created perhaps the most loathsome U.S. president ever portrayed in popular culture—a figure who is obviously meant to conjure up memories of Richard Nixon, but who in the end makes "Tricky Dick" look like Mr. Nice Guy by comparison. Logan turned out to be literally a traitor to the United States, colluding with the Russians and countenancing a terrorist strike against American citizens in a conspiracy that would have shocked even Fox Mulder. Looking carefully at *24,* one would conclude that the spirit of *The X-Files* is very much alive in American popular culture in the post-9/11 era.

At a party celebrating the conclusion of the broadcast run of *The X-Files,* Sandy Grushaw paid tribute to its creator: "Chris Carter didn't just create a show for our time, but for all time."[31] A Fox executive is not exactly the most objective judge of one of his own network's series, and Grushaw's evocation of Ben Jonson's famous encomium to Shakespeare may be a trifle over the top. As with all cultural products, only time will tell how enduring the achievement of *The X-Files* will turn out to be in the history of television. But I think that it is already safe to say that the rumors of its death in 2002 were exaggerated. The continuing relevance of *The X-Files* is a tribute to the vitality of popular culture and its ability to perform a gadfly role in American society. The pilot episode of *The Lone Gunmen* is a powerful reminder that popular culture may sometimes glimpse truths that have eluded those in power who are supposed to be on the lookout for just such truths. I am not shocked to find that creative artists can be more imaginative than government bureaucrats. The critics of *The X-Files* in 2001–2002 mistook political dissent for cynicism about politics. In political terms, popular culture is at its best when it provides not a chorus unanimously singing the praises of the United States and its values, but lone voices raising the questions that must be asked if freedom is to continue to flourish in democratic America.

10

UN-AMERICAN GOTHIC

The Alien Invasion Narrative and Global Modernity

> Human communities have long proved to be permeable by alien influence, but the liberal societies are unique in incorporating their permeability in their definition. They cannot do otherwise while remaining faithful to their commitment to freedom. If there is a tension between the liberal dedication to freedom and liberal openness to whatever threatens it, the perfect resolution of that tension has yet to be found.
>
> —Joseph Cropsey, "The End of History in the Open-Ended Age?"

Many critics of globalization discuss the process as if it involved only the Americanization of the globe. Given the United States' position as the only global superpower today, this view is understandable, especially since American military might undergirds various forms of political, economic, and cultural influence as well. To see Coca-Cola, McDonald's, KFC, and other U.S. brand names wherever one travels around the world today can easily lead one to believe that Earth is rapidly being made over into a gigantic American strip mall. But if one looks at a typical American strip mall these days, one might begin to form the opposite impression. It might very well contain a Jamaican restaurant, a Mexican grocery, a Tae Kwan Do academy, a Chinese acupuncture clinic, and perhaps even a Buddhist or a Baha'i temple. As recently as twenty years ago, if you went into a restaurant in, say, South Dakota and asked for wine, the waiter would likely have stared at you in disbelief. Today the chances are that even a semi-upscale restaurant in the backwaters of America will have a wine list, perhaps featuring bottles from France and maybe from as far away as Australia and South Africa, chosen on the basis of the latest recommendations from the *Wine Advocate* or the *Wine Spectator.* The globalization of the American palate may seem like a trivial development, but it is no more so than the burgeoning worldwide taste for Big Macs and fries. In short, if we are what we eat, the globalization of America is proceeding apace with the Americanization of the globe. And that means that Americans are developing the same anxieties about global-ization that people all over the world are experiencing. The globalization of America has occurred so rapidly and included such extensive and deep changes that it has unsettled and unnerved the American people.

The New Gothic versus the Old

This unease has been mirrored in American popular culture in some obvious and not-so-obvious forms. I will discuss the ways that fears about immigra-tion and the porousness of U.S. borders have surfaced in American television programs, reflecting a deep-seated concern that the very integrity of Ameri-can identity is being eroded. These fears often take the form of nightmare images of alien invasions and alien-human hybrids—the birth of a mode in popular culture that might be called Un-American Gothic.[1] The Gothic traditionally embodied a fear of the past; and, as we saw in chapter 7, its images of horror accordingly took the form of decaying castles, graveyards, and the Undead. Born in the eighteenth century, the Gothic mode expressed the Enlightenment's fear of all the reactionary forces, the remnants of an undemocratic past, that were blocking progress. Science fiction would at first sight appear to be the opposite of the Gothic. With its spaceships, time travel, and miraculous cures for diseases, science fiction seems to embrace the future as a glorious realm, a technological paradise. In the original *Star Trek* (1965–1969), for example, the heroes represent the liberating potential of science and technology. They continually fight aristocratic and theocratic pockets of resistance to the spread of enlightened modernity.

But paradoxically, science fiction has been shadowed from its begin-ning by images of horror, and it has often blended with the Gothic mode. Mary Shelley's *Frankenstein* may be the first science fiction novel, but it is also one of the great horror stories of the nineteenth century. Other pioneer works of science fiction, such as Robert Louis Stevenson's *Dr. Jekyll and Mr. Hyde* and H. G. Wells's *The Island of Doctor Moreau*, also combine elements of the Gothic. In science fiction, the traditional Gothic fear of the past is transformed into a fear of the future. Authors such as Shelley, Stevenson, and Wells question whether science is a purely benevolent force, and they uncover the dark side of the Enlightenment, its ability to generate its own monsters. Over the years, science fiction writers have contemplated the horrors that unbridled science may unleash on an unsuspecting world, forces that threaten to obliterate traditional ways of life. The new Gothic nightmare is of weapons of mass destruction, irresistible plagues, and genetically engineered, freakish mutations. As we will see in this chapter, in the past two decades, television shows reflect deep anxieties about challenges to the United States coming from both beyond and within its borders, ultimately a fear that traditional American institutions and values are being undermined by an increasingly powerful global technocracy.

The Cultural Contradictions of Imperialism

To many it looks as if America and Americans have conquered the world, and U.S. popular culture sometimes reflects this sense of triumph. But many television programs do not give the impression that Americans feel that they are sitting on top of the world. Rather they seem to live in fear that sinister forces somewhere out there in the world are about to conquer them. The seemingly paradoxical experience of the conqueror feeling conquered is by no means unprecedented in world history. It seems to be integral to the experience of empire, as the example of Rome illustrates. Ancient Rome dominated the Mediterranean world in many ways more fully than the United States dominates the globe today. Where today local natives may cringe at the sight of a McDonald's going up in their neighborhood, Gauls or Judeans would have balked at the sudden appearance of a Roman amphitheater in their midst. With its military, political, and economic power, Rome projected its cultural influence more forcefully and unashamedly than the United States ever has. The Romans openly proclaimed themselves to be conquerors and forced the people they ruled to acknowledge them as masters.

But even as Rome entered its imperial age, some of its best thinkers began to feel uneasy about maintaining their Roman identity intact. Virgil's *Aeneid* celebrates the imperial triumphs of Augustus Caesar, but in its portrait of his great rival, Mark Antony, it suggests that a Roman conqueror might succumb to the very forces he thought he had conquered. Toward the end of Book VIII, Virgil portrays an Egyptianized Antony, overwhelmed by oriental forces, seduced by the Egyptian queen Cleopatra, and linked with the bestial gods of the East:

And facing them, just come
From conquering the peoples of the dawn,
From the red shores of the Erythraean Sea—
Together with barbaric riches, varied
Arms—is Antonius. He brings with him
Egypt and every power of the East
And farthest Bactria; and—shamefully—
Behind him follows his Egyptian wife. . . .
. . . Every kind of monster
God—and the barking god, Anubis, too—
Stands ready to cast shafts against Minerva
And Venus and at Neptune.[2]

Antony's story illustrates the cultural contradictions of imperialism: campaigning in foreign lands exposes the conqueror to alien ways of life, which may end up subverting his attachment to his own people. Military victory may turn into cultural defeat. Moreover, as Roman armies marched into lands all around the Mediterranean, foreigners from those same lands poured back into the city of Rome, attracted to the center of empire and eager to embrace Roman citizenship for all it was worth. This explains how an Egyptian pyramid came to be built in downtown Rome by a man named Cestius, who evidently felt it would be fashionable to go to his grave like a pharaoh. The pyramid of Cestius is an early example of what is jokingly referred to in postcolonial studies as the "Empire Strikes Back" motif. As if in anticipatory revenge for all those alien amphitheaters Rome was to go on to construct around the Mediterranean, the imperial metropolis got an Egyptian pyramid that stands to this day as part of its Aurelian walls—an eternal monument to the way Rome was orientalized even as it tried to Romanize the world around it.

Rome as a distinct community dissolved into the vastness of its own empire. Once a neatly walled-in city with its horizons narrowly focused on war and the warrior virtues, Rome turned into an imperial cosmopolis embracing a wide range of ways of life and cultural options. To be a Roman in the age of the Empire was something very different from being a Roman in the early days of the Republic.[3] Among other transformations, Rome eventually metamorphosed into a Christian community, the ultimate example of how the subjugated East ended up conquering the seemingly dominant West in the ancient world.

The history of Rome lays bare the inexorable logic of empire: unlimited military expansion is inevitably linked to unlimited immigration from the imperial frontiers. The price an empire pays for trying to extend its control over the whole world is to have to absorb a sampling of the whole world's population within its borders. The imperial state necessarily becomes a multinational community, or at least a multiethnic one, and thus has trouble maintaining its traditional communal identity. The history of the British Empire tells the same tale as the Roman, culminating in the image of an orientalized London—the Londonstan that Salman Rushdie has presented brilliantly in novels such as *The Satanic Verses*. In one of the most imaginative passages in the book, Rushdie has his hero, Gibreel Farishta, fantasize about the results of a tropicalized and therefore totally transformed London:

> Institution of a national siesta, . . . higher-quality popular music. . . . Improved street-life, outrageously coloured flowers. . . . better cricketers; higher emphasis on ball-control among professional footballers, the traditional and soulless English commitment to "high workrate" having been rendered obsolete by the heat. Religious fervour, political ferment. . . . No more British reserve; hot-water bottles to be banished forever, replaced in the foetid nights by the making of slow and odorous love. . . . Spicier food.[4]

Having chosen Imperial Rome as a model for their own empire, the British ended up with a similar experience, watching citizens in the homeland adopt the manners and mores of their formerly colonized subjects in India.

The United States has not pursued empire as directly or openly as Rome or Great Britain did, but it has nevertheless ended up exercising a kind of global hegemony and is having to face the domestic consequences in ways that closely resemble the earlier Roman and British experiences. The pressures of immigration, especially of Hispanic peoples, have become acute in the United States, straining medical, educational, welfare, and other resources and leading many Americans to feel that their way of life is fundamentally under attack. The United States has dealt with immigration problems throughout its history, but in the larger context of an overall globalization of America, the current situation seems to be especially disturbing to people around the country. In economic terms, Americans are concerned that domestic jobs are being outsourced to foreign shores, while jobs that remain at home are being taken by illegal immigrants. As a result, immigration has become a heated political issue in the United States, with many people calling for the government to close its borders, especially with Mexico, to immigrants of any kind. The ongoing and contentious debate over bilingualism in the United States is only one cultural reflection of these concerns. Whatever one's attitude may be regarding the rights and wrongs of immigration, it is a simple fact that the American people are deeply troubled by the issue.

The X-Files and Alien Invaders

It is hardly surprising, then, that fears about immigration have begun to feature prominently in American popular culture. A classic case is *The X-Files* (1993–2002). The show is especially significant because of the way it relates the problem of immigration to the problem of globalization and links both to what might be termed the larger problem of empire. At its science-fiction–conspiracy-theory core, *The X-Files* presents as dark a picture of globalization as has ever appeared in American popular culture—a paranoid nightmare of globalizing forces run amok and riding roughshod over American traditions and institutions.[5] The premise of the series is that alien beings plan to invade and colonize Earth. They have entered into a conspiracy with a shadowy syndicate of political and business leaders from around the globe to help prepare for the alien takeover, which requires the creation of alien-human hybrids. The hero and heroine of the series are two FBI agents, Fox Mulder (David Duchovny) and Dana Scully (Gillian Anderson), who gradually learn that the pillars of the American regime—the FBI itself, the Department of Justice, the Congress, the Presidency—are not what they seem. Those who appear to be in charge turn out to be just taking orders; they are puppets manipulated from behind the scenes by members of the syndicate, who are working for—although at times against—the aliens. The sources of the syndicate's power are kept vague, but it is obviously international in character, associated with multinational corporations and multinational organizations, including the United Nations. What is clear in *The X-Files* is that the United States and its government are no longer in control of their own destiny.

To explain how this loss of control came about, *The X-Files* offers a revisionist history of America since World War II, which suggests that in its quest for global power, the United States, much like the Roman Empire, became the mirror image of the forces it was trying to contain and combat.

The history emerged in bits and pieces over the course of several seasons, but chronologically arranged, it begins with the end of World War II, when, according to the series, the United States used captured German and Japanese scientists to pursue the agenda of its own military-industrial complex. *The X-Files* presents this development as a Faustian bargain. For the sake of power, America joined up with the very forces it had been fighting as the embodiment of evil in the world. The series takes a similar view of the Cold War. Several episodes point to covert links between American and Russian science and technology. The way *The X-Files* ties all this together is to connect the German, Japanese, Russian, and American scientists to experiments involving alien-human hybrids. In short, the whole invasion/conspiracy plot connecting the aliens, the syndicate, and the U.S. government symbolizes the way that America's military and imperial aspirations led to its being caught up in a system of international power relations in which it came to resemble the enemies against whom it claimed to be defining and defending itself. *The X-Files* suggests that to a large extent the United States created this system, but eventually it became a prisoner of its own creation, subject to the dictates of an amoral and inhuman science, whose unbridled use in totalitarian regimes it had condemned. In *The X-Files,* the way the United States gradually becomes assimilated to its purported opposites is the heart of the problematic of empire and the most sinister aspect of globalization.

The X-Files thus represents a cultural backlash against globalization, especially the globalization of America, in the 1990s. For decades, Americans had felt confident that their country was projecting its power outward into the world and in a way that was unequivocally good—a confidence reflected in popular culture in TV series such as the original *Star Trek,* in which American democratic institutions are being spread not just around the globe, but throughout the whole galaxy.[6] In *The X-Files,* however, the American Empire appears to be imploding, as alien forces unleashed in the course of imperial expansion now strike back, subverting and replacing the duly constituted government of the United States. This fictionalized situation reflected an increasing sense among Americans in the 1990s that they were no longer sure who was running their lives—their own government and institutions, or mysterious forces from beyond their borders. In the 1990s, a number of theorists from different fields developed a thesis that came to be known as "the end of the nation-state."[7] They argued that after centuries of being the dominant political institution, at least in the West, the nation-state in the late twentieth century was losing ground to all sorts of alternative forms of economic, cultural, and even political organizations—from supranational organizations like the European Union, to economic trading areas like the one created by the North American Free Trade Agreement (NAFTA), to newly emerging economic and cultural units like the Pacific Rim, to the increasing power and independence of multinational corporations. These developments all have positive aspects, especially in economic terms, and many of the "end of the nation-state" theorists hail them as the wave of the future. But from the traditional perspective of the nation-state and the patriotism it seeks to create, all these developments appear to be subverting its authority and hence look sinister. In a variety of ways, *The X-Files* makes reference to all the "end of the nation-state" phenomena, especially the way that economic and cultural forces no longer respect national borders.

The X-Files became famous for offering a remarkably negative portrait of the American government, but really its point is that the government is no longer *American* in the traditional sense. It has been taken over by alien forces and no longer represents the will of the American people. *The X-Files* shows the constitutional civil liberties of the American people being taken away by a global technocracy. The projected triumph of the aliens is linked to an Orwellian and even Foucauldian vision of an administered world gone global, in which institutions, including hospitals, clinics, schools, laboratories, research facilities, prisons, asylums, nursing homes, orphanages, and corporations, compile information about human beings in order to exercise control over them.[8] *The X-Files* suggests that in the second half of the twentieth century a new threat to freedom emerged. The danger is no longer traditional despotism, a tyrant like Hitler or Stalin who rules with a strong and cruel hand and openly advertises that he is in command and brooks no opposition. Generally *The X-Files* deals with what Alexis de Tocqueville calls "soft despotism," a new form of seemingly democratic tyranny in which the government, in the guise of a benevolent provider, gradually takes over the lives of its citizens and turns them into passive subjects, dependent on government bureaucracies to care for them from the cradle to the grave.[9]

Although conventional despots like Saddam Hussein are occasionally mentioned in *The X-Files,* the "tyrant" in the show is more likely to take the form of a man in a white coat, calmly asking you to submit to an examination or an inoculation. The underlying fear in *The X-Files* is that the world is now being run by experts, who lay claim to rule based on their scientific and technological know-how, not their political and military victories. This claim is difficult for ordinary people to challenge, especially since these technocrats do not look particularly evil—indeed, they give the appearance of being trained professionals who genuinely care for humanity. And yet, *The X-Files* suggests, they are increasingly taking control of our lives away from us and attempting to regulate all aspects of our existence in the name of our health, safety, and welfare. Among the most ominous words a character in *The X-Files* can hear are "This is for your own good." It usually means that he or she is about to be injected with an experimental virus and has at most an episode to live before experiencing a gruesome death in the name of science.

At the core of *The X-Files* is the experience of alien abduction. Mulder's sister was abducted, and so is Scully in the second season, as a well as a host of other characters in the series. The show was able to tap into a fear that had already become widespread in American pop culture, reflected in best-selling books, cheesy movies, and television appearances by self-proclaimed abductees.[10] The standard alien abduction narrative features one striking moment: the abductee is strapped down in some kind of apparatus in a medical facility and subjected to intrusive probes by strange, frightening, and alien equipment. It is remarkable how often alleged abductees tell the exact same story of what happened to them. If one chooses not to explain the consistency of these narratives by the possibility that they might actually be true, one needs to find some common experience that might lie behind them. I would argue that these nightmares of imaginary medical examinations are generated—and I hope that this is not too much of a stretch—by fear of real medical examinations. The proliferation of alien abduction narratives coincides roughly with the moment when ordinary Americans were increasingly finding themselves subject to increasingly intrusive—and "alien"—medical procedures, including all sorts of exotic technologies. The most nightmarish aspect of the alien abduction experience is the feeling of utter helplessness and passivity, of being subject to humiliating manipulation by cold and unfeeling strangers. For all its benefits, modern medicine often produces just this experience.[11]

Alien abduction narratives epitomize the feeling that *The X-Files* dwells on in all aspects of modern life—the sense that human beings have become passive subjects in a worldwide technocracy, manipulated at will by faceless experts who have the right, for example, to experiment with their bodies and even their minds. In their day-to-day activities, ordinary people feel that they no longer know who they are really dealing with. They do not interact face to face with the people who affect their lives. When confronted with financial or educational or legal or political institutions, the average individual finds them impersonal and remote—in short, alien.[12] In the world of global modernity, personal relationships are continually being replaced by institutional relationships. The major vocations—medicine, law, teaching, business, and so on—become increasingly professionalized, subject to various forms of testing, licensing, accreditation, and regulation by the nation-state and even international organizations. Modern professionals are less likely than their nineteenth- or early twentieth-century counterparts to act on their own as individuals. They are more likely to function as part of some larger organization—a hospital, a corporation, a university—which is organized bureaucratically and substitutes routines and standard operating procedures for individual judgment and initiative.

The modern professional ends up working directly for the state, or in an organization that is in effect an extension of the state, which is itself becoming part of a global technocracy. This progressive absorption of traditionally independent institutions into the state apparatus is at the heart of *The X-Files*.[13] It is, in fact, what *The X-Files* images as an alien takeover of America. The characters in *The X-Files* keep discovering that the professionals who dominate their lives and are supposedly responsible for their safety and welfare—especially the doctors, the professors, the scientists, the police, the military, and the politicians—are involved in a global conspiracy to take away their freedom, if not their very identities and lives. That is the deepest meaning of alien invasion in *The X-Files*.

In a further ominous development in the series, technology increasingly produces substitutes for aspects of human life that were once thought to be natural. In particular, *The X-Files* repeatedly portrays government efforts to usurp the power of human reproduction, to take it away from the family, where it has traditionally belonged, and to place it instead in the laboratory, where cloning and other artificial means of breeding can be used by the state to manufacture its own population to order.[14] In *The X-Files* an inhuman—and un-American—science becomes the instrument of global power and tries to eradicate human freedom.

The X-Files links these fears about globalization with fears about immigration. The series rests on a fundamental pun on the word *alien*. In science-fiction terms, the word of course refers to extraterrestrial beings, the little green—or in this case gray—men, of whom we get tantalizing glimpses in many episodes. But *The X-Files* also uses *alien* in the sense we mean when we speak of "illegal aliens."[15] Several episodes deal with the plight of foreigners who have entered the United States under suspicious circumstances, either illegally or just surreptitiously. In all cases, *The X-Files* stresses the fact that the immigrants are racially or at least ethnically distinct from the American mainstream, and yet usually their goal—and often their threat—is to sneak into that mainstream. Immigrants in *The X-Files* include African Americans, Mexican Americans, and Chinese Americans, as well as figures from Eastern Europe and India.[16] The typical immigrant in *The X-Files* is presented as a hybrid figure, half American and half something else. Here is the most important link between the alien as extraterrestrial and the alien as immigrant. The extraterrestrial aliens also frequently appear as hybrids, half human and half something else. The issue of hybridity becomes central in *The X-Files* and is connected to anxieties about globalization. Hybridity of identity is the alternative to homogeneity of identity. The fear of hybrids in *The X-Files* reflects Americans' concerns that, in an era of globalization, they can no longer count on any kind of cultural homogeneity in their country.[17] Gone are the days of America as the great melting pot, when immigrants—or, at least, their children—were expected to assimilate into the mainstream of society as fully Americanized citizens. Instead, in an age of multicultural ideology, immigrants are in effect urged to cling to what makes them different from the American mainstream, including languages other than English.

Thus Americans have come to worry that their very identity as a distinct people is in jeopardy, and *The X-Files* mirrors this fear with its sinister alien-human hybrids. The hybrid is at once a monster and "just like us." One of the chief concerns about both the immigrant aliens and the extraterrestrial aliens in *The X-Files* is that, while maintaining their foreign identity, they may be able to pass for ordinary Americans, blending right into society and thus able to carry out in secret whatever nefarious schemes they may have in mind. At the same time, *The X-Files* presents that hybridity as monstrous, a mixing together of what is meant to be kept apart. Episodes are often devoted to forcing one form of alien or another to come out of its shell, either literally or figuratively, and reveal its truly alien—and hence monstrous—character.

The aliens in *The X-Files* are typical migrants—loners, outcasts, and misfits—often refugees from some form of political oppression who are forced to lead a gypsy-like existence. A particularly threatening aspect of the alien immigrants in *The X-Files* is that they tend to be stateless people and therefore are poised to subvert America as a nation-state. Having experienced persecution under various forms of state tyranny, these migratory people have learned strategies for avoiding government control. In particular, they

have developed fluid identities that help them to blend into strange circumstances and escape state surveillance. They become quick-change artists, as it
were, able to adapt immediately to new situations and thus to wriggle out of
efforts to entrap and imprison them. Their ultimate goal as stateless people
is to become "invisible" to the state, a goal which a number of alien figures
in *The X-Files* manage to achieve in one form or another.[18] The best study of
stateless people is James C. Scott's *The Art of Not Being Governed,* and, as if
echoing *The X-Files,* he repeatedly speaks of them as "shape-shifting."[19] Scott
explains that people fleeing political oppression often retreat to frontiers and
end up caught between rival and possibly hostile states. They thus have to
develop hybrid identities to deal with such dangerous situations. They tend
to become multilingual and readily change their religion and other seemingly fundamental beliefs and customs in order to be able to negotiate a path
between the different ethnic communities with which they must contend.

Scott points out that, given their versatility, resourcefulness, and mobility, stateless people frequently succeed very well as immigrants in more
tolerant nations, such as the United States. But the nomadic habits they
develop during generations of statelessness often make it hard for them to
integrate fully into the stable community of a nation-state, with its fixed
laws and institutions. Both the illegal aliens and the extraterrestrial aliens
in *The X-Files* are frequently presented as shape-shifters. Shape-shifting has
always been a staple of horror movies and provides one of the most common plot motifs in *X-Files* episodes. Scott explains why: the alien as shape-
shifter speaks to the most profound fear of any traditional community: that
foreigners can move in its midst and appear to be native, while remaining
alien—and monstrous—"deep down inside."

Fears about immigration in *The X-Files* are thus the mirror image of
fears about globalization, and the show in effect explores the immigration
problems of an imperial regime. The logic of empire produces a multinational community at home, rife with the potential for ethnic and cultural
strife. In both immigration and globalization, something non-American
and even un-American is taking over America, usually by masquerading
as American while embodying principles that are alien to the United States.
The immigrants in *The X-Files* are all associated with traditional ways of life
native to their home countries, customs quite alien to the American way
of life. They typically practice voodoo, witchcraft, exorcism, or other forms
of magic quite foreign to the enlightened world of contemporary America.
Their supernatural powers hark back to the pre-Enlightenment past, when

religion ruled society.[20] Scully and Mulder have to use all the resources of modern science to meet the challenge that old-time religion poses to contemporary America. Yet Mulder has a great interest in and respect for the occult, and the triumph of scientific modernity over traditional beliefs is often presented as involving significant losses (for example, *The X-Files* displays a great admiration for the traditional religious beliefs and practices of Native Americans).[21]

In portraying the clash between American modernity and foreign ways rooted in the past, *The X-Files* often seems to be lamenting the destruction of traditional ways of life around the world (another unfortunate consequence of globalization). In the manner of many horror movies, the show is often quite sympathetic to the "monsters" it portrays, dwelling on the difficulty anyone who is different will inevitably have adjusting to the mainstream of society and its limited sense of what is "human." *The X-Files* often seems to be suggesting that monstrousness is in the eye of the beholder and that society actually creates the monsters it then seeks to expel from its ranks.[22] Mirroring the confusion of the American people themselves, the show seems unable to decide whether the United States should open or close its borders. At many points, *The X-Files* appears to celebrate ethnic and other forms of difference and to fear nothing more than the homogenization of humanity in a global state (symbolized by the experiments with cloning and other unnatural forms of reproductive uniformity throughout the series). But at the same time, *The X-Files* displays a marked tendency to gothicize difference, to present the alien as truly monstrous and incompatible with the normal—and normative—American way of life.[23]

The X-Files thus presents globalization as a process that affects all nations, including the one that appears to be exercising global hegemony. Although the imperial center thinks that it is exercising control over the periphery, the imperial frontier reacts back upon the center, threatening through such processes as immigration to create cultural blowback and blur the distinction between colonizer and colonized. For a television show, *The X-Files* develops a surprisingly sophisticated understanding of globalization, one that seems very relevant to the world situation today. Yet some have argued that *The X-Files* is dated, a relic of the 1990s, made obsolete by the events of 9/11, which pundits at the time supposed would turn the American people from skeptics about their government into believers in it as their protector (as did in fact happen to some extent, at least initially).[24] But it seems odd to dismiss the continuing relevance of a show that in retrospect has proved to be so prophetic. As we saw in chapter 9, in an eerily accurate anticipation of 9/11, the pilot episode of the *X-Files* spin-off *The Lone Gunmen*, which aired on March 4, 2001, deals with a terrorist attempt to fly a commercial airliner into the World Trade Center. In general, at a time when most people were still thinking that threats to America would continue to come from foreign nations, *The X-Files* was already suggesting that in the future they would become more amorphous and hence more difficult to deal with. The central image of a foreign threat in *The X-Files* is an infection, with an unidentifiable source, an unknown cure, and the ability to spread unchecked in any direction. *The X-Files* offered an early warning about the emergence of terrorism, particularly bioterrorism, as one of the most dangerous consequences of globalization.

The Attack of the *X-Files* Clones

As if in recognition of the continuing relevance of *The X-Files*, the fall 2005 television season might have been dubbed "The Return of Scully and Mulder." At least six shows making their debuts drew upon the Fox series as a predecessor: *Bones* (2005–), *Supernatural* (2005–), *The Night Stalker* (2005), *Invasion* (2005–2006), *Threshold* (2005), and *Surface* (2005–2006).[25] Some of these shows involved people who had worked on *The X-Files*, and these series all referred to the earlier show, either in their scripts or in their publicity material. For example, in the opening episodes of both *Bones* and *Supernatural*, one character turns to his partner and says, "If you're Scully, I'm Mulder." Three of these shows—*Invasion, Threshold,* and *Surface*—explore the same thematic material that *The X-Files* does. Although post-9/11 popular culture was supposed to become uniformly patriotic, these shows revived the political paranoia of *The X-Files*, dealing with government conspiracies and cover-ups and chronicling the erosion of civil liberties in the United States. They portray the American government spying on its own people and imprisoning and interrogating them in a less than constitutional manner.[26] Moreover, the three titles—*Invasion, Threshold,* and *Surface*—all point to the issue of borders and the unnerving possibility of their being violated. The shows are remarkably similar in conception, suggesting that they reflect significant concerns of the American people. *Invasion* deals with a monster hurricane that hits the east coast of Florida and brings with it some kind of alien force that takes possession of people's bodies (or rather re-creates them), turning them into alien-human hybrids. *Threshold* deals with an alien force that descends upon a ship at sea, turning its crew into alien-human hybrids, who then try to spread the "infection" throughout the U.S. population. *Surface* deals with strange hybrid creatures that suddenly appear in the ocean and go on to threaten the mainland United States in a giant tsunami that overwhelms the Mid-Atlantic coast.

Because these three shows did not make it beyond a first season—*Threshold* did not even complete one full season—it is difficult to interpret any of them without knowing where they were headed. After the first season of *The X-Files,* for example, we knew virtually nothing about the conspiracy between the aliens and the syndicate. In fact, we were not even sure if the aliens really existed and were not just figments of Mulder's hyperactive imagination. But even in their brief runs, the three television series offer interesting material for analysis, and they hark back to *The X-Files* in the way they reflect anxieties about the porousness of U.S. borders and the threat of immigration to the integrity of the American way of life. All three shows raise the theme of hybridity, and they present it as something monstrous. *Invasion* even jokes about bringing up this issue. At one point, when the hero of the series uses the term *hybrid* with one of the aliens, the alien replies, "I heard that's what you're calling us. It's very trendy."[27] Americans, all three shows seem to say, no longer have a simple and straightforward identity. They are becoming hybrids, and the new admixture is a foreign or an alien element that makes them fundamentally different from what they were before and poses a threat to the continuation of their traditional way of life as Americans.[28]

In all three shows the alien threat is associated with, and comes out of, the ocean. This motif was used earlier in *The X-Files,* in which a number of episodes deal with ships' crews infected at sea, and the mysterious alien black oil is transported by oceangoing vessels. In the typical science fiction movie or television show in the 1950s or '60s, alien threats tended to come from the sky—most famously, of course, in flying saucers.[29] This motif obviously reflected Cold War anxieties about nuclear weapons, strategic bombers, intercontinental ballistic missiles, and the space race between the United States and the Soviet Union. During the Cold War, Americans had a great deal to worry about—above all, nuclear annihilation—but at least they were confident that they knew who their enemies were. Threats from the sky seem to suggest, "At least we'll see them coming." But threats from the ocean are harder to identify. They can suddenly well up and hit at any time and any place; moreover, in *Invasion* and *Surface,* they masquerade as natural disasters. The shift from invasion from the sky to invasion from the ocean seems to register a change in Americans' perception of the world, a recognition of the way the rules of the international game changed in the 1990s: "We didn't know where the real threat was coming from. We thought it was from one nation, the U.S.S.R., but now it's more complicated. Something is coming across our borders and we don't know what, where, or when." I am perhaps formulating this point too explicitly, but it does seem significant that *Invasion, Threshold,* and *Surface* all suggest that, whatever the threat to the United States may be, it can no longer simply be identified as a fleet of invading spaceships but is something much more nebulous and harder to spot. In a globalized world, where national borders no longer have the same force, an invasion may easily be confused with more benign or natural processes.[30]

Moreover, in American mythology, the ocean has always been identified as the route of immigration. Today more people may come to the United States by plane than by boat, but the image of immigration in popular culture is still the tired, the hungry, the huddled masses yearning to breathe free docking at Ellis Island in New York Harbor. The aliens landing in flying saucers in science fiction movies of the 1950s looked more like an invading army than huddled immigrants. By contrast, alien creatures washing up on our shores come closer to the immigrant archetype—another reason why the ocean may figure so prominently in *Invasion, Threshold,* and *Surface.* Of the three, *Invasion* is the show that most systematically confronts the issue of immigration. Since it is also by far the best of the three artistically and the one that most fully harks back to *The X-Files,* I will concentrate on *Invasion,* with occasional references to the other two shows.[31]

Hybrids and Hurricanes

Because *Invasion* is set in southern Florida, in the vicinity of the city of Homestead and Everglades National Park, it is easy for the series to bring up the issue of immigration. The opening shot in the pilot episode features a Hispanic woman with her son, and at many points during the series we hear Spanish spoken (the hero is a Cuban refugee). A scene deleted from the broadcast pilot but available on the DVD set features a Hispanic police-woman trying to get an old man to seek shelter from the coming hurricane. Refusing her help, he tells her, "You go, Gomez—go back to Havana." She denies that she is an immigrant: "I'm not Cuban, Earl. I'm from Pensacola. Pensacola, Florida." When he replies, "Pensacola, my ass; you're a damn alien" (#1), the show humorously introduces the same pun on which *The X-Files* is based. Throughout *Invasion,* we hear of aliens in the sense of extraterrestrials and aliens in the sense of immigrants, illegal or otherwise; often characters turn out to be aliens in both senses at once. Given the Florida setting, it is natural for Cuba and Cubans to come up often in the series, but the show also contains references to countries in Central America (Honduras), the Caribbean (Haiti), and South America (Venezuela and Brazil).

For one plot reason or another, the show keeps picturing what look like, and in fact are, refugee camps, either on the mainland or in the Florida Keys. The rising tide of the hurricane brings a flood of refugees to the shores of Florida who must be dealt with and who quickly strain the combined resources of local and federal authorities. *Invasion* was well into production before Hurricane Katrina struck the Gulf Coast; what was a disaster for New Orleans turned out to be a stroke of good fortune for the TV series. It seemed extremely timely when it made its debut on September 21, 2005, just a few weeks after Katrina devastated New Orleans. The show made excellent use of the political controversy surrounding Katrina. The fourth episode, "Alpha Male," features a substantial and pointed debate over the way the government dealt with the hurricane disaster depicted in the series, which closely echoes the actual complaints made by the American public, especially about the inadequate and inept response by the Federal Emergency Management Agency (FEMA is referred to negatively in episode 19).[32] Just as we saw in *Mars Attacks!* in chapter 4, *Invasion* suggests that ordinary people working together on their own might be better able to deal with a crisis than government authorities.[33] In fact, the show portrays government intervention only making matters worse. Residents of the town complain bitterly to the sheriff about the quarantine he has imposed, which, they insist, keeps out the very help they need to rebuild their lives. Playing upon the insecurity and fears of its citizens, the government exploits a natural disaster to clamp down on their freedom of movement and exert control over their everyday activities. In its obsession with immobilizing its citizens, herding them together in safety zones, it prevents them from acting on their own to protect themselves and improve their conditions. In short, government often stands in the way of its citizens improvising and taking the initiative to solve their problems themselves.

Like *The X-Files, Invasion* displays a strong antigovernment streak. It eventually reveals that the federal government, and above all the military, are mixed up in the alien invasion, or at least are trying to cover it up. *Invasion* strongly suggests that ordinary Americans do not want their shores invaded by aliens, while the federal government is indifferent to their concerns and perhaps is even aiding the aliens for its own dark purposes. At one point the military is shown experimenting on the aliens to discover and presumably exploit their superpowers—a plot development reminiscent of the story of the government supersoldiers in the final seasons of *The X-Files*.

One of the clearest indications that *Invasion* is dealing with American anxieties about immigration is the extraordinary fertility of the aliens. The women whose bodies have been taken over by the aliens do not just have babies; they evidently have litters. As the first season drew to its conclusion, the show increasingly focused on the situation of a number of hybrid women who have become pregnant and are facing the prospect of an uncertain and extremely painful childbirth. Unfortunately the series ended without clarifying what exactly the alien births would involve, but it is clear that they would be multiple. The show strongly suggests that the aliens are indifferent to the fate of the mothers and care only about the propagation of their own species. One of the standard fears about immigrants is that they reproduce rapidly and without restraint. This anxiety goes to the heart of the fundamental fear that the immigrant population will displace the mainstream population by overwhelming it numerically. Alien pregnancy turned out to be the most Gothic element in *Invasion*. In the best horror-movie tradition à la *Rosemary's Baby* (1968), it takes a legitimate fear women experience ("Will my baby be normal?") and gothicizes it with monstrous images of grotesquely distended, pulsating bellies and the sonogram promise of abnormally multiple births. In this respect, *Invasion* echoes *The X-Files*, which also generates fears concerning alien methods of reproduction, especially the genesis of twins, triplets, and other forms of mass reproduction, including cloning. The widespread Gothic images of birth in American popular culture would also seem to reflect anxiety about all the new forms of reproductive technology that have been developed and put into practice in recent decades. People evidently have become afraid that natural/traditional methods of reproduction are being replaced by novel technologies, the full consequences of which for human welfare cannot be foreseen.

The larger issue of alien-human hybridity in *Invasion* gets complicated. When a human drowns or otherwise ends up in ocean waters, he or she may be taken over by one of the alien beings (more precisely, the original human body is discarded, while the alien makes a kind of clone of it). In terms of outward appearance, the resulting alien-human hybrid is indistinguishable from the original, although blood tests and other medical indicators can discriminate a hybrid from a real human being. More significantly, subtle psychological changes point to the difference between the new hybrid and the old human. For example, early in the series, the young daughter of a hybridized woman intuitively senses that her mother is no longer the same person. The most pronounced changes brought about by hybridization occur in women, who begin to lose interest in their children and sometimes cease to care about them at all. One young hybridized mother abandons her baby and refuses even to acknowledge that it is hers. Whatever the invasion may ultimately be, it chiefly seems to constitute a threat to the nuclear family.

This motif ties in with the central plot line of *Invasion*, which centers on a broken family, or rather two broken families. The hero, a park ranger named Russell Varon (Eddie Cibrian), is divorced and has remarried. His new wife is named Larkin Groves (Lisa Sheridan). His ex-wife, Mariel (Kari Matchett), a medical doctor, is now married to Tom Underlay (William Fichtner), the town's sheriff (both, as it turns out, have been hybridized). Mariel's two children with Russell, Jesse (Evan Peters) and Rose (Ariel Gade), are now chauffeured back and forth between the two households in a variety of SUVs, getting lost in transit with alarming frequency. Sheriff Underlay has a daughter named Kira (Alexis Dziena) from a previous marriage, and Larkin is newly pregnant with Russell's child. All this may sound like a soap opera, and it is. Take away the science-fiction trappings, and *Invasion* is a good old-fashioned soap opera about divorce, remarriage, sexual jealousy, broken families, custody of the kids, and all the emotional mayhem that results. Mariel sums it all up when she tells her son, "Divorce sucks, Jesse" (#7).

The emotional core of *Invasion* is the trauma of a broken family for all concerned, and the characters are constantly struggling to protect their families from external forces that threaten to tear them apart. They are repeatedly faced with situations in which they must choose between protecting their families and performing their professional duties (as sheriff, park ranger, doctor, or, more generally, savior of the world). What does all this have to do with globalization? The suggestion seems to be something like this: the increasing complexity of the modern globalized world makes increasing demands on the time and energy of modern professionals, forcing them to neglect their families. The force with which Hurricane Eve slams into the Florida coast may be a symbol for the impact of the global on the local. People can no longer pay sufficient attention to their immediate and local concerns—their families and their neighborhoods—because they are distracted by all sorts of global concerns that demand their attention.

In *Invasion* the pressing need to deal with what amounts to an immigration crisis—the flood of refugees into southern Florida—prevents the main characters from adequately dealing with a number of personal and family crises they are facing. In the midst of all the hurricane-induced chaos, the children repeatedly complain that they have been abandoned by their parents. As Jesse says at one point, "So basically we have no parents now" (#18). *Invasion* reflects Americans' fears that with their new concern with global issues—saving the world—they are losing sight of what is right before their eyes and closest to their hearts: their own families. Russell speaks for all the central characters in the series when he says of the crisis around him, "I care about how this affects my family" (#2). Later, when he is asked if he is ever going to tell the world what he knows about the invasion, Russell replies, "When I know it's not going to hurt my kids" (#11). Larkin, who is a TV journalist, concludes a live report with this observation about what she has learned from the hurricane experience: "What's really important is family and the people we love" (#13). The extent to which the characters in *Invasion* come to focus on their families may reflect their guilt about the way they have been neglecting their children— in particular, their sacrificing their families in the name of their careers.

The tension between the global and the local, specifically the threat to the nuclear family, is common to all the shows we have been discussing. *The X-Files* developed into a chronicle of three dysfunctional nuclear families—the Mulders, the Scullys, and the Spenders, the family of the infamous Cigarette-Smoking Man (William B. Davis).[34] In various episodes characters' involvement in the alien conspiracy forces them to sacrifice members of their family; and, particularly in the later seasons, the series explores the ways in which Mulder's and Scully's careers prevent them from having families of their own.[35] In *Threshold,* the absence of families, normal or otherwise, is striking. The cast of characters is a rather unattractive crew of emotional and even sexual misfits, who seem incapable of and uninterested in having families. The youngest (and most sympathetic) member of the Threshold team is engaged to a woman, and later in the series we learn that he has secretly married her, but his commitment to fighting the alien invasion prevents him from having a normal relationship with her and almost costs him his life (or his human identity). The plot of *Surface* also involves several broken families and custody battles. To carry on her crusade against the alien creatures, the heroine must break off contact with her children, while the hero in his obsessive quest for the creatures ends up with his wife demanding a divorce. The pattern in these series is extraordinarily consistent. (For the record, *Bones, Supernatural,* and *The Night Stalker* all deal in one way or another with broken families as well.) The main thing that gets sacrificed in response to global threats is the nuclear family and, above all, the children, who are left to fend for themselves while their parents go off, either to conspire with or fight against an alien invasion. *Invasion* and these other shows suggest that the great fear among Americans at the moment is that the integrity of the home and the nuclear family is being threatened, and that threat is somehow linked to America's increasing global commitments.[36]

The Return of the Pod People

Alien-human hybridity has many other meanings in *Invasion,* so many that one might call it overdetermined as a symbol. When hybrids begin to take over the local high school, the show, following in the tradition of *Buffy the Vampire Slayer,* makes something Gothic out of normal adolescent anxieties. The teenage hybrids behave like bullies, form cliques that exclude the remaining humans, and generally act like jerks—more precisely, jocks. In one scene on a basketball court, the high school hybrids perform perfectly as a team, able to pass the ball around without dropping it, even though they have their eyes shut. This is one of the many respects in which the hybrids develop abilities superior to those of normal human beings. More generally, they experience a much deeper community spirit, but that comes at the expense of their sense of individuality. Perhaps *Invasion* is harking back to some of the antitotalitarian science fiction allegories of the 1950s. It seems to owe a great deal to *Invasion of the Body Snatchers* (1956) and pays homage to that classic movie with its many references to "pod people" in episode 9 (which also contains a mention of "body-snatched people"). Critics have interpreted this film in different ways, but one obvious reading views it as a Cold War parable of a communist takeover of America.[37] The pod people think the same way, feel the same way, and act the same way—all contrary to the spirit of American individualism. With specific references to Cuba, the Bay of Pigs, and Fidel Castro in *Invasion,* it might be interpreted as an anticommunist allegory.

But in many ways, the hybrids seem more fascist than communist. They are associated with the local police force—Sheriff Underlay is one of their leaders—and they become linked up with the U.S. military and form their own paramilitary group. There is one pointed reference to Nazism in the series, when Jesse says, "I feel like I'm in occupied France, the trains are roll-ing, and nobody's doing anything to stop them" (#19). Perhaps *Invasion* is exploring the possibility of homegrown fascism in the United States. But in the end, whether the show is attacking left-wing or right-wing totalitarian-ism may be immaterial. What is important is that it is antigovernment in general and more specifically antiauthoritarian. The show seems to lament the way the hurricane and the invasion behind it become an excuse for a massive increase in local and federal government intrusion into the lives of ordinary citizens in Florida. Perhaps the hurricane/invasion can be read as a symbol not of immigration, but of the new terrorist threat in post-9/11 America (these two sources of anxiety are, of course, related). Although *Invasion* focuses on Hispanic characters and the Latin American world, there are a few pointed references to Iraq in the series, including a strange moment when Russell learns of the two hybrid leaders: "If Underlay is Sad-dam, Szura is Zarkawi" (#13).

If terrorism is at issue in *Invasion,* then the series may be suggesting that the United States has overreacted and sacrificed its fundamental liberties in the course of trying to protect them.[38] The show seems to be critical of the increasing militarization of American society since 9/11, particularly the use of the military in civilian situations. Episode 21 offers a very negative portrait of security control by the military, with a particularly ugly scene included in the DVD set that conjures up all the nastiness of airport security measures these days (including cute little Rose having her pet cat taken away from her by a heartless soldier). In episode 22, Russell says bitterly, "When it comes to national security, we're pretty good about justifying anything." The problem of terrorism is even more central in *Threshold,* and the issue of the sacrifice of civil liberties keeps coming up in that show, although most of the time it seems to endorse the choice of security over liberty.[39] The stance of *Invasion* seems more libertarian, but one must remember that the military forces in episode 21 are, in fact, hybrids masquerading as the U.S. Army; and, in the end, the real Air Force comes to the rescue of the endangered humans. Perhaps the show is suggesting that our government is protecting us against alien terrorists after all.

Still, in support of a libertarian reading, *Invasion* repeatedly presents negatively the way the hybrids band together to assert their authority and form various kinds of goon squads. Several scenes portray the hybrids com-ing together in a local church with a priest who is himself hybridized, and again the show seems to be criticizing the groupthink of this community and the way they gang up on outsiders, which is to say, normal human beings. But it is not clear that *Invasion* is portraying organized religion as a force for evil in the United States. The priest insists that the group is simply using his church building as a meeting place and that he is not conducting religious services or in any way serving in his capacity as a priest with them. Rather than religious services, the meetings in the church seem more like a support group with a twelve-step program. The hybrids refer to themselves as "survivors," give testimony to their survival experiences, and encourage one another's personal growth as if they were members of "Aliens Anonymous." Perhaps the show is criticizing New Age movements and the popular ideology of self-help and self-development, which leads people to turn their backs on their families, especially their children, in the name of self-actualization.

All this may sound confusing, and perhaps the show is itself confused on these issues, but perhaps confusion is the point. *Invasion* may be portraying the confusion that results from the globalization of America. It begins with a typical American small town, with typical small-town values, chiefly traditional family values. This tightly knit community is suddenly invaded by a wide range of new ideological and religious possibilities, as well as new varieties of people who challenge its self-definition. All these developments place strains on the small town, as it tries to rebuild itself and reform its sense of community. The remaining humans increasingly come to feel that their way of life is fundamentally threatened, and they try to find ways to fight back against what they view as a hostile takeover of their homeland. At the most general level, *Invasion* is about social change and whether people are going to resist it or embrace it. For example, in episode 9, Underlay says of his wife Mariel, "She doesn't exactly embrace change. . . . She's afraid of letting go of the past." Here the same Gothic dynamic is at work as in *The X-Files*. The hybrids are passing as normal human beings, which helps them gradually extend their control over society and remake it, especially given their allies in high places and, above all, their links to the military. But although they look like humans, we keep getting hints that the hybrids are monstrous and will destroy the America we know. They are abnormally attracted to water and can survive underneath it for prolonged periods of time; they give birth in an alien way; indeed, in one of the final revelations in the series, we learn that the hybrid women must give birth in water. At many points, *Invasion* gives the impression that the very survival of the human species is at stake and that a failure to stop the alien invasion will mean the extermination of humanity. If we are to associate the invasion with the globalization of

America and the consequent transformation of the country, *Invasion* gives almost as negative a portrait of the process as *The X-Files* does.

But in its concluding episode, *Invasion* offers a twist on this dark vision. Faced with the prospect of a number of hybrid women giving birth, Mariel Underlay insists on saving their lives and helping them—partly because she is a doctor, partly because she is a woman, and partly because she is a hybrid herself (and pregnant, too). She even succeeds in getting her ex-husband and confirmed alien fighter, Russell Varon, to assist the process and help the pregnant hybrids to the water. This plot development reflects a fundamental ambiguity in the way the aliens are presented in *Invasion*. Most of the time, the hybrids are pictured as monsters and treated as deeply un-American, specifically in their collectivist attitudes. But just as happens in *The X-Files*, *Invasion* at times treats the aliens sympathetically. It even raises the possibility that they may be the legitimate next stage in human evolution (this idea comes up in *Threshold,* too). The series is filled with references to Darwin and the language of evolution, with phrases like "survival of the fittest" and "Cambrian explosion" appearing frequently and episodes entitled "Unnatural Selection" (#5), "Origin of Species" (#10), and "Re-Evolution" (#18). Larkin's brother, Dave (Tyler Labine), describes the situation of humans vis-à-vis aliens this way: "like we're the Neanderthals and they're us" (#18).

In certain physical and mental respects, the hybrids are improvements over the human species. They heal from wounds much faster, for example, and are even able to regenerate limbs. Over the course of the season, Tom Underlay as leader of the hybrids becomes an increasingly sympathetic figure. He starts out as sinister—the seeming villain of the show—poised in opposition to Russell Varon as the hero. But as we learn more about his past history, we come to empathize with Underlay's plight as a hybrid. In the last episodes he joins up with Varon to fight a renegade group among the hybrids and thus becomes a kind of hero himself.[40] We will never know where *Invasion* was heading ultimately in its treatment of the hybrids, but it is clear that even in its one completed season, it went from treating them as pure monsters—the "pod people"—to considering the possibility that they might have a good side and perhaps even represent the future of humanity.

This ambiguity is evident in the rhetoric of the show. At times, *Invasion* could not be more xenophobic in its language, as characters basically voice versions of the traditional attitude "The only good alien is a dead alien." But at times the rhetoric of *Invasion* becomes distinctly multicultural in spirit. Sometimes the hybrids are allowed to speak eloquently of their right to be different and, paradoxically, to be treated as human beings. In the final episode, for example, when Mariel defends the pregnant hybrids' right to give birth, she says, "Whatever's inside them may be different, but it doesn't mean that it's bad. And it doesn't mean that it's dangerous—it's just different" (#22). This defense of difference is a recurring motif in the series.[41] Earlier Dave, who is fully human, says, "Just because something is different doesn't necessarily make it bad" (#10), and Underlay echoes this phrasing when he says, "Just because someone's different doesn't make them a monster" (#14). Like *The X-Files, Invasion* is deeply suspicious of hybridity, but it tries to remain open to the possibility that hybridity, as an alternative to homogeneity, may be something good. Both shows generally tend to gothicize difference, but they have their moments of celebrating it as well. In this ambiguity, they perhaps reflect something about the American people—they may be anxious and even frightened about globalization, but at the same time they appear to be eager to embrace what might be its good aspects.

The Aliens Keep Coming

The fact that *Invasion, Threshold,* and *Surface* never made it past their first seasons might seem to call into question my claim that they reflect the mood of the American people. Dealing with this objection leads into the murky question of why a given TV show succeeds or fails. The ideological content of a show is rarely if ever the decisive factor in whether it stays on the air. Television is an entertainment medium, and entertainment considerations are more likely to explain the cancellation of *Invasion, Threshold,* and *Surface* than some hypothetical inability to get in sync with the Zeitgeist. *Surface* was a silly show and deserved to be canceled. *Threshold* had an intriguing premise and solid production values, but the characters were largely unlikable, and the show committed a cardinal sin in television terms: it failed to develop any sexual tension between its female lead and any of the male leads (one of the keys to the long-term success of *The X-Files* was the audience's fascination with the possibility of a romance between Mulder and Scully). I cannot point to any artistic faults in *Invasion,* and I believe that it deserved to be renewed. In fact, ABC did not cancel the show until the last possible moment. Sometimes the success or failure of a given show is simply a matter of luck.

The two *X-Files* clones that did survive their first seasons and in fact went on to become hits, *Bones* and *Supernatural,* have less of the ideological content of their model and more of its entertainment values. Both shows stress sheer horror elements—the "grisly corpse of the week" motif—and both draw more than *Invasion, Threshold,* or *Surface* did on sheer star power. Moreover, *Bones* and *Supernatural* succeeded in developing a chemistry between their leads. *Supernatural* is a classic on-the-road buddy story, featuring two handsome young brothers and a cool car. *Bones* copies the *X-Files* formula exactly, with the underlying sexual tension between its male and female leads serving as a principal source of its audience appeal.

The 2005–2006 TV season brought us probably as close as we will ever come to a controlled experiment in television programming. With several shows imitating various aspects of *The X-Files,* we have some evidence for the claim that entertainment values trump ideological content when success on television is at stake. The two shows that imitated the more superficial aspects of *The X-Files* did better than the three that drew more deeply upon its content. But a "controlled experiment" by television standards hardly meets real scientific criteria—above all, one cannot control for quality. Still I feel justified in tentatively concluding that the mere fact that a show was canceled does not necessarily mean that its ideological content was responsible for the cancellation. In any case, even though *Invasion, Threshold,* and *Surface* ultimately failed, they were originally scheduled by the networks in prime time and therefore were watched with interest by millions of viewers, many of whom complained bitterly about their cancellation. Thus these shows probably did reflect the concerns of the American people.

In support of this view, fears about globalization, terrorism, and immigration continue to surface in television series, and *The X-Files* continues to spawn imitations. At least three shows on the air in the 2010–2011 regular season were forms of invasion narrative with clear ties to *The X-Files: The Event, V,* and *Fringe. The Event* (2010–2011) tells a story of extraterrestrials who have already invaded Earth and infiltrated important positions in government and society. Many of the aliens are being held at a secret government base in Alaska. As the story opens, despite strenuous objections from his advisors, the president of the United States, Elias Martinez (Blair Underwood), is about to inform the American public about the existence of this base and the captive aliens. But he is prevented from doing so by an assassination attempt against him, which reveals deep divisions within the U.S. government, involving various conspiracies and cover-ups (the show goes on to portray the vice president as having participated in the plot against Martinez). All these developments are reminiscent of *The X-Files;*

we also learn of a division among the aliens, just as in the earlier series. As if to acknowledge its *X-Files* pedigree, the show in part revolves around the abduction by shadowy forces of the sister of one of its main characters; she is named Samantha, just as Mulder's famously abducted sister was. In true *X-Files* fashion, much of the dramatic tension in *The Event* grows out of attempts to reunite a broken family in the midst of national, international, and interplanetary turmoil. And with all the palace intrigue the series portrays going on in the White House, *The Event*, like *The X-Files*, suggests that the government of the United States is no longer under its citizens' control. In fact, for several episodes, the aliens succeed in controlling the presidency.

The Event is mainly interesting as what seems to be the first attempt in American pop culture to portray Barack Obama in fictional terms. President Martinez is a Cuban American, and the producers originally intended to cast a Hispanic actor in the role. But perhaps the decision to give the African American actor Blair Underwood the part started them thinking about parallels to President Obama. Martinez begins as an idealist. Like Obama, he has evidently made campaign promises about transparency in government and, in particular, has pledged to make public the facts about the government prison in Alaska. This containment facility in Alaska seems to be a stand-in for the U.S. base in Guantánamo Bay, Cuba, in which terrorist suspects have been held for years and about which Obama made promises similar to those of Martinez during his campaign. As a man of peace, Martinez tries to deal diplomatically with the aliens, even when his advisors recommend a more belligerent response and the aliens start wreaking havoc in America. *The Event* quickly becomes a story of the education of an idealistic president in the practical realities of a hostile world. In the early episodes, Martinez appears weak, indecisive, and ineffectual; he is duped, manipulated, and outmaneuvered by the aliens and barely able to keep the U.S. military in line. In one episode, we see him tied up and helpless in the White House in what appears to be a coup—only to learn that this is a dream sequence. Still, the episode makes its point: Martinez needs to toughen up to fulfill his duties as president.

Disillusioned by the treachery of the aliens, who have broken promise after promise to him, Martinez becomes a war president and orders military strikes against them, even in a civilian setting. The March 21 episode, "A Message Back," offered a surprisingly erudite debate among the president's cabinet about the posse comitatus law of 1878. Like *Invasion, The Event* seems to be raising questions about the increasing militarization of homeland security in response to terrorism; but perhaps, like *Threshold,* it approves of this development. Somewhat surprisingly, it is the chairman of the Joint Chiefs of Staff who invokes the posse comitatus act and objects to the use of U.S. military forces against civilians. A newly toughened Martinez responds, "Thank you, general. I'm well aware of the federal law. I'm also aware that when Congress passed the posse comitatus 130 years ago, they weren't accounting for the threat we're facing right now." This kind of argument became familiar after 9/11; supposedly, unprecedented historical developments have made traditional legal and constitutional safeguards of civil liberties obsolete. To justify the president's tough actions, *The Event* evokes the specter of 9/11 on several occasions, most memorably when the aliens use their superior technology to destroy the Washington Monument. The series seems to be portraying all the new anxieties and challenges to freedom that Americans face in the post-9/11 environment. For example, it includes alien-human hybrids, since some of the aliens who have infiltrated American society have married and had hybrid children. The worry that one can no longer tell true Americans from false is central to the series.[42] Again and again, *The Event* plays on post-9/11 fears that the terrorists are now living among us. Aliens in our government form the ultimate sleeper cells.

Hoping to transfer the whole population of their home planet to Earth, the aliens are working to eradicate the human race, or at least massively to reduce its numbers. As in *The X-Files,* they intend to use an airborne virus (bred in an alien-human hybrid) to accomplish their nefarious purposes (it is said to be a variant of the Spanish Flu of 1918). As in several other invasion narratives, *The Event* constantly contrasts loyalty to family with loyalty to some higher and less personal cause. Sophia Maguire (Laura Innes), the leader of the aliens, tells one of her lieutenants, Michael Buchanan (Scott Patterson), "You've never let your feelings about your [human] family get in the way of what needs to be done" (she is referring to the plan to take over Earth). By contrast, Vicky Roberts (Taylor Cole), one of the principal fighters against the aliens, says, "I'm just doing this to protect my family, the people I love." Like *Invasion, The Event* seems to present devotion to one's family as the true measure of humanity and to regard devotion to some grander, world-embracing cause as alien to the spirit of America. In defending their families and their loved ones, ordinary Americans acting outside the law and as maverick heroes in *The Event* do at least as well as the federal government in tracking down the aliens and defeating their plans.

V (2009–2011) is a remake of a 1983 TV series of the same name. It begins with the arrival of a fleet of massive spaceships, commanded by an alien queen named Anna (Morena Baccarin), who exerts a strange fascination over the population of the United States and the rest of Earth. Her charismatic impact is aided by favorable attention from the media, spearheaded by an ambitious television news reporter named Chad Decker (Scott Wolf), who colludes with Anna to make her look good and in the process advance his own career. With the promise of bringing change for the better to humanity by sharing their advanced technology, the queen and the Visitors she leads cause a sensation, especially among young people, who flock to their spaceships when given the chance and who treat Anna like a rock star. In particular, the Visitors ingratiate themselves with humanity by providing what is referred to as "universal health care" and later offer to solve such problems as global warming and air pollution with something called "blue energy." They propose what Decker describes as a "world-wide urban renewal project." Called Concordia, it is touted as a way to create "real jobs in a harsh economy."

Although the terms "stimulus package," "shovel-ready jobs," and "quantitative easing" never come up and the energy is blue, not green, it was inevitable, given all these details, that commentators would draw a parallel between the Visitors and the Obama administration.[43] Despite denials from the show's creators, it is difficult to believe that they were not responding to current events and specifically to the hopes and fears generated by the Democratic Party's agenda under President Obama.[44] The violent protests depicted in the series against the Visitors point in the direction of the Tea Party movement. It is particularly interesting that one of the main leaders of the opposition to the Visitors is a Catholic priest, Father Jack Landry (Joel Gretsch).[45] Like *The X-Files, V* explores the problematic place of religion in the modern technological world, especially the tension between spiritual faith and soulless science. In fact, the Visitors are using all their scientific power to locate the human soul and eradicate it. As in *The X-Files,* traditional religion appears to be a main site of resistance to the triumph of technological modernity in *V.*

In another parallel to *The X-Files* and the other alien invasion narratives discussed in this chapter, *V* presents the extraterrestrials as a threat to the nuclear family. Anna is using her beautiful daughter Lisa (Laura Vandervoort) to lure a teenage boy named Tyler Evans (Logan Huffman) away from his human mother. The boy comes from a broken home; his estranged father is played by none other than Nicholas Lea, who portrayed the infamous triple or quadruple agent Krycek in *The X-Files.* The aliens have already modified Tyler's DNA in an attempt to create an alien-human hybrid. Moreover, the Visitors have interfered with a number of human pregnancies, just as the aliens in *The X-Files* did. And like the aliens in *Invasion,* the Visitors reproduce on a massive scale. Their queen is, in fact, a kind of queen bee, who is able to generate hundreds of soldiers at a time. This motif in *V* points to the typical anxieties associated with immigration. A hostile news reporter says of the Visitors, "When newcomers arrive on your shores, you have to be careful." Once again, alien immigrants threaten to overwhelm the native population.

Thus, like *The X-Files, V* shows the traditional American way of life, here epitomized by a nuclear family and a local church parish, threatened by invading aliens and the global technocracy they represent. This technocratic regime hopes to generate its own population by a form of mass reproduction and thus substitute docile subjects for independent American citizens. The aliens appear to be offering a deal to humanity: "Give up your freedom and your traditional institutions, like the family, and with our technology we will cure your diseases, solve all your problems, and take care of your welfare." As a queen, Anna is a perfect symbol of the nanny state.[46] Again and again she relies on her people's advanced technology to win her battles against traditional forms of resistance to would-be omnipotent government power. When Anna goes to the Vatican, she secures the official support of the Catholic hierarchy by threatening the cardinals with demonstrating that the miracles of science can overwhelm and undercut the miracles of faith. The anxiety about globalization in *V* centers on the way a new leader turns up in the United States and insists on speaking to all nations at once. Anna seems concerned about humanity as a whole, not just America. This motif in *V* is reminiscent of an idea much discussed at the time of Obama's election, that he represents something new in American politics, a sort of postmodern, postnational president who will focus on global concerns to the exclusion of narrowly national ones.[47]

Like *Invasion* and *The Event, V* occasionally portrays its aliens sympathetically. Some of them develop human emotions and rebel against Anna. Just as in *The Event,* the "good" aliens are the Visitors who have been secretly living among human beings for years and have married humans and had children with them. Both the humans and the Visitors display a marked tendency to put family concerns above the interest of their nation or even their species. The characters are repeatedly willing to betray their closest comrades in the struggle against Anna in order to protect a loved one in their families. This tendency is in sharp contrast with a standard motif in World War II movies—the most famous being *Casablanca* (1942)—in which heroes and heroines are expected to put patriotism and saving the world above any personal considerations.[48] Like the characters in *Invasion,* those in *V* tend in the opposite direction; they seem to be making up for their past neglect of their loved ones by now turning the family into an absolute value. The need to protect their families justifies any breach of faith with supposedly higher principles.[49]

The aliens are, then, at their most "human" when they worry about their children. But despite such humanizing touches, *V,* like *The X-Files* and *Invasion,* has a strong tendency to gothicize difference. It shows that deep down the aliens are lizards—literally. Strip off their artificial human skin—as happens several times in the series—and they are revealed to be monstrous. *V* leaves no doubt that most of the aliens are malevolent. The Visitors intend to eliminate human beings and replace them with their own kind. Ultimately *V* presents as frightening an image of immigration, globalization, and technocracy as *The X-Files* does.[50]

Beyond the Fringe

Fringe (2008–) is arguably the most successful clone of *The X-Files,* both artistically and commercially; it has already made it to a fourth season.[51] From its standard opening scene of some horrific and mysterious happening to its stylish opening credits, *Fringe* is a blatant copy of *The X-Files.*[52] It pairs a female FBI agent named Olivia Dunham (Anna Torv) with a slacker-genius named Peter Bishop (Joshua Jackson) and has developed the kind of sexual tension and chemistry between them that Scully and Mulder generated. Like *The X-Files,* the show is obsessed with multinational corporations, and features one, Massive Dynamic, which often seems to be more powerful than the U.S. government. As a series, *Fringe* follows the pattern of *The X-Files* by offering a mixture of stand-alone episodes and ongoing mythology episodes. Olivia and Peter often investigate isolated cases of bizarre phenomena ("fringe science") with the aid of Peter's father, Walter Bishop (John Noble), a brilliant but mentally unstable scientist. But these cases frequently are linked with a larger plot, called initially the Pattern, which includes various government cover-ups and conspiracies. At its emotional core, *Fringe* tells the story of an abducted child and the resulting

"Maybe we should have brought our hazmat suits," thinks Agent Olivia Dunham (Anna Torv) as she leads Walter and Peter Bishop (John Noble and Joshua Jackson) to investigate the latest bioterrorist attack on *Fringe*. (Fox Broadcasting/Photofest)

broken family, thereby clearly calling to mind *The X-Files.*[53] *Fringe* has taken to copying specific episodes of *The X-Files,* and even seemed to imitate the second *X-Files* movie, *I Want to Believe* (2008), in an especially well-written third-season story called "Marionette" (3.9).[54]

Fringe is another invasion narrative, but the invaders are from a parallel universe rather than another planet, and we are as likely to invade their world as they are ours (a good image of the way that globalization is a two-way street: America is being globalized even as it Americanizes the globe). Each human being in our world has a counterpart in the alternate universe, with the differences between them arising from the accidents of their personal histories, which have sent them on divergent paths of development. More generally, *Fringe* reveals several significant differences between the two universes that apparently must be traced to key events that either did or did not take place in one or the other. For example, in the alternate universe, evidently the *Hindenburg* did not burn in 1936, because we see zeppelins as an ordinary and much-used mode of transportation in contemporary New

York. Similarly, we know that in that world the 9/11 attacks did not succeed in destroying the World Trade Center, because we see it still standing at the end of the first decade of the twenty-first century (in the alternate universe, the White House was destroyed, and the Obamas are pictured moving into its replacement). Among many other significant historical differences between the two universes is the fact that in the alternate one, John Kennedy was not assassinated (we hear on a radio news report that he is leaving his post as U.S. Ambassador to the United Nations to accept another position in the Obama administration). The fact that we hear of a Nixon Highway in the alternate New York and that Nixon's image appears on a silver dollar strongly suggests that the Watergate scandal never occurred there.

With its parallel universe, *Fringe* evokes all the anxieties about globalization and immigration we have been analyzing. It treats modern science and the global world it is creating as sources of both hope and fear. Technological forces may save us or destroy us. *Fringe* dwells as obsessively as *The X-Files* does on horrific scenes in hospitals and specifically in operating rooms, repeatedly blurring the line between medical treatment and medical experimentation.[55] The name *Fringe* is similar to *Surface* or *Threshold,* and evokes the same worry about the porousness of U.S. borders that the earlier series embodied. In the alternate New York, the Department of Defense is located on the same island as the Statue of Liberty, suggesting that the traditional American symbol of open borders has been repurposed to police and close them. In that world, Lady Liberty no longer welcomes immigrants with open arms. The militarization of police activity that is so striking in the other shows we have examined is very much on view in *Fringe* as well. The FBI rarely shows up in an episode without aerial surveillance, full-body armor, and a SWAT team. Concern about foreigners and other alien and subversive forces, specifically terrorists, has blurred the line between the military and the police. Throughout the show, federal authorities intervene without hesitation in what appear to be purely local jurisdictions.

In *Fringe,* people on our side are the first to penetrate into the other universe, with disastrous consequences for that world. At the points of contact, the very fabric of reality begins to dissolve in the parallel universe. Its authorities have had to learn how to cordon off and quarantine areas where breaches between the two universes have occurred. This is Homeland Security with a vengeance. In the jargon of the series, most of Boston has been "ambered," encased with a fluid that quickly solidifies, leaving the people thus trapped in a state of suspended animation. "Ambering" is a powerful symbol of the way government operates. To protect its citizens, it freezes them in place, so that they can do no harm. Unfortunately, in such circumstances, they cannot do anything at all. Here in its purest form is the paradox of government power: to protect its citizens, it feels that it needs to take all the life out of them. *Fringe* presents ambering as a controversial government policy. We repeatedly see crowds of protesters, carrying signs with slogans such as "Release the Ambered" and "Amber Is Death" ("Olivia," 3.1). Evidently the amber controversy ended up in court, with the frozen citizens declared legally dead, even though we learn in "Amber 31422" (3.5) that they can be revived.

Throughout *Fringe,* governments are hostile to the freedom and mobility of their own people. As its name indicates, the series portrays governments obsessed with people on the fringe of society. Like *The X-Files,* it focuses on migrants, loners, outcasts, misfits, and other kinds of stateless people, who often strive for and achieve some form of invisibility or otherwise drop "off the map" ("6955 KHZ," 2.6) or "off the grid" ("Concentrate and Ask Again," 3.12) . Often, as in *The X-Files,* these shadowy figures are shape-shifters.[56] The aim of the Fringe Division is to identify and locate these disturbingly mobile figures and clamp down on their suspicious and subversive activities.

But as the series repeatedly shows, the technologies that allow a government to exert and maintain control over its citizens also give them the possibility of eluding and escaping its authority. *Fringe* consists of a battle on both sides of the parallel-universe divide between government efforts to keep track of citizens' movements and their efforts to evade this monitoring and control. This aspect of the series becomes especially dramatic in the third season, when Olivia is trapped in the parallel universe and becomes a homeless, stateless person there. She even lacks the obligatory identity card—called a Show Me—and must rely for help on the ultimate symbol of perpetual mobility: a cabdriver. Several episodes focus on her struggles to elude the efforts of the parallel Fringe Division to capture her. In an *X-Files*–style reversal, she was the hunter in our world, but becomes the hunted in the other. In particular, she is trying to avoid medical experimentation on her by "Walternate," Walter Bishop's counterpart in the parallel universe. In *Fringe,* medicine is as much the villain as in *The X-Files,* and for the same reason: it represents the triumph of an inhuman and inhumane science over fellow feeling and family warmth. In our universe, Walter had already subjected Olivia when she was a child to horrific experiments, forcing dangerous and untested drugs on her in an effort to develop her mental powers.

She becomes the key to traveling between the universes and hence is of great importance to both governments in their efforts to police and sometimes cross the borders.

A parallel universe would seem to be a government's worst nightmare. It cannot tolerate the idea that there is a space in which its citizens might be free of its authority and even oblivious of its very existence. What is worse, these people obey a different government. In that sense, they are "aliens" and pose a threat to the original government. The very notion of a parallel universe suggests that any one government is limited. No matter what it claims, its authority is never universal. It keeps bumping against the borders of other governments, which open up different possibilities for their citizens. The parallel-universe idea represents the core of freedom—the perennial human ability to imagine the world as other than it is, to dream of a world in which events have turned out differently. The imagination is the most powerful weapon that can be used against any given state—one can fantasize it out of existence by envisioning an alternate world.[57] The state likes to present itself as inevitable, the unavoidable outcome of history. Its official chronicles portray its emergence as not a contingent but a necessary development that culminates in and justifies the nation-state exactly as it is (in American history, this concept is known as "manifest destiny"). "Accept no substitutes" is the fundamental claim of every state; "There is an alternative" is the fundamental idea behind the notion of parallel universes.

Altered States

Fringe even maps the alternate United States differently. In "The Plateau" (3.3), we learn that in the parallel universe Texas is divided into two states, North and South. A prominent map in Walternate's Liberty Island office can be freeze-framed to reveal all sorts of cartographic anomalies.[58] The alternate America evidently does not include Alaska and Hawaii; a substantial portion of California has disappeared (presumably into the Pacific as a result of a catastrophic earthquake); North and South Carolina are united into one state called simply "Carolina"; the Upper Peninsula of Michigan is not part of the United States (presumably because it is part of Canada); and so on. A map is a nation-state's most basic image of its stable identity. But *Fringe* reminds us that the political borders drawn on a map are conventional, unstable, and mutable. Had history taken a different course, the borders within and around America might have been drawn differently. In this fundamental geographic sense, the identity of the United States would have been altered.

Over the course of *Fringe,* its characters increasingly develop the ability to move between the two universes and thereby to escape the power of one government or the other. The series in effect deals with the fringe areas Scott explores in his *The Art of Not Being Governed,* the borderlands between different regimes, in which people can carve out a zone of freedom by playing off one government against the other. *Fringe* repeatedly portrays life on the margin; and, although it usually presents marginalized figures as freakish and dangerous, like *The X-Files,* it often treats them sympathetically. As a parent tells a child in "Do Shapeshifters Dream of Electric Sheep?" (3.4), "Sometimes monsters aren't all that bad." Fringe phenomena are precisely those that challenge government control. Despite concerted efforts by authorities in both universes, they seem to be losing the battle against fringe phenomena, as the fabric of both universes begins to fray and tear apart at the margins. *Fringe* creates an effective image of the new borderless world of globalization, in which nation-states can no longer secure their frontiers. As traffic increases between the universes, a country's native citizens in effect become immigrants, aliens in its midst who are, in fact, alienated from the regime. That is a striking symbol of what it is for a nation-state to be globalized and see its traditional sense of its national identity weakened and undermined.

At its core, *Fringe* portrays what happens when a government views its own people as its worst enemy because they refuse to stay in place and be counted. The government does everything it can to track and control their movements and shut down any contingent and unpredictable developments in society. The conjunction of the parallel universes brilliantly illustrates this idea. Our side distrusts and hunts down the people coming from the other side. The other side distrusts and hunts down the people coming from our side. *And yet they are the same people.* The two governments even end up suspicious of their own agents, who have a strong propensity to act like traitors when they cross between universes and sometimes even when they do not. *Fringe* portrays a society that has turned in on itself in total paranoia, living on the principle, to use the famous line from *Pogo,* "We have met the enemy and he is us."[59] Or, as Walternate tells Olivia's counterpart in the other universe (known in the show's jargon as "Fauxlivia"), "I told you there would be invaders coming over here from the other side, but I didn't tell you they would be us" ("Over There, Part 2," 2.22).

Fringe depicts the disturbing results when a nation-state becomes obsessed with the idea that its greatest enemies are freely moving among the ranks of its own citizens. The fact that the series shows both universes crumbling is a powerful image of the way this attitude leads to a society's implosion and self-destruction. The two worlds of *Fringe* are criss-crossed by "shatter zones," to use one of Scott's basic terms. He could well be describing the TV series when he defines the term: "It is perhaps one of the features of shatter zones located at the interstices of unstable state systems that there is a premium on the adaptability of identities. Most hill cultures have, as it were, their bags already packed for travel across space, across identities, or across both."[60] For *Fringe,* one would, after the third season, have to add "across time," but otherwise this passage goes right to the heart of the show. It explains the mutability of identity that is one of the hallmarks of its characters, and, above all, it aptly characterizes its political setting. *Fringe* takes place in "shatter zones located at the interstices of unstable state systems," the fault lines between warring regimes. Under the pressure of their own paranoia, the regimes in *Fringe* are fragmenting and literally falling apart. The characters in *Fringe* seem to be faced with the sad choice of living under one authoritarian regime or another, both dominated by a technocratic medical science and a military-industrial complex. But the series seems to show, in Scott's terms, that if people could learn to move between the two parallel universes in a gypsy-like existence—to dwell in the cracks, as it were, between the two regimes—they might achieve a minimal degree of freedom and independence.

Yet freedom proves to be elusive in *Fringe,* even though its very premise seems to point to the contingent nature of human existence. Several events that are often held responsible for turning history in the wrong direction in our world did not happen in the other world, including two of the most regrettable incidents in American history, the Kennedy assassination and the Watergate scandal. Many people dream of just such a world and speculate how much better it would have turned out. And yet, *Fringe* shows, somehow the government in the other world became just as authoritarian as our government, if not more so. *Fringe* seems to suggest that no matter what happens in history, governments will struggle against freedom because ultimately their enemy is history itself, the contingent, spontaneous, and unpredictable unfolding of human action over time. In both universes, the government takes credit for, and bases its authority on, protecting its people from their enemies. But, deep down, *Fringe* suggests that the greatest enemy of the people may be their own government. The opposition between the two parallel universes covers over a deeper and more fundamental opposition—that between each government and its society. In fact, in both universes the government uses the threat of "aliens" to increase its surveillance of and control over its own society. Apparently at war with each other, the two universes are really at war with the freedom of their own people.

Fringe epitomizes the way in which contemporary invasion narratives differ from the 1950s flying saucer movies described in chapter 4. Those films reflected a Cold War mentality: the threat to America clearly came from external enemies; the Martians generally stood in for the Soviets. Fear of internal subversion usually focused on communist infiltration, and thus could still be linked to a particular foreign power. In *Fringe*, Walter looks back nostalgically to the good old days when he worked for the CIA and the Department of Defense in the clear-cut struggle against the "commies" and the "pinkos" (see, for example, "Earthling," 2.6). In contemporary invasion narratives since *The X-Files*, the enemy cannot be as easily identified, and is as likely to come from inside the U.S. borders as from outside them.[61] And what is frightening about the invaders is not their difference, but their sameness. This in part reflects the distinction between the Cold War and what has come to be known as the War on Terror, which is a much more open-ended and nebulously defined conflict, with no clear enemies, and sleeper cells a major concern. Shows such as *The X-Files* and *Fringe* go so far as to suggest cynically that in the absence of real enemies to underwrite its authority the government will, if necessary, fabricate them.

At first sight, a government would seem to be threatened by the existence of a parallel universe as an alternate to its authority. But a parallel universe might provide a way for a government to prop up its authority. It might conjure up the specter of a parallel universe to frighten its citizens into tame submission to its rule. If a government can no longer exploit the threat of external enemies, it can generate fears that the enemy comes from among its own citizens. The official message of the parallel universe idea runs something like this: "Look around you. The ordinary people who seem to be just like you—your neighbors, the people you trust—may be aliens, they may be from another world, intent on destroying you. Report any suspicious activities."[62] Or, as signs in the alternative universe put it, "Report Anomalies." The notion of a parallel universe provides a way for a government to divert its people's attention from its authoritarian rule by fixating them on their own fellow citizens as their worst enemy. The complex mythology of *Fringe* may ultimately represent the way governments legitimate themselves as their citizens' only line of defense against their own society, which is to say, against themselves. For all the Byzantine complexities of its plot, in one respect *Fringe* may be the most direct of all the series we have examined. Several of the others hint darkly that the aliens they portray somehow reflect aspects of the American political system, especially its potential for a technocratic despotism. Only in *Fringe,* with its idea of a parallel universe, is the suggestion clear that when we look at Walternate's maximum security regime, we are looking into a mirror.

Fringe seems deeply pessimistic about politics. It would be pointless to ask if its viewpoint is right-wing or left-wing when its central idea is that, in Orwellian fashion, warring regimes are really mirror images of each other. They may seem to be political opposites, but deep down they are united in their obsessive need to control their own populations. *Fringe* portrays the hope for a better government as utopian and even quixotic. We may fantasize that if only events had worked out differently, government might have become benevolent, but that is to misunderstand its nature. *Fringe* frustrates the utopian impulse that is often at work in science fiction.[63] We can try to imagine a better world, but it turns out to be only marginally different from our own. We may get zeppelins and two states of Texas for the price of one, but we still live under what looks a great deal like a police state. For all the fun that the creators of *Fringe* had coming up with an alternate universe, what is striking is how little difference all the changes end up making in world history. The famous butterfly effect does not seem to operate on the political level in *Fringe.*[64] For example, the survival of the *Hindenburg* evidently did not somehow result in a German victory in World War II—that sort of development often happens in parallel universe stories. All the differences in the alternate United States do not seem to add up to a fundamental change in the American regime. On both sides of the cosmic divide, an imperial technocratic state prevails.

According to *Fringe,* the basic impulse of government is imperialistic: to keep expanding the sphere of its authority in the ultimate hope of wiping out "parallel universes." But as we saw in discussing the real empires of Rome and Britain, and the logic of empire in *The X-Files,* as empires expand, they eventually reach a limit, ingesting new matter until they bite off more than they can chew, as it were, and develop indigestion, unable to assimilate new forces without weakening their sense of their own distinct identity. Fortunately for human freedom, empires always fray at their margins when they rub up against other empires (again symbolized in *Fringe* by parallel universes). Because of the instability and permeability of empires at their frontiers they cannot eradicate human freedom.[65] That is why in the series the most interesting characters always dwell on the fringe of society—and not just the motley assortment of shape-shifters, rebels, criminals, mad scientists, computer nerds, psychopaths, lunatics, freaks, and other aberrant individuals who liven up the plots and create all the mysteries. The main characters are fringe figures, too. In an interview, executive producer Jeff Pinkner said about the series: "The reason the show is called *Fringe* is because ultimately it's about these characters who are the fringe of society."[66] As Walter says in "Night of Desirable Objects" (2.2), "We're all mutants." Peter, for example, is described as a "misfit" and a "nomad" in the first episode—and a "high school dropout" to boot.[67] In "Johari Window" (2.11), Olivia says that, as a result of her job, "[I feel] like I was a freak, like I had suddenly grown a third eye. Doing this job makes you less and less normal."[68] Olivia, Peter, and Walter may be devoted to protecting the mainstream of society, but they have to stand well outside its currents to be able to do so. Ostensibly the series portrays the defense of the center of society against the fringe, but it always shows that the fringe is more interesting than the center.

Bowling Alone

Olivia, Peter, and Walter do not lead normal lives. Although they may crave nothing more than to settle down into ordinary family life, their careers and missions prevent them from doing so (here again is the choice between family and a larger cause that we have seen throughout these alien invasion narratives).[69] Olivia's childhood had to be sacrificed so that she could develop the unusual powers that make it possible for her to travel between the universes. Peter has been singled out to save one universe or the other or both, but only at the cost, it appears at the end of season three, of his very existence. The way he fuses with the Doomsday Machine provides a powerful image of the individual being absorbed into the state apparatus. In one way or another, both Olivia and Peter work for the federal government, and it ends up destroying their lives as ordinary human beings, specifically their ability to create a family of their own.[70] The main characters in *Fringe* apparently do not have lives outside of the institutions they work for—whether government agencies, corporations, or universities. Olivia's cute and precocious niece, Ella Blake (Lily Pilblad), seems to represent the value of family life as an alternative to a government career, and yet we learn in the flash-forward episode "The Day We Died" (3.22) that she too will end up working for the FBI when she grows up. Civil society—any sphere of activity independent of the government—seems weak in the world of *Fringe*. When Harvard professor Robert Putnam was looking for an image of the weakening of civic association in contemporary America, he chose "bowling alone."[71] Sam Weiss (Kevin Corrigan)—the man who mentors Olivia and restores her confidence in season three—operates a bowling alley in Boston. It is virtually empty whenever we see it, with at most one bowler at a time. When Olivia goes there, she goes alone.

Walter Bishop perfectly embodies the way in which the margin comes to occupy the center in *Fringe*. He is a loner and a misfit. His taste for LSD helps define his place at the Timothy Leary end of the social spectrum. For years he was institutionalized for mental instability, and he remains emotionally fragile even when released in his son's custody. He carries an enormous burden of guilt, first of all in personal terms, for his abuse of both Peter and Olivia as children. But he also feels like a criminal, responsible for destroying one or both universes because of his reckless experiments. In "The Day We Died" we see Walter convicted as a criminal and imprisoned—he has, in fact, become identified in public as "the most reviled man in the universe."

Yet this criminal outcast is often the only person who can solve the fringe-science mysteries, and he has to come up with ways of dealing with the threats from the parallel universe. In the other United States, his counterpart, Walternate, is secretary of defense, a pillar of the community who is charged with protecting it.[72] John Noble does a brilliant job of playing both roles, capturing perfectly the unnerving instability of the one and the reassuring stability of the other. That the two Walter Bishops are ultimately one may be the most profound comment *Fringe* has to make on the nature of government. What from one angle looks like a calm, reliable government official from another looks like a mad scientist. At the center of government over here is a refugee from its own carceral institutions, while over there, Walternate turns out to be as much of a mad scientist as Walter Bishop when it comes to his treatment of Olivia. At times, one gets the feeling in *Fringe* that the inmates are running the asylum. No one else seems capable of handling the craziness of the universe, or rather universes. In a typical moment in *Fringe,* in "The Last Sam Weiss" (3.21), Walter says of one of his schemes, "I know it sounds crazy, but it's our only viable option." Craziness is so basic to the operation of the Fringe team that Peter says in "Olivia" (3.1), "I'm sure tomorrow will bring the usual insanity." A regularized insanity is about the best *Fringe* has to offer when it comes to achieving order in the world.

Just as we saw in *The X-Files* and *24* in chapter 9, in *Fringe* the government is incapable of protecting its citizens if it sticks to its own bureaucratic rules and procedures. In "What Lies Below" (2.12), Walter says that he has "little patience for small-minded bureaucrats." In the first season, *Fringe* went out of its way to show federal bureaucracy impeding the efforts of the Fringe Division, above all with the series' portrait of an obnoxious, intrusive, and genuinely repellant representative of Homeland Security, who conducts a personal vendetta against Olivia and keeps thwarting her efforts to fight crime. The Fringe team operates as a rogue outfit within the U.S. government. As in *The X-Files* and *Threshold,* the representative branch of the federal government cannot be trusted in *Fringe*. In "Do Shapeshifters Dream of Electric Sheep?" (3.4), for example, a U.S. senator turns out to be a mole from the parallel universe. The Fringe team cannot depend on any other agents of the government to support or protect them. Olivia repeatedly relies on her unusual psychic powers to solve mysteries that would otherwise baffle the FBI. She chafes under the restrictions the FBI places on her and is always asking her boss to cut through red tape to enable her to act immediately on her instincts and her intuitions. Peter has a shady criminal past and many disreputable associates. He often must step outside the law to do what the FBI is forbidden to do. And of course Walter never respects the ordinary rules of hospital procedure, especially when it comes to his use of untested and dangerous drugs on his "patients." *Fringe* shows again and again that one cannot uphold the law without breaking it.

In sum, *Fringe* portrays a world in which government tries desperately to normalize society, to protect the mainstream from any subversive forces on its fringes. Just as in *The X-Files,* we see the whole array of governmental or quasi-governmental institutions that seek to impose normality on its citizens: the police station, the prison, the laboratory, the university, the elementary school classroom, the corporation, the clinic, the hospital, the insane asylum, and so on. But society cannot get along without its "lunatic fringe." Even the most oppressive government depends on maverick individuals like Olivia, Peter, and Walter. Without their ability to think outside the box and act outside the law, the government would be powerless to deal with fringe phenomena. Freedom is in a very precarious position in the series, but it nevertheless turns out to be essential to human life.[73]

The Show Heard 'Round the World

When both *The Event* and *V* were canceled in the spring of 2011 just as I was writing about them, I began to wonder whether my analyzing a TV show had become the kiss of death (and whether I could find some way to exploit this uncanny power in the service of rival networks). The renewal of *Fringe* for a fourth season gave me some hope that a show could survive my critical scrutiny, and, before I could start worrying that the alien invasion narrative had become moribund in American pop culture, TBS announced *Falling Skies* (2011–) for the summer season. Steven Spielberg is an executive producer of the series; he is generally credited with knowing what the American people want to see in film and television. And *Falling Skies* is yet another alien invasion narrative. The story begins six months after space aliens have invaded Earth and nearly exterminated humanity. The series focuses on a group of refugees who have linked up with some remaining military forces to fight the aliens in Massachusetts. In what may well be a television first, the hero is a Boston University professor, and, since his subject is history, the show is filled with pointed comparisons to past events.

Given its setting, the show's most prominent historical reference point is the American Revolution. At one point, Professor Tom Mason (Noah Wyle) informs his followers, "The battles of Lexington and Concord were fought not too far from here. A small force of colonists against the entire might of the British Empire." *Falling Skies* relates its alien invasion narrative to the problem of empire and freedom. The imperialist ambitions of the aliens to conquer Earth trigger a freedom movement among the surviving humans, who, in a familiar historical pattern, "take to the hills" and become guerrilla fighters. The ruins of civilization they roam through could once again be described in James Scott's terms as a "shatter zone," where the U.S. government has ceased to exert any authority and the alien empire has yet to establish its control. Seeking a precedent in American history for refusing to give in to the invaders, Mason quotes Patrick Henry: "The battle is not to the strong alone; it is to the vigilant, the active, the brave." The evocation of Patrick Henry—most famous for saying, in the same speech, "Give me liberty or give me death"—sounds the keynote of the show, a celebration of American freedom. The remaining humans are housed for a while in a school named after John Kennedy and bearing this motto: "Education Is a Better Safeguard of Liberty Than a Standing Army."[74] Like *Deadwood, Mars Attacks!, Invasion, The Event,* and *V, Falling Skies* explores whether a small group of ordinary Americans can organize on their own to defend their freedom against powerful forces working to deny them liberty.

Falling Skies features the by-now standard alien-human hybrids. The aliens enslave human children by placing them in a kind of biological harness, which gradually transforms them into something other than human. The professor manages to rescue two boys from the aliens, one of whom is his own son. In a parallel to *V,* the alien biotechnology turns out to have cured the disease of one of the boys and makes both physically stronger. But the price they pay for this improvement in their health is that they lose their freedom to the aliens. Their attachment to their families weakens, and one of the boys, even after he has been liberated from the harness, longs to return to his alien masters and actually tries to escape to rejoin them. Yearning for the feeling of solidarity they gave him with their species, he rejects his link to an individual human family. Like *Invasion* and many other sci-fi narratives, *Falling Skies* appears to allegorize the choice between American individualism and the alien spirit of collectivism.

As a Spielberg production, the series focuses even more obsessively on the nuclear family than any of the other narratives we have examined.[75] Among the remaining humans, everything must be done with the children in mind. The alien invasion has torn apart many families, but we also learn that several of them were broken even before the spaceships arrived. The characters make a major effort to reconstitute their nuclear families, and a lot of substitute parenting goes on in the series. As is typical of Spielberg's work, father-son bonding is at the emotional heart of *Falling Skies.* In a familiar pattern, the characters are repeatedly placed in situations in which they must choose between saving their own children and saving the larger world from the aliens.

Another historical reference point in *Falling Skies* is the Western. One of the characters says of the lawlessness in the wake of the alien invasion, "It's the Wild West out there." Because the aliens have damaged or destroyed much of American civilization (the Internet, for example), the surviving humans are in effect plunged back into a frontier existence. In chapter 2, we looked at a number of cases of genre-crossing. *Falling Skies* is another example of the sci-fi Western, a sort of *Deadwood* without the cuss words. It explores the same problem that fascinated David Milch: whether it is possible to achieve order without law. In the wake of the alien destruction, the characters of *Falling Skies* must try to survive without the state that used to organize their community and provide them with security. They are in effect returned to the state of nature. Or rather, in view of their knowledge of American history, they enter what in chapter 3 I called the postpolitical condition. In their struggle to survive, they are familiar with political institutions and work to reconstitute them. In particular, they can draw on the resources of surviving remnants of the U.S. military. But *Falling Skies* is rooted in the older American idea of a civilian militia. Its heroes are citizen-soldiers, not professional military figures, as their links to Lexington, Concord, and the American Revolution suggest.

With no nation-state to guide them, the characters in *Falling Skies* are perpetually on the move and lead a gypsy-like existence. They must continually scramble for the basic necessities of life, including food, shelter, and medicine. They have to learn how to defend themselves against their enemies, the aliens, who have many high-tech surveillance methods at their disposal and the usual superior weaponry. But the survivors must also figure out how to protect themselves against each other. In a glimpse of a Hobbesian world, the series offers many examples of criminals who seek to rob, rape, and generally injure any helpless humans they can find. *Falling Stars* also features traitors to the human species, individuals who are in cahoots with the aliens and eager to turn over children to their clutches or to report the movements of humans so that the aliens can capture or kill them. Many of the difficulties the human survivors face involve sorting out a chain of command and balancing civilian against military interests. As is typical of the frontier and particularly reminiscent of *Deadwood,* they practice a kind of rough justice, occasionally behaving like vigilantes but on the whole proving adequate to the task of organizing their community by themselves. *Falling Skies* suggests just what we saw in chapter 4 in *Mars Attacks!*—ordinary American people could do a good job of dealing with an alien invasion in the absence of help from the federal government.

With most of them coming from a comfortable urban existence in Boston, the characters generally miss big-city life. But there are compensations for their having been thrust into a kind of small-town life. In contrast to what we saw in chapter 2 in *Have Gun–Will Travel, Falling Skies* embraces the traditional American ideal of the small town. In the absence of the big city, the characters experience a greater sense of community, and, as we have seen, they learn anew the value of family (this is, after all, a Spielberg production). They reassume many of the functions that people earlier turned over to government. For example, they now are, in effect, homeschooling their children, with apparently positive results (the children seem to enjoy school for a change). They have to make do without modern medical facilities. But in return, they get their own family doctor. Not only does Dr. Anne Glass (Moon Bloodgood) make house calls, she even lives in the same house with the main characters. The big-city, research-oriented, hospital-based surgeon they begin with is killed off early in the series by an alien. They are then left with a female doctor who is a "mere" pediatrician, but at least she genuinely cares for their welfare on an individual basis and is not interested in experimenting on them. Besides, if the children are their main concern, who is better to have as a doctor than a pediatrician? As with education, the survivors learn the advantages of securing their own health care in the absence of state support. If I am remembering correctly, no one in the series ever has to fill out a form in triplicate, make a copayment, or worry about meeting a deductible.

For all the sci-fi premise of the series, *Falling Skies* contains many elements of domestic Westerns, such as *Little House on the Prairie* (1974–1982) and *Dr. Quinn, Medicine Woman* (1993–1998). One clever reviewer referred to the show as "watching the Walton family at the end of the world."[76] *The Waltons* (1972–1981) was the quintessential series celebrating old-style rural existence in America and its family values. There is something oddly nostalgic about *Falling Skies.* The characters lose the benefits of modern civilization, but, in an almost Rousseauian spirit, they are freed from many of its drawbacks as well. Forced back on their own resources, they regain a sense of community and a sense of independence with the satisfaction of knowing that for once they are relying on themselves, not the state, to save them. As self-reliant citizen-soldiers, the characters recapture the spirit of the old frontier. Living in the shadow of Lexington and Concord and acting out a kind of eastern Western, they rediscover the traditional American values of freedom and independence.

Globalization and Freedom

Perhaps because I had not yet begun to write about it, *Falling Skies* was renewed for a second season. But whether individual programs are renewed or canceled, alien invasion narratives and the mode I call Un-American Gothic have become firmly ingrained in American popular culture. From what we have seen in *The X-Files, Invasion, Threshold, Surface, The Event, V, Fringe,* and *Falling Skies,* American television seems to be returning obsessively to plots about porous borders, alien invasions, threats to the traditional

American way of life, the hybridization of identity in a globalized world, the dissolution of the nuclear family, and the dangers of a global technocracy. *The X-Files* pioneered this mode, and all these later shows owe a great debt to its creator, Chris Carter, and his staff (many of whom have worked on these *X-Files* clones). Far from having been made irrelevant by 9/11, *The X-Files* led American pop culture into the twenty-first century with formulas well suited to dealing with such issues as terrorism, globalization, and the emerging threat of a worldwide technocratic elite.

As for the relation of the problem of globalization to the problem of freedom, many aspects of globalization have actually contributed to the growth and diffusion of freedom. As an economic phenomenon, globalization involves such developments as free trade and the free movement of capital. In this respect, globalization has helped loosen the grip of nation-states on their citizens and worked to free the productive energies of human beings around the world. But economic globalization is not the same as political globalization. To the extent that globalization has created supranational political units, it becomes more difficult for individuals to escape the ever enlarging and tightening net of government. Beginning with *The X-Files,* almost all the TV shows we have examined in this chapter deal with the increased surveillance capabilities of modern government, its determination to spy into every aspect of its citizens' lives, and its ability to do so because of new technologies. *The Event,* for example, features airborne surveillance drones and many scenes of government officials using satellite coverage to track people's movements in real time. Viewing these shows, you get the impression that, in a Foucauldian nightmare of the panoptical state, your government knows exactly where you are at every moment of the day.

Domestic espionage on the part of government agencies is only one aspect that these shows expose of the dangerous alliance between the modern nation-state and modern science. Biotechnological manipulation of natural functions such as reproduction is another obvious example. These shows convey a sense that modern science is in the service of the state and the modern state is in the service of science.[77] Science created an image of the world as being perfectly predictable, and, with its computer models of everything from hurricanes to business cycles, it fuels the hope of governments to be able to predict the future and thus control the activities of their citizens.[78] Science also claims to be a universal authority and thus points the state in the direction of universality. When the power of government extends beyond the borders of the nation-state, its threat to freedom only becomes greater. Many have feared that a world government might achieve the greatest tyranny in history, by eliminating all alternatives to and refuges from its rule.[79] The global conspiracies orchestrated by alien invaders in a number of these programs may be an image of the danger of world government.

The concern that all these shows reflect is that globalization and freedom may be at odds with each other, if what globalization means is the triumph of a worldwide technocracy, the universal rule of experts. Alien invasions are almost by definition associated with advanced technology. How else could the aliens get to Earth? Thus, the aliens in these narratives tend to represent the power of modern technology and allow the shows to explore its impact on human life and, in particular, the way it poses a threat to freedom. The alien invasion narratives often link a superior technology that offers to solve all the world's problems with a demand for the surrender of individual freedom in return.[80] Reduced to their essentials, all these shows seem to reflect a pervasive feeling among Americans that their government is alien to them, and they are alienated from it. It has become remote from their interests and fails to represent their will. Judging by these shows, one would conclude that Americans no longer feel that they are governing themselves. All the lower-level and local institutions that used to mediate between them and their national government—epitomized by the New England town meeting that is, in effect, recreated in *Falling Skies*—have become lost in the large scale of modern regimes, which reach beyond national borders with international and global agendas. The individual citizen feels dwarfed in such a global context. That explains why these shows, whose stories take a global perspective appropriate to a forward-looking genre like science fiction, nevertheless at the same time focus on the local and the traditional, subjects we associate with a backward-looking genre like the Western. Paradoxically, these programs, with flying saucers, mad scientists, and alien-human hybrids, nostalgically look back to such old-fashioned phenomena as small-town America, religious faith, and, above all, the nuclear family—forces that foster personal independence by creating local centers of gravity to counteract the pull of the giant nation-state.

In one way or another, all these shows juxtapose the old and the new, the local and the global—indeed, they show these forces in conflict. As we saw in chapter 3 on *Deadwood* and chapter 4 on *Mars Attacks!*, turning away from the nation-state to the self-organizing power of ordinary people on the local level may be the best way to preserve freedom. The programs we have examined in this chapter impress us with their futuristic visions of the kinds of worldwide problems we encounter in our age. But they may be more important for reminding us that, even in the era of globalization, individual human beings can still make a difference, starting at the local level. That may be the reason why these invasion narratives focus on the struggles of individual men and women against worldwide conspiracies of seemingly omnipotent alien forces. Again and again, these programs show that the odds may be heavily stacked against humanity, but individuals continue to fight heroically for their freedom. Throughout this book we have seen two antithetical visions of the American people in popular culture. In one, they are pictured as the passive and helpless victims of one apocalyptic scenario after another—alien invasions, terrorist attacks, viral plagues, natural disasters like hurricanes. Unable to fend for themselves, ordinary people panic easily and would destroy themselves if they were not taken care of by their government and the elite corps of experts it commands. In the other vision, the American people band together spontaneously to overcome the obstacles in their way. They are able to respond to crises on their own and deal with their problems, provided that they are allowed to use their inventiveness and Yankee ingenuity. Fighting for what is most dear to them—their homes and families—these ordinary people make up for their lack of expertise with their courage, determination, common sense, and common decency. Only in this second vision are Americans viewed as capable of living as free and independent men and women.

At the very end of the first season of *Falling Skies,* the aliens, speaking through a human child, reveal that they "didn't expect resistance on this level—they find that interesting." This almost clinical response—what strange specimens these human beings are!—might represent the failure of technocratic elites to appreciate the power of the ordinary human desire for freedom. At many points in this book, we have seen that elites have a tendency to underestimate the resilience and the resourcefulness of ordinary people.[81] Speaking in the grand American tradition of resisting tyranny in all forms, even a global technocracy, Tom Mason stands up for Yankee rebelliousness: "You thought this was gonna be easy?" *Falling Skies* is by no means the best of these programs, but it is exactly right to associate the struggles of its characters with America's first battle for liberty. What these shows have in common is the realization that efforts to subvert and destroy freedom are profoundly alien to the original spirit of America. These alien invasion narratives thus epitomize what we have been exploring throughout this book—the way popular culture has wrestled with the problematic nature of freedom while continuing to affirm its value as the American way of life.

ACKNOWLEDGMENTS

Since this book continues the project I began in *Gilligan Unbound,* I refer my readers to its acknowledgments for a fuller record of my debts to all the people who have, over the years, encouraged and supported my work on popular culture.

I want to thank James Pontuso, William Irwin, and Michael Valdez Moses for reading versions of this book in its entirety and making very useful suggestions for improving it. At the University Press of Kentucky, Stephen Wrinn and Anne Dean Watkins heartened me from the beginning with their enthusiasm for this project and have helped me at every stage of my progress. I also thank Allison Webster and Donna Bouvier for their assistance in getting this book into its final shape.

I am deeply grateful to all the editors listed below, who aided in the earlier publication of many of the chapters of this book. Stephen Cox, of *Liberty* magazine, made a special effort to republish my essay on *South Park.*

Over the past decade, I have had the valuable opportunity to present the substance of these chapters as papers at conferences and as lectures at colleges and universities all over the United States. It would take too long to list the many people who sponsored and facilitated these appearances, but I thank them all for the chance to develop my ideas in public and to benefit from lively exchanges with a wide variety of audiences. I should single out the Politics, Literature, and Film section of the American Political Science Association and the Ludwig von Mises Institute for hosting me on numerous occasions.

A special word of gratitude goes to Peter Hufnagel and Andrea Dvorak, who have in recent years joined the small circle of friends who put up with my sometimes impossibly weird taste in pop culture. Being much younger than I am, they have listened wide-eyed to my improbable tales of the ancient days when there were but three networks on television and programming ceased at 1:00 a.m. Being able to draw upon their fresh perspectives has helped me keep in touch with the latest developments in pop culture. I think they were trying to tell me something when they gave me a Blu-ray player for Christmas. Having said a sad farewell to my VCR in the dedication of *Gilligan Unbound* and replaced it with a DVD player for this book, I am prepared to take the next step and follow my young friends' lead bravely into the new world of twenty-first-century entertainment technology.

The introduction was published in an earlier version under the same title in *Philosophy and the Interpretation of Pop Culture,* ed. William Irwin and Jorge J. E. Gracia (Lanham, MD: Rowman & Littlefield, 2007), 161–186.

Chapter 1 was published in an earlier version under the same title in *Print the Legend: Politics, Culture, and Civic Virtue in the Films of John Ford,* ed. Sidney A Pearson Jr. (Lanham, MD: Lexington, 2009), 101–131.

Chapter 3 was published in two earlier (and different) versions: one under the same title in *The Philosophy of the Western,* ed. Jennifer L. McMahon and B. Steve Csaki (Lexington: University Press of Kentucky, 2010), 113–147; the other under the title "The *Deadwood* Dilemma: Freedom versus Law," in *Damned If You Do: Dilemmas of Action in Literature and Popular Culture,* ed. Margaret S. Hrezo and John M. Parrish (Lanham, MD: Lexington, 2010), 21–39.

Chapter 5 was published in an earlier version under the title "Flying Solo: *The Aviator* and Libertarian Philosophy," in *The Philosophy of Martin Scorsese,* ed. Mark T. Conard (Lexington: University Press of Kentucky, 2007), 165–187.

Chapter 6 was published in two earlier (and different) versions: one under the title "The Invisible Gnomes and the Invisible Hand: *South Park* and Libertarian Philosophy," in *South Park and Philosophy: You Know, I Learned Something Today,* ed. Robert Arp (Oxford, UK: Blackwell, 2007), 97–111; the other under the title "Cartman Shrugged: *South Park* and Libertarianism," *Liberty* 21, no. 9 (2007): 23–30.

Chapter 7 was published in an earlier version under the same title in *The Philosophy of Horror,* ed. Thomas Fahy (Lexington: University Press of Kentucky, 2010), 137–160.

Chapter 8 was published in an earlier version under the title "Film Noir and the Frankfurt School: America as Wasteland in Edgar Ulmer's *Detour,*" in *The Philosophy of Film Noir,* ed. Mark T. Conard (Lexington: University Press of Kentucky, 2006), 139–161.

Chapter 9 was published in an earlier version under the same title in *Homer Simpson Marches on Washington: Dissent through American Popular Culture,* ed. Timothy M. Dale and Joseph Foy (Lexington: University Press of Kentucky, 2010), 75–96.

Chapter 10 was published in an earlier version under the title "Un-American Gothic: The Fear of Globalization in American Popular Culture," in *The Impact of Globalization on the United States,* vol. 1, *Culture and Society,* ed. Michelle Bertho (Westport, CT: Praeger, 2008), 109–127.

NOTES

Preface

My epigraph (spoken by the character Jack Cade) is from William Shakespeare, *Henry VI, Part Two*, IV.ii.189–190, in *The Riverside Shakespeare*, ed. G. Blakemore Evans (Boston: Houghton Mifflin, 1974).

1. See Joseph A. Schumpeter, *Capitalism, Socialism and Democracy* (New York: Harper, 1975), 81–86.

2. The person most responsible for popularizing the term *libertarian* was Murray Rothbard. See especially his book *For a New Liberty: The Libertarian Manifesto* (New York: Macmillan, 1978).

3. This libertarian strain is, for example, present in nineteenth-century American fiction, notably in Mark Twain. Many of the characteristics I find in contemporary American popular culture are already evident in Twain. In particular, several of the charges made against contemporary pop culture were made against his work during his lifetime—that his books are vulgar, obscene, blasphemous, sloppily written, and not fit to be read by decent people, let alone children. And now those books are regarded as American classics. On the question of what constitutes the greatness of America, Twain has his hero make a telling observation at the beginning of chapter 33 of *A Connecticut Yankee in King Arthur's Court*, where he condemns the foolish disposition of countries like England to honor their worthless political elites at the expense of the private enterprise inventors who actually benefit humanity: "With the spirit of prophecy upon me, I could look into the future and see [England] erect statues and monuments to her unspeakable Georges and other royal and noble clothes-horses, and leave unhonored the creators of this world—after God—Gutenberg, Watt, Arkwright, Whitney, Morse, Stephenson, Bell." Mark Twain, *A Connecticut Yankee in King Arthur's Court* (Oxford: Oxford University Press, 1997), 257. With their celebration of the entrepreneur, these words are very much in the spirit of *The Aviator* and *South Park*; this passage appropriately comes at the beginning of a chapter that defends free trade; and, of course, the Yankee ingenuity Twain's hero embodies is just another name for entrepreneurship. For more on Twain and American pop culture, see chapter 6, on *South Park*.

4. On this subject, see Lawrence W. Levine, *Highbrow/Lowbrow: The Emergence of Cultural Hierarchy in America* (Cambridge, MA: Harvard University Press, 1988), and LeRoy Ashby, *With Amusement for All: A History of American Popular Culture since 1830* (Lexington: University Press of Kentucky, 2006).

5. For a case study of government regulation of television, see my essay "The Road to Cultural Serfdom: America's First Television Czar," in *Back on the Road to Serfdom: The Resurgence of Statism*, ed. Thomas E. Woods Jr. (Wilmington, DE: ISI, 2010), 171–187, 216–219.

6. Paul Hindemith once confessed to his fellow composer Otto Luening that 80 percent

of his musical compositions were bad. When Luening asked why Hindemith tolerated this failure rate, the creator of masterpieces such as *Mathis der Maler* replied, "Because without the 80 percent, there would never have been the 20 percent." Quoted in Richard Taruskin, *The Danger of Music and Other Anti-Utopian Essays* (Berkeley: University of California Press, 2010), 60. Hindemith is unusually candid in admitting that artistic creation is a hit-or-miss proposition and that a large number of failures is the precondition for a small number of successes. If anything, Hindemith probably underestimates the proportion of failures to successes in cultural production. The aim of criticism is to separate the wheat from the chaff, but in the process critics often forget that the wheat could not come into being without the chaff. They end up with a vision of elite culture as a realm of pure, isolated masterpieces wholly cut off from, and unrelated to, any broader cultural context.

7. I cite examples of this kind of criticism and develop a further critique of the Frankfurt School in chapter 8, on Ulmer's *Detour.*

8. Thus, I differ from Frankfurt School theorists when I discuss the presentation of capitalist entrepreneurs in works such as *The Aviator* and *South Park.* Instead of analyzing the creators of these works as lackeys of capitalism, compelled by the commercial nature of the media to support commerce, I examine the ways in which their works effectively make a cogent argument for free enterprise. This option is not open to Frankfurt School theorists because they do not believe that a cogent defense of free enterprise is possible. The Frankfurt School theorists do not deal with an obvious objection to their view of American pop culture as pro-capitalist: the fact that capitalists are so often portrayed as villains in films and television shows. I discuss this matter in chapter 5, on *The Aviator,* and chapter 6, on *South Park.*

9. See Svetlana Alpers, *Rembrandt's Enterprise: The Studio and the Market* (Chicago: University of Chicago Press, 1988), 59–60: "[Rembrandt was] the head of a large studio operation. He certainly had over fifty students and/or assistants during the course of his career. And others were attracted to his style. He engendered, nurtured, and sold the Rembrandt mode to the Dutch public. . . . From our new knowledge of his studio entourage, we can conclude that for most of his life Rembrandt was not a lone genius but the setter of a certain (and, for a while, a fashionable) pictorial style." For a discussion of the case of *The Man with the Golden Helmet,* see 1–6, 121–122.

10. Janet McTeer, as quoted in Jane Wollman Rusoff, "Bad Shakespeare Is 'Good Fun,'" *CityTalk,* May 25, 2001. See also V. F. Perkins, *Film as Film: Understanding and Judging Movies* (New York: Da Capo, 1993), 161: "The belief that popularity and excellence are incompatible dies hard. It survives in the pejorative undertones of the word 'commercial' and in the equation of significance with solemnity and obscurity. It survives in the blanket condemnation . . . of whole genres of popular cinema, from Biblical spectacles to horror movies, from science fiction pictures to Westerns. It survives, particularly, in the notion that the cinema offers two distinct phenomena, one, important, called art, and the other, trivial, known as entertainment. In its crudest form it amounts to the belief that the quality of a film is inversely proportional to the size of its audience."

11. Vanessa Thorpe, "Salman Rushdie Says TV Dramas Comparable to Novels," *The Observer,* June 12, 2011, http://www.guardian.co.uk/2011/jun/12/salman-rushdie-write-tv-drama (consulted June 23, 2011). For more examples of serious novelists writing for television, see Craig Fehrman, "The Channeling of the Novel," *New York Times,* December 16, 2011.

12. Mickey Rapkin, "They Killed Kenny . . . and Revolutionized Comedy," *GQ*, February 2006, 146.

13. I discuss the attachment of aesthetic theorists to the silent medium in my essay "The Fickle Muse: The Unpredictability of Culture," in *American Culture in Peril*, ed. Charles W. Dunn (Lexington: University Press of Kentucky, 2012), 55–77.

14. I have also tried not to burden this book with theoretical analysis of the nature of popular culture or arguments against alternative views. For my thoughts on these matters, with responses to specific theorists in the area, see my essays "The Art in the Popular," *Wilson Quarterly* 25, no. 1 (Summer 2001): 26–39 (with specific reference to Plato); "Is There Intelligent Life on Television?" *Claremont Review of Books*, Fall 2008: 56–59 (with specific reference to Adorno and Horkheimer); and "Get with the Program: The Medium Is Not the Message," *Academic Questions* 23 (2010): 435–449 (with specific reference to Marshall McLuhan). For more theoretical reflections on the study of popular culture and the special difficulties involved, see "Notes on Method" in my book *Gilligan Unbound: Pop Culture in the Age of Globalization* (Lanham, MD: Rowman & Littlefield, 2001), xxix–xli.

15. I am setting aside the issue of deliberate forgery, although even it raises some interesting philosophical questions about art. See, for example, Denis Dutton, *The Art Instinct: Beauty, Pleasure, and Human Emotion* (New York: Bloomsbury, 2009), 177–188.

16. For a fuller discussion of the relevance of Darwinian biology to understanding artistic form, see my essay "The Poetics of Spontaneous Order: Austrian Economics and Literary Criticism," in *Literature and the Economics of Liberty: Spontaneous Order in Culture*, ed. Paul A. Cantor and Stephen Cox (Auburn, AL: Ludwig von Mises Institute, 2009), 21–62.

17. One of the most judicious of American auteur theorists, Andrew Sarris, is eloquent on just this point: "The fascination of Hollywood movies lies in their performance under pressure. Actually, no artist is ever completely free, and art does not necessarily thrive as it becomes less constrained." *The American Cinema: Directors and Directions, 1929–1968* (New York: Da Capo, 1996), 31. See also Perkins, *Film as Film*, 172: "John Huston said: 'Some of the worst pictures I've made, I've made since I've had complete freedom.' Creative freedom does not guarantee, nor does industrial production rule out, a good result. In the cinema we are involved with a product, not a system of production. We can reach a judgment without knowing how a film was made."

18. The irony, of course, is that the Victorian novel and nineteenth-century Italian opera were the pop culture of their day and resulted from a largely commercial system of production. Only time has elevated the Victorian novel and nineteenth-century Italian opera to the level of elite culture and led many critics to forget their commercial roots. As we have seen, Shakespeare also worked in the chief medium of commercial pop culture of his era. It is remarkable how many of the works that are now regarded as artistic masterpieces grew out of what was viewed—and often condemned—as vulgar pop culture in their day. There have been important artistic movements that were elitist even at their origin, such as French neoclassical drama or modernist poetry, painting, and music. One might call this "the hothouse model of culture." In the alternate model, cultural works grow out of the same soil, only some flourish and come to tower over the others. In the elitist model, true works of art must be developed in isolation from the cultural mainstream, under fundamentally different (chiefly noncommercial) conditions. Whether this elitist model generates works superior in quality to those with popular origins is a very interesting question, which I leave to my readers to ponder.

Introduction

My epigraph is from V. F. Perkins, *Film as Film: Understanding and Judging Movies* (New York: Da Capo, 1993), 160.

1. This principle was the cornerstone of the New Criticism. See, for example, Cleanth Brooks, *The Well Wrought Urn* (New York: Harcourt Brace, 1947), where he defends "the proposition that *every word* in a poem plays its part" (221; italics in the original). The New Critics did not, of course, invent this principle, and it has in fact often been embraced by authors themselves. See, for example, a letter Ernest Hemingway wrote on March 31, 1925, to his publisher, Horace Liverwright, warning him not to make any changes in the text of his collection of short stories, *In Our Time:* "It is understood of course that no alterations of words shall be made without my approval. . . . [T]he stories are written so tight and so hard that the alteration of a word can throw an entire story out of key. . . . There is nothing in the book that has not a definite place in its organization. . . . If cuts are made . . . , it will be shot to pieces as an organism." *Ernest Hemingway: Selected Letters, 1917–1961,* ed. Carlos Baker (New York: Charles Scribner's Sons, 1981), 154–155.

2. For a real-life example of this kind of practical reality in the motion picture business, see Tom Weaver, "An Interview with Shirley Ulmer," in *The Films of Edgar G. Ulmer,* ed. Bernd Herzogenrath (Lanham, MD: Scarecrow, 2009), 272. Ulmer's wife reports of the director's habits on a movie set: "He always got to a point where he would suddenly say, 'Well, it's getting towards the end of the day. I'm gonna *cheat—and* you're gonna cheat along *with* me. We're gonna go *fast,* we're gonna do one take.' They would call him 'One-Take' Ulmer" (italics in the original).

3. For more on this bit of television history, see my book *Gilligan Unbound: Pop Culture in the Age of Globalization* (Lanham, MD: Rowman & Littlefield, 2001), xxxv–xxxvi. See also Brian Lowry, *The Truth Is Out There: The Official Guide to the X-Files* (New York: Harper, 1995), 23–25, 64–65.

4. For general discussions of the relation between popular culture and elite culture, see Harriett Hawkins, *Classics and Trash: Traditions and Taboos in High Literature and Popular Modern Genres* (Toronto: University of Toronto Press, 1990); Herbert J. Gans, *Popular Culture and High Culture: An Analysis and Evaluation of Taste* (New York: Basic Books, 1999); Russell Nye, *The Unembarrassed Muse: The Popular Arts in America* (New York: Dial, 1970), 1–7; and Richard Keller Simon, *Trash Culture and the Great Tradition* (Berkeley: University of California Press, 1999). On this specific point, Gans writes (37): "the freedom of creators depends less on whether they are in high or popular culture than on whether they are working in an individual or group medium. A novelist can create a finished product by himself, but playwrights, filmmakers, and musicians are inevitably involved in group enterprises, and their work is often changed by other group members who also participate in creating the finished product." On this point, see also Jack Stillinger, *Multiple Authorship and the Myth of Solitary Genius* (Oxford: Oxford University Press, 1991), 163; and Perkins, *Film as Film,* 158–159, 169.

5. See David Bevington, "General Introduction," in Bevington, ed., *The Complete Works of Shakespeare* (New York: Addison-Wesley, 1997), lxvii.

6. *Poetics,* 1451a. The key passage comes at the end of section 8: "And the parts of the events ought to have been put together so that when a part is transposed or removed, the

whole becomes different and changes. For whatever makes no noticeable difference if it is added or not added is no proper part of the whole." *Aristotle: On Poetics*, trans. Seth Benardete and Michael Davis (South Bend, IN: St. Augustine's Press, 2002), 26.

7. Gary Saul Morson, "The Prosaics of Process," *Literary Imagination* 2 (2000): 379. Aristotle does say that some authors have "discovered not by art but by chance" the right subjects for tragic treatment (*Poetics* 1454a, in Benardete and Davis, 36), but here he is referring to the genesis, not the form, of works of art. Elsewhere Aristotle makes it clear that in a good plot, things will appear to happen not by chance, but in accord with some design: "it will be more wondrous than if they come to be spontaneously or by chance, since even among chance things those seem most wondrous which appear to have come to be as if for a purpose" (*Poetics* 1452a, in Benardete and Davis, 28).

8. This contrast, originally formulated by German critic August Schlegel, was famously articulated by Samuel Taylor Coleridge in his lectures on Shakespeare: "The form is mechanic when on any given material we impress a pre-determined form, not necessarily arising out of the properties of the material. . . . The organic form . . . is innate; it shapes as it develops from within." Quoted in David Perkins, ed., *English Romantic Writers* (New York: Harcourt Brace, 1967), 500.

9. For a brilliant and concise account of these developments in aesthetics, see Martha Woodmansee, *The Author, Art, and the Market: Rereading the History of Aesthetics* (New York: Columbia University Press, 1994).

10. On Coleridge's plagiarism in general, see Norman Fruman, *Coleridge, the Damaged Archangel* (New York: George Braziller, 1971); for a discussion of the specific issue of organic unity and Coleridge's relation to the Schlegel brothers, see ibid., 205–214.

11. For examples of the influence of Coleridge on the New Criticism, see Brooks, *Well Wrought Urn*, 7–8, 26–27, 258. For the idea of the "structure of the poem as an organism" in New Criticism, see 213. See Woodmansee, *Author, Art, and the Market*, 98, for a more general connection between Romanticism and the New Criticism.

12. For further discussion of this point, see my essay "The Primacy of the Literary Imagination, or, Which Came First: The Critic or the Author?" *Literary Imagination* 1 (1999): 133–137.

13. Woodmansee, *Author, Art, and the Market*, 4, 28.

14. For the historical background to these developments, see Neil McKendrick, John Brewer, and J. H. Plumb, *The Birth of a Consumer Society: The Commercialization of Eighteenth-Century England* (Bloomington: Indiana University Press, 1982).

15. Alvin Kernan, *Samuel Johnson and the Impact of Print* (Princeton, NJ: Princeton University Press, 1987), 293. Gans, *Popular Culture*, 66, gives a similar account of the "creators of what was now explicitly described as high culture": "The decline of the court reduced their prestige, their source of support, and their privileges. The rise of a huge market for the popular arts meant for them not only a severe reduction of cultural standards but also a loss of control over the setting of standards for publics of lower status and education. In this process the artists forgot the subordination and humiliation that they often suffered at the hands of their patrons and failed to appreciate the freedom and dignity that they acquired even as they lost their guaranteed audience and its economic support. They solved the problem of their audience by denying that they needed one; they created only for themselves and their peers who could appreciate their work. Consequently, they had only contempt for

the new publics on whom they depended for economic support, even though these offered artists greater rewards and more freedom than they had had before. The cult of the artist as genius, later transformed into the romantic image of the artist, provided culture with the prestige it lost when it was no longer associated with the aristocracy." On this point, see also Lee Erickson, *The Economy of Literary Form: English Literature and the Industrialization of Publishing, 1800–1850* (Baltimore: Johns Hopkins University Press, 1996), 104–105. For a thorough critique of the Romantic ideology of the autonomous creative genius, see Jerome J. McGann, *The Romantic Ideology: A Critical Investigation* (Chicago: University of Chicago Press, 1983) and *A Critique of Modern Textual Criticism* (Chicago: University of Chicago Press, 1983), 8, 40, 42.

16. For one of the earliest attempts in English to condemn the emergence of mass culture, see William Wordsworth's preface to the 1800 second edition of *Lyrical Ballads:* "For a multitude of causes, unknown to former times, are now acting with a combined force to blunt the discriminating powers of the mind, and, unfitting it for all voluntary exertion, to reduce it to a state of almost savage torpor. The most effective of these causes are the great national events which are daily taking place, and the increasing accumulation of men in cities, where the uniformity of their occupations produces a craving for extraordinary incident, which the rapid communication of intelligence hourly gratifies. To this tendency of life and manners the literature and theatrical exhibitions of the country have conformed themselves. The invaluable works of our elder writers, I had almost said the works of Shakespeare and Milton, are driven into neglect by frantic novels, sickly and stupid German Tragedies, and deluges of idle and extravagant stories in verse." *Selected Poems and Prefaces by William Wordsworth,* ed. Jack Stillinger (Boston: Houghton Mifflin, 1965), 449. This brief passage contains the germ of the critique of popular culture developed by the Frankfurt School in the twentieth century in such books as *Dialectic of Enlightenment* by Max Horkheimer and Theodor Adorno. For more on the Frankfurt School, see chapter 8, on *Detour.* For a discussion of the importance of the Wordsworth passage, see Woodmansee, *Author, Art, and the Market,* 113–114. She traces it back to German thinking on the subject; earlier she quotes Friedrich Schiller: "There is now a great gulf between the *elect* of a nation and the *masses*" (74).

17. On the connection between the idea of genius and the idea of organic form, see Woodmansee, *Author, Art, and the Market,* 53–54.

18. For the critical hostility to the novel, see ibid., 89–92. Woodmansee cites a number of negative responses to the so-called "reading epidemic," including this one from a writer named Johann Adam Bergk: "the majority of readers devour the most wretched and tasteless novels with a voracious appetite that spoils head and heart. By reading such worthless material people get used to idleness that only the greatest exertion can overcome again" (89). For further examples of nineteenth-century critiques of novel reading, see Jennifer Hayward, *Consuming Pleasures: Active Audiences and Serial Fictions from Dickens to Soap Opera* (Lexington: University Press of Kentucky, 1997), 6, 26–27; and Erickson, *Economy of Literary Form,* 139–141. For a full treatment of the subject, see John Tinnon Taylor, *Early Opposition to the English Novel: The Popular Reaction from 1760 to 1830* (New York: King's Crown, 1943). Going through all these accounts, one is struck by the fact that in the nineteenth century, reading novels was criticized for exactly the same reasons for which watching television is criticized today.

19. On this point, see Erickson, *Economy of Literary Form,* 15, 105, 171–172.

20. Woodmansee, *Author, Art, and the Market,* quotes Schiller as lamenting that "the German public forces its writers to choose according to commercial calculations rather than the dictates of genius" (80) and: "I now know that it is impossible in the German world of letters to satisfy the strict demands of art and simultaneously procure the minimum support for one's industry" (84). For the continuation of this attitude in the present world, see Gans, *Popular Culture,* 191.

21. For some examples, see Cantor, *Gilligan Unbound,* xxxvii and especially 214n6.

22. Ibid., xxxvii, 215n8. For specific examples of *X-Files* writers praising Chris Carter's intervention in their work, see Brian Lowry, *Trust No One: The X-Files* (New York: Harper, 1996), 227–229, and Andy Meisler, *The X-Files: I Want to Believe* (New York: Harper, 1998), 122.

23. Jack Stillinger has assembled a wide range of evidence on this subject; and, as the title of his book—*Multiple Authorship and the Myth of Solitary Genius*—indicates, he uses it to call the Romantic aesthetic into question. For his list of prominent examples of multiple authorship in the history of British and American literature, see 204–213.

24. Stillinger, *Multiple Authorship,* 164–169.

25. Michael Mangan, *Christopher Marlowe: Doctor Faustus* (London: Penguin, 1989), 21: "We know from the evidence of Henslowe's papers that in 1602 he paid two lesser-known writers, William Bird and Samuel Rowley, four pounds, 'for ther adicyones in doctor fostes.'"

26. G. Blakemore Evans, *The Riverside Shakespeare* (Boston: Houghton Mifflin, 1974), 1683–1700; and Scott McMillin, *The Elizabethan Theatre and the Book of Sir Thomas More* (Ithaca, NY: Cornell University Press, 1987), 135–159.

27. For example, Coleridge wrote the opening line of Wordsworth's "We are Seven" and Wordsworth wrote lines 19–20 of the original version of Coleridge's "The Rime of the Ancyent Marinere" (lines 15–16 of the later "The Rime of the Ancient Mariner"). For a detailed study of another example of literary collaboration in the nineteenth century, see Lillian Nayder, *Unequal Partners: Charles Dickens, Wilkie Collins, and Victorian Authorship* (Ithaca, NY: Cornell University Press, 2001).

28. For a full account of Pound's contribution to Eliot's poem, see the chapter "Pound's *Waste Land*" in Stillinger, *Multiple Authorship,* 121–138.

29. Stillinger, *Multiple Authorship,* 146. For further discussion of the Wolfe–Perkins collaboration, see McGann, *Textual Criticism,* 53, 78–79. For further discussion of the general issue of authors working with editors and publishers, see McGann, *Textual Criticism,* 34–35, 42–44, 52–53, 75.

30. Paul Delany offers a particularly trenchant critique of government attempts to subsidize art under socialism in his *Literature, Money and the Market* (London: Palgrave, 2002). See especially 122: "institutions that seek to by-pass the market are not likely to be any more successful in promoting high art on demand. The Soviet writers' unions, for example, specified a preferred literary form (socialist realism) and paid creators directly to make examples of the desired works. The effects of this command economy included a complete collapse of Russian fiction from its earlier achievements, much more dramatic than any decline of the novel in the West." See also ibid., 172–174, for a further critique of government subsidy of the arts and a detailed discussion of how the system functioned, or rather failed to function, in the Soviet Union.

31. See Stillinger, *Multiple Authorship,* 173: "because the product comes to us as a whole entity, we have mistakenly assumed that it was created whole in the first place."

32. Samuel Johnson provides an excellent example of an author who seemed to need deadlines to get him to write; see Kernan, *Samuel Johnson,* 94–96. For another example, see Alan C. Dooley, *Author and Printer in Victorian England* (Charlottesville: University Press of Virginia, 1992), 40, where he discusses William Makepeace Thackeray's "repeated references in his letters to writing frantically against deadlines." For a discussion of Dostoevsky and deadlines, see Gary Saul Morson, *Narrative and Freedom: The Shadows of Time* (New Haven, CT: Yale University Press, 1994), especially 202–203: "the ecstasy of risk also partially accounts for Dostoevsky's habit of accepting money in advance for novels he promised to provide in an impossibly short time. The most famous such incident occurred on July 2, 1865, when he signed a contract with the unscrupulous entrepreneur Stellovsky to provide a novel by November 1, 1866. Stellovsky was counting on the forfeit provisions, which allowed him nine years to publish all Dostoevsky's works for free. Dostoevsky went abroad, played roulette, borrowed more money, and worked on *Crime and Punishment* until it became clear he could not finish it on time. At last, with only a month remaining, he hired a stenographer and in twenty-eight days dictated another novel, completed one day before the deadline. Perhaps not just because of its topic, he entitled the work *The Gambler.*" In addition to reminding us that we owe some great works of literature to publishers' deadlines, this incident shows that some authors, for good or ill, share the risk-taking spirit of the entrepreneur.

33. Sarane Alexandrian, *Surrealist Art* (New York: Thames and Hudson, 1985), 140–150.

34. Morson, "Prosaics," 386.

35. For examples of these sorts of contemporary references in television soap operas, see Hayward, *Consuming Pleasures,* 187–188. Hayward discusses analogous contemporary references in the serialized novels of the nineteenth century (30, 44), including cases of Charles Dickens working from newspaper incidents (47). An example of this sort of contemporary reference early in the history of the English novel is the way Henry Fielding worked the Jacobite Rebellion into the plot of *Tom Jones.* See Lennard J. Davis, *Factual Fictions: The Origins of the English Novel* (Philadelphia: University of Pennsylvania Press, 1996), 203–205, especially 203: "It has been suggested that Fielding did not originally intend to include the rebellion in his work but that he inserted the event at the last moment because it was happening just when he was writing book six."

36. Morson, "Prosaics," 381, and "Sideshadowing and Tempics," *New Literary History* 29 (1998): 608–609.

37. For many examples of this phenomenon, see Dooley, *Author and Printer*—he shows how the mechanics of book production in the nineteenth century introduced all sorts of elements of contingency into the final product. As he puts it in one case, "stereotype plates were subject to an insidious typographical entropy through which textual changes that nobody intended could occur" (4). See also 160, 164. For some specific examples of authors failing to spot textual changes introduced by mistake during the printing process, see 40, 45, and 48 (George Eliot), 40 (William Makepeace Thackerary), and 41 (Charles Dickens). As Dooley sums up the situation (85): "An author may have had complete control over every detail of a text right up to the moment printing began, but once the machines began to turn, faulty readings could appear and slip through without detection, or be noticed and erroneously repaired."

38. Morson, "Sideshadowing," 599–600. Morson says of his distinctive approach to literature, which he calls "tempics" as opposed to "poetics": "In literature and elsewhere,

tempics, as a way of reading that takes time and contingency seriously, should help us to read experience without making a poem of it, and yet find meaning in it" (601).

39. For an example early in the history of the English novel, see Lennard Davis's discussion of the procedures of Samuel Richardson, in *Factual Fictions,* 189: "The method he chose for writing his works was to pass various drafts around to his correspondents and ask for criticism, revisions, and so on." Davis compares this to "writing by committee" and speaks of "spontaneous reactions" to "spontaneous writing," concluding that from its inception "the novel had the possibility of becoming a kind of circulating news/novel-letter, a work perpetually in progress, perpetually added to" (190). For a later example of this kind of literary feedback, involving Tennyson, see Dooley, *Author and Printer,* 21, 52.

40. For a provocative discussion of the problematic aspects of efforts by the Modernist movement to shield artists from commercial pressures, see Lawrence Rainey, *Institutions of Modernism: Literary Elites and Public Culture* (New Haven, CT: Yale University Press, 1998), especially 40, 148–149, 168. In particular, Rainey analyzes the case of the poet H.D. (Hilda Doolittle), who was relieved of commercial publishing pressures by the generous patronage of a woman named Winifred Ellerman (pen name: Bryher). Rainey describes this situation as "a modernist dream—or perhaps nightmare—come true" and characterizes H.D.'s nonfiction prose after 1942 as "a kind of writing that suggests the solipsistic reverie that became her habitual state under Bryher's benevolent but narcotic and claustral care" (156). See Delany, "Paying for Modernism" and "T. S. Eliot's Personal Finances, 1915–1929" in *Literature, Money and the Market,* 146–171, for analysis of other attempts to "establish a modernist literary economy in isolation from the literary marketplace" (146). In the Eliot essay, Delany does a particularly good job of demolishing what he calls Ezra Pound's "myth of the economic martyrdom of modernist writers" (162).

41. Lowry, *Truth Is Out There,* 140; and Cantor, *Gilligan Unbound,* 167–168.

42. In the crisp formulation of Franco Moretti, "The Slaughterhouse of Literature," *Modern Language Quarterly* 61 (2000): 219n12: "if it is perverse to believe that the market always rewards the better solution, it is just as perverse to believe that it always rewards the worse one!"

43. For some concrete examples, see Cantor, *Gilligan Unbound,* xxxvi; and Hayward, *Consuming Pleasures,* 154.

44. See Hayward, *Consuming Pleasures,* 170, and 174–185 for a detailed study of the development of one character in a television soap opera in response to audience feedback.

45. For discussion of some of the aspects and implications of serial publication, see Erickson, *Economy of Literary Form,* 158–168, and Morson, "Prosaics," 385–386. For a fuller discussion of the serial novel and the theoretical problems it raises for understanding literature, see my essay "The Poetics of Spontaneous Order: Austrian Economics and Literary Criticism," in *Literature and the Economics of Liberty: Spontaneous Order in Culture,* ed. Paul A. Cantor and Stephen Cox (Auburn, AL: Ludwig von Mises Institute, 2009), especially 37–76.

46. For examples of Dickens expanding the role of his characters or killing them off in response to sales figures, see Hayward, *Consuming Pleasures,* 58–59, 61; see especially 58: "he greatly expanded Sam Weller's role in *Pickwick Papers,* when sales jumped to forty thousand after Sam's first appearance." In the most extreme case of negative feedback in serialization, the publication of a novel might simply be stopped in mid-career if the public failed to respond favorably to it. See Erickson, *Economy of Literary Form,* 158.

47. Hayward, *Consuming Pleasures,* 2–3.

48. For the various forms of audience feedback in television soap operas, see ibid., 165.

49. See ibid. for examples of both discontinuity in Victorian serial novels (82) and the greater potential for character development (37, 50).

50. See Friedrich Hayek, *Law, Legislation and Liberty,* 3 vols. (London: Routledge, 1982), 1: 9–10, 26–27, and *The Fatal Conceit: The Errors of Socialism* (Chicago: University of Chicago Press, 1988), 24.

51. On the theological model in Romantic aesthetics, see Woodmansee, *Author, Art, and the Market,* 18–19.

52. Let me stress that I am talking about an analogy here, not an identity. Forms of biological and cultural evolution both involve a process of variation and then selection from among the variants by some kind of feedback. But the process of feedback in the two cases is fundamentally different. Darwin founded his theory of the origin of species on the principle of what he called "natural selection," by which he meant to emphasize the fact that conscious choice by something resembling the human mind is nowhere involved in the process. In all forms of cultural evolution, the human mind does of course come into play, and at some point conscious choices must be made. Faced with the range of possible jokes a brainstorming session of comedy writers has developed, the head writer or the comedian has to choose which will be featured in the show's opening monologue. Faced with a wide array of programming, television viewers have to choose which shows to watch. What makes these processes "evolutionary" is that they are not planned out completely in advance; they still involve feedback and hence development over time. In fact, these examples of cultural evolution resemble Darwin's chief analogy for his theory of natural selection—the domestic breeding of animals. The first chapter of *Origin of Species* is entitled "Variation under Domestication" and shows how species change over time when human beings set out deliberately and consciously to alter them. This chapter makes it clear that Darwin himself recognized that evolution can occur as a result of either conscious or unconscious processes. And he recognized the different outcomes involved; domestic breeding, for example, produces results much faster than the unconscious process of natural selection. So does cultural evolution because, unlike biological evolution, it is decidedly "Lamarckian"—in phenomena such as language, acquired characteristics *can* be inherited (which is to say that cultural traditions are deliberately passed down to new generations). For further discussion of the differences between biological and cultural evolution, see Hayek, *Fatal Conceit,* 23–28.

53. For Franco Moretti, see "On Literary Evolution," *Signs Taken for Wonders: Essays in the Sociology of Literary Forms* (London: Verso, 1988), 262–278; *Modern Epic: The World System from Goethe to García Márquez* (London: Verso, 1996), 20, 22, 94, 150, 177–178, 184, 188–191; and "Slaughterhouse of Literature," 207–227. For Gary Saul Morson, see *Narrative and Freedom;* "Sideshadowing and Tempics" and "Contingency and Freedom, Prosaics and Process," *New Literary History* 29 (1998): 599–624, 673–686; and "Prosaics," 377–388.

54. For the element of contingency in Darwinian biology, see Stephen Jay Gould, *Wonderful Life: The Burgess Shale and the Nature of History* (New York: W. W. Norton, 1989), especially 51, 283–291, 299–301, 317–318.

55. Gould, *Wonderful Life,* 300–301. For the application of these ideas to literature, see Morson, "Sideshadowing," 618–621.

56. See the introduction to *Origin of Species,* where Darwin writes, "This is the doc-

trine of Malthus, applied to the whole animal and vegetable kingdom." Charles Darwin, *The Origin of Species,* ed. Gillian Beer (Oxford: Oxford University Press, 1996), 6. For the influence of Smith and classical economics on Darwin, see Hayek, *Law, Legislation and Liberty,* 1: 20–22, 152–153n33; and *Fatal Conceit,* 24–25, 146–147. If Hayek seems biased in favor of a fellow economist, the point is confirmed by a natural scientist: see Stephen Jay Gould, *The Structure of Evolutionary Theory* (Cambridge, MA: Harvard University Press, 2002), 121–125, especially 122: "the theory of natural selection is, in essence, Adam Smith's economics transferred to nature."

57. For Hayek's understanding of spontaneous order, see "Reason and Evolution" and "Cosmos and Taxis," chapters 1 and 2 of the first volume, *Rules and Order,* of his trilogy *Law, Legislation and Liberty,* 1: 8–54. See also "The Theory of Complex Phenomena" and "The Results of Human Action but not of Human Design" in his *Studies in Philosophy, Politics and Economics* (New York: Simon & Schuster, 1967), 22–42, 96–105. For a brief but comprehensive survey of the development of the idea of spontaneous order, see Steven Horwitz, "From Smith to Menger to Hayek: Liberalism in the Spontaneous-Order Tradition," *The Independent Review: A Journal of Political Economy* 6 (2001): 81–97. For more on the concept of spontaneous order and its application in the realm of culture, see the essays in Cantor and Cox, *Literature and the Economics of Liberty,* especially 1–97.

58. For a discussion of contingency and television, see Umberto Eco, "Chance and Plot: Television and Aesthetics," in *The Open Work,* trans. Anna Cancogni (Cambridge, MA: Harvard University Press, 1989), 105–122. Eco deals chiefly with the distinctive phenomenon of live television broadcasts.

59. For the importance of the time element in serial forms, see Hayward, *Consuming Pleasures,* 136.

60. The classic statement of this view can be found in Percy Shelley's *A Defence of Poetry:* "When composition begins, inspiration is already on the decline, and the most glorious poetry that has ever been communicated to the world is probably a feeble shadow of the original conception of the poet." *Shelley's Poetry and Prose,* ed. Donald H. Reiman and Sharon B. Powers (New York: W. W. Norton, 1977), 504. For a critical assessment of this understanding of literary composition, see Dooley, *Author and Printer,* 171, and McGann, *Textual Criticism,* 102–103.

61. For citation of some of these critics (including Theodor Adorno) and further critique of the idea that television has inherent limitations as a medium, see my essays "Is There Intelligent Life on Television?" *Claremont Review of Books,* Fall 2008: 56–59, and "Get with the Program: The Medium Is Not the Message," *Academic Questions* 23 (2010): 435–449.

62. Hayward, *Consuming Pleasures,* 62. I have been concentrating on television, but as Hayward demonstrates, everything I have said about the virtues of multiple authorship and improvisation in this medium applies equally well to the other media of popular culture, including film. I have in effect been arguing against the famous auteur theory of moviemaking, a late descendant of Romantic aesthetics that views films as being created solely by their directors. Indeed, some auteur critics credit certain directors with possessing quasi-divine creative power in shaping their movies into perfect organic wholes. For a good exposition of the auteur theory, see Andrew Sarris, *The American Cinema: Directors and Direction, 1929–1968* (New York: Da Capo, 1996), especially 19–37, 269–278. (As in any judicious presentation of a theory, Sarris makes many reasonable qualifications of its claims and sig-

nificant concessions to its critics.) For a concise and incisive critique of the auteur theory, see the chapter "Plays and Films: Author, Auteurs, Autres," in Stillinger, *Multiple Authorship*, 163–181. I apply my arguments in this introduction about the conditions of television production to the case of a famous movie in my essay "'As Time Goes By': *Casablanca* and the Evolution of a Pop-Culture Classic," in *Political Philosophy Comes to Rick's: Casablanca and American Civic Culture*, ed. James Pontuso (Lanham, MD: Lexington, 2005), 9–24. In the specific case of *Casablanca*, I show how multiple authorship and improvisation managed to produce a cinematic masterpiece, not the botched result auteur theory would have predicted. For the best analysis I know of the issue of authorship in movies and the director's role, see Perkins, *Film as Film*, 158–186. In a balanced discussion, Perkins manages to give the director pride of place in the creation of movies while still acknowledging the role of many others in the process.

63. This is another example of how cultural evolution differs from biological—another case where, in the "selection" phase of evolution, the intervention of a conscious mind is necessary. But notice that this is still a case of spontaneous order. Producers do not perfectly plan the production process from the beginning—they just recognize the "perfect" outcome of a relatively unplanned process when they see it. This is exactly what Hayek is talking about under the formula "the results of human action but not of human design."

64. For a critique of FCC chairman Newton Minow and his famous idea of television as a "vast wasteland," see my essay "The Road to Cultural Serfdom: America's First Television Czar," in *Back on the Road to Serfdom: The Resurgence of Statism*, ed. Thomas E. Woods Jr. (Wilmington, DE: ISI, 2010), 171–187, 216–219.

65. For a comprehensive treatment of this possibility, see Tyler Cowen, *In Praise of Commercial Culture* (Cambridge, MA: Harvard University Press, 1998). See also Perkins, *Film as Film*, 161–162.

1. The Western and Western Drama

My epigraphs are from Aeschylus, *The Oresteia*, trans. Robert Fagles (New York: Viking Penguin, 1975).

1. Ford himself described *The Searchers* as "a kind of psychological epic." Tag Gallagher, *John Ford: The Man and His Films* (Berkeley: University of California Press, 1986), 333. For other uses of the word *epic* in conjunction with the film, see J. A. Place, *The Western Films of John Ford* (Secaucus, NJ: Citadel, 1974), 169, 171–172; Joseph McBride and Michael Wilmington, *John Ford* (New York: Da Capo, 1975), 147; and Richard Waswo, *The Founding Legend of Western Civilization: From Virgil to Vietnam* (Hanover, NH: Wesleyan University Press, 1997), 302. Ford also said of *The Searchers*, "It's the tragedy of a loner" (quoted in Peter Bogdanovich, *John Ford* [Berkeley: University of California Press, 1978], 92); he commented that he wanted to make "a tragedy, the most serious in the world, that turned into the ridiculous" (quoted in McBride and Wilmington, *Ford*, 153); and he explained, "The situation, the tragic moment, forces men to reveal themselves, and to become aware of what they truly are. . . . What interests me are the consequences of a tragic moment—how the individual acts before a crucial act, or in an exceptional circumstance" (quoted in Martin M. Winkler, "Homer's *Iliad* and John Ford's *The Searchers*," in *The Searchers: Essays and Reflections on John Ford's Classic Western*, ed. Arthur M. Eckstein and Peter Lehman [Detroit: Wayne State

University Press, 2004], 163). For other uses of the words *tragic* or *tragedy* in connection with the film, see Waswo, *Founding Legend,* 305; and Gary Wills, *John Wayne's America: The Politics of Celebrity* (New York: Simon & Schuster, 1997), 261. Frank Nugent's screenplay for *The Searchers* (Suffolk, UK: Screen Press, n.d.) describes the faces of the two heroes as "etched by wind and privation and cold into tragic, fanatic masks" (46); this suggests that Nugent also had Greek tragedy in mind.

2. Place says of the role of Monument Valley in *The Searchers,* "Ford uses it as Homer used the sea" (*Western Films,* 171).

3. The only sustained efforts I have found that discuss *The Searchers* in terms of Greek epic and tragedy are both by Martin M. Winkler: "Homer's *Iliad,*" 145–170; and "Tragic Features in John Ford's *The Searchers,*" in *Classical Myth and Culture in the Cinema,* ed. Martin M. Winkler (Oxford, UK: Oxford University Press, 2001), 118–147. Winkler uses the *Iliad* as a basis of comparison, but not the *Oresteia.* For a broader effort to set Ford's work in the context of the epic tradition, see the two chapters on Ford in Waswo, *Founding Legend,* 295–324.

4. Although I focus on the *Oresteia* in my attempt to bring out the classical aspects of *The Searchers,* I also refer frequently to the *Iliad* and the *Odyssey,* and ultimately I wish to show an epic as well as a tragic dimension to Ford's film. I am not claiming that Ford consciously used either the *Oresteia* or the Homeric epics as models for his film; although some influence, direct or indirect, is possible, we are basically talking about similar material generating similar themes.

5. Mera J. Flaumenhaft, *The Civic Spectacle: Essays on Drama and Community* (Lanham, MD: Rowman & Littlefield, 1994), 38–39.

6. Ibid., 42–43.

7. The phrase was coined by critic Thomas Rymer in 1678 in his *The Tragedies of the Last Age Consider'd.*

8. See R. P. Winnington-Ingram, "Clytemnestra and the Vote of Athena," in *Greek Tragedy: Modern Essays in Criticism,* ed. Erich Segal (New York: Harper & Row, 1983), 101; and Bernard Knox, *Word and Action: Essays on the Ancient Theater* (Baltimore: Johns Hopkins University Press, 1979), 65, 68.

9. Flaumenhaft, *Civic Spectacle,* 7–8, 19.

10. Hegel's writings on tragedy are conveniently collected, in English translation, in Anne Paolucci and Henry Paolucci, *Hegel on Tragedy* (New York: Harper & Row, 1975). This volume contains, as an appendix, A. C. Bradley's helpful essay "Hegel's Theory of Tragedy."

11. For Hegel's view of *Antigone,* see Paolucci and Paolucci, *Hegel,* 178.

12. For the conflict between Christianity and the revenge ethic in *Hamlet,* see Paul A. Cantor, *Shakespeare: Hamlet* (Cambridge, UK: Cambridge University Press, 2004), 25–49.

13. For an excellent discussion of the historical moment of Aeschylus and Greek tragedy in general, see Jean-Pierre Vernant and Pierre Vidal-Naquet, *Myth and Tragedy in Ancient Greece,* trans. Janet Lloyd (New York: Zone, 1990), 23–28.

14. Jeanne Heffernan, "'Poised between Savagery and Civilization': Forging Political Communities in Ford's Westerns," *Perspectives on Political Science* 28 (1999): 147.

15. Several critics mention anachronistic elements in the *Oresteia.* Richmond Lattimore speaks of the anachronistic presence of tyranny in the trilogy; see his "Introduction to the *Oresteia,*" in *The Complete Greek Tragedies,* ed. David Grene and Richmond Lattimore (Chicago: University of Chicago Press, 1959), 1: 11n6. Walter Kaufmann says of *The Eumenides,*

"to us Delphi seems a long way from the prehistoric Peloponnesus, and in the second half of this play we proceed to Athens, leaving behind the dark world of irrationality and myth." Kaufmann, *Tragedy and Philosophy* (Garden City, NY: Anchor, 1969), 218. See also Flaumenhaft, *Civic Spectacle*, 10, 31, 36. For the general tension between an archaic heroic world and the modern city in Greek tragedy, see Vernant and Vidal-Naquet, *Myth and Tragedy*, 26–27.

16. Aeschylus may not have known exactly when Agamemnon lived, but he certainly knew that it was centuries before his own day. In effect, the *Oresteia* asks us to believe that an Athenian court was founded barely one generation after the end of the Trojan War.

17. For the way the new legal thought and vocabulary in fifth-century Athens influenced the tragedies written in the city, see Vernant and Vidal-Naquet, *Myth and Tragedy*, 25.

18. See, for example, *Agamemnon*, 52, lines 1224–27. I quote the *Oresteia* from the Robert Fagles translation. Future citations will be incorporated into the body of the essay, with the first numbers indicating the pages and the second the line numbers in Fagles.

19. For Hegel's views on the *Oresteia*, see Paolucci and Paolucci, *Hegel*, 68–69, 177–178, 185–186. For passages in Aeschylus that seem to anticipate Hegel's theory, see *Agamemnon*: "Each charge meets counter-charge./ None can judge between them" (the Chorus at 167, lines 1588–89); *The Libation Bearers*: "Now force *clash* with force—right with right!" (Orestes at 197, line 448); and the exchange between Clytemnestra: "Watch out—the hounds of a mother's curse will hunt you down" and Orestes: "But how to escape a father's if I fail?" (218, lines 911–912).

20. Bernhard Zimmermann, *Greek Tragedy: An Introduction*, trans. Thomas Marier (Baltimore: Johns Hopkins University Press, 1991), 43; and Flaumenhaft, *Civic Spectacle*, 20.

21. In Book XVIII of the *Iliad*, the community at peace on Achilles' shield contains an image of a court arbitration and thus looks forward to the world of the polis: see Jenny Strauss Clay, *The Wrath of Athena: Gods and Men in the Odyssey* (Princeton, NJ: Princeton University Press, 1983), 183–184. Homer's Troy is nominally a city, but he presents it basically as one big family, governed by Priam like a large household; a remarkable number of the important Trojan men we see are Priam's sons. For a contrary view, see Edith Hall, *Inventing the Barbarian: Greek Self-Definition through Tragedy* (Oxford, UK: Clarendon Press, 1989), 14: "The central institution of the Homeric poems is the polis."

22. For Achilles' view of lying, see *Iliad*, Book IX, lines 379–380; I cite the *Iliad* from the translation of Robert Fagles (Harmondsworth, UK: Penguin, 1990). For the differences between Achilles and Odysseus as heroes, see Clay, *Wrath of Athena*, 96–112, 184–185. Homer's treatment of Odysseus shows that, long before Aeschylus, he was aware of the problematic character of the revenge ethos. His portrayal of Achilles' reconciliation with Priam in Book XXIV of the *Iliad* is a recognition of the limits of revenge and an appreciation of the fact that true nobility may require moving beyond vengeance.

23. Lattimore, "Introduction," 8–9.

24. For a thorough comparison of Homer's treatment of Agamemnon's story with Aeschylus', see Kaufmann, *Tragedy*, 199–204.

25. Winnington-Ingram, "Clytemnestra," 90; and Zimmermann, *Greek Tragedy*, 45.

26. Hall, *Inventing the Barbarian*, 1–13.

27. For a thorough analysis of the differences between the Achaeans and the Trojans, see Seth Benardete, *The Argument of the Action: Essays on Greek Poetry and Philosophy* (Chicago:

University of Chicago Press, 2000), 20–27; and *Achilles and Hector: The Homeric Hero* (South Bend, IN: St. Augustine's, 2005), 18–28.

28. This contrasts sharply with the way Muslim warriors are portrayed in the Christian epics of the Middle Ages, such as the *Song of Roland*: they are generally shown to be worshipping demons or false idols; only the Christian warriors worship the true God. On the matter of Greek-Trojan parallels, Hall shows that they have similar political institutions in the *Iliad* (*Inventing the Barbarian*, 14–15).

29. See, for example, James M. Redfield, *Nature and Culture in the Iliad: The Tragedy of Hector* (Durham, NC: Duke University Press, 1981); he argues that Hector is "the true tragic hero of the poem" (109).

30. The Greek word *barbaros* (meaning "barbarian") does not appear in Homer. But Hall points out that "there is one sign in the Homeric poems of the term *barbaros,* in a compound adjective *barbarophonos,* 'of foreign speech,' used of the Carians in the Trojan Catalogue (*Il.* 2. 867)" (*Inventing the Barbarian*, 9).

31. Book IV, lines 498–509.

32. For the general contrast between cowboys and Indians in Ford, see Place, *Western Films*, 233; Gallagher, *Ford*, 249; and Waswo, *Founding Legend*, 316–317.

33. See Redfield, *Nature and Culture,* 123–127, for the ways in which Hector is superior to Achilles in what we would call the domestic virtues.

34. See Winkler, "Tragic Features," 127–128; Edward Buscombe, *The Searchers* (London: British Film Institute, 2000), 21; and Robert B. Pippin, *Hollywood Westerns and American Myth* (New Haven, CT: Yale University Press, 2010), 121.

35. It might be argued that the barbarian elements in Agamemnon are to be traced to the Asiatic origins of the House of Atreus. The glossary in Fagles's edition of the *Oresteia* describes Tantalus as "a Lydian king and founder of the line of Pelops, Atreus, Agamemnon, and Orestes. His Asian origin perhaps implied a streak of un-Greek brutality in him and his descendants" (334). But Aeschylus does not mention the Asiatic origins of Tantalus anywhere in the *Oresteia;* he makes the barbarian elements in Agamemnon a matter of character, not of race.

36. Hall gives specific examples of what these stereotypes were and shows how they actually appear in "oriental" (Near Eastern) literature in the ancient world (*Inventing the Barbarian*, 205–207).

37. Fagles's translation is hardly literal, but the word "barbarian" does occur in the original Greek in this passage. For a more literal translation, see Hall: "Do not pamper me like a woman nor grovel before me like some barbarian with wide-mouthed acclaim" (*Inventing the Barbarian*, 206).

38. Benardete, *Argument,* 101; and Hall, *Inventing the Barbarian,* 206–208.

39. Lattimore, "Introduction," 17–18; Winnington-Ingram, "Clytemnestra," 88; and Vernant and Vidal-Naquet, *Myth and Tragedy,* 265.

40. Hall, *Inventing the Barbarian,* 208–209.

41. Lattimore, "Introduction," 10–11n6.

42. Hall, *Inventing the Barbarian,* 204–205.

43. Flaumenhaft, *Civic Spectacle,* 52: "It is no accident that the Furies so often remind us of the Dionysian maenads in Euripides' *Bacchae.*"

44. See, for example, *The Eumenides,* 237–238, lines 151–157. On this point, see Lattimore, "Introduction," 30.

45. Hall, *Inventing the Barbarian*, 205.

46. Christian Meier points out that *The Eumenides* "is the only time, as far as we know, that Aeschylus sets his action in his own city." Meier, *The Political Art of Greek Tragedy*, trans. Andrew Webber (Baltimore: Johns Hopkins University Press, 1993), 105; see also 131. See also Vernant and Vidal-Naquet, *Myth and Tragedy*, 265.

47. Flaumenhaft, *Civic Spectacle*, 27, 32.

48. Meier, *Political Art*, 113–114; and Flaumenhaft, *Civic Spectacle*, 34–35.

49. Eva Brann, "The *Eumenides* of Aeschylus: Whole-Hearted Patriotism and Moderated Humanity," *St. John's Review* 50 (2008): 28–29, 33–34.

50. Meier, *Political Art*, 134–135.

51. See Flaumenhaft's discussion of Athens' ability to assimilate foreigners (*Civic Spectacle*, 36).

52. Lattimore, "Introduction," 31; Meier, *Political Art*, 114; Flaumenhaft, *Civic Spectacle*, 37; and Brann, "*Eumenides*," 34–35.

53. Meier, *Poliltical Art*, 121.

54. *Civic Spectacle*, 27; see also Brann, "*Eumenides*," 24–25.

55. Flaumenhaft, *Civic Spectacle*, 51.

56. Kaufmann, *Tragedy*, 207, 209; and H. D. F. Kitto, *Greek Tragedy: A Literary Study* (Garden City, NY: Anchor, n.d.), 98.

57. To understand Ethan, it helps to read Herman Melville's characterization of the American frontiersman: "The backwoodsman is a lonely man. He is a thoughtful man. He is a man strong and unsophisticated. Impulsive, he is what some might call unprincipled. At any rate, he is self-willed; being one who less hearkens to what others may say about things, than looks for himself, to see what are things themselves. If in straits, there are few to help; he must depend upon himself; he must continually look to himself. Hence self-reliance, to the degree of standing by his own judgment, though it stand alone." *The Confidence-Man: His Masquerade* (1857; rpt. New York: W. W. Norton, 1971), 125. Chapters 25–27 of *The Confidence-Man*, which deal with what Melville calls "The Metaphysics of Indian-hating," in effect provide a fascinating commentary on *The Searchers* and show that Ford's film has deep roots in a classic American subject, one that is reflected in its greatest literature.

58. Winkler is perhaps the most negative of Ethan's critics; he argues that Ford uses the "standard iconography of westerns" to portray Ethan as a villain ("*Iliad*," 153–154). But elsewhere Winkler compares Ethan to "the tragic sufferer of the Greek stage" ("Tragic Features," 128). Arthur M. Eckstein, in "Darkening Ethan: John Ford's *The Searchers* (1956) from Novel to Screenplay to Screen," *Cinema Journal* 38 (1998), makes similarly contradictory statements about Ethan; he is correct to say that Ethan "is *not* a traditional western hero" (5), but he goes along with Winkler in overemphasizing the "villainous" aspects in his character (11). In his summation of Ford's attitude toward Ethan, Eckstein writes, "It was negative: Ethan has great power and frontier expertise, but Ford intended him to be a psychologically damaged, tragic figure" (17). According to this logic, Shakespeare's attitude toward figures such as Hamlet, Othello, and King Lear would be negative too, and yet these are among the greatest tragic heroes in world literature. Macbeth is perhaps the best example of a figure who would be regarded as a villain in conventional moral terms, but he rises to heroic stature in Shakespeare's complex, tragic portrayal. Winkler and Eckstein make the same error: they begin with the simplistic distinction between heroes and villains in conventional Westerns,

and then, when they find that Ethan does not fit that definition of a hero, they conclude that Ford must think of him as a villain. But a Ford Western is closer to a Shakespearean tragedy than it is to a Tom Mix or a Hopalong Cassidy movie. Ford's heroes became increasingly complicated and complex, culminating in Ethan Edwards, who displays the same sort of mix of virtues and vices typically found in a Shakespearean tragic hero. McBride and Wilmington come closer to the truth than Winkler or Eckstein when they describe Ethan this way: "Ethan is both hero and anti-hero, a man riven in two by his passions, radically estranged from his society and yet driven to act in its name. His strengths and failings, like the promise and danger of the land around him, are inextricable" (*Ford,* 148). See J. David Alvis and John E. Alvis, "Heroic Virtues and the Limits of Democracy in John Ford's *The Searchers,*" in *Print the Legend: Politics, Culture, and Civic Virtue in the Films of John Ford,* ed. Sidney A. Pearson Jr. (Lanham, MD: Lexington, 2009), for the way *The Searchers* departs "from the black-and-white plot of the typical western film" (135) and for their view of Ethan as "Ford's study in the tragic combination of qualities that make civilization possible and yet at the same time threaten to undermine its achievements" (141).

59. On this point, see Alvis and Alvis, "Heroic Virtues," 145. I have transcribed all quotations from *The Searchers* from the Warner Home Video Ultimate Collector's Edition DVD (2006); in some cases, I have consulted the Frank Nugent screenplay (although it often differs in wording from the film Ford shot).

60. *Agamemnon,* 130, lines 714–730. The image of the lion cub reared in a house is usually taken to refer to Helen—an interpretation that fits the immediate context in this choral ode. But in a brilliant reading of the passage, Knox, in *Word and Action,* has shown that the image applies equally well to Agamemnon, Clytemnestra, and Aegisthus (31), and, above all, to Orestes: "In each generation, the children of the house have gone through the cycle of the parable, from auspicious beginning to bloody end" (36). The story of the lion cub becomes emblematic of the whole tragedy of the House of Atreus and hence of the tragic hero in general (see also Vernant and Vidal-Naquet, *Myth and Tragedy,* 253).

61. Buscombe, *Searchers,* 18.

62. For precedents in American literature for Ethan's quest for revenge against Indians, see Leslie A. Fiedler, *The Return of the Vanishing American* (New York: Stein and Day, 1968), 125–126, especially his discussion of Judge Hall's chronicle of Colonel Moredock.

63. McBride and Wilmington speak of "Ethan's craziness" (*Ford,* 158); Gallagher says that "he goes insane" (*Ford,* 335); Eckstein refers to the "near-psychotic Ethan" ("Darkening Ethan," 18); Winkler has a whole section on his "Journey into Madness" ("Tragic Features," 128–132).

64. On the parallel with Achilles, see Alvis and Alvis, "Heroic Virtues," 150. Of course this parallel does not make Ethan's actions "right" in any conventional moral sense, but it does suggest that in a Homeric framework, Ethan's actions are compatible with being a hero, albeit a tragic hero. For other comparisons of Achilles with Western heroes, see John G. Cawelti, *The Six-Gun Mystique,* 2nd ed. (Bowling Green, OH: Bowling Green State University Popular Press, 1984), 83–84; Pippin, *Hollywood Westerns,* 20–21; and Peter A. French, *Cowboy Metaphysics: Ethics and Death in Westerns* (Lanham, MD: Rowman & Littlefield, 1997), 79–80.

65. Wills, *Wayne's America,* 257–258.

66. Critics such as Winkler ("Tragic Features," 127; "*Iliad,*" 155) and Eckstein ("Darkening Ethan," 5), who regard Ethan as a villain, make much of the way he shoots Futterman—in

the back. But they evidently forget that Futterman was coming with two accomplices to kill Ethan while he slept. Winkler refers to this as an "ambush scene" (*"Iliad,"* 166n13), which is correct, but only if one realizes that Futterman was coming to ambush Ethan, not vice versa. Ethan may not behave like a conventional hero in this scene, but his actions are hardly criminal and indeed fit the harsh code of the West. Although Captain Clayton wants Ethan to appear in the state capitol to answer charges that have been made against him in connection with Futterman's death, the Texas Ranger evidently thinks that Ethan will be able to acquit himself of the charges. For a contrary view of this incident, see Pippin, *Hollywood Westerns,* 135.

67. For example, as soon as Brad Jorgensen learns that the Comanches have raped and killed Lucy Edwards, the woman he loved, he races off to attack their camp in an utterly fruitless attempt at revenge and gets himself killed in moments. Brad is young and impulsive; Ethan's wariness as an avenger is clearly the product of his age and experience.

68. There is talk in the film of legal authorities in the state capitol, but they are too remote to aid Ethan.

69. See Place, *Western Films,* 173, and McBride and Wilmington, *Ford,* 158–159.

70. Ethan thus illustrates the traditional epic problem of the hero by nature (a superior warrior) being subordinate to a conventional ruler (an inferior warrior)—what might be called the Achilles-Agamemnon problem. On this issue, see W. T. H. Jackson, *The Hero and the King: An Epic Theme* (New York: Columbia University Press, 1982), 7–14.

71. Place, *Western Films,* 172–173.

72. Ibid., 162. For the Western's hostility to Christianity, and the femininity and domesticity with which it is associated, see Jane Tompkins, *West of Everything: The Inner Life of Westerns* (New York: Oxford University Press, 1992), 32–33, and Fiedler, *Vanishing American,* 141–142. In *Cowboy Metaphysics,* French argues at length that the Western develops a worldview fundamentally antithetical to Christianity's.

73. The Civil War hovers in the background of *The Searchers* much the way the Trojan War does in the *Oresteia.* In both works, the way in which order inevitably breaks down during war serves to recreate the prepolitical situation in which the revenge ethic flourishes. The Civil War background is even more prominent in the Alan Le May novel on which the movie is based; see Le May, *The Searchers* (New York: Berkeley, 1985), 4–5, 80–81, 175, 300.

74. Place, *Western Films,* 164.

75. Buscombe, *Searchers,* 21–23.

76. A third liminal figure is Martin Pauley, who is one-eighth Cherokee and thus also provides a bridge between cowboys and Indians in the story; see Thomas Schatz, *Hollywood Genres: Formulas, Filmmaking, and the Studio System* (Boston: McGraw-Hill, 1981), 75. He enters the film riding a horse bareback like an Indian. Ethan distrusts Martin as a "half-breed"; at one point he says to him in disgust, "That's the Injun in you." But in many respects Pauley emerges as the most virtuous character in the film in conventional terms—and he evidently is to be rewarded with a marriage into white society as the film ends. The fact that Ford makes the "half-breed" Pauley such an admirable character is perhaps the strongest evidence that he does not accept the conventional cowboys-versus-Indians opposition (see Place, *Western Films,* 164; Buscombe, *Searchers,* 47).

77. Buscombe, *Searchers,* 22.

78. See McBride and Wilmington, *Ford,* 159.

79. Ibid., 147.

80. Ibid., 152.

81. Again Melville's portrayal of the frontiersman sheds light on the character of Ethan: "Though held in a sort a barbarian, the backwoodsman would seem to America what Alexander was to Asia—captain in the vanguard of conquering civilization. Whatever the nation's growing opulence or power, does it not lackey his heels? Pathfinder, provider of security to those who come after him, for himself he asks nothing but hardship" (*Confidence-Man*, 126).

82. See McBride and Wilmington, *Ford*, 148; Waswo, *Founding Legend*, 330; and Schatz, *Hollywood Genres*, 75–76. For particularly thought-provoking readings of this scene, see Pippin, *Hollywood Westerns*, 137–140; and Alvis and Alvis, "Heroic Virtues," 141–142.

83. Place, *Western Films*, 170–171.

84. Winkler, "Tragic Features," 145–146.

85. For an extended analysis of this psychologically complex moment, see Pippin, *Hollywood Westerns*, 128–131.

86. Let me make it clear: not all men in *The Searchers* are barbarians, but all barbarians are men. The women among the Indians are tame and submissive; the squaw Martin inadvertently "marries" exerts a kind of domesticating influence on him. And contrary to Ethan's deepest fears, even Scar has not succeeded in turning Debbie into a "savage." In general, Aeschylus does not present women in the *Oresteia* as positively as Ford does in *The Searchers*. After all, Clytemnestra is the chief villain of the trilogy, precisely because she is a woman who tries to act like a man (Lattimore, "Introduction," 13; Winnington-Ingram, "Clytemnestra," 84–87; Zimmermann, *Greek Tragedy*, 39; and Hall, *Inventing the Barbarian*, 204–205). Although Athena clearly is a positive figure, she was not born of woman, but sprang directly from Zeus's head. Nevertheless, the female element of the Furies, with their concern for hearth and home, must be incorporated into the Athenian regime at the end of the trilogy. Ford presents civilization as involving a precarious balance between masculine and feminine elements, and Aeschylus ultimately does the same by having Apollo and the Furies reconciled in the *Oresteia*. As both an Olympian and a female, Athena is well positioned to mediate between the Olympian Apollo and the feminine Furies (Brann, "*Eumenides*," 26–27). In the end, the passionate and irrational Furies plead for balance and measure (*Eumenides*, 254, line 541). In Winnington-Ingram's interpretation, Aeschylus very much resembles Ford in the way he presents women; see especially "Clytemnestra," 102: "It is, indeed, striking how interest and sympathy are concentrated upon the women in the *Agamemnon*, where, to set against Iphigeneia, Clytemnestra, and Cassandra, we have the humiliated Agamemnon and the ignominious Aegisthus" (102).

87. This point has been made by many critics; see, for example, Place, *Western Films*, 162; Buscombe, *Searchers*, 7–9; Eckstein, "Darkening Ethan," 16; and Winkler, "Tragic Features," 129. But the critics who regard Ethan as a villain talk as if his love for Martha were a burning passion and an active threat to her marriage; Eckstein, for example, claims that Ethan constitutes "a serious threat to the family" ("Darkening Ethan," 6) and later speaks of "the threat of incestuous adultery" Ethan creates. This seems to me to be a misreading of how Ethan and Martha feel about each other. Their love is very much a thing of the past, and both have accepted that fact; there is something wistful about the way they regard each other. Nugent's screenplay describes Ethan and Martha this way: "Then for a moment their eyes meet and hold—and a world of sadness and hopelessness is in their look" (13). This is not the description of an active, passionate love affair. Whatever else one may say about

Ethan, he is not about to break up his brother's family. For a similar view, see Pippin, *Hollywood Westerns*, 115, 173n10.

88. For this parallel, see Pippin, *Hollywood Westerns*, 115.

89. On the mixture of tragedy and comedy in *The Searchers,* see McBride and Wilmington, *Ford,* 147; Buscombe, *Searchers,* 47; Winkler, "Tragic Features," 144–145n60; and especially Alvis and Alvis, "Heroic Virtues," 150–151.

90. Place, *Western Films,* 171; and McBride and Wilmington, *Ford,* 155.

91. Place, *Western Films,* 162–163.

92. Martin's Indian blood is emphasized in this scene in the Nugent screenplay: he is described as "fighting like an Indian" (97); Ethan comments on his behavior, saying, "Comanches don't use their fists" (98); later, Charlie gives Martin an Indian blanket and tells him, "You fight like a Comanch. . . . Maybe this'll help ya pass as one" (105).

93. Schatz, *Hollywood Genres,* 72–73.

94. In Le May's novel *The Searchers* (67) virtually the same words are spoken by the Ethan figure (who is named Amos in the book). For comparisons of the novel and the movie, see Buscombe, *Searchers,* 45; and Eckstein, "Darkening Ethan," 6–8.

95. See Kaufmann, *Tragedy,* 208; and Winkler, "Tragic Features," 141. On the possibility of reconciliation at the end of a tragedy in Hegel's theory, see Paolucci and Paolucci, *Hegel,* 57, 74.

96. But see Flaumenhaft for a sense of loss at the end of *The Eumenides:* "But thoughtful members of that audience—and today's—might sense that, with the triumph of Athens and the successful assimilation of the Furies into a city that makes even foreigners familiar, something has gone out of the world. Despite the colorful procession, the clarified political language of the last play seems flat, less vibrant, less powerful, than that at the start of the trilogy. After Orestes departs, the only humans on stage are a crowd of anonymous Athenians. Compared to Clytemnestra, Agamemnon, and even Aegisthus, these people must feel smaller" (*Civic Spectacle,* 37–38).

97. This is the central theme of Ford's later classic, *The Man Who Shot Liberty Valance* (1962), in which John Wayne again plays the heroic but flawed warrior who must incorporate some of the barbarism that threatens civilization in order to combat it. He dies rejected and neglected by the very community he saved, because it cannot make room for a man of his roughness and toughness. Instead, the community embraces—and makes a hero out of—the Jimmy Stewart character, who represents the virtues of law and education (he is an educated lawyer), although he is clearly less of a man than the John Wayne figure (the Stewart character is feminized by working in a restaurant, and he even wears an apron at one point in the film). For an interpretation of this film along these lines, see Heffernan, "Savagery and Civilization," 148–149. For further discussion of the film, see Pippin, *Hollywood Westerns,* 61–101. For a particularly probing analysis, see French, *Cowboy Metaphysics,* 135–150. French uses the *Oresteia* as an important point of reference in discussing *The Man Who Shot Liberty Valance;* see ibid., 146. For further use of the *Oresteia* in analyzing the film and a serious attempt to relate it to philosophical thinking, see Vittorio Hosle and Mark W. Roche, "Vico's Age of Heroes and the Age of Men in John Ford's Film *The Man Who Shot Liberty Valance,*" *Clio* 23 (1994): 131–147.

98. See Place, *Western Films,* 163–164; McBride and Wilmington, *Ford,* 151–152; Wills, *Wayne's America,* 258; and Schatz, *Hollywood Genres,* 74–75.

99. See Meier, *Political Art,* 132.

2. The Original Frontier

My epigraph from Kennedy's acceptance speech is available at http://130.18.140.19/stennis/JFK-Nomination.htm (consulted August 15, 2011).

1. For the Cold War politics of *Star Trek,* see "Shakespeare in the Original Klingon: *Star Trek* and the End of History" in my book *Gilligan Unbound: Pop Culture in the Age of Globalization* (Lanham, MD: Rowman & Littlefield, 2001), 35–64, especially 48–49. I develop a fuller interpretation of the series in that essay than I am able to do here and discuss specific episodes at length.

2. On the origin of this phrase, which variously appears as "Wagon Train in the sky" or "Wagon Train in space," see Joel Engel, *Gene Roddenberry: The Myth and the Man behind Star Trek* (New York: Hyperion, 1994), 39, 63–64, 228.

3. Indeed, the quotation from Kennedy's nomination speech at the beginning of this chapter reads like a mission statement for the starship *Enterprise.*

4. For a brief survey of Roddenberry's pre–*Star Trek* career as a TV writer, see David Alexander, *Star Trek Creator: The Authorized Biography of Gene Roddenberry* (New York: Penguin, 1994), 154; for a complete list of his screenwriting credits, see ibid., 557–566.

5. J. Fred MacDonald, *Who Shot the Sheriff? The Rise and Fall of the Television Western* (New York: Praeger, 1987), 59.

6. An early *TV Guide* review perceptively called the show "self-consciously arty." Quoted in Martin Grams Jr. and Les Rayburn, *The Have Gun–Will Travel Companion* (Arlington VA: OTR, 2000), 45. See also Russell Nye, *The Unembarrassed Muse: The Popular Arts in America* (New York: Dial, 1970): "*Have Gun, Will Travel* was undoubtedly the most literate and sophisticated of television Westerns" (411).

7. See Grams and Rayburn, *Have Gun Companion,* 53, for Sam Rolfe's comment: "Paladin is really a Shakespearean-type character anyway, he comes from King Arthur and the Round Table."

8. I cite both *Have Gun* and *Star Trek* episodes by the standard numbering given in both the DVD sets and the various published guides to the shows. "The Ballad of Oscar Wilde" was written by, of all people, the novelist Irving Wallace.

9. See MacDonald, *Who Shot the Sheriff?,* 62–63.

10. To complete the parallels, we now know that this trait characterized JFK as well.

11. For a memo from Roddenberry comparing Paladin and Spock as superheroes, see Alexander, *Star Trek Creator,* 333.

12. See ibid., 244 for a memo in which Roddenberry describes Spock this way: "Spock's weakness is an intellectual superiority complex. He finds it hard to hide his look of smugness when others decide questions on the basis of anything less than cold logic." The fact that Roddenberry goes on to speak of Spock as a "half-breed" in this memo shows that he is thinking about the character in Western terms.

13. On this subject, see Will Wright, *Sixguns & Society: A Structural Study of the Western* (Berkeley: University of California Press, 1975), 152–153.

14. For example, Roddenberry has Paladin recite an entire Shakespeare sonnet in "Maggie O'Bannion" (#67). This episode represents the pinnacle of Paladin's career as a literary critic. When O'Bannion says of Shakespeare, "I think he's terribly common," Paladin corrects her: "He deals with common ideas, but in language of most uncommon beauty." Presenting

Shakespeare as superior to Shelley and Tennyson as a lyric poet, Paladin offers Sonnet 18 as "one of the finest passages in the English language." On the use of Shakespeare in *Star Trek,* see Cantor, *Gilligan Unbound,* 60–64, and my essay "From Shakespeare to Wittgenstein: 'Darmok' and Cultural Literacy," in *Star Trek and Philosophy: The Wrath of Kant,* ed. Jason T. Eberl and Kevin S. Decker (Chicago: Open Court, 2008), 3–17.

15. Quoted in Alexander, *Star Trek Creator,* 332. Alexander adds a note to this passage, correcting Roddenberry: "Gene wrote 24 episodes [of *Have Gun–Will Travel*] over its five-year [*sic*] run but according to Sam Rolfe, creator of the program, there was no such position as head writer on the show." See also ibid., 154n10.

16. As Roddenberry liked to put it, "It's not *Star Trek* unless I say it's *Star Trek*" (Engel, *Gene Roddenberry,* 206).

17. Alexander, *Star Trek Creator,* 462–463.

18. Grams and Rayburn, *Have Gun Companion,* 65.

19. Patrick Stewart, the actor who played Captain Picard, neatly summed up *Star Trek*'s contradictory stance on feminist issues in the eulogy he spoke at Roddenberry's memorial service: "Infuriatingly, *Star Trek* remains simultaneously liberated and sexist" (Alexander, *Star Trek Creator,* 552). Its willingness to show women in positions of authority culminated in *Star Trek: Voyager* (1995–1996), where a woman finally becomes captain of the *Enterprise.* As for *Have Gun–Will Travel,* in Roddenberry's "Maggie O'Bannion," for example, a woman gets to run a cattle ranch—although only with Paladin's help and careful tutelage.

20. A good example of such an episode is "Hey Boy's Revenge" (#31, written by Albert Aley). According to Grams and Rayburn, in *Have Gun Companion*: "This script was daring for its time. [Producer] Julian Claman had to argue and fight with the network censors to allow the broadcast" (46). Another episode sympathetic to Chinese culture is "The Hatchet Man" (#103, written by Shimon Wincelberg).

21. Paladin's familiarity with Indian culture is stressed in Roddenberry's episode "Yuma Treasure" (#14), in which he says, "I've lived with the Yumas." The chief of the Yumas tells Paladin, "You know our ways." More generally, an army major says of Paladin, "He can get an escort from any tribe. . . . He's even ridden with Cochise himself." The episode of *Have Gun* perhaps most sympathetic to Indians, and one of the most dramatically effective in the entire series, is "Return to Fort Benjamin" (#98, written by Robert E. Thompson). For the record, the Association of American Indian Affairs, while deploring the general representation of Indians on television, approved the way the subject was treated on *Have Gun;* see MacDonald, *Who Shot the Sheriff?,* 114.

22. For this kind of episode, see, for example, "Fight at Adobe Wells" (#104).

23. For an account of this episode, "Plato's Stepchildren" (#67), that lays to rest a number of popular myths about the famous kiss, see Alexander, *Star Trek Creator,* 292–296.

24. For a typical example of a cultural studies approach to *Star Trek,* which predictably condemns the show as racist, see Daniel Leonard Bernardi, *Star Trek and History: Race-ing toward a White Future* (New Brunswick, NJ: Rutgers University Press, 1998), especially 26–28.

25. Five of the six seasons of *Have Gun–Will Travel* are currently available on DVD; that means that I have been able to view nineteen of the twenty-four episodes Roddenberry wrote. That gives me a substantial and representative sample to work from. Of those, I have chosen six to discuss in detail, and I refer to most of the remaining ones at various points in this chapter. I have transcribed all the quotations from the series myself. Confining

myself in this chapter largely to *Have Gun* episodes written by Roddenberry risks giving the impression that I regard him as having had a special status among the show's writers or being largely responsible for its success. As I explain elsewhere in the chapter, this is by no means my assessment of Roddenberry's role in the show. In fact, many of my favorite *Have Gun* episodes are by writers other than Roddenberry.

26. On Roddenberry's tendency to project his sexual fantasies into *Star Trek,* see Engel, *Gene Roddenberry,* 84–85.

27. The *Star Trek* "Elaan of Troyis" episode (with a story credit to Roddenberry) is a kind of "taming of the shrew" script Roddenberry evidently liked to write. The equivalent in *Have Gun* is a Roddenberry script called "Ella West" (#17), in which Paladin must use all his skill and all his strength to tame the extremely unladylike female star of a Wild West show. The episode contains a typical Roddenberry line from Paladin: "There's one wild thing that men will never civilize—women."

28. See Alexander, *Star Trek Creator,* 154n10.

29. Roddenberry was still using the phrase "robber barons" in a memo he wrote in 1987 describing the most capitalistic species in the universe, the infamous Ferengis of *Star Trek: The Next Generation;* of the Ferengis he writes: "their idea of 'fair' is that which profits them the most" (Engel, *Gene Roddenberry,* 248).

30. The classic anticapitalist episode of *Star Trek* is "The Trouble with Tribbles" (#42). On this episode, see Cantor, *Gilligan Unbound,* 180. Roddenberry's hostility to capitalism is an example of a central Hollywood paradox—writers who make enormous sums of money condemning the very system that makes their wealth possible. But there is a certain logic to this behavior. Although Hollywood pays writers huge sums of money, they never feel that it is enough or, more generally, that their talent is sufficiently rewarded. Moreover, most Hollywood writers, Roddenberry among them, believe that the business interests of Hollywood interfere with their creativity. For Roddenberry's condemning the "Robber Baron reasoning" in Hollywood, see Alexander, *Star Trek Creator,* 305. See ibid., 390–391, for an even more revealing comment from Roddenberry: "Also, to be honest, I vary between regarding businessmen as saber-tooth tigers and Builders of America. This usually depends on the status of my continuing fight with several studios over the difference between their gross and my net profits." Few writers have been so candid about the capitalistic source of their anticapitalism. For other anticapitalist and anticommercial statements from Roddenberry in Alexander's book, see 386, 422, 465–466. On 452, Roddenberry spotlights the impulse that feeds the anticapitalist ire of many writers: "I wish this were a better world, in which people pressed money on artists and said, 'Go out and be an artist, I'll invest in that.'" Roddenberry was famous for his ability to imagine utopian worlds; here he imagines one in which artists would have no obligations whatsoever to the people who fund their creativity. For a contrary view on this issue—gratitude toward the financial backers of film and television—see chapter 4, on *Mars Attacks!* and chapter 6, on *South Park.*

31. The classic example of this kind of *Star Trek* episode is the second season "Who Mourns for Adonais?" (#32), in which the *Enterprise* crew comes upon the Greek god Apollo on a distant planet and must figure out the secret source of his power—and destroy it. On this episode, see Cantor, *Gilligan Unbound,* 44–45.

32. For the anti-McCarthyism of *The Crucible,* see Richard A. Schwartz, *Cold War Culture: Media and the Arts, 1945–1990* (New York: Checkmark, 2000), 70–71.

33. Anti-McCarthyism was a pervasive theme in *Have Gun–Will Travel,* not just a preoccupation of Roddenberry. Perhaps the most pointed treatment of McCarthyism is in the third-season "Night the Town Died" (#99), in which a community destroys itself by attempting to hunt down—and lynch—"traitors" in its midst. For Roddenberry speaking of "Edward R. Murrow's courageous stand against Senator Joe McCarthy," see a 1968 letter in Alexander, *Star Trek,* 353–354.

34. For another use of *Macbeth* in a Roddenberry episode of *Have Gun,* see the second-season "The Return of Roy Carter" (#71). In perhaps the most bitter and cynical script Roddenberry ever wrote, a just man dies to save the life of a criminal, provoking Paladin to use Macbeth's nihilistic words to characterize human life: "It is a tale / Told by an idiot, full of sound and fury / Signifying nothing." The noble hero of this episode is named Robert April (Larry Blake)—the same name Roddenberry originally proposed for the captain of the *Enterprise.*

35. A classic example is the second-season "Catspaw" (#30), a Halloween episode of *Star Trek.* The series' one "Western," a third-season episode called "Spectre of the Gun" (#56), which involves a recreation of the famous Gunfight at the OK Corral, is also a story of learning how to see through artificially created illusions.

36. See Grams and Rayburn, *Have Gun Companion,* 58.

37. See, for example, Roddenberry's "The Hanging of Roy Carter" (#43).

38. For insight into the significance of lynch mobs in the Western, see Leslie A. Fiedler, *The Return of the Vanishing American* (New York: Stein and Day, 1968), 139.

39. A good parallel in *Star Trek* would be the calm way Spock defends himself when he is on trial for mutiny in "The Menagerie" (#16).

40. The motif of coolly facing down an angry lynch mob and calling them cowards can earlier be found in chapter 22 of Mark Twain's *Adventures of Huckleberry Finn* (1884).

41. In "The Hanging Tree," the townspeople do the right thing not as an organized body, but as individual Christians. That is, they are not led by a sheriff, marshal, or other government official; in fact, to the extent that they are following any lead, it comes from Paladin's eloquent Christmas Eve speech.

42. Early in "Posse" the saddle tramp, Dobie, questions Paladin's lack of trust: "Look, just 'cause two strangers meet, they don't gotta be suspicious of each other." But as the episode quickly demonstrates, in the world of *Have Gun–Will Travel,* the clear Hobbesian lesson is precisely that when two strangers meet they have to be suspicious of each other because they lack a common authority to which they are both subject. For a rejection of this purely Hobbesian understanding of the world, see chapter 3, on *Deadwood.*

43. Cf. Engel's characterization of Roddenberry's imaginative stance in *Star Trek:* "Roddenberry often positioned himself as the outsider, alone on an intergalactic parade stand, watching the world from a perspective not shared by any other human" (*Gene Roddenberry,* 201).

44. See ibid., 106 and 109, where Engel quotes Dorothy Fontana saying of Roddenberry, "He identified with his captains."

45. On this aspect of Roddenberry's fantasy life, see ibid., 24, 244–245. One of the most obvious pairings between *Have Gun* and *Star Trek* episodes is "Les Girls" (#81) in the former (written by Roddenberry) and "Mudd's Women" (#4) in the latter (story credit to Roddenberry): both reflect Roddenberry's fascination with beautiful and exotic women.

In "Les Girls," Paladin escorts three French women to be married to farmers in Oregon; in "Mudd's Women," Kirk escorts three interplanetary beauties to be married to miners on a remote planet. In Roddenberry's notes on this episode (one of the potential pilots for *Star Trek*), he acknowledged the Western origins of the plot: "Duplicating a page from the 'Old West'; hanky-panky aboard [the *Enterprise*] with a cargo of women destined for a far-off colony" (Engel, *Gene Roddenberry*, 50).

46. For an insightful analysis of the paradoxes of liberalism, see Harvey C. Mansfield Jr., *The Spirit of Liberalism* (Cambridge, MA: Harvard University Press, 1978), especially 10–14, 39–40, 60–61, 104.

47. I will compound this heresy for *Star Trek* fans by going on record with the opinion that *Have Gun–Will Travel* is on balance the better series. Generally speaking, it is better written, better acted, and better produced. Despite the fact that it involved twice as many seasons and nearly three times the number of episodes, *Have Gun* maintained a remarkable consistency of quality that *Star Trek* could not match. And one must truly marvel at the ability of the *Have Gun* writers, including Roddenberry, to tell complex stories in the space of the mere twenty-four minutes available to them on average for each episode. I do not wish to offend *Star Trek* fans, but I realize that, given the way I have set up this essay, I may seem to be arguing that *Have Gun–Will Travel* should be remembered merely as a kind of prelude to *Star Trek*. It was much more than that.

48. MacDonald is particularly critical of the violence in *Have Gun*; see *Who Shot the Sheriff?*, 74–75.

49. For a list of all Roddenberry's writing credits for *Star Trek*, see Alexander, *Star Trek Creator*, 564–565. He had a total of six writing credits for the three seasons, and one for the first pilot, and in addition had five story credits. The issue of getting writing and story credit in Hollywood can be complicated, often involving arbitration by the Screen Writers' Guild. For a sample of some of the disputes Roddenberry got involved in with other writers for the series, see Alexander, *Star Trek Creator*, 284–290.

50. For detailed examples of Roddenberry's rewriting of *Star Trek* scripts, which often became obsessive, see Engel, *Gene Roddenberry*, 86–95, and Alexander, *Star Trek Creator*, 245.

51. For a detailed summary of what others contributed to the development of the basic concepts of *Star Trek*, see Engel, *Gene Roddenberry*, 87–88, especially this comment from Dorothy Fontana, who was in a position to know: "Over the years a lot of people have swallowed the line that Gene Roddenberry was the sole creator of *Star Trek*. And it's not true. If you look at the development of the scripts along the way, you see all the elements that were contributed by other writers. The base was there, the bones were there, the skeleton was there; maybe even the flesh. All the rest, the laying on of the weight and the muscle, was done by others."

52. For more on this issue, see Engel, *Gene Roddenberry*, 60, 146, 208; and Grams and Rayburn, *Have Gun Companion*, 61.

53. For some specific examples of this tendency, see Engel, *Gene Roddenberry*, 88–89, 118–119.

54. Examples include Sam Peeples, Shimon Wincelberg, and Sam Rolfe himself. The list of actors and directors who worked in both *Have Gun* and *Star Trek* is remarkably long. Hollywood is a small town.

55. For Boone's exceptionally active role in shaping the series, see Grams and Rayburn, *Have Gun Companion*, 70–77.

56. In a 1968 memo sent to all those involved in the series, Roddenberry himself acknowledged Nimoy's role in the evolution of Spock as a character: "We all worked very hard to build him into a fully dimensional character, and a lot of people, including Leonard Nimoy, deserve credit" (quoted in Alexander, *Star Trek Creator,* 317).

57. See the introduction to this book.

58. Alexander, *Star Trek Creator,* 219.

59. Cf. Engel's summation of Roddenberry's contribution to *Star Trek:* "Roddenberry's real accomplishments were constructing *Star Trek's* parameters, selling the series, seeking quality writers, and often recognizing brilliance when he saw it" (*Gene Roddenberry,* 88).

60. See Alexander, *Star Trek Creator,* 31–32, 35, 119, 132–137, 188, 397.

61. See Engel, *Gene Roddenberry,* 42–44. A convincing piece of evidence in favor of Engel's view is the fact that of all the TV scripts Roddenberry had sold before *Star Trek,* not a single one was a science fiction story. A key figure in this whole debate is Roddenberry's friend and fellow writer, Sam Peeples; even Alexander admits that Roddenberry asked Peeples if he could consult his "huge collection of old science fiction magazines" when he was working up *Star Trek* (*Star Trek Creator,* 203). Alexander writes, "Gene took somewhere between fifty and a hundred photographs of old science fiction magazine covers, searching for ideas for the design of the *Enterprise*" (204). It was Peeples who came up with the phrase "where no man has gone before" in connection with *Star Trek* (Alexander, *Star Trek Creator,* 228).

62. Alexander, *Star Trek Creator,* 249; italics in the original.

63. For other examples of Roddenberry telling writers to forget about science fiction in writing for *Star Trek,* see Engel, *Gene Roddenberry,* 74, 93.

64. Alexander, *Star Trek Creator,* 249.

65. Desilu Studio executive Oscar Katz, in his account of how he and Roddenberry sold NBC on the idea of *Star Trek,* reveals that Western patterns were on everybody's minds. He says that they told NBC of one archetypal *Star Trek* plot: "First, the spaceship is out for a five-year mission on some sort of 'police action.' It gets word that on some planet where there's some rare mineral being mined there is some claim jumping. So we go to the planet and settle the dispute, whatever. We said, 'That's very much like *Gunsmoke.* The sheriff or marshal settles the problem.'" Katz explains another analogy they used: "'That's very similar to *Wagon Train,*' which was a very big hit then on the air. . . . We always compared it with current hit shows before we got into the more esoteric parts of the format" (Alexander, *Star Trek Creator,* 196). Wherever one looks in the genesis of *Star Trek,* one finds Westerns.

66. Ibid., 241; italics in the original.

67. Ibid.; italics in the original.

68. Ibid., 354; italics in the original.

69. For the details, see William Boddy, "The Western," in *The Television Genre Book,* ed. Glen Creeber (London: BFI, 2001), 14–17.

70. MacDonald's *Who Shot the Sheriff?* is devoted to analyzing the decline of the Western on American television and offers these ideological reasons for what happened; see especially 12, 28, 112, 136–137. For the connection between the classic Western and capitalism, see Wright, *Sixguns & Society,* 15, 173–179.

71. See Schwartz, *Cold War Culture,* 327; MacDonald, *Who Shot the Sheriff?,* 104; and John H. Lenihan, *Showdown: Confronting Modern America in the Western Film* (Urbana:

University of Illinois Press, 1980), 47–54, 148–176. For the New Western in the American novel, beginning in the 1960s, see Fiedler, *Vanishing American,* especially 150–187.

72. A well-known example of this pattern is Theodore Dreiser's novel *Sister Carrie* (1900). On the "American's long-standing distrust of the city," see Nye, *Unembarrassed Muse,* 36.

73. See Wright, *Sixguns & Society,* 52–53.

74. For an episode of *Have Gun* written by Roddenberry that reflects these ideas, see "Alice" (#182). In this story, Paladin exposes the corruption that lies behind the respectable façade of a small town and in the process teaches a lesson in the relativity of values. This episode works to deconstruct a standard Western myth. A town that claims to have left its Wild West days behind it and achieved civilization is shown to be founded on a lie and the suppression of the truth about its past.

75. At roughly the same time that *Have Gun* was on CBS, a series with the apt name *Maverick* (1957–1962) flourished on ABC. Its hero (played by James Garner) was an itinerant gambler—another case of a traditional Western villain stereotype transformed into a hero. On *Maverick,* see MacDonald, *Who Shot the Sheriff?,* 63. Oddly enough, the two series shared an episode about an ex-army camel, "The Great Mojave Chase" (#3) in *Have Gun* (written by Roddenberry) and "Relic of Fort Tejon" in *Maverick* (teleplay by Jerry Davis, from a magazine story by Kenneth Perkins).

76. Although the show leaves the matter sketchy, Paladin's roots are clearly in the East Coast establishment; he went to West Point, for example. For Roddenberry's own "bicoastalism," see a letter he wrote in 1983, in which he specifically contrasts the lack of sexual liberation in "the South" with what "can be seen happening very rapidly in New York and on the West Coast" (Alexander, *Star Trek Creator,* 474). For a similar bicoastal contempt for the American heartland in Edgar Ulmer, see chapter 8, on *Detour.* For a critique of this elitism, see chapter 4, on *Mars Attacks!*

77. From what we saw in chapter 1, *The Searchers* can help define what is new in *Have Gun–Will Travel.* In the traditional Western, the hero is often shown to be a loner, a misfit, or an outcast; in that respect, Paladin resembles Ford's Ethan Edwards. But Ethan is still a man from the community he defends in a way that Paladin is not. Ethan is an avenger—that means that his cause is personal and he had relatives, loved ones, and friends in the community he fights for. In the end, he senses that he cannot fit into that community, but he does not view it with contempt or think of it as beneath him. If anything, he probably wishes that he could belong, but realizes that his experience has unfitted him for doing so. Ethan does not laugh at the little community he leaves at the end. For all Ford's efforts at comic relief in the film, Ethan's story remains fundamentally tragic. He is torn between civilization and a form of barbarism. Paladin's story is, by contrast, fundamentally comic. Unlike Ethan, he has a place to go at the end of each episode, and it is rather pleasant; he is frequently portrayed at the ends of episodes returning to the high life back in San Francisco. Many of the *Have Gun* episodes are comic, or have significant comic moments. Paladin frequently has a good laugh at the expense of the communities he visits and cleans up. The reason is that, unlike Ethan or the traditional Western hero generally, Paladin comes to the Western frontier like a visitor from another planet, or like a time traveler. In his terms, he comes from a sophisticated and modern world, and he generally looks down with contempt on the backwardness of the frontier West. One cannot imagine Ethan going to an opera or dining on gourmet food. Ethan feels like an outcast when he has to leave the community he defended. Paladin

feels a sense of relief to get back to the modern world of San Francisco. Occasionally he has old friends in the towns he visits, but no one who could tie him down in such primitive backwaters. Paladin is *not* an avenger; his cause is rarely personal, and he often speaks out against the spirit of revenge. He is a modern professional and presents himself as effective precisely because he is not acting out of personal motives. That is why, for all the seeming similarities between Paladin and the traditional Western gunfighter, he in fact represents a complete reconception of the role. More generally, Ford's films embody a conception of the American small town that is at odds with the vision of *Have Gun*. Ethan must be sacrificed to create the peace on the frontier that will allow small towns to develop and prosper—and to deal with their problems largely on their own. In *Have Gun,* Paladin's rugged individualism is still needed even after the frontier has been basically pacified because small towns are not capable of handling their own affairs justly.

78. Paladin embodies a Hollywood lifestyle before Hollywood existed. He gets to go to cultural premieres, wines and dines in the best circles of society, and is surrounded by beautiful women. And, in the fulfillment of every Hollywood writer's dreams, he manages to combine this hedonistic existence with the moral satisfaction of going forth every week to save the world.

79. For references to the Civil War in a Roddenberry script, see "Juliet" (#59); for *Have Gun* episodes by other writers, see "Night the Town Died" (#99), "The Unforgiven" (#86), "One Came Back" (#93), "The Prophet" (#94), and "Lady with a Gun" (#108).

80. The most famous *Star Trek* episode dealing with racial prejudice and civil rights issues is the third-season "Let That Be Your Last Battlefield" (#70).

81. In Roddenberry's formulation, the keynote of *Star Trek* is "infinite diversity through infinite combinations" (quoted in Engel, *Gene Roddenberry,* 247).

82. In the way Paladin works behind the scenes—at one point literally in the dark—to aid the new marshal unseen, this episode anticipates John Ford's *The Man Who Shot Liberty Valance* (1962).

83. The most famous Western movie dealing with a town unable and unwilling to defend itself is *High Noon* (1952). The relevance of this film to various left-wing causes in Hollywood, especially anti-McCarthyism, was widely perceived at the time. See Schwartz, *Cold War Culture,* 138. John Wayne objected to the film's ideology, as did Howard Hawks. They claim to have made *Rio Bravo* (1959) as a kind of answer to *High Noon*. See Lenihan, *Showdown,* 119, 125.

84. The title and the subject matter of the episode recall a well-known *Playhouse 90* script by Rod Serling, "A Town Has Turned to Dust" (1958), which deals with "racism and lynchings in the South" (Engel, *Gene Roddenberry,* 73). The drama starred none other than William Shatner.

85. What I say about television applies equally well to the Western films of the 1950s. They were not, as many critics have claimed, uniformly conservative in their ideology. In his remarkably comprehensive and judicious survey of the Western in American film, John Lenihan argues: "The relevance of so many Westerns to the problems of racial equality and the Cold War suggests that popular culture after World War II cannot be easily dismissed as escapist pap or as a reflection of public complacency. Nor was the Western's relevance limited to headline issues. Rather, it encompassed much of the social criticism usually considered peculiar to the country's intelligentsia" (*Showdown,* 90; see also 116). Not assuming that all

Westerns are alike, Lenihan studies them one by one and demonstrates how varied their ideological positions are. As a result, he finds continuities between 1950s and 1960s Westerns: "Westerns of the 1960s would offer less a new picture of society than one that would accentuate the societal viciousness and banality depicted in the fifties Westerns and would glorify less ambiguously the hero's violence and alienation. This in turn renders questionable the tendency of many historians to interpret the disenchantment of the sixties as a sudden departure from what they presume to be a decade of public apathy and contentment. The social criticism in Westerns of the fifties suggests that, even though Americans in that time were less inclined to riot or protest, they were nonetheless aware of, and disturbed by, the shortcomings of their society" (147).

86. A study of cross-pollination among different pop culture genres would be very interesting. The Dirty Harry movies of the 1970s and '80s are an excellent example of the urban Western, in which many of the generic conventions of the traditional Western are transferred to a contemporary city setting. The fact that the Western star Clint Eastwood played the "urban gunfighter" in this series helped make the generic connections clear. On this subject, see Lenihan, *Showdown,* 172–173. Another example of the urban Western is the modern vigilante movie, epitomized by the *Death Wish* series (1974, 1982, 1985). These movies also feature a star identified with Westerns, Charles Bronson; and the fact that they are called "vigilante" movies also indicates their link to the Western. As for television, Dennis Weaver, who played Chester in *Gunsmoke* (1955–1975), starred in an urban Western called *McCloud* (1970–1977). Sam McCloud is a modern deputy marshal transported from Taos, New Mexico, to New York City, where he uses his frontier skills and savvy to deal with urban crime. As for the confluence of the Western with science fiction, a good example is the movie *Outland* (1981), a remake of *High Noon* set on one of Jupiter's moons. An example of a sci-fi–Western hybrid on television is Joss Whedon's show *Firefly* (2002). For another sci-fi Western, see my discussion of *Falling Skies* (2011–) in chapter 10. For the migration of the Western into TV science fiction, see Schwartz, *Cold War Culture,* 327. Perhaps the most systematic attempt to blend the conventions of science fiction and the Western is the film *Cowboys and Aliens* (2011), which pits a stereotypical Western grouping of outlaws, cattlemen, and Indians against space invaders prospecting for gold. For the view that science fiction and the Western do not mix well, see Peter A. French, *Cowboy Metaphysics: Ethics and Death in Westerns* (Lanham, MD: Rowman & Littlefield, 1997), 144.

87. See Grams and Rayburn, *Have Gun Companion,* 34–35, 135.

88. Alexander, *Star Trek Creator,* 185. Engel quotes TV writer Christopher Knopf saying of this proposed series, "There's no question in my mind this idea was absolutely the philosophical forerunner to *Star Trek*" (*Gene Roddenberry,* 38).

89. In the wake of the success of *Deadwood,* there are some signs of the Western making a comeback on television; see "A Return of the Wild West," *TV Guide,* Sept. 26–Oct. 2, 2011, 8.

3. Order Out of the Mud

My epigraphs are from David Milch, *Deadwood: Stories of the Black Hills* (New York: Melcher Media, 2006), 135; and Neil Postman, *Amusing Ourselves to Death: Public Discourse in the Age of Show Business* (New York: Penguin, 1986), 7.

1. John Locke, *Two Treatises of Government,* ed. Thomas Cook (New York: Hafner, 1947), 139.

2. Ibid., 145.

3. Thomas Hobbes, *Leviathan,* ed. C. B. MacPherson (Harmondsworth, UK: Penguin, 1968), 187. On the importance of America in Hobbes's thought (with some reference to Locke as well), see Pat Moloney, "Hobbes, Savages, and International Anarchy," *American Political Science Review* 105 (2011): 189–204.

4. Jean-Jacques Rousseau, *The First and Second Discourses,* ed. and trans. Roger D. Masters (New York: St. Martin's, 1964), 224.

5. I am speaking of the Rousseau of the *Second Discourse* here. In later works, especially *The Social Contract,* he tried to show how freedom and law could be made compatible in the form of a self-legislating community. In even later works, such as *The Reveries of a Solitary Walker,* he returned to his preference for freedom over law. The relation between freedom and law is in many respects the central issue in Rousseau's thought, and one on which he explored several possibilities.

6. See Bernard Bailyn, *The Ideological Origins of the American Revolution* (Cambridge, MA: Harvard University Press, 1967), 27–29. On the separation of powers specifically, see Harvey C. Mansfield Jr., *America's Constitutional Soul* (Baltimore, MD: Johns Hopkins University Press, 1991), 115–134. For a comprehensive treatment of the subject, see Thomas L. Pangle, *The Spirit of Modern Republicanism: The Moral Vision of the American Founders and the Philosophy of Locke* (Chicago: University of Chicago Press, 1988).

7. The ABC television series *Lost* (2004–2010) actually featured characters named Locke and Rousseau.

8. Milch has an exceptionally distinguished academic background. He graduated Phi Beta Kappa from Yale, received an MFA from Iowa, and went on to teach creative writing at Yale, where he worked with such noted scholars as Robert Penn Warren, Cleanth Brooks, and R. W. B. Lewis. In his comments about *Deadwood* and in the series itself, he displays an extraordinarily wide range of knowledge in many cultural areas, including philosophy. Season 3, episode 10 of *Deadwood,* for example, contains a learned if somewhat irreverent discussion of Socrates and Alcibiades. In season 2, episode 9, one character mentions both David Hume and Karl Marx. Several references to "Leviathan" suggest that Milch had Hobbes specifically in mind when creating the series (although the Bible and *Moby-Dick* are obviously alternate sources of these references).

9. For example, Daniel Salerno has said of the show, "No television program—or film, for that matter—that I can recall has done such marvelous things with the English language. . . . Television critics and viewers have often referred to it as Shakespearean." "'I Will Have You Bend': Language and the Discourses of Power in *Deadwood,*" *Literary Imagination* 12 (2010): 190.

10. Television is a collaborative medium, and Milch himself would not claim sole responsibility for creating the whole of *Deadwood.* In the cumulative screen credits for the three seasons the show ran, a total of fourteen different directors and sixteen different screenwriters are named. In his commentaries, Milch makes it clear that he worked closely with the individual actors in creating the characters they were playing. Nevertheless, all the evidence suggests that *Deadwood* is essentially the product of David Milch's imagination; he maintained creative control over all aspects of the production. When asked point-blank in

an interview, "Do you write the show alone?" Milch did not simply deny it: "I have a pretty heavy hand. I work on pretty much every scene. First they [the other writers] do drafts, and then I work on them." See http://dir.salon.com/story/ent/feature/2005/03/05/milch/print. html (consulted September 9, 2008).

11. I have transcribed all quotations from *Deadwood* from the Home Box Office DVDs (season 1, 2004; season 2, 2006; season 3, 2007). I will cite them by the season number and episode number in parentheses (so that this citation would read: 1.1).

12. Milch, *Black Hills,* 121.

13. The quotation from Brown is from the bonus feature commentary "The Wedding Celebration" in the second-season set of DVDs of *Deadwood.* For a similar statement of the central question of the series, see Erin Hill, "'What's Afflictin' You?': Corporeality, Body Crises and the Body Politic in *Deadwood,*" in *Reading Deadwood: A Western to Swear By,* ed. David Lavery (London: I. B. Taurus, 2006), 181: "the central question of *Deadwood* . . . is whether or not residents can be trusted to handle their business themselves without being regulated by a larger power, or, put more simply, whether order is possible without law." This understanding of the Old West is not unique to popular culture; it is, in fact, common among historians; it is one of the central themes, for example, of Frederick Jackson Turner: "Western democracy included individual liberty, as well as equality. The frontiersman was impatient of restraints. He knew how to preserve order, even in the absence of legal authorities." Turner, *The Frontier in American History* (New York: Henry Holt, 1953), 212; see also 343–344. For an excellent discussion of order in the Old West, with a useful bibliography, see Ryan McMaken, "The American West: A Heritage of Peace," *Mises Daily Article,* February 12, 2004, http://www.mises.org/fullstory.asp?control=1449 (consulted February 12, 2004).

14. The quotation from Milch is from the bonus feature commentary "The New Language of the Old West" in the first-season set of *Deadwood* DVDs.

15. The phenomenon Milch is examining—the self-organizing power of society—has a venerable intellectual history, going at least as far back as the Scottish Enlightenment and Adam Smith's idea of the invisible hand. Perhaps the best label for what Milch is talking about is "spontaneous order," a term made popular by Friedrich Hayek. See his *Law, Legislation and Liberty* (London: Routledge and Kegan Paul, 1982), especially 1: 72–123. Hayek argues that in the British common-law tradition judges "discover" the rules that have already evolved in commercial and other social transactions, and articulate and codify them as law in the course of their case-by-case decisions. This is a perfect example of what Milch means by "retrospectively apply[ing] the sanction of the law to the things we do to maintain order." Hayek contrasts this kind of common law, which as it were bubbles up out of society, with positive law, legal codes devised by legislatures and imposed on society from above. For another analysis of a Western in terms of Hayek's concept of spontaneous order, which also draws upon Hobbes and Locke, see Aeon J. Skoble, "Order without Law: *The Magnificent Seven,* East and West," in *The Philosophy of the Western,* ed. Jennifer L. McMahon and B. Steve Csaki (Lexington: University Press of Kentucky, 2010), 139–147. For another vision of the self-organizing power of society, rooted in Alexis de Tocqueville's understanding of America, see chapter 4, on Tim Burton's *Mars Attacks!*

16. Hobbes, *Leviathan,* 223–224.

17. For Hobbes's basic indifference on the issue of forms of government, see *Leviathan,* 238–240.

18. See, for example, Paul Wright and Hailin Zhou, "Divining the 'Celestials': The Chinese Subculture of *Deadwood*," in Lavery, *Reading Deadwood*, 157, 166.

19. Hobbes, *Leviathan*, 186.

20. This quotation is from the bonus feature commentary "An Imaginative Reality" in the first-season set of *Deadwood* DVDs.

21. On the artificiality of the state, see Hobbes, *Leviathan*, 226.

22. Ibid., 185.

23. Ibid., 184.

24. Ibid., 185.

25. Ibid.

26. Milch says of Dority and Turner, "They are champions who represent their masters" (Milch, *Black Hills*, 157).

27. See Leo Strauss, *Natural Right and History* (Chicago: University of Chicago Press, 1953), 234–235; and Robert A. Goldwin, "John Locke," in *History of Political Philosophy*, ed. Leo Strauss and Joseph Cropsey (Chicago: Rand McNally, 1963), 492.

28. Hobbes, *Leviathan*, 188; see also 234. The word *propriety* meant the same as "property" when Hobbes was writing.

29. For Hobbes on property, see Richard Pipes, *Property and Freedom: The Story of How through the Centuries Private Ownership Has Promoted Liberty and the Rule of Law* (New York: Alfred Knopf, 1999), 32. This book gives an excellent overview of the issue of property throughout history.

30. Locke, *Two Treatises*, 134.

31. Ibid., 184. For Locke on the sanctity of property, see Pipes, *Property*, 35.

32. Locke, *Two Treatises*, 186.

33. Ibid., 134.

34. Ibid., 136.

35. Ibid., 139.

36. See Strauss, *Natural Right*, 242–245, and Pierre Manent, *An Intellectual History of Liberalism*, trans. Rebecca Balinski (Princeton, NJ: Princeton University Press, 1995), 43–46.

37. On the absence of all commercial activity in the state of nature, see Hobbes, *Leviathan*, 186: "In such condition, there is no place for Industry; because the fruit thereof is uncertain: and consequently no Culture of the Earth; no Navigation, nor use of the commodities that may be imported by Sea; no commodious Building; no Instruments of moving, and removing such things as require much force; no Knowledge of the face of the Earth; no account of Time; no Arts; no Letters; no Society."

38. Locke, *Two Treatises*, 130. The sharp contrast between Hobbes and Locke on the state of nature begins to blur once one looks beneath the surface in their writings, that is, once one accepts Leo Strauss's argument that Locke was an esoteric writer. Given Hobbes's notoriety as, among other things, an atheist, Locke had every reason to exaggerate his differences from his predecessor and to minimize his agreements—if he had any hope of seeing his political ideas accepted by his contemporaries. A careful reading of the *Second Treatise* shows that Locke ultimately accepts Hobbes's characterization of the state of nature as a state of war, or at least he admits that an original state of nature must necessarily develop into a state of war once property disputes multiply. That is why Locke, like Hobbes, views as inevitable the establishment of a government to settle the disputes that develop in the state of nature. On

the buried similarities between Hobbes and Locke on the state of nature, see Strauss, *Natural Right,* 224–228; Manent, *Liberalism,* 47–48; and Paul A. Rahe, *Republics Ancient and Modern* (Chapel Hill: University of North Carolina Press, 1994), 2: 258, 268–271. See especially Pangle, *Modern Republicanism,* 246: "Locke exaggerates (especially in the first half of the *Second Treatise*) the peaceful and reasonable possibilities of the precivil condition in order to mask the extent of his agreement with the unpalatable Hobbesian conception of human nature: he thus seduces most of his readers into accepting or entertaining the essentials of that account without being shocked into quite realizing what they are doing" (see also 131, 170–171). But whatever the esoteric meaning of the *Second Treatise* may be, its exoteric message is clear: Locke is offering an alternative to Hobbes's view of the state of nature. Since it was that exoteric message that functioned in eighteenth-century political discourse, I am safe in drawing a sharp contrast between Hobbes and Locke in discussing their influence on America and, by extension, Milch's *Deadwood.*

39. For an excellent discussion of how the problem of staking out mining claims in the absence of legal authorities was actually handled in the Old West, see Terry L. Anderson and Peter J. Hill, *The Not So Wild, Wild West: Property Rights on the Frontier* (Stanford, CA: Stanford University Press, 2004), 104–119. As the title indicates, this book is a revisionist history of the West, showing that it was much less violent and contentious than popular culture has pictured it. This book does the best job of providing the historical background for anyone interested in *Deadwood* and Milch's theme of order without law. For example, in discussing the relatively peaceful development of the fur-trapping trade in the Old West, Anderson and Hill quote historian Hiram Chittenden: "It might be concluded . . . that, as the country was literally lawless, or without means of enforcing laws, lawlessness and disorder would be the rule. Such was not the case. . . . It will be found that life, liberty, and the right to property, were as much respected in the depths of the wilderness as within the best regulated of cities" (89).

40. Milch, *Black Hills,* 99. Contemporary sociological studies have confirmed Milch's intuitions in this respect, especially Hernando de Soto's work on squatter communities in Peru. He reports that his research "found no evidence to bear out the charge that life in informal settlements is anarchic and disorganized. On the contrary, it found a set of extralegal norms which did, to some extent, regulate social relations, offsetting the absence of legal protection and gradually winning stability and security for acquired [property] rights." He goes on to conclude that his research "shows that people are capable of violating a system which does not accept them, not so that they can live in anarchy but so that they can build a different system which respects a minimum of essential rights." *The Other Path: The Invisible Revolution in the Third World,* trans. June Abbott (New York: Harper & Row, 1989), 19, 55. De Soto is describing Lima, Peru, but he might as well be describing Milch's Deadwood. On the role of squatters in the development of the West, see Turner, *Frontier,* 101, 122–123, 137.

41. When the community puts the assassin of Hickok on trial, the hastily assembled jury is told that without a proper court or legal procedures they "must rely on common custom" (1.5).

42. When Alma Garrett's husband is murdered and she inherits his rich claim, Whitney Ellsworth must be brought in to work it actively in order for her to maintain her claim to the property.

43. See Pangle, *Modern Republicanism,* 308n5, where he speaks of "the truly amazing speed with which Locke's conception of property permeated and radically transformed English

common law. By 1704 (six years after the publication of the *Two Treatises!*) Locke's notions begin to appear as the standard or orthodox notions in legal commentary. I believe it is safe to surmise that Locke's influence on the legal and hence political thinking of the American colonists in subsequent years, by way of this transformation in legal thinking, was enormous." On the importance in general of federal policies for turning public lands into private property, see Turner, *Frontier*, 170, 211, 259, 272–273, 276, 293. See especially 27, where Turner quotes Senator Scott of Indiana describing the federal government's land policy as "merely declaratory of the custom or common law of the settlers." This is another example of what Milch means when he speaks of "retroactively apply[ing] the sanction of law to the things we do to maintain order." The great hope of the citizens of Deadwood is that the territorial authority will simply ratify the mining claims they have already established on their own. Anderson and Hill discuss historical precedents for such ratification: "In 1851, California passed the Civil Practice Act, which established a judicial system and basically codified the agreements that had been reached in the mining camps. The justices, in deciding mining cases, were to admit as evidence 'the customs, usages, or regulations established or enforced at the bar or diggings embracing such claims'" (*Wild West*, 114).

44. Consider Salerno's hyperbolic—but perhaps prophetic—comment on Swearengen as an artistic creation: "The character is already legendary—beloved by modern audiences and critics—and if there is real justice, he will still be as studied and beloved in 400 years as Falstaff and Iago—his closest Shakespearean analogues—are today" ("Discourses of Power," 197).

45. For Milch's own formulation of the paradox of Swearengen, see *Black Hills*, 17: "He is a very good man with none of the behaviors of goodness. He's a whoremongering murderer who protects the whores he abuses."

46. On this point, see David Drysdale, "'Laws and Every Other Damn Thing': Authority, Bad Faith, and the Unlikely Success of *Deadwood*," in Lavery, *Reading Deadwood*, 142.

47. Milch, *Black Hills*, 213.

48. Ibid., 41. Cf. Locke's treatment of barter and money in *Two Treatises*, 144: "And thus came in the use of money—some lasting thing that men might keep without spoiling, and that by mutual consent men would take in exchange for the truly useful but perishable supports of life."

49. For an excellent historical analysis of the positive role of commerce in the American West, especially of the way it worked to overcome prejudice and created economic opportunities for ethnic minorities, see Bradley J. Birzer, "Expanding Creative Destruction: Entrepreneurship in the American Wests," *Western Historical Quarterly* 30 (Spring 1999): 45–63.

50. Milch, *Black Hills*, 55.

51. Hearst follows an old prospector's custom of referring to gold as "the color."

52. Locke stresses the fact that commodity money originally develops independently of any government activity: "This partage of things in an inequality of private possessions men have made practicable out of the bounds of society and without compact, only by putting a value on gold and silver, and tacitly agreeing in the use of money; for, in governments, the laws regulate the right of property, and the possession of land is determined by positive constitutions" (*Two Treatises*, 145). On this point in Locke, see Joseph A. Schumpeter, *History of Economic Analysis* (New York: Oxford University Press, 1954), 291. Locke's commodity theory of money was not fully developed until the late nineteenth century, in Austrian economics, which emphasizes the idea that money develops naturally out of a barter economy, with no

need for government intervention; see Carl Menger, *Principles of Economics,* trans. James Dingwall and Bert F. Hoselitz (Grove City, PA: Libertarian Press, 1994), 257–271. Apropos of the Western, Menger argues that one of the earliest forms of money was cattle (263–265). As for commodity money in Deadwood, since it is a gold-rush town, it naturally operates on the gold standard. When Alma Garrett opens the first bank in town, her "full faith and credit" is founded on the gold reserves on her property.

53. Milch, *Black Hills,* 142.

54. Rousseau, *Discourses,* 102.

55. Milch writes, "The men who came to Deadwood craved a new beginning, a chance to break their ties to civilized institutions and forms of meaning" (*Black Hills,* 15). But this implies that these people were already shaped by those civilized institutions. Try as they may, they cannot totally escape their links to the East Coast and the European Old World (after all, some of the characters are not even American but British).

56. This quotation is taken from the bonus feature commentary "The New Language of the Old West" in the first-season set of *Deadwood* DVDs.

57. See E. Hill, "'What's Afflictin' You?,'" 182.

58. James C. Scott, *The Art of Not Being Governed: An Anarchist History of Upland Southeast Asia* (New Haven, CT: Yale University Press, 2009), 337.

59. Ibid., 118; see also 335.

60. Rousseau, *Discourses,* 130.

61. See E. Hill, "'What's Afflictin' You?,'" 181.

62. Rousseau, *Discourses,* 140.

63. Ibid., 150–151. The Western offers the opportunity to explore this Rousseauian possibility of a community halfway between the undeveloped state of nature and the over-developed modern nation-state. Sometimes this happy medium takes the form of a Native American community (just the sort of "savages" Rousseau himself offers as an example of this intermediate state). Milch may be offering Deadwood prior to its absorption into the United States as another form of happy medium.

64. For Rousseau's negative view of property, see *Discourses,* 141–142, 151–152, 156–157.

65. See ibid., 134, 137.

66. See especially the important discussion in note i of the *Second Discourse,* 201–203.

67. On this idea in Rousseau, and his relation to John Milton, see "A Discourse on Eden" in my book *Creature and Creator: Myth-making and English Romanticism* (Cambridge, UK: Cambridge University Press, 1984), 1–25.

68. Jean-Jacques Rousseau, *The Social Contract and Other Later Political Writings,* ed. and trans. Victor Gourevitch (Cambridge, UK: Cambridge University Press, 1997), 41.

69. For a similar view in a traditional historian, see Turner, *Frontier,* 205.

70. For similar views of the series, see Drysdale, "Unlikely Success," 139–141; and Amanda Ann Klein, "'The Horse Doesn't Get a Credit': The Foregrounding of Generic Syntax in *Deadwood*'s Opening Credits," in Lavery, *Reading Deadwood,* 99–100. Scott provides a trenchant critique of the standard account of civilization as progress; see especially *Not Being Governed,* 7–8 and 188: "What the schema portrays is not simply a self-satisfied normative account of progress but a gradient of successive stages of incorporation into state structure. Its stages of civilization are, at the same time, an index of diminishing autonomy and freedom" (188). This is a perfect formulation of the theme of "civilization and its dis-

contents" in *Deadwood*.

71. Hearst has the same attitude toward small towns that Paladin exhibits in *Have Gun–Will Travel;* see chapter 2. Both come from San Francisco; they seem to represent the big-city elites who have no respect for small towns and the small businesses that operate there. Unlike Gene Roddenberry, Milch believes that small towns can run themselves and overcome deep-rooted problems, such as prejudice, on their own—even and especially small towns run by businesspeople.

72. For a detailed comparison of Swearengen and Hearst, see Salerno, "Discourses of Power," 202–203.

73. For other critiques of the collusion between big business and big government, see chapter 5, on *The Aviator,* and chapter 6, on *South Park*.

74. For a similar defense of ordinary people and local interests against the national government, see chapter 4, on *Mars Attacks!*

75. Milch, *Black Hills,* 143.

76. Ibid., 135.

77. As a sign of the importance of state-of-nature thinking to the genre, one might be able to classify Westerns as basically Hobbesian, Lockean, or Rousseauian in spirit. The majority of American Westerns tend to be Lockean. As shown by the title of a famous example—*How the West Was Won* (1962)—American Westerns generally portray the victory of civilization over various forms of frontier barbarism. By contrast, the Italian Western—the so-called Spaghetti Western created by Sergio Leone—is usually Hobbesian in spirit, portraying the West as profoundly lawless and truly a war of all against all. Westerns like Kevin Costner's *Dances with Wolves* (1990), which romanticize the world of Native Americans and celebrate the virtues of a prepolitical way of life, could be called Rousseauian in spirit. For an analysis of the portrayal of Native Americans in Westerns, with specific reference to *Dances with Wolves* and a discussion of the background in Rousseau, see Michael Valdez Moses, "Savage Nation: Native Americans and the Western," in McMahon and Csaki, *Philosophy of the Western,* 261–290. The best Westerns, such as *Deadwood* and the films of John Ford, seem to combine elements of Hobbes, Locke, and Rousseau in creative tension. For the view that Westerns alternate between the poles of Locke and Rousseau, see John Marini, "Defending the West: John Ford and the Creation of the Epic Western," in *Print the Legend: Politics, Culture, and Civic Virtue in the Films of John Ford,* ed. Sidney A. Pearson Jr. (Lanham, MD: Lexington, 2009), 10, 17nn10–11. For other attempts to apply state-of-nature thinking to popular culture, see Dean A. Kowalski's analysis of the 2006 film *V for Vendetta* in "R for Revolution: Hobbes and Locke on Social Contracts and Scarlet Carsons," in *Homer Simpson Goes to Washington: American Politics through Popular Culture,* ed. Joseph J. Foy (Lexington: University Press of Kentucky, 2008), 19–40; and Claire P. Curtis, *Postapocalyptic Fiction and the Social Contract* (Lanham, MD: Lexington, 2010)—Curtis draws on Hobbes, Locke, and Rousseau.

4. *Mars Attacks!*

My epigraph is taken from http://en.wikiquote.org/wiki/William_F._Buckley,_Jr. (consulted June 13, 2011). This quotation appears in different wording in different places; I have chosen the wording offered on Wikiquote because, to me, this sounds more like Buckley than the other versions do.

1. Kenneth Turan, "*Mars Attacks!* Tim Burton's *Plan 9,*" *Los Angeles Times,* December 13, 1996, as cited in the Wikipedia article on the film, http://en.wikipedia.org/wiki/Mars_Attacks! (consulted on June 16, 2011).

2. One can view the complete set of the fifty-five original *Mars Attacks!* trading cards, produced by the Topps Company in the early 1960s, at: http://www.flickr.com/photos/31558613@N00/sets/72157625601126001/ (consulted on June 16, 2011).

3. Bill Warren, "Tim Burton Attacks!," in *Tim Burton: Interviews,* ed. Kristian Fraga (Jackson: University Press of Mississippi, 2005), 111.

4. For a concise overview of science fiction films and their relation to the Cold War, see Richard A. Schwartz, *Cold War Culture: Media and the Arts, 1945–1990* (New York: Checkmark, 1998), 114–115, 276–277. For a detailed analysis of 1950s invasion movies, see Marc Jancovich, *Rational Fears: American Horror in the 1950s* (Manchester, UK: University of Manchester Press, 1996), 10–79. See also Joyce A. Evans, *Celluloid Mushroom Clouds: Hollywood and the Atomic Bomb* (Boulder, CO: Westview, 1998), especially 117–126; and M. Keith Booker, *Monsters, Mushroom Clouds, and the Cold War: American Science Fiction and the Roots of Postmodernism, 1946–1964* (Westport, CT: Greenwood, 2001), especially 105–137.

5. I discuss the portrayal of the FBI in American popular culture during the Cold War in my book *Gilligan Unbound: Pop Culture in the Age of Globalization* (Lanham, MD: Rowman & Littlefield, 2001), 115–117. Elsewhere in that book, I discuss other examples of the impact of the Cold War on American pop culture, specifically in the cases of *Gilligan's Island* (1964–1967) and the original *Star Trek* television series (1966–1969), as well as the movie *Star Trek VI: The Undiscovered Country* (1991).

6. The program was inaugurated by President Dwight Eisenhower in his speech "Atoms for Peace" given to the United Nations General Assembly on December 8, 1953.

7. As a pupil in the New York City public school system in the 1950s, I remember being taught—incessantly—that the two greatest achievements in the history of humanity were atomic energy and the United Nations (both credited to Franklin Delano Roosevelt, incidentally). Like most baby boomers, I can still recall being shown the 1957 Disney film *Our Friend the Atom* in school.

8. For the relationship between science and the federal government throughout American history, see James T. Bennett's highly polemical and provocative book, *The Doomsday Lobby: Hype and Panic from Sputniks, Martians, and Marauding Meteors* (New York: Springer, 2010); for the Cold War era in particular, see chapter 3, especially 45–46, 49, 53, 59, and 76–77.

9. This motif appears at least as early as Edgar G. Ulmer's *The Man from Planet X* (1951). The idea of aliens taking over the minds of humans reflects Cold War anxieties about the brainwashing of U.S. soldiers captured during the Korean War. See David J. Skal, *The Monster Show: A Cultural History of Horror* (New York: Faber and Faber, 2001), 251; and Booker, *Monsters,* 121.

10. *Invaders from Mars* may be suggesting that the way the space invaders subvert the family and the police is precisely what is sinister about them. The film may be another allegory of a takeover of American institutions by communism. Still, the negative light in which it casts the family and local institutions was noted at the time by no less an authority than the Parent-Teacher Association, as Skal reports: "PTA representatives were not pleased about *Invaders from Mars.* Wrote one: 'Here, in science fiction form, is an orgy of hate and fear and futility, with no hope of escape, no constructive element whatsoever. The child with

whom one is asked to identify is bereft of any security from father and mother, from constituted authorities, and the adults burst into meaningless violence'" (Skal, *Monster Show*, 251; his citation reads, "Transcript of 1953 PTA reports on *Invaders from Mars*, Billy Rose Theatre Collection, New York Public Library for the Performing Arts at Lincoln Center"). This description of the film may sound laughably alarmist to us today, but it shows that flying saucer movies were taken seriously and read for their political meaning even when they were first released.

11. On this point, see Schwartz, *Cold War Culture*, 151.

12. I have transcribed all quotations from *Earth vs. the Flying Saucers* from the Columbia Pictures DVD (2002).

13. There is some debate over who really directed the movie. According to Chris Steinbrunner and Burt Goldblatt, "Officially Howard Hawks was only the producer of *The Thing*, but for years it has been rumored that he also directed large portions of it." Steinbrunner and Goldblatt, *Cinema of the Fantastic* (New York: Galahad, 1972), 224. Most commentators treat *The Thing* as a typical Howard Hawks tale of male comrades facing danger together on a frontier, with the genre switched from Western to science fiction.

14. See Schwartz, *Cold War Culture*, 331–332; and Booker, *Monsters*, 119–120. Treating the film in the context of Hawks's career, Steinbrunner and Goldblatt write, "Often, in the routine science fiction films of this period and later, the world is saved by, say, the Marines, but in no other film is the heroism, the professionalism, and the effectiveness of 'our side' so earnestly and dramatically portrayed" (*Cinema*, 224). For a different interpretation of *The Thing*, see Jancovich, *Rational Fears*, 34–41.

15. Schwartz, *Cold War Culture*, 75, and Booker, *Monsters*, 133–134. Another pacifist film from this era is Jack Arnold's *It Came from Outer Space* (1953), based on a story by Ray Bradbury. The "invading" aliens in this film turn out to have merely crashed on Earth and just need time to repair their spaceship so that they can go about their cosmic business. Only an amateur astronomer (Richard Carlson) is willing to help them against a mob of fearful and angry townspeople. Once again, the scientist is the lone voice of reason in a paranoid world; in this case, the film seems to be criticizing America's Cold War hostility to foreigners. *It Came from Outer Space* is unusual for films of its type because the national government (in the form of the army) refuses to get involved at all in the investigation of the crash of the UFO. Instead, the movie focuses on the conflict between the scientist and a local sheriff, thus again celebrating a scientific elite at the expense of local authorities. Only the disinterested scientific expert can rise above local prejudices. On this point, see Jancovich, *Rational Fears*, 171–176.

16. This plot formula was so widespread at the time that it even appears in a Japanese flying saucer movie, Toho Studio's *The Mysterians* (1957). In this film, the common people of Japan can be saved from the devastation wrought by alien invaders only by prompt action from their government, their military, and their scientists. As in *Earth vs. the Flying Saucers*, the Japanese authorities develop technological countermeasures against the Mysterians with remarkable speed. But in a twist that shows that science may be evil as well as good, one of the Japanese scientists turns traitor to his species and collaborates with the Mysterians because of their superiority in science. As the only people ever to have been bombed by nuclear weapons, the Japanese had a special reason in the 1950s to be skeptical about the power of science, and many of their sci-fi movies, from *Godzilla* (1954) on, reflect their concerns about

nuclear weapons. If *The Mysterians* is a political allegory, it seems to express Japanese unease about U.S. military forces occupying their soil after World War II. Having landed near Mt. Fuji, the Mysterians make two demands: (1) to be given a small plot of land for their base on Earth; and (2) to be permitted to intermarry with Japanese women of their choosing. The contemporary relevance of these plot details seems unmistakable. On this point, see Booker, *Monsters,* 173n15; and Jerome F. Shapiro, *Atomic Bomb Cinema: The Apocalyptic Imagination on Film* (New York: Routledge, 2002), 280–281.

17. This motif is evident in Wells at least as early as his "atomic bomb" novel *The World Set Free* (1914) and is a principal theme of his later book, *The Shape of Things to Come* (1933) as well as of the movie he made from it with William Cameron Menzies, *Things to Come* (1935).

18. Jancovich provides an insightful analysis of *The Day the Earth Stood Still* (*Rational Fears,* 41–46). He is especially good on its hostility to freedom: "Klattu [*sic*] claims that this solution to war does not involve any loss of freedom, except the freedom to behave 'irresponsibly.' But there is a problem with the word 'irresponsible': it is not as easy to define as Klattu implies. What may be irresponsible to one person may not be to another. . . . Klattu's proposal does not reject violence, but places it firmly within the hands of the state. Nor is it presented as an option. He informs the scientists that there is no alternative. . . . The film demands rigid conformity to the universal order, an order from which there can be no valid dissent" (45–46). For the contrary view, that "Klaatu's ultimatum does not violate anyone's rights," see Aeon J. Skoble, "Technology and Ethics in *The Day the Earth Stood Still,*" in *The Philosophy of Science Fiction,* ed. Steven M. Saunders (Lexington: University Press of Kentucky, 2008), 91–101.

19. George Pal's *Destination Moon* (1950) may be unique in its day for the way it expresses some skepticism about the federal government's competence and champions the free enterprise system. It pointedly suggests that only private companies could successfully put men on the moon. The film's lunar project is led by a Howard Hughes figure (he has set speed records in planes and owns both an aircraft manufacturing company and an airline), and it is supported by a variety of corporate sponsors. In order to launch their rocket, these entrepreneurs must overcome obstacles created by government bureaucracies overly concerned with safety regulations. The fact that the famous science fiction writer Robert Heinlein was heavily involved in this movie may explain what appears to be its libertarian slant. But even *Destination Moon* foresees a reconciliation between government and private enterprise. The entrepreneurs plan on eventually selling their rockets to the U.S. government. Moreover, the story clearly takes place in a Cold War context. The Hughes figure wins over his fellow entrepreneurs to the project when he invokes the challenge of the space race. American entrepreneurs must finance a rocket to the moon before unnamed foreign powers get there first. On this film, see Booker, *Monsters,* 109–110.

20. Christine Spines, "Men Are from Mars, Women Are from Venus," in Fraga, *Burton,* 127.

21. Warren, "Tim Burton Attacks!," in Fraga, *Burton,* 108.

22. Ibid., 109.

23. Spines, "Men Are from Mars," 120.

24. Gems quoted in ibid.

25. Mark Salisbury, ed., *Burton on Burton* (London: Faber and Faber, 2000), 145.

26. Ibid., 146.

27. This cinematic tradition was evident in the silent era, well represented in Mack Sennett's Keystone Kops films. Sennett himself explained these films in anarchistic terms: "Authority had been ridiculed! That was exactly the artistic effect I was after. . . . Nearly everyone of us lives in the secret hope that someday before he dies he will be able to swat a policeman's hat down around his ears." Quoted in LeRoy Asbhy, *With Amusement for All: A History of American Popular Culture since 1830* (Lexington: University Press of Kentucky, 2006), 171. For more on the antielitism of silent comedies, see ibid., 172–173.

28. Salisbury, *Burton*, 153.

29. I have transcribed all quotations from *Mars Attacks!* from the Warner Home Video DVD (1997).

30. Given Burton's sympathy for marginalized figures, one might expect him to be sympathetic to multiculturalism, and indeed he often speaks in favor of openness to different cultures. But Burton appears to become suspicious of multiculturalism when it becomes a political ideology. As I explain later in this chapter, Burton questions multiculturalism as an abstract slogan, but champions it in the practical life of the American people.

31. The film is, of course, satirizing Decker as well for his militarism, but at least his view of the Martians proves to be correct.

32. In fact, the Martians do misinterpret a human gesture of peace at the greeting ceremony—the release of a dove—as an aggressive act. Evidently, the Martians do not like birds.

33. By contrast, in the *Mars Attacks!* trading card series, the American military, although it suffers initial defeats, quickly responds to the Martian threat by invading Mars, taking the fight to the Martians, and destroying them on their home soil.

34. For the contrast between the big city and the small town in American popular culture, see chapter 2, on *Have Gun–Will Travel*.

35. On this subject, see William A. Galstone, "Civil Society and the 'Art of Association,'" *Journal of Democracy* 11, no. 1 (January 2000): 64–70. In a view similar to what we saw in the case of Locke in chapter 3, Tocqueville thought that civil society can be conceived as independent of government, logically, if not necessarily historically, prior to it.

36. Alexis de Tocqueville, *Democracy in America,* trans. Harvey C. Mansfield and Delba Winthrop (Chicago: University of Chicago Press, 2000), 489–490.

37. Ibid., 491.

38. As odd as it may sound, I have speculated in print as to what Tocqueville would think of Las Vegas if he could revisit America today. See my "Postmodern Prophet: Tocqueville Visits Vegas," *Journal of Democracy* 11, no. 1 (January 2000): 111–118.

39. Tocqueville, *Democracy in America,* 491–492.

40. See Friedrich Hayek, *The Road to Serfdom* (Chicago: University of Chicago Press, 1944).

41. Here I am referring to *Democracy in America,* vol. 2, part 4, chapters 6–8. On this subject, see Paul A. Rahe, *Soft Despotism, Democracy as Drift: Montesquieu, Rousseau, Tocqueville, and the Modern Project* (New Haven, CT: Yale University Press, 2009).

42. These words were spoken by then presidential candidate Barack Obama in a fundraising speech delivered in San Francisco on April 11, 2008; he was referring to Americans in small towns in Pennsylvania and the Midwest. The text of the speech can be found by Googling "cling to guns and religion," as, for example, at this site: http://inkslwc.wordpress.com/2008/04/12/barack-obama-bitter-pennsylvanians-cling-to-guns-or-religion/ (consulted June 16, 2011).

43. Strictly speaking, the Americans of *Mars Attacks!* do not create associations in the formal sense that Tocqueville speaks of in *Democracy in America.* They spontaneously act alone or in small groups. Nevertheless, the film does point to exactly the self-reliance in Americans that impressed Tocqueville. *Mars Attacks!* does include several scenes of ordinary Americans who panic when faced with the Martian invasion. The film does not claim that all Americans are capable of dealing with disaster; it shows only that some are, but that is enough to deflate claims for government omnicompetence.

44. As the prototype of all subsequent Martian invasion stories, *The War of the Worlds* already contains many of the motifs that were to be developed in later book, movie, and television versions. Wells wrote the novel as a lesson to the British Empire. In 1898, the British were sitting on top of the world, confident that their military and technological superiority would prevail in the twentieth century and continue to secure their hegemony over their colonies. Wells showed that a militarily and technologically superior force from Mars could do to the British Empire what it had been doing to non-European peoples around the world. In that sense, *The War of the Worlds* can be read as an antigovernment novel. Nevertheless, the novel betrays Wells's growing socialist convictions and celebrates the centralized power of strong governments. Wells appears to admire the tight organization of the invading Martian forces, especially their ability to coordinate their movements perfectly and pursue a campaign planned in advance with single-minded devotion. By contrast, Wells shows human beings panicking as they flee the Martian invaders. He thus established what has become a convention of this genre: portraying the chaotic response of ordinary people to an alien invasion. Their only hope seems to lie in help from their government and its military; Wells pictures them as utterly incapable of organizing themselves or of responding rationally to the Martian threat. He has particular contempt for any free-enterprise responses to the plight of the refugees; he has great disdain for the private boat operators who come to rescue people—because they charge exorbitant sums for the service. As in much of his science fiction, Wells's socialist belief in central government planning as the only solution to human ills shines through in *The War of the Worlds.*

45. The one exception to this rule occurs near the end of the film, when the president's daughter, evidently the only surviving member of the Washington establishment, awards the Congressional Medal of Honor to Richie for saving the world. With the characteristic modesty of ordinary people, Richie says, "There's a lot of people in the world that have done a lot more than I have, and they're the ones who should be here now, getting a medal."

46. Burton must like this song; he had used it earlier in *Edward Scissorhands.*

47. The film's iconoclasm is evident in the way it treats its own Hollywood stars with sublime disrespect. Burton reports, "I just thought it would be fun to see big stars getting blown away. It's like all those movies that they used to make where you never know who's going to make it. I remember seeing Robert Wagner on fire in *The Towering Inferno.* I didn't expect Robert Wagner to be on fire. It's kind of cathartic in a way" (Spines, "Men Are from Mars," 121). The stars in *Mars Attacks!* become part of Burton's debunking of the American elite. They compete as to who can die more ignominiously (Glenn Close's death by chandelier may take the prize). Burton treats his stars as just more American icons who need to be smashed. As he says elsewhere, "I've always loved those Irwin Allen films—those 'Celebrities Getting Killed' movies. That's a genre unto itself. . . . It seemed like a good idea just to blow away celebrities with ray-guns" (quoted in Salisbury, *Burton,* 148). Once again, we see

Burton's urge to liberate the American people from idol worship of their elites. For a similar debunking of the Hollywood elite in *South Park,* see chapter 6.

48. For some reason, DeVito's character did not merit a name in the script; he is identified in the cast simply as "Rude Gambler."

49. That racial issues are in the background of the film is suggested by the way President Dale's final appeal to the Martians echoes Rodney King's famous words "Can we all get along?" in his May 1, 1992, attempt to calm things down during the L.A. riots (see http://en.wikipedia.org/wiki/Rodney_King; consulted June 25, 2011). I am indebted to Michael Valdez Moses for calling this echo to my attention. The line "Can't we all just get along?" recurs in a clearly racial context in Burton's *Planet of the Apes* (2001), spoken by Limbo (Paul Giamatti).

50. For the democratic character of Las Vegas as a cultural phenomenon, see my "Postmodern Prophet" article.

51. On this subject, see LeRoy Ashby, *With Amusement for All: A History of American Popular Culture since 1830* (Lexington: University Press of Kentucky, 2006).

52. Kristine McKenna, "*Playboy* Interview: Tim Burton," in Fraga, *Burton,* 155. For more on Burton as auteur, see Jenny He, "An Auteur for All Ages," *Tim Burton* (New York: Museum of Modern Art, 2009), 16–23.

53. Quoted in Warren, "Tim Burton Attacks!," 115.

54. In this regard, the audio commentary provided by Burton and Paul Reubens (the actor who created Pee-wee Herman) on the DVD of *Pee-wee's Big Adventure* (Warner Home Video, 2000) is instructive. They continually talk about the movies they imitated in their film, and Burton brings up the subject of genre again and again; for him, making the movie was an exercise in "another day, another genre."

55. Salisbury, *Burton,* 151. Cf. a similar statement by Trey Parker, one of the creators of *South Park:* "The boundaries are part of the fun" (*Reason,* December 2006, 64).

56. Quoted in Salisbury, *Burton,* 109.

57. McKenna, "*Playboy* Interview," 161.

58. Storyboards, a kind of cartoon version of a film that allows the production team to visualize what it will look like and work out problems in advance, were first used by the Walt Disney Studio in the 1930s. Several auteurs, such as Alfred Hitchcock and Akira Kurosawa, are famous for their use of storyboards. A generous sampling of the storyboards for *Pee-wee's Big Adventure* is available in the Special Features bonus on the DVD ("Production Sketches and Storyboards"). Having worked in the Disney studio and trained as a cartoonist, Burton makes good use of storyboards, but his increasing sense of the messiness of movie production has led him to rely on them less and less, as he says in an interview about *Ed Wood:* "The problems of making a movie is [*sic*] really such a goofy thing. It's not an exact science and many things can go wrong. . . . That's great, because that's what makes it kind of fun. . . . I've gotten more away from storyboards. . . . Obviously on a [*sic*] effects picture you board a lot more. On a picture like this [*Ed Wood*] I find you don't need to storyboard. You're working mainly with actors, and there's no effects going on, so it's best to be more spontaneous. We did this one a little more on the spot. The approach I took was to start with the concept. Who the characters are and so forth, then just sort of do it. It's got an episodic, matter-of-fact approach. We didn't want to impose too much of a style on it. Let the people be the focus and the style will come out of that." Lawrence French, "A Meeting of Minds: Tim Burton's *Ed Wood,*" in Fraga, *Burton,* 104. Many critics speak of Burton imposing his distinctive style

on every movie he makes, but here he claims that the style emerges spontaneously from his material as he and other people (including the actors) work on the film. Burton appears to view filmmaking as a form of spontaneous order.

59. See McKenna, "*Playboy* Interview," 160–161, for Burton's speaking of his tendency to identify with Wood: "I'm like Ed Wood in that I go into every movie with the same mixture of optimism, enthusiasm, and denial."

60. Many people choose *Citizen Kane* as the greatest film of all time, but not, as it happens, Tim Burton. His comments on Welles and *Citizen Kane* may surprise the critics who think of him as working in the art-film tradition. When asked in an interview whether he admires Welles's work, Burton replied, "I never really saw *Citizen Kane*. The Welles films sort of passed me by. I haven't seen *The Lady from Shanghai*. I have seen *The Third Man*, and I guess I must have seen *Citizen Kane*. Yes, I'm sure I've seen *Citizen Kane*" (French, "A Meeting of Minds," 105). This statement does not suggest that Welles was a great influence on Burton's development. If he has a personal pantheon of filmmakers, it seems to include Ed Wood, Ray Harryhausen, and Irwin Allen rather than Orson Welles, Ingmar Bergman, and Jean Renoir. (He does, however, express admiration in his interviews for such auteurs as Frederico Fellini and Roman Polanski.) In a moment in the *Playboy* interview even more troubling to elitist auteur theorists, Burton pays tribute to commercial television: "As far as the work that influenced me, I'm a child of television and I grew up on monster movies, *The Twilight Zone*, and *The Outer Limits*" (McKenna, "*Playboy* Interview," 169). And here is perhaps Burton's most telling admission: "Growing up as part of the television generation, I probably veer toward bad taste" (quoted in Salisbury, *Burton*, xv).

61. Quoted in Salisbury, *Burton*, 153. Note again the way Burton is always thinking of movies in terms of genres.

62. Ibid.

63. For a discussion of the continuing fascination with alien invasion narratives in American pop culture and their ideological significance, see chapter 10, "Un-American Gothic."

5. Flying Solo

My epigraph is from Ludwig von Mises, *The Anti-Capitalistic Mentality* (Princeton, NJ: D. Van Nostrand, 1956), 108.

1. In an interview, Scorsese says of Hughes, "He became the outlaw of Hollywood in a way." See http://movies.about.com/od/theaviator/a/aviatorms121004.htm (consulted May 9, 2006; hereinafter cited as "Internet interview").

2. For the record, all the Scorsese characters mentioned thus far—Travis Bickle, Rupert Pupkin, Max Cady, and Jake LaMotta—are played by Robert De Niro.

3. "Introduction," *The Aviator: A Screenplay by John Logan* (New York: Miramax Books, 2004), vii. In the Internet interview, in response to the question "Do you see any parallel between Howard Hughes's obsessions and yours?" Scorsese says, "I have [had] over the years, some close friends and acquaintances who have said, who have described me at one point, 'Don't go in the room. He's got the tissue boxes on his feet.' . . . But basically I couldn't presume to say I've been like Howard Hughes. Howard Hughes was this visionary. . . . I usually like to lock myself in the screening room and just screen. That's maybe the only similarity I see." In an Internet interview, Leonardo DiCaprio is more candid when asked

whether he could relate to Hughes: "The *Hell's Angels* sequence, being a part of films that have gone on for many, many months and you're sitting there with the director trying to get things perfect and do things over and over and over again, that was something that I think Scorsese and I immediately identified with." See http://movies.about.com/od/theaviatorld/a/aviatorld121004.htm (consulted May 9, 2006).

4. A perfect example of Hollywood's negative portrayal of the businessman is the cruel banker Mr. Potter in Frank Capra's classic *It's a Wonderful Life* (1946). For a comprehensive survey of the portrayal of businessmen in American popular culture, see the chapter "The Culture Industry's Representation of Business" in Don Lavoie and Emily Chamlee-Wright, *Culture and Enterprise: The Development, Representation and Morality of Business* (London: Routledge, 2000), 80–103. Lavoie and Chamlee-Wright provide representative figures from media studies: "Of all the antagonists studied in over 30 years of programming, businessmen were twice as likely to play the role of antagonist than any other identifiable occupation. Business characters are nearly three times as likely to be criminals, relative to other occupations on television. They represent 12 percent of all characters in identifiable occupations, but account for 32 percent of crimes. Forty-four percent of all vice crimes such as prostitution and drug trafficking committed on television, and 40 percent of TV murders, are perpetrated by business people" (84). For examples of negative television portrayals of businessmen, see chapter 2, on *Have Gun–Will Travel*. There I also explore the reasons why Gene Roddenberry as a creative artist criticized capitalism, despite the ways he benefited from it.

5. On the hostility to business in the general culture, see F. A. Hayek, *The Fatal Conceit: The Errors of Socialism* (Chicago: University of Chicago Press, 1988), 89–105; and Mises, *Anti-Capitalistic Mentality*. Mises offers an interesting analysis of the psychology of detective stories on 52–55.

6. The Hollywood archetype of the idealistic senator who takes on the business interests in his state and fights corruption, even in the Senate itself, is found in Frank Capra's *Mr. Smith Goes to Washington* (1939).

7. Scorsese, "Introduction," *The Aviator*, viii. In the Internet interview, Scorsese says of the movie, "The approach on this material really, really comes from John Logan, the writer."

8. For the sake of convenience, I have quoted from the published version of the screenplay, even though the spoken dialogue occasionally departs in minor ways from the text. Page numbers are given in parentheses in the body of the essay. All italics in the quotations from *The Aviator* are in the original text.

9. Ludwig von Mises, *Human Action: A Treatise on Economics* (New Haven, CT: Yale University Press, 1949), 303. On this point, see also Adam Smith, *An Inquiry into the Nature and Causes of the Wealth of Nations*, 2 vols. (1776; rpt. Indianapolis, IN: Liberty Classics, 1981), 1: 454, 456.

10. For speculations on why people in Hollywood generally condemn capitalism, see Mises, *Anti-Capitalistic Mentality*, 30–33.

11. Patrick Goldstein, "The Big Picture," *Los Angeles Times*, January 26, 2005.

12. The bowdlerization in the brackets is courtesy of the *Los Angeles Times*. My guess is that what DiCaprio really wrote was "balls."

13. See Charles Higham, *Howard Hughes: The Secret Life* (New York: G. P. Putnam's Sons, 1993), 179.

14. See DiCaprio's "Foreword" to *The Aviator*, vi. In the Internet interview, in response to

the question "Do you think Howard Hughes would have been the genius that he was without the OCD?" DiCaprio replied, "I think they're a direct result of one another. It's like he would have not been as obsessed about making the largest plane ever built. He wouldn't have been obsessed about breaking every speed record. He wouldn't have been obsessed about flying around the world faster than anyone else. He wouldn't have been obsessed about reshooting *Hell's Angels* for sound, having that movie go on for four years. . . . It was all completely a part of his obsessive nature and his OCD that made him have such an amazing, astounding life." For the theme of madness in *The Aviator,* see Jerold J. Abrams, "The Cinema of Madness: Friedrich Nietzsche and the Films of Martin Scorsese," in *The Philosophy of Martin Scorsese,* ed. Mark T. Conard (Lexington: University Press of Kentucky, 2009), 87–89.

15. Mises, *Human Action,* 582.

16. For Scorsese's comments on Hughes as a visionary, see the interview on *The Aviator* in Richard Schickel, *Conversations with Scorsese* (New York: Alfred A. Knopf, 2011), 241.

17. Higham, *Hughes,* 24.

18. See, for example, Mises, *Anti-Capitalistic Mentality,* 44–45. For further discussion of what Mises calls "parlor socialists," see 25–28, where he provides an astute sociological analysis of why people who have inherited wealth may turn against capitalism. Joseph Conrad's novel *The Secret Agent* provides a brilliant analysis of aristocratic socialism and also traces the convergence of the extreme left and the extreme right in a hatred of capitalism.

19. For a parallel in another Scorsese film, one might look to the treatment of Abraham Lincoln in *Gangs of New York.* With its suspicion of federal war policies—especially the draft—the film seems to sympathize with the hostile response of New Yorkers to a stage representation of Lincoln. American presidents who vastly expanded the power of the federal government do not fare well in Scorsese's movies.

20. Scorsese and DiCaprio agree on this point in their Internet interviews. Scorsese says, "Ultimately, what I really liked was the way the story developed into a struggle between [Hughes] and the government and Pan Am. I thought that was interesting. I think it has a lot of resonance for today, particularly the investigation committee smearing people." DiCaprio says, "How the hell do you make this situation with Juan Trippe and Pan American Airways and this Senator become a sympathetic situation towards Howard Hughes? . . . I realized . . . it has to do with corporate takeover and the involvement of huge corporations with our government, and they're in cahoots and it's going on today with the Enron scandals and numerous other things. That's what really made me say, 'Okay, here's this one man, he's his own boss, he is rich but he is a stand-up individual and here he is with all these horrible things going on with himself mentally, standing up in front of the Senate and battling the Senate to stop the monopoly on international travel.' I think, ultimately, people kind of got behind that. . . . They really loved this one individual taking on the entire system, taking on the government, taking on huge monopolies and corporations."

21. Let me reiterate here that I am not talking about the historical facts of this case, only about the way in which *The Aviator* presents them.

22. Specifically, Scorsese seems to have in mind the great Senate hearing scene in Francis Ford Coppola's *The Godfather, Part II* (1974). Although we are sympathetic to Michael Corleone (Al Pacino), there can be no question that he is in fact guilty of the crimes that the Senate committee is investigating. Given Scorsese's lifelong rivalry with Coppola, it is difficult to believe that he was not trying to show that he could create a Senate hearing scene

as powerful as the one by his fellow Italian American director. A number of the details in Scorsese's scene—Hughes's consultation with his consigliere Noah Dietrich, his reading of a prepared statement, his appeal to his patriotism, the confusion and consternation among the senators when the hearing fails to go the way they planned—all point to Coppola's corresponding scene in *Godfather II*. Both scenes take place just after World War II; even the cinematography of Scorsese's scene echoes Coppola's. Read against Coppola's Senate scene, Scorsese's takes on added meaning—Scorsese is showing that the senators are the gangsters. Coppola's film already hints in this direction; one of the senators on the investigating committee, Pat Geary (G. D. Spradlin), is shown to have ties to the Corleone family. *Tucker: The Man and His Dream* (1988) is another Coppola film that presents a U.S. senator as a villain and invites comparison with *The Aviator*. It tells the story of Preston Tucker (Jeff Bridges), a visionary entrepreneur who seeks to build "the car of tomorrow." He takes on the Big Three automobile companies in Detroit and is ruined by a conspiracy orchestrated on their behalf by a corrupt senator named Homer Ferguson (Lloyd Bridges). In an eerie anticipation of *The Aviator*, *Tucker* includes a scene with Howard Hughes (Dean Stockwell), staged in the ghostly presence of the real Spruce Goose and presenting Hughes as also a victim of Ferguson's machinations. *Tucker* shares many ideas and themes with *The Aviator*, but in this film Coppola does not match Scorsese in artistic quality. *Tucker* is almost cartoonish, with caricatures rather than fully developed characters and a relentlessly upbeat tone that glosses over the serious issues the film raises. As tended to happen at this stage of Coppola's career, he emphasizes visual style at the expense of dramatic substance. Still, it is interesting to see that, like Scorsese with Hughes, Coppola identifies with Tucker as a creative genius battling the corporate establishment. By focusing on Tucker's marketing efforts, Coppola assimilates the automobile industry to the entertainment industry. Like Scorsese, Coppola speaks up for the entrepreneur's freedom from government interference, especially in Tucker's eloquent challenge at his trial for stock fraud: "If Benjamin Franklin were alive today, he'd be arrested for flying a kite without a license."

    23. Smith, *Wealth of Nations*, 1: 493–494.

    24. Ibid., 1: 493.

    25. Ibid., 1: 456.

    26. Ibid., 1: 26–27.

6. Cartman Shrugged

My epigraph is from Mark Twain, *"1601" and "Is Shakespeare Dead?"* (New York: Oxford University Press, 1996), iv.

    1. *Symposium*, 221E–222A, in *Plato: Lysis, Symposium, Gorgias*, trans. W. R. M. Lamb, Loeb Classical Library (Cambridge, MA: Harvard University Press, 1925), 239.

    2. For more on the relation between *South Park* and Plato, see William W. Young III, "Flatulence and Philosophy: A Lot of Hot Air, or the Corruption of Youth?" and William J. Devlin, "The Philosophical Passion of the Jew: Kyle the Philosopher," in *South Park and Philosophy: You Know, I Learned Something Today*, ed. Robert Arp (Oxford, UK: Blackwell, 2007), 5–7, 88–89.

    3. *The Clouds*, lines 392–394, in *The Clouds*, trans. William Arrowsmith (New York: New American Library, 1962), 45.

4. For some of the same reference points, see Toni Johnson-Woods, *Blame Canada! South Park and Contemporary Culture* (New York: Continuum, 2007), 91.

5. In a book in which I repeatedly stress the viability of multiple authorship as a mode of production in popular culture, I will simply note that everybody seems to accept Parker and Stone as the co-auteurs of *South Park* without worrying how they work together and how their contributions to the show might be distinguished. I wonder if many viewers of the show could even tell them apart. In the terms of English Renaissance drama, they are the Beaumont and Fletcher of contemporary cartoons.

6. See M. M. Bakhtin, *Rabelais and His World,* trans. Hélène Iswolsky (Bloomington: Indiana University Press, 1984); and *The Dialogic Imagination: Four Essays,* trans. Caryl Emerson and Michael Holquist (Austin: University of Texas Press, 1981). On the relevance of Bakhtin, Rabelais, and the carnivalesque to *South Park,* see Johnson-Woods, *Blame Canada!,* xii–xvi, 75–76; and Alison Halsall, "'Bigger Longer & Uncut': *South Park* and the Carnivalesque," in *Taking South Park Seriously,* ed. Jeffrey Andrew Weinstock (Albany: State University of New York Press, 2008), 23–37.

7. For anyone unfamiliar with the characters of *South Park,* I will state briefly that the four main characters are children named Eric Cartman, Kyle Broflovski, Stan Marsh, and Kenny McCormick (Parker and Stone voice all four, as well as other characters in the show). For a detailed discussion of the four boys, as well as the other main characters in *South Park,* see Johnson-Woods, *Blame Canada!,* 163–186. For the variant spellings of *Broflovski,* see ibid., 185n5.

8. Like Shakespeare's Falstaff, Cartman is ultimately derived from a stock character of Roman comedy: the braggart captain (*miles gloriosus*). Besides his love of boasting and lying, Cartman shares with Falstaff a tendency to cowardice; both characters like to act tough in front of their friends, but quickly back down when challenged.

9. François Rabelais, *Gargantua and Pantagruel,* trans. J. M. Cohen (New York: Viking Penguin, 1955), 63.

10. Ibid., 67–68. Rabelais reveals his debt to Plato's *Symposium* in the author's prologue to book 1 of *Gargantua and Pantagruel,* where he refers to the same Silenus passage I quote at the beginning of this chapter.

11. The profanity in *Deadwood* serves a similar purpose.

12. Jonathan Swift makes use of the same satiric technique in *Gulliver's Travels,* especially with his diminutive Lilliputians and gigantic Brobdingnagians. For the way "the theme of gigantic dimensions serves Rabelais for perspectivistic effects of contrast, which upset the reader's balance," see Erich Auerbach, *Mimesis: The Representation of Reality in Western Literature,* trans. Willard R. Trask (Princeton, NJ: Princeton University Press, 2003), 272–276.

13. Rabelais, *Gargantua,* 181.

14. I cite *South Park* episodes by the standard numbers given in the Warner Home Video DVD sets.

15. Nick Gillespie divines the connection when he says that South Park will "prove every bit as long-lived in the American subconscious as Mark Twain's Hannibal, Missouri." Gillespie, "*South Park* Libertarians," *Reason* 38, no. 7 (December 2006): 60. A Google search for "Twain and *South Park*" did not yield meaningful results, except for an attempt by Brown University students to organize a course on "*South Park,* Mark Twain, and Finding an American Culture" posted on March 16, 2011.

16. For many seasons of *South Park,* the boys' closest confidante was the African American cook at their school, known as Chef (voiced by Isaac Hayes). This might be regarded as a recreation of the Huck-Jim pairing. The boys learn many lessons about life from Chef that nobody else at their school is willing to teach them, and he repeatedly proves to be a liberating influence on them.

17. Mark Twain, *Adventures of Huckleberry Finn* (Oxford, UK: Oxford University Press, 1999), 127 (chapter 21), 130 (chapter 21), and 189 (chapter 31). These and like passages elsewhere in *Huckleberry Finn* and other works by Twain shed light on David Milch's use of profanity in *Deadwood.* Twain is unable to use the kind of language Milch wrote into his show, but he indicates that such language was readily spoken in nineteenth-century America, especially on the frontier.

18. Twain, *1601,* ix. As if to suggest the pedigree of his work, Twain has Queen Elizabeth mention that she met Rabelais when she was fifteen years old.

19. Twain, *1601,* v (italics in the original). It is possible that *1601* gives us a glimpse of what Twain's prose might have looked like if he had published in a more liberal climate of opinion. On this point, see Erica Jong's introduction to this edition of *1601* "[Twain] could not fill *Huckleberry Finn* with farts, pricks, and cunts, but he could play in *1601* and prepare his imagination for the antisocial adventures he would give his antihero in the other book" (xxxviii). And more generally, in words relevant to *South Park,* Jong writes: "in Mark Twain's case, pornography was an *essential* part of his oeuvre because it primed the pump for other sorts of freedom of expression" (xxxiii).

20. See Lawrence W. Levine, *Highbrow/Lowbrow: The Emergence of Cultural Hierarchy in America* (Cambridge, MA: Harvard University Press, 1988), 212.

21. *Huckleberry Finn* is a particularly interesting case because it is often still banned in libraries and school districts because of its racist language.

22. See Aristotle, *Poetics,* 1448a and 1449a in the standard numbering (sections 2 and 5 of Book I).

23. On this point, see Johnson-Woods, *Blame Canada!,* 82–84. The people who wish to see *South Park* taken off television would probably have tried to get Mark Twain's books banned if they had lived in the nineteenth century. Some of them might still want to see Twain's books banned today.

24. On *South Park* finding "the most potent taboos in American society and thus the most sacred of cows to satirize," see Matt Becker, "'I Hate Hippies': *South Park* and the Politics of Generation X," in Weinstock, *Taking South Park Seriously,* 150.

25. As several commentators have pointed out, this fight sequence closely mimics one in John Carpenter's movie *They Live* (1988). See Johnson-Woods, *Blame Canada!,* 223; and Brian L. Ott, "The Pleasures of *South Park* (An Experiment in Media Erotics)," in Weinstock, *Taking South Park Seriously,* 44.

26. For a good analysis of this episode, see Becker, "'I Hate Hippies,'" 155–156.

27. For a politically correct critique of *South Park,* see Robert Samuels, "Freud Goes to South Park: Teaching against Postmodern Prejudices and Equal Opportunity Hatred," in Weinstock, *Taking South Park Seriously,* 99–111. Reading this essay gives a good sense of the ideological positions Parker and Stone are combating. As his title indicates, Samuels takes as his pedagogical goal inoculating his students against the harmful influence of *South Park.*

28. For a critique of the "equal opportunity offensiveness of *South Park*," see Stephen Groening, "Cynicism and Other Postideological Half Measures in *South Park*," in Weinstock, *Taking South Park Seriously,* 113–129. Like Samuels and several of the other authors in the Weinstock volume, Groening tries to deflect or dilute the critique of liberal and left-wing causes in *South Park* by falling back on the claim that the show criticizes everything. He then accuses the show of breeding political apathy: "Viewers may see themselves as participants in a society rife with injustice but with no immediately viable solutions and prefer the uncommitted cynical irony of *South Park*'s parodic satire" (124). The same point is made in another essay in the volume: Lindsay Coleman, "Shopping at J-Mart with the Williams: Race, Ethnicity, and Belonging in *South Park*," 131–141. Coleman concludes, "Although Parker and Stone satirize the powerful, the hypocritical, and the stridently bigoted, they do not provide solutions to society's problems or provide the keys to social harmony" (141). With criticism such as this, I can only wonder whether it is asking too much of a TV cartoon to expect it to "provide solutions to society's problems or provide the keys to social harmony." I applaud the title of the volume these essays appear in, but this may be a case of taking *South Park* too seriously. Ultimately, the authors in the Weinstock collection complain not that *South Park* does not offer solutions to social problems, but that it does not offer their own liberal or left-wing solutions. As "Cripple Fight" demonstrates, *South Park* does not simply jump back and forth randomly between conservative and liberal positions. Rather, it offers its own solutions to problems by appealing consistently to libertarian principles.

29. For example, in an interview, Matt Stone said, "We're libertarians. Which is basically: Leave me alone—and I'm okay with drugs and gays." Mickey Rapkin, "They Killed Kenny . . . and Revolutionized Comedy," *GQ,* February 2006, 146. Many commentators have noted the libertarianism of *South Park;* for a well-balanced account of the show's politics, see Johnson-Woods, *Blame Canada!,* 203–215.

30. As quoted in Brian C. Anderson, *South Park Conservatives: The Revolt against Liberal Media Bias* (Washington, D.C.: Regnery, 2005), 178.

31. Quoted in Gillespie, "*South Park* Libertarians," 66.

32. For an analysis of why such groups turn against capitalism, see Ludwig von Mises, *The Anti-Capitalistic Mentality* (Princeton, NJ: D. Van Nostrand, 1956), especially 30–33 for the turn against capitalism in Hollywood.

33. See especially chapter 5, note 4.

34. As quoted in Anderson, *South Park Conservatives,* 82. On the treatment of celebrities in *South Park,* see Johnson-Woods, *Blame Canada!,* 187–199, 210–211; and Damion Sturm, "Omigod, It's Russell Crowe!": *South Park*'s Assault on Celebrity," in Weinstock, *Taking South Park Seriously,* 209–215, especially 215, where he analyzes in the case of George Clooney the way the show "dismantles star power."

35. Mises, *Anti-Capitalistic Mentality,* 2.

36. George Bernard Shaw offers this interpretation of Alberich; see his *The Perfect Wagnerite* (1898) in George Bernard Shaw, *Major Critical Essays* (Harmondsworth, UK: Penguin, 1986), 198, 205.

37. For the way H. G. Wells uses invisibility as a symbol of capitalism, see my essay "*The Invisible Man* and the Invisible Hand: H. G. Wells's Critique of Capitalism," in *Literature and the Economics of Liberty: Spontaneous Order in Culture,* ed. Paul A. Cantor and Stephen Cox (Auburn, AL: Ludwig von Mises Institute, 2009), 293–305.

38. F. A. Hayek, *The Fatal Conceit: The Errors of Socialism* (Chicago: University of Chicago Press, 1988), 90, 91, 93.

39. Several e-mail responses to an earlier version of this chapter argued that the gnomes' diagram is making fun of the sketchy business plans that flooded the initial public offering (IPO) market in the heyday of the dot-com boom in the 1990s. Having helped write a few such documents myself, I know what these correspondents are referring to, but I still think that my interpretation of this scene fits the context better. If the gnomes' business plan is simply satirizing dot-com IPOs, then it has no relation to the rest of the episode. I seem, however, to be fighting a losing battle over this interpretation. The "sketchy business plan" interpretation is going viral. See, for example, Art Carden, "'Underpants Gnomes' Political Economy," http://blogs.forbes.com/artcarden/2011/07/14/underpants-gnomes-political-economy (consulted August 9, 2011).

40. Adam Smith, *An Inquiry into the Nature and Causes of the Wealth of Nations,* 2 vols. (1776; rpt. Indianapolis, IN: Liberty Classics, 1981), 1: 456.

41. Thus, I am not about to get drawn into disputes over the quality of Starbucks' products. In fact, this chapter is about Harbucks, that is, the fictional form in which *South Park* represents Starbucks, not the actual retail chain. As with Howard Hughes in chapter 5, I am analyzing a fictional representation of a historical reality, not the reality itself. For a defense of the real Starbucks, see Jackson Kuhl, "Tempest in a Coffeepot: Starbucks Invades the World," *Reason,* January 2003, 55–57.

42. This attitude is epitomized by a very peculiar passage in the works of Marxist thinker Theodor Adorno, in which he laments the fact that the modern market economy has made cheap reproductions of all sorts of cultural artifacts readily available to large numbers of people. He complains that young radicals fill their dwellings with works of elite culture: "On the walls the deceptively faithful colour reproductions of famous Van Goghs like the 'Sunflowers' or the 'Café at Arles.' . . . Added to this the Random House edition of Proust—Scott Moncrieff's translation deserved a better fate, cut-price exclusivity even in its appearance. . . . All cultural products, even non-conformist ones, have been incorporated into the distribution-mechanisms of large-scale capital. . . . Even Kafka is becoming a fixture in the sub-let studio." Adorno, *Minima Moralia: Reflections from Damaged Life,* trans. E. F. N. Jephcott (London: Verso, 1978), 207. Perhaps Adorno could afford original Van Goghs and first editions of Proust (and high-rent apartments), but one wonders why he begrudges poor students their access to elite culture, even in cheap reproductions. I discuss Adorno's snobbery further in chapter 8.

43. This line of argument is characteristic of the Frankfurt School of Marxism; I analyze it further in chapter 8.

44. Rapkin, "They Killed Kenny," 146.

45. As with Harbucks/Starbucks, I am mainly interested in Wall Mart rather than Wal-Mart. That is, my analysis once again deals with the representation of Wal-Mart in *South Park,* not with the actual retail chain. For a defense of the real corporation and its practices, see Paul Kirklin, "The Ultimate pro-WalMart Article," *Mises Daily Article,* June 28, 2006, http://mises.org/daily/2219 (consulted August 4, 2011).

46. Several commentators fail to understand the media sophistication of *South Park* and miss the humor in moments like this. See, for example, Johnson-Woods, *Blame Canada!,* 153–154, 205. She thinks that the horror elements are the show's way of characterizing Wal-

Mart, not its way of characterizing the common misperception of Wal-Mart. Parker and Stone evidently have their personal doubts about Wal-Mart, but they are mainly concerned with the absurd extent to which its critics go in demonizing it. On this episode, see also Becker, "'I Hate Hippies,'" 157.

47. Quoted in Gillespie, "*South Park* Libertarians," 63.

48. The episodes in question were pulled only from the repeat rotation; they were allowed to air originally, and they are now once again available in the DVD sets of the series.

49. This incident has been widely discussed. See, for example, Jeffrey Andrew Weinstock, "*Simpsons* Did It!": *South Park* as Differential Signifier," in Weinstock, *Taking South Park Seriously,* 91–93; Kevin J. Murtagh, "Blasphemous Humor in *South Park,*" in Arp, *South Park and Philosophy,* 29–39, especially 33; and David R. Koepsell, "They Satirized My Prophet . . . Those Bastards!: *South Park* and Blasphemy," in Arp, *South Park and Philosophy,* 131–140, especially 138.

50. In this case, the images of Mohammed were not made available on the DVD version of the episodes. For discussion of another *South Park* episode dealing with Muslim themes, "Osama bin Laden Has Farty Pants" (#509), see chapter 9, on *The X-Files* and 9/11.

51. Quoted in Gillespie, "*South Park* Libertarians," 64.

7. The Fall of the House of Ulmer

My epigraph is from Gary D. Rhodes, "'Tremonstrous' Hopes and 'Oke' Results: The 1934 Reception of *The Black Cat,*" in *Edgar G. Ulmer: Detour on Poverty Row,* ed. Gary D. Rhodes (Lanham, MD: Lexington, 2008), 303. Laemmle, the founder and head of Universal Pictures, was responding to questions about why *The Black Cat* did not follow the Edgar Allan Poe story on which it claimed to be based.

1. For a concise account of the European Gothic tradition and its transformation in nineteenth-century American fiction, see the chapter "Charles Brockden Brown and the Invention of the American Gothic" in Leslie A. Fiedler, *Love and Death in the American Novel* (Normal, IL: Dalkey Archive, 1997), 126–161.

2. For an overview of Universal's contribution to the horror movie genre, see Tom Weaver, Michael Brunas, and John Brunas, *Universal Horrors: The Studio's Classic Films, 1931–1946,* 2nd ed. (Jefferson, NC: McFarland, 2007); and John T. Soister, *Of Gods and Monsters: A Critical Guide to Universal Studio's Science Fiction, Horror, and Mystery Films, 1929–1939* (Jefferson, NC: McFarland, 1999).

3. See, for example, Stefan Grissemann, *Mann in Schatten: Der Filmmacher Edgar G. Ulmer* (Vienna: Paul Zsolnay, 2003), 67; Gregory William Mank, *Karloff and Lugosi: The Story of a Haunting Collaboration* (Jefferson, NC: McFarland, 1990), 56, 81–82; Chris Steinbrunner and Burt Goldblatt, *Cinema of the Fantastic* (New York: Galahad, 1972), 81, 87–88; Don G. Smith, "*The Black Cat,*" in *Bela Lugosi,* ed. Gary J. Svehla and Susan Svehla (Baltimore: Midnight Marquee, 1995), 67–68, 71; and Weaver, Brunas, and Brunas, *Universal Horrors,* 95.

4. See Smith, "*Black Cat,*" 65; and Mank, *Karloff and Lugosi,* 80.

5. See Smith, "*Black Cat,*" 64–65; and Mank, *Karloff and Lugosi,* 80.

6. Like all commentators on the film, I treat *The Black Cat* as the creation of Edgar Ulmer. But, as is the case with almost all movies, especially one coming out of a Hollywood studio, *The Black Cat* was a collaborative effort. On the role of Ulmer's screenplay writer,

George Carroll Sims (pen names: Peter Ruric and Paul Cain), see Dennis Fischer, "*The Black Cat,*" in *Boris Karloff,* ed. Gary J. Svehla and Susan Svehla (Baltimore: Midnight Marquee, 1996), 94–95. For more on the complicated history of the development of the script for *The Black Cat,* see Weaver, Brunas, and Brunas, *Universal Horrors,* 88–89. Due to a series of accidents, studio intervention in the making of *The Black Cat* was initially minimal, and Ulmer had an unusual degree of artistic freedom in originally shaping the film. On this subject, see Fischer, "*Black Cat,*" 97. Universal did, however, intervene after Ulmer produced the rough cut and forced him to recut the film and reshoot several scenes. Taking into account all these factors, critics nevertheless regard *The Black Cat* as the work of Ulmer and assume that it reflects his peculiar artistic interests and obsessions. See, for example, John Belton, *The Hollywood Professionals,* vol. 3, *Howard Hawks, Frank Borzage, Edgar G. Ulmer* (London: Tantivy, 1974), 149.

7. See Paul Mandell, "Enigma of *The Black Cat,*" in *The Cinema of Adventure, Romance and Terror,* ed. George E. Turner (Hollywood, CA: ASC, 1989), 184.

8. See ibid., 192–193.

9. On the score, see Mank, *Karloff and Lugosi,* 56, 80; Mandell, "Enigma," 193–194; Weaver, Brunas, and Brunas, *Universal Horrors,* 93; and Alison Peirse, "Bauhaus of Horrors: Edgar G. Ulmer and *The Black Cat,*" in Rhodes, *Edgar G. Ulmer,* 283. Ulmer's love of classical music is evident throughout his films, most famously in *Carnegie Hall* (1947). One of Ulmer's lesser films, *Isle of Forgotten Sins* (1943; also known as *Monsoon*), is redeemed only by its musical score, which is filled with quotations from Richard Wagner's operas; its deep-sea divers discover an underwater treasure of gold to the tune of the Rheingold motif from Wagner's *Das Rheingold.* Typically, Ulmer turns a B-movie into a rewriting of Wagner's Ring Cycle. For a detailed analysis of the use of Wagner in the film, see Andrew Repasky McElhinney, "A World Destroyed by Gold: Shared Allegories of Capital in Wagner's *Ring* and Ulmer's *Isle of Forgotten Sins,*" in *The Films of Edgar G. Ulmer,* ed. Bernd Herzogenrath (Lanham, MD: Scarecrow, 2009), 109–124. For more on Ulmer and classical music, see chapter 8.

10. Mank reports that on the set of *The Black Cat,* Ulmer's nickname was "the aesthete from the Alps" (*Karloff and Lugosi,* 47). Ulmer's daughter remarked in an interview, "My mother always tells the story that when she married him, their honeymoon was like three weeks of her being locked in a room with him, and with him educating her! Even though she had had a very fine, 'normal' American education, it was nothing like his European culture." Tom Weaver, "Her Father's Keeper: Arianné Ulmer Cipes," *Video Watchdog* 41 (1997): 41.

11. For the "clashing cultural dynamics" of *The Black Cat,* see Christopher Justice, "Edgar G. Ulmer: The Godfather of Sexploitation?," in Rhodes, *Edgar G. Ulmer,* 33; and Bernd Herzogenrath, "Ulmer and Cult/ure," in *Edgar G. Ulmer: Essays on the King of the B's,* ed. Bernd Herzogenrath (Jefferson, NC: McFarland, 2009), 23, 29. For a general study of Ulmer as an émigré and of the theme of exile in his films, see Noah Isenberg, "Perennial Detour: The Cinema of Edgar G. Ulmer and the Experience of Exile," *Cinema Journal* 43 (2004): 3–25; and Isenberg, "Permanent Vacation: Home and Homelessness in the Life and Work of Edgar G. Ulmer," in Herzogenrath, *Films of Edgar Ulmer,* 1–20.

12. On the importance of World War I, see Herbert Schwaab, "On the Graveyards of Europe: The Horrors of Modernism in *The Black Cat,*" in Herzogenrath, *Films of Edgar Ulmer,* 39.

13. I have transcribed all quotations from *The Black Cat* from the DVD version available in Universal's *The Bela Lugosi Collection* (2005).

14. On the issue of the shock value of *The Black Cat* and the role of censorship in its production, particularly Universal's initial benign neglect and later intervention in reshaping the film, see Mank, *Karloff and Lugosi*, 55, 70, 79; Mandell, "Enigma," 181–182, 184–185, 188; and Fischer, "*Black Cat*," 91–92, 97. Ulmer had to meet with the infamous Hollywood censor Joseph Breen before going ahead with the film. On this point, see David J. Skal, *The Monster Show: A Cultural History of Horror* (New York: Faber and Faber, 1993), 178; and Mark A Vieira, *Sin in Soft Focus: Pre-Code Hollywood* (New York: Harry N. Abrams, 1999), 175. Even with the cuts and reshooting ordered by Universal, *Variety* called the screen version of *The Black Cat* "a truly horrible and nauseating piece of sadism" (quoted in Fischer, "*Black Cat*," 110). When the film was shown later in Great Britain, it was censored even further, with the devil worshipers improbably refashioned into "sun worshipers" (Fischer, "*Black Cat*," 112). For more on Ulmer and Breen, see Gregory William Mank, "*The Black Cat*," in Herzogenrath, *Edgar G. Ulmer*, 96. Mank points out that *The Black Cat* was banned in Austria, and he cites the reason given by the authorities: "religious feelings are hurt by the broad showing of the devil service and by the fact that one main figure, an Austrian, is shown as [a] military traitor and main criminal, thus offending the national feeling of the people" (101).

15. Although Karen Werdegast is technically only Poelzig's stepdaughter, the incestuous implications of their marriage are very strong.

16. See Skal, *Monster Show*, 180.

17. See Grissemann, *Mann in Schatten*, 80; Skal, *Monster Show*, 177; and Dion Tubrett, "The Devil's Contract: The Satisfaction of Self-Destruction in Edgar G. Ulmer's *The Black Cat*," in Rhodes, *Edgar G. Ulmer*, 297–298.

18. Quoted in Peter Bogdanovich, *Who the Devil Made It* (New York: Alfred Knopf, 1987), 576 (italics in the original).

19. Ulmer himself said of *The Black Cat*, "It was very much out of my Bauhaus period" (quoted in Bogdanovich, *Who the Devil Made It*, 576). See also Grissemann, *Mann in Schatten*, 70; and Bret Wood, "Edgar G. Ulmer: Visions from the Second Kingdom," *Video Watchdog* 41 (1997): 28. On the architecture in the film, see Mandell, "Enigma," 186, 193; and Peirse, "Bauhaus of Horrors," 278–281.

20. Ulmer's fullest study of the aesthetic temperament and its potential for horror is *Bluebeard* (1944), the story of an artist who feels compelled to murder the beautiful models he paints. In its portrait of an artist living in poverty, forced to work for a dealer who makes more money than he does from his work, *Bluebeard* may be Ulmer's most autobiographical movie, an allegory of his own career in the film business. Steffen Hantke, "Puppets and Paintings: Authorship and Artistry in Edgar G. Ulmer's *Bluebeard*," in Rhodes, *Edgar G. Ulmer*, 190, discusses the tensions in *Bluebeard* "between the economic necessity to serve the culture industry on the one hand, and artistic ambitions on the other." For more on the relation of *Bluebeard* to *The Black Cat*, see Grissemann, *Mann in Schatten*, 195–207; and Herzogenrath, "Ulmer and Cult/ure," 30–36.

21. Mank reports that the original shooting script of the film speaks of "Poelzig's embalming room, where he immortalizes the bodies of his women after having immortalized their souls in other, perhaps gentler ways" (*Karloff and Lugosi*, 63).

22. On Count Cenci as a vampire, see James B. Twitchell, *The Living Dead: A Study of the Vampire in Romantic Literature* (Durham, NC: Duke University Press, 1981), 79–92.

23. For a detailed study that links Stoker's Dracula specifically to the Anglo-Irish aristocracy, see Michael Valdez Moses, "The Irish Vampire: *Dracula,* Parnell, and the Troubled Dreams of Nationhood," *Journal X* (Autumn 1997): 66–111.

24. Thus, this time Lugosi got to play the Van Helsing part to Karloff's Dracula. Determined to change his screen image, Lugosi insisted on playing a "good guy" in *The Black Cat.* See Grissemann, *Mann in Schatten,* 68; and Mank, *Karloff and Lugosi,* 53.

25. On the differences in the original script, see Mank, *Karloff and Lugosi,* 69; Mandell, "Enigma," 188; and Fischer, "*Black Cat,*" 91–92, 104, 106.

26. On the characterization of the Americans in the film, see Tubrett, "Devil's Contract," 291–293.

27. According to Mank, the movie originally contained a breakfast scene in which Peter Alison, like the typical Ugly American, "insults the house, Poelzig, the Hungarian language, Hungary, the food, and the servants." *Karloff and Lugosi,* 69.

28. Another way of viewing *The Black Cat* is as a reverse invasion narrative. Many horror stories deal with the United States being invaded by sinister forces from abroad (see chapter 10). By contrast, in *The Black Cat,* ordinary figures from the United States "invade" the sinister world of Central Europe. In a paradoxical way, the innocent Americans trigger a series of events that end up destroying the figures who come out of the European Gothic tradition.

29. See Skal, *Monster Show,* 178. Americans had, of course, participated in World War I, and many had been scarred by the experience. But the fact that the war had not taken place on American soil meant that its psychological impact on the United States never approached the devastating effect it had on Europe, and the United States was spared the divisive nationalism and ethnic disputes that played out, especially in central and eastern Europe, in the wake of World War I.

30. I may seem to be giving Ulmer too much credit for prophetic powers and political seriousness in *The Black Cat.* But Mandell reports that in Ulmer's original draft of the story, a character named Frau Goering was to be included in the Black Mass scene, described as "to be played by a man, the dark fuzz on her lip suggesting Hitler's moustache" ("Enigma," 190). This detail casts a new light on *The Black Cat* and suggests that it may have been more of a political allegory than has been supposed. As a Jewish émigré from the German-speaking world in Europe, Ulmer was undoubtedly aware of what was happening in Berlin in 1934. That fact may add a new layer of meaning to Ulmer's story of Europeans haunted by their defeat in World War I, seeking revenge for the wrongs done to them and turning to a satanic cult leader for salvation—and ultimately being destroyed in the process. The connections to Hitler in *The Black Cat* have been noted by several critics; for example, Grissemann quotes J. Hoberman, echoing a famous book by Siegfried Kracauer and describing *The Black Cat* as "from Caligari to Hitler in one lurid package." *Mann in Schatten,* 82. See also Tubrett, "Devil's Contract," 293. For more on connections between *The Black Cat* and Nazism, see Herzogenrath, "Ulmer and Cult/ure," 30: "Ulmer, as a Jew, was definitely highly sensitive to what was going on in Germany at the time—note that the historic Marmoros was a Jewish district, close to Mateszalka, where one of the biggest concentration camps in Hungary was built ten years later."

31. As Fischer points out, the author of the screenplay of *The Black Cat,* George Carrol

Sims, wrote for Hollywood under the pen name Peter Ruric, but also wrote mystery stories under the pen name Paul Cain (*"Black Cat,"* 94–95). On Sims/Ruric/Cain, see also Mandell, "Enigma," 183.

32. Cf. Belton, *Hollywood Professionals,* 154. See Fiedler on the symbolism of the upper and lower levels of the Gothic castle (*Love and Death,* 132).

33. There are undocumented claims that Ulmer studied architecture in his youth in Vienna. *The Black Cat* even contains an architectural history in-joke: the Karloff character is named after the well-known German architect Hans Poelzig. See Isenberg, "Perennial Detour," 4, 10. Herzogenrath, "Ulmer and Cult/ure," adds that "Hans Poelzig . . . designed the film-sets for *The Golem,* [and] . . . , as an architect, was the teacher of Albert Speer, and built the IG-Farben building in Frankfurt" (30). As for Ulmer's knowledge of psychoanalysis, his wife reports that Ulmer and Karloff used to talk about the subject on the set of *The Black Cat* and casually mentions that "Edgar was a Jungian." She adds that Lugosi "mistrusted the Krafft-Ebbing conversations Boris enjoyed with Ulmer" (quoted in Mank, *Karloff and Lugosi,* 67–68). Ulmer later said of his film *Strange Illusion* (1945), "I was fascinated at that time with psychoanalysis, and this story was about a father-son relationship" (quoted in Bogdanovich, *Who the Devil Made It,* 596).

34. For general reflections on this subject, see Massimo Cacciari, *Architecture and Nihilism: On the Philosophy of Modern Architecture,* trans. Stephen Sartarelli (New Haven, CT: Yale University Press, 1993).

35. For a reading of *The Black Cat* in terms of Freud's concept of the death instinct, see Tubrett, "Devil's Contract," 289–300.

36. The ordinariness of the cult members comes across in the screen version of the movie; the shooting script, by contrast, called for them to be "as odd and freakish as possible—all to have the suggestion of some kind of abnormality about them. Members, for the most part, of the decadent aristocracy of the countryside" (Mank, *Karloff and Lugosi,* 71). See also Mandell, "Enigma," 190.

37. This aspect was emphasized more strongly in the original version of the script. See Mandell, "Enigma," 188.

38. *The Black Cat* transforms traditional Gothic symbolism. The lower regions of Poelzig's house are in effect the dungeons of the haunted castle of the old European Gothic tradition and represent the frightening power of the past to haunt the present and prevent the characters from escaping ancient crimes and guilt. The gleaming, modernist house Poelzig has erected on the ruins of old Fort Marmaros represents a new kind of Gothic, what one might call the Gothic of the future. It symbolizes the new forces abroad in the modern world, including psychoanalysis, modern architecture, and modernism itself, which may be just as destructive as the evils of the past. *The Black Cat* points to another form of genre crossing, reconfiguring the Gothic in science fiction, a subject I examine in chapter 10.

39. On modernism in the film, see Schwaab, "Graveyards of Europe," 40–42; and especially Herzogenrath, "Introduction," in Herzogenrath, *Films of Edgar Ulmer,* xix: "Making clear references to the traumatic experience of World War I, especially in one scene in which the camera roams aimlessly and elegantly through the vaults of a former fortress, the film could be read as a weird reflection on modernism. . . . Ulmer's film seems to blame modernism as the source of moral decay."

40. Throughout *The Black Cat* "melodrama" functions as a negative pole. Earlier in the film, Poelzig reproaches Werdegast: "Of what use are all these melodramatic gestures?" Contrasting elite with pop culture, Ulmer seems intent on distinguishing his tragic story from vulgar melodrama.

41. On Europeans versus Americans in the film, see Schwaab, "Graveyards of Europe," 40, 49.

42. In a variant of a pattern we saw in *Mars Attacks!* in chapter 4, in *The Black Cat* ordinary Americans in effect triumph over a European elite.

43. Mandell, "Enigma," 192; see also Mank, *Karloff and Lugosi,* 78

44. On postmodernism in the film, see Grissemann, *Mann in Schatten,* 77.

45. Cf. Stefan Grissemann's comment on the Kino DVD documentary *Edgar G. Ulmer: The Man Off-Screen* (2004): "He loved European culture, especially high culture, which brought strange dissonances into his trivial American films."

46. For Tocqueville's view of culture in the United States, see part 1 of book 2 of *Democracy in America,* especially chapters 9–19.

47. For an excellent survey of the way European philosophers and intellectuals have viewed America, see James W. Ceaser, *Reconstructing America: The Symbol of America in Modern Thought* (New Haven, CT: Yale University Press, 1997). I explore Ulmer's relation to the Frankfurt School at length in chapter 8. There I argue that *Detour* (1945) presents a more negative view of America than *The Black Cat* does precisely because, in Frankfurt School fashion, Ulmer measures it against the standard of European elite culture, for example, contrasting jazz unfavorably with classical music, much the way Theodor Adorno did. The theme of Europe versus America recurs throughout Ulmer's career. *Carnegie Hall* again sets up a contrast between European classical music and American jazz, but offers a more hopeful outcome, a synthesis of the two musical traditions in a Gershwin-like rhapsody that the hero is able to perform in the venerable concert hall at the end of the film. On this subject, see Tony Tracy, "'The Gateway to America': Assimilation and Art in *Carnegie Hall,*" in Rhodes, *Edgar G. Ulmer,* 211–223. One of Ulmer's last and most peculiar films—his 1958 contribution to the "nudie" genre, *The Naked Venus*—also turns on the differences between European and American culture, this time much to the disadvantage of the latter. In France people appreciate the finer things in life, including classical music, painting, and nudity, whereas Americans, in Ulmer's view, are enmeshed in puritanical attitudes that are destructive of all true art. On this subject, see Justice, "Edgar G. Ulmer," 31–34.

48. For a detailed analysis of Heidegger's view of America, see Ceaser, *Reconstructing America,* 187–213.

49. Martin Heidegger, *An Introduction to Metaphysics,* trans. Ralph Manheim (Garden City, NY: Anchor, 1961), 31.

50. Ibid., 37–38.

51. Nietzsche is undoubtedly the common link in their thought. For Nietzsche on the perilous state of Europe, particularly the menace from Russia, see, for example, section 208 of his *Beyond Good and Evil.*

52. Johann Wolfgang von Goethe, "To the United States," trans. Stephen Spender, in *The Permanent Goethe,* ed. Thomas Mann (New York: Dial, 1953), 655. For the German original, see *Insel Goethe: Werkausgabe,* ed. Walter Höllerer (Frankfurt: Insel, 1970), 1: 224–225.

8. America as Wasteland in *Detour*

My epigraph is from W. H. Auden, *Lectures on Shakespeare*, ed. Arthur Kirsch (Princeton, NJ: Princeton University Press, 2000), 57.

1. See, for example, R. Barton Palmer, *Hollywood's Dark Cinema: The American Film Noir* (New York: Twayne, 1994), 108, who calls *Detour* "undoubtedly the finest example of a purely noir thriller." Greil Marcus says that "*Detour* is as severe and displacing, as austere and thrilling, as any film Hollywood has ever turned up." Marcus, *The Shape of Things to Come: Prophecy and the American Voice* (New York: Farrar, Straus and Giroux, 2006), 144. Noah Isenberg points out that "in 1992, [*Detour*] was declared worthy of inclusion in the National Film Registry at the Library of Congress, the only B-picture to have earned the honour." Isenberg, *Detour* (London: British Film Institute, 2008), 20. Isenberg's book is part of the BFI Film Classics, a series reserved for the likes of *Citizen Kane* (1941), *The Search-ers* (1956), and *The Wizard of Oz* (1939), "a series of books that introduces, interprets and celebrates landmarks of world cinema" (1).

2. The constraints under which Ulmer labored while making *Detour* have become the stuff of Hollywood legend. I have seen the budget placed at as low as $20,000, but for the accurate figures, see Isenberg, *Detour*, 39: "*Detour* was budgeted at $87,579.85—and came in eventually at $117,226.80 . . . giving it possibly the smallest production budget in the entire canon of classic film noir." There is some controversy over the length of the shooting sched-ule, but Isenberg concludes that the film probably was shot, as Ulmer claimed, in just six days. For some of the unfortunate results of this haste and the low budget, see ibid., 45–46.

3. For the elements that make *Detour* an example of film noir, see ibid., 74–75; and Scott Loren, "Dead Fathers and Other Detours: Ulmer's *Noir*," in *Edgar G. Ulmer: Detour on Poverty Row*, ed. Gary D. Rhodes (Lanham, MD: Lexington, 2008), 62.

4. Alain Silver and Elizabeth Ward, eds., *Film Noir: An Encyclopedic Reference to the American Style*, 3rd ed. (Woodstock, NY: Overlook, 1992), 90.

5. On the symbolic significance of California in the film, see Isenberg, *Detour*, 76–81; Phillip Sipiera, "All Wrong Turns: Tracking Subjectivity in *Detour*," in Rhodes, *Edgar G. Ulmer*, 148–19; and Dana Polan, "*Detour's* History/History's *Detour*," in *Edgar G. Ulmer: Essays on the King of the B's*, ed. Bernd Herzogenrath (Jefferson, NC: McFarland, 2009), 147.

6. See Palmer, *Dark Cinema*, 114. In part 1, we saw the central role that the West plays in the American imagination, especially as the site of freedom and independence. As a critique of the idea of the West in popular culture, *Detour* strikes at the heart of America's self-conception as the land of the free.

7. I quote *Detour* from the Alpha Video DVD of the film (2002).

8. See Palmer, *Dark Cinema*, 114, 117; and Hugh S. Manon, "See Spot: The Parametric Film Noirs of Edgar G. Ulmer," in Rhodes, *Edgar G. Ulmer*, 102.

9. Isenberg has researched the Production Code Administration files on *Detour* at the Margaret Herrick Library and reports that the office of Joseph Breen (the notorious Hol-lywood censorship czar) was very concerned about the film's portrait of the movie industry. Isenberg quotes a Breen memorandum: "If you decide to lay this story in Hollywood, it is important that [the actors] be so characterized as not to reflect discredit on the Motion Picture industry" (*Detour*, 81).

10. See, for example, ibid., 67–73.

11. Gregory William Mank, *Karloff and Lugosi: The Story of a Haunting Collaboration* (Jefferson, NC: McFarland, 1990), 81.

12. For a representative collection of Frankfurt School writings, see Andrew Arato and Eike Gebhardt, eds., *The Essential Frankfurt School Reader* (New York: Continuum, 1982). For a good but brief overview of the Frankfurt School, see the chapter "The Frankfurt School and 'Critical Theory,'" in Leszek Kolakowski, *Main Currents of Marxism: Its Origins, Growth and Dissolution,* trans. P. S. Falla (Oxford: Oxford University Press, 1978), 3: 341–395. For a fuller treatment, see George Friedman, *The Political Philosophy of the Frankfurt School* (Ithaca, NY: Cornell University Press, 1981).

13. On the emigration of the Frankfurt School to the United States, see Laura Fermi, *Illustrious Immigrants: The Intellectual Migration from Europe, 1930–41,* 2nd ed. (Chicago: University of Chicago Press, 1971), 332–333; and Lewis A. Coser, *Refugee Scholars in America: Their Impact and Their Experience* (New Haven, CT: Yale University Press, 1984), 90–101. On Adorno in particular, see Anthony Heilbut, *Exiled in Paradise: German Refugee Artists and Intellectuals in America, from the 1930s to the Present* (New York: Viking, 1983), 160–174.

14. See Nico Israel, *Outlandish: Writing between Exile and Diaspora* (Stanford, CA: Stanford University Press, 2000), 85–86. Israel points out that Horkheimer's home became the site of the "West Coast Institute for Social Research."

15. For a history of the reception of the German émigrés in Hollywood, see John Russell Taylor, *Strangers in Paradise: The Hollywood Émigrés, 1933–1950* (New York: Holt, Rinehart and Winston, 1983). A good deal of oral and visual archival material from this period is available in the DVD *Shadows in Paradise: Hitler's Exiles in Hollywood* (Kultur, 2008).

16. Max Horkheimer and Theodor W. Adorno, *Dialectic of Enlightenment,* trans. John Cumming (New York: Continuum, 1986), 139. All future quotations from this work will be from this edition, with page numbers in parentheses in the body of the chapter.

17. Theodor Adorno, *Minima Moralia: Reflections from Damaged Life,* trans. E. F. N. Jephcott (London: Verso, 1978), 43. All future quotations from this work will be from this edition, with page numbers in parentheses in the body of the chapter.

18. On this point, see Kolakowski, *Main Currents,* 3: 377: "Whereas socialists formerly denounced capitalism for producing poverty, the main grievance of the Frankfurt school is that it engenders abundance and satisfies a multiplicity of needs, and is thus injurious to the higher forms of culture."

19. This argument is particularly odd in view of Toscanini's courageous and unwavering opposition to fascism in Italy and elsewhere.

20. See Horkheimer and Adorno, *Dialectic,* 139: "If most of the radio stations and movie theaters were closed down, the consumers would probably not lose so very much. . . . The disappointment would be felt not so much by the enthusiasts as by the slow-witted, who are the ones who suffer for everything anyhow."

21. Walter Benjamin, *Illuminations,* trans. Harry Zohn (New York: Schocken, 1969), 217–251.

22. For an example of this argument, see Kolakowski, *Main Currents,* 3: 379.

23. Lombardo was a band leader who specialized in syrupy musical arrangements; he and his group, the Royal Canadians, offered the "sweetest music this side of heaven."

24. For a critique of Adorno's view of jazz, see Heilbut, *Exiled,* 127–128, 167–168. For a largely implicit but at times pointedly explicit critique of Adorno's understanding of twen-

tieth-century music in general, see Alex Ross, *The Rest Is Silence: Listening to the Twentieth Century* (New York: Picador, 2007).

25. On classical music in the film, see Isenberg, *Detour*, 67–68.

26. All statements about Ulmer by his daughter, and quotations from her, are taken from her discussions with Tag Gallagher as reported in his essay "All Lost in Wonder: Edgar G. Ulmer," http://www.latrobe.edu.au/screeningthepast/firstrelease/fr0301tgafr/2a.htm (consulted April 21, 2005).

27. Mank, *Karloff and Lugosi*, 56, reports that it was "Ulmer's idea to score *The Black Cat* with classical motifs." When Carl Laemmle heard the score, he was, according to Mank (80), "apoplectic, hating the idea of the classical music; he wanted to rescore the entire picture." Fortunately, Laemmle's son backed Ulmer, and the remarkable score was left alone. The score was actually written by the German émigré composer Heinz Roemheld. Roemheld may have provided a model for Al Roberts's musical career: he "had spent two almost destitute years in Washington, D.C., playing piano in the lobby of the Shoreham Hotel" (ibid., 56).

28. Benjamin, *Illuminations*, 256.

29. Mank, *Karloff and Lugosi*, 47. James Naremore, in *More Than Night: Film Noir in Its Contexts* (Berkeley: University of California Press, 2008), calls Ulmer a "true aesthete of the lower depths" and "a self-described 'art-obsessed' intellectual who felt an affinity with Bertolt Brecht and the Bauhaus" (144).

30. For this view of the film, see Palmer, *Dark Cinema*, 110.

31. Given Ulmer's sense of alienation, it was almost inevitable that when he turned to the genre of science fiction in the 1950s, he created one of the first examples of the "lonely, misunderstood visitor from another planet" motif. In *The Man From Planet X* (1951), people from Earth fail to communicate properly with a space alien, and in their effort to exploit his strange powers they nearly trigger a planetary apocalypse.

32. Israel, *Outlandish*, 200n37.

33. See Kolakowski, *Main Currents,* 3: 376, 395. For an example of cultural nostalgia in *Dialectic of Enlightenment,* see 132–133, where the Marxists Horkheimer and Adorno end up praising the cultural policies of Wilhelmine Germany. For the "aristocratic (or imitatively aristocratic)" character of European critiques of America, see Russell A. Berman, *Anti-Americanism in Europe: A Cultural Problem* (Stanford, CA: Hoover Institution, 2004), 42. But Berman argues that Adorno himself is not anti-American; see 134–145.

34. Israel, *Outlandish*, 90.

35. From his daughter's description, Ulmer sounds more broad-minded than Adorno, and more tolerant of American popular culture: "He loved this country, baseball, hot-dogs, Jackie Gleason, jazz, Sid Caesar, Jimmy Durante, and Bar BQs." In *Carnegie Hall*, the young hero who chooses a career as a jazz pianist over one as a classical musician is vindicated in the end by an appearance at the famous concert hall, introduced by no less than Leopold Stokowski. The movie seems to present positively a jazzed-up version of the same Chopin waltz Roberts plays "straight" in *Detour*. For a full discussion of *Carnegie Hall* as a film about immigrant experience, see Tony Tracy, "'The Gateway to America': Assimilation and Art in *Carnegie Hall*," in Rhodes, *Edgar Ulmer*, 211–223.

36. The southwestern deserts through which the camera in *Detour* moves are broadly speaking the same landscapes that John Ford features in his Westerns, including *The Searchers*. In *Detour*, these areas are truly empty—a space that simply must be traversed in order

to get anywhere meaningful (such as Los Angeles). The corresponding landscapes in Ford's Westerns, and the Western in general, seem similarly devoid of life and do come across as threatening. Nevertheless, they contain pockets of human settlement; and, as we saw in chapter 1, Ford believes that these empty spaces can eventually be won for civilization. In Ulmer, the American desert is simply a void; in Ford, it is a frontier, a world of danger but also of human possibility. The wide-open spaces that the American Western typically embraces look suspicious and inhospitable to Ulmer's European eyes.

37. For a similar vision of America from a Russian émigré, see Vladimir Nabokov's novel *Lolita*. On this parallel, see Sipiera, "All Wrong Turns," 150, 160, 162n20.

38. For a detailed analysis of this episode, see my book *Gilligan Unbound: Pop Culture in the Age of Globalization* (Lanham, MD: Rowman & Littlefield, 2001), 172–177.

39. This kind of bicoastal vision of America can be homegrown, as we saw in the case of Gene Roddenberry in chapter 2. The most cosmopolitan areas of America have understandably always been the two coasts, and American elites headquartered in New York and California have often shared with Europeans a disdain for the heartland.

40. For the definitive Frankfurt School analysis of Donald Duck, see Horkheimer and Adorno, *Dialectic*, 138.

41. For a further critique of the Frankfurt School thinkers as cultural outsiders, see my essay "Is There Intelligent Life on Television?," *Claremont Review of Books* 8, no. 4 (Fall 2008): 56–59.

42. Palmer, in *Dark Cinema*, 108, stresses the roots of *Detour* in American fiction.

43. This point becomes clear if one looks at the chronological development of film noir. In the chronology in Silver and Ward, *Film Noir* (Appendix B, 333), ten of the first fifteen examples they give of the genre (from the period 1927–1941) were directed by men born in Europe. Thus, in its crucial formative stages as a genre, film noir was shaped by European directors. For the argument that film noir was developed by European directors, see Taylor, *Strangers*, 63, 193–205. On this point, see also Isenberg, *Detour*, 82–86, especially 85: "In the end, Ulmer took Goldsmith's material [the novel on which *Detour* is based] and infused it with a European sensibility, one shaped by the canon of classic Weimar cinema, avant-garde art, music, and literature." For a thorough development of the thesis that film noir has a dual origin in both American hard-boiled fiction and the work of émigré directors, see Bruce Crowther, *Film Noir: Reflections in a Dark Mirror* (London: Columbus, 1988), chapters 2 and 3, especially 39: "The ties which bind American *film noir* of the mid-1940s to the German Expressionist cinema of the 1920s are visually self-evident."

44. See, for example, Nicholas Christopher, *Somewhere in the Night: Film Noir and the American City* (New York: Free Press, 1997), especially 12: "film noir is an utterly homegrown modern American form." In a review of Christopher's book, I develop further the thesis that film noir has European roots; see "Film Noir Politics: The Ideology of a Movie Genre," *Weekly Standard*, June 30, 1997, 34–35.

45. On this point, see Heilbut, *Exiled*, 249.

46. For a comprehensive account of intellectual anti-Americanism, see James W. Ceaser, *Reconstructing America: The Symbol of America in Modern Thought* (New Haven, CT: Yale University Press, 1997). For more on this subject, see chapter 7, on *The Black Cat*.

47. For an overview of this literary tradition, see Russell Nye, *The Unembarrassed Muse: The Popular Arts in America* (New York: Dial, 1970), 255–265; and LeRoy Ashby, *With Amuse-*

ment for All: A History of American Popular Culture since 1830 (Lexington: University Press of Kentucky, 2006), 303–309.

48. Martin Goldsmith, *Detour* (1939; rpt. Lexington, KY: Blackmask, 2006), 60.

49. *Scenario* 3, no. 2 (Summer 1997): 1. Future quotations from this text are given in parentheses in the body of the chapter.

50. Isenberg, *Detour,* 13. For yet another account of the genesis of the script of *Detour,* see David Kalat, *"Detour's Detour,"* in *The Films of Edgar G. Ulmer,* ed. Bernd Herzogenrath (Lanham, MD: Scarecrow, 2009): "[Goldsmith] worked with Ulmer and PRC producer Martin Mooney to summarize the story as a screenplay treatment in October of that year [1944]. The extent of Mooney's role in the process is opaque—neither Ulmer nor Goldsmith showed much inclination to share the limelight with a mere pencil-pusher—yet it was Mooney's name on the sixteen-page treatment submitted to the Production Code of America's office for approval" (150). If, as Kalat claims, Ulmer was involved at the treatment stage of *Detour,* he likely did have a major role in shaping the plot. Kalat does not know what to conclude: at one point (151), he seems to be giving all the credit to Goldsmith; at another (154), he reserves some for Ulmer. Unfortunately for media scholars, this case is typical of how difficult it is to sort out the truth of Hollywood history. Too many egos are involved and too much money is at stake when it comes to such matters as screenwriting credits. As a scholar of Renaissance literature, I have long been used to dealing with questions of authorship in Elizabethan drama, most famously with the question, who wrote Shakespeare's plays? (Short answer: a man named Shakespeare.) We would not expect events that happened as recently as 1944–1945 to be shrouded in mystery the way events from Shakespeare's day are. But rather than lacking evidence, as happens with Elizabethan history, in the twentieth century we have too much evidence, that is, contradictory accounts from interested parties to the disputes. Kalat complicates the matter of the authorship of *Detour* even further by crediting the most famous Hollywood censor with shaping the movie's plot in a crucial way: "Joseph Breen, the chief censor for the motion-picture business, replied that PRC had to be out of its ever-lovin' mind if it thought the PCA would give its stamp to a dirty-minded story about prostitutes and murderers. Changes would have to be made: Sue could not be seen to sleep around. . . . Ulmer and Goldsmith decided that the simplest solution to that dilemma was to drop the Sue subplot altogether and leave the story focused on Al and Vera" (150–151). All of these historical details show how difficult it is to apply the single-author model of creation to the motion picture industry. And yet *Detour* remains a minor masterpiece.

51. Stefan Grissemann, *Mann in Schatten: Der Filmmacher Edgar G. Ulmer* (Vienna: Paul Zsolnay, 2003), 217. If it is talking about the same document, *Scenario* puts the length at 141 pages (181).

52. Grissemann, *Mann in Schatten,* 218.

53. Quoted in Peter Bogdanovich, *Who the Devil Made It* (New York: Alfred Knopf, 1989), 597.

54. Isenberg, *Detour,* 100n22.

55. See Grissemann, *Mann in Schatten,* 218.

56. Goldsmith, *Detour,* 28, 90.

57. Goldsmith, *Detour* (screenplay), from *Scenario,* 134. One can almost hear both Ulmer and Mooney saying simultaneously: "Lose the vulture."

58. As Grissemann points out, Goldsmith's novel is filled with domestic scenes, with

Al and Sue briefly living together in his small apartment (*Mann in Schatten,* 222, 359n48). In the part of the novel that the film omits entirely, Sue lives with a female roommate and shares intimacies with an actor-lover in Hollywood (named, of course, Raoul). The novel also mentions Al's father and Sue's mother. Thus we see that the film emphasizes the loneliness and isolation of the characters in a way the novel does not. In assessing Ulmer's status as the "auteur" of *Detour,* we must focus not on what he took from Goldsmith's novel, but on what he deliberately chose to omit. As is true in all branches of the arts, the act of omission can be a creative act.

59. Remember that the auteur theorists emphasize the visual style of a film, not its thematic content. Indeed, they emphasize the way directors impose their distinctive visual style on any material. From this perspective novelists almost by definition cannot be auteurs of films; at most they can provide the material on which auteur directors perform their magic.

60. Goldsmith, *Detour,* 38.

61. Ibid., 42. For other presentations of Hollywood as a world of illusions in the novel, see 37, 70–71, 88.

62. See, for example, Silver and Ward, *Film Noir,* 331.

63. Goldsmith, *Detour,* 63.

64. See Goldsmith, *Detour* (screenplay), from *Scenario,* 148. On this point, see Polan, "*Detour*'s History," 141–142. Polan provides an excellent analysis of the relations among the three versions of the *Detour* story and uses the case of Ulmer to raise serious doubts about the validity of the auteur theory. The Rhodes volume contains another essay questioning the wisdom of viewing Ulmer as an auteur: Stefanie Diekmann, "Products of Circumstance," in Rhodes, *Edgar G. Ulmer,* 206–214. Diekmann offers a judicious assessment of Ulmer's virtues and limitations as a filmmaker. For more skepticism about the auteur theory, based on a study of Ulmer, see Kalat, "*Detour*'s Detour," 142–146.

65. For the relation of Hitchcock's *Psycho* (1960) to Robert Bloch's 1959 novel of the same name, see Mark Janovich, *Rational Fears: American Horror in the 1950s* (Manchester, UK: University of Manchester Press, 1996), 253–258, 300.

66. For Ulmer's comments on the director's role in creating visual images and the director's superiority to the novelist in this regard, see Bogdanovich, *Who the Devil Made It,* 602 (Ulmer is specifically referring to *Detour* here).

9. The Truth Is Still Out There

My epigraph is from the final episode of *The X-Files,* "The Truth" (2002).

1. For example, NBC Entertainment president Jeff Zucker was quoted in "The Robins Report" in *TV Guide,* October 13, 2001, as saying, "This is a watershed moment, where everything in popular culture changes" (37).

2. I quote the article from http://time.com/time/printout/0,8816,175112,00.html (consulted July 13, 2008).

3. See, for example, Suzanne Fields, "A Reformed Hollywood? More Wholesome Entertainment Poised to Sell," *Washington Times,* October 1, 2001, A21. In many ways, these responses resemble the concerns about American pop culture that surfaced immediately after Pearl Harbor in 1941. On this subject, see LeRoy Ashby, *With Amusement for All: A History of American Popular Culture since 1830* (Lexington: University Press of Kentucky, 2006),

263–271. For the connection between Pearl Harbor and 9/11, see Marcia Landy, "'America under Attack': Pearl Harbor, 9/11, and History in the Media," in *Film and Television after 9/11,* ed. Wheeler Winston Dixon (Carbondale: Southern Illinois University Press, 2004), 79–100.

4. For a detailed article on how one show, *The Agency* (2001–2003), struggled to adapt to the post-9/11 environment, including script and cast changes, see Stephen Battaglio, "Tactical Maneuvers," *TV Guide,* December 15, 2001, 43–44, 60–61. For attempts by the Bush administration to influence Hollywood production after 9/11, see Dana Calvo and Rachel Abramowitz, "Hollywood May Enlist in Unconventional Warfare," *Los Angeles Times,* November 10, 2001, A6, which discusses a meeting between Bush's senior advisor Karl Rove and high-level Hollywood executives, such as Sandy Grushaw of Fox and Sherry Lansing of Paramount.

5. For the way TV comedians reacted to 9/11, see Matt Roush, "Reality Check," *TV Guide,* October 20, 2001, 28–32. The article quotes late-night host Conan O'Brien: "I have no idea how we're going to get back to doing this [comedy] again. I make a living acting like an ass, generally. No one's looking to me to put this in perspective" (29). At the time, only Jon Stewart of Comedy Central's *The Daily Show* (1999–) seemed willing to challenge the "end of irony" thesis: "Maybe we should wait to make pronouncements about what will happen to us culturally until the fire is completely put out. Why did irony have to die? Why couldn't puns have died? Or would that have been too devastating to Mr. Al Yankovic?" (ibid., 30). Just a month later, however, *TV Guide* was reporting a return to normalcy among TV comedians (Mark Laswell, "Laughing Matters," *TV Guide,* November 20, 2001, 24–28). The article ends with a heavy dose of irony about the end of irony: "*Vanity Fair* editor Graydon Carter, whom many blame for starting the epidemic of eulogies for contemporary humor, has since issued a deft retraction in the *Washington Post.* 'Only a fool would declare the end of irony. I said it was the end of the age of ironing,' Carter said, adding a new wrinkle to the debate" (28). For more on the putative end of irony, see my article "Irony Survives," http://mises.org/daily/837 (substantial portions of this article have been incorporated into this section of this chapter).

6. Robert Siegel, ed., *The Onion Ad Nauseam: Complete News Archives,* vol. 13 (New York: Three Rivers, 2002), 235, 241–242.

7. See http://en.wikipedia.org?wiki/Saturday_Night_Live_(season_27) (consulted February 25, 2011).

8. For an extended discussion of this episode, as well as a complete transcription of its text, see Sebastian J. Westphal, *American National Identity after September 11: Post-9/11 Experience as Mirror Narrative* (Berlin: Wissenschaftlicher Verlag, 2007), 63–82, 97–112. This book gives an excellent overview of American reactions to 9/11, especially in popular culture.

9. Allan Johnson, "Secret Agents Won't Reveal All in the Finale of *The X-Files,*" *Chicago Tribune,* May 19, 2002, Arts & Entertainment (section 7), 5.

10. Andrew Stuttaford, "The Ex-Files: Mulder and Scully's Exit," *National Review Online,* May 17, 2002, http:www.nationalreview.com/stuttaford/stuttaford051702.asp (consulted January 6, 2006). Among media pundits taking this line on the demise of *The X-Files* at the time (indeed, on the very same day), I notice in my files an authority I generally find unimpeachable: "Paul A. Cantor, a University of Virginia English professor, said that the end of the series reflects a change in the mood of the country, which has less cynicism about the government after Sept. 11 than it did during the drama's heyday" (Greg Braxton, "Closing the Files," *St. Petersburg Times,* May 17, 2002, F30).

11. As early as February 12, 2000, Matt Roush was writing in *TV Guide* of *The X-Files* that "an exhaustion factor has set in among fans" (20). In his predictions in the September 9, 2000, issue of *TV Guide* for the start of the eighth season of *The X-Files*, he wrote, "this seems like an excellent opportunity for Carter to find a way for Duchovny and Anderson to bow out gracefully" (8). Responding to Carter's decision to end the series, Roush wrote in the February 9, 2002, *TV Guide*: "Nothing on TV lasts forever, not even a landmark like Fox's marvelously inventive *The X-Files*. . . . Yes, I will miss the show when it signs off in May after nine seasons, a wise but overdue decision. The sorry fact is that I've been missing the series—at least as it was in its prime—for some time. The decline dates back to the fatal decision last season to continue without Duchovny's full-time services . . . , a move that coincided with the unsatisfying announcement of Scully's miracle pregnancy: two 'jump the shark' moments for the price of one" (10). On Duchovny's absence causing the show's decline, see also Johnson, "Secret Agents," 5.

12. For a discussion of several later shows that refer to *The X-Files*, see chapter 10.

13. Rick Lyman, "Horrors! Time for an Attack of the Metaphors? From Bug Movies to Bioterrorism," *New York Times*, October 23, 2001, E3.

14. Paul A. Cantor, *Gilligan Unbound: Pop Culture in the Age of Globalization* (Lanham, MD: Rowman & Littlefield, 2001), 184–185. This book contains a long analysis of the show in the chapter "Mainstreaming Paranoia: *The X-Files* and the Delegitimation of the Nation-State," 111–198. The scholarly literature on *The X-Files* has become quite extensive. I know of three collections of essays on the show: David Lavery, Angela Hague, and Marla Cartwright, eds., *"Deny All Knowledge": Reading the X-Files* (Syracuse, NY: Syracuse University Press, 1996); Dean A. Kowalski, ed., *The Philosophy of The X-Files* (Lexington: University Press of Kentucky, 2007); and Sharon R. Yang, *The X-Files and Literature: Unweaving the Story, Unraveling the Lie to Find the Truth* (Newcastle, UK: Cambridge Scholars, 2007). Of the many valuable essays on the show, see especially Michael Valdez Moses, "Kingdom of Darkness: Autonomy and Conspiracy in *The X-Files* and *Millennium*," in *The Philosophy of TV Noir*, ed. Steven M. Sanders and Aeon J. Skoble (Lexington: University Press of Kentucky, 2008), 203–227; and Christy L. Burns, "Erasure: Alienation, Paranoia, and the Loss of Memory in *The X-Files*," *Camera Obscura 45* (2001): 195–225. For an excellent analysis of *The X-Files* in a broad cultural and political context, see Peter Knight, *Conspiracy Culture: From the Kennedy Assassination to The X-Files* (London: Routledge, 2000). Knight notes the diffusion of power in *The X-Files*: "Paradoxically, then, the more *The X-Files* promises to reveal a traditional humanist conspiracy of top-down control, the more it seems to paint a Foucauldian portrait of decentered power which is everywhere in the system but in no particular location" (220).

15. I have transcribed all quotations from "Pilot" from the 20th Century Fox DVD set *The Lone Gunmen: The Complete Series* (2004). The quotations from the producers are from either their commentary on the pilot episode or the retrospective feature "The Making of *The Lone Gunmen*" in that collection.

16. By their nature, these conspiracy theories are of dubious provenance and questionable in terms of both authority and motive—and they are mostly to be found on the Internet. I hesitate to dignify them by citation, especially since some of them involve anti-Semitic claims. Nevertheless, in the interests of scholarship, and because some of them offer excerpts from the relevant moments in the *Lone Gunmen* pilot, I cite three of the sources I consulted: http://www.cloakanddagger.de/media/LONE%20GUNMEN/Killtowns.htm, http://www

.thetruthseeker.co.uk/print.asp?ID=1130, and http://www.davidcogswell.com/MediaRoulette/ LoneGunmen.html (all consulted July 13, 2008). If one is interested in the subject, all one need do is Google "Lone Gunmen and 9/11."

17. I can confirm this account based on a conversation I had with Vince Gilligan when he appeared at the Virginia Film Festival in Charlottesville on November 7, 2010.

18. The pilot was not the only episode of *The Lone Gunmen* that conjured up images that came to be associated with 9/11. "Tango de los Pistoleros" contains this remarkable line about a Department of Defense composite material that confers invisibility: "Saddam Hussein could build a Cessna out of this stuff and fly it right into the White House." The imaginations of *The Lone Gunmen* staff were evidently in high gear in 2001 and attuned to the Zeitgeist.

19. See, for example, Jesse Walker, "X-Files, R.I.P.," *Reason Online,* May 20, 2002, http:// www.reason. com/news/printer/32603.html (consulted May 29, 2008).

20. For another way Guantánamo is represented in American pop culture, see the discussion of *The Event* (2010–2011) in chapter 10.

21. I have transcribed all quotations from "The Truth" from the 20th Century Fox DVD set *The X-Files: The Complete Ninth Season* (2004). The quotations from the producers are from either their commentary on this episode or the documentary "The Making of 'The Truth'" in that collection.

22. George W. Bush, "Address on Initial Operations in Afghanistan," http://www .americanrhetoric.com/speeches/gwbush911initialafghanistanops.htm (consulted July 21, 2008).

23. I owe this insight to Michael Valdez Moses, who has often guided me through the mysteries of *The X-Files.*

24. One of the post-9/11 predictions that turned out to be off the mark was the widespread opinion that the attacks spelled the doom of reality shows on TV—the subject of two editions of the Robins Report in *TV Guide* (October 13 and 20, 2001). One "senior network executive" was quoted as saying of reality television, "My gut tells me it's over. After what's happened here, the audience is going to want uplifting programming—not endless faux reality, where people succeed by screaming and double-crossing." Tom Wolzien, a senior media analyst at the investment-research firm Sanford C. Bernstein & Co., made this comment: "Millions of Americans watched thousands of people die in ghastly terrorist attacks in their own backyard. After this kind of unprecedented horror, you have to wonder if anybody will want these reality shows the networks have bet so much on." USA Network president Doug Herzog joined the chorus: "We know we've entered a whole new terrain. . . . You have to ask if the values people want to see now are represented in a lot of these reality programs. Do we still want to see people stabbing each other in the back to win a million dollars?" (The three preceding quotations are taken from the Robins Report, *TV Guide,* October 13, 2001, 37–38.) Polls at the time seemed to confirm these predictions. J. Max Robins reported that a poll taken by Initiative Media "found that since September 11, 57 percent of those surveyed say their taste for these types of [reality] shows has diminished." ABC Entertainment cochairman Lloyd Braun said, "The pettiness and interpersonal dynamics of people are one of the really interesting parts of these shows. But you have to wonder, after September 11, whether people will look at that now and say, 'Please, we don't care.'" (The two preceding quotations are taken from the Robins Report, *TV Guide,* October 20, 2001, 57–58.) All these reports of the death of reality programming on TV proved to be premature; in fact, the genre is now flourishing more than ever. With the benefit of several years' hindsight, it is easy for

us today to laugh at the confidence with which these experts made their predictions about the demise of reality TV, but I can understand why they made them at the time. Still, the way all these commentators woefully misread the future of reality TV is good evidence for the wisdom of Jon Stewart's caution at the time not to rush to judgment and, literally and figuratively, to wait for the dust to settle before making apocalyptic pronouncements about the future course of pop culture.

25. For a concise overview of post-9/11 pop culture, see Ashby, *Amusement for All,* 495–500. Ashby concludes, "Within a relatively short time, it seemed that the immediate effects of 9/11 on entertainment were, in fact, negligible or, at best, ephemeral" (498). For a more upbeat assessment of pop culture responses to 9/11, see the Biography Channel program "How Pop Culture Saved America: A 9/11 Story" (first broadcast September 5, 2011). For more views on this subject, see Dixon, *Film and Television after 9/11,* especially Wheeler Winston Dixon, "Introduction: Something Lost—Film after 9/11," 1–28; Rebecca Bell-Metereau, "The How-To Manual, the Prequel, and the Sequel in Post-9/11 Cinema," 142–162; and Jonathan Markowitz, "Reel Terror Post 9/11," 200–225.

26. In the first movie in this series, *Batman Begins* (2005), the hero goes to the Orient to perfect his fighting skills at the mountain retreat of Ra's Al Ghul (Ken Watanabe), a religious fanatic who heads an international terrorist organization (obviously pointing in the direction of Osama bin Laden). This plot development suggests an equivalence between U.S. forces and the Asian terrorists they are combating. On this subject, and further analysis of this film in light of 9/11, see Michael Valdez Moses, "Blockbuster Wars: Revenge of the Zeitgeist," *Reason Online,* September 30, 2005, http://www.reason.com/hod/mvm093005.shtml (consulted September 30, 2005).

27. Debate over the question of whether *The Dark Knight* comments on U.S. foreign policy quickly came to focus on the issue of whether the film's Batman is a portrait of George Bush and, if so, whether it is a favorable or unfavorable portrait. See, for example, Andrew Klavan, "What Bush and Batman Have in Common," *Wall Street Journal,* July 25, 2008, A15. In Chris Nashawaty, "Knight Fever," *Entertainment Weekly,* August 1, 2008, 24, the director of *The Dark Knight,* Christopher Nolan, quotes Michael Caine, the actor who plays Batman's butler, making what I regard as the single most intelligent comment on the film: "Superman is the way America sees itself, but Batman is the way the world sees America."

28. Steve Warren, "Indiana Jones and the Kingdom of the Crystal Skull," *The Hook,* July 10, 2008, 60. Notice that *The X-Files* continues to be a reference point in popular culture even in 2008.

29. In reviewing the movie blockbusters of the summer of 2008 I cannot, alas, include *The X-Files: I Want to Believe.* In fact, the movie did poorer-than-expected business at the box office, perhaps effectively ending the franchise. The disappointing showing of the film might be taken as strong evidence for the claim that *The X-Files* has become irrelevant in the post-9/11 world. But the situation is more complicated than it at first appears. Having themselves bought into the "*X-Files* and 9/11" thesis, the producers went out of their way to avoid any possible element of government conspiracy in the new film and dropped most of the trademark themes of the TV series. The advance publicity for the film stressed the absence of antigovernment sentiment in it. For example, in a prerelease interview, Frank Spotnitz assured the potential audience, "I don't think you're going to worry about the government in this one" (quoted in Whitney Pastorek, "The Truth Is in Here," *Entertainment Weekly,* August

1, 2008, 36). It is ironic that, even as the genuine summer blockbusters were presenting the U.S. government in an extremely negative light, the *X-Files* film deliberately blunted its political edge and may have thereby destroyed its chances for success. There were other reasons for the film's poor showing at the box office. It had the misfortune of opening one week after the new Batman film *The Dark Knight*, which emerged as one of the greatest box-office successes of all time and no doubt drained some of the potential audience for a new *X-Files* film. Moreover, *I Want to Believe* is an extremely dark, unnerving, and depressing film, with almost none of the humor or light touches that brought comic relief to many of the TV episodes. With very few of the characters remaining alive from the series, the film offered little to die-hard fans other than the chance to see Mulder and Scully reunited and a glimpse of Skinner coming to the rescue. *I Want to Believe* may have been an excellent movie—a serious reflection on profound issues of religion and science—but it was not a good *X-Files* movie. Therefore, it would be unfair to judge the relevance of the original TV series to our world on the basis of how this theatrical film performed at the box office. For a review of *I Want to Believe* that makes a strong case for the quality of the movie and its intellectual depth, see Michael Valdez Moses, "Modern Day Frankensteins: The Return of Mulder and Scully," *Reason Online*, August 11, 2008, http://www.reason.com/news/show/128028.html (consulted September 29, 2008).

30. For an analysis of *24* in relation to 9/11, see Ina Rae Hark, "'Today Is the Longest Day of My Life': *24* as Mirror Narrative of 9/11," in Dixon, *Film and Television after 9/11*, 121–141.

31. This quotation is from the *X-Files* DVD documentary "The Making of 'The Truth.'"

10. Un-American Gothic

My epigraph is from Joseph Cropsey, "The End of History in the Open-Ended Age? The Life Expectancy of Self-Evident Truth," in *History and the Idea of Progress,* ed. Arthur M. Melzer, Jerry Weinberger, and M. Richard Zinman (Ithaca, NY: Cornell University Press, 1995), 105.

1. For a brief overview of the significance of invasion narratives in American culture, see Eric Mottram, "Out of Sight but Never Out of Mind: Fears of Invasion in American Culture," in *Blood on the Nash Ambassador: Investigations in American Culture* (London: Hutchinson Radius, 1989), 138–180.

2. Virgil, *The Aeneid,* trans. Allen Mandelbaum (New York: Bantam Dell, 2004), Book VIII, lines 888–895, 908–911.

3. I discuss this contrast as Shakespeare presents it in his Roman plays in my book *Shakespeare's Rome: Republic and Empire* (Ithaca, NY: Cornell University Press, 1976). As often happens, Shakespeare anticipates the great problems of later ages. In particular, *Antony and Cleopatra* is in effect a study of globalization, and Shakespeare explores the connection between the pursuit of empire and the undermining of a distinct sense of national identity.

4. Salman Rushdie, *The Satanic Verses* (New York: Viking Penguin, 1988), 355.

5. On paranoia in *The X-Files,* especially about government institutions, see Douglas Kellner, "*The X-Files* and Conspiracy: A Diagnostic Critique," in *Conspiracy Nation: The Politics of Paranoia in Postwar America,* ed. Peter Knight (New York: New York University Press, 2002), 205–232.

6. For a discussion of the galactic politics of *Star Trek,* see the chapter on the series in my book *Gilligan Unbound: Pop Culture in the Age of Globalization* (Lanham, MD: Rowman & Littlefield, 2001), 35–64.

7. See, for example, Kenichi Ohmae, *The End of the Nation State: The Rise of Regional Economies* (New York: Free Press, 1995); Jean-Marie Guéhenno, *The End of the Nation-State,* trans. Victoria Elliott (Minneapolis: University of Minnesota Press, 1995); and Martin van Creveld, *The Rise and Decline of the State* (Cambridge, UK: Cambridge University Press, 1999).

8. See Michael Valdez Moses, "Kingdom of Darkness: Autonomy and Conspiracy in *The X-Files* and *Millennium,"* in *The Philosophy of TV Noir,* ed. Steven M. Sanders and Aeon J. Skoble (Lexington: University Press of Kentucky, 2008), 203–204, 213–214. This essay does an excellent job of showing Michel Foucault's relevance to *The X-Files.* I have drawn heavily upon it in developing my argument in this chapter.

9. On Tocqueville and "soft despotism," see his *Democracy in America,* vol. 2, part 4, chapters 6–8, and Paul A. Rahe, *Soft Despotism, Democracy as Drift: Montesquieieu, Rousseau, Tocqueville, and the Modern Project* (New Haven, CT: Yale University Press, 2009).

10. Alien abduction accounts are usually traced back to the story of Barney and Betty Hill in 1961, as described in John C. Fuller's book *The Interrupted Journey* (New York: Dell, 1966). Two of the most widely read accounts of alien abductions were published in 1987, Whitley Strieber's *Communion* (New York: Avon, 1987), and Budd Hopkins's *Intruders* (New York: Ballantine, 1987). For a detailed analysis of the alien abduction phenomenon and its political implications, see Jodi Dean, *Aliens in America: Conspiracy Cultures from Outerspace to Cyberspace* (Ithaca, NY: Cornell University Press, 1998). Dean's book is controversial because she takes seriously the possibility that alien abduction narratives might be true.

11. I am old enough to remember the days of the family doctor, when a physician dressed in street clothing would come to your home to examine you with only the instruments he could carry in a small and rather homey-looking bag, filled with devices no more threatening than a stethoscope. The almost complete transfer of medicine to hospitals and clinics, with their antiseptic atmosphere and their massive batteries of machines, has transformed the experience of being diagnosed and treated into something far more menacing than the practice of the friendly family doctor. It is well known that horror stories work best when they tap into real-world fears. The power of *The X-Files* to frighten its audience was fueled by the way it drew upon ordinary fears of modern medicine. The program reveled in showing autopsies and other examples of modern medicine at its most frightening and gruesome— and its most inhumane. Peter Knight, *Conspiracy Culture: From the Kennedy Assassination to The X-Files* (London: Routledge, 2000) offers a similar analysis of the significance of alien abduction narratives in popular culture, with an explanation of why women specifically feature in them: "The prevalence of alien abduction narratives which feature invasive gynecological procedures speaks to concerns about rapidly changing reproductive technology, in a decade whose political terrain has been scarred by battles over abortion, and fertility treatments such as surrogacy and cloning. Unlike body-snatching invasions of the 1950s when scientists (often in collaboration with the military) saved the day, alien abduction narratives in the 1990s express fears about medical science's invasion of the body as the source of danger" (171). As Knight suggests, alien abduction narratives may be a kind of collective nightmare about frightening developments in modern medical technology that are seldom discussed openly in America because they are so controversial politically.

12. Dean makes a similar argument that alien abduction narratives reflect widespread insecurity in America about modern technology and technocracy: "When the server at the colleges where I teach crashes, or when my answering machine intersperses month-old mes-

sages with today's calls, I feel abducted by technology. . . . [For the American people], there must be an explanation for the lack of control, the insecurity, the helplessness [they feel]. . . . The 'magic' of technology, its unpredictability, its failure to live up to their expectations, its inability to protect them, marks the alien reality in which they live. . . . Abductees express a lack of agency. . . . [Their stories] bear witness to a lack of control, insecurity, and violation, to a lack of response from those who are supposed to protect and care. . . . Should I trust my doctor? My insurance company? Pharmaceutical manufacturers?" (*Aliens in America*, 111–112, 122, 124). All these everyday and perfectly understandable anxieties about modern technology are transformed into Gothic horrors in *The X-Files* and other alien invasion narratives we will examine in this chapter.

13. As we saw in chapter 4, on *Mars Attacks!*, this government takeover of the institutions—the associations—of civil society is what Tocqueville feared for America's future and the core of what he described as soft despotism.

14. See Moses, "Kingdom of Darkness," 219; and Linda Badley, "The Rebirth of the Clinic: The Body as Alien in *The X-Files*," in *"Deny All Knowledge": Reading the X-Files*, ed. David Lavery, Angela Hague, and Marla Cartwright (Syracuse, NY: Syracuse University Press, 1996), 150–154.

15. On the link between the two senses of *alien*, see Dean, *Aliens in America*, 155–157; Knight, *Conspiracy Culture*, 51; and Christy L. Burns, "Erasure: Alienation, Paranoia, and the Loss of Memory in *The X-Files*," *Camera Obscura* 45 (2001): 195–225, especially 196–200.

16. I discuss in detail the theme of immigration in *The X-Files* and analyze the treatment of these different ethnic groups in the chapter on the series in my book *Gilligan Unbound*, 122–148.

17. On the issue of alien-human hybridity, especially its relation to racial anxieties, see Dean, *Aliens in America*, 165–166.

18. The invisibility of Mexican migrant workers is the subject of an *X-Files* episode called "El Mundo Gira"; note the comment of writer-producer John Shiban: "These people are invisible. We see them, but we don't see them." Quoted in Andy Meisler, *The Official Guide to the X-Files: I Want to Believe* (New York: Harper Prism, 1998), 122. On the importance of "El Mundo Gira," see my *Gilligan Unbound*, 139–141; and Jan Delasara, *PopLit, PopCult, and The X-Files: A Critical Exploration* (Jefferson, NC: McFarland, 2000), 202–203.

19. See James C. Scott, *The Art of Not Being Governed: An Anarchist History of Upland Southeast Asia* (New Haven, CT: Yale University Press, 2009), 210–211, 219, 230, 256, and 321.

20. See Knight, *Conspiracy Culture*, 217, on *The X-Files*: "The paranormal episodes usually take place in the dark forests and small towns of the gothic imagination. They represent the anachronistic remnants of an older world that has somehow escaped the inexorable process of modernity and rationalization."

21. The frequent appearance of Native Americans in *The X-Files* is thus related to the theme of immigration. The show in effect treats them paradoxically as "native immigrants." (On Native Americans in *The X-Files*, see my *Gilligan Unbound*, 156–164.) As nomadic people, Native Americans either are denied full integration into the United States or deliberately resist it. They display all the characteristics of stateless people as Scott describes them, and in particular appear as shape-shifters (see the first-season episode called "Shapes") and are linked at many points in the show's mythology to the extraterrestrial aliens. *The X-Files* gives a similar portrait of various other migratory groups in the U.S. population, including the kind

of "trailer trash" discussed in chapter 4 (see the fourth-season episode called "Home" and my *Gilligan Unbound*, 206–211) and the hill people of Appalachia (see the seventh-season episode called "Theef" and *Gilligan Unbound*, 202–203). These various groups in the United States have much in common with the Southeast Asian hill people Scott discusses in *The Art of Not Being Governed*. They can also be compared to the "hill people" of *Deadwood;* see chapter 3, where I treat the show's characters as "stateless" in Scott's sense. For the idea that *The X-Files* associates immigrants from foreign shores with marginalized groups within the United States, see M. Keith Booker, *Strange TV: Innovative Television Series from The Twilight Zone to The X-Files* (Westport, CT: Greenwood, 2002), 134–136. In general, migrants or nomads are a challenge to the hegemony of the nation-state. They refuse to stand still and be counted. *The X-Files* repeatedly juxtaposes the efforts of the nation-state to enumerate and categorize its citizens (for the purpose of controlling them) with the evasiveness and elusiveness of shape-shifting nomads.

22. On this point, see Kellner, "*X-Files* and Conspiracy," 216.

23. On this point, see Karen Backstein, "Flexing Those Anthropological Muscles: *X-Files*, Cult TV, and the Representation of Race and Ethnicity," in *Cult Television*, ed. Sara Gwenllian-Jones and Roberta E. Pearson (Minneapolis: University of Minnesota Press, 2004), 131–134. This is one of the best treatments of the theme of immigration in *The X-Files*.

24. See, for example, Andrew Stuttaford, "The Ex-Files: Mulder and Scully's Exit," NRO (National Review Online), May 17, 2002, http:www.nationalreview.com/stuttaford/stuttaford051702.asp (consulted May 17, 2002). For more on this subject, see chapter 9, on *The X-Files* and 9/11.

25. In the October 24, 2005, *TV Guide*, in an article entitled "Scared Yet? Rating TV's new creepshows," Matt Roush links together all of these shows (except *Bones*) and compares them to *The X-Files* (30). One of the stars of *Supernatural*, Jared Padlecki, described the show this way: "It's *X-Files* meets *Route 66*" (*TV Guide*, November 14, 2005, 38).

26. These shows may not be quite as paranoid about the government as *The X-Files* is, but *The X-Files* sets a high standard of political paranoia. *Invasion* and *Surface* seem on the whole to take a dim view of the American government. *Threshold* seems to be largely pro-government, but only because its premise is that a set of experts has in effect taken over the federal government in a time of crisis, and institutions such as Congress are no longer in control. In fact, *Threshold,* much like the series *24* (2001–2010), suggests that the normal operations of the federal government, including bureaucratic standard operating procedures and congressional oversight, can only get in the way of dealing with today's crises. If *Threshold* is pro-government, it is not in favor of anything recognizable as traditional American government. In one episode, the Threshold team gets authorization to have blown out of the sky a plane carrying a U.S. senator because the team members have evidence that he has become hybridized into an alien. So much for congressional oversight as far as this series is concerned. For more on this issue, see note 39 below.

27. I have transcribed all quotations from *Invasion* from the DVD set (Warner Home Video, 2006) and will cite them simply by episode number. This line is from episode 14; in the future, I will place the number of the episode in parentheses in the text. Later in the series, *Invasion* plays with hybridity again when the same character says while pointing at a street full of aliens, "They're hybrids. The people—not the cars" (#19).

28. *Surface* does not pursue this theme as clearly as the other two shows. Its hybrid

creatures are not extraterrestrial, but have been created by scientists working for a mysterious corporation (a plot motif reminiscent of *The X-Files*). However, the teenage hero of the series, Miles (Carter Jenkins), raises one of the hybrid creatures from an aquatic egg, and as a result the human and the hybrid become very attached to each other. After being bitten by his pet, Nim (short for Nimrod), Miles begins to assimilate the creature's alien nature and develops some of its superpowers. In this plot motif, *Surface* begins to parallel *Invasion* and *Threshold* and thus can be reasonably categorized with them.

29. For more on flying saucer movies, see chapter 4, on *Mars Attacks!*

30. To make my point, I have exaggerated the difference between contemporary TV shows and earlier popular culture. Threats from the ocean occasionally appear in 1950s and '60s popular culture—for example, in the movies *The Beast from 20,000 Fathoms* (1953), *It Came from Beneath the Sea* (1955), and *The Giant Behemoth* (1959). By the same token, a sort of spaceship does appear in *Threshold,* and the alien creatures in *Invasion* drop from a stormy sky as bright lights. Nevertheless, the fundamental reorientation in spatial symbolism I discuss in this paragraph does seem to be occurring in recent popular culture. *Invasion* at times insists that the aliens are not in fact extraterrestrial but may be somehow native to Earth. In a globalized world it is harder to trace a threat to a clearly foreign source. This reorientation is strikingly evident in Steven Spielberg's 2005 remake of the classic *War of the Worlds* story. In contrast to what happens in all earlier versions, in Spielberg's the Martians do *not* suddenly appear in spaceships. Rather it turns out that they have already buried their war machines in American soil, and they simply pop up to wreak destruction (in the area of New York City). This reworking of the story seems to reflect new fears about terrorist sleeper cells: the enemy is already in our midst, and we just do not know it. For an insightful discussion of fears of terrorism in recent popular culture, including Spielberg's *War of the Worlds,* see Michael Valdez Moses, "Blockbuster Wars: Revenge of the Zeitgeist," which appeared on *Reason Online* on September 30, 2005, http://www.reason.com/hod/mvm093005shtml (consulted September 30, 2005).

31. The creator of *Invasion* is former teen heartthrob Shaun Cassidy, whose subsequent career as a writer and producer has proven that he is more than a pretty face. Apropos of my topic, he created another remarkable TV series called *American Gothic* (1995), which also did not deserve to be canceled after one season. I am not sure that I would rank Cassidy with Chris Carter or David Milch as a series creator, but his unhappy track record of canceled shows is proof that Hollywood does not always reward artistic success. I want to make sure that my defense of commercial culture in the United States is not mistaken for the claim that it never makes errors.

32. FEMA is a recurrent villain in *The X-Files,* especially in the first movie, *Fight the Future* (1998).

33. In the case of an invasion of flying saucers, as in *Mars Attacks!,* one might legitimately hesitate to rely on ordinary people to save the day; some sort of coordinated military response seems called for. No one would ever credit Burton's movie with being realistic in offering Slim Whitman's music as humanity's salvation. But *Invasion* mirrors events that actually happened. In the case of the Katrina disaster, legitimate and well-documented arguments have been made that the highly centralized government responses failed, while spontaneous efforts by local people and seemingly disorganized and unprofessional volunteers did succeed in improving conditions. For a concise summary of these arguments, see Neille Ilel, "A

Healthy Dose of Anarchy," *Reason* 38, no. 7 (December 2006): 48–56. Apropos of what we have been saying about maverick heroes in America, Ilel writes of the small groups of rescue and reconstruction volunteers in New Orleans: "When necessary, they simply ignored the authorities' wrongheaded decisions: pushing supplies through closed checkpoints, setting up in unapproved areas, breaking the rules when it made more sense than following them" (51). Like Ilel's article, *Invasion* points to the spontaneous order of ordinary Americans as the best way of responding to a disaster, rather than the supposedly coordinated efforts of government agencies (which are remote from local needs and concerns, tangled up in bureaucratic standard operating procedures, and pursuing agendas of their own). Ilel provides a more realistic validation of the reliance on ordinary people that we saw in *Mars Attacks!* For a fuller and more detailed account of the Katrina disaster, see Rebecca Solnit, *A Paradise Built in Hell: The Extraordinary Communities That Arise in Disaster* (New York: Penguin, 2010), 231–304. Ilel might be accused of a libertarian bias, but Solnit is by her own account a utopian socialist. Nevertheless, Solnit comes to conclusions identical to Ilel's: that centrally organized government responses to disasters normally fail, while the spontaneous efforts of ordinary citizens have a much better chance of succeeding. Solnit refers to both state-of-nature thinking and pop culture myths in her account, as in this passage: "Often in disaster, the government is at least inadequate to the crisis; not infrequently, it is so disorganized as to be irrelevant or almost nonexistent. . . . Then the citizens are on their own, as they are when bureaucracy and red tape keep institutions from responding urgently enough. In the absence of government, people govern themselves. Everyone from Hobbes to Hollywood filmmakers has assumed this means 'law of the jungle' chaos. What in fact takes place is another kind of anarchy, where the citizenry by and large organize and care for themselves" (152). Solnit's book is required reading for anyone who wants to assess the relative competence of ordinary people and government authorities to deal with disasters. In case after case, from the San Francisco earthquake of 1906 to 9/11, she documents the ways in which elites failed the ordinary people they were supposed to protect and in many instances made matters worse. She also cites a number of sociologists who have studied disaster scenarios and have come up with the fascinating concept of "elite panic." As one concluded: "to heck with this idea about regular people panicking; it's the elites that we see panicking. The distinguishing thing about elite panic as compared to regular-people panic, is that what elites will panic about is the possibility that we will panic. . . . It's a very paternalistic orientation to governance. It's how you might treat a child" (129; see also 127). The concept of elite panic is well illustrated in *Mars Attacks!*, as we saw in chapter 4.

34. I discuss the crisis of the nuclear family in *The X-Files* in *Gilligan Unbound*, 204–211. On the importance of, and threats to, the nuclear family in *The X-Files*, see Moses, "Kingdom of Darkness," 220–221.

35. Scully's miraculous pregnancy in season eight turns out to be the exception that proves the rule. Even when she has a child, Scully is forced to give it up for its own safety in season nine.

36. This same pattern is evident in another show that could easily be included under the rubric "Un-American Gothic": *Buffy the Vampire Slayer* (1997–2003). Buffy (Sarah Michelle Gellar) is a teenage girl singled out for the task of saving the world from evil forces. Her mission threatens to destroy her nuclear family in several ways and prevents her from living the carefree life of an ordinary high school (later college) student. On the most basic

level, the show allegorizes the impact of feminism on the life of young American women—their new sense of mission interferes with the traditional goals of finding a proper husband, marrying, and raising a family; they gain a sense of empowerment, but pay a price in terms of ordinary happiness. In the fourth season, in an *X-Files* turn, Buffy gets involved with a covert and sinister government operation and also must deal with a hybrid figure, this time a human-demon-robot hybrid named Adam (George Hertzberg). Strictly speaking, *Buffy* is not an alien invasion narrative, although it does involve all sorts of demons trying to cross the threshold between hell and earth. It thus incorporates many of the motifs we have been examining in this chapter.

37. See, for example, Richard A. Schwartz, *Cold War Culture: Media and the Arts, 1945–1990* (New York: Checkmark, 1998), 151; Mark Jancovich, *Rational Fears: American Horror in the 1950s* (Manchester, UK: University of Manchester Press, 1996), 64–65; and Knight, *Conspiracy Culture,* 173–174.

38. For more on the issue of terrorism and civil liberties, see chapter 9 on *The X-Files* and 9/11.

39. In an article on the show entitled "Threshold of a Hit" in the November 7, 2005, *TV Guide,* Craig Tomashoff says rather casually of the Threshold team, "They're not above squashing a civil liberty or two." He then compares the show to *The X-Files* and goes on to quote Brannon Braga, its executive producer: "In *The X-Files,* the government conspiracy was the shadowy enemy. In our show, the heroes *are* the conspiracy." This quotation seems to mark a post-9/11 change in attitude toward covert government activities in *Threshold.* Charles Dutton, one of the actors in the series, describes it as "playing into what's happening in this country today with Homeland Security and the Patriot Act." Tomashoff continues, "And when aliens attempt to infect our food supply in an upcoming episode, Braga notes, there is definitely 'a parallel to the terrorist threat that strikes a primal fear'" (all these quotations are from p. 52 of the article). By contrast, when a high-ranking military official in *Invasion* says, "I promise, we're all patriots here" (#8), the show appears to be treating the remark skeptically.

40. The notion of renegades among the aliens comes straight out of *The X-Files.*

41. For another example of this kind of rhetoric of difference, see chapter 2, on Gene Roddenberry. For satire of this kind of rhetoric, see chapter 4, on *Mars Attacks!*

42. For the prevalence in American pop culture of narratives about people leading secret lives, see Stephen Marche, "What's With All the Secrets and Lies?," *Esquire,* September 2010, 102–104. Marche cites *The Event* as one example of this trend.

43. See, for example, Troy Patterson, "Guess Who's Coming to Eat Us for Dinner: The Classic '80s Series *V* Gets a Post-9/11 Update," http://www.slate.com/id/2234470/; Lisa de Moraes, "ABC Executives Sound Coy about New TV Series' Political Edge," http://www.washingtonpost.com/wp-dyn/content/article/2009/08/09/AR2009080901970_pf; and "*V* aims at Obamamania," http://www.chicagotribune.com/enterainment/chi-tc-tvcolumn-v-1102-1103nov03,0, 62487 (all three consulted February 6, 2011).

44. In an interview in the feature "Breaking Story: The World of *V*" on the Warner Home Video DVD set of the first season of *V* (2010), one of the producers, Scott Rosenbaum, insists that the original creator of the series "had the Bush administration in mind." One of the actors, Logan Huffman, says in the same feature, "I think there's a strong distrust of the inner workings of all government."

45. *V* seems to go out of its way to suggest that the opposition to the Visitors is based in

426 Notes to Pages 328–329

religion. One of the other main opponents is identifiably Jewish, an ex-Mossad agent named Eli Cohn (Oded Fehr).

46. In the original 1983 version of *V,* the leader of the Visitors was male. The change of gender in the new series no doubt reflects the greater feminism of contemporary television, the desire to show women in positions of authority. But it also works to associate the aliens with everything we mean when we speak of the nanny state. In *The Event,* the aliens' leader is also female. Laura Innes does an especially good job of playing Sophia with an almost perpetual look of pained concern on her face. Caring only about the welfare of her people, she cannot understand why the American government refuses to take orders from her and follow her instructions to the letter. Innes captures perfectly the patronizing attitude of such do-gooders everywhere—their smugness, self-satisfaction, and self-righteousness. Sophia cannot comprehend how anyone could question her motives. And yet, like many do-gooders, she is willing cold-bloodedly to kill hundreds, thousands, and millions of people to save her world. In an interview in the feature "The Making of *The Event*" on the NBC Universal DVD set (2011), Innes compares Sophia to Nelson Mandela. An executive producer of the show, Jeffrey Reiner, more accurately describes the character as an "Irish terrorist crossed with the Dalai Lama."

47. On Obama as postnational president, see, for example, Jeffrey T. Kuhner, "The Post-National Candidate," http://www.washingtontimes.com/news/2008/aug/03/the-post-national-candidate/?page=1 (consulted February 15, 2011). Moraes ("Political Edge") and Patterson ("Eat Us for Dinner") speculate that, if Anna stands for Obama, then *V* is playing into the belief many have expressed that Obama is an "alien," that is to say, he was not born in the United States and therefore is not eligible to be president. *The Event* also deals with the controversy over Obama's origins, but cleverly displaces it onto the president's wife, Christina Martinez (Lisa Vidal). The issue of her immigration status comes up early in the show. When her husband finds inconsistencies in the record of her life, he begins to suspect that she may be one of the many aliens masquerading as human beings. She quiets his suspicions by admitting that her immigration records are indeed falsified; but she gives a plausible explanation: her parents came from Santo Domingo but claimed to be from Cuba to get refugee status. It turns out, however, that Christina *is* an alien after all. In the very last moment of the series, when the alien planet mysteriously appears in Earth's sky and the Martinez boy asks his mother, "What is it?" she replies, "Home." That two TV programs in 2011 may have brought up covertly the dispute over Obama's birth status is an interesting example of the way pop culture mirrors contemporary controversies. *The Event* even includes a female senator from Alaska who makes trouble for President Martinez—she may be a stand-in for Sarah Palin.

48. In the famous words of *Casablanca,* spoken by Rick Blaine (Humphrey Bogart), "I'm no good at being noble, but it doesn't take much to see that the problems of three little people don't amount to a hill of beans in this crazy world." Howard Koch, *Casablanca: Script and Legend* (Woodstock, NY: Overlook, 1992), 219.

49. Hollywood is famously a place where people put their careers above their families; witness its high divorce rate. Perhaps the reverse behavior in so many characters in these TV shows reflects guilt feelings in the Hollywood community.

50. In its 2009 Fall Preview issue, *TV Guide* discusses *V* as dealing with the "theme of a paranoid post-9/11 society" (Sept. 14–20, 2009, 37).

51. In his roundup of the best TV shows of 2011, Matt Roush lists *Fringe* at number 8

and calls it "a more than worthy successor to *The X-Files*." See "Matt Roush's Top 10," *TV Guide*, Dec. 19, 2011–Jan. 1, 2012, 13. Ten years after 9/11, *TV Guide* is still offering *The X-Files* as a touchstone of quality in American pop culture.

52. The similarities between *Fringe* and *The X-Files* are so obvious that the issue has haunted the show from before its broadcast debut, and its production team has continually been on the defensive in interviews. See *TV Guide*, July 14, 2008, 33–34, where one of the show's writers, Robert Orci, admits, "*The X-Files* was an inspiration"; and *TV Guide*, September 8, 2008, 42, where its creator-producer, J. J. Abrams, tries to differentiate his show from *The X-Files* in a rather lame fashion: "But I do think that a government agent investigating weird stuff is kind of where the similarities end." See also James Hibberd's *The Live Feed* for July 14, 2008, where the *Fringe* team may protest a bit too much that they have not copied *The X-Files* (http:www.thrfreed.com/2008/07/fringe-x-files.html; consulted September 17, 2008). For an excellent comparison of *Fringe* with *The X-Files*. see Michael Curtis Nelson, "'Fringe': Every Generation Gets the 'X-Files' It Deserves," http://www.popmatters.com/pm/tools/print/125503 (consulted October 4, 2011). Other recent shows have been honest from the beginning about their roots in *The X-Files*. Jonathan Nolan, the creator of *Person of Interest* (2011–) says of his hero and heroine that he "imagines the pair as a latter-day Mulder and Scully. *The X-Files* is definitely something we had in mind." Mike Flaherty, "Taking a Byte Out of Crime," *TV Guide*, Oct. 24–Nov. 6, 2011, 39.

53. In this regard, the two series are mirror images of each other. In *The X-Files*, Mulder's father sacrifices his sister to alien abduction as part of a plan to save the world; in *Fringe*, Walter Bishop saves his son (or rather a double of his son) by abducting him from another universe and thereby endangers our whole world. In the feature "The Mythology of *Fringe*" on the DVD set of the second season (Warner Home Video, 2010), writer-producer Jeffrey Vlaming claims that the *Iliad* is the real parallel to *Fringe*: the abduction of Helen of Troy is the mythic analogue of Walter's abduction of Peter. The abduction of Samantha Mulder, however, seems to be a much closer parallel. On *Fringe* as family drama, executive producer Jeff Pinkner says, "The best television is, in one way or another, family drama masquerading as something else. . . . This is a family drama masquerading as a science-fiction show." Quoted in http://whosnews.usaweekend.com/2010/09/fringe-producers-on-alternate-universes-and-a-third-season-we%E2%80%99re-interested-in-world-building/ (consulted February 15, 2011). The same might be said of *The X-Files*.

54. I cite *Fringe* by season and episode numbers. I take all numbering and quotations from the Warner Home Video DVD sets (season one, 2009; season two, 2010; season three, 2011). As for parallels between the two series, in *Fringe* "White Tulip" (2.17) uses a plot device from a sixth-season *X-Files* episode called "Monday." In both episodes, the characters get caught in what threatens to become an endless time loop. "Johari Window" (2.11) calls to mind a fourth-season *X-Files* episode called "Home." In both episodes, the FBI agents come upon mutant freaks generated in the claustrophobic atmosphere of a Gothic small town. As the second season of *Fringe* opens, forces in Washington are threatening to shut down the Fringe division, just as they are always trying to do in *The X-Files*. The parallels between *Fringe* and *The X-Files* go on and on. The fact that a veteran of *The X-Files*, Darin Morgan, served as a consulting producer in the first season of *Fringe* may help explain the way it continually drew upon the earlier series. Jeffrey Vlaming also worked on *The X-Files*.

55. Like *The X-Files*, *Fringe* is constantly mixing genres, a fact not lost on one of its stars,

Anna Torv: "*Fringe* sort of slides seamlessly among quite a few different genres." Quoted in Damian Holbrook, "Weird Science," *TV Guide,* Oct. 20, 2008, 28. While basically a science fiction show, it combines elements of a procedural drama (solving a mysterious crime each week) and a medical drama (a remarkable number of its scenes take place in hospitals, clinics, asylums, or other medical facilities; and, when all else fails, Walter is always ready to conduct impromptu autopsies in his Harvard lab). With Gothic horror thrown in for good measure, both *The X-Files* and *Fringe* gain dramatic power by drawing upon many of the popular TV genres. On the mixing of genres in *The X-Files,* see Kellner, "*X-Files* and Conspiracy," 212.

56. As we learn in "Momentum Deferred" (2.4), the "official" shape-shifters in *Fringe* are "mechano-organic hybrids" sent over from the other side to prepare the way for its people to invade our universe. Technically speaking, then, these are not alien-human hybrids, but they play roughly the same role in *Fringe* that their counterparts do in *The Event* and *V.* In the tradition of *Invasion of the Body Snatchers,* these hybrids create doubles of people in our world and replace them, often infiltrating into positions of power in our government—as a U.S. senator, for example, in "Do Shapeshifters Dream of Electric Sheep?" (3.4). In the same episode, we discover that some of the hybrid shape-shifters develop an attachment to their human families, just as happens in *The Event* and *V.*

57. The importance of the imagination is the reason why Walter turns to children in his experiments to gain access to the alternate universe; the power of their imaginations has not yet been tamed by the adult world. In the key episode about Walter's experiments, "Subject 13" (3.15), a young Peter tells a young Olivia, "You gotta imagine how you want things to be. And then you can try and change them." Later in the same episode, Peter's mother tells him, "Sometimes the world we have is not the world we want. But we have our hearts and our imaginations to make the best of it." In "Os" (3.16), the chief operating officer of Massive Dynamics, Nina Sharp (Blair Brown), speaks of Walter's "imagination," his "boundless creativity."

58. This map can be best viewed in "6:02 AM EST" (3.20). For the details, see Patrick Lee, "Secrets of the Alternate U.S.A. from Fox's *Fringe,*" http://blastr.com/2010/05/secrets-of-the-alternate.php (consulted February 15, 2011).

59. See http//en.wikipedia.org/wiki/Pogo_(comic_strip) (consulted August 18, 2011). For this motif in *The X-Files,* see Knight, *Conspiracy Culture,* 178.

60. Scott, *Not Being Governed,* 329.

61. I have deliberately overstated this contrast. As we saw in chapter 4, on *Mars Attacks!,* Cold War paranoia extended to the fear of internal subversion in the United States, and as we saw earlier in this chapter, *Invasion of the Body Snatchers* particularly anticipated the kind of invasion narrative epitomized by *Invasion,* in which the aliens masquerade as ordinary Americans. In his *Rational Fears,* Jancovich interprets the 1950s flying saucer movies as developing the same themes we have seen in TV shows from the 1990s and later. Thus, he concludes, "Indeed, 1950s horror does not seem to have disappeared, but is constantly reworked and reshown within the present. . . . *The X-Files* continually and self-consciously reworks the narratives of this period" (303). Jancovich makes a good case for his view, but I would argue that he is reading 1950s invasion narratives through the lens of more recent films and television shows. He may be correct that a fear of global technocracy is already evident in 1950s pop culture; he may, however, in some cases be mistaking what are in fact

favorable portrayals of a military-scientific elite for criticism because he is reading his own views back into the earlier works.

62. This hypothetical formulation is not all that far from routine public service announcements in American airports these days, or other forms of Homeland Security propaganda.

63. See Jean Baudrillard, *Simulacra and Simulation,* trans. Sheila Faria Glaser (Ann Arbor: University of Michigan Press, 1994), 121–127, for related speculation on the disappearance of utopian vision in contemporary science fiction, especially 122–123, where Baudrillard claims that science fiction models now "leave no room for any kind of imaginary transcendence. . . . We can no longer imagine any other universe." In Baudrillard's terms, the other universe in *Fringe* is not truly a parallel universe (125); it is merely a simulacrum of our universe, which in turn is merely a simulacrum of it. Neither universe is truly real, but only a simulation. For Baudrillard, in the modern world of the media, government has become all image with no substance. There is no authentic politics anymore, only a simulacrum of politics. Hence, in terms of *Fringe,* the apparent differences between the parallel universes become insignificant in light of the fact that they are both just simulacra. It does not matter whether the images differ if both worlds are no more than mere images generated by governments to maintain control over their citizens. As should be clear from the date of his book, Baudrillard is not referring to *Fringe,* but I believe that his argument is relevant to the series.

64. In the terms of *Fringe,* this might be called the firefly effect. "Firefly" (3.10) is devoted to showing that seemingly insignificant and unrelated events, if altered, could add up to produce major changes in personal histories (a recurrent theme in the series; it comes up, for example, in "White Tulip" and "The Plateau"). But in political terms, *Fringe* asks us to believe both that the sequence of U.S. presidents since the 1960s could have been altered, and that Barack Obama would still have been elected president in 2008.

65. One of the best illustrations of the permeability of empires on their frontiers can be seen when they attempt literally to wall themselves in (Hadrian's Wall, the Great Wall of China). As the archaeological record shows, these would-be impenetrable barriers erected between civilization and barbarism become sites of commerce, cultural exchange, and even intermarriage between citizens and aliens. Even when walled, the frontiers of empire come to resemble cell membranes, where interchange between inside and outside becomes the norm.

66. This quotation is from http://whosnews.usaweekend.com/2010/09/fringe-producers-on-alternate-universes-and-a third-season-we%E2%80%99re-interested-in-world-building/ (consulted February 15, 2011).

67. In "Brown Betty" (2.19), Nina Sharp says, "Peter Bishop is a con man with many talents and many identities, all of them suspect."

68. This episode deals with a government experiment that has gone awry and resulted in turning a whole town into freaks. The clear implication is that the government has ended up doing the same thing to Olivia and the other agents who work for it. As often happens in *Fringe,* the specific story of the week parallels the ongoing story of the main characters. A central idea in the series is that the government creates the very monsters it then must fight against, a motif familiar from *The X-Files.*

69. In this respect, the main characters of *Fringe* experience the same dilemmas facing Scully and Mulder. Olivia as a single woman is contrasted with her more conventional sister, who has a child to take care of. In "The No-Brainer" (1.12), when Olivia is suddenly called away by duty, her sister tells her, "Go. Save the world." Olivia is a kind of adult Buffy. She has

been singled out for the mission of saving the world and has had to give up family life and ordinary happiness to do so. Many of the characters in *Fringe* are forced to choose between saving their families and saving the world. For example, in "Earthling" (2.6), the head of the Fringe Division, Phillip Broyles (Lance Reddick), reveals, "I took this job to make the world a safer place for my family. Instead I lost them." As we have seen, Walter Bishop started all the problems by saving his son at the risk of destroying the entire universe. In the course of the series, he has to learn to accept the idea of sacrificing Peter in order to save the universe.

70. The issue of broken and thwarted families lies at the emotional heart of *Fringe*. Although Peter and Olivia fall in love, they are never able to have a child together, even in the flash-forward episode "The Day We Died" (3.22), which portrays them as married in the future. Olivia is reluctant to bring a child into a world on the verge of destruction, even though Peter reassures her that "people still have families." Ironically, Peter *is* able to have a child with Olivia's counterpart from the other universe. When Fauxlivia crosses over to spy on our world, part of her plan is to seduce Peter, and she gets pregnant as a result. But she discovers that fact only when she returns to the parallel universe. Since the child becomes the key to Walternate's plan for destroying our universe, Fauxlivia's pregnancy is accelerated by artificial means. "Bloodline" (3.18) thus features the kind of Gothic pregnancy and birth sequence we have seen in many of these alien invasion narratives. Fauxlivia's mother refers to the birth as a "miracle," recalling Scully's miraculous pregnancy in *The X-Files*. As of the end of season three, Peter and Fauxlivia, despite having had a child together, do not get to form a happy family. On the "high price" Scully and Mulder "pay for their vocational commitments in *The X-Files*," see John A. McClure, "Forget Conspiracy: Pynchon, DeLillo, and the Conventional Counterconspiracy Narrative," in Knight, *Conspiracy Nation,* 256.

71. See Robert D. Putnam, *Bowling Alone: The Collapse and Revival of American Community* (New York: Simon and Schuster, 2001). Putnam's point is that Americans, who used to show their public-spiritedness by bowling in teams, have come increasingly to bowl alone as isolated individuals.

72. In "Subject 13" (3.15), a TV news report refers to Walternate as "the architect of the famed Star Wars defense system that protects our nation." Agonizing over Peter's abduction, Walternate tells his wife, "They're about to point out how ironic it is that the Safety Czar couldn't protect his own child." This irony goes right to the core of what *Fringe* has to say about the world of contemporary politics.

73. I offer this interpretation of *Fringe* with some hesitation. The show is still in progress, and there are indications that it may be changing direction in its upcoming fourth season (for the record, I am writing this chapter in August 2011). The creators have introduced a time-travel motif that is evidently going to allow them to rewrite its history next season. For example, the character of Peter disappeared out of our universe at the end of the third season, and he has been written out of the lives of all the other characters—they evidently do not know that he ever existed. It is possible that a fourth or subsequent season of *Fringe* will invalidate what I claim in this chapter. Such are the perils of writing about pop culture as it unfolds. For the moment all I can do is to offer the most consistent interpretation of *Fringe* that I can currently work out.

Postscript: On May 11, 2012, just as this book was about to be set in type, *Fringe* completed its fourth season with an episode entitled "Brave New World" (4.22). So successful was the season that in the *TV Guide* 2012 "Fan Favorites" poll, viewers voted *Fringe* their favorite drama, much to the surprise of the magazine, which began its report of the results with these words: "No, you're not in an alternate universe" (*TV Guide*, April 16–29, 2012, 20). Thanks in part to its fans' enthusiasm, *Fringe* was renewed for an abbreviated, thirteen-episode fifth season. The fourth season tended to avoid the political themes of the earlier seasons, concentrating instead on developing the reconfigured personal relationships of its main characters in an altered timeline. Thus, I found nothing in the fourth season that led me to change my interpretation of the series. But one major plot development might seem to contradict my account of *Fringe*. In the end-of-season cliffhanger, we learned that Peter is finally going to have a child with a reasonable facsimile of the original Olivia. Still, I suspect that my claim that Peter and Olivia will never experience normal family life together will not be refuted in the fifth season. I do not foresee that *Fringe* will suddenly transform into *Walter Knows Best*.

The one markedly political episode of the fourth season, "Letters of Transit" (4.19), offers strong support for a libertarian reading of the series. The episode flash-forwards to the year 2036, when faceless (and hairless) bureaucrats from an even more distant future (2609) have traveled back in time to impose a tyranny on the United States. The episode contains many Orwellian touches, including ubiquitous posters of these tyrants (known as Observers) in full "Big Brother Is Watching You" mode. The libertarian thrust of the episode is emphasized in the opening credits. Normally at this point, *Fringe* flashes on the screen the names of the weird phenomena it usually portrays: Quantum Entanglement, Viral Therapy, Gravitons, Time Paradox, Psychogenesis, Bilocation, Psychic Surgery. But "Letters of Transit" begins with a very different list of phenomena: Community, Joy, Individuality, Education, Imagination, Private Thought, Due Process, Ownership, Free Will. The opening credits culminate in a stark image of one word, "Freedom," encased behind barbed wire. The inclusion of the word "Ownership" in the opening credits strikes a particularly libertarian note. "Letters of Transit" also contains a quotation from the British television series *The Prisoner* (1967–1968), well known for its libertarian themes. When a security guard addresses Walter as a prisoner, he replies with the famous words of *The Prisoner*'s mysterious Number Six (Patrick McGoohan): "I am not a number; I am a free man." *Fringe* thus pays tribute to a great libertarian precursor on television.

In addition, "Letters of Transit" seems to point to a controversy that erupted over bureaucratic overregulation in the European Union in November 2011. When Broyles is offered a drink of water by one of the Observers, the *Fringe* agent turns it down: "It's water; it doesn't do anything for me." (Coming from a future Earth depleted of all its natural resources, the Observers evidently relish the opportunity to drink pure water.) The Observer answers Broyles: "It hydrates you." This peculiar exchange, which seems to come out of nowhere, probably refers to a bizarre ruling by the European Food Standards Authority (EFSA) that purveyors of bottled water may not claim that it can be used to combat dehydration. Many commentators at the time—not just libertarians—seized on this moment as the *reductio ad absurdum* of governmental regulation. See, for example, Victoria Ward and Nick Collins, "EU bans claim that water can prevent dehydration," *The Telegraph*, November 18, 2011, http://www.telegraph.co.uk/news/worldnews/europe/eu/8897662/EU-bans-claim-that-water-can-prevent-dehyration.html. As the epitome of the kind of rule by technocratic elites that *Fringe* criticizes, the EU is a likely target of satire in "Letters of Transit." For several seasons *Fringe* presented the Observers as detached and disinterested technocrats (always dressed in business suits). In "Letters of Transit," the show reveals these seemingly benign figures to be members of a self-indulgent elite, concerned only with their own power and eager to subjugate whole populations to their technocratic rule. But at least, in contrast to their EU counterparts, the Observers are willing to acknowledge that water hydrates.

74. These words were spoken by the famous nineteenth-century American orator Edward Everett.

75. When asked by an interviewer why "so many of your works have centered on family," Spielberg replied, "It's a theme I harken back to a lot because it's something I believe in. . . . I tend to always come back to the family as a touchstone for audiences to get into these bizarre stories." Spielberg refers to *Falling Skies* as a "postapocalyptic story with a 21st century [spin on the] spirit of '76" and adds, "I've always been interested in how we survive and how resourceful we are as Americans." Quoted in Ileana Rudolph, "Look! Up in the Skies," *TV Guide*, July 4–10, 2011, 19–20.

76. Michael Hale, "Television Review: Falling Skies," *New York Times*, June 17, 2011. See http: en.wikipedia.org/wiki/Falling_skies (consulted August 20, 2011).

77. On this point, see chapter 4, on *Mars Attacks!*, and James T. Bennett, *The Doomsday Lobby: Hype and Panic from Sputniks, Martians, and Marauding Meteors* (New York: Springer, 2010).

78. In the other universe in *Fringe*, one government expert uses computers to assign exact mathematical probabilities to any contingent human action. The premise of "The Plateau" is that the human mind, if artificially enhanced, would be able to calculate the outcome of even the most complicated series of seemingly unrelated events.

79. See, for example, Leo Strauss, *On Tyranny* (Chicago: University of Chicago Press, 2000), 211.

80. As *The X-Files* shows, this Faustian bargain, which may seem so fantastic and imaginary, is actually epitomized by modern medicine, which induces us to surrender the freedom of our bodies to technicians in return for their promise to cure our diseases and ultimately, perhaps, to make us immortal. Beginning roughly in the second half of the twentieth century, modern medicine began to make its own Faustian bargain with the modern state, gradually ceding control to the state in return for its financial support. The direct and personal relation between doctor and patient began to be broken by all sorts of intermediary institutions, including insurance companies, corporations, and the state itself. In the process, the fundamental nature of medicine has been transformed. For most of human history, medicine was thought of as an art, the healing art, practiced by "medicine men," wise practitioners who drew upon years of personal experience to treat their patients individually. Only in the twentieth century did medicine become a science, in which university-trained professionals apply principles derived from clinical research in the treatment of patients as "case studies," individual examples of general rules. In this new conception of "medical science," the science becomes more important than the individual doctor, and doctors become effectively interchangeable. Under these circumstances, it is no accident that health care has emerged as a contentious political issue, and in varying ways the shows we have discussed reflect these controversies. People increasingly feel that medicine is no longer under their control and is just one more aspect of their lives that has become "alien" to them. That explains the persistent association of medicine with aliens in these invasion narratives. In fact, in virtually all the shows we have discussed, the greatest anxiety and the greatest horror are generated by scenes in hospitals, chiefly involving heartless doctors and exotic medical technologies put

to sinister purposes. The ultimate "invasion" in these programs seems to be invasive medicine. For the perfect distillation of the alien invasion narrative in American pop culture, with medicine at its most invasive, see the pilot episode of *South Park*, "Cartman Gets an Anal Probe" (1997, #101). For the connection between the politics of health care and the modern scientific project, see Tom Merrill, "Health Care and the Technological Project," *Perspectives on Political Science* 40, no. 1 (January–March 2011): 1–8.

81. This tendency is evident in the way professional psychologists concluded after 9/11 that the event would cause significant damage to Americans' mental and even physical health. See Sharon Jayson, "Americans Are Resilient, Even after Tragedies as Big as 9/11," *USA Today*, August 4, 2011, D1: "Ten years after the Sept. 11 attacks, the American psyche has bounced back better than psychologists predicted. . . . Psychologists overestimated the number of people who would suffer long-term effects—and underestimated the resilience humans can muster in the wake of tragedy." Professional psychologists, like many experts, have a vested interest in viewing ordinary people as mentally fragile and incapable of dealing with disasters and crises. Only under such conditions will the services of such experts be in demand. For a critique of the trauma theories of psychologists, see Solnit, *Paradise Built in Hell*, especially 99 and 219. For a remarkable documentary about the resilience of ordinary people on the very day of 9/11, see "Boatlift, An Untold Tale of 9/11 Resilience," http://www.youtube.com/watch?v=MDOrzF7B2Kg (consulted October 2, 2011). See also Alvin Powell, "In Praise of Ordinary People," http://news.harvard.Edu/gazette/story/2011/09/in-praise-of-ordinary-people/?utm_source= alumniaffairs@utm_medium=hagemail&utm_campaign=sept11 (consulted September 20, 2011), which quotes Isaac Ashkenazi, director of the Urban Terrorism Preparedness Project at the Harvard School of Public Health: "This country is a superpower . . . because of the people. This country was established and developed bottom up by resilient individuals. The real first responders are the bystanders. . . . The government should use the people as an asset and not an obstacle. . . . People are not victims; they are active bystanders."

INDEX

Page numbers in *italics* refer to illustrations and captions.

ABC, 323, 417n24
Abrams, J. J., 427n52
absolute sovereignty, doctrine of, 101, 105–6, 144
Adorno, Theodor, 219, 248–52, 255–58, 402n42, 408n47
Adventures of Tom Sawyer (Twain), 195–96
advertising, 204–5
Aeneid (Virgil), 301–2
Aeschylus, 26–27, 31, 36. See also *Agamemnon; Eumenides, The; Libation Bearers, The; Oresteia; Searchers, The* (film; 1956), *Oresteia* compared to
Afghanistan, 196, 275, 282, 291–92, 293
Agamemnon (Aeschylus), 31, 32, 38–39, 41–42, 366n19, 369n60
Alda, Alan, 173
Alexander, David, 87, 375n30, 378n61
Aley, Albert, 374n20
Alice in Wonderland (film; 2010), 160
alien abduction narratives, 307–8, 420–21nn10–12, 427n53
alien invasion narratives: in American popular culture, 344–45, 423n30; family as portrayed in, 338–39, 430n70; flying saucer movies compared to, 336, 428–29n61; globalization fears as portrayed in, 307–8, 344–47; medical technology in, 432–33n80; ocean as source of threat, 423n30; polarities in, 346–47

aliens, double meaning of, 308–9
Allen, Irwin, 393n47, 395n60
Alpers, Svetlana, xix, 354n9
Amazing Transparent Man, The (film; 1959), 215, 254
American dream, 244–46
American Gothic (TV series), 423n31
American Gothic fiction, 223
American heartland: absence of, in *Detour*, 260; elitist contempt for, 29, 92–94, 202, 379n76, 412n39; Hughes's origins in, 167; self-reliance of, in *Mars Attacks!*, 134, 151–52; as site of prejudice, in *Have Gun–Will Travel*, 29, 92–94, 202. See also small-town America
American people: in American popular culture, 347; economic illiteracy of, 207–8; as "innocents abroad," in *Black Cat*, 221, 233–38; mobility of, 256–58; as multicultural, 158–59; 9/11 and, 433n81; self-reliance of, 134, 151–54, 315, 346–47, 393n43, 433n81; spontaneous order provided by, 423–24n32
American Revolution, 341, 343
Americans with Disabilities Act, 199
anarchism, 97, 146, 385n40, 392n27, 424n33
Anasazi peoples, 291–92
Anderson, Gillian, 282, 284, 304, 416n11
Anderson, Terry, 385n39, 386n43
anthrax scare, 285–86
antibusiness trends, 169, 202, 205–6, 396n4, 396n6